THE
MINISTER'S MANUAL

EIGHTY-FIRST ANNUAL ISSUE

THE MINISTER'S MANUAL
2006

Edited by

JAMES W. COX

JOSSEY-BASS
A Wiley Imprint
www.josseybass.com

Editors of THE MINISTER'S MANUAL
G. B. F. Hallock, D.D., 1926–1958
M. K. W. Heicher, Ph.D., 1943–1968
Charles L. Wallis, M.A., M.Div., 1969–1983
James W. Cox, M.Div., Ph.D.

THE MINISTER'S MANUAL FOR 2006. Copyright © 2005 by James W. Cox.

Published by Jossey-Bass
A Wiley Imprint
989 Market Street, San Francisco, CA 94103-1741   www.josseybass.com

Jossey-Bass books and products are available through most bookstores. To contact Jossey-Bass directly call our Customer Care Department within the U.S. at 800-956-7739, outside the U.S. at 317-572-3986, or fax 317-572-4002.

Jossey-Bass also publishes its books in a variety of electronic formats. Some content that appears in print may not be available in electronic books.

Library of Congress Cataloging Card Number

25-21658
ISSN 0738-5323
ISBN 0-7879-7922-8

Printed in the United States of America
FIRST EDITION
HB Printing
10 9 8 7 6 5 4 3 2 1

CONTENTS

PREFACE

This is the final volume of *The Minister's Manual* under my sole editorship. The next volume will be edited by myself and Dr. Lee McGlone, a pastor and teacher with many talents and wide experience. He assisted me in various ways with several volumes of the *Manual,* and his contributions have all been of the highest order. I am grateful to the staff of Jossey-Bass Publishers for their careful attention to all aspects of this annual volume.

As I have indicated in previous volumes, *The Minister's Manual 2006* presents sermonic contributions from a wide range of preachers, teachers, and writers. They come from many geographical, denominational, and theological backgrounds. Although they do not always agree on every issue, they speak responsibly and their thoughts merit careful consideration. They share our common faith and enrich our personal understanding and devotion. Nevertheless, the contributors speak for themselves, and their views do not necessarily represent those of the publisher, the editor, or the Southern Baptist Theological Seminary.

I am grateful to the seminary, where I have taught since 1959, for providing valuable secretarial assistance in producing the manuscript. Again, I wish to thank Linda Durkin for her faithful and efficient assistance and Katie Law for her aid in preparing this volume. I also wish to thank the authors and publishers from whose works I have quoted. It is hoped that the rights and wishes of no one have been overlooked. Again, I am deeply grateful.

James W. Cox
The Southern Baptist Theological Seminary

SECTION I

GENERAL AIDS AND RESOURCES

CIVIL YEAR CALENDARS FOR 2006 AND 2007

2006

January						
S	M	T	W	T	F	S
1	2	3	4	5	6	7
8	9	10	11	12	13	14
15	16	17	18	19	20	21
22	23	24	25	26	27	28
29	30	31				

February						
S	M	T	W	T	F	S
			1	2	3	4
5	6	7	8	9	10	11
12	13	14	15	16	17	18
19	20	21	22	23	24	25
26	27	28				

March						
S	M	T	W	T	F	S
			1	2	3	4
5	6	7	8	9	10	11
12	13	14	15	16	17	18
19	20	21	22	23	24	25
26	27	28	29	30	31	

April						
S	M	T	W	T	F	S
						1
2	3	4	5	6	7	8
9	10	11	12	13	14	15
16	17	18	19	20	21	22
23	24	25	26	27	28	29
30						

May						
S	M	T	W	T	F	S
	1	2	3	4	5	6
7	8	9	10	11	12	13
14	15	16	17	18	19	20
21	22	23	24	25	26	27
28	29	30	31			

June						
S	M	T	W	T	F	S
				1	2	3
4	5	6	7	8	9	10
11	12	13	14	15	16	17
18	19	20	21	22	23	24
25	26	27	28	29	30	

July						
S	M	T	W	T	F	S
						1
2	3	4	5	6	7	8
9	10	11	12	13	14	15
16	17	18	19	20	21	22
23	24	25	26	27	28	29
30	31					

August						
S	M	T	W	T	F	S
		1	2	3	4	5
6	7	8	9	10	11	12
13	14	15	16	17	18	19
20	21	22	23	24	25	26
27	28	29	30	31		

September						
S	M	T	W	T	F	S
					1	2
3	4	5	6	7	8	9
10	11	12	13	14	15	16
17	18	19	20	21	22	23
24	25	26	27	28	29	30

October						
S	M	T	W	T	F	S
1	2	3	4	5	6	7
8	9	10	11	12	13	14
15	16	17	18	19	20	21
22	23	24	25	26	27	28
29	30	31				

November						
S	M	T	W	T	F	S
			1	2	3	4
5	6	7	8	9	10	11
12	13	14	15	16	17	18
19	20	21	22	23	24	25
26	27	28	29	30		

December						
S	M	T	W	T	F	S
					1	2
3	4	5	6	7	8	9
10	11	12	13	14	15	16
17	18	19	20	21	22	23
24	25	26	27	28	29	30
31						

2007

January						
S	M	T	W	T	F	S
	1	2	3	4	5	6
7	8	9	10	11	12	13
14	15	16	17	18	19	20
21	22	23	24	25	26	27
28	29	30	31			

February						
S	M	T	W	T	F	S
				1	2	3
4	5	6	7	8	9	10
11	12	13	14	15	16	17
18	19	20	21	22	23	24
25	26	27	28			

March						
S	M	T	W	T	F	S
				1	2	3
4	5	6	7	8	9	10
11	12	13	14	15	16	17
18	19	20	21	22	23	24
25	26	27	28	29	30	31

April						
S	M	T	W	T	F	S
1	2	3	4	5	6	7
8	9	10	11	12	13	14
15	16	17	18	19	20	21
22	23	24	25	26	27	28
29	30					

May						
S	M	T	W	T	F	S
		1	2	3	4	5
6	7	8	9	10	11	12
13	14	15	16	17	18	19
20	21	22	23	24	25	26
27	28	29	30	31		

June						
S	M	T	W	T	F	S
					1	2
3	4	5	6	7	8	9
10	11	12	13	14	15	16
17	18	19	20	21	22	23
24	25	26	27	28	29	30

July						
S	M	T	W	T	F	S
1	2	3	4	5	6	7
8	9	10	11	12	13	14
15	16	17	18	19	20	21
22	23	24	25	26	27	28
29	30	31				

August						
S	M	T	W	T	F	S
			1	2	3	4
5	6	7	8	9	10	11
12	13	14	15	16	17	18
19	20	21	22	23	24	25
26	27	28	29	30	31	

September						
S	M	T	W	T	F	S
						1
2	3	4	5	6	7	8
9	10	11	12	13	14	15
16	17	18	19	20	21	22
23	24	25	26	27	28	29
30						

October						
S	M	T	W	T	F	S
	1	2	3	4	5	6
7	8	9	10	11	12	13
14	15	16	17	18	19	20
21	22	23	24	25	26	27
28	29	30	31			

November						
S	M	T	W	T	F	S
				1	2	3
4	5	6	7	8	9	10
11	12	13	14	15	16	17
18	19	20	21	22	23	24
25	26	27	28	29	30	

December						
S	M	T	W	T	F	S
						1
2	3	4	5	6	7	8
9	10	11	12	13	14	15
16	17	18	19	20	21	22
23	24	25	26	27	28	29
30	31					

Church and Civic Calendar for 2006

January

1	New Year's Day
5	Twelfth Night
6	Epiphany
10	League of Nations Anniversary
13	Baptism of the Lord
16	Martin Luther King Jr.'s Birthday, observed
17	St. Anthony's Day
25	Conversion of St. Paul

February

1	National Freedom Day
2	Presentation of Jesus in the Temple
12	Lincoln's Birthday
14	St. Valentine's Day
	Race Relations Sunday
20	President's Day
22	Washington's Birthday
24	St. Matthias, Apostle
28	Shrove Tuesday

March

1	Ash Wednesday
5	First Sunday in Lent
12	Second Sunday in Lent
14	Purim
17	St. Patrick's Day
19	Third Sunday in Lent
25	Feast of Annunciation
26	Fourth Sunday in Lent

April

2	Fifth Sunday in Lent
9	Passion Sunday
	Palm Sunday
9–15	Holy Week
13	Maundy Thursday
14	Good Friday
16	Easter
25	St. Mark, Evangelist
31	Law Sunday

May

1	Law Day
	May Day
	Loyalty Day
	St. Philip and St. James, Apostles
1–5	Cinco de Mayo Celebration
1–7	National Family Week
14	Mother's Day
25	Ascension Day
29	Memorial Day, observed

June

2	Shavuot
4	Pentecost
11	Trinity Sunday
	Children's Sunday
	St. Barnabas, Apostle
18	Father's Day
	Corpus Christi, observed (US)
24	St. John the Baptist
29	St. Peter and St. Paul, Apostles

July

1	Canada Day
4	Independence Day
22	St. Mary Magdalene
25	St. James, the elder, Apostle

August

7	Civic Holiday (Canada)
14	Atlantic Charter Day
15	Mary, Mother of Jesus
24	St. Bartholomew, Apostle
26	Women's Equality Day

September

4	Labor Day
21	St. Matthew, Evangelist and Apostle
23	Rosh Hashanah (Jewish New Year)
29	St. Michael and all Angels

October

1	World Communion Sunday
2	Yom Kippur (Day of Atonement)
7	First Day of Sukkoth
	St. Luke, Evangelist
23	St. James, Brother of Jesus
24	United Nations Day
31	Reformation Day
	National UNICEF Day

November

1	All Saints Day
2	All Souls Day
11	Veterans Day
	Armistice Day
12	Stewardship Day
	Remembrance Day (Canada)

19–26	National Bible Week
	National Family Week
23	Thanksgiving Day
30	St. Andrew, Apostle

December

3	First Sunday of Advent
10	Second Sunday of Advent
15	Bill of Rights Day
17	Third Sunday of Advent
25	Christmas
26	Boxing Day (Canada)
	St. Stephen, Deacon and Martyr
27	St. John, Evangelist and Apostle
28	The Holy Innocents, Martyrs
31	New Year's Eve
	Watch Night

The Revised Common Lectionary for 2006

The following Scriptures are commended for use by various Protestant churches and the Roman Catholic Church and include first, second, and Gospel readings, and Psalms, according to Cycle B from January 1 to November 27 and according to Cycle C from December 3 to December 31.[1]

Jan. 1: Isa. 61:10–62:3; Ps. 148; Gal. 4:4–7; Luke 2:22–40

Epiphany Season

Jan. 8: Isa. 60:1–6; Ps. 72:1–7, 10–14; Eph. 3:1–12; Matt. 2:1–12
Jan. 15: 1 Sam. 3:1–10 (11–20); Ps. 139:1–6, 13–18; 1 Cor. 6:12–20; John 1:43–51
Jan. 22: Jon. 3:1–5, 10; Ps. 62:5–12; 1 Cor. 7:29–31; Mark 1:14–20
Jan. 29: Deut. 18:15–20; Ps. 111; 1 Cor. 8:1–13; Mark 1:21–28
Feb. 5: Isa. 40:21–31; Ps. 147:1–11, 20c; 1 Cor. 9:16–23; Mark 1:29–39
Feb. 12: 2 Kings 5:1–14; Ps. 30; 1 Cor. 9:24–27; Mark 1:40–45
Feb. 19: Isa. 43:18–25; Ps. 41; 2 Cor. 1:18–22; Mark 2:1–12
Feb. 26: 2 Kings 2:1–12; Ps. 50:1–6; 2 Cor. 4:3–6; Mark 9:2–9

Transfiguration Sunday

Lenten Season

Mar. 1 (Ash Wednesday): Joel 2:1–2, 12–17; Ps. 51:1–17; 2 Cor. 5:20b–6:10; Matt. 6:1–6, 16–21

Mar. 5: Gen. 9:8–17; Ps. 25:1–10; 1 Pet. 3:18–22; Mark 1:4–15

Mar. 12: Gen. 17:1–7, 15–16; Ps. 22:23–31; Rom. 4:13–25; Mark 8:31–38

Mar. 19: Exod. 20:1–17; Ps. 19; 1 Cor. 1:18–25; John 2:13–22

Mar. 26: Num. 21:4–9; Ps. 107:1–3, 17–22; John 3:14–21; Eph. 2:4–20

Apr. 2: Jer. 31:31–34; Ps. 51:1–12; Heb. 5:5–10; John 12:20–33

Holy Week and Easter Season

Apr. 9 (Palm/Passion Sunday): Liturgy of the Palms—Matt. 21:1–11; Ps. 118:1–2, 19–20; Liturgy of the Passion—Isa. 50:4–9a; Ps. 31:9–16; Phil. 2:5–11; Matt. 26:14–27:66

Apr. 10 (Monday): Isa. 42:1–9; Ps. 36:5–11; Heb. 9:11–15; John 12:1–11

Apr. 11 (Tuesday): Isa. 49:1–7; Ps. 71:1–14; 1 Cor. 1:18–31; John 12:20–36

Apr. 12 (Wednesday): Isa. 50:4–9a; Ps. 70; Heb. 12:1–3; John 13:21–32

Apr. 13 (Thursday): Exod. 12:1–4 (5–10), 11–14; Ps. 116:1–2, 12–19; 1 Cor. 11:23–26; John 13:1–7, 31b–35

Apr. 14 (Good Friday): Isa. 52:13–53:12; Ps. 22; Heb. 10:16–25; John 18:1–19

Apr. 15 (Holy Saturday): Job 14:1–14; Ps. 31:1–4, 15–16; 1 Pet. 4:1–8; Matt. 27:57–66

Apr. 16 (Easter Vigil): Gen. 1:1–2:4a; Ps. 136:1–9, 23–26; Gen. 7:1–5, 11–18, 8:6–18, 9:8–13; Ps. 46; Gen. 22:1–18; Ps. 16; Exod. 14:10–31, 15:20–21; Exod. 15:1b–13, 17–18; Isa. 55:1–11; Isa. 12:2–6; Prov. 8:1–8, 19–21, 9:4b–6; Ps. 19; Ezek. 36:24–28; Ps. 42–43; Ezek. 37:1–14; Ps. 143; Zeph. 3:14–20; Ps. 98; Rom. 6:3–11; Ps. 114; Matt. 28:1–10

Apr. 16 (Easter): Acts 10:34–43; Ps. 118:1–2, 14–24; 1 Cor. 15:1–11; John 20:1–18; (Easter Evening): Isa. 25:6–9; Ps. 114; 1 Cor. 5:6b–8; Luke 24:13–49

Apr. 23: Acts 4:34–35; Ps. 133; 1 John 1:1–2:2; John 20:19–31

Apr. 30: Acts 3:12–19; Ps. 4; 1 John 3:1–7; Luke 24:36b–48

May 7: Acts 4:5–12; Ps. 23; 1 John 3:16–24; John 10:11–18

May 14: Acts 8:26–40; Ps. 22:25–31; 1 John 4:7–21; John 15:1–8

May 21: Acts 10:44–48; Ps. 98; 1 John 5:1–6; John 15:9–17

May 28: Acts 1:15–17, 21–26; Ps. 1; 1 John 5:9–13; John 16:6–19

June 4 (Pentecost): Ezek. 37:1–14 or Acts 2:1–21; Ps. 104:24–34, 35b; Rom. 8:22–27; John 15:26–27, 16:4b–15

June 11 (Trinity): Isa. 6:1–8; Ps. 29; Rom. 8:12–17; John 3:1–17

June 18: 1 Sam. 15:34–16:13; Ps. 20; 2 Cor. 5:6–10 (11–13), 14–17; Mark 4:26–34

June 25: 1 Sam. 17:(1a, 4–11, 19–23) 32–49; Ps. 9:9–20; 2 Cor. 6:1–13; Mark 4:34–41

July 2: 2 Sam. 1:1, 17–27; Ps. 130; 2 Cor. 8:7–15; Mark 5:21–43

July 9: 2 Sam. 5:1–5, 9–10; Ps. 48; 2 Cor. 12:2–10; Mark 6:1–13

July 16: 2 Sam. 6:1–5, 12b–19; Ps. 24; Eph. 1:3–14; Mark 6:14–29

July 23: 2 Sam. 7:1–14a; Ps. 89:20–37; Eph. 2:11–22; Mark 6:30–34, 53–56

July 30: 2 Sam. 11:1–15; Ps. 14; Eph. 3:14–21; John 6:1–21

Aug. 6: 2 Sam. 11:26–12:13a; Ps. 51:1–12; Eph. 4:1–16; John 6:24–35

Aug. 13: 2 Sam. 18:5–9, 15, 31–33; Ps. 130; Eph. 4:25–5:2; John 6:35, 41–51

Aug. 20: 1 Kings 2:10–12, 3:3–14; Ps. 111; Eph. 5:15–20; John 6:51–58

Aug. 27: 1 Kings 8:(1, 6, 10–11) 22–30, 41–43; Ps. 84; Eph. 6:10–20; John 6:56–69

Sept. 3: Song of Songs 2:8–13; Ps. 45:1–2, 6–9; James 1:17–27; Mark 7:1–8, 14–15, 21–23

Sept. 10: Prov. 22:1–2, 8–9, 22–23; Ps. 125; James 2:1–10 (11–13), 14–17; Mark 7:24–37

Sept. 17: Prov. 1:20–33; Ps. 19; James 3:1–12; Mark 8:27–38

Sept. 24: Prov. 31:10–31; Ps. 1; James 3:13–4:3, 7–8a; Mark 9:30–37

Oct. 1: Esther 7:1–6, 9–10, 9:20–22; Ps. 124; James 5:13–20; Mark 9:38–50

Oct. 8: Job 1:1, 2:1–10; Ps. 26; Heb. 1:1–4, 2:5–12; Mark 10:2–16

Oct. 15: Job 23:1–9, 16–17; Ps. 22:1–15; Heb. 4:12–16; Mark 10:17–31

Oct. 22: Job 38:1–7 (34–41); Ps. 104:1–9, 24, 35a; Heb. 5:1–10; Mark 10:35–45

Oct. 29: Job 42:1–6, 10–17; Ps. 34:1–8 (19–22); Heb. 7:23–28; Mark 10:46–52

Nov. 5: Ruth 1:1–18; Ps. 146; Heb. 9:11–14; Mark 12:28–34

Nov. 12: Ruth 3:1–5, 4:14–17; Ps. 127; Heb. 9:24–28; Mark 12:38–44

Nov. 19: 1 Sam. 1:4–20; Ps. 16; Heb. 10:11–14 (15–18), 19–25; Mark 13:1–8

Nov. 26 (Christ the King): 2 Sam. 23:1–7; Ps. 132:1–12 (13–18); Rev. 1:4b–8; John 18:33–37

Advent and Christmas Season

Dec. 3: Jer. 33:14–16; Ps. 25:1–10; 1 Thess. 3:9–13; Luke 21:25–36

Dec. 10: Mal. 3:1–4; Luke 1:68–79; Phil. 1:3–11; Luke 3:1–6

Dec. 17: Zeph. 3:14–20; Isa. 12:2–6; Phil. 4:4–7; Luke 3:7–18

Dec. 24: Mic. 5:2–5; Luke 1:47–55; Heb. 10:5–10; Luke 1:39–45

Dec. 25 (Christmas, Proper 1): Isa. 9:2–7; Ps. 96; Titus 2:11–14; Luke 2:1–14 (15–20); (Proper II): Isa. 62:6–12; Ps. 97; Titus 3:4–7; Luke 2:(1–7) 8–20; (Proper III): Isa. 52:7–10; Ps. 98; Heb. 1:1–4 (5–12); John 1:1–14

Dec. 31: 1 Sam. 2:18–20, 26; Ps. 148; Col. 3:12–17; Luke 2:41–52

Four-Year Church Calendar

	2006	2007	2008	2009
Ash Wednesday	March 1	February 21	February 6	February 25
Palm Sunday	April 9	April 1	March 16	April 5
Good Friday	April 14	April 6	March 21	April 10
Easter	April 16	April 8	March 23	April 12
Ascension Day	May 25	May 17	May 1	May 21
Pentecost	June 4	May 27	May 11	May 31
Trinity Sunday	June 11	June 3	May 18	June 7
Thanksgiving	November 23	November 22	November 27	November 26
Advent Sunday	December 3	December 2	November 30	November 29

Forty-Year Easter Calendar

2006 April 16	2010 April 4	2014 April 20	2018 April 1
2007 April 8	2011 April 24	2015 April 5	2019 April 21
2008 March 23	2012 April 8	2016 March 27	2020 April 12
2009 April 12	2013 March 31	2017 April 16	2021 April 4

2022 April 17	2028 April 16	2034 April 9	2040 April 1
2023 April 9	2029 April 1	2035 March 25	2041 April 2
2024 March 31	2030 April 21	2036 April 13	2042 April 6
2025 April 20	2031 April 13	2037 April 5	2043 March 29
2026 April 5	2032 March 28	2038 April 25	2044 April 17
2027 March 28	2033 April 17	2039 April 10	2045 April 9

Traditional Wedding Anniversary Identifications

1 Paper	7 Wool	13 Lace	35 Coral
2 Cotton	8 Bronze	14 Ivory	40 Ruby
3 Leather	9 Pottery	15 Crystal	45 Sapphire
4 Linen	10 Tin	20 China	50 Gold
5 Wood	11 Steel	25 Silver	55 Emerald
6 Iron	12 Silk	30 Pearl	60 Diamond

Colors Appropriate for Days and Seasons

White. Symbolizes purity, perfection, and joy and identifies festivals marking events in the life of Jesus, except Good Friday: Christmas, Epiphany, Easter, Eastertide, Ascension Day; also Trinity Sunday, All Saints Day, weddings, funerals. Gold may also be used.

Red. Symbolizes the Holy Spirit, martyrdom, and the love of God: Good Friday, Pentecost, and Sundays following.

Violet. Symbolizes penitence: Advent, Lent.

Green. Symbolizes mission to the world, hope, regeneration, nurture, and growth: Epiphany season, Kingdomtide, Rural Life Sunday, Labor Sunday, Thanksgiving Sunday.

Blue. Advent, in some churches.

Flowers in Season Appropriate for Church Use

January: carnation or snowdrop
February: violet or primrose
March: jonquil or daffodil
April: lily, sweet pea, or daisy
May: lily of the valley or hawthorn
June: rose or honeysuckle
July: larkspur or water lily
August: gladiolus or poppy
September: aster or morning star
October: calendula or cosmos
November: chrysanthemum
December: narcissus, holly, or poinsettia

Quotable Quotations

1. Love is the only weapon we need.—Rev. H.R.L. Sheppard
2. When you are down and out something always turns up—and it is usually one of your friends.—Orson Welles
3. Race prejudice is as thorough a denial of the Christian God as atheism, and a far more common form of apostasy.—Harry Emerson Fosdick
4. Age is not all decay; it is the ripening, the swelling of the fresh life within, that withers and bursts the husk.—George Macdonald
5. Compromise does not mean cowardice.—John F. Kennedy

6. Calvary is the key to an omnipotence which works only and always through sacrificial love.—Michael Ramsey

7. The bitterest tears shed over graves are for words left unsaid and deeds left undone.—Harriet Beecher Stowe

8. We are the Bibles the world is reading; we are the creeds the world is needing; we are the sermons this world is heeding.—Billy Graham

9. From acquaintances, we conceal our real selves. To our friends we reveal our weaknesses.—George Basil Hume

10. The martyrs shook the powers of darkness with the irresistible power of weakness.—John Milton

11. Only the sinner has the right to preach.—Robert Morley

12. I know! I have had the experiences of being gripped by something stronger than myself. Something that people call God.—Carl Gustav Jung

13. Security is mostly a superstition. It does not exist in nature. . . . Life is either a daring adventure or nothing.—Helen Keller

14. An atheist is a man who has no invisible means of support.—John Buchan

15. We know what happens to people who stay in the middle of the road. They get run down.—Aneurin Bevan

16. I have no problem with retirement. I'd much rather be put out to pasture than under it.—Robert Orben

17. Oh, what a tangled web do parents weave/when they think their children are naïve.—Ogden Nash (1902–1971)

18. If a man hasn't discovered something that he will die for, he isn't fit to live.—Martin Luther King Jr.

19. When I can no longer bear to think of the victims of broken homes, I begin to think of the victims of intact ones.—Peter DeVries

20. The afternoon of a human life must have a significance of its own, and cannot be merely a pitiful appendage to life's morning.—Carl Jung

21. The thing that impresses me most about America is the way parents obey their children.—Edward VIII (1894–1972)

22. Charity is the power of defending that which we know to be indefensible. Hope is the power of being cheerful in circumstances which we know to be desperate.—G. K. Chesterton

23. The paradoxical—and tragic—situation of a man is that his conscience is weakest when he needs it most.—Erich Fromm

24. Insanity is hereditary—you get it from your children.—Sam Levenson

25. Genius is one percent inspiration, ninety-nine percent perspiration.—Thomas Alva Edison

26. There is only one thing in the world worse than being talked about, and that is not being talked about.—Oscar Wilde

27. The great act of faith is when a man decides he is not God.—Oliver Wendell Holmes Jr.

28. All great virtues bear the imprint of self-denial.—William Ellery Channing

29. The young man who has not wept is a savage, and the old man who will not laugh is a fool.—George Santayana

30. I've developed a new philosophy—I only dread one day at a time.—Charles Schulz
31. Technology . . . the knack of so arranging the world that we don't have to experience it.—Max Frisch (1911–1991)
32. There were times my pants were so thin I could sit on a dime and tell if it was heads or tails.—Spencer Tracy
33. A pessimist is a man who looks both ways before crossing a one-way street. —Laurence J. Peter (1919–1990)
34. An honest man's the noblest work of God.—Alexander Pope
35. God's a circle whose center is everywhere and whose circumference is nowhere. —Empedocles (5th century B.C.)
36. Discovery consists of seeing what everybody has seen and thinking what nobody has thought.—Albert Szent Györgyi
37. There is one big problem with the road to success—no rest areas.—Robert Orben
38. Preaching is personal counseling on a group basis.—Harry Emerson Fosdick
39. The realities of faith lie outside the realm of psychology.—Carl Gustav Jung
40. The intention of Christianity was to change everything.—Sören Kierkagaard
41. A fanatic is one who can't change his mind and won't change the subject. —Winston Churchill
42. To do evil that good may come of it is for bunglers in politics as well as morals. —William Penn
43. Thoroughly to teach another is the best way to learn for yourself.—Tryon Edwards
44. Father, your sermons are like water to a drowning man.—Churchgoer
45. The things taught in schools are not an education but the means of an education. —Ralph Waldo Emerson
46. Work is more fun than fun.—Noel Coward
47. We work to become, not to acquire.—Elbert Hubbard
48. There are only two lasting bequests we can hope to give our children. One of these is roots, the other, wings.—Hodding Carter
49. The only thing I can't stand is discomfort.—Gloria Steinem
50. All cruelty springs from weakness.—Seneca
51. A decent provision for the poor is the true test of a civilization.—Samuel Johnson
52. When you sit with a nice girl for two hours, you think it's only a minute. But when you sit on a hot stove for a minute, you think it's two hours. That's relativity. —Albert Einstein

Questions of Life and Religion
1. How does the Golden Rule apply in life today?
2. What are the evidences of the presence of God in our lives?
3. Does violence in movies and TV influence the behavior of children?
4. How is God different from us?
5. What is the purpose of baptism?
6. How is the Bible an authority for us today?
7. Are there prayers that God doesn't answer?
8. What is the role of music in worship?

9. What should a Christian do who backslides?
10. Can we explain suffering?
11. Is participation in the political process a Christian duty?
12. How can we make holidays more bearable for lonely people?
13. What can we do to find the will of God for our personal life?
14. What, to you, are some of the most important verses of the Bible?
15. Are there Christian standards of courtesy?
16. When is anger appropriate?
17. How can our children cope with the menace of drugs?
18. What does nature tell us about God?
19. Are religion and psychiatry friends or enemies?
20. Does "positive thinking" contribute to physical health?
21. What should be our attitude toward other religions?
22. What causes religious doubt?
23. Is divorce ever right?
24. How can Jesus be our example today?
25. What should we pray for?
26. What is love?
27. Who is a saint?
28. Can conscience be a good guide?
29. Is God a person?
30. What was the purpose of Jesus' miracles?
31. Why do we observe the Eucharist or Lord's Supper?
32. How did we get the Bible in its present form?
33. What are the abiding lessons from the Reformation?
34. How should a congregation try to determine God's will for its actions?
35. How can we make worship more meaningful?
36. How can we determine if we should enter a religious vocation?
37. In what sense is the Bible the Word of God?
38. What are some basic guidelines for telling right from wrong?
39. What sort of people should lay leaders in the church be?
40. Should the biblical doctrine of election cut the nerves of evangelism and missions?
41. In what ways does God reveal himself?
42. Is suffering always or ever a punishment for sin?
43. Is doubt a normal part of Christian experience?
44. What makes a happy marriage?
45. When is confrontation of an adversary a Christian duty?
46. Why was the Book of Revelation written?
47. "What must I do to be saved?" (Acts 16:30).
48. What will heaven be like?
49. In what sense does the Bible have authority over us today?
50. What does it mean to be "born again"?
51. Is it Christian to be patriotic?
52. What is the meaning of Easter?

Biblical Benedictions and Blessings

The Lord watch between me and thee when we are absent from one another.—Gen. 31:49

The Lord our God be with us, as he was with our fathers; let him not leave us nor forsake us; that he may incline our hearts unto him, to walk in all his ways and to keep his commandments and his statutes and his judgments, which he commanded our fathers.—1 Kings 8:57–58

Let the words of my mouth and the meditation of my heart be acceptable in thy sight, O Lord, my strength and my redeemer.—Ps. 19:14

Now the God of patience and consolation grant you to be like-minded one toward another according to Christ Jesus; that ye may with one mind and one mouth glorify God, even the Father of our Lord Jesus Christ. Now the God of hope fill you with all joy and peace in believing, that ye may abound in hope, through the power of the Holy Ghost. Now the God of peace be with you.—Rom. 15:5–6, 13, 33

Now to him that is of power to establish you according to my Gospel and the teaching of Jesus Christ, according to the revelation of the mystery, which was kept secret since the world began but now is manifest, and by the Scriptures of the prophets, according to the commandments of the everlasting God, made known to all nations for the glory through Jesus Christ forever.—Rom. 16:25–27

Grace be unto you, and peace, from God our Father, and from the Lord Jesus Christ.—1 Cor. 1:3

The grace of the Lord Jesus Christ and the love of God and the communion of the Holy Ghost be with you all.—2 Cor. 13:14

Peace be to the brethren, and love with faith, from God the Father and the Lord Jesus Christ. Grace be with all them that love our Lord Jesus Christ in sincerity.—Eph. 6:23–24

And the peace of God, which passeth all understanding, shall keep your hearts and minds through Christ Jesus. Finally, brethren, whatsoever things are true, whatsoever things are honest, whatsoever things are just, whatsoever things are pure, whatsoever things are lovely, whatsoever things are of good report; if there be any virtue, and if there be any praise, think on these things. Those things which ye have both learned and received, and heard and seen in me, do; and the God of peace shall be with you.—Phil. 4:7–9

Wherefore also we pray always for you, that our God would count you worthy of this calling and fulfill all the good pleasure of this goodness, and the work of faith with power; that the name of our Lord Jesus Christ may be glorified in you, and ye in him, according to the grace of our God and the Lord Jesus Christ.—2 Thess. 1:11–12

Now the Lord of peace himself give you peace always by all means. The Lord be with you all. The grace of our Lord Jesus Christ be with you all.—2 Thess. 3:16–18

Grace, mercy, and peace, from God our Father and Jesus Christ our Lord.—1 Tim. 1:2

Now the God of peace, that brought again from the dead our Lord Jesus, that great shepherd of the sheep, through the blood of the everlasting covenant, make you perfect in every good work to do his will, working in you that which is well-pleasing in his sight, through Jesus Christ, to whom be glory for ever and ever.—Heb. 13:20–21

The God of all grace, who hath called us unto his eternal glory by Christ Jesus, after that ye have suffered a while, make you perfect, establish, strengthen, settle you. To him be glory and dominion for ever and ever. Greet ye one another with a kiss of charity. Peace be with you all that are in Christ Jesus.—1 Pet. 3:10–14

Grace be with you, mercy, and peace from God the Father, and from the Lord Jesus Christ, the Son of the Father, in truth and love.—2 John 3

Now unto him that is able to keep you from falling, and to present you faultless before the presence of his glory with exceeding joy, to the only wise God our Savior, be glory and majesty, dominion and power, both now and ever.—Jude 24:25

Grace be unto you, and peace, from him which was, and which is to come; and from the seven Spirits which are before his throne; and from Jesus Christ, who is the faithful witness, and the first begotten of the dead, and the prince of the kings of the earth. Unto him that loved us, and washed us from our sins in his own blood, and hath made us kings and priests unto God and his Father, to him be glory and dominion for ever and ever.—Rev. 1:4–6

SECTION II

SERMONS AND HOMILETIC AND WORSHIP AIDS FOR FIFTY-TWO SUNDAYS

SUNDAY, JANUARY 1, 2006

Lectionary Message

Topic: The Children of God

TEXT: Gal. 4:4–7

Other Readings: Isa. 61:10–62:3; Ps. 148; Luke 2:22–40

Every day parents somewhere experience the rebellion of a son or daughter. In going against the wishes of their parents, the children make a mess of their lives. I remember well one time in my ministry receiving a call from frantic parents asking me to come to their home. Their teenage son had time and time again abused alcohol and drugs. He had failed time and time again in school and work. When I arrived, he was sitting on the stairs to the second floor with a rifle, threatening to kill his parents and anyone else who might stand in his way of leaving the house. Fortunately, the gun was not loaded when I was able to take it away from him. Although the parents' lives had been in danger from his confused state, these parents did not respond in anger but in love and sorrow. He was still their son, and no matter what he had done with his life they loved him. With someone else they probably would have had him arrested. Sonship made the difference.

Out of love God sent his Son to redeem the world and to adopt those who would trust in Christ. We become heirs with Christ—yes, joint heirs.

The Scriptures affirm this promise in God:

"But as many as received him, to them gave he the power to become the sons of God." (John 1:12)

"For as many as are led by the Spirit of God, they are the sons of God." (Rom. 8:14)

"Listen, my beloved brothers and sisters. Has not God chosen the poor in the world to be rich in faith and to be heirs of the kingdom that he has promised to those who love him?" (James 2:5)

Because God has made a promise does not mean one is automatically a child of God. We are all God's creation, but not all are the sons and daughters of Christ. It is essential that the Holy Spirit be present in our lives, both before and after the salvation experience. The Holy Spirit convicts us of our sinful nature and our need of Christ to redeem us. Then the Holy Spirit wants to be our guide and to empower us, as Christians, to fulfill the will of God.

How can we know that God has spiritually adopted us and made us heirs of his Kingdom? Let me mention several characteristics that will be present in our lives.

The Scriptures tell us: "Believe in the Lord Jesus, and you shall be saved, you and your household" (Acts 16:31). As our faith and trust in Christ grows, we will have more and more assurance that we have been saved. We will be changed people, and others will see this change in us.

As children of God, we have a peace that helps us become stable people in an unstable world. We know in whom we have believed and are not blown about with the latest religious fad or the old false doctrines.

To heirs of God, the Church is a vital part of life; they are not "church hoppers" when things don't go their way. Children of God will stand for their convictions and feel the presence of God supporting them. They will not be shy in the face of ridicule.

Heirs of Christ will be honest, genuine, and forthright. There will be no mixture of hypocrisy in their lives. Children of God will be very transparent and will not leave doubt about where they stand on the issues of life. There will be no confusion or flip-flopping about their yes or no. People will be aware that they are living from the heart and not for show.

There are some who try to impress others with syrupy words. The gentleness and courtesy of Christians will be a consistent part of their lives. They will not be individuals who go to church on Sunday and sing "Holy, Holy, Holy" and then during the week live "Helly, Helly, Helly." Christians are to be caring, and others will know that they have been with Jesus.

The child of God will follow the motto of Paul: "Therefore, my beloved, be steadfast, immovable, always excelling in the work of the Lord, because you know that in the Lord your labor is not in vain" (1 Cor. 5:58). A Christian is steadfast in prayer. Prayer is not a button to push to summon God but a way of talking to God all the time about everything from expressing love to seeking forgiveness of sins.

A son or daughter of God is steadfast in not only reading but studying God's Word. It becomes a source of strength and revelation from God.

God expects his children to be steadfast in service. We need to be willing to sacrifice, if need be, to do the things God wants us to do here on Earth. It is not a payment program for what he has done for us but a way to express our love for him.

We live in a very uncertain time. So much of our society seems to be on the edge of disaster. We, as children of God, are not unconcerned about the everyday problems around us, but in the midst of problems we feel the everlasting arms of God around us, assuring us that he is walking beside us. Being a child of God does not take away the problems of the world, but we do have the assurance that we shall, in the end, be delivered up into his presence.

Are you a son or daughter of God? Do you enjoy the life of being an heir of God and a joint heir with Christ?

Receive Christ and be led of the Spirit!—William Cubine

ILLUSTRATION

HE CAME TO ME.   He who has found and experienced that Jesus really is the one who was to come and that we do not wait for another will have to say this: "It was not the seeking of my heart that led to success; nor hardheadedness that brought me to peace. No—he has *given* me all that. He came to me! I would not even have sought him if he had not found me beforehand—and everything is true that he had promised me no matter how much of an adventure it sounded like for a beginner in faith."—Helmut Thielcke[1]

SERMON SUGGESTIONS

Topic: Praise the Lord
TEXT: Ps. 198
(1) The command: *praise* defined; the duty distributed. (2) The motivation: God's transcendence (v. 13); God's grace toward his people (v. 14).

Topic: Forever God!
TEXT: Gen. 1:1
(1) What God began. (2) What happened to God's creation. (3) God's response then, now, ultimately.

WORSHIP AIDS

CALL TO WORSHIP.   "The Lord is in his holy temple; let all the earth be silent before him" (Hab. 2:20 NIV).

INVOCATION.   Our times are in your hands O Lord; our steps are well ordered, thus do we pray to be faithful servants all through this year, ones who honor and serve the Lord of Hosts.—E. Lee Phillips

OFFERTORY SENTENCE.   "This is the thing that the Lord has commanded: Take from among you an offering to the Lord; let whoever is of a generous heart bring the Lord's offering" (Exod. 35:4–5 NRSV).

OFFERTORY PRAYER.   Generous Lord, allow our first offering of the New Year to be the continuation of a pattern that never stops giving, as our Lord never stops giving.—E. Lee Phillips

PRAYER.   "In the beginning was the Word. . . ."

That in the beginning your Word was present, creating a cosmos out of chaos—
That at the dawn of history your Word of covenant should be spoken to your people, Israel, calling them to a world purpose—
That in these latter days you should call Jesus of Nazareth at *his* baptism to be your Word—your Light—to all peoples in all times—
That through him—his life, ministry, passion—living again, you established the Church to be and to be prophetic of that communion and community your Word proclaims for all—
That through the ages you have called Luthers and Calvins to re-form and re-new the Church in mission—
That in this time and place *we* should be called to be your Church—

---

[1]*Faith: The Great Adventure* (Philadelphia: Fortress Press, 1985), p. 115.

That on this occasion we should be privileged to be together to celebrate Word and
Sacrament, we praise you and give you thanks.

We pray for those who have heard your call through our "life together" and have come
today in commitment and re-commitment to your love purpose in Christ. With them, may
we be faithful to the gospel of reconciliation, to which we all are called.

In the power of your love to heal, may we embrace those among us who are ill, those facing the loneliness of bereavement, those discouraged with failure, those made anxious with
difficult decisions.

We pray for the family of faith. We pray, too, for *our* families, in which our lives are most
intimately set. To these we bear a special responsibility to the Gospel, but often we are hesitant, even reluctant. Increase your love in us, strengthen our faith, empower us with your
Spirit to do what we know.

We pray, too, for the family of humankind. How can we worship *you*, Parent of us all,
except our brother and sister be with us? We thank you for all who affirm and celebrate your
Word, your intention, from the beginning—one world, one people. We pray for the United
Nations, where this dream is precariously and painfully nurtured. We pray for leaders and
field workers who persevere in seeking to bring order out of chaos and who seek to pass
bread to those who hunger. With them may we all give and labor with the confidence that
there is a grace at work that can fashion wholeness in the face of all of man's brokenness—
the grace of our Lord Jesus Christ.—John Thompson

SERMON
Topic: If This Were My Last Sermon
TEXT: John 3:16

During my thirty-five years of teaching, the focus of my attention has been on the Gospels. I
guess you could say that this is the part of the Bible of which I am least ignorant. My main
area of study has concentrated on what are called the Synoptic Gospels, that is, the Gospels
of Matthew, Mark, and Luke. Of these, I am least ignorant of Mark. Yet my text this morning
does not come from Mark or Luke, or even from Matthew. It comes, rather, from the fourth
Gospel—the Gospel of John. It is a well-known text. In fact, it may be the best-known verse
in all the Bible. I know that as a child it was the first Bible verse I ever learned. It is found in
the third chapter of John and is verse 16. If you have a Bible or New Testament with you this
morning, I encourage you to turn with me to John 3. If you did not bring a Bible, please take
the one in the chair in front of you and turn to page 73 in the New Testament section. Would
you please stand with me as I read this great text of Scripture:

> For God so loved the world, that He gave His only begotten Son, that whoever believes in him
> shall not perish, but have eternal life.

The context of this verse involves a conversation between Jesus and a man named Nicodemus. In the opening verses of John 3, we read [read John 3:1–2 aloud]. Nicodemus is described
quite positively in verse 1. He is a Pharisee, that is, a member of the most influential Jewish
sect. (Today we would probably call it a denomination.) The Pharisees have a bad reputation

among Christians. There are several reasons for this. According to Matthew 23, there were numerous hypocrites among the Pharisees, and some of them bitterly opposed the ministry of Jesus. Some tended to be quite legalistic in their thinking. Yet religious hypocrisy and legalism are usually a parasitic growth that feeds off the finest and noblest piety.

As with Christians today, religious hypocrisy and legalistic thinking are usually associated with religious groups that take their religion very seriously and earnestly seek to keep God's commandments. This was also true in Jesus' day. Nicodemus is portrayed as a devout and pious Pharisee. He is not in any way portrayed negatively in our account. He is also described as a ruler of the Jews. This indicates that he was a member of the Sanhedrin, the ruling body in Israel that consisted of seventy leaders of the people and the high priest. Today he would be something like a senator.

He is also referred to in verse 10 as not just "a" teacher in Israel but as "the" teacher of Israel, that is, *the* well-known and respected teacher of Israel. In John 7:45–52, we read that Nicodemus protested against the desire of some fellow Pharisees to condemn Jesus, and in 19:38–42 he is described as having assisted Joseph of Arimathea in the burial of Jesus. In verse 2, he is described as coming to Jesus "by night," and this may indicate that he did so because of fear of the Jews (cf. 19:38).

If we were seeking to publish a red-letter edition of the Bible in which the words of Jesus are printed in red, our account in John 3 would create some serious difficulties. There is no doubt, for instance, that verses 3, 5–8, and 10 should be printed in red, but after this it is not easy to decide. It is unclear whether at times John is commenting about Jesus or whether Jesus is speaking about himself. For example, in verse 11 the words "we" and "our" (not "I" or "my") raise questions, but once again in 12, where we have "I" and "you," we would want to print this in red. But then in verses 15–18 we have once again "him" instead of "me." Whether in John 3:16 we have Jesus' own words or whether they are the inspired words of John, ultimately does not make any difference. If they are John's own interpretative words, they are the infallible and inerrant Word of God, written under Divine inspiration. If they are Jesus' words, they are also the infallible and inerrant Word of God, recorded by the Divinely inspired apostle. I remember speaking to a person once who told me, "When I read the Bible, it is meaningful, but I really feel I am reading the Word of God when I read Jesus' words found in the red parts of the Gospels."

Now if John was inspired to write infallible and inerrant Scripture, Jesus' words cannot be more infallible or more inerrant. You cannot be more infallible than infallible, and you cannot be more inerrant than inerrant, any more than you can be more perfect than perfect. Thus whether our text is John's own inspired commentary on God's love and his sending his Son to die for the sins of the world, or whether it is Jesus' inspired commentary, does not really change anything. We must also remember that the discussion between Jesus and Nicodemus is recorded in the Greek language, not in Aramaic—the language that Jesus and Nicodemus actually spoke. It is through the inspired writings of John and the other Gospel writers that we have access to the words and thoughts of Jesus and the significance of his life, death, and Resurrection.

The greatness of John 3:16 is evident for a number of reasons. For one, it is a wonderful summary of the biblical message encapsulated into just twenty-five words in the NASB translation, as well as in the Greek text. Its greatness is also due to the fact that it talks about the three most important beings in the entire world: *God*, *Jesus* (the Son of God), and *us*—created as we are in the image of God. What it teaches about God, Jesus, and us is extremely important. We know this because this teaching is repeated time and time again throughout the New Testament.

I. Let us look first of all at what it says about us. It says that

1. We are the kind of people for whom Christ had to die.

Our present generation is much concerned with the need for people to have a good self-image. We emphasize that we need to feel good about ourselves. Shame and guilt are feelings and thoughts that we are told to avoid because they lead to low self-esteem. And there is some truth in this. Self-hate—despising oneself—can lead to all sorts of personal and social problems. It causes us to do things that harm us, as well as others.

Yet within our great text, we learn an important truth about ourselves that is repeated throughout the Bible. As Jesus himself says in Mark 2:17, "I did not come to call the righteous, but sinners"; in Luke 19:10 he says, "For the Son of man has come to seek and to save that which was lost." And in our text, we read that the Son came in order that we "shall not perish." The dreadful state in which we find ourselves is not merely something that is future. Already now we stand condemned before God. Look what John writes in the following verses [read 3:17–18 and 36 aloud].

C. S. Lewis, the great British spokesman for the Christian faith during the middle of the twentieth century, has rightly said, "[Christianity] . . . has nothing (as far as I know) to say to people who do not know they have done anything to repent of and who do not feel that they need any forgiveness."[2] Christianity is for sinners.

Christianity is, however, for all people, because Paul states

That "all have sinned and fall short of the glory of God" (Rom. 3:23 NIV)
That "all [are under the power of] sin" (Rom. 3:9)
That "[t]here is none righteous, not even one" (Rom. 3:10)

Does this Christian teaching lead to a negative self-image? It does if our self-image is based on a false understanding of ourselves. The fact is, our text tells us that

1. We are the kind of people for whom Christ had to die.

We are the kind of people Jesus tells Nicodemus in verses 3 and 7 that need to be "born again." A realistic, Christian self-image should not be based on a false impression of our own goodness but on the fact that, despite our being sinners, we are loved by God. John 3:16 allows us to have a realistic and undeniably positive self-image. This is not based on an untruth of our own, supposedly good character, which is all too often far from praiseworthy, but it is based on the great truth, found in our text, that God loves us. It is God's undeniable love for us that provides us with a true sense of worth. This, however, is not so much a self-worth but, more important, a "God-worth."

---

[2]*Mere Christianity*, Book I, chap. 5.

II. The second important truth that our text teaches us is about God. It tells us that

2. God loves the world.

People like to talk about "God's love." It is a popular theme, and no one will get into trouble preaching about God's love for the world. For many people, however, the content—the way in which God loves the world—has little to do with how the Bible says God loves the world. Society tends to think of God's love as some undefined, noncondemning, sentimental feeling of goodwill that permeates the air we breathe. In our text, God's love is described rather specifically: God loves the world "so" . . . Although many tend to interpret "so" to mean "so much" (God loves the world so very much that he gave his only begotten Son), "so" actually refers not to the *degree* of God's love but the *manner* of his love. In other words, "so" describes not the *amount* of God's love but *the way* in which God loves us. The word *so* is used fourteen times in the Gospel of John and never refers to the degree or amount or "how much" but always describes "the way in which" something is done. It is used twice more in chapter 3. In 3:8, "so" describes that just as one cannot see the wind but only hear its sound, "so" in a similar manner one does not see the Spirit entering into the life of the believer but only the resultant, changed life brought about by the Spirit. In 3:14, "so" describes that just as Moses during the exodus lifted up an image of a serpent for people to see and believe and thus be healed from their poisonous snakebite, "so" in like manner the Son of Man would be lifted up on a cross and people who believed in him would be saved from the condemnation of sin.

In John 3:16, "so" describes "how," that is, the way in which God loved the world. He loved the world in this manner: "He gave his only Son." When the New Testament writers talk about the love of God, it does not refer to some ambiguous and amorphous atmosphere of divine love permeating the cosmos. On the contrary, it is a specific love revealed in the greatest act of love the world has ever known. Listen to how this love is described elsewhere:

In Romans 5:8 we read, "But God demonstrates [or proves] his own love toward us, in that while we were yet sinners, Christ died for us."

In 1 John 4:9 we read, "By this the love of God was manifested in [or among] us, that God sent his only begotten Son into the world so that we might live through him."

In 1 John 4:10 we read, "In this is love, not that we loved God, but that he loved us and sent his Son to be the propitiation for our sins." (Refer also to 1 John 3:16: "We know love by this, that he laid down his life for us. . . .")

Our text this morning tells us, "For God so loved the world, that he gave his only begotten Son, that whoever believes in him shall not perish, but have eternal life." The New Testament knows nothing about God's love for the world that is not in some way connected to his sending his Son to die for our sins.

On our first sabbatical my wife, Joan, our children, and I spent the year in Heidelberg, Germany. Our two oldest children, Julie and Keith, attended Bunsen Gymnasium, named after the inventor of the Bunsen burner. Our youngest son, Steve, attended Grundschule in the village of Schlierbach. One day while in downtown Heidelberg I had some time, so I visited some of the old churches there. Often there is a cemetery next to the churches, and on this particular day I walked in the cemetery looking at the various gravestones and their inscriptions. As I did so, I came across one gravestone that not only mentioned the name and dates of the person buried there but it had a Bible verse inscribed on the tombstone. It was our text—John 3:16—written, of course, in German. I was very upset, however, because someone had desecrated the stone with bright red paint. This made me quite angry, but my anger quickly turned to sadness as I read what the person had written on the tombstone. He had written the words *mich liebt kein gott: mich* (me), *liebt* (loves), *kein* (no), *gott* (God): "No God loves me."

I became sad and wanted to tell him, "Friend, look up. Look up! Look at the top of the church steeple. Do you see the cross? God loves you. God has proven his love for you. Christ has died for you." Our text tells us that God loves us. He loves the whole world, and this involves not just some of the world. He loves the whole world. The term *world* in our text is not exclusive but inclusive. It involves not just a small percentage of the world but the whole world. And it involves you and me, here this morning. God loves the world and does not want any to perish but that all should come to repentance and faith in his Son (2 Pet. 3:9).

Friend, every time you see a cross from this day forward, whether on a church steeple, on a necklace, in a painting, or whatever, remember that this proves God loves us.

> "But God demonstrates [or proves] his own love toward us, in that while we were yet sinners, Christ died for us."
>
> "For God loved the world in this manner, that he gave his only begotten Son, that whoever believes in him shall not perish, but have eternal life."

III. The third and final point that we need to look at in our text involves what it says about Jesus Christ, the Son of God. Out text tells us that

3. Jesus Christ, God's Son, died for us.

God gave his only Son for us. This brief summary does not tell us how the death of the Son of God is able to keep us from perishing and give to us eternal life, but this is made clear enough in the rest of Scripture. Listen to how the New Testament explains this:

> "[God] made him who knew no sin to be sin on our behalf, so that might become the righteousness of God in him." (2 Cor. 5:21)
>
> "He himself bore our sins in his body on the cross, so that we might die to sin and live to righteousness; for by his wounds you are healed." (1 Pet. 2:24)
>
> "For Christ also died for sin once for all, the just for the unjust, so that he might bring us to God." (1 Pet. 3:18)
>
> "For even the Son of Man did not come to be served, but to serve, and to give his life a ransom for many." (Mark 10:45)

Theologians can explain this much better than I, but I love the way the hymn writer puts it: "In my place condemned he stood, sealed my pardon with his blood, Hallelujah what a Savior!"

Well, I haven't shared anything new with you this morning—anything you haven't heard before. There has been no unique insight into something hidden for two thousand years. But if this were the last sermon I would ever preach, I would want to share with you "the old, old story of Jesus and his love." I would want to share with you the glorious gospel that has once and for all time been delivered to the world. Our text is very well known, but please don't let its familiarity blind you to the wonder of its message. Well-known texts of the Bible are usually well known because they contain great and important biblical truths.

Our text tells us, first of all, about our awful and desperate situation:

1. We are the kind of people for whom only the death of the Son of God could bring forgiveness and eternal life.
2. God loves the whole world, and he has demonstrated once and for all time that he loves us in this manner: he sent his Son to die on our behalf.
3. Jesus, God's Son, by his death on the cross, brought eternal life for all who believe and trust in him.

Listen once again to our wonderful text: "For God so loved the world, that he gave his only begotten Son, that whoever believes in him shall not perish, but have eternal life."—Robert H. Stein

SUNDAY, JANUARY 8, 2006
Lectionary Message

Topic: Seeking and Finding
TEXT: Matt. 2:1–12
Other Readings: Isa. 60:1–6; Ps. 72:1–7, 10–14; Eph. 3:1–12

Fourteen days ago we celebrated the birth of Jesus. We call it Christmas. By now most of the visible signs of this celebration have been taken down and stored until November or December of this year.

The Wise Men saw a visible part of Christmas—the star in the East that guided them in the search for Jesus. But they wanted more! They asked, "Where is he?" They wanted to experience this person God had sent into the world.

So many who believe in the Christmas event do not understand that what they so often see in the nativity scene is not accurate. The Wise Men were not present on the night Christ was born. Matthew 2:1 says, "In the time of King Herod, after Jesus was born in Bethlehem of Judea, wise men from the East came to Jerusalem."

In December we experienced various parts of the outside of Christmas. We heard it in church, watched it on television, listened to it on the radio. We saw it in the faces of children, the lights surrounding us, the gifts with the bright wrappings, the special messages on greeting cards, the beauty of sanctuaries with Advent reminders, and many other creative expressions of Christmas.

But there is more to experiencing the celebration of the birth of Christ than these outside expressions. The heart of celebrating Christmas is Christ himself. To experience his presence, to worship him, to exchange our love with him—this is what the Wise Men were seeking—and found. They worshiped him and presented their gifts to him.

These men had been preparing for this encounter for a long time, but there is a contrast between the shepherds and the Wise Men. They all were following God's leadership; however, one group followed in simple faith and found Christ on the night of his birth. The Wise Men found Christ after his birth, following a long search.

How can a person in this era of history find Christ in the manner of the Wise Men? Christmas is over, and a whole year of opportunities is ahead. Wise persons today will seek to know the truth by actively seeking God's will in their lives. And wise persons will spend a significant amount of time alone with God. Contemplation is a difficult task for most of us. We are so often caught up in the hustle and bustle of everyday life that we do not stop and acknowledge God.

How will you know that something spiritual is happening in your life? You will experience forgiveness of sins, peace in the midst of chaos, strength for the day, and hope for tomorrow. God wants to bless you with many hours and days in this New Year. It is left to you whether you will allow God to bless you.

Here is a very inspiring and challenging statement.

One Solitary Life
He was born in an obscure village, the child of a peasant woman.
He grew up in another village, where he worked in a carpenter shop until he was thirty.
Then for three years he was an itinerant preacher.
He never wrote a book.
He never held an office.
He never traveled more than two hundred miles from the place he was born.
He did none of the things one usually associates with greatness.
He was only thirty-three when the tide of public opinion turned against him.
He was turned over to his enemies and went through the mockery of a trial.
He was nailed to a cross between two thieves.
When he was dead, he was laid in a borrowed grave.
Nineteen centuries have come and gone, and today he is the central figure of the human race and the leader of mankind's progress.
All the armies that ever marched,
All the navies that ever sailed,
All the kings that ever reigned
Have not affected the life of man as much as that
One Solitary Life.[3]

The Wise Men found this "One Solitary Life!" They were guided by God back to their homes via a different route than they had come. Will you be wise and let God guide you this year?—William Cubine

SERMON SUGGESTIONS

Topic: Ideal Virtues of a Nation's Leader
TEXT: Ps. 72
(1) Justice for all. (2) Care for the poor, needy, and oppressed. (3) Inspiration of international cooperation. (4) A true representative of God.

Topic: God's "Therefore"
TEXT: Exod. 20:1–17
(1) God's grace toward us (v. 1). (2) Our response of faith, love, and obedience (vv. 2–17).

---

[3]Author unknown.

WORSHIP AIDS

CALL TO WORSHIP.   "From the rising of the sun to its setting my name is great among the nations" (Mal. 1:11 RSV).

INVOCATION.   Merciful God, we pause amid the rush and haste of the day to sing praises unto our God, to pray and wait. Surprise us in the waiting and lead us in the praying to commit ourselves anew to the Christ of Calvary.—E. Lee Phillips

OFFERTORY SENTENCE.   "Give unto the Lord the glory due unto his name: bring an offering and come before him: worship the Lord in the beauty of holiness" (1 Chron. 16:29).

OFFERTORY PRAYER.   O Giver of all, may *our* giving be gracious—not out of any sense of compulsion but in joyous response to the fullness of your grace in Christ. In whose name *we* give and live.—John Thompson

PRAYER.   Father, every one of us here has received the wonder of your grace. Not one has been without some indication of your favor, and each of us has been granted at least one talent to use as we choose. Grant us this morning the wisdom to use our talents well and for your purpose and glory.

How thankful we are that no one has been left empty-handed in life. We come this morning thankful for one another's gift. Thank you for the one who can teach our children, for the one who has the gift of easy friendship, for the one who can make money and consecrate it to good causes. We thank you for public leaders who can administer the affairs of the community for the public good. We thank you for the ones who manage the machinery we use, who repair it and understand its technological mysteries. We thank you for the ones who clean our homes and communities and make of them splendid places. We thank you for those who can pray deeply, those who can sing joyfully and with great meaning, those who can inspire us to be active in doing good. We thank you for the way in which our gifts supplement another's, helping us to know that we are members of one another. We are deeply grateful that in exercising our talents, we can give glory to you and make this world a brighter, better, and happier world for all people everywhere.

We cannot come to you this morning, Father, without bringing those whose lives feel useless to them because of loss and sickness and inability to function fully day by day. Give them a sense of purpose, even in their present dilemmas, and restore them to joy, we pray. We all come today aware that our sins and failures have hindered the coming of your Kingdom to another. Let forgiveness be real to us, as we commit ourselves, as we are, to your care and keeping, and send us from this hour with purpose and joy because we have gathered here for a brief moment in Jesus' name.—Henry Fields

SERMON

Topic: The Faith That Can Change the World

TEXT: Rom. 1:14–17

Karl Marx once said, "Philosophers have only interpreted the world differently; the point is, however, to change it."

We live in a world today that desperately needs to be changed. All around us we see the stark evidence of a world gone bad: school shootings, kidnappings, terrorism, and rampant immorality. Things don't look much better in the Church: attendance is down, divorce is up, and the number of unevangelized people in the world hovers near 1.7 billion.

Given these circumstances many people are asking themselves, "Where is God?" The question that should be asked is, "Where are God's people?"

What we need, to quote the U.S. Marine Corps, is "A Few Good Men (and women)." We need people like the apostle Paul. We need Christians with a world-changing faith.

Having given his salutation to the Christians in Rome in verses 1 through 8, Paul explains his desire to visit the imperial capital in verses 9 through 13. Then, beginning in verse 14 and running through verse 17, Paul finishes his introduction to the book of Romans by explaining his heartfelt desire to bring the gospel to Rome.

I. *Model for world-changing faith.* It is here, in Paul's description of his motives, that we see modeled a Christian with a world-changing faith. And it is this model that we must follow if we want to have an impact on the world in which we live.

(a) *Share your faith.* As we look to verse 14, we can sense Paul's overwhelming desire to share his faith. In fact, he speaks of this as an "obligation." Such an obligation could be described as being two-fold. First, Paul understood that his obligation was to God as a result of his salvation and his appointment as apostle. Already in verse 1, Paul has said that he is "a bond-servant of Christ Jesus" who has been "set apart for the gospel of God." Paul clearly understood the Great Commission of Matthew 28:18–20 to be a Great Commandment (see also Eph. 3:8; 1 Cor 9:16–17).

(b) *Share your faith with everyone.* The second obligation to which Paul felt bound was the one he mentions in verse 14. Here Paul writes that he is obligated to "Greeks and to barbarians," "to the wise and to the foolish"; that is, Paul, entrusted with the gospel itself, is obliged to take it to all Gentiles, regardless of race or social level. Paul echoes this thought in Romans 12:10, where he writes, "For there is no distinction between Jew and Greek. . . ." Unfortunately, according to George Barna, only 32 percent of evangelical Christians share Paul's sense of obligation.

(c) *Share your faith willingly.* One must note, however, in verse 15 that this obligation was not fulfilled reluctantly. Rather, Paul says, "I am eager to preach the gospel." Fulfilling the Great Commission is not a burden but a joy for Christians with a world-changing faith. Jesus told the apostles, "If you love me, you will keep my commandments" (John 14:15). Thus fulfilling the Great Commission becomes a responsive act of love as well as obedience.

Underlying Paul's eagerness to preach to those "in Rome" is Jesus' exhortation in Acts 1:8 to "be my witnesses both in Jerusalem, and in all Judea and Samaria, and even to the remotest part of the earth." Such unbridled enthusiasm also reveals Paul's commitment to share his faith at all costs, even in the face of potential danger, both physical and emotional, whether by potential imprisonment or intellectual ridicule. As he would later write, "To live in Christ and to die is gain" (Phil. 1:21).

(d) *Share your faith willingly because there is no other way to be saved.* Paul then boldly states that he is "not ashamed of the gospel" (1:16). Paul could confidently proclaim that he was not ashamed of the gospel because he understood that, apart from the gospel, there is no hope of salvation. As Paul goes on to state in verse 16, "it is the power of God for salvation to everyone who believes."

How different an attitude this is from the multitudes of professing Christians who sit in our pews week after week, yet never share their faith. Again, according to pollster George Barna, only 40 percent of professing Baptists share their faith in any given year. Many reasons could be proffered for such a dismal level of obedience to the clear command of Christ (Matt. 28:18–20; Acts 1:8). One such reason, revealed in surveys, is that many Christians simply do not understand the nature and content of the gospel message itself.

II. *The gospel's message.* At this point the preacher would do well to briefly explain the gospel. From our text we see three crucial elements to its message: (1) it is the work of God; (2) it leads to salvation; (3) it requires faith.

First, the gospel is "the *power of God* for salvation to everyone who believes"; that is, it is the work of God. All humanity desperately needs spiritual help (Rom. 3:23). Yet Paul writes that no one seeks it (Rom. 3:10–18). Many texts could be cited to document God's mighty role in salvation, but two familiar verses go a long way toward explaining it. John 3:16 speaks of God's loving motivation, while Ephesians 2:8 tells of his gracious work in our lives.

Second, we recognize that the gospel leads to "*salvation* [for] everyone who believes." Salvation, like so many other subjects in theology, can be spoken of in an already-not-yet fashion. Those who believe are saved from the sins of their past (Rom. 6:23). They are saved from the power of sin in the present (Rom. 6:17–18), and they are saved for the future (1 John 3:2).

Third, it is apparent in this text that salvation is for everyone "*who believes.*" The kind of faith that Paul speaks of is more than mere knowledge or mental assent to the facts of Christ's life. The demons possess such knowledge, yet they will not be spared God's wrath (James 2:19; 1 Pet. 2:4). Paul calls for the kind of belief that results in trusting God to do what man cannot. One must "confess . . . Jesus as Lord" and "believe that God raised him from the dead" (Rom. 10:9–10). That kind of faith only comes from the Lord (Eph. 2:8). And it is that kind of faith that is absolutely necessary, for "whoever will call on the name of the Lord will be saved" (Rom. 10:13).

There is no doubt that our world needs changing. The answer cannot be found in deprivation or legislation but in evangelization. Evangelist D. L. Moody said, "The gospel is like a lion—just open the door and get out of the way."

Are you standing in the way of the gospel, or do you have a world-changing faith?—Peter Beck

SUNDAY, JANUARY 15, 2006
Lectionary Message

Topic: Follow Me
TEXT: John 1:43–51
Other Readings: 1 Sam. 3:1–10; Ps. 139:1–6, 13–18; 1 Cor. 6:12–20

A large automobile assembly plant announced it was closing in ten days. Immediately, the workers and community raised the question, Why? The chair of the board explained that the full workforce was only producing five automobiles a day. No company could stay in business with this production level. No wonder the community was so concerned after receiving those facts.

But how many churches are concerned with the low number of individuals coming to Christ through their efforts? After all, isn't gaining new converts one of the main functions of a church? I do not believe in production-line evangelism or any other method that leaves out the work of the Holy Spirit.

To know about Jesus is not enough. Salvation does not come until we have a personal relationship with Christ—until we know him. God loves the world and is constantly seeking to relate himself redemptively to all people. When we personally walk with Christ, there will be the challenge to share our saving experience with others. It is both a privilege and a responsibility to tell others about the grace of God in Christ. Jesus said, "As the Father has sent me, even so I send you" (John 20:21).

At the beginning of this message, I want you to ask yourself several questions:

1. *Do you fully understand what it means to have a personal relationship with Christ?* Jesus said, "Those who love me will keep my word, and my Father will love them, and we will come to them and make our home with them" (John 14:23).
2. *Is Christ your friend?* "I do not call you servant any longer, because the servant does not know what the master is doing, but I have called you friend, because I have made known to you everything that I have heard from my Father" (John 15:15).
3. *Do you want to share your walk with Christ?* Both Peter and John answered them, "Whether it is right in God's sight to listen to you rather than God, you must judge for we cannot keep from speaking about what we have seen and heard" (Acts 4:19–20).

Philip was one of the group of witnesses for Christ. He was the one who found Nathanael and told him about Jesus. The name Nathanael means "God has given" and is not found in the first three Gospels. This person in John's Gospel may have been the Bartholomew of Matthew, Mark, and Luke. His reply to Philip was not a warm response. Philip did not debate Nathanael but said, "Come and see." Jesus does not need to be defended, but shared with others.

The first recorded activity of Jesus in Galilee was the calling of Philip and Nathanael. Philip, Andrew, and Peter were from Bethsaida, which was located in Lake Galilee. When Jesus was enlisting these four men, he did not give them any outrageous claims about himself. He simply said, "Come and see." He wanted them to be willing followers who responded by their own choice.

Jesus was not one who avoided giving positive affirmations. He knew some of the strong traits of Nathanael and did not hesitate to verbalize them. We, too, should be aware that those we seek to help in their spiritual journey have good characteristics, as well as weak ones.

Jesus was an individual who had insight into people's lives. He saw that Simon was a strong potential servant if he submitted to the power and leadership of God in his life. When he observed Nathanael, he saw this man's character and religious devotion. Jesus said of Nathanael, "Behold, an Israelite indeed, in whom is no guile" (John 1:47). Jesus also saw in him that he was a student of the Scriptures and one who had prayerful habits. He showed that he was an open person who was willing to change his mind in the light of evidence. He said in faith, "Rabbi, you are the Son of God! You are the King of Israel!" (John 1:49). It is in Jesus that God seeks man, and in Jesus man finds God.

We see that men who came to Jesus understood and accepted his call to devotion and commitment, responded to his leadership, and went forth to give witness to Christ. Christ still calls individuals—men and women, young and old—to follow him. We must first make him Lord in our lives, and then we can become worthy to go and tell others about Christ. He does not want individuals to *talk* about him but not be willing to *live* him. The key factor for witnessing comes from the Christian's personal relationship with Christ as Savior and Lord.

Will you come and see what Christ has done for us? What he will do for you? Then go and follow the Light of Christ!—William Cubine

SERMON SUGGESTIONS

Topic: Can You Believe It?
TEXT: Ps. 139:1–6, 13–18
(1) God knows all about us as we are. (2) God is working out an eternal plan for us, in spite of the things we have done and what we are.

Topic: What It Means to Be Holy—Today
TEXT: Lev. 19:36b
(1) *Holiness* defined. (2) Holiness exemplified in changed and changing circumstances. (3) Holiness motivated.

WORSHIP AIDS

CALL TO WORSHIP.   "I was glad when they said unto me, Let us go into the house of the Lord" (Ps. 122:1).

INVOCATION.   Gracious Lord, may the joy of our gathering together in your name not only lift us toward you but also spill over into the lives of those about us every day.

OFFERTORY SENTENCE.   And he said to them all, "If any man will come after me, let him deny himself, and take up his cross daily, and follow me" (Luke 9:23).

OFFERTORY PRAYER.   Lord, let the gifts of our hands reflect the dedication of our hearts for the sake of Christ and his Kingdom.—E. Lee Phillips

PRAYER.   Father, this morning we come to you troubled by events that stir around us. We cannot understand them completely, for the causes and reasons for them are deeper than we can see. But we do know that many lives are disrupted by man's inhumanity to man. We do know that injustice and a lack of understanding as to what is just creates a dangerous climate that readily explodes with violence. And we do know that innocent people are forever being hurt or killed and that the burden of the pain rests on those who would change matters, were they able.

This morning we pray that you will send your Light on these troublesome times. Remind us anew that we are brothers and sisters together in this family of life. Remind us again that we have a responsibility for each other that goes beyond the physical concerns of life. Remind us that we are our brothers' keeper and must shoulder that responsibility and insist that it be carried out by people at every level of life. How we need to be taught anew that we are to love one another, even as Christ has loved us! Somehow this morning, make these more than words that we have heard until familiarity has worn them thin. Make them the sum and substance of our reason for reaching out to one another in our times of need.

And as we reach out, deliver us from being selective and exclusive. Make us aware that Christ died for all mankind and that we, who are his people, must live to serve all mankind. Close our eyes to economic difference, social difference, class difference, and color difference, and open our eyes to need in every life and heart that we meet. Then grant us the courage to be busy about your business everywhere we are.

Focus our eyes on the wonder of life that lasts forever, we pray. Keep us aware that so much that is disruptive is passing; it does not come to stay. But may we never forget that some values are eternal and must claim us above all else. This morning make us into good soldiers of the cross. May we not cringe from duty. May we not surrender to temptations to take the easy way when life becomes difficult. May we look ever to Jesus, the author and finisher of our faith, for strength and direction as we seek to do his will in all things among all people, we pray in his most Holy Name.—Henry Fields

SERMON

Topic: God Is Great; God Is Good

TEXT: Job 42:1–9

I. The child's prayer, "God is great; God is good," is the most basic and most profound statement that we can make about God. The child's prayer is also the philosopher's question. Following clear logic and the abundant evidence of human suffering, E. S. Brightman was among a class of philosophers who declared that you can't have it both ways. God cannot be both great and good, all-powerful and all-loving. Either God is able to relieve human suffering but does not care, or God cares but is not able. Given the choice, Brightman concluded that God must be limited in power and knowledge.

Rabbi Kushner concludes: "God can't do everything." In *When Bad Things Happen to Good People,* the chapter on God's limits focuses on the teachings of the Talmud about improper prayers—the sort of things we should not ask of God, like changing the rules of nature or doing for us what we are capable of doing for ourselves.

J. B.—a "play in verse" by Archibald MacLeish—is a modern setting of the book of Job; it is somewhat cynical and irreverent. The setting is a dark corner of a circus tent, a sideshow stage. There are times when most of us see life as a three-ring circus. The roles of God and Satan are played by Mr. Zuss and Nickles—two circus vendors—and sometimes the roles seem reversed. After the scene introducing J. B., Mr. Zuss offers a satanic quip: "Well, that's our pigeon."

Zuss observes that someone is always playing Job in the world. Nickles seems almost compassionate in his response: "Millions and millions of mankind burned, crushed, broken, mutilated, slaughtered, and for what? For thinking! For walking round the world in the wrong skin, the wrong-shaped noses, eyelids: Sleeping the wrong night wrong city—London, Dresden,

Hiroshima." Nickles then chants the little jingle that defines the conflict, the dilemma of a sleepless humanity: "If God is God he is not good, If God is good he is not God."

Job is more than a solitary figure. Job is everyone, a multitude. Although Job is personal and often appears to be like a reflection in our own mirror, he is also global.

J. B. was first produced in New York in 1958. The world was still emerging from World War II. The full impact of the Jewish Holocaust was sinking in, and the U.S. civil rights movement was under way. No one really mistook the uneasy truce in Korea for world peace. The cold war and the nuclear arms race were on, and another war in Southeast Asia was about to start up. The hard realities of history raised serious questions about the evolutionary moral progress of the world.

II. Every corner of the globe and every age are involved in meaningless, futile suffering. Our question today is whether we can pray, with the children, "God is great; God is good."

(a) *God is great.* I am sure that you have seen the TV commercial: the guy is watching a football game on videotape that has come down to a deciding field goal. The ball is placed and kicked in the air on the way to the goalposts. Suddenly, he pauses the action, runs out of the house, drives to the church, kneels at the altar and prays, makes the sign of the cross, then drives back home to hit the "play" button. The ball goes through the uprights, the game is won, and a celebration ensues.

I confess to getting a chuckle out of the scene, and I have asked myself why I am not offended with the ridiculous and sacrilegious picture of prayer. The whole picture is less about prayer than it is about the way technology has changed our ways of thinking—even about prayer. I have watched ball games on videotape. However, I never recall praying for a change in the outcome of an event that has already been concluded. That is ridiculous. In fact, I do not recall praying for God to change the course of a live ball game. I do not wish to be sacrilegious here, but I doubt that God has a favorite in the Superbowl.

Why then do I pray for and with people who are dealing with cancer and plead with God to change the course of the disease? I assume something about the loving nature of God. I believe that God cares about human suffering. God cares that we are dust. I cannot really separate the goodness from the greatness of God. I have been Job. I have sat with Job in the ashes, and I have prayed with Job, and I have sometimes felt, with Job, abandoned to fate by a god who either does not care or cannot help. "If God is God," I assume that God is in control of the universe and the primary cause of all events. Because I believe that God is God, I pray for change in the course of events that I perceive to be in contradiction to the nature of God.

I believe that God is Lord of nature, but I have had to adjust my expectations. I do not attribute everything that happens in the world to God. We have learned from Jesus to pray, "Our Father." The role of father means something to me. There was a time with my children when it seemed that I was the Lord, able to do all things. They looked to me for the basic necessities of life and sometimes assumed that I could do far more than I was able. How often and how painfully I had to say, "No, we cannot afford that," or "No, I do not believe you need that." Sometimes I had to say, "I can't fix it. It is broken beyond repair. We will have to do without." The Fatherhood of God is a metaphor, an image of God. Certainly, God is not limited as I am limited, yet I do believe that the same kind of exchange goes on between the Father and the children of God. We have a child's-eye view of the world.

(b) *God is good.* The final chapter of Job may be a disconnected addition to the story—a fairytale ending where "they all lived happily ever after." I see an essential correction to the course of faith. This story began with a capricious deity making deals in heaven with the Satan to test Job, as one would kick the tires on a used car. The God we meet in the whirlwind is the God of Creation, who transcends all human understanding, including the crass picture of God in the first two chapters. Finally, it seems that Job bows before the revelation of God and acknowledges that God is great, but translators are not sure whether he resigns to mortality or repents to being dust-defiant to the end.

We almost get a fat rewind to the beginning in the final restoration of Job's wealth, health, and family. Something inside of me wants to stop the action and yell, "Foul!" This is inconsistent with reality. I know too many Jobs who have lost everything and never recovered. I have seen a few people recover from bankruptcy and from cancer, but I have never seen anyone replace dead children. It is absurd, almost like saying to someone whose child has died, "It's OK. You can get another one." Our families are not like ice-cream cones that can be replaced when we drop them on the sidewalk.

In the end, God blesses Job's challenge to the crass idea that God is playing games with humanity. God blesses the angry cries of the tormented soul who believes in justice and mercy. God vindicates Job's questioning faith, and Job sees better days. It is interesting that the friends are sent off to make amends for their wrong-headed ideas about Job and about God. The end is the ultimate. We live toward final things—eschatology.

The man in agony in the garden of Gethsemane prays, "Abba Father, for you all things are possible; remove this cup from me; yet, not what I want, but what you want" (Mark 14:36); then he goes out to face the cross. There he cries out with Job to God, "Why have you abandoned me?"

Jesus knew the goodness of God. If God is not good, God cannot be great. The jingle of Nickles is cute but not quite right. If God is God, God must be good. The greatness and the goodness of God are inseparable. Whatever else I might question or wonder about God, I believe that God is love.—Larry Dipboye

SUNDAY, JANUARY 22, 2006

Lectionary Message

Topic: A Universal Requirement of God

Text: Mark 1:14–20

Other Readings: Jon. 3:1–5, 10; Ps. 62:5–12; 1 Cor. 7:29–31

A student takes a test in a history class and scores a failing grade. The student takes the test home and says to his parents, "I am sorry! I am sorry I failed the test." For the parent to believe that the student is really sorry, he must make a change in his study habits and be better prepared for the next test.

For many, the concept of repentance just means being sorry. The Greek word for repentance is *metanoia,* which means a change of mind or direction. The word *repentance* is used at least seventy times in the New Testament and was part of the message of Christ when he began his public ministry.

In some interpretations, repentance is not based on biblical theology; it is not remorse or feeling sorry about our sins. Judas was probably remorseful for his betrayal of Jesus, but it did not lead him to a right relationship with God. And it is not self-condemnation and hate for self. We can dislike some of our actions, but it does not mean we will change. It is not penance when we voluntarily suffer as punishment for our sins and does not necessarily carry with it a change in character or conduct.

In our society today, individuals are using a multitude of excuses for their mistakes and are not willing to accept responsibility. But Jesus gave a command to repent in order to have a right relationship with God.

There are clearly some elements in repentance we need to understand if there is to be a change in the direction of our lives. We must have a sense of conviction about what is right and what is wrong. If repentance is changing direction, then we need to understand what we are deliberately rejecting and replacing in our lives. One of the works of the Holy Spirit is to convict us of sin. It is a time of reminding us that we are on the wrong path.

Paul states in 2 Corinthians 7:10, "For godly grief produces a repentance that leads to salvation and brings no regret." Contrition or grief for having sinned is very important. Some have referred to this feeling as godly sorrow. It is not a superficial emotion. It is a time when one is totally broken and weeps from the inside out for the wrongdoing in his or her life.

Along with conviction, contrition means a change in ideas. The mind, attitude, and way of life make an about-face; there is a 180-degree turn in a person's life. It becomes evident to others that Christ is now in control.

We see all around us individuals who do not wish to accept responsibility for their actions. They want to blame their parents, church, school, society, and anyone else or anything for the mistakes they make.

When repentance takes place in people's lives, it becomes an intellectual experience. They admit that they have done wrong and want to correct their way of life and the hurt to others they have caused. There is emotion to repentance. Remorse and sorrow are real experiences when repentance occurs. The will is part of the repentance experience: we must willingly decide to change our way of living.

John the Baptist's preaching called for repentance, and he promised forgiveness of sins to those who repented. It still implies today, as it did then, a change of mind and a turning from evil. It means a change of allegiance and an inner turning around. God is made King of our life. Repentance will inspire outward change of conduct; it is the process of turning from sin and turning to God in faith.

The New Testament sets forth repentance and faith as the conditions of salvation. True repentance and saving faith are inseparable. The New Testament refers sometimes only to repentance (Acts 2:38, 17:30) and sometimes only to faith (Acts 16:30–31; Eph. 2:8–9), but the emphasis on one always assumes the other. Paul followed Jesus when he proclaimed "repentance toward God and faith toward our Lord Jesus Christ" (Acts 20:21).

John not only said to repent but to believe the good news. What is the "good news?" It is the good news of hope (Col. 1:23), the good news of peace (Eph. 6:15), the good news of truth (Gal. 2:5), the good news of immortality (2 Tim. 1:10), the good news of God's promise (Eph. 3:6), and the good news of salvation (Eph. 1:13).

It is time to turn and learn what great things God has for you!—William Cubine

ILLUSTRATIONS

A modern analogy may capture some (not all) dimensions of the preaching of Jesus. In a crowded airline terminal, hundreds of persons are scurrying in dozens of directions. Above the steady buzz of noise, a voice booms through a loudspeaker, "Flight 362 is now arriving at gate 23. Will passengers holding tickets for New York please check in at gate 23; you will be boarding soon." Some people, of course, never hear the announcement and continue on their way. Others hear it but, having reservations on another flight, pay no attention. Some, however, who want to go to New York and who have been nervously awaiting such an announcement, look up expectantly, check their ticket for the flight number, gather their baggage, turn around and set out with some urgency for gate 23.—Lamar Williamson Jr.[4]

One of my most moving pastoral experiences came when a young man lay dying in a suburban Maryland hospital. On his last day on Earth, with life ebbing away, his mother was with him for support. She was a longtime member of a fundamentalist church in another state. Her pastor there was harsh in his judgment of her son. I am not aware that she felt the full effect of her church's moralistic theology, but it did not matter. Hour after hour, she sat by her son's bedside, cradling his head in her arms, bathing his fevered forehead with a cool cloth, speaking quietly and tenderly. I do not know that I have witnessed as pure an expression of the grace of God as I did in that hospital room. And it was also a needed reminder that there are times when it is possible for people to rise above their narrow theological principles into the realm of God's grace. She was certainly an inspiration to me.—J. Philip Wogaman[5]

SERMON SUGGESTIONS

Topic: Getting Along with God

TEXT: Ps. 62:5–12

(1) By recognizing that God is in control (vv. 6–7). (2) By staying in touch with God (v. 8). (3) By considering the consequences of wrongdoing (vv. 9–10). (4) By trusting God to reward a life of obedience and service (vv. 11–12).

Topic: In the Wilderness

TEXT: Num. 21:5–9

(1) Our inevitable trials and complaints. (2) God's unfailing proffered mercies. (3) God's special resolution of our basic need (John 3:14–15).

WORSHIP AIDS

CALL TO WORSHIP.   "Know therefore that the Lord thy God, he is God, the faithful God, which keepeth covenant and mercy with them that love him and keep his commandments to a thousand generations" (Deut. 7:9).

---

[4]*Mark* (Atlanta: John Knox Press, 1983), p. 43.
[5]*An Unexpected Journey* (Louisville, Ky.: Westminster John Knox Press, 2002), pp. 58–59.

INVOCATION.   Almighty God, whom to know is to love and to love is to serve, we come before you to be met by you in this sacred hour. Stir our souls here this morning so that our voices will sing your praise. Open our minds to truth that we may be able to ponder your precepts. Claim our wills so that in us your will shall be done as we are led by the Holy Spirit through the love of Christ, even as were those first followers who learned from him to pray: [repeat the Lord's Prayer].—Henry Fields

OFFERTORY SENTENCE.   "God is able to make all grace abound toward you; that ye, always having all sufficiency in all things, may abound to every good work" (2 Cor. 9:8).

OFFERTORY PRAYER.   Thank you, Father, that we are all in the ministry of serving Christ together. Remind us that our giving of tithes and offerings is one vital way to serve others in his name. Lead us to be generous as we give that missions may be done, ministries funded, your house of worship sustained, and the gospel proclaimed everywhere. We pray in Jesus' name.—Henry Fields

PRAYER.   In the glory of this beautiful Sunday morning we come to you, Father, to worship in your presence. With us we bring a lot of baggage that we hope to leave in the back room of your care where forgiveness and restoration are managed. We also bring with us our hope and dreams of doing life better, praying that they might find fulfillment through your grace and power.

Then there are the things we need to confront in life, which only you can reveal clearly to us. So we ask that you open our eyes to truth as we gather before you today. Open our minds to reality as we ponder long thoughts of your ways. Open our hearts to receive the wonder of your presence and love.

Forgive us for our limited vision, when we could see a broader and longer view so easily. Forgive us for being earthbound, when you have called us to live amid the very heavens of eternity. Forgive us for the narrow boundaries we set for ourselves and others, when we have the broadness of your eternal creative presence in which to live. Forgive us for our failure to heed your revelation, given through your Word. Forgive us, Father, for our insistence that we be the center of Creation, when we are intended to focus on you as Maker and Giver of all things.

Now in these moments speak to our hearts, we pray. Call us to higher life and make us your own, we plead in Jesus' name.—Henry Fields

SERMON
Topic: Rich in America
TEXT: Luke 12:48b

A retired maintenance worker won the $270,000,000 lottery this week. I do not play the lottery, but like many of you I have often dreamed of what I would do if I hit the jackpot—won a multi-million-dollar lottery. I would certainly pay off *all* my bills and some of my family's bills. I would buy my mother a house, and I would certainly travel. I would travel a lot. But after I had bought some toys and had a lot of fun, I would devote myself—my time and my new-found wealth to making a difference in this world.

I. I want you to consider this morning that all of us sitting in this room have won the lottery. It may not seem that way, but it is certainly true. There are six billion people on this earth, and three billion of them have never made or received a phone call. If your household earns $50,000 a year, you are in the top 5 percent of all wage earners in America and in the top .5 percent of all wage earners in the world. The truth is, being born in America and having an education and having a profession, as most of us do, makes us winners in the lottery of life.

And I wonder what God would say to those of us who sit in this room, having won the lottery of life, and call ourselves serious followers of Christ.

I may be making you feel uncomfortable. We don't like being called rich, because most of us don't feel rich. Some of us don't want to think about our money. Or maybe you have sat under so many preachers who have condemned you and made you feel guilty for working, progressing, earning money, and living in a capitalistic system. Yes, I have sat there, too.

II. I have a different approach. First, I want to talk about what God would say to the rich here in America and to the rich sitting right here in this room.

(a) *Growth is the natural order.* The first thing that God would say to you and me is that growth is the natural order of life and that growth is good. I do not know why, but God has not put one thing into this world in full bloom. First, there is a seed, then a blade, then a flower. First, there is a newborn, then a child, then a teenager, then an adult, then an older adult. By simply observing nature we can see this principle in place. There is a natural order of this world, and growth is that natural order.

And God would say to us that growth is good. The desire you have to get better, to do more than you have done, to be in a job that makes a difference and, yes, to have more tomorrow than you have today and to pass on to your children more than you had is good. It is God-given.

There should be no stopping your growth. The question we need to ask is, How high will a tree grow? The answer: As far as possible.

We also should grow as far as possible, in all areas of our lives—professionally, educationally, in travel, experiences, and yes, financially. But let us not stop there.

(b) God would also be careful to remind us, "What does it profit you if you gain the entire world and lose your own soul?" The answer: it does not profit you at all. So let's make sure that we grow in more than in work and money. Let us also grow where it really matters; let us grow in the things that will be eternal; let us grow in love, in compassion, in our relationship with God, and in doing good work.

The message of the Bible from the story of David and Solomon to the stories of Jesus and the disciples is that God is more interested in who you are, where you are going, and your being in relationship with him. Who you are as a person of love is important. Who you are in relationship with Jesus Christ is important. God loves you and wants to see your spiritual growth be more important than your physical growth.

(c) The Jewish people have a philosophy that we must "be about repairing the earth." We should do things that help people grow, help the planet heal, and help the poor improve. Many of us do this in our jobs as nurses, doctors, and teachers. Many of us do this with our wealth, by giving to organizations that make a difference.

I want to suggest that we can be about repairing the Earth with a little more intention. Our growth as individuals and as spiritual people is not just for growth's sake. It has a purpose.

We can bring the Kingdom of God here on Earth by making sure that we pass along the knowledge that we have gained. We can use our volunteer hours to make a difference and not just to pass time. We can make sure that every dime we give goes to helping people. We can slowly shape our actions by asking the question, Will this help to repair the Earth?

Many people look at the rich of our country and condemn them (us) at every turn. They put us down for having a job, for growing, and for our talents and abilities. If you are rich, it does not mean that God does not love you. And it is not true that God loves poor people more than rich. Our wealth is not our sin. It is a responsibility that we have to honor God with our wealth, to be about repairing the Earth, and to remember that nothing is more important than our relationship with God.—Conway Stone

SUNDAY, JANUARY 29, 2006
Lectionary Message

Topic: Don't Be a Stumbling Block
TEXT: 1 Cor. 8:1–13
Other Readings: Deut. 18:15–20; Ps. 111; Mark 1:21–28

"I really don't care what others think about me!" Many individuals today have this philosophy of life, but it is not the attitude of a Christian who wants to be a positive witness for Christ.

Paul faced a problem with the new Christians in Corinth over the matter of eating meat that had been offered to idols. The offering of animal sacrifices was common and an essential part of pagan worship. Most of the time, the priest would use only a small portion in the ritual, and the remainder of the meat was used in various ways. Some was sold in the marketplace and some at the temple feast to the general public. Paul deals more at length with this issue in 2 Corinthian 8–10. It was not a trivial matter in that day.

Paul stated some principles that will be a guide for the Christian. These pronouncements concerning what is right and wrong on gray questions of our behavior are still relevant for the Christian in our present society.

I. *The Corinthians were very proud of their knowledge and wisdom.* Paul says in verse 2, "Knowledge makes arrogance, but love edifies." Persons who think they know it all may be the ones who are really ignorant. Individuals who are truly brilliant are the least conscious of their learning.

Love is the most important essential of life, not knowledge. "But anyone who loves God is known by him" (v. 3). Paul makes it clear that there is only one God—the source and center of life and one Lord Jesus Christ as the Savior of the world. Without him, nothing was made.

Some Christians were not in any way affected by eating meat sacrificed to idols. But others, because of their ancestry, upbringing, and religious teachings, could not accept this connection to idols. Even today there are Christians who want to hold on to tradition rather than rethink new ideas.

Paul states in verse 8: "Food will not bring us close to God. We are no worse off if we do not eat, and no better off if we do." It was not a moral issue. However, Paul says that they should consider how their actions would influence others. They were told not to cause a weaker Christian or seeker to stumble. Paul was aware that a sin against another Christian was a sin against Christ.

Paul has a very simple and clear solution to the problem. "Therefore, if food is a cause of their failing, I will never eat meat, so that I may not cause one of them to fail." The principle of love is greater than the principle of knowledge. Christians may have to sacrifice things that are not wrong in themselves so that others will not develop a perception that harms our witness.

Paul writes a clear statement concerning how we can live an effective Christian life before others. In Romans 12:1 he says, "I appeal to you therefore, brothers and sisters, by the mercies of God, to present your bodies as a living sacrifice, holy and acceptable to God, which is your spiritual worship." Christianity has not failed, but we who claim the name of Christ have failed because we are not willing to sacrifice to share the Light of Christ.

II. You may be asking yourself, "How can I keep from being a stumbling block in someone's life?" It starts with your being honest about your relationship with God.

We all need to have, from time to time, a spiritually refreshing experience with Christ. I believe that we change when we put Christ in the center of our lives. When Christ is the center of our lives, we relate differently to our family, church, work, friends, enemies, and all other contacts we have daily. With Christ at the center and God the Holy Spirit guiding and empowering us, all things become possible.

We must reach out in love to those around us. This does not mean we compromise our convictions and ethics. We send the wrong message when we say one thing and then do another. Christ died for us that we might live for him. We need to look closely at all phases of life and ask what might be right for us but is a problem to others who are weak in the faith.

Give serious prayer to some of the following activities you may enjoy and are not bad in themselves, then pray for God's direction in your practice of them:

Participating in sports activities on Sunday
Shopping on Sunday
Doing yard and home repairs on Sunday

One test might be to ask yourself, "Would I want my minister to do what I am doing?"

It all comes down to how much you love God and what you feel is your spiritual responsibility as an extension of Christ here on earth.—William Cubine

ILLUSTRATIONS

One of the great church people in this hemisphere is Archbishop Helder Camara of Recife, Brazil. I once heard him say, with a broad smile and in a heavy accent: "Right hand, left hand—both belong to ze same body but ze heart is a little to ze left."

I tell you this story because I too believe that "ze heart is a little to ze left." You don't have to give socialist answers, but you do have to press socialist questions. These are the ones that point toward greater social justice.

In religious faith, simplicity comes in at least two distinct forms. One lies on the near side of complexity. Those of us who embrace this kind of simple faith dislike, in fact are frightened by, complexity. We hold certainty dearer than truth. We prefer obedience to discernment. Too many of us bear out Charles Darwin's contention that ignorance more frequently begets confidence than does knowledge. And apparently such religious folk were as abundant in Jesus' time as they clearly are in ours. Also in Jesus' time, as in ours, conventional religious wisdom stressed correct belief and right behavior.

Then there is the religious simplicity that lies on the far side of complexity. That's where, I believe, we must look for Jesus and his message. I believe that when all is said and done, when every subtle thing has been dissected and analyzed every which way, Jesus' message remains incredibly simple, unbelievably beautiful, and as easy to translate into action as for a camel to pass through the eye of a needle.—William Sloane Coffin[6]

I remember April 6, 1968. I was participating in an international "Theology of Hope" conference at Duke University when Harvey Cox stormed into the hall and cried, "Martin Luther King has been shot!" The conference ended immediately, and the participants returned home because many cities in America were burning that night. I left a few days later for Tübingen, and I promised my American friends that whenever I returned to their country, I would not speak about the theology of hope any more but of the cross:

> In a civilization that glorifies success and happiness and is blind for the suffering of others, people's eyes may be opened to the truth, if they remember that at the center of the Christian Faith stands the assailed, tormented Christ, dying in forsakenness. The recollection that God raised the Crucified one and made him the "Hope of the world" must lead churches to break their alliances with the violent and enter into solidarity with the humiliated.

—Jürgen Moltmann[7]

SERMON SUGGESTIONS

Topic: The Story of the Lord
TEXT: Ps. 111
(1) The story unfolds in power and grace from Genesis to Revelation (vv. 2–4). (2) The story touches life in God's care of his people: providing for everyday needs (v. 5); sustaining in crisis times (v. 6); clarifying his expectations (vv. 7–8); rewarding those who revere him and go his way (vv. 9–10).

Topic: The Way to Real Success
TEXT: Deut. 8:1–20
(1) *Then:* The story of Moses told of God's saving acts. (2) *Always:* Humanity's perennial problems with a loving, gracious God: forgetfulness; pride. (3) *Now:* Examples from the world, the nations, and individual experience; the remedy—remembering, obeying.

WORSHIP AIDS
CALL TO WORSHIP.   "For thus saith the high and lofty One that inhabiteth eternity, whose name is Holy; I dwell in the high and holy place, with him also that is of a contrite and humble spirit, to revive the spirit of the humble, and to revive the heart of the contrite ones" (Isa. 57:15).

---

[6]"The Politics of Compassion." In *Just Preaching: Prophetic Voices for Economic Justice* (St. Louis: Chalice Press, 2003), edited by André Resmer Jr. for Family Promise, p. 47.
[7]*Passion for God* (Louisville, Ky.: Westminster John Knox Press, 2003), pp. 71–72.

INVOCATION.   Lord, in the stillness we would know you are our God; in prayer we would commune with you; in worship we wait and are not the same. Amen.—E. Lee Phillips

OFFERTORY SENTENCE.   "Therefore, my beloved brethren, be ye steadfast, unmoveable, always abounding in the work of the Lord, forasmuch as ye know that your labor is not in vain in the Lord" (1 Cor. 15:58).

OFFERTORY PRAYER.   Now we give and now we share, O Lord, for now the hour of opportunity is wedded with the moment of need and the glad sharing of the saints.—E. Lee Phillips

PRAYER.   Almighty Father of us all, we thank thee for these associations and rejoicings and psalms of praise, and for this place of prayer. We rejoice that we are all understood here by one whose eye never faileth, whose pity is everlasting, and whose sympathy is as large as all the universe, dominated by the throne of our great Father, our God.

We are here this morning with so many needs, such intricate ways, such complex and serious problems that only the divine hand may touch our wound in safety; only the divine kindness that moves amidst many sicknesses with stillness; only a love that remembers our griefs and would not make them more agonizing; only the power to redeem that may save the lowliest—only this we ask for, the presence of thyself, O God, in Christ Jesus, our Lord.—Frank W. Gunsaulus

SERMON
Topic: Who Determines Who You Are?
TEXT: Matt. 3:17

In Charles Schulz's comic strip *Peanuts,* Charlie Brown is saying to Linus, "I can't talk to that little red-haired girl because she's *something* and I'm *nothing.*"

Whether it is a redhead, or a blonde, or a brunette, or something else entirely, there are forces at work in life that tend to intimidate us and keep us from being something—from being the something for which we have been created. But it is not only Charlie Brown who suffers from an identity crisis. Perhaps this comic strip has had such popularity because Charlie Brown is Charles Schulz's "Everyman."

Interviewing the singer Tom Jones, Dinah Shore mentions his wife and their long marriage. She asks, "Doesn't all your popularity among women 'rock' your wife?" Tom Jones answers, in effect, "No. It doesn't bother her. She does not get jealous. She enjoys *the security of knowing who she is.*" We all need the poise that comes from knowing who we are.

Who determines who you are?

No generation in recent times, or probably no generation in history, has been so tormented by the *identity question* as has our own. The way this nagging question has haunted modern man is illustrated in the story of a young soldier who was wounded and lost his memory. He did not remember who he was. One night he was presented at the boxing ring between bouts in hopes that someone would recognize him and identify him. Momentarily, there was silence, but then, almost in desperation, the soldier cries, "Will nobody tell me who I am?" Is this not the secret cry of thousands who do not know who they are and are not convinced that anyone really cares: "Will nobody tell me who I am?"

Who tells me who *I* am? Who determines who *you* are?

The answer to these questions is posed in the baptism and temptation experience of Jesus, as read in our New Testament lesson. These two incidents belong together. Too often they are considered separately.

Who determines who you are? I am convinced that the answer to this question is discovered in one's baptism—or should be. It was answered for Jesus in his baptism; there was the Voice from heaven saying, "You are my beloved son, in whom I am well pleased."

The answer to one's identity is present in the sacrament of baptism, whether one is brought to it by parents as an infant or whether, at a discretionary age, the person presents him- or herself for baptism. If baptism is more than a mere social custom, parents should be hearing, on behalf of their child: "You are my son." "You are my daughter." In bringing their child they are responding to the covenant God made with Abraham through whom all future generations were to be blessed. The water on the forehead is a public sign that this child is not just the son of John and Mary Jones but he is a son of God. It is God who has called him into being. It is not just the minister but God who speaks his name. The responsibility of the parents, of the godparents, and of the congregation is to love and nurture this child in a way that when he has reached an age of conscious and deliberate decision, he will declare who he is in making his own confession of faith. The parents do not determine who their child is. From the beginning God has ordained who he is. In his baptism, they come to acknowledge this fact, to affirm it, to celebrate it.

Who determines who you are? Your parents? A brother or sister? Your high school counselor? Your wife? Your husband? A friend? Baptism is a symbol for every person answering that question. When Jesus was baptized, there came a Voice from heaven saying, "This is *my* beloved Son in whom I am well pleased."

This Voice is portrayed as coming from heaven, for God had taken the initiative in making his covenant with men. God, out of his love, in the meaning of his grace, spoke to Abraham at the dawn of recorded history, and this Voice is heard again at baptism, as someone is proclaimed his son or daughter—heirs of the same promise. Baptism *is* a time when heaven and Earth meet. There is mystery here, to be sure—the mystery of God's presence.

There is another reason the Voice heard in baptism is portrayed as coming from heaven: the discovery of who one is is a revelation from beyond. The Voice that is pictured as coming from above is actually the Voice of God within the person. As one of the writers of Genesis puts it, man is created "in the image of God." God is present in each of us. He speaks to us in the deepest recesses of who we are as persons. The place where God is most fully present is in our uniqueness, in our self, in our person, in our soul.

In this sense every person is *immaculately* conceived. In the birth of the person, there is more here than meets the eye. There is more than biology can explain. God breathed into Adam—man—the breath of life, and so he breathes into every person the breath of life. The God who was present in the beginning is present in *your* beginning. With God you are no accident, you are no afterthought, you are his creative purpose from the outset.

But in the Voice we hear at baptism, there is the clamor of many voices from this direction and that, enticing us from the one who has heralded our true identity. Straightway from the waters of baptism, Jesus found himself in the wilderness besieged by the Deceiver, tempting him to succumb to all kinds of popular images of who the Messiah should be. The *wilder-*

ness symbolizes the loneliness of temptation for every person. It is a battle that no one else can fight for us. It is in the solitude of our own mind and heart that we win or lose.

To sin is to *miss* the mark. It is to be distracted from the main business of life by the ways in which the world has come to define life: by bread (materialism), by popularity (success), by ownership (power). These were the temptations that came to Jesus. It was not Jesus' purpose to gain a following by any means but to do the will of God, to be a true son of the Father. And these are the temptations that crowd into *our* lives, as we are bombarded by all kinds of ways to strike it rich, to be popular, to be successful, to be powerful. But they are distractions from the agenda we heard announced for our life in baptism.

T. S. Elliot aptly describes what temptation is for modern man: "distracted by distraction upon distraction." Sin is to live by the distractions rather than by the call of God.

Temptation entices us from our true call to be a person—to be there, to be present, to answer the roll when our name is called. *"John Jones!"* Where is he? He is never at home. He is never at home long enough *to find out who he is.*

This is Willy Loman's predicament in Arthur Miller's outstanding play, *The Death of a Salesman.* Willy was all the time extroverting to make a sale. No wonder in a moment of insight he should confess, "I feel kind of temporary about *myself."* We *do* feel temporary about ourselves if we do not experience the security that comes with knowing who we are. Do you recall the epitaph that Biff, one of the sons, spoke over his father's grave: "He never knew who he was." How pathetic to spend a lifetime but never respond to the call of who you are! This drama is aptly titled, *The Death of a Salesman.* But it was not "the death of Willy Loman," for Willy Loman had never really lived.

This play is haunting because Willy symbolizes so strikingly the lostness of modern man—a loss of identity. He does not know who he is. He is no longer a person. As someone has characterized his predicament, God created him to love people and use things, but contemporary man has got it all turned around: he loves things and uses people. He has become a slave to his own technology and is rapidly becoming its victim. With all of his time-saving gadgets, life itself has escaped him. Life is not nearer, but *death* is. He has but found more sophisticated ways of destroying himself. It is all very clean, very antiseptic; all he has to do is push a button while wearing gloves. There will be no fingerprints left to betray man as the culprit.

There is a real sense in which the person, the nation, the civilization that loses its way has to get back on where it got off. Repentance, it seems to me, is a turning, a returning to our roots. As an Old Testament prophet puts it, "Look unto the Rock from whence you are hewn." How we need to return to the waters of *our* baptism to know who we are!—John Thompson

SUNDAY, FEBRUARY 5, 2006
Lectionary Message
Topic: Bad News, Good News for People in Exile
TEXT: Isa. 40:21–31
Other Readings: Ps. 147:1–11, 20c; 1 Cor. 9:16–23; Mark 1:29–39

I. Isaiah 40 is one of the best-known and best-loved chapters of the Bible. It speaks to a common human reality—our sense of weariness and exhaustion as life overpowers us with problems and pressures. At such times we feel we are in exile, cut off from home, from everything that gives life meaning. So to read that those who wait upon the Lord will find renewed strength is indeed good news, and it is no wonder we return again and again to this comforting, hopeful passage.

(a) *Before the good news.* However, these words are so familiar to us that we may not notice the way the prophet comes to this affirmation of renewal. Frederick Buechner says the gospel is bad news before it is good news, because the way to the good news (we are reconciled) is through the bad news (we are sinners). The author of Isaiah 40 understands this need to confront bad news before we can affirm the good. The prophet's bad news is aimed both at worldly rulers, who think their power is ultimate, and Israel in exile, whose whining despair shows she has forgotten who her God is.

The Oscar-winning "best picture" of 1981, *Chariots of Fire*—the story of the British Olympic team at the 1924 Paris games—makes it very clear that Isaiah 40 takes us through a dark valley before leading us to the light. One of its star runners is Eric Liddell, an evangelical Presbyterian missionary, home from China to get his degree from the University of Edinburgh. Eric uses his success as a runner to glorify God and spread the gospel. But the scheduling of his qualifying heat on a Sunday almost derails his drive for Olympic gold. To run on Sunday would violate the fourth Commandment, so Eric refuses. Instead, on that day he goes to the Scottish Church of Paris and preaches a sermon at the time he would have run this race.

We don't hear his sermon, but we do hear his text: Isaiah 40, beginning at verse 12 and continuing intermittently to the end of the chapter. What makes this reading such a dark experience is not merely Eric's somber demeanor but the way the film uses parallel editing to connect this reading with the fate of the British runners on that day. Every one of them fails miserably. The implication that God sits in judgment of the British team for violating the Sabbath is hard to avoid.

(b) *Two kinds of temptations.* Before we can hear the good news that God will renew our strength when we are weary, we need to hear the bad news that all our attempts to live on our own terms will fail. Even the most powerful of us will come to naught. The temptation of rulers, with their earthly power, is to think that they can make the rules themselves, as this film shows when the British Olympic Committee (including the Prince of Wales, the future King Edward VIII) tries to pressure Eric to violate his conscience. God judges such hubris and declares it nothing. Princes and rulers will be carried off suddenly and unexpectedly, like plants uprooted by a mighty wind.

Most of us are not rich and powerful enough to be tempted by such hubris. However, we may be tempted to think that God has forgotten us in our lowly estate. We are like grasshoppers, the prophet says, so why should the Creator of the world show concern for or even notice us? We are too insignificant for God to take up our cause or put things right for us. This is Israel's complaint: "My way is hidden from the Lord, and my right is disregarded by my God." They are in exile, without land, Temple, or Davidic king. How can Yahweh see or care for them?

(c) *Good news out of bad.* This accounts for the exasperated tone of the prophet's rhetorical questions: "Have you not known? Have you not heard? Have you not understood?" The answer is, "Of course you have!" Of all the peoples of the Earth, Israel knows that the God she worships is the Creator of all things, incomparable in power, who never grows faint or weary, and who can redeem any situation, regardless of how hopeless it seems. How can Israel say that God has disregarded her? God sees her plight, even in exile.

The great paradox of human reality is that we are simultaneously a little lower than the angels yet are made from the dust of the ground. Shakespeare's Hamlet puts it this way: we are "the beauty of the world, the paragon of animals," and also the "quintessence of dust." The rulers of the Earth are tempted to overemphasize our angelic beauty, while the rest of us are tempted to stress our quintessential dust. Exiled Israel says she is nothing; she no longer counts in God's eyes. But the prophet says no to all this self-pity. The God Israel worships has unsearchable understanding, and no situation is beyond God's power to redeem. What Israel really needs to hear again is what she already knows: those who wait upon God—the source of all strength and vitality—will find their strength renewed.

In a world that seems out of control, that exhausts us with its demands and wearies us with false claims of security in power or possessions, we need to hear this message, given to exiles 2,500 years ago. Whatever our exile may be, we can know yet again the God who creates, judges, and renews all things. By waiting upon and trusting God's ultimate goodness toward us, we will find our strength renewed so that we can soar and run and walk.

We have already known, heard, and understood this good news. Do we have the ears to hear it yet again?—Bill Thomason

ILLUSTRATIONS

Still, let us *wait on the Lord*. It is by bare trust in him that we *renew our strength, put forth wings like eagles, run and not weary, walk and not faint.*

Put forth wings—run—walk! Is the order correct? Hope swerves from the edge of so descending a promise, which seems only to repeat the falling course of nature—that droop, we all know, from short ambitions, through temporary impulsiveness, to the old commonplace and routine. Soaring, running, walking—and is not the next stage, a cynic might ask, standing still?

On the contrary, it is a natural and true climax, rising from the easier to the more difficult, from the ideal to the real, from dream to duty, from what can only be the rare occasions of life to what must be life's usual and abiding experience.

. . . Let hope rejoice in a promise, which does not go off into the air, but leaves us upon solid earth; and let us hold to a religion, which, while it exults in being the secret of enthusiasm and the inspiration of heroism, is daring and divine enough to find its climax in the commonplace.[1]

I saw and knew that his marvelous and utter goodness brings our powers to their full strength. At the same time I saw that he is at work unceasingly in every conceivable thing, and that it is far greater than anything we can imagine, or guess, or think. Then we can do no more than gaze in delight with a tremendous desire . . . and to delight in his goodness. . . .

---

[1]George Adam Smith, *The Book of Isaiah*, Vol. 2 (London: Hodder & Stoughton, n.d. [late nineteenth century]), pp. 102–103, 105. Cited in *Resources for Preaching and Worship—Year B: Quotations, Meditations, Poetry, and Prayers*, compiled by Hannah Ward and Jennifer Wild (Louisville, Ky.: Westminster John Knox Press, 2002), p. 62.

This is achieved by the grace of the Holy Spirit, both now and until the time that, still longing and loving, we die.[2]

SERMON SUGGESTIONS

Topic: Some Wonderful Works of God
TEXT: Ps. 147:1–11, 20c
(1) God brings his people together (v. 2). (2) God heals the brokenhearted (v. 3). (3) God brings a sense of the stability and permanence of his Creation (vv. 4–5). (4) God makes the consequences of moral choice clear: support for the struggler (v. 6a); defeat for the ungodly (v. 6b).

Topic: The Choice Is Yours
TEXT: Joshua 1:1–9
(1) God's purpose (vv. 1–3). (2) God's promise (v. 5). (3) God's command (v. 9a).

WORSHIP AIDS

CALL TO WORSHIP.   "O send out thy light and thy truth: let them lead me; let them bring me unto thy holy hills, and to thy tabernacle" (Ps. 43:3).

INVOCATION.   Lord of life, let this hour of worship be special for us, a time of taking stock, a time of listening to God's word, a time of renewal in Christ's name.—E. Lee Phillips

OFFERTORY SENTENCE.   "So then every one of us shall give account of himself to God" (Rom. 14:12).

OFFERTORY PRAYER.   Gracious God, grant that when we give an offering, genuine love may accompany what we present before the course of your Kingdom.

PRAYER.   Lead us, O Lord, through the difficult and crooked ways of our world. Help us to make wise decisions; save us from our prejudices, and give us the grace to listen to people who differ from us, if we can see that they are sincere and honest in what they want, in what they think. Bind us together in one great family, with many different opinions and many different ways of life, and unite us in our effort to show men in some specific way the compassion that was once in Christ Jesus.—Theodore Parker Ferris

SERMON
Topic: If God Be for Us
TEXT: Rom. 8:31–39

Abraham was one hundred years old at the birth of Isaac. The boy was the gift of God's promise in covenant with the old man and a gift of joyous laughter for Sarah. Finally, God

---

[2]Julian of Norwich, *Revelations*, translated by Clifton Wolters (Harmondsworth: Penguin, 1966), p. 129. Cited in Ward and Wild, *Resources*, p. 62.

came through with the promise, and it seems that the story of Abraham was getting to the part about living happily ever after. Then comes the horrible decree: "Take your son, your only son Isaac, whom you love, and go to the land of Moriah, and offer him there as a burnt offering."

This is one of those passages we would like to rip from our Bibles. Even with the happy ending (God provides the sacrifice and spares the child), it is a horrible story—hardly bedtime reading for children. The English Baptist scholar G. Henton Davies could not accept as simple history that God had ordered the sacrifice of Isaac, and Baptists burned his commentary on Genesis over it. Davies raised the rhetorical question—the right question: "Did God make, would God in fact have made, such a demand upon Abraham or anybody else except himself?" Then he left to Abraham's psychoanalysis the source of the horrible decree.

In your worst nightmare can you imagine hearing such a horrible command as a word from God? It is one of the few episodes of mental illness in the Bible that is frightening for its suggestive content. In *When Religion Gets Sick,* Wayne Oates notes the suggestive sickness in the gross images of cutting off an offending hand or plucking out an offending eye. The story just hangs there in Genesis 22. You don't have to like it or to read it, but you can't erase it either. The embarrassing interlude says nothing we want to hear about God. It consumes an inordinate amount of theological energy from scholars trying to understand or to justify its existence in the Bible. Finally, most scholars interpret Genesis 22 as a correction to the practice of human sacrifice sometimes found among neighbors to the Jews.

The good news—and most certainly the teaching of the passage—is that God provides an alternative to human sacrifice. The Jews offered animal sacrifices to Yahweh. Human sacrifice was repugnant, unnecessary, and unacceptable—until, of course, we come to a second Abraham-Isaac story in the new covenant with God we call our New Testament. Perhaps Genesis 22 is a prelude and hint of what is to come in the continuing saga of salvation. Only the Son of God, that later son of Abraham, is acceptable to God as human sacrifice. The message is in Paul's letter to the Romans: "He who did not withhold his own Son, but gave him up for all of us, will he not with him also give us everything else?" God would not permit from Abraham what God has given in Christ.

I. *God is for us.* In my senior year at Baylor, Dr. James C. K. Mau came from Hong Kong to the university as a guest professor. He had a doctorate in English law and served as pastor of a Baptist church in Hong Kong. I became his volunteer assistant and chauffeur. I persuaded the pastor of the little church where I served to invite Dr. Mau as a missions speaker one Sunday morning. His English was difficult to follow, but everyone knew the story of the sacrifice of Isaac. The congregation squirmed with discomfort in the slow, tedious, broken English describing the trek of Abraham and Isaac to Mount Moriah, and I wondered how he was going to get us out of the closed box he was constructing. I kept thinking I was responsible. After all, he was my friend and my idea for a speaker. I prayed for Dr. Mau and maybe for my own rescue. Finally, he got to the point of the sermon and the ram in the thicket. He pointed to the side of the room as he declared, "There is the Christ! The ram is the Christ!" This was not a new interpretation, but for me that day it was a revelation. In the painful struggle to understand where this sermon was going, I came to a new understanding of the direction of the biblical drama of redemption. Treating the cross of Christ as a sacrifice to God is no less appalling than the offering of Isaac.

The cross was obviously a major obstacle for early Christians, forced to find a positive place for the public humiliation and execution of Jesus, and Christians continued to struggle with the sadistic cruelty of this bloody sacrifice as a statement from God. In the twelfth Christian century, Anselm of Canterbury wrote in *Cur Deus Homo* that the death of Jesus was an act of human sacrifice to satisfy the justice of God. It made perfect sense. All of the pieces of the legal puzzle fell into place, but the grace of God disappeared in the cold logic known as the "satisfaction theory of the atonement." What possible justification could anyone find for the sacrifice of Isaac or of Jesus?

We view the cross from two directions—from Lent and from Easter. Although the Passion narratives never lose sight of the Resurrection, during Lent the approach to Good Friday is a slow death march into the dark regions of human suffering and evil. After Easter, the cross takes on new meaning. It becomes the touchstone of grace. The suffering and death of Jesus is evidence of God's solidarity with our suffering and death—the clear word that God is love. For suffering humanity the Word of God is, "Nothing can separate us from the love of God."

II. *Nothing can separate us*. My first real job was working for the city swimming pool as a lifeguard. It was a baby-sitting task. I taught swimming to children in the morning and watched over them in the afternoon. To qualify for the job, I had to be certified by the Red Cross in water safety and rescue. I carried two symbols of my responsibility: a "Senior Lifesaving" patch on my black uniform-swimsuit and a whistle on a string around my neck. In training, I learned personal survival skills, water rescue techniques, and basic first aid for drowning victims. Certification required mastering basic swimming strokes, better-than-average swimming ability, and endurance.

As a young man I enjoyed the macho image, but I was surprised to learn that the first rule for the rescuer was to avoid heroics. The first choice for rescue was the buoy and hook. A heroic leap into the water is a leap into danger and should only be attempted as a last resort to avoid a double drowning.

(a) *Resurrection suggests rescue*. Sometimes the Christian gospel is only a word of rescue. The popular notion is that from the safe distance of transcendence God will throw us a rope to pull us out of the water of evil and suffering. In some interpretations of eschatology (the last things), God will abandon the evil world to destruction while all of the chosen are taken safely away.

But salvation is more than rescue. The gospel is, "God so loved the world." Nothing less than the redemption of the whole Creation is in the scope of the divine love. The gospel of Christ is about the God who sends the Son into the deep waters of evil and suffering in order to redeem the water, as well as the victim. To use popular parlance, the incarnation of God in Christ was bigger than chasing alligators. He came to drain the swamp. Christ suffers with us. Christ was willing to drown with us, that we might live in him.

Sacrifice, suffering, and death are only symptoms of the larger problem. We struggle with separation, with abandonment. What we fear most is not death but dying alone and without hope. Paul has been trying to explain evil, to justify suffering, and to build a case for the continuing problem of bad things happening to good people. Finally, he declares victory:

"If God is for us, who is against us?"
"In all these things we are more than conquerors through him who loved us."

Standing in the cemetery with the cold wind in our faces and a flower-covered box containing the earthly remains of our beloved, we suddenly face the finality of separation, and the Word of God resounds. Nothing in all Creation can separate us from the love of God in Christ Jesus our Lord. This is the gospel of Christ!—Larry Dipboye

SUNDAY, FEBRUARY 12, 2006
Lectionary Message

Topic: Moved with Compassion
TEXT: Mark 1:40–45
Other Readings: 2 Kings 5:11–14; Ps. 30; 1 Cor. 9:24–27

I. The story in Mark 1 of Jesus healing a leper is at the midpoint of a larger sequence of miracle stories. None of these is told for its own sake. All are told to say something about Jesus and what he has come to do.

(a) *Lifted up, restored to service.* The healing of Peter's mother-in-law, the first and shortest of these miracles, appears to offer nothing but a bare account of the event. After Jesus begins his public ministry at Capernaum, he retires to the house of Peter's mother-in-law. She is to host Jesus and the disciples, providing nourishment and a place to stay (hospitality is one of the most important roles women play in this society). But to everyone's consternation, she is in bed with a fever. The disciples tell Jesus. He goes to her, takes her hand, and lifts her up. The fever leaves, and she begins to serve them.

Mark's use of the verb "lift up" apparently has more than descriptive significance. Other New Testament writers use it for Jesus' Resurrection. Her healing is, in a sense, a resurrection to new life. Jesus lifts her out of her lost condition, her loss of honor, and her social disgrace and gives life back by restoring her to her rightful role.

As we might expect, this story gets around Capernaum, inundating Jesus with requests for healing. Consequently, Jesus tells the disciples he will proclaim his message in other towns, "for that is what I came out to do." Healings are important, but proclaiming the message is more important. Understanding the message will keep people from misunderstanding the healings. Hearing is the beginning of healing.

(b) *Compassionate anger.* But as our reading today shows, Jesus cannot get away from requests for healing. A leper approaches, begging Jesus, "If you choose, you can make me clean." *If* you choose: does that little conjunction "if" imply previous rejections by would-be healers? This man knows Jesus *can* heal him but is afraid Jesus *won't*. These words move Jesus to "pity," our translation says. "Pity," however, does not capture this word's full force. Some say the translation should be "anger." Literally, it means "having one's intestines turn."[3] Jesus so identifies with this man that he is physically affected. This

---

[3]Walter Grueggemann, and others, *Texts for Preaching: Year B* (Louisville, Ky.: Westminster John Knox Press, 1993), p. 150.

is what the Bible means by compassion: an identification with another so complete that we feel what they feel.

But why would Jesus be angry, if that is Mark's meaning? Perhaps he is angry with the man for doubting his willingness to help. That does not seem likely, so it may be that Jesus is angry because the man implies others could have helped but refused. Or a third possibility is that Jesus is angry that there are such things as leprosy, which have the power to separate one human being from another. We can't be sure if this man's condition is what we today call Hansen's disease. But it doesn't matter; his malady was sufficient to cut him off from human society, and that is what I think affects Jesus so strongly.

Jesus' response is immediate, forceful, and effective. It is also shocking, because the first thing Jesus does is touch the man, something forbidden by the Law and dangerous, since touch could communicate disease. Then Jesus says, "I *do* choose [to make you clean]. Be made clean!" And the man is healed.

Is it Jesus' touch or his words that heal the man? We don't know, but the manner of healing is not important. The focus in miracle stories is Jesus—that he has the power to do such things and is moved by compassion to do them. Jesus warns the man to say nothing about his healing and commands him to present himself to the priest in accordance with the Law to be certified as healed. Literally, these two commands are contradictory, since the man will have to explain to the priest what happened to him. In any case, the man disobeys the command to silence, and the multitudes flock to Jesus, forcing him out of towns into the deserted countryside.

(c) *Salvation.* Such stories could easily sidetrack us into arguments about whether or not miracles are possible. That is an important question for theologians to ponder but is not the point of the story. Mark's purpose is to point to the character of the one who performs the miracle. Jesus cures the sick because he is compassionate. He never asks, "Why are you sick?" His only question is, "How can I help?" To everyone who says, "If you choose, make me clean," Jesus responds, "I *do* choose!"

The other important point about Jesus' miracles is that they are stories of salvation, which is not some other-worldly phenomenon we experience after death. Rather, it occurs here and now, because it is essentially a restoration of relations broken by sin, disease, class, and race. Peter's mother-in-law recovers from her fever to serve. She has been restored to right relations with others. Jesus tells the leper to get priestly certification. Then he can be reintegrated into his community, to be cut off from which is to be lost. Healing mends not only diseased bodies but broken relationships.

In the same way that Jesus healed with no conditions, our compassion should be unconditional. Following Jesus means helping people in need. But our compassion also needs to be effective. Genuine compassion will restore right relations.

We cannot cure the sick merely by touch or by saying words of healing. But we can be agents of reconciliation, moved to compassion for those in need.—Bill Thomason

ILLUSTRATIONS

The New Testament evidence is that both Jesus and the Christian community prayed for the sick and laid hands on them when they prayed. We know in our daily lives that it is often touch, the hand on the shoulder, the hug of a friend, the cuddle of a child, that lets us know that we are loved. Touch, often more than words, is a way of giving physical expression to our prayers and concern for each other.[4]

In his concern for [humankind's] history of suffering, for publicans and sinners, for the poor, the lame and the blind, for the dispossessed and those alienated from themselves by "evil spirits," Jesus is a living parable of God: this is the way in which God looks on [humankind]. The story of God is told in the story of Jesus. It is God himself who in the life story of Jesus discloses to us a new world, another way of experiencing reality. . . . The church becomes a community in which those who have opened themselves to the critical force of the parable of Jesus' life tell stories round a shared table. In this way we too can listen to Jesus' story today. We are simply asked whether we will stake our life on it.[5]

SERMON SUGGESTIONS

Topic: Cocksure to Cringing—and Then?

TEXT: Ps. 30

(1) We can draw presumptuous conclusions from our "good luck" (v. 6). (2) Then appalling reversals can shake our faith (v. 7). (3) But rejoicing is possible: through earnest prayer (v. 8); through calm reasoning (v. 9); through total trust (vv. 10–12).

Topic: God's Ventricle Stroke That Makes a Minus a Plus

TEXT: Judg. 5:1–5

(1) The mixed message of a universe where there is pain and tragedy. (2) The reliable fact of God who is Lord of all and brings victory out of mystery and tragedy.

WORSHIP AIDS

CALL TO WORSHIP.   "He that dwelleth in the secret place of the most High shall abide under the shadow of the almighty. I will say of the Lord he is my refuge and my fortress: my God, in him will I trust" (Ps. 91:1–2).

INVOCATION.   O God, you have shown us how we should behave toward one another. Today show us that pattern again. May the grace of our Lord Jesus Christ truly change our hearts.

OFFERTORY SENTENCE.   "The earth is the Lord's, and the fullness thereof; the world, and they that dwell therein" (Ps. 24:1).

OFFERTORY PRAYER.   Gracious Lord, we acknowledge your ownership of all the Earth and everything and everyone in it. What we confess with our lips may we prove with our deeds. Through him who gave his all for our salvation.

---

[4]*The Pattern of Our Days: Liturgies and Resources for Worship,* edited by Kathy Galloway (Glasgow: Wild Goose Publications, 1996), p. 47. Cited in Ward and Wild, *Resources,* p. 68.
[5]Edward Schillebeeckx, *God Among Us: The Gospel Proclaimed,* translated by John Bowden (London: SCM Press, 1983), p. 31. Cited in Ward and Wild, *Resources,* p. 69.

PRAYER.   We thank thee, Almighty God, for the rich heritage of this good land; for the evidences of thy favor in the past; and for the Hand that hath made and preserved us a nation. We thank thee for the men and women who, by blood and sweat, by toil and tears, forged on the anvil of their own sacrifice all that we hold dear. May we never lightly esteem what they obtained at a great price. As we are grateful for rights and privileges, may we be conscious of duties and obligations.

On this day, we thank thee for the inspiration that breathes in the memory of Abraham Lincoln, and we pray that something of the spirit that was his may be ours today. Like him, may we be more concerned that we are on thy side, than that thou art on ours. In our hearts may there be, as there was in his, malice toward none and charity for all; that we may, together, with thy blessing and help, "bind up the nation's wounds, and do all which may achieve and cherish a just and lasting peace among ourselves and with all nations."—Peter Marshall

SERMON
Topic: The Most Important Invitation
TEXT: Matt. 11:28–29

Jesus said, "Come to me, all who labor and are heavy laden, and I will give you rest. Take my yoke upon you, and learn from me; for I am gentle and lowly in heart, and you will find rest for your souls. For my yoke is easy, and my burden is light."

What an inviting offer!

At times, we have all been weary from bearing heavy burdens—the burdens of ill health, the burdens of family strife, the burdens of job unhappiness, or the burdens of excessive demands in our lives.

Here Jesus offers to lighten our burdens. This is indeed a wonderful invitation!

This is the only time in all of Scripture when Jesus directly invites us to receive relief from the heaviness of our burdens by taking on the yoke of discipleship in his name.

In Old Testament and Jewish tradition, the image of a "yoke" was commonly used to represent servitude and obedience. It was a large wooden collar used to connect two animals of labor, especially oxen.

The rabbis of Jesus' day often spoke of the "yoke of the Law" or the "yoke of the commandments." They meant one should take on the laws of a legalistic religion, just as one would take on a yoke, and wear them as a part of oneself.

Jesus uses the same image of wearing a yoke as if it bound one to something, but this time it is to bind oneself to the yoke of God's grace in Christ Jesus instead of the yoke of strict obedience to the Law.

This invitation could only come from one source, only from the Incarnate God, from Christ himself. Jesus' invitation is "come to me"—not to a book, not to a set of laws, not to a set of behavioral prescriptions. "Come to me," says Jesus. St. Augustine said that he found no such invitation anywhere else! When Jesus says his yoke is easy and not burdensome, he doesn't mean that life will be easy and burden-free. He is not saying his yoke leads to a life of comfort and ease. The rest he promises will not be a vacation. The root word for "vacation" is the same as for the words "vacant" and "vacuum"—in other words, emptiness! The rest and relief offered by Jesus is the Sabbath rest, the rest that only God can give, the rest that comes from the presence of God in our lives. It is an invitation to receive spiritual food and strength through his presence in our lives. People who have shared the same experience have closeness—a kind of bond and rapport.

One of the first times I saw this dramatically acted out was during seminary. It was early in my seminary training. I was the pastor of a small church down in eastern North Carolina, about an hour's drive from the seminary. I would go there each Friday night and return to school on Sunday night. Word came to me one Wednesday that an old farmer in that congregation had passed away, and I was asked to come and conduct his funeral. I was a young minister and had not had much experience with bereavement and grief. I had no idea what it was like to love intensely and live with someone most of your life and then lose that person.

Before going down on Tuesday to meet with the widow and family, I went to my books on pastoral care, trying to learn what I should say to be of comfort. I drove down and went to the house to see the widow and her children. I remember going in and trying as best I could to empathize with her in her grief. Even though she was very gracious, it was very clear to me that my words were very theoretical and that I was speaking out of a lack of any sense of what she was experiencing. I only knew about, I did not know from within, what she was experiencing. While I was there, an older woman came into the room. Someone said to me that a few months before, her husband had died. I will never forget the way she went across the room and tenderly embraced this freshly grieving widow. She said simply, "I know my dear, I know," and just held her close. I could immediately see a bridge of understanding and comfort between these two widows. They had shared a common experience, and they knew what the other was going through. That bond of common experience was the basis for the kind of relationship I could never have had with her at that stage of my life.

Jesus is saying that God is no longer distant and aloof but is close to us, in a way that can only come from having lived life as we live. This message is indeed comforting. That is why these very words are part of the "Comfortable Words" following the confession and absolution in Rite I. Those who are weary and burdened will receive rest in Christ. God is saying, "I have been there. I have been there living as you are living. I understand!" Henry Nouwen, the distinguished Jesuit priest, teacher, and spiritual guide, was once asked to distill the gospel of Jesus to its purest expression. Nouwen reflected for a moment and then said two words: "Come close! Come close!" Nouwen contended that God was saying to the world in Jesus, "Come close."

Jesus was saying to all who would hear him, "Come close." This is the invitation of all invitations, and it is constantly there for each and every one of us. "Come close." Throughout Christian history, the witness of those who have come to be recognized as saints has always been, primarily, a testimony to the closeness of their lives with Jesus Christ—not good works, not great learning, not even service to the needy, but the heart of their spirituality was always based on personal closeness to him! "Come to me, all who labor and are heaven laden, and I will give you rest."

This is the most important invitation ever extended! It is extended to each and every one of us, personally, and that is indeed good news!—Cannon Dick Brown

SUNDAY, FEBRUARY 19, 2006

Lectionary Message

Topic: God's "Yes" to Us

TEXTS: Isa. 43:18–25; 2 Cor. 1:18–22; Mark 2:1–12

Other Reading: Ps. 41

I. Two weeks ago we heard from Isaiah 40 that we can depend on God, who never grows faint or weary. But today the same prophet says Israel has wearied God with her iniquities. Which is it? Does God never grow weary? Or can we weary God with our sin?

(a) *God of the unexpected.* The answer to this apparent contradiction lies in a distinction. In one sense, we *do* weary God. God offers us new life, but we prefer our own way. So God's weariness is like the exasperation of a good parent with a stubborn child. All parents know times when they want to throw up their hands and throw in the towel. But good parents *don't*. The weariness of parental exasperation doesn't lead to that of parental exhaustion. We can weary God to exasperation by insisting on our own way but not to exhaustion so that God ever gives up on us.

Instead, God says to Israel, "Don't remember the former things, or consider the things of old. I am about to do a new thing." The things of old are Israel's sin that led to exile. God's new thing is Israel's redemption, which will make a way in the desert for her to go home. The desert symbolizes Israel's hopelessness. How could they survive this journey? Yahweh answers, "I will make a way in the wilderness and rivers in the desert." Yahweh, who judged Israel for her sin, will now redeem Israel by turning the desert into a highway and a river. God's exasperated weariness has not exhausted God's love. This is something new and unexpected.

(b) *The unexpected Jesus.* Of all the new things God is doing, Jesus is the most unexpected. Jesus' healing of the paralytic in Mark 2 illustrates this truth, because it is full of unexpected twists and turns. It is the culmination of Mark's introductory portrait of Jesus, answering the question of who Jesus is. This introduction begins with Jesus' baptism and temptation, his calling disciples, and his teaching, preaching, and wonder-working. "What is this?" the amazed people ask. "A new teaching—with authority!" This authority includes power to heal the sick and cast out demons. Who can this be?

Healing the paralytic adds to this wonder but also moves us closer to the answer. Jesus has returned to Capernaum and is teaching in a house. A large crowd gathers, blocking the doorway, prohibiting anyone from entering. Consequently, four men carrying a paralytic are unable to bring the man to Jesus. They take a radical step, giving the story a comic element. They carry the man onto the roof of the house and tear a hole in it large enough to lower him into Jesus' presence. (Homes in Palestine were made of mud and sticks, with flat roofs accessed by any outside staircase.) When Jesus sees the faith of these men, he says to the paralytic, "Son, your sins are forgiven."

This story puzzles us, raises questions for us. Couldn't these men find some way to get to Jesus other than by destroying a neighbor's house? Did the people inside panic when the ceiling began falling on them? Why did Jesus forgive the man's sins before healing him? Why is this forgiveness predicated on the *friends'* faith, not the paralytic's?

We are not the only ones to ask questions. Scribes present in the room say to themselves, "[This] is blasphemy! Who can forgive sins but God alone?" And now we see the point of Mark's story. We understand the new layer of meaning he adds to his portrait of Jesus. He has already shown Jesus as an authoritative teacher of a new thing. He has already shown Jesus as a wonder-worker with power over natural illnesses and supernatural demons. He now shows us a Jesus who can forgive sins, and as the scribes said, "Who can forgive sins but God alone?" If Jesus of Nazareth can in fact forgive sins, then God is doing something new, unique, and unexpected.

(c) *God's "yes" to us.* Mark has already told us who Jesus is. He is the Son of God (1:1), the beloved with whom God is very pleased (1:11), the Holy One of God (1:24). The scribes' question, ironically, speaks a truth they do not believe. Jesus, knowing their skepticism, says out loud what they are thinking, then offers evidence of his right to forgive sin: "Which is easier, to say . . . , 'Your sins are forgiven,' or to say, 'Stand up and take your mat and walk'?" The scribes dare not answer this question, because if they do and Jesus heals the man, they will have to admit something they don't believe. Jesus turns to the paralytic and finally does what we have expected him to do all along. He tells the man to stand, take his mat—he will carry it now, instead of it carrying him—and go home. His sins had been forgiven because of his friends' faith. In being healed, however, the man demonstrates his own faith, because in obedience he does what Jesus tells him to do. Can there be any doubt that Jesus is who Marks says he is?

God's new thing for Israel freed them to go home from exile. Jesus' healing of this man frees him, too, to find his way home. In Jesus, God is doing a new thing—forgiving our sins without the need of sacrificial intermediaries. In Jesus, God is always saying yes to us—not yes to all our wants but yes to all our deepest needs. The paralytic's deepest need was forgiveness. In saying yes to that need, Jesus also made possible the healing of his body. By obeying Jesus, this man said "yes" back to Jesus. This response to Jesus is the only way to forgiveness and healing and home.—Bill Thomason

ILLUSTRATION

We have come off a certain ordering of social reality that has been long established and which seemed right—a relation of privilege and poverty, of power and pain—and we learned how to manage that arrangement. It does seem as though the lid has blown off it, though: the old privileges of wealth and power lack credibility, the old authority of whites and males is trembling, the old advantage of European roots and all the rest is in deep jeopardy. And it makes us very frightened.

God is indeed doing a new thing among us. God is fashioning a new pattern of social relations in which privilege will have to attend to poverty, in which power will have to submit to pain, in which advantage will have to be recruited for compassion, in which old priorities will have to be repositioned in order to let in people long kept out. God is doing a new thing.[6]

SERMON SUGGESTIONS

Topic: God's Surprises

TEXT: Ps. 41

(1) We may be more important to God than rivals or enemies think (vv. 1–3). (2) We still may be more undeserving than we think (vv. 4–9). (3) Yet God will give us a final opportunity to prove our integrity and win with him (vv. 11–13).

---

[6]Walter Brueggemann, *The Threat of Life: Sermons on Pain, Power, and Weakness*, edited by Charles L. Campbell (Minneapolis: Fortress Press, 1996), p. 60. Cited in Ward and Wild, *Resources*, p. 72.

Topic: Love and Loyalty

TEXT: Ruth 1:16–18

(1) The racial problems Ruth faced. (2) The power of love to overcome prejudice. (3) The role of Naomi and Ruth in the genealogy of David and Jesus.

WORSHIP AIDS

CALL TO WORSHIP.   "Oh that men would praise the Lord for his goodness, and for his wonderful works to the children of men! For he satisfieth the longing soul, and filleth the hungry soul with goodness" (Ps. 107:8–9 KJV).

INVOCATION.   Allow all that we need to be met by all you desire for us in worship today, O Lord, so that the routine of our lives may be encountered by the holiness of heaven and the redeeming power of the Christ.—E. Lee Phillips

OFFERTORY SENTENCE.   "For every beast of the forest is mine, and the cattle upon a thousand hills" (Ps. 50:10).

OFFERTORY PRAYER.   We are yours, O God. You have created us. You have redeemed us. You have given us the power to gain the fruits of our labors. And know that we bring as offerings of gratitude and love only what is already truly yours.

PRAYER.   We thank you, O God, for these sixty minutes that can change one's life. We thank you for life, for health, for grace that we have this blessed privilege of worship. So often we do not appreciate the preciousness of life until it is threatened by disease or accident. How selfishly we grasp it, how carelessly we squander it, how thoughtlessly we neglect it.

Life is not the paltry thing that many of us spend our days in. We are afraid to live. We fear life more than we fear death. When we choose security rather than adventure, we choose death rather than life. Why do we live in the winter of discontent when you call us to the springtime of a perennial hope? To choose life, whatever the risk, is to believe in the Resurrection.

How often we miss the here-and-nowness of your teaching—the immediacy of your Resurrection power to make all things new.

We pray that we may hear your Word in a fresh and new way that we may catch a vision of the new Heaven and the new Earth of which Christ, as Risen Lord, is the harbinger.

We pray for our nation in its many opportunities to give leadership in the community of nations. We pray for the president, for members of his cabinet, and for Congress, that this opportunity to make a difference in our nation and the life of the world will not be squandered in partisan politics. May they have such faith to be discerning of the new things you are doing in our day.

We pray for all those who would lead an earnest seeking for the truth that makes for justice, for the order that makes for peace, for the compassion that leads to life.

Where there is any brokenness among us—in health, in sorrow, in love, in disappointment, in failure—we pray the healing of the grace of our Lord Jesus Christ who is here as Risen Lord, teaching us as he taught his apostles to pray and live.—John Thompson

SERMON
Topic: Hints to the Christian Life
TEXT: Matt. 5:1–12

Somewhere Mark Twain observes that the sections of the New Testament giving him the most trouble are not those he cannot understand but rather the section he can. And George Bernard Shaw echoes Mark Twain when he remarks that "Christianity would probably be a good thing if it were ever tried." They may be on to something. "We will wrangle for religion, write for it, fight for it, die for it, anything but live for it," says Charles Caleb Colton. There's the nub of it. The Christian life is not so much a matter of doctrine, dogma, systems of belief, ideas, and worldviews. It blossoms as an expression of our lives, a quality of being. It reflects a certain radiant style, a quality of joy, a tilt of disposition anchored in the Eternal.

I believe each of us deeply yearns for a quality of life like that. I believe most of us seek it everywhere but in the grace and release of the gospel.

Where, then, do we discover clues to this promised quality of life? Indeed, what hints does the gospel provide, enabling us to live more closely attuned to the pattern of our Lord? Talk about hints to the Christian life! Those Beatitudes provide a crystalline description of life rooted and grounded in the grace of the only security sticking with us through life and death: the all-embracing, undergirding love of God that we know through Christ Jesus.

Now *reorientation* really means a whole new world for us. This surrender to the sovereignty of the God of Jesus Christ creates a fresh arena for our lives. Let me offer an analogy. September 11, we know, changed your world and mine. We perceive—we feel in our viscera—dramatic variation in our global context, our national and perhaps personal identity.

Just as with the arrival in our world of Jesus of Nazareth, the New Testament testifies to an event bearing catastrophic impact. We confess Jesus as Christ, not simply an itinerant Nazarene stumbling along the dusty roads of Palestine. Jesus comes as a decisive historical presence qualitatively changing human existence. A teacher he is, but more than that.

A prophet he is, but more, much more. Do we see in him an image of bodies healed, souls mended, futures blown open? Indeed! Jesus, as Christ, bears healing, mending, and future renewal—now! Does Jesus point toward a community where resentments dissolve and hostility dissipates, a community where mercy, kindness, and justice suffuse human encounters? Jesus embodies that kind of world among us—now. Does Jesus promise a city where race, culture, neighborhood, creed, and gender no longer pit us against one another but where, rather, everyone serves as diverse components in forging a whole and reconciled community? Yes! Indeed, the design for the common life of our city emerges from the love and hope incarnate in the life and death of Jesus. He breaks through into our history, not simply as a brilliant moralist, a religious genius, an original prophet, another Socrates, Moses, Buddha. No, Jesus breaks through as the harbinger of a new age, a new world, a new quality of life. Matthew is convinced that Jesus bears the gracious, healed, reconciling, transfigured human future of God among us—now!

Wow! Now, finding ourselves citizens of this new setting, this new ethos, this new realm ruled by the grace and peace of Jesus Christ situated amid this old world of ours, the Beatitudes become descriptions of our moral life in Christ's new world.

Take that first Beatitude, for instance: "Blessed are the poor in spirit, for theirs is the kingdom of heaven." That Beatitude describes our posture before God when we surrender our lives to Christ's new realm. It declares simply that, like the economically impoverished, like the poor in material things who have nothing to lean on, no goods to prop up their lives, no cash to hide their desperation, the poor in spirit come before God with nothing. They come— dare I say?—*we* come with no claim of success in business, academia, politics, salary schedule. No, nothing. We stand before God with zero, zilch, zippo—but with a desperate eagerness to participate in the triumph of kindness. We let go of every claim to special identity, except as Christ claims us for humble and gracious service.

You see, to be poor in spirit is not a demand. It is not an imperative. It is not something we are under obligation to live up to, a moral challenge we are supposed to meet. To be poor in spirit is simply the way it is alongside Jesus Christ.

And astounding! Alongside Christ we will not only be poor in spirit, we will at the same time know the realm of heaven. Yes, the realm of heaven! Pie in the sky? Golden streets and angel music? Not on your life. The realm of heaven is not some vague afterlife beyond the clouds up in the wide blue yonder but a new reality, a new community, a fresh network of relationships marked by mutuality, solidarity, and service. It breaks in on us, even as we come before God with nothing but open hearts and hands.

You see, living in the realm of heaven means we are no longer ruled by the sovereignties of this world tearing us apart, stressing us out, eating us alive, worrying us to death. It means we gain our full humanity; we are saved, sustained, empowered, enabled, renewed, recreated, not by our income or our job, our gender or our race, not by our designer clothes, our power-food diet, our esoteric therapists. Nothing this world offers as a key to value and self-worth provides anything but illusion, fraud, and seduction to fruitless striving. No, insists the New Testament—the Beatitudes—the key to health, to wholeness, to integration, to coherence—the key to our full humanity—lies in rendering ourselves open before the gracious empowering spirit of the crucified Christ, allowing Christ finally to rule our lives and shape our identities. "Blessed: deeply, profoundly joyous, God-embraced and supported—yes blessed are the poor in spirit for theirs is the realm of heaven."

And what about those other Beatitudes? How do they surface in our lives? Their expression hinges to a great degree on the first. They reflect what life is like when we surrender to the sovereignty of Christ's new realm. Listen: our first loyalty being to Jesus Christ, we mourn for a broken Creation riddled with illness, hostility, wars, and rumors of war. We weep over the injuries we inflict on one another. We grieve over untimely death and are sickened and saddened by the tragedy of the world. But yes—*yes!*—alongside Christ we find comfort and consolation by one who himself suffers and knows we suffer, too.

Or again, walking alongside Jesus Christ we are meek—no, not whimpering, tail-between-the-legs, compliant milk-toast wimps but men and women able to manage and transform suffering to walk the second mile, to absorb humiliation without resort to vengeance. We possess a serenity impossible to ruffle, embitter, or enrage. We conquer with kindness and live assured—everything to the contrary—assured of God's deigning the triumph of kindness.

Yet again, shoulder-to-shoulder with Christ, we hunger and thirst for righteousness. We know of our inadequacy to right the world all by ourselves. We do not labor under any illusions of our own gifts and talents. We starve for the nourishment of fairness, the feast of justice, the cuisine of peace, the rich tonic of reconciliation, strengthening us to bear up under the worst, slaked and satiated by the vision and vitality of the promised, graced community.

And yes, walking with Jesus Christ, surrendering to Christ's realm, we discover ourselves merciful. In a world riddled with getting even, paying the piper, calculating this, weighing that, sinking hairline-deep into litigation, blowing the enemy out of the water. In driving the opposition to the wall, mercy is the order of the day. We experience mercy in our own lives from the forgiveness and openhandedness of Jesus Christ, and we offer mercy to others, exercising the very character of God.

Of course, even again, being loyal to the gracious realm of Christ, we find ourselves pure in heart. That does not mean we are prissy or prudish. It surely does not mean we hide from the corruption and scandal of the world or harbor a harsh, narrow, moralistic approach to life. Purity of heart means, rather, we live without dissimulation before or diversion from the healing, reconciling will of our God. It means we stand with integrity, our whole persons committed and loyal to the world Christ Jesus creates among us.

And yes, those who surrender to the realm of Christ will know the joy of peacemaking. To be sure, that is bringing together two parties in conflict, but it is more. Peacemaking entails reaching out, identifying and empathizing with and reconciling the alienated, the marginalized, the outsider. It means moving through and across dividing lines, embracing the estranged, the enemy.

And we dare never forget, insists this revelatory offering: by surrendering to Christ we incur the disbelief, cynicism, mockery, laughter, and resistance of the world.

O friends, I have not just delivered a catalog of what we will do as we live the Christian life. I have offered hints as to how the Christian life unfolds. Should we take the plunge, we will discover for ourselves the living truth of these illustrative hints and perhaps add some of our own to Matthew's luminous list, a consequence of following Jesus.—James W. Crawford

SUNDAY, FEBRUARY 26, 2006

Lectionary Message

Topic: Shrines, Transfiguration, and Listening

TEXT: 2 Kings 2:1–12; Mark 9:2–9

Other Readings: Ps. 50:1–6; 2 Cor. 4:3–6

The Old Testament readings and the Gospel today are stories of wondrous experiences called "theophanies." Theophanies reveal Divinity to us and have contradictory effects. They terrify us, bringing us face-to-face with God, whose power and glory threaten to overwhelm us. But they also draw us to them with an attraction like that of absolute beauty: this power and glory are the very source of our well-being.

I. *Theophanies and crisis.* Theophanies are rare. When they occur they come at crucial moments for God's people, as Elijah's translation illustrates. For years, Elijah had spoken for Yahweh, but the time had come for him to depart. Will Elisha, his successor, faithfully speak God's word? How can Israel be sure? Elijah had promised that Elisha would receive a double portion of God's spirit, if he (Elisha) witnessed Elijah's translation. So Elisha sticks with his friend as though they were physically joined and sees the fiery chariot and whirlwind. As Elijah ascends, his mantle falls from his shoulder, landing at Elisha's feet: Elijah's authority has passed to Elisha, answering Israel's anxious questions.

The mantle, a loose outer garment, carries symbolic meaning. On the way to this theophany, Elijah had used it to cross the Jordan River, striking the water with it and causing the river to part, making a path of dry ground. This parting of the Jordan recalls the great foundational event of Israel's history: the exodus from Egyptian slavery, when Moses parted the Red Sea. The power that had saved Israel then had been at work in Elijah. Now the mantle has passed to Elisha, and when he comes to the Jordan, he also parts the waters and crosses on dry ground. In Elisha, Yahweh will continue to defend, protect, and save Israel.

II. *Shrines and Transfiguration.* Mark surely has this story in mind as he relates the Transfiguration. If so, he means his story to be a culmination of that begun with Moses (the Law) and continued with Elijah-Elisha (the prophets). Jesus takes Peter, James, and John to the top of the mountain. A blinding light engulfs him, turning his clothes a dazzling white. In the midst of this, Moses and Elijah appear, talking with Jesus. The disciples are struck dumb, until Peter stammers out the foolish suggestion that they build booths on that very spot. Farmers in Israel built booths in their fields during harvest as shelters, so they could spend the night there. So important was the harvest that Israel had enshrined it in one of her three major festivals—the Feast of Booths. Peter was saying, "Let's do something to commemorate this, build a shrine to show where it happened, create a liturgy we can celebrate every year to remember."

Peter's motivation is the very human impulse to hang on to whatever manifestations of the Divine we have. Shrines are permanent, visible, objective. Transfigurations are not. They are dynamic, pointing beyond themselves. Like Jesus' miracles, the Transfiguration doesn't happen for its own sake. So Peter's suggestion shows he has missed the point. If we are granted a theophany, we cannot cling to or hold on to it. Theophanies are for the sake of making God known to us and others. Peter's suggestion would drain the dynamic reality of this event and turn it into a lifeless museum.

This glory is too much for the disciples. A cloud overshadows this terrifying, beautiful brightness, obscuring the figures. A Voice says: "This is my Son, the Beloved; listen to him!" A heavenly Voice had spoken these words at Jesus' baptism, but apparently only Jesus had heard them. Now the Voice speaks for the disciples to hear, because the command is to them. Then the theophany ends. As Jesus and the disciples descend the mountain, he commands them not to tell anyone about this until after that other Transfiguration we call the Resurrection.

III. *Listening.* The Voice from the cloud implies that the disciples have not been listening. When Jesus asked, "Who do you say that I am?" Peter blurted out, "You are the Messiah," speaking the truth but not understanding it. When Jesus began to teach them that he would suffer, Peter had objected, prompting Jesus' harsh rebuke: "Get behind me, Satan!" Peter had not been listening.

Transfiguration shakes us up, demonstrating that the God we worship cannot be pinned down, domesticated, tamed, objectified. This is why the second Commandment forbids idols. This is why Jesus refused to sign up for Peter's booth-building project. Theophanies demand that we pay attention to, that we *listen* for, what the Transfiguration means and how it can change lives. This is hard to hear, because we are pragmatic people who put results above everything else. We value doers over thinkers any day. Like Peter, when we witness a Transfiguration, we want to do something. God also wants us to do something, but not before we're ready to do it. Jesus knows the disciples aren't ready and (like 2 Isaiah with exiled Israel) Jesus asks them, "Have you not known? Have you not heard? Listen!"

What about us? Have we acted before we have listened? We who are one in Christ are nevertheless divided by all sorts of conflicts. What should we be saying to the world about war? Capital punishment? Abortion? The rights of gay, lesbian, and transgendered people in the Church and in society? Environmental degradation? Economic disparity between haves and have-nots? Equally devout Christians can be diametrically opposed to one another on such issues.

Could it be that many of us are not actually listening to Jesus before making up our minds? Perhaps the heated, sometimes un-Christian character of our conflicts arises because we have been so dazzled by the glory of the Transfiguration, the numinous power of chariots of fire, that we forget the first and most important thing: to listen to Jesus.—Bill Thomason

ILLUSTRATIONS

The movie *Chariots of Fire* gets its title from that strange, fear-inspiring story of Elijah's translation. The connection between the movie and 2 Kings 2 is that both stories are about the passing of the mantle of leadership and authority to a new generation. In the movie, that new generation is the class matriculating in 1919 at Cambridge University, the first class after World War I had decimated a generation of British youth. The film focuses on the two star runners on the British team for the 1924 Paris Olympics—Harold Abrahams, son of a Jewish immigrant from central Europe, and Eric Liddell, a Presbyterian missionary from China in Edinburgh to get his degree. Both are fiercely competitive, and both are motivated by religious concerns. Harold uses his athletic stardom to force the British class system to overcome its anti-Semitism and accept him as a social equal. Eric uses his fame to glorify God and spread the gospel.

The personalities of these men are very different. Harold is driven to find acceptance and flagellates himself over his every failure, both real and imagined. Eric, in contrast, is serene and self-confident, his one brush with angst being his temptation to violate the fourth Commandment when his qualifying heat at the Games is scheduled for a Sunday. Eric is also a contrast to his fellow Calvinists, who see God as a benevolent dictator. Eric's desire to glorify God does not grow out of a sense of duty or fear, but rather a joy in pleasing God. We learn the secret of Eric's faith in a scene he has with his sister, Jennie, who frets that his preparations for the Olympics have distracted him from his preaching of the gospel.

Eric tells Jennie that he is going back to China as a missionary. But, he says, "I've got a lot of running to do first. Jennie, Jennie . . . you've got to understand. I believe that God made me for a purpose. For China. But he also made me *fast*. And when I run, I feel his pleasure. To give it up would be to hold him in contempt. . . . To win is to honor him."

Jesus, *the* Son of God, is beloved, the object of God's pleasure. Eric Liddell, *a* son of God, also pleases God by running fast, by exercising his God-given natural abilities. All children of God need to learn the lesson Eric Liddell had learned: when we are most truly ourselves, we most truly please God.—Bill Thomason

Faith is the touching of a mystery, it is to perceive another dimension to absolutely everything. . . . In faith, the mysterious meaning of life comes alive. Beneath the simple, explicable, one-dimensional surface of things their genuine content begins to shine. . . . To speak in the simplest possible terms: faith sees, knows, senses . . . the presence of God in the world.[7]

SERMON SUGGESTIONS

Topic: God Makes Himself Known—Again
TEXT: Ps. 50:1–6
(1) Through the visible universe (v. 1). (2) Through his special revelation (v. 2). (3) Through dramatic signs of judgment (v. 3). (4) Through renewal of vows made to God in earlier days (vv. 4–5).

Topic: When We Make Demands of God
TEXT: 1 Sam. 12:19–25
(1) God lets us have our way, even when our way is wrong. (2) Consequences often make us see that we have been foolish and evil. (3) Nevertheless, God can work out his sovereign purpose: as God hears the prayers of those who care; as God uses the witness of those who champion and teach his truth and will.

WORSHIP AIDS

CALL TO WORSHIP.   "Jesus answered and said unto him, If a man love me, he will keep my words: and my Father will love him, and we will come unto him, and make our abode with him" (John 14:23).

INVOCATION.   Today, our Father, increase our love for you that we may know more of your infilling presence and in turn share in a greater way with the world the good news of your salvation.

OFFERTORY SENTENCE.   "The silver is mine, and the gold is mine, saith the Lord of hosts" (Hag. 2:8).

OFFERTORY PRAYER.   What we bring to your treasury, O God, we bring with an awareness of our stewardship. Help us to reflect on every aspect of our living, working, and saving, to the end that we shall make our lives richer toward you.

PRAYER.   O Lord, amid all threats to our security we look to thee to protect us. We would not dictate the terms of your providence. You know what is best. If our loyalty to you means that we shall be misunderstood, disliked, or even persecuted, then give us the grace to bear patiently and creatively this burden of our obedience. But grant that we shall never, through lack of love or lack of courtesy or lack of tact, bring on ourselves needless burdens and call them your will.

As we look back across the years of our lives, we can see how, again and again, we have been spared through your mercy. You have, again and again, set our feet upon a rock and put

---

[7]Alexander Schmemann, *Celebration of Faith* (Crestwood, N.Y.: St. Vladimir's Press, 1991), pp. 59–60. Cited in Ward and Wild, *Resources*, p. 82.

a song on our lips. Give us the faith to feel that solid foothold and sing that song, even before the deliverance comes. For it befits us who believe in you to stand firmly and sing joyfully, even before the fruition of our salvation. So renew our hearts in praise and gratitude.

SERMON

Topic: The Original Shepherd's Guide
TEXT: 1 Pet. 5:1–4

You've heard the jokes. They're usually shared between folks who are serving in the local church. Usually, they're facing some sort of difficulty—real or perceived. Maybe there's something they know that their church should be doing differently and they just can't seem to get the people moving in a new direction. Maybe the congregation isn't moving fast enough for these twenty-first-century Spurgeons. So they share knowing looks and speak of their congregations in lofty, biblical terms. They talk about their flocks and their fields. Then they chuckle and comfortingly remind themselves that sheep are notoriously stupid animals—and they stink, too.

In a day and age of short pastoral tenures, theological compromise, moral failure, and all-too-frequent church division, it is time for God's churches and his people to look, not at the sheep but the shepherds. Like the rulers of ancient Israel in the time of Ezekiel and the religious leaders of Jesus' day, bad shepherding is surely to blame for many of the Church's problems.

Peter, drawing on the colorful biblical imagery of shepherding, writes to the elders of the Church, exhorting them to "shepherd the flock of God" (1 Pet. 5:2). Building on this familiar picture, Peter calls them to follow the example of the Good Shepherd. To ensure that those who lead the flock are properly qualified for this vital task, Peter encourages us to consider our calling, our motivation, and our example.

(a) *Consider your calling.* If you serve in any capacity in the Church of God, you must ask yourself periodically, "Why do I do it?"

Compulsion to serve is not a valid reason. Nor should one do it simply because "someone" must. That is not true servanthood. As Peter says in verse 2, shepherding God's flock should be done voluntarily, without coercion—parental, pastoral, or otherwise (1 Pet. 5:2a). Godly shepherds are to exercise oversight of the flock out of love for the Lord and his work, and a clear sense of divine calling—plain and simple.

Some debate exists as to the meaning of the phrase "according to the will of God" in this verse. One possible meaning is that one volunteers of his own free will, according to the plan of God. However, since "the will" has been supplied in the English translation, another possibility exists. The meaning of the shorter phrase, "according to God," could be that one is to exercise pastoral oversight in the same manner as God. In either case, the motivational emphasis that Peter calls for is one of self-sacrifice like that of the Good Shepherd who came to lay down his life for his sheep (John 10:11, 15, 17–18).

(b) *Consider your motivation.* Another test that Peter suggests to ensure that one is properly shepherding the "flock of God" is to check one's motivation.

Just as compulsion is an inappropriate reason to shepherd God's flock, "sordid gain" must also be ruled out (1 Pet. 5:2b). The one who shepherds for this reason is no better than the hired hands in the parable of the Good Shepherd or those who take advantage of the flock in Ezekiel. The bad shepherds in both of these examples, John 10 and Ezekiel 34, saw the flock only for what profit the sheep could bring them. The Puritan Matthew Poole writes, "It is a shameful thing for a shepherd to feed the sheep out of love [for] the fleece." Rather, a true shepherd will serve "with eagerness," out of a deep love for Christ, the kind of love that Peter affirmed by the side of the sea (John 21:15–17).

A shepherd of the Church has been entrusted with eternal riches; he must not focus on temporal gold. While every minister deserves his or her salary, money must not be the primary focus. Unfortunately, we have to ask, How many pastors in our churches today serve only for the paycheck? How many of the pastors who move from church to church to church every couple of years do so to fill their wallets? Perhaps these shepherds love the fleece more than the sheep. Jesus said, "Seek first his kingdom and his righteousness, and all these things will be added to you" (Matt. 6:33).

(c) *Consider your example.* Finally, the shepherd must not "lord it over those allotted to [his] charge but [prove] to be examples to [his] flock" (1 Pet. 5:3).

The pastor or elder possesses real authority, but he is not to abuse it as did the Gentiles that Jesus condemns in Luke 22 or the "shepherds of Israel" who abused their sheep in Ezekiel 34:4. Instead, good shepherds concern themselves with continually "proving to be examples to the flock." Just as the people of the Church look to God and Christ for direction, they also look to their human leaders for an example. The people called of God to lead his flock must live lives worthy of being emulated. In others words, the shepherds of the Church are to lead their people unto righteousness rather than drive them from the fold.

Paul expected as much from himself. He endured hardships and persecution in his drive to share the gospel. He was stoned and left for dead. He was shipwrecked and jailed. This man loved the Lord, and those who met him knew it. Because of this, Paul could humbly call them to follow his example (Phil. 3:17; 1 Thess. 1:7; 2 Thess. 3:7, 9).

Shepherds of the modern Church, realize that your flock is watching you. Are you setting a godly example?

In the end, if the shepherds of the Church are faithful and true to the example of Christ, the "Chief Shepherd" will reward them for their diligence (1 Pet. 5:4). Rather than being ejected from the flock or running away from it, they will be honored by the Master Shepherd with an "unfading crown of glory" when their job on earth is done.

Shepherding God's flock can be a dirty job, but the benefits are great. If you follow Peter's advice, you can be confident that it's not you that stinks.—Peter Beck

SUNDAY, MARCH 5, 2006
Lectionary Message

Topic: Of Faith, Water, and Wood
Text: 1 Pet. 3:18–22
Other Readings: Gen. 8:9–17; Ps. 25:1–10; Mark 1:4–15

The setting: a classroom in then-apartheid Durban, South Africa. New Testament scholar John H. Elliott, author of the magisterial nine-hundred-page commentary on 1 Peter and one in whom academic rigor has not extinguished evangelical fire, looks out upon a sea of black faces, the students distant, withdrawn. There is no eye contact. And Elliott begins by asking,

"How many of you would be interested in hearing of a N.T. book that addresses an audience of original inhabitants who have been uprooted and dispossessed by invaders of a foreign occupying power and its alien culture?"

Now all eyes are *glued* on the speaker, and Elliott is off and running on 1 Peter, written, he told me by phone, as a word of encouragement to a people living in the eastern reaches of the Roman empire and, increasingly, victims of Rome's economically and culturally oppressive drive eastward. And for 1 Peter the urgent question is: How does one live out the gospel in such a place and time? How does one live as an exile in one's native land? Further examples (also Elliott's): How today as a small farmer? Or as one, even a veteran, sleeping on the streets of any major American city? As the working poor? As a Native American? 1 Peter is addressed to such exiles, as well as all open to seeing the world from their basement window or refrigerator box.

I. The sweet fruit of a Christian life in community:

(a) *Godward.* 1 Peter calls upon a community of exiles to be obedient, to evidence the genuineness of faith, to believe in him, to discipline yourselves (repeated), to trust in the God who raised Christ from the dead, to show faith and hope set on God, to long for spiritual milk, to grow into salvation, to come to him, to be built into a spiritual house, to believe (three references), to seek purity and reverence, in your hearts to sanctify Christ as Lord; when suffering, to entrust yourselves to a faithful creator.

(b) *Humanward.* 1 Peter sounds such notes as these: be holy in conduct; show genuine mutual love; love one another deeply from the heart; be a holy priesthood; proclaim God's mighty acts; *live as aliens and exiles* [italics mine]; conduct yourselves honorably [as outsiders]; let others [insiders who, tragically, wish to fit in this fallen world] see your honorable deeds; be capable of genuine moral seriousness (4:7); be hospitable; serve one another with whatever gift you have received from Christ; speak as if speaking the word of God.

II. Bitter fruit to be avoided:

(a) The "lower" wrong road (that is, wrongs any moral person might censure) includes the following: malice (something outsiders could be especially vulnerable to); guile, insincerity, slander; the desires of the flesh (a morally lax community will seldom have the time, focus, or credibility to live out a difference of moral stature). Do not suffer as a murderer, a thief, a criminal, *or even a mischief maker* (italics mine—a hazard also of otherwise good people).

(b) The "higher" wrong road: Do not be conformed (but at some point who *doesn't* want to conform? to fit, and thus to belong?); do not be ignorant (aliens and exiles must also *outthink* the dominant culture). Rembrandt painted St. Matthew *thinking* and even portrayed the apostle Paul in prison *with piles of parchments, deep in thought;* Botticelli painted St. Augustine *in his study,* and paintings of St. Jerome in his study were common. What church today would want a religious picture of anyone merely *thinking*? But can C-level thinking ever result in A-level witness? The early Church also *outthought* Rome.

III. The rewards of good fruit eaten, spoiled fruit avoided:

(a) 1 Peter's catalog, itself of panoramic sweep, like the opening music to "Out of Africa," includes these rewards: that you are sprinkled with his blood; new birth; the salvation of your souls; born anew; "a chosen race, a royal priesthood, a holy nation, God's own people"— aliens and exiles. (Yes, as reward! In such a world, wear it proudly, if not always happily.) Repeatedly: "You will endure. . . ."; a quiet and gentle spirit; nothing will hinder your prayers (in our 24/7, six-places-at-once culture, *think* about that one!); you will inherit a blessing, see good days; the face of the Lord will not be against you (the unstated contrast is sobering!); you will not be intimidated (Christian moxie!); a clear conscience, you will have the element of surprise (*true* "shock and awe"); you will be a people who knows what time it is ("the end of all things is near"); your love will cover a multitude of sins; God will be glorified. Even your suffering will be no disgrace but rather in accordance with God's will. The terms pound upon the heart like the sound of a surf at incoming tide.

IV. The apple does not fall far from the tree; the foundations of piety in 1 Peter:

(a) *Foundations in Christ's passion.* "Put to death in the flesh." The term *sarx* designates the tissue, muscle, or fleshly part of one's anatomy, in contrast to bones, blood, and internal organs. When contrasted, as here, to *spirit,* it refers more generally to the physical (and mortal) dimension of one's life (Elliott).

The foundation is in itself infinitely moving, consoling, and empowering: for example, Bach's "O sacred head, now wounded." The German actually translates, "Oh, head full of blood and wounds." Another example: Michelangelo's "Pieta"—Mary holding the dead Christ, Mary's face, even in marble, pulsing with sorrow. And Rembrandt's painting of the entombment of Christ (Munich) is so powerful that art restorers say they cannot work on it more than about twenty minutes at a time. And there are the hymns, such as "Were You There?"

Faith's foundations in the death of Christ also protect us from founding faith upon deaths, or the *use* of deaths that is *not* life-giving. Note the *use* made by some of September 11, the use *all* war makes of its dead, the use high-risk sports enthusiasts and others make of their mentors.

(b) *Visit to spirits in prison.* (Luther: "a strange text and certainly a more obscure passage than any other . . . in the N.T."). Whatever the author meant, the image of Christ visiting spirits in prison is rich with possibilities. Choose your own. What a gulag of misery, with endless columns of abjects trudging off to prison—prisons spiritual, moral, economic, ethnic and national, mental, physical, even DNA—is challenged in this *tour de force* of the Son of God who breaks imprisoned spirits out of darkness and into beauteous heavenly Light.

(c) *Baptism prefigured in the story of Noah.* The flood story is, in truth, a grim tale. A thirteenth-century miniature depicts a crow feeding on the upturned neck of the floating, bloated corpse of a horse; a medieval woodcut depicts the ark with no sails. The message: with water everywhere, where should one go? There will be no port in this storm. Hans Baldung Grien, in *The Flood* (1525), "pays great attention to portraying the agony of the people that illustrate their superhuman efforts to stay alive."[1]

Michelangelo's work in the Sistine chapel is equally grim—men, women, and children desperately seeking high ground, climbing trees, a boat loaded with people about to capsize. Rembrandt, in a simple drawing, depicts Noah and his family trudging up the ark's gangplank with heavy hearts, a study in infinite grief and loss, like the Holocaust survivors they are.

And yet—"Noah is a figure of Christ, who has regenerated us by water, and faith, and wood" (that is, *the cross.*) Thus does Justin Martyr (110–165 A.D.) ponder the flood and Christ's saving work. "For Christ, being the first-born of every creature, became again the chief of

---

[1]*Old Testament Figures in Art,* the J. Paul Getty Museum.

another race regenerated by himself through water, and faith, and wood, containing the mystery of the cross; even as Noah was saved by wood when he rode over the waters with his household."—Peter Fribley

ILLUSTRATIONS

"For righteous Noah, along with the other mortals at the deluge, i.e., with his own wife, his three sons and their wives, being eight in number, were a symbol of the eighth day, wherein Christ appeared when he rose from the dead, for ever the first in power. . . . Accordingly, when the prophet says, 'I saved thee in the times of Noah,' . . . he addresses the people who are equally faithful to God, and possess the same signs. . . . But the whole earth, as the Scripture says, was inundated, and the water rose in height fifteen cubits above all the mountains: So that it is evident that this was not spoken to the land, but to the people who obeyed him: for whom also He had before prepared a resting-place in Jerusalem, as was previously demonstrated by all the symbols of the deluge; I mean, that by faith, water, and wood, those who are afore-prepared, and who repent of the sins which they have committed, shall escape from the impending judgment of God."[2]

A prayer from the 1662 *Book of Common Prayer* of the Church of England, to be read at times of storm at sea, captures the dichotomy of life and death in the Flood prefiguring baptism:

> O most glorious and gracious Lord God, who dwellest in heaven, but beholdest all things below: Look down, we beseech thee, and hear us, calling out of the depth of misery, and out of the jaws of this death, which is ready now to swallow us up: Save us Lord, else we perish. The living, the living shall praise thee. O send thy word of command to rebuke the raging winds, and the roaring sea; that we, being delivered from this distress, may live to serve thee, and to glorify thy Name all the days of our life. Hear, Lord, and save us, for the infinite merits of our blessed Savior, thy Son, our Lord Jesus Christ. *Amen*

The prayer immediately follows the Psalms, where for centuries sea captains could readily find it!

A prayer based on Luther's "flood-Baptism" prayer:

> Holy God, mighty Lord, gracious Father: We give you thanks, for in the beginning your Spirit moved over the waters and you created heaven and earth. By the gift of water you nourish and sustain us and all living things.
>
> By the waters of the flood you condemned the wicked and saved those whom you had chosen, Noah and his family. You led Israel by the pillar of cloud and fire through the sea, out of slavery into the freedom of the promised land. In the waters of the Jordan your Son was baptized by John and anointed with the Spirit. By the baptism of his own death and resurrection your beloved Son has set us free from the bondage to sin and death, and opened the way to the joy and freedom of everlasting life. He made water a sign of the kingdom and of

---

[2]Justin Martyr, *The Ante-Nicene Fathers,* Vol. 1, p. 268.

cleansing and rebirth. In obedience to his command, we make disciples of all nations, baptizing them in the name of the Father, and of the Son, and of the Holy Spirit.

Pour out your Holy Spirit, so that *those* who *are* baptized may be given new life. Wash away the sin of *all those* who *are* cleansed by this water and bring *them* forth as *inheritors* of your glorious kingdom.[3]

SERMON SUGGESTIONS

Topic: A Pilgrimage of Prayer
TEXT: Ps. 25:1–10
(1) Begin with trust (vv. 1–3). (2) Ask for guidance (vv. 4–5). (3) Confess your sins (vv. 6–7). (4) Walk humbly in the paths God shows (vv. 8–10).

Topic: "Friendship Unsurpassed"
TEXT: 2 Sam. 1:25–26
(1) The friendship of David and Jonathan (1 Sam. 20:1–42). (2) Friendship today: it fulfills important needs; it is subject to loss and grief; it may be used by God in creative and redeeming ways.

WORSHIP AIDS

CALL TO WORSHIP.   "The hour cometh and now is, when the true worshippers shall worship the Father in spirit and in truth: for the Father seeketh such to worship him" (John 4:23).

INVOCATION.   We remember how our Savior suffered, that we may, by faith, live the life abundant. In that hope we pray that our worship will be God-honoring, fully committed, and ever-informed by the cross of Christ.—E. Lee Phillips

OFFERTORY SENTENCE.   "Seek ye first the Kingdom of God and his righteousness, and all these things shall be added unto you" (Matt. 6:33).

OFFERTORY PRAYER.   Our Father, we have trouble establishing our priorities in life. Help us to know what really counts in the end, so that we may give our hearts to matters of first importance. Let no earthly love stand between us and our doing what life is all about. In the name of him who loved us, lived for us, and died for us.

PRAYER.   (Lent) God, it is never easy to lead others in prayer, but it is even more challenging in Lent when we are confronted with the Master's "Follow me," as in no other season. Lent is no Sunday school picnic; it is the challenge to choose the road less traveled. Lent is a time of threshing and winnowing, a time of pruning and sacrifice, a time of discipleship and the bearing of a cross. Lent is not so much a time for giving up something as giving oneself to something, not a time to pull back but commit, not a time to withhold but to be generous—to give to the uttermost.

---

[3]"Holy Baptism," *Lutheran Book of Worship*, 1978, p. 122.

O God, grant us faith to stay the course, to trust love in the face of life's contradictions, to discover the joy that comes through the agony of pain.

Help us to realize, O God, that no casual following, no sauntering along with our hands in our pockets, no half-hearted commitment will suffice when Jesus confronts us: "Are you able to drink of the cup of which I am about to drink and be baptized with the baptism with which I am to be baptized?"

We thank you for what we have witnessed this morning: the celebration of the sanctity of the family in the sacrament of baptism. May what we have seen and heard renew in us that covenant that you made with our Father Abraham at the dawn of recorded history.

In covenant we pray for one another: where there is any discouragement may the family of faith encourage; where there is loneliness, may we befriend; where some letter is needed, may we be the thoughtful writer; where ill health threatens body, mind, or soul, we pray for the grace that makes whole, no matter what.

Bless him who is the Servant of the Word on this occasion with the mighty power of Your Spirit.

For the troubled areas of this world we pray your peace—for life, not death.

Through him who prays from a cross, "Father, forgive them for they know not what they do" and is here as Reconciler, teaching *us* to pray.—John Thompson

SERMON

Topic: Which Way to Heaven?

Text: Matt. 7:13–14

It matters which road you take in life. In Jesus' day a narrow way could be a road winding left to right up a mountain toward a walled city on top of the mountain. The strait gate was the entrance into the city. The walk was tough because it went up the mountainside. Most people chose to remain in the valleys to walk the broad and easy way.

I. The road most traveled is the way worst traveled—"Wide is the gate and broad is the way that leads to destruction, and there are many who go in by it" (Matt. 7:13).

(a) We live in an undisciplined age, for the easy way costs no sacrifice.

1. A river flows along crooked channels, and it takes the way of least resistance.
2. You may believe in heaven without it affecting your life down here.
3. None can "yawn self to heaven with an idle wish" (Richard Cecil).

(b) The easy way, instead of bringing freedom, restricts and limits life.

1. You become a slave to comfort, pleasure, and selfishness.
2. You will search for happiness and never find it.
3. You will try to avoid problems and suffering only to find more pain.

(c) The easy way leads to the wide gate of destruction and despair.

1. No matter how many are in the crowd, the broad way of sin leads to destruction.
2. Lot and company found this when they took the low road to Sodom.
3. No one is predestined to hell, but God knows the human inclination to sin.

II. The way less traveled is the way best traveled—"Because narrow is the gate and diffi-cult is the way which leads to life, and there are few who find it" (7:14).

(a) Cost and sacrifice is rewarded with growth, direction, and meaning.

1. Salvation is both God's gift and God's demand.
2. Nothing great in life was ever achieved without discipline.
3. Jesus never begged for disciples; he merely laid down the rules and asked us follow him.

(b) The way of discipline expands and enriches life.

1. Jesus was neither a legalist nor a libertine. He could see truth wherever it was.
2. The narrow road and strait gate of Jesus opens the door to new possibilities, so Jesus is not talking about having a narrow mind that limits God.
3. A train must travel narrow tracks to see the countryside—a narrow bridge; across a canyon is safety.

(c) This way leads to the narrow gates of life in heaven.

1. A "gate" here refers to entrance into heaven.
2. As we walk the narrow road, a vision of heaven becomes clearer.
3. Jesus is the "Door" through whom we must enter heaven.

III. The road you take will make all the difference in your life.

(a) In Robert Frost's poem "The Road Less Traveled," he said that he "took the road less traveled, and it made all the difference."

(b) Each of us comes to a crossroads calling for a decision. We must make a choice.

(c) Jesus walks with us as our companion along the narrow road.

Where will you end up if you keep traveling the way you are going? John Bunyan's clas-sic book *Pilgrim's Progress* opens with: "As I walked through the wilderness of this world. . . ." Bunyan describes alternate roads, one hard and one easy to travel. Pilgrim chose the hard road leading to life. At the end of the journey Pilgrim says, "I am going to my Father's, and tho' with great difficulty. . . . I do not repent of all the Trouble I have been at to arrive where I am. . . . My Marks and Scars I carry with me, to be a witness . . . that I have fought his Battles who now will be my rewarder." Bunyan concludes his book with, "So he passed over, and all the Trumpets sounded for him on the other side." At the end of the road we find rest from our travels in Christ.—Ron Blankenship

SUNDAY, MARCH 12, 2006
Lectionary Message

Topic: The Great Reversal
TEXT: Mark 8:31–38
Other Readings: Gen. 17:1–7, 15–16; Ps. 22:23–31; Rom. 4:13–25

Today's lesson immediately follows Jesus' question, "Who do people say that I am?" and, after others' false starts, Peter's answer: "You are the Messiah." One would expect, as it were, the house lights to come up and for there to be great applause, even a standing ovation. But what *does* follow is, in fact, Jesus' prediction of his own suffering and death. And he says all this quite openly; it should come as no surprise.

I. "He said all this quite openly." Historically, the Church, for all its backsliding, for all its monuments to pomp and power, for all its banked fires of cooled passion for its Lord, *has* borne witness that the Son of Man must suffer, and that in this regard the Church is not above its Master.

(a) The Church has "said all this quite openly" in its music. Each preacher will cite that music to which he and his people resonate. A few obvious examples are Passion music: Bach's St. Matthew's Passion and St. John's. There is an entire history of Requiem masses, among them masses by Mozart, Schubert, Haydn, Brahms, and Faure. I heard Faure's "Pie Jesu" ("Blessed Lord Jesus"), from Faure's "Requiem," sung after 9/11 at the funeral of FDNY firefighter Thomas Patrick Cullen III. It was sung in Latin in a Park Avenue Catholic church in New York City and, *in Latin*, was deeply understood by those rows and rows of firefighters with the "thousand-yard stare." And nowhere is witness to Christ's suffering and to our sharing it proclaimed more openly in music than in Negro spirituals.

(b) The Church has "said all this openly" in its art. The tormented painter Caravaggio, himself a murderer, depicted grim scenes of Christ's Passion, the figures of which come from real persons in his own time. And Matthias Gruenewald's "Eisenheim altarpiece," with its harrowing portrayal of Christ on the cross, shows the nails through his hands. North European Gothic sculpture repeatedly portrays in oak the limp body of Christ, in one case held in God the Father's arms. In a Lutheran church in Luther's Saxony, the pastor, from a high pulpit, looks straight across at a large cross with a corpus on it. The message: preach Christ, and him crucified. Rembrandt, in his paintings of the Crucifixion, by putting himself quite recognizably in the picture could not have made the message more clear: we share in Christ's sufferings, as well as his Crucifixion.

(c) The Church has "said all this openly" in its most revered saints. It has affirmed the tie between its life and Christ's life in its choices of classic saints: from St. Stephen (the first martyr) and St. Paul and St. Peter to William Tyndale; Bishop Polycarp, martyred at eighty-six; and, all over Europe, now in museums but once in churches, statues to the first conscientious objector, St. Sebastian, his young torso tied to a post and arrows piercing his chest. (Sebastian had been a Roman soldier, but upon becoming a Christian, came to believe military service incompatible with his new-found faith.)

Of modern examples that "say all this openly," there is also no shortage: Bishop Helder Camera; Dietrich *and* Klaus Bonhoeffer; Martin Luther King Jr.; Father Michael Judd, FDNY chaplain, the first death certificate issued by New York City after September 11; "the four chaplains" of World War II—two Protestants, one Catholic, one a rabbi—all of whom gave their life jackets to others and went down with the S.S. Dorchester (depicted on a three-cent postage stamp).

II. But Peter took Jesus aside and began to rebuke him. To which Jesus replies that Peter's mind is set on earthly things, not heavenly things. (Note body language, as well as verbal rebuke.)

(a) Is Peter an isolated case and, in any event, uniquely under the influence of the Devil? In both cases, the answer is no.

Peter does not speak for himself only but also for the community. In this regard, note that Jesus, after his initial reply, speaks to the crowd and his disciples, not Peter only.

Peter's words are not put on his lips by some outside power; they are human words and quite his own, quite as much his own as his later denial.

(b) What are some of the human things upon which we, like Peter, set our minds? This Lenten season may be as good a time as any to use, as a sort of grid of self-examination, a brief overview of one or more of the Seven Deadly Sins. For note that "Square 1"—first base, in Jesus' reconstruction of life's focus—is *not* to take up your cross but to *deny* yourself. Yet there is a no more countercultural proposition than that one should deny oneself.

Pride—once a deadly sin, even *the* cardinal sin; one now seldom hears the word except with approval. Legitimate positive use aside, what did classical religious thinkers see as its pitfalls? Can its classical understanding be retrieved? Thomas Aquinas cataloged four deadly wrong foundations of pride: (1) some people consider themselves the cause of their achievements and talents (heard *anything* wrong with that on some talk radio?). (2) Others, though acknowledging their gifts as from God, believe they deserve them (in saying that, can one avoid saying that I *deserve* my DNA, or that I *deserve* not having died in the jungles of Vietnam or being killed by a drunk, and so on? I don't see how). (3) And there are those who boast of qualities they do not possess. (4) Finally, there are those who, by way of calling attention to their uniqueness, despise others who lack the qualities they possess.

The deadly sins of greed, envy, and gluttony are enjoying a heyday (not that anger, lust, or sloth are languishing!). A classic parable of envy: someone is told that he will be given anything he wishes but that his enemy will be given that gift twofold. And the person wishes to be blind in one eye. A tale of greed: Solomon Schimmel, in *The Seven Deadly Sins*, underscores how our culture masks greed with such euphemisms as "financial success," "the good life," or "having it all." (Masks? Not always. There is a game called GREED, complete with dice spelling the word. Gluttony is a brand of chocolate, and so on.) Why do people pursue wealth? Schimmel says for hedonistic impulses, for prestige, for "the challenge of the chase," as an instrument of power, as a result of envy, due to pressure from a spouse, to alleviate anxiety, for devout Calvinist Protestants, out of religious belief. A few do it out of altruism. "The classical moralists consider inordinate efforts to acquire possessions as avaricious when our motives are selfish or hedonistic, our means unjust, and we put our trust in riches."[4]

The story of Midas shows how greed dehumanizes. Princeton economist Paul Krugman cites the story of Midas as a parable of flawed economic theory, wherein nothing is valued but tangibles. Thomas Aquinas distinguishes two ways in which greed may mean a failure in moderation: it may directly harm one's fellow man, or it may corrupt one's inner attitude toward wealth. (When friends cleared out Father Michael Judd's monastic quarters after 9/11, they found they had little to attend to; he had already given most of his few possessions away. He was ready to die.) "Our gluttony, lust, greed, pride, and envy are stimulated and serviced by the greed of certain businesses and advertising agencies."[5] Yet seventeenth-century divine Jeremy Taylor writes: "The happiest people are those who help others rather than those who focus on helping themselves."[6]

---

[4]Solomon Schimmel, *The Seven Deadly Sins: Jewish, Christian, and Classical Reflections on Human Psychology.*
[5]Schimmel.
[6]Schimmel.

III. "The happiest people": living the cross.

(a) The paradox of betrayal as witness: the Church, in confessing its calling to bear witness to Christ's suffering and to share that suffering, while at the same time confessing that it falls far short of doing so, need not simply be seen as trapped in a cycle of failure, guilt, and remorse. Paradoxically, by this self-indicting confession, it keeps Christ, and not itself, central. It bears witness, rare in this high-fiving, chest-thumping day, to a power beyond itself.

(b) The legitimate reward of honest confession: the Church confesses the one in whom it is *not* ashamed (Mark 8:38). Nearly by default, the Church invites others to join in its worship of the one about whom none need be embarrassed, none need apologize. Taking then, inevitably, its place at the "lower place" of the banquet of its Lord, it confidently awaits the word, "Friend, go higher." This is not presumption but the promised fruit of the tree of authentic piety.

(c) The stories of unsung saints: parables of fidelity in the everyday. Some years ago, on a wintry day, an airliner crashed into the Potomac River. Passengers struggled in the icy waters, and out of that chaos there emerged one person, an ordinary businessman, who pulled numerous passengers to safety before succumbing to the cold. He was, overnight, a hero. But who was he before then? I suggest that he was *exactly* who he was before, only no one knew it, not even himself. There are many who quietly live a life of fidelity to God and neighbor. God may have a firmer grip on you than you know. Yes. But be careful: a *false* humility may also belittle the power of God. Lighten up and give thanks for that power. The Son of Man will give more thanks yet "when he comes in the glory of his Father with the holy angels." By God's grace, insofar as you are "an apple that has not fallen far from the tree," by all means give thanks to God for the tree. But also for the good fruit that *you* are. Rest assured, *God* does.—Peter Fribley

ILLUSTRATIONS

In the course of sending over twelve thousand used paperbacks to GIs in Iraq, I have corresponded by e-mail with a number of service personnel. (My e-mail address is in each book, together with the message, "Whoever you are reading this book, we pray for your safe return.") There is no correspondence I treasure more than that from Staff Sgt. James Genco. (I have permission to tell his story.) Jim, utterly unaware of self in his writing, has come to symbolize, for me, the nobility of the ordinary person who does his duty, seeks not to gain his life but to lose it for others. I quote:

10/09/03

Peter

This is a hard place to work and keep the peace a side note a few months back I was delivering the dinner meal to a line unit a crowd of people were at the gate as we tried to enter a person came through the crowd with an AK47 firing away myself and two gate guards turned and fired the person dropped . . . he was 10 years old said the father a short time later as he cursed us for taking his son I don't know if I did it I had to protect my men and my unit. The boy injured one soldier and some civilians I did not want to do it my son is not much older this place is strange at times.

Jim

Das Gewissen steht aug (The Rise of Conscience), a book published in the 1950s, gives the biographies of sixty-four martyrs against the Nazi regime and is organized in an unusual way: by motive. First, appropriately, is "The confession of youth." There the open, quiet face of Jonathan Start, Jehovah's Witness, looks out at the viewer. He was, the guards said, the talk of the whole camp. When the guards trembled as they put the noose about his neck, he told them, "Why do you tremble; stand fast for Jehovah and Gideon." Those were his last words. Sophie Scholl, a young student, did the insane thing of throwing anti-regime leaflets about.

The second category: "Lived learning." Elisabeth von Thadden's last words were from a hymn by Paul Gerhard, "End, O Lord, bring to an end all our need." Third: "Word and sacrifice for others." Fourth: "The state and right," among whom was attorney Klaus Bonhoeffer. Fifth: "The sense of tradition." Sixth: "In the spirit of Christ," with Dietrich Bonhoeffer. Seventh: "Freedom and order."

Chaplain (Colonel) Charles F. Kriete, retired, a long-time friend of mine, tells of his CO's first words to him upon arriving in Vietnam: "There are two kinds of persons here, those who expect to die and those who expect to live. If you are in the former category, you will be of no use to me." What his commander meant was that only if my friend was able to put death behind him, would he be of use. Only if, way inside, he died to the fear of death. (The CO had won a Silver Star in WW II in the South Pacific at age sixteen. He knew whereof he spoke.)

Recently, I called on an elderly, retired former missionary educator to Madagascar. She recounted that in the early days mail could take six months, and there was no cable. "You put your loved ones in the hands of the Lord," she said, "and they did the same with you." How much trust in God have we lost because, with better communication, we no longer think we need place one another in God's hands?

There is no writer on the Seven Deadly Sins more respected than the sixth-century pope, Gregory the Great:

> Gregory did not include pride as one of the seven cardinal sins, but rather believed that it breeds the seven, which in turn breed a multitude of other vices. . . . The arrogant person who thinks so highly of himself . . . expects deference and is thus easily *angered.* Assuming himself superior to others, he is especially prone to *envy,* which is a response to threats to one's self-esteem. Being self-satisfied, he does not feel compelled to bestir himself in pursuit of spiritual goals and so commits the sin of *sloth.* He will easily trample over the rights of others, as is so frequently done by the *greedy,* the *gluttonous,* and the *lustful.* It is not that pride inevitably leads to these vices, but since this is frequently the case, Gregory designated pride the mother and Queen of all vices.[7]

> Pride is unique among the seven deadly sins in that we are frequently unaware of our arrogance, whereas we tend to know when we are angry, greedy, gluttonous, and so on. Moreover, unlike the other six sins, when our pride is pointed out to us we often do not even realize that it is a vice. This is because it is difficult for us to admit that we are of less worth than we imagine ourselves to be, and because our culture values high self-esteem and fails to appreciate humility or even modesty.[8]

---

[7]Schimmel, pp. 33–34.
[8]Schimmel, p. 36.

Medieval artists and poets depicted pride with a variety of symbols which capture the many facets of the proud sinner. Pride was a queen or king (lord of the vices), helmeted with spear in hand, mounted on a white steed, attacking the virtues. Pride was a lion, king of the beasts, an eagle, flying above all others in the sky, a peacock arrogantly calling attention to its glorious feathers, and a woman vainly admiring her reflection in a mirror.[9]

—Peter Fribley

SERMON SUGGESTIONS

Topic: From Cross to Resurrection
TEXT: Ps. 22:23–31
Jesus quoted this psalm (v. 1) as he was dying on the cross. (1) God rules (v. 23). (2) Despite all our sins, hesitations, and fears, he hears our desperate prayers (v. 24). (3) God's victory in our lives is a source of praise everywhere and forever (vv. 25–31).

Topic: Wisdom Then and Wisdom Now
TEXT: 1 Kings 3:7–28; Gal. 6:7–8
(1) The amazing wisdom of Solomon. (2) How we can match and surpass the wisdom of Solomon.

WORSHIP AIDS

CALL TO WORSHIP.   "Rend your heart, and not your garments, and turn unto the Lord your God: for he is gracious and merciful, slow to anger, and of great kindness, and repenteth him of the evil" (Joel 2:13).

INVOCATION.   Father of our Lord Jesus Christ, we beseech thee to engender in us during these holy days of Lent such spiritual understanding that we may remember the life and labor of our Lord, not vainly as a thing long gone, but fruitfully, seeing in our own days the same eternal Spirit which in him revealed the glory of thy great love to me, bearing the cross for our sakes.—Samuel H. Miller

OFFERTORY SENTENCE.   "Unto whomsoever much is given, of him shall be much required: and to whom men have committed much, of him they will ask the more" (Luke 12:48).

OFFERTORY PRAYER.   O God, some of us have been given much, yet we are afraid some calamity will overtake us. Our anxiety has made us untrusting and poor stewards of thy bounty. Increase our faith, allay our fears, and open the wellsprings of generosity in our hearts, so that our giving may not be decided by our worries but by thy expectations.

PRAYER.   O God, we turn to thee in the faith that thou dost understand and art very merciful. Some of us are not sure concerning thee, not sure what thou art, not sure that thou are at all. Yet there is something at work behind our minds. In times of stillness, we hear it, like

---

[9]Schimmel, p. 34.

a distant song; there is something in the sky at evening time, something in the face of man. We feel that 'round our incompleteness flows thy greatness, 'round our restlessness, they rest. Yet this is not enough.

We want a heart to speak to, a heart that understands, a friend to whom we can turn, a breast on which we may lean. O that we could find thee. Yet could we ever think these things unless thou had inspired us? Could we ever want these things unless thou were very near?

Some of us know full well, but we are sore afraid. We dare not yield ourselves to thee, for we fear what that might mean. Our foolish freedom, our feeble pleasures, our fatal self-indulgence suffice to hold us back from thee, though thou art our very life, and we so sick and needing thee. Our freedom has proved false; our pleasures have long since lost their zest; our sins—oh, how we hate them.

Come and deliver us, for we have lost all hope in ourselves.—W. E. Orchard

SERMON
Topic: Baptized with Sinners
TEXT: Matt. 3:13–17

The paradox of Christ in the Gospels leaves an element of mystery for us to ponder, and the logical contradictions begin at the beginning with the baptism of Jesus. The Gospel of John passes over the baptism entirely. The baptizer is a forerunner who identifies Jesus as "the Lamb of God" and reports the descent of the Spirit on Jesus, but the fourth Gospel never mentions the baptism of Jesus. In the other Gospels, the baptism is something of an embarrassment. The message of John the Baptist was confrontational, and his baptism was a sign of repentance from sin. In Luke, the people ask, "What then should we do?" John speaks directly to the people, including Pharisees, Sadducees, tax collectors, and soldiers, about specific signs of selfishness, extortion, and violence. Jesus was guilty of none of these things. Why should he submit to baptism by John and be found among the notorious sinners of his day, acting out a ritual of repentance and cleansing from sin? The puzzle continued to perplex Christians long after the Gospels were written. Jerome refers to a Gospel to the Hebrews in which Mary suggested that the whole family go to John and be baptized. Jesus protested: "In what have I sinned that I should go and be baptized by him? Unless, perhaps, what I have just said is a sin of ignorance."

Matthew alone attempts to explain. When John protested, "I need to be baptized by you," Jesus replied, "it is proper for us in this way to fulfill all righteousness." Christian baptism begins with John, but we must follow Christ far beyond John. When we do, we get beyond the damnation of John to the redemptive note of grace in Christ. For Christians, the meaning of baptism extended beyond the negative rite of cleansing and repentance in John's ministry. In Christ, baptism became a positive act of commitment to the will of the Father, an affirmation of the faith journey.

(a) *Baptism stands at the beginning of the Christian life.* Life begins with baptism. Just as baptism was the first act of the saving mission of Jesus, baptism is the first act of the Christian life. Dale Moody stressed the importance of baptism as a door to the Church. He liked to tell of the excavation of an ancient church building from the first Christian centuries. A baptismal pool was found, not at the front where we like to place our baptistery but at the door of the church as a symbol of entrance into the Christian life.

One day a very important man approached Jesus in the privacy and secrecy of the evening to pursue questions about the Kingdom of God that Jesus preached. Jesus identified the beginning of the Christian life with birth: "You must be born from above." Nicodemus was confused. He had already been born. Physically, we cannot repeat the event through which our lives began. Jesus enlarged the vision to include life in the Spirit. Jesus repeated, "No one can enter the Kingdom of God without being born of the water and the Spirit." Since we begin life in the amniotic fluid of the womb, we are physically born of water. Because the Christian life begins in the waters of baptism, we are also born spiritually in the water.

(b) *Baptism is a matter of choice.* The most important presence in the baptistry is the faith of the new Christian. Jesus chose to be baptized of John. It is highly unlikely that the disciples would have concocted a story that they had so much trouble explaining. Jesus was not compelled by John or by any necessity to submit to baptism. We can only guess at the source in John's experience of baptism. The Essenes practiced a rite of washing that may have provided the key, and John himself might have come from this sect to begin preaching around the Jordan. Jesus could have gone to the source, to the Essenes. He might have baptized himself, considering that no one, including John, was really worthy of such a task.

John Smythe and Thomas Helwys are credited with the beginnings of English Baptists in Amsterdam, Holland. The British Crown would not allow separated sects to practice their faith, so the Baptists packed up and left. Smythe was reported to have baptized himself before administering the rite to the rest of the congregation. He later had problems of conscience over self-baptism and resigned the sect. Helwys was left to lead the new congregation back to England.

Later in Baptist history, J. R. Graves attempted to make a case for baptismal succession based on tracing one's baptism through ministers all the way back to Christ and the apostles. Smythe and Graves missed it. The authenticity of baptism is in the commitment of the believer, not the holiness or historical pedigree of the minister. That is why we talk in the baptistery. Someone asked me recently who authorizes baptism? I realized that I never say, "by the authority vested in me." The focus is on the believer, "Upon your confession of faith in Jesus Christ as Savior and Lord."

(c) *Baptism is a mark of identity.* In baptism you are marked for life as a child of God and disciple of Christ. Baptism is an extension of birth. I have stuffed away in a file an ancient copy of my birth certificate. I was born in my grandparents' home, delivered by a country doctor, Dr. Dean, whose operating room was usually found in the kitchen or bedroom of a farmhouse. He had no connection or significant obligation to the state and no hospital or office staff to back his work. My parents had to go to the local courthouse and testify to my birth. Purely on the basis of their witness, I was certified to be male, live, and the child of Walter and Dessa Dipboye. On occasions when I wonder about my existence, I can pull out the document and find my identity from the beginning.

In baptism Jesus identified himself with the sinful humanity he came to save; 2 Isaiah's Suffering Servant was counted with the transgressors, despised and rejected: "the LORD has laid on him the iniquity of us all." The scandal of baptism for Jesus was also the scandal of the cross. He counted himself as one of us. He not only chose baptism, he chose each of us. As Jesus counted himself in the human family of mortals through baptism, in baptism we sinners anchor our identity in Christ.—Larry Dipboye

SUNDAY, MARCH 19, 2006

Lectionary Message

Topic: The Cleansing of the Temple: A Work in Progress

Text: John 2:13–22

Other Readings: Exod. 20:1–17; Ps. 19; 1 Cor. 1:18–25

I. Viewing the Temple: Beginnings Seen Through the Prism of Endings

(a) The fourth Gospel places the story of Jesus' cleansing of the Temple at the outset of Jesus' ministry, whereas the other Gospels put the story at the end, at Jesus' Passion. Since it seems unlikely that, having cleansed the Temple, Jesus would have been able to move about freely for the next three years, it would seem that, factually, the other Gospels got it right and thus that John, who on occasion *appears* to play more loose with history, once again got it wrong.

(b) But not so fast! We often look at beginnings through the lens of their endings and often better understand because we do. There is reason and historical support for placing events out of factual sequence. And we are especially prone to look at beginnings through the lens of endings when the ending has not been peaceful but violent or tragic.

For example, the person may have been a great historical figure. Those haunting scenes of JFK—the young sailor, the young man sailing, those scenes with his children—and our pride and joy as he declares, *"Ich bin ein Berliner"*—but all, for us, forever seen against a late-November day in Dallas.

Another example: as tourists, we wander through the rooms of some historical figure's home: Emily Dickinson's home, Eisenhower's in Kansas, Custer's quarters at Fort Riley. Or we tour the Wright brothers' bicycle shop in Dayton, Ohio, or African American poet Paul Lawrence Dunbar's home in that same city, and, above all, Jerusalem, city of David and our Lord.

(c) But the figures may be so-called ordinary people who, for us, are now forever framed by their ending.

Here's an example: a little girl, her diary, her family's small apartment in Amsterdam, a retrospective of some sixty of her adoring father's photographs, his shadow often in the picture, and always that other shadow—the Holocaust. Anne Frank.

And another: at one of several FDNY firefighters' funerals I attended immediately following 9/11, in Brooklyn, at the back of the church of largely Hispanic Catholics, the usual collection of the deceased's photographs, among them several of a little boy, proudly seated in his toy fire truck. The poignant, sometimes heartbreaking and truly revealing prism of endings turned on beginnings.

And who, watching an old rerun of, say, "Law and Order," can catch a glimpse of the World Trade Center against the nighttime New York City skyline and *not* view those proud towers through their fiery end? The fourth Gospel knows what it is doing.

II. Cleansing the Temple

(a) What is frequently said (but wrong)? It is frequently said that in the Temple scene Jesus, by becoming angry, even "losing it," shows his humanity. Here, it is said, is not the sallow-faced, "indoor" Jesus of some Sunday school curricula; here is not the passive, hand-wringing "Now children, be *nice*" Jesus of some Christian exhortation. Here is no naïve avoidance of the necessity of the gospel to confront power. Here, by gum, is a *man. Here,* in showing his violent anger, Jesus demonstrates that he is human.

(b) Anger in Jesus' hands is one thing but in ours often quite another. Anger is still one of the Seven Deadly Sins. Like dynamite used to tunnel through a mountain, anger can be used for constructive social purposes. But too often it isn't. Thomas Aquinas likened anger—a deadly sin—either to one who hears, but not well and thus gets it wrong, or to an elderly man being led by the nose through the guile of a young mistress.

To focus on Christ's anger as a *sign* of his humanity is, in effect, to seek after signs. But Jesus' *entire life,* and not especially this outburst, is expressive of his humanity. Moreover, *to single out anger* and gladly affirm *anger* as expressive of his humanity, versus, for example, Jesus at the marriage of Cana, which immediately precedes our text and at which Jesus is the life of the party, probably says more about us than about our Lord.

(c) "Warmer," but still off the mark: the cleansing of the Temple as an attack on, and an attempt to reform, organized religion. Jesus does attack the religion of his day, and in the fourth Gospel with special vitriol against the Jews. Thus in the Temple scene John would appear to remind us that religion should serve as a means to an end—the love of God and neighbor, the upright, Godward life commended in Psalms 1 and 15 and everywhere in Scripture—and not as an end in itself. But in John, especially, what you see is often not what you get, or at least not what John wants you to get. John's cues and verbal puns and double entendres can be as subtle and veiled as the facial expressions of a high-stakes poker player. An attack on organized religion with the end to reform it? Warmer, but once again, as with the focus on Jesus' anger, still off the mark.

III. Raising the Temple

(a) The temple Jesus speaks of is his body, and if we get past the barrier of too-easy familiarity with the story—our "of course, he means" response—Jesus' claim is scarcely easier for us to hear than it was for John's first hearers, including the Jews.

A modern-day parable: I pastored a small rural church near 225-foot, million-dollar wind generators; the foundation of one was not solid, and the tower began to tilt. What to do? Guy the tower? Simply hope for the best? No, the entire tower had to be taken down, a new foundation poured a distance away, and the tower re-erected.

On what sinking sand is the Church founded today? Opinions will differ. But John's agenda is no mere reform, however wide-sweeping. That would be *cleansing* the Temple, *guying* the wind generator. But one "leaning tower of Pisa" is enough, and it is justly famous only because it is still there, not because it is a good idea.

(b) What, then, is our response? Seek to embody Christ's full humanity, his "life of the party" at Cana as fully as his anger at the money changers? By all means. Reform, yes. And much more, but for that, other texts at other times. Here, rather, something quite different—something as simple as reform is complex and as quiet as humanity is noisy.

Remember—remember to your bones. Remember when you have as good as forgotten all those hymns, perhaps especially those most beloved to you. Remember as parents, suddenly finding yourselves in a quiet home, your noisy teenager newly off to college. Remember, as I do, the god-awful quiet late at night in the orthopedic ward of a military hospital filled with GIs, all of them amputees, fresh off a four-engine air-ambulance from Vietnam. (I tried to welcome one man home at the plane by shaking his right hand, only to find he didn't have one—or legs. Another man, in a wheelchair, on his first phone call home, kept apologizing, through tears, to his mother—for losing his legs.) Remember with all the filledness of that pregnant silence that immediately follows the performance of a great orchestral work.

Remember Jesus. Jesus was speaking of the temple of his body. And when some crane of time has gently laid all the towers of your hopes on the ground, the foundations themselves being fatally flawed, or simply, like Jesus' own old age, somehow not to be, remember Jesus.

Jesus was speaking of the temple of his body.

"After he was raised from the dead, *his disciples remembered* that he said this; and they believed the Scriptures and the word that Jesus had spoken."

ILLUSTRATIONS

The artist Cecco del Caraavaggio's "The Cleansing of the Temple, 1610–1615," depicts a Jesus in centered, steely anger, coming down a flight of stairs, lashing out with a handful of braided rope, chasing nine money changers, some fleeing headlong in fear, some, though fleeing, looking back in anger. The money changer's board rests on a pagan altar. One figure, fallen on the ground, attempts to gather up scattered coins, symbolizing human greed. All the figures are portrayed in the garb of the artist's own time, as is the style of the Temple. The artist very accurately set the scene in the portico of the Temple of Jerusalem's outside courtyard. How would this scene be portrayed in the setting and figures of *our* time? (See *Gospel Figures in Art*, p. 249—a lovely, small, and affordable publication of the J. Paul Getty Museum.)

Following 9/11, I attended the funerals of eight FDNY firefighters and one NYPD officer and subsequently worked as a Red Cross chaplain, first on the graveyard shift with emergency personnel at Ground Zero, later at Pier 94 and 51 Chambers St., with survivors of the Trade Center as they waited, often through long hours, for assistance. Over coffee, FDNY personnel told me that, in responding to the Trade Center tragedy, they knew well enough what could lie ahead. One told of a "probie" (probationer) who was ordered off a fire truck as it left the station house. "This is a bad one," he was told. Not you, not this time. Mike Cammerata, also a probie, was not so fortunate. He was the youngest of the 343 fallen; I attended his funeral at Our Lady Queen of the Sea on Staten Island. He was promoted to firefighter posthumously. Port Authority officer Brian Verardi told of his friend Christopher Amoroso. Amoroso actually made it out; there are photos of him frantically assisting an Asian American woman to safety. But he went back in. Verardi worked eighty days, seventy-two-hour weeks, in that smoldering graveyard before his friend's remains were found. "It was an honor," he said. One firefighter, trapped in a stairwell in his bunker gear, exposed to intense heat but not flame, was mummified. They rehydrogenated his fingers to get prints.

At 51 Chambers Street a woman told me of coming down the stairs, flight after flight, and being haunted by all those faces, many young, climbing their cross as she came down. Taking a risk, I suggested to her that, right as survivor's guilt is, she could perhaps also take with her the legacy of their mute witness to her infinite worth and in some small measure seek, in her life, to honor that legacy. Hours later she came back to me, her eyes moist, thanked me, and kissed me discreetly on the cheek.

Like Jesus, in some measure these rescue personnel are now raised up and reign forever, in glory and in our consciousness, from their cross. May we all honor their legacy.

Is there genetic or DNA or archaeological evidence for the truth of the way of the cross? Bryan Sykes's *Adam's Curse: A Future Without Men* could be dismissed as science fiction were it not for the author's credentials: Professor of Genetics at the Institute of Molecular Medicine at Oxford. Sykes traces the decline of the male gene and its eventual extinction about 7,500 generations hence. He also traces the no-holds-barred, testosterone-pumped aggression of the modern world to the advent of settled agriculture a mere 13,000 years ago, with its hugely heightened rewards of greed and rise of wealth, property, and power—and, in brief compass, the enslavement of women, children, and less dominant males. With the advent of agriculture, one finds skeletons of women (and women only) with unmistakable signs of osteoarthritis, damaged vertebrae, and curvature of the thighbone, coupled with long outgrowths of the kneecaps; all are injuries consistent with a life tied to kneeling at the grindstone.

How different from all this "clashing of antlers," with its supporting cast of adoring females, is the way of the cross. How different was Jesus' attitude toward women and children and toward those *without* wealth, property, or power. ("Blessed are the *gentle*, they shall inherit the earth!") How different is this life, lifted high and glorified in an outpouring of sacrificial love for others. DNA-genetic-archaeological evidence for the truth of the way of the cross? I think so.—Peter Fribley

SERMON SUGGESTIONS

Topic: God's Story
TEXT: Ps. 19
(1) God's story in a law-abiding universe (vv. 1–6). (2) God's story in the challenges of human behavior: the perfection of God's requirements (vv. 7–10); the personal value of these requirements (vv. 11–13). (3) The resolution of the tensions in God's unfolding story (v. 14).

Topic: A Delicate Sign
TEXT: 2 Kings 25:27–30 (see also Heb. 11–12; Ezek 37:1–14; Isa. 14:24–27)
(1) There is hope. (2) Not all the alien power of the empire can crush that hope. (3) The hope always comes in fragile, precarious ways, always at the brink of being snuffed out.[10]

WORSHIP AIDS
CALL TO WORSHIP.   "The sacrifices of God are a broken spirit: a broken and a contrite heart, O God, thou wilt not despise" (Ps. 51:17).

INVOCATION.   By the touch of your fire, kindle our spirit, Father, that we may become lights in this community, guiding others into faith in Jesus and his truth. Enable us to shed his light in the world, not to glorify ourselves, nor for the glory of any person, only for your glory. Give us the fire of true religion, Father—religion like that which came upon the apostles at Pentecost and enabled them to live the prayer Jesus taught them to pray: [repeat the Lord's Prayer].—Henry Fields

OFFERTORY SENTENCE.   "It is required in stewards, that a man be found faithful" (1 Cor. 4:2).

OFFERTORY PRAYER.   By the Holy Spirit multiply each gift and bless every life affected by these gifts, our Maker and our God. Amen.—E. Lee Phillips

---

[10]Walter Brueggemann, *2 Kings: Knox Preaching Guides, John 14* (Atlanta: John Knox Press, 1982), p. 101.

PRAYER.   We come to you this morning, Father, as children peering, as it were, through a glass that is darkly tinted. We long to see what lies beyond this vale in which we walk, these moments where we stand. In reality we can see but little, either with eye, mind, or faith. So much is hidden from us, and that by your love and providence. Yet we see and know and believe enough to understand that our priorities are not aligned with your purposes in every measure of life.

You created us to be in harmony with you and thereby at peace with each other, but we have too often sought to be gods unto ourselves and have sought our own slice of the pie. We have eaten selfishly, not only from our own plates but from those of others as well. We have fattened our self-indulgences and in the process have sacrificed families, destroyed friendships, abandoned communities, and forgotten covenants.

Help us beginning today, Father, with our gigantic problems of vision. Help us to take our eyes off those things that are passing—things of momentary distraction—and focus on eternal values and truth. Let us perceive that when we see double for ourselves, we are not truly focused on being new creations in Christ Jesus. Oh, Father, the old Adam is yet alive in us; we have not died to him and been made completely alive in Christ Jesus. Renew a right heart within us this morning, Father. Bring us to that point in our lives when we can pray with all completeness and sincerity, "Not my will, but yours be done on earth as it is in heaven." Then we can walk in light, not in darkness. Then we can reflect the presence of Christ to illuminate every dark corner of life. Then we can be beacons for others as they struggle, seeking a way to truth and love and eternal life. So visit us here this morning that we might each lift the fallen, comfort the sorrowing, care for the dying, weep with those who weep, and rejoice with those who rejoice because we have here been met by your Holy Presence and given courage and strength to do your will through Christ, in whose name we pray.— Henry Fields

SERMON
Topic: One in Christ
TEXT: Gal. 3:28

Early in his letter to the Galatians (Gal. 1:11–12), Paul describes a confrontation he had with the apostle Peter. Peter, who was a Jewish Christian, came to Antioch and ate at the table with Christians of Greek culture. Then a group of Christian Jews arrived from Jerusalem. They told Peter that if he continued at the Greek table he would lose credibility among Jews. In response, Peter separated himself from the Greeks. Paul says he told Peter that Peter's initial community with the Greeks condemned his separation.

Why did Peter walk away? In our text, Paul says it was because we are "Jew or Greek, male or female, slave or free." Paul uses "Jew or Greek" in the sense of cultural identities. They are mental impressions, like images and stereotypes. Identities occur in pairs, with opposites that are seen as adversaries. The power of separation that is in all of us works through the cultural identities and their opposites—and against community.

Community is a relationship of whole persons. We are larger than any of our several identities and larger than all of them together. Community can develop when people meet face-to-face as whole persons, like Peter's meals with the Greeks. Community involves an interlocking bond of support for the community as an entity and support for moral principles. Communities provide relationships among whole persons and promote unity. The only fulfilling identity is an identity in community.

When we rely ultimately on an identity, perhaps for security or fulfillment, we define ourselves by it and other individuals by its opposite. When Peter assumed his Jewish identity, he saw the individuals at his table as "Greeks." Given the history, the Greek identity in Peter's mind might have included images of "cultural aggressor" or "religiously unclean." In that moment, Peter saw the Greeks as opposed to Peter-as-Jew, and that vision of opposed identities compelled him to reject his opposites. Of course, we do not know Peter's mind, but this seems to be implied by the idea of opposed identities. The power of separation working through cultural identities always is driving us toward rejection and toward breaking community.

Today, science and technology promise to provide the ultimate answers and the ultimate reality that will end all disagreement and conflict. But beware! Social scientists are concerned that our culture of technology works against community. Technology began its rise in the 1970s, replacing heavy industry. At the same time, our individual work in the institutions that build community began a dramatic decline. Yardsticks such as the number of people taking a leadership position in a civic organization indicate that our participation has dropped by 50 percent. What could be behind the change?

The production and consumption of technology bring pressures against participation in community. Production demands longer hours. It also widens the income gap between those with high and low technology skills. The culture of technology produces an intense assumption that we will consume the products of technology we can afford and that we will consume them to create our own identities. The task of the consumer is to select products that relate to the consumer, so we create self-centered identities. When we rely on them, we become closed to community. We have created a new set of opposed identities: "consumer or community."

The culture of technology's strong assumption that we will consume products carries over into relationships. Consumers select relationships by reducing other individuals to identities. The opposition between traditional identities gets worse. The young and the old each have consumed their lives into significant separation. Churches that rely on cultural identities in struggling to be community for "young or old" feel the power of that separation. Jesus' own ministry was concerned with "rich or poor." Consumers have purchased homes that are separated by income level and separated from the homes of low-skilled workers. Low-skilled workers are left alone with schools that do not teach adequate technology skills, with violent neighborhoods, and with city tax bills.

We are "hardwired to connect," but our connections have tended not to create community. We have connected with others primarily in small groups and associations; small groups offer mutual support. But when consumers see the group as an identity of support, they become dependent. The group turns inward and opposes the broader community. Associations include AARP, mass celebrity events, and community service projects. Meetings of consumers in associations involve selected identities that are only a facet of their personalities. Bonds of support do not develop.

The culture of technology puts us in tension. The more we seek fulfillment by acting as consumers toward others, the more we oppose them as whole persons and limit them to identities. We do not establish community or gain fulfillment, for community is the necessary context of fulfillment. It is not surprising that we tell therapists and counselors that we have a deeply felt need to belong. We know that our relations with others are not what they should be. Our need to belong is a plea: How can the power of separation in our lives be overcome?

Paul gives the Christian answer: "one in Christ Jesus." All humanity in all of its identities is unified in Christ. It is a simple answer, and we should be certain that we know its saving power. How can we possibly be one with those who oppose us and one with the community, when the consumption that our culture demands is an agent of our separation?

We are one in Christ Jesus because the crucified and resurrected Christ is reconciling love. The power of acceptance in Christ's reconciling love overcomes the power of separation. In life and on the cross, Jesus overcame the rejection of individuals because of their identities. He became one with the whole persons whom the righteous called sinners and criminals. In Jesus Christ's reconciling love, we join him in being crucified to the opposition between cultural identities and in being resurrected in victory over the power of separation.

We are one in Christ because Christ's love reconciles us with our true selves in God and to all humanity. In Second Corinthians (2 Cor. 5:18–19), Paul says, "In Christ God was reconciling the world to himself" and giving us "the ministry of reconciliation." In the power of acceptance in Christ's love, we see others and ourselves as Christ sees us: as whole persons. In our true selves in Christ, we experience our essential unity with all humanity, in constructive harmony and perfect community. In this union, we find ultimate fulfillment. When we look out from the experience of unity onto the separation in our lives, the power of separation is broken. The reconciling love of Jesus Christ draws us into our future of unity in Christ. We can see how the past—our past, with all of its separation—can be a foothold for a step toward community and family in the next moment of our lives. We can see that every inch we move toward community is like a mustard seed that God can grow into God's Kingdom.

Peter's initial move into fellowship with Greeks at Antioch showed us what the power of Christ's reconciling love means in our lives. It was an example for Paul's great announcement that in the faith of Jesus Christ, there is no longer Jew or Greek, male or female, consumer or community, young or old, or rich or poor. No longer does the power of separation limit us to seeing individuals as identities that distort and break our relationships. No longer are our connections with others closed to whole persons and community. When we are open to Christ's reconciling love, our connections with others—in associations and small groups, and at work and in family—are opened to a new meaning. The new meaning is the power of acceptance in the unity of Christ, bringing into our existence the reality of reconciliation with whole persons and transformation into community.—J. Kendrick Wells III

SUNDAY, MARCH 26, 2006
Lectionary Message

Topic: God So Loved the World
TEXT: John 3:14–21
Other Readings: Num. 21:4–9; Ps. 67:1–3, 17–22; Eph. 2:4–20

The account of Nicodemus coming to Jesus by night is, to borrow election terminology, the run-up to today's lesson. So let's briefly review that story.

I. Nicodemus comes to Jesus.

(a) Give Nicodemus credit. He comes with questions. Pharisee, teacher, leader of the Jews, he would nonetheless seem to come with an open mind. Not easy for one with all his learning. Not easy socially, either; he has a position to maintain.

(b) Give him credit also in that his questions turn on the basics—that Jesus is a teacher come from God and that Jesus mediates the presence of God. And consider all that Nicodemus does *not* ask: Rabbi, how can *I* perform miracles? Have a piece of the action? Help my church grow? But simply, *"Rabbi, we know that you are a teacher come from God; for no one can do these signs that you do apart from the presence of God."* He knows that religion has centrally to do with a sense of the presence of God.

(c) But what about this business of Nicodemus coming to Jesus by night out of fear of the Jews. Traditionally, that has been held against him. But what if Nicodemus also comes by night because he is genuinely open to answers he does not want and may dread sharing *or* bottling up inside him? After all, Pharisees who had their minds made up were happy enough to challenge Jesus in broad daylight. But here? Perhaps better a fearful soul with an open mind than that bravery which is the byproduct of a closed one.

II. Jesus tells Nicodemus that no one can see the Kingdom of God without being born from above—that one must be born of water and the Spirit.

(a) Briefly, a word study: "born from above"—in Greek, *anothen*—also translates as "born again." The word *anothen must* carry both meanings. No one English word can do that. But lose the double meaning and you muck up the whole thing.

(b) Nicodemus's question, "Can one reenter one's mother's womb?" is usually taken to indicate that he is thick as a board. But the widespread use (one must say, misuse) of this text to support saying "born again" without hearing "from above" suggests that our own self-congratulation as to better understanding is likewise premature. And the last words fall from Nicodemus's lips: "How can this be?" The words do, in fact, lead us to the unfathomable depths of Jesus' teaching, whether intended or not. By contrast, sole focus on "born again" reduces the transcendent grandeur of "from above" and "born of water and the Spirit" to a subjective personal experience. In theological terms, it substitutes anthropology for Christology; in plain English, humankind for God. In its own way, it is a reductionist humanism—a low ceiling indeed.

III. Like sunrise, God's offer of new life is an unmerited gift. Like sunrise, it has a life of its own.

(a) God's gift of new life, born of water and the Spirit, comes of infinite love: "God so loved the world. . . ." We struggle to paraphrase what this means. But when eminent New Testament scholar Rudolf Schnackenburg, author of a magisterial three-volume commentary on the Gospel of John, simply says that the best treatment of what John means is found in 1 John 4:9ff., we will gladly follow suit: "God's love was revealed among us in this way: God sent his only Son into the world so that we might live through him. In this is love, not that we loved God but that he loved us and sent his Son to be the atoning sacrifice for our sins. Beloved, since God loved us so much, we ought to love one another."

(b) Of love and will: "that he gave. . . ." At the risk of boring you, allow me to note the difference between *send* and the word used here—*gave.* The fourth Gospel frequently speaks of God as *giving,* and by this means to speak of God as the source of what Jesus offers the world.

But when John speaks of Jesus as coming from God, he uses two Greek verbs meaning "to send" (3:17, 4:34, 5:23–24, 30, 36–37, 6:38). God *sent* Jesus. By contrast, John 3:16 is the only place in the fourth Gospel that says God "gave" his Son to the world. The difference? To "send" Jesus is more clearly associated with God's *will* for the world, whereas *didomi*, to *give*, seems to be used "to underscore that the incarnation derives from God's *love* for the world as well as from God's will."[11]

A simple human analogy: you may *send* your sweetie flowers or chocolate, but you'd best *give* her an engagement ring. With no need of Greek or scholarship or even literacy, African American slaves understood all this and more in the Negro spiritual, "*Give* Me Jesus." In Paul Scherer's phrase, "God came down the stairs of heaven with a child in his arms, and *gave.* . . ."

(c) God so loved *the world.* Once again Rudolf Schnackenburg, the old priest, has not forgotten what Christian learning is about, namely, the nurture of the faithful.

Here, as whenever the mission of the Son is spoken of, the notion of "world" is neither quite neutral nor quite negative. The "world" is not simply the place where men live but is all of sinful mankind, which has turned away from God. Still, it is not yet the specific term for *mankind,* insofar as it rejects the divine envoy and pursues him with enmity and hatred. It is the "world" far from God and yet profoundly longing for him and sensing its need for redemption—the "world" that is the object of God's infinite love and mercy.[12]

"Far from God yet profoundly loving for him, and sensing its need of redemption. . . ." For whom, pray tell, does that *not* speak? Far from God. When were you or I especially close? Are you close now but know that can change—and, in any event, "profoundly longing for him"? "Profoundly" (*de profundis*), "out of the depths," the psalmist says. Out of what depths comes your longing and mine? Depths-of-life narrative? Depths of childhood—good, bad, and awful? Depths of adult relationships? Depths of religious practice? And out of that depth wherein the whole is greater than the sum of the parts. "Out of two sounds a third sound, and out of three sounds, not a fourth sound, but a star." Out of what "not a fourth sound"? "Sensing its need of redemption."

Never mind the church stereotypes. Redemption as the retrieval of soul *and body*—John's earlier "born of *water* and Spirit" refers to birth waters as well as baptism. No out-of-body spirituality here; Nicodemus was not all wrong. Redemption, then, is the retrieval of life, soul, *and body* from destructive forces going nowhere fast, seemingly with a life of their own, like a car in an uncontrollable skid. Redemption is a sense of nearness where there was distance, a fullness where there was emptiness, and of the joy of a beloved's arrival, where before there was only the stale air and drawn blinds of an inexpressible longing.

IV. A gift freely given is not a "free lunch," cannot be, given the nature of the gift, but to those who accept the gift, it will be seen that your deeds have been done in God, and you will reign with Christ.

(a) *The gift is not a "free lunch."* John warns that, although God did not send the Son to condemn the world, those who prefer darkness to light, because their deeds are evil, are

---

[11]IDB loc. cit.

[12]Rudolf Schnackenburg, *The Gospel According to St. John,* Vol. 1 (New York: Crossroad, 1982), p. 399.

condemned. "People loved darkness rather than light." Important as belief in Christ is, the proof is in the pudding: *deeds*. Plural. "If you love me, you will keep my commandments." "Those who have my commandments and keep them are those who love me." Plural. But time and again the fourth Gospel takes the plural back to the singular, the branches to the trunk: *love*. "If you love me." "Greater love hath no man than this that he lay down his life for a friend."

(b) *Your deeds are seen of God.* Who else will see them, or honor them if they do, is not said. Given the world's darkness, one cannot be sure.

(c) *We come full circle.* The first verse of our lesson reads, "Just as Moses lifted up the serpent in the wilderness, so much the Son of Man be lifted up, that whoever believes in him may have eternal life." For John, with his stress on Jesus' glory, "lifted up" refers to the Crucifixion. Christ is not exalted on the third day only, but already on the cross. And in this world, criss-crossed with darkness and light, one may reign with Christ in seeing signs of the coming of the Kingdom, or like the two thieves. More likely, one will move from one to the others. In either event, the Lutheran benediction and response is apt: "L: Go in peace, serve the Lord. R: *Thanks be to God.*" In either event, one will share Christ's glory. And soon or late, "it will be seen that your deeds have been done in God."

ILLUSTRATIONS

A collection of letters to Fred Rogers of "Mister Rogers' Neighborhood," from children and parents, with Fred's replies, is titled *Dear Mister Rogers;* the collection catches the warm, very real person I knew both personally and through his GPTV television program. The letters range an amazing gamut:

Do you ever get angry? (*Answer:* "Of course, and it is important to find a good outlet when you do. I pound hard on the piano or swim hard.")

Do you ever poop? Do you like being famous? (*Answer:* "I don't think of myself as an entertainer.")

Why do you feed the fish? (*Answer:* "To teach responsibility, and ever since a girl wrote saying how distressed she was when I did not *say* that I fed the fish, since she was blind, I always also *say* that I feed the fish.")

(From a five-year-old) Why don't wishes come true? (The answer dealt with the place of pretending but also that "everyone has to learn to deal with disappointment. I'm proud of you for starting now.")

Perhaps the most touching letter came from a mother whose five-and-one-half-year-old daughter had an inoperable brain tumor and for whom the only hope was radiation. But when the daughter learned that she would have to be in a room by herself, she screamed and cried. Even sedation did not help. The staff and her mother kept saying that it would take only one minute. "What is a minute?" the daughter asked. The mother pondered how to explain and finally began singing, "It's a beautiful day in the neighborhood" through the intercom. And the minute was up, even before finishing Mr. Rogers's song. "It is very embarrassing," the mother wrote, "but I do it gladly for her. By now, every doctor and technician in Radiation Therapy knows your song" (p. 68), "God so loved the world."

Fred was so *unaware* of self, so focused on each child, "just one little buckaroo," as Gabby Hayes had taught him, was so able *himself* to become as a child, while every inch the professional, that the Word became flesh. He did not send love; he gave it, of himself, and richly. He was, incidentally, ordained specifically to his television ministry, having studied for the ministry over eight years during lunch hours. He continued the study of New Testament Greek with his beloved mentor, professor Bill Orr, until Dr. Orr's death late in Fred's life.

Klaus Bonhoeffer, brother of Dietrich Bonhoeffer, and also involved in the July 20 plot against Hitler, knowing he would be hanged in the morning wrote his children a letter. I quote from an excerpt (the translation is my own):

> The people you encounter. Take otherwise as they are. Do not force yourself against what is strange or what displeases you, and keep an eye out for the good side. Then you will not only be more in the right, but also protect yourself from narrow-heartedness. In the garden grow many flowers. Tulips bloom beautifully, but have no scent; and the rose has its thorns. An open and appreciative eye also rejoices in unassuming green. In the same way one discovers persons' mostly hidden better sides when one puts oneself in a position to do so. But believe me, children, life opens itself up, whether in intimate or larger circles, when you think not of yourself only, but of others, when you share the lot of others. He who in singing sets store only by his own voice, or even refuses to hear himself, everything escapes such a person. What is at stake is not only to be ready to come to another's assistance here and there. . . . But he who is genuinely thankful often gives more.[13]

"The guilt of God is certainly not a Christian dogma, and yet it is an emotionally inescapable implication of the Christian myth, visible and audible in countless works of Christian art. The pathos of those artistic enactments—those masses and oratorios, passion plays and memorial liturgies, and above all those painting and sculptures in which the unspeakable is left unspoken—is inseparable from the premise that God is inflicting this pain on himself for a reason. 'The real reason,' as Albert Camus wrote in his haunting novel *The Fall*, 'is that he himself knew he was not altogether innocent.'"[14]

A rural American folk hymn from the early nineteenth century captures this pathos in words of striking simplicity.

> What wondrous love is this, O my soul, O my soul?
> What wondrous love is this, O my soul?
> What wondrous love is that that caused the Lord of Bliss
> To bear the awful curse for my soul, for my soul,

---

[13]Klaus Bonhoeffer, from *Das Gewissen steht auf* (Frankfurt/Main: Mosaik Verlag, 1954), p. 131ff.
[14]Jack Miles, *Christ: A Crisis in the Life of God* (London: William Heinemann, 2001), p. 5.

To bear the awful curse for my soul?
To God and to the Lamb I will sing, I will sing,
To God and to the Lamb I will sing.
To God and to the Lamb who is the great I AM,
While millions join the theme, I will sing, I will sing,
While millions join the theme, I will sing.

—Peter Fribley

SERMON SUGGESTIONS

Topic: Something to Talk About

TEXT: Ps. 107:1–3, 17–22

(1) God is unfailingly good and kind (vv. 1–3). (2) God reaches out to people in the extremes of need: self-inflicted suffering (vv. 17–18); desperate prayer (v. 19); healing word (v. 20). (3) Appropriate response: thanksgiving (v. 21); songs of rejoicing (v. 22).

Topic: Why David Praised the Lord

TEXT: 1 Chron. 16:9–22

(1) Because of the Lord's wonderful acts (vv. 9–13). (2) Because of the Lord's judgments (vv. 14–22).

WORSHIP AIDS

CALL TO WORSHIP.   "I acknowledge my transgressions: and my sin is ever before me" (Ps. 51:3).

INVOCATION.   Lord, as we worship today, let all pretense drop, let all falseness and shame be done away. Allow the mystery of the power of your grace for sinners to so overwhelm us that we respond in faith believing, through Jesus, our Elder Brother.—E. Lee Phillips

OFFERTORY SENTENCE.   "Each one as a good manager of God's different gifts must use for the good of others the special gift he has received from God" (1 Pet. 4:10 TEV).

OFFERTORY PRAYER.   Generous God, accept these gifts we bring, testimonies of our stewardship gladly give through the power of the Holy Spirit to save and sanctify.—E. Lee Phillips

PRAYER.   You are the Good Shepherd calling us from the far country with memories of a love that does not let us go. Help us to comprehend the nature of our *lostness;* it is not that we have lost some*thing,* but we have lost some*one.* We have set out to gain the world and we have lost ourselves; we do not know who we are, for we have forgotten from whence we have come. May we return to the waters of our baptism, to listen, to hear—the Voice of the Beyond that is within: you are my son; I created you; I love you. You are my daughter, my lovely one, how I love you.

Father, what manner of love you have shown to us that we should be your children. Praise be to Thee!—John Thompson

SERMON
Topic: Beyond Optimism
TEXT: Rom. 8:28–30

To speak of going "beyond optimism" should not be interpreted as a call to pessimism. If that's what you glean from what I will be saying, then perhaps, together, we have missed the point. For the pessimist, this is a world without a positive point. If it goes anywhere, its destination is harm, injury, defeat. There is no point, no cause for optimism; to use the title of Jean Paul Sartre's play, there is "no exit." But even without being a thoroughgoing card-carrying pessimist, it is not difficult to constantly see the dark side, the foreboding possibility in daily events. There was such a man who was dejected when his pastor came around for a final visit before departing for a new assignment in another church. The pastor, looking at the bright side said, "It is likely that the next pastor will be far better than I have been." But the man would not be convinced; he replied, "That's what they said last time."

This is a common form of pessimism—believing that all things get worse. There is another variety, and that is anticipating trouble. George Shinn, in his book *Good Morning Lord,* tells of a woman who asked her husband on the first night in their new home to go downstairs and look for a burglar. "Jim, I'm sure there is a burglar downstairs." He looked and there was no burglar. This went on for seventeen years, with no results except a real strain on the marriage. Then one night, the same request; his response was that he had been looking for seventeen years, but he looked, and there was a burglar! Jim caught him in the act of rifling the place. He said, "Go on my friend, take anything you want. I'm not going to call the police. But when you are finished, do me one favor. Come upstairs with me. I want to introduce you to my wife. She's been looking for you for seventeen years." One form of pessimism is that we look for trouble and eventually we find it.

So if I have to choose between a pessimistic viewpoint and an optimistic one, it is not a contest. For much of it is in the way we see things. A person with more insight than formal education once said, "My eyes are getting troublesome. I'll have to go to an optimist." And I must agree, I'm on the side of optimism; pessimistic people pull me down, cloud my horizons. Like the person in the story, I look for an optimist.

Now having said all of this and, I hope, putting myself clearly on the side of the optimist, I want to ask an important question: Is thoroughgoing, see-the-bright-side optimism enough? Is an assurance that all things (if seen properly) are good, or that *all* things work together for good, a firm foundation for our lives? We are not so sure. Voltaire, in his play *Candide,* said, "Optimism is the madness of maintaining that everything is right when it is wrong." If that is optimism, or if optimism as an end in itself can become this, then we must move beyond it. Can we use a text of Scripture to assert that everything is right when it isn't? If so, then we have abused words that have given hope and meaning to millions.

Some years ago a pastor wrote an article called "The Use and Abuse of Romans 8:28." He quoted a man in his congregation who had lost his wife in an accident. "A lot of people have recited this verse to me, but I don't think they really know what it means." Nine years ago I read that sentence, but how many times before and since that time I have seen similar scenes acted out. We want to be of help and comfort, to encourage faith. So without realizing it, we imply that everything that happens comes directly from God. Furthermore, it suggests that all events work out for the best. Is that the promise of God to a person who has lost a loved one, is without a job, or singularly seeks to hold a family together?

No, the promise of God is not that all that happens to us is good or that all events can be seen through the eyes of faith as working together for good. This seems to deny the reality of evil. Scott Peck, a psychiatrist, has written a book, *The People of the Lie,* that deals with the reality of evil in human life. The book is a graphic reminder of the danger of pretending that evil does not exist or can be ignored. Now I know there is the opposite extreme of associating every problem, failure, or setback with the devil, but that's another sermon. What is clear enough for the subject at hand is that not all things, even if accepted in faith or seen in an optimistic light, are good. To believe in a gracious and powerful God does not demand such intellectual suicide. It does not require calling that which is destructive, or even evil, good.

The promise is not that by saying the right words, or having a bright outlook, or giving a positive confession, bad magically becomes good. The promise is that God does not abandon us, even as we experience the consequences of a fallen world, poor choices, or of sin; God is there. *In everything, God works for Good.* That is what this famous verse of Scripture is saying; the subject is not all things or everything, but *God.* Paul is not saying blink twice, smile, blink again, and all will be well. We are not asked to deny the existence of evil. We are not required to view faith as only a state of mind or say that injustice and sin have their good side. No, the promise is not that these things don't exist or that they are really beneficial in the long run. The promise is that they do not have the final victory. They are real but not the final reality. They can be faced because there is a power greater than all of these that denies them the final word. It is the power of love.

This is not some arcane belief, some disposable doctrine. Here is the heart of living Christianity. Was it God's ultimate, loving purpose that Jesus be given over to the outstretched hands of our passions and prejudices, spit upon, rejected, by those of us he came to save? No. But the circumstances of a fallen world where people do reject love and deny the power of forgiveness could only be won by evil apparently winning the day. They buried the Light in a borrowed grave, but it was not the final victory. God was there, raising the one who prayed that the cup of death be passed from him; yet, accepted it because he believed that such evil as unjust verdicts, jealousy, and hatred could not triumph. God whom he saw as a loving Father would have the final word. Indeed, Jesus the Messiah *was* the final word, the Saving Word that offers life to you and me when we despair of going on, when one foot will not go in front of the other.

Can that promise be for you and me? The promise is for all who love God and are called according to his purpose. You say, "I am not sure I qualify. I want to believe that God has a plan and that I am called to be a part of it. I want to love God, if such a thing is possible." In the invitation to the Lord's table, we sometimes say "to those who love God a little and would love him more . . ." It is a process; it does not happen all at once. It begins in wanting to believe in God's love and loving purposes for us. One step of faith can begin an incredible journey. We can begin to trust ourselves to that love, which did not desert Christ on the cross and turned defeat into victory. Then we are able to see those events that seem to say "no exit" or "all is lost" or "no point in going on" as less than the final word.

Teilhard de Chardin, the French priest and paleontologist, captured that promise for me when he said, "Like an artist making use of a fault or an impurity in the stone he is sculpting, or the bronze he is casting, so as to produce more exquisite lines or a more beautiful tone, God without sparing us the partial deaths or the final death, which form an essential part of our lives transfigures them by integrating them in a better plan . . . provided we trust lovingly in him."

Now there is a cause for optimism, not of the blind, careless variety. We are called to a chastened optimism, a *redeemed optimism.* It is not pretending that all, in itself, is good but that if we love God and trust his loving purposes, he works with us for good in *all* things. That is God's promise.—Gary D. Stratman

SUNDAY, APRIL 2, 2006
Lectionary Message

Topic: After Darkness, Light!

TEXT: Jer. 31:31–34

Other Readings: Ps. 5:1–12; Heb. 5:5–10; John 12:20–33

I. *The miracle of God's promise.* Salvation comes only on the far side of disaster. That is the promise of the Lord, given to Jeremiah. Only after the Lord has "plucked up and pulled down, destroyed and overthrown" will he "build and plant" (1:10). The land will be desolate. Just as God's people have forsaken him, so he shall forsake them and send them away into exile, where their desire to serve other gods will be fulfilled (5:19). The Lord's repeated appeals to his people to repent have gone unheeded: the pliable clay that might have been re-formed turns out to be a clay pot, which the Lord shall shatter (18:1–19:15). The people stubbornly have followed their own evil will (7:24, 11:8, 16:12). Their heart is uncircumcised, perverse, "more crooked than anything" (9:26, 17:9). The Lord, therefore, is bringing darkness and disaster on the land (13:15–17). All those social institutions to which one might look for help and security shall fail: the political leaders, the king and his advisers, the temple, and most of all the prophets (cf. 9:23–24). Indeed, the prophets and the powerful represent the greatest temptation, since they hold out the false hope that disaster will not come, that the nation would be spared. For them, any word to the contrary is regarded as treason.

The promise given to Jeremiah calls the hearers to believe in the miracle of restoration beyond disaster, to believe, in effect, in the resurrection of the dead: "the days are coming," says the Lord, "when I shall make a new covenant." The people shall find grace, but they shall find it only in the wilderness (31:2). That is the message of the cross, which the prophet here anticipates: only after Good Friday does Easter morning arrive; only after the servant of the Lord has suffered shall he find satisfaction; only then shall he savingly justify the many (Isa. 53:10–12). "It is necessary for the Son of Man to suffer many things" (Luke 9:22). The experience of ancient Israel and Judah anticipates the suffering of the Messiah, who came to bear judgment in place of Israel, and all the nations.

The cross of Christ and the experience of Israel, which foreshadowed it, have their echo in the lives of Christians. Life has its times of trial and difficulty. They come to every one of us, in differing ways and in differing measures. And ultimately, each of us must face the end of life, when for us, too, "every earthly prop gives way." Then for us God in Christ must and shall be "all our help and stay" (Edward Mote).

II. *The new work of God.* It is not merely our experience of trial, however, that brings us closer to God. The troubles we encounter in life might just as well drive us away from God as drive us to him. Not everyone who faces difficulty encounters God's saving presence there. It is not simply Israel's exile from the land that was to bring the people back to God. It was a miracle of grace. It was an unmerited word and act of God, unanticipated and unexpected, even though already announced: "I will make a new covenant with the house of Israel and the house of Judah" (31:31).

It proved impossible for the people to keep the former covenant made at Sinai. Their evil hearts led them astray. Now God promises something entirely new: he will no longer meet them from without, as a covenant-partner who calls for their loyalty. He now takes upon himself the whole of the covenant duty: he himself shall remake their heart so that they gladly keep his commands. The Law will no longer stand outside them on stone tablets. It shall be written in their hearts. The prayer of the prophet—"*you* heal me, Lord, and I shall be healed" (Jer. 17:14)—now finds its answer. God and God alone must save his people—and the nations as well.

According to the witness of the New Testament, this promise of a new covenant was fulfilled in the death and Resurrection of Jesus Christ. In him, God makes us to be new creatures, who freely and spontaneously do his will. Of course, that does not mean that Christians have arrived at final salvation! The old reality of our fallen self remains with us until the grave (Rom. 7:7–25). Yet the "new obedience" is present with us as a life-determining reality. We live under the lordship of another, in whom the Law of God has come to its fulfillment.

III. *The new people of God.* A new situation arises from God's saving work. All of Israel shall know the Lord. There will be no longer any need for instruction or admonition. Everyone shall know the Lord immediately and directly: "they shall all be taught of God" (Isa. 54:13; John 6:44; 1 Thess. 4:9). And they shall *know* him, not merely know *about* him. The Lord promises a vital, living relationship with all who belong to him. Above all else, the Lord promises that his people shall know him as the God who forgives sin and by that forgiveness makes them into new creatures who love him and do his will.

The New Testament teaches us that although the days are yet to come in which this promise arrives in its fullness *with* us, the promise has decisively arrived *for* us in Jesus Christ. The day has dawned. In him, we who believe taste the new realities that the Lord has promised. This tasting, in fact, is the essence of the Christian life, in which we make progress day-by-day. Who would not wish to taste afresh this goodness of God?

ILLUSTRATION

Perhaps the best illustration to use here may be drawn from the book of Jeremiah itself: the potter's vessel, which is shattered beyond repair (19:11), shall yet be mended by the hand of its Creator. So it is with the human heart: only God can make us new, as he has done in Jesus Christ (10:86)—Mark Seifrid

SERMON SUGGESTIONS

Topic: From Awful to Awesome

TEXT: Ps. 51:1–13

(1) David's sin (2 Sam. 11, 12). (2) David's repentance (vv. 1–9). (3) David's future (vv. 10–12).

Topic: Praying for the Right Things

TEXT: 2 Chron. 1:7–13

(1) Solomon recognized his potential (vv. 8–9). (2) Solomon recognized the price of achievement (vv. 10–12a).

WORSHIP AIDS

CALL TO WORSHIP.   "To the Lord our God belong mercies and forgiveness, though we have rebelled against him; neither have we obeyed the voice of the Lord our God, to walk in his laws, which he set before us by his servants the prophets" (Dan. 9:9–10).

INVOCATION.   God of love, God of judgment, we are reminded again of our rebellion and disobedience. Show us your mercy and your forgiveness today, so that our lives and our words may truly praise you.

OFFERTORY SENTENCE.   "And the children of Israel brought a willing sacrifice unto the Lord, every man and woman, whose heart made them willing to bring for all manner of work, which the Lord had commanded to be made by the hand of Moses" (Exod. 35:29).

OFFERTORY PRAYER.   Gracious Father, you have set before us many ways to do your work in the world. Though not all of us can preach or teach, most of us can bring an offering from the fruits of our daily work. As we present to you our gifts, open new channels of blessing to others through what we bring.

PRAYER.   In this sanctuary, away from the usual demands of life, we come to thank you for the family of faith and for one another, Father. How we rejoice that you set us in families, not just the blood-kin clan but the family of the Church, the family of the nation, the human family. Often we become so enmeshed in the troubles of the families that we fail to see the strengths of the families to which we belong. Enable us to focus on what brings us together rather than what tears us apart. Show us how to manage the disruptions in such a way that they will be redemptive for everyone. Teach us how to love our neighbor as we love ourselves. Help us to relearn the art of forgiveness and the way to forgetfulness of wrongs inflicted on us by others. But may we never forget our responsibility to set right the wrongs that we do to others. Imbue us with the courage to stand for what is right, even when what is right is not popular in the family. Help us to grow a character that will be worthy of our kinship with Christ and an asset to those with whom we live and among whom we walk.

So often, Father, we isolate ourselves in our own small individual worlds, believing that what we do does not really matter to anyone else or is none of their business. Remind us that we are our brothers' and sisters' keeper, and everything we do in some way has an effect on all those around us who are part of the human family. Show us that because of our withdrawal, a part of your purpose is left undone, for each of us is here to do your will, something else we forget too quickly. Today cleanse us, Father, of our unrighteousness. Open our hearts to your grace, that the evil in the world may be overcome in us and through us. We come to you now, that we might be saved from our sins and from ourselves and our selfishness. Here, now, in quietness and confidence, help us to renew our strength. We pray in Jesus' name.—Henry Fields

SERMON
Topic: The Chasms We Cannot Cross
TEXT: Luke 16:19–31

This unusual parable has profound insight into our relationships with each other and with God. Its base, of course, is Jesus' earlier teaching in Luke: "Blessed are you who are poor, for yours is the kingdom of God. . . . But woe to you who are rich, for you have received your consolation" (6:20, 24). The parable is not an accusation but an application. The parable is about our human situation.

In his heart, the rich man knew he should have cared for Lazarus. The books of Moses and the prophets require just and generous dealing with the poor. The devout Jews of the day understood the Scriptures to command love of our neighbors as ourselves, as we know from Luke's account of the conversation between Jesus and a lawyer (10:28). The parable itself indicates that the rich man should have acted from love and compassion. Jesus' description of Lazarus makes us cry out, "Care for him!" In conversation with Abraham, the rich man volunteers that he should have.

Why did he not care? The answer is not that he is unaware of Lazarus at his gate. He calls Lazarus by name. The answer of the parable is that a great chasm separates them. The chasm is between Heaven and Hades. It also lies between the rich man and Lazarus. The great chasm is the separation between the realities of the rich man and Lazarus. It is the same chasm the rich man dug in life, as he created a separated reality and at death it became fixed. The first verse of the parable describes the rich man's reality. In literal translation, he was "splendidly making merry daily."[1] He created his merry reality by using his wealth as a consumer. Consumers use their power to select and control objects, and his request that Abraham send Lazarus to care for him shows that he had reduced Lazarus to an object for consumption. He had generalized, abstracted, and moralized the suffering person of Lazarus into a concept that was not worthy of compassion.

Who are the rich today? The answer is that all of us who consume are the rich man's brothers. The culture of technology gives people at all income levels an unprecedented power to consume, as well as pressures to use our power of consumption to create personal realities. We embrace technology because of its genuinely great promise to improve life for all humanity. It could feed the hungry of the world. Yet it is our consumption that realizes technology,

---

[1]Joseph A. Fitzmyer, *The Gospel According to Luke (X-XXIV). The Anchor Bible* (Garden City, N.Y.: Doubleday, 1985), p. 1131.

and we have consumed it for entertainment, celebrations, and other products that build a twenty-four-hour reality of harmony and merriment. As consumers, we select products that relate to ourselves, and the realities we create are self-centered and separated. As consumers, we reduce other individuals to objects for consumption.

Who is on the other side of the great chasm? Libby Babcock is the wife of an accomplished man who developed bipolar disease and has been suicidal. She writes, in a published letter, that society accepts mental illness only as a concept. Society's concept understands the mentally ill as people who are in therapy and may take antidepressant medication. "But," she says, "that is pretty much where the acceptance ends. Bring out the seriously mentally ill and the attendant social, financial and administrative problems and prepare to be met with embarrassment, avoidance and fear. . . . To people who have not been forced to deal with mental illness in their own lives, it never becomes a reality."[2]

Concepts also separate us from the suffering realities of the homeless, of prisoners, of low-skill workers who can afford only violent neighborhoods with schools that teach inadequate skills, of poor pregnant women for whom an abortion is the only chance for a productive life, of the elderly who are ill and alone, of gays who long for acceptance of their lives in communities of faith, and of a poor family in a housing project who did not know the difference between lavatory and toilet. This does not advocate any particular policy on these issues, but it does assert that a just social policy should account fully for affected realities. In small groups, I tell my story about the family in the housing project. Usually, someone denies it. That denial is a mark of the chasm.

How can we cross the chasm? The resounding answer of the parable is that we cannot (16:26). The rich man had not responded in faith to Moses and the prophets. His ultimate concern was the use of his power to consume reality. The power to consume only can acquire more objects for its self-centered reality.

We are not always consumers, we protest. We follow modern codes of ethics that require us to aid those in need. In the face of such giving, the parable's answer is the same. Jesus Christ is in the giving of time and money for these in need, but our concern for the Christ is not the dominant motive. When it is not, we make the poor our objects of consumption in a reality dedicated to our own happiness. The parable offers no list of broken ethics for the rich man. It teaches that the chasm existed because he did not love his neighbor as himself.

The ability to overcome the power of the chasm comes only from God, and it comes to us through him who first spoke the parable. It is the acceptance of the power of reconciliation, in the faith of Jesus Christ, that separates our realities. It comes to us when our ultimate concern is Jesus Christ.

The crucified and Resurrected Christ comes to us as reconciling love—reconciling us to God, to ourselves, and to others. Like the rich man, we dig chasms between others and us that turn out to be chasms between God and us. The power of acceptance in God's power of reconciliation reunites us with God. In union with God, we can see that all are children of God. We can see the separation of our realities and know the pain we have caused by reject-

---

[2]*The Courier Journal Forum Page*, 2004. (In possession of the author)

ing the realities of those to whom we ought to have ministered. Then we can experience God's unconditional acceptance and its power in us through Jesus Christ—power that, for the first time, enables us to love our neighbors as ourselves.

The reconciling love of Jesus Christ in us does not cross the great chasm between realities. It removes the chasm by transforming our separated reality into a new reality. In the healing faith of Jesus Christ, we experience others as the Christ sees them—as ourselves, together in unity. When we look out from the unity of Jesus Christ, the power that separates our realities is broken. The power of reconciliation and acceptance in the Christ gives us the power to accept others, not as concepts but as whole persons, and to perceive them in our reality as brothers and sisters. The reconciling love of Christ comes to us as our future, and for the first time we can see our separated situation in the world and its possibilities for reconciliation into a new reality of healing and community.

Let us be embraced, ultimately, by the new reality of the Christ that heals us, with all humanity, into the family of God.—J. Kendrick Wells III

SUNDAY, APRIL 9, 2006
Lectionary Message

Topic: Shattered Hopes?
TEXT: Matt. 21:1–11
Other Readings: Ps. 118:1–2, 19–29; Isa. 50:4–9a; Ps. 31:9–16; Phil. 2:5–11; Matt. 26:14–27:66

I. *High expectations.* Nothing could have seemed more certain to Jesus' disciples on this day of his triumphal entry than the impending revelation of Jesus as Messiah. That is not to say that they did not have their fears (10:32)! But their expectations had been raised very high. James and John had already attempted to stake a claim to priority in the coming Kingdom (10:35–45). Moreover, as Jesus drew near to Jerusalem, the crowds that followed him increased (10:46; 11:8). In the healing of blind Bartimaeus, there was a visible sign that Jesus would make himself known as the Son of David then and there in Jerusalem (10:46–52). Their hopes must have soared! Jesus' incredible foreknowledge about the colt he required for his entry into Jerusalem would have had the same effect on them. Everything took place precisely in the way that Jesus had said that it would (11:1–6).

Surely, the significance of Jesus' action did not escape them either. The prophet Zechariah had foretold that Israel's king would come to Jerusalem mounted on the colt of a donkey (Zech. 9:9). Here before their eyes, Jesus performed this decisive messianic act: he entered the city riding on a donkey. The joy of the crowds was wild and exuberant, as they acclaimed Jesus as the coming Messiah: "Hosanna! Blessed is the One who comes in the name of the Lord!" (11:9; Ps. 118:25). The Kingdom of God was about to appear: "Blessed is the coming kingdom of our father David!" (11:10). The disciples' fears were cast aside for the moment. Triumph was at hand.

II. *Shattered hopes.* Their hopes were shattered, of course. Three times, according to Mark, they had heard Jesus' predictions of his suffering and death, but they did not and could not grasp them (8:31–33, 9:30–32, 10:32–34). They could not see what was coming. They interpreted Jesus' words and actions with a "hermeneutic of glory," which obscured from them the reality and necessity of the cross. They saw only triumph in Jesus' entry into Jerusalem. They didn't really see the one on the donkey and the self-chosen humility of the coming King. They participated in the event as those who were deaf and blind, who still needed healing from Jesus in order to awaken to the moment. Their slumber in Gethsemane was only an outworking of this slumber of their minds and hearts.

We who live in the light of Easter must not be quick to congratulate ourselves on our more privileged perspective on the cross. Doesn't the same blindness still plague our living and thinking, even though through the gospel we have caught a glimmer of light? Don't we find ourselves all too ready to set our hopes on immediate victories, on swift deliverance from trial, on easy and pleasant paths? The cross of Christ brings with it the cross of the Christian. None of us who belong to him can escape it. We must ask ourselves if our reading of Scripture, our prayer, our thinking also has remained captured to a "hermeneutic of glory" or whether we reckon with the cross. Postmodern thought has rightly underscored that all human thinking is perspectival, dependent on our time and place in the world. Scripture teaches us that, ultimately, there are only two "places" in which the human being stands. Either we stand at the cross, or we attempt to take flight from it into a "heaven" of our own vain imaginations.

III. *Jesus' expectation.* In the midst of all the excitement about him, Jesus moved boldly, deliberately—and quietly. The end of the day must have been something of a letdown for the disciples. Jesus did nothing. He looked about him, at all that was going on in the Temple, and then inconspicuously departed for Bethany where he was lodging. All those who imagined that the Kingdom would come that day were severely disappointed.

Jesus alone recognized what was about to come upon him. He alone grasped the meaning of the moment, with its temporary joy and impending sorrow. He saw through the crowd to the cross and accepted it, took it on himself. That means, of course, that he knew and accepted the false hopes of his disciples, which were about to be shattered. He knew their weakness, their radical, fatal weakness of false calculations and unbelief. He would shortly hear Peter's empty protestation that he would never abandon Jesus. He could see well beyond it. That was why he had come, after all, to give his life to redeem Peter and all the rest from their idle, unbelieving dreams. Indeed, his promise of restoration—"after I am raised, I will go before you into Galilee"—preceded Peter's oath never to forsake him (14:28–29).

IV. *Hope fulfilled.* The failure of the disciples was included in Jesus' acceptance of his cross. Their false expectations were already comprehended within his knowledge of what was coming upon him. With that knowledge he carried them, pronouncing the forgiveness that they—especially Peter—would need, before they needed it. Their misdirected expectations were overcome by his larger, although more painful, purpose. In a way that John's Gospel makes clear for us, the disciples spoke better than they knew. The one whom they acclaimed did triumph in Jerusalem. The Kingdom for which they hoped did arrive decisively in his cross—and in his Resurrection. That for which they longed was given to them, not in the way they expected but in a far greater and fuller sense than they could have imagined. So, too, the Risen Lord deals with each of his disciples. Our hopes, our expectations, which often lie shattered at our feet, remain safe and sure in the hand of the one who will cleanse them from sin and fulfill them beyond all our imagining.—Mark Seifrid

SERMON SUGGESTIONS

Topic: Unavoidable Celebration

TEXT: Ps. 118:1–2, 19–29

(1) Timeless affirmation (vv. 1–2). (2) Timely experience (vv. 19–29): access (vv. 19–20); confirmation of God's victory (vv. 21–23); appropriate rejoicing (vv. 24–25). (3) Focal leadership (vv. 26–29).

Topic: The Distant Cross Comes Near

TEXT: Ps. 31:9–16

(1) A picture of pain, sorrow, and rejection (vv. 9–13) (see Matt. 27:46). (2) A picture of trust (vv. 14–16) (see Luke 23:46).

WORSHIP AIDS

CALL TO WORSHIP.   "Jesus said to His disciples, 'If any one wishes to come after Me, let him deny himself, and take up his cross, and follow Me'" (Matt. 16:24 NASB).

INVOCATION.   O Christ, we are following. We often falter, we fall far behind, we fail to see, to understand, but we try. We want to know, we want to do, we want to be the kind of person in whom you can live and love and save some of the world's suffering.—Theodore Parker Ferris

OFFERTORY SENTENCE.   "All shall give as they are able, according to the blessing of the Lord your God that he has given you" (Deut. 17:17 NRSV).

OFFERTORY PRAYER.   Lord, allow this offering to bring many to saving faith in the name of the Father, the Son, and the Holy Spirit.—E. Lee Phillips

PRAYER.   O Father, as we begin this Holy Week commemorating the coming of the Lord with power to establish his Kingdom among us, keep us from a casualness that would cause us to think that we can pass through these days as innocent bystanders. Make us as sensitive to the fickleness of our own lives as we are to the vacillating ways of a Pontius Pilate or a betraying Judas, or the denying ways of a Simon Peter.

Grant us courage to follow Jesus, so that in his Passion we may discover the truth that we can have eternal life. In these days before us, keep us at the cross until its deep mysteries unfold, at least in part, for our own life. Teach us through that horrible event that we really are only sinners, but sinners who are loved by God in Christ Jesus and who can be saved by his grace and by the sacrifice made on our behalf.

During the week before us, teach us anew that the agonies of this world are the agonies that you feel and that you are dying a thousand deaths that people may be reconciled to you and to one another. Inspire us through all the meaning of Eastertide to be faithful to our high calling of being instruments of your love and reconciliation. Unite us in a fellowship that rejoices with those who rejoice and weeps with those who weep. Grant to those who are sick in mind, body, or spirit the mercy of your healing. Grant to those who are lonely, bereft of loved ones or friends, a sensitivity to the companionship of your abiding presence. Grant to the stranger within our gates a sense of oneness with your people. Grant to the lost the light of your searching that they may be found.

In the days ahead may your highest aspiration for your Church be confirmed in and through us, and on every front may the kingdoms of this world become the Kingdoms of our God and of his Christ.—Henry Fields

SERMON
Topic: The Ambivalence of Palm Sunday
TEXT: Mark 14:1–15:47

When Jesus rode into Jerusalem the Sunday before he died, no one knew he was coming. No one had invited him. Neither the governor nor the high priest was on hand to welcome him. The people had no time to prepare either themselves or the city for his arrival. Some of the pilgrims who were in town for the festival improvised a reception. They cut down branches from the trees to wave as he passed by, and some of them put their garments on the donkey that he rode and even spread them in the way as they would for a king. But the city as a whole was taken completely by surprise. Suddenly, unannounced, uninvited, he appeared. There he was!

Things often happen that way. You are lost, either literally or figuratively. Frantically, you try to find your way out. You try this door and that door, this person and that person, this doctor and that doctor, this religion and that religion, all to no avail. Suddenly, where you least expect it, when you are ready to give up, a door opens of its own accord. There is a way out. You are in the clear. You have been found.

Or you are looking for a mate. As you crave food, you crave companionship, and not only the casual companionship of friends that come and go but the lifelong companionship of a mate. You begin to look for the perfect person; you make dates, you go to parties and join clubs. Suddenly, when you are not looking, when you are not thinking about it, someone appears. Here is your mate. This is the one!

Life works in a strange, mysterious way, doesn't it? For on the one hand, it says to you: If you want me, you have to look for me, work for me, search for me, find me for yourself. But when it comes to the great things in life (at least, it seems so to me, and it is confirmed more and more in my experience), life says to you: Here I am! An opportunity drops in your lap, unbidden, unexpected; there it is! You did not seek it; it singled you out, so to speak. A book is left on a bedside table in a room where you are spending the night. You read it and, as you read, it is as though a new planet swims into your ken. A person walks across your path and changes the whole direction of your life. A vision flashes across your horizon, and the entire world is different from that moment on.

That is the way it happened then. The people were looking for a king, a real king—a king with authority, with power, who could lead them out of the morass, both political and spiritual, in which they were caught. They looked everywhere. They searched the Scriptures for generations to see where he might be born, and when. They combed the ranks of the royal family, defunct though it was, to see if there might be someone there who would fill this role. Some, believing that this could be no earthly figure, scanned the sky for a heavenly being who would come to be their king. And when they couldn't find him, they prayed to God and asked him to send one to them.

Then one day when they were not looking, when they were not thinking abou' streets of Jerusalem, on the steps of the Temple, there stood a King! He was nothing like a. king they had ever seen or heard of before, or ever dreamed about; he had none of the things that they associated with royalty, but there was something kingly about him, nevertheless, and even the most insensitive of them were aware of it and knew instinctively that he had the right to rule. There he stood, without notice, without warning—young, plain, yet imperious. They had done nothing to bring him there; he simply had come.

He made no attempt to force himself upon them, no attempt whatever to take the city by storm. There was nothing that resembled in any way a coup d'état, nothing like the great conquerors of the past who rode into a city and took it by force. With Alexander, Napoleon, and Hitler, Jesus had absolutely nothing in common. Nothing! He was the King of a Kingdom as different from theirs as day is from night. There he was, and they were absolutely free to accept him or to reject him.

That, too, is the way things happen. Life allows us an amazingly large margin of freedom, and the great things, when you stop to think about it, life seldom forces upon anyone. They are presented, but they do not have to be taken in. Bach made music, for instance—music such as no one had ever heard. People were free to listen to it or not to listen to it. Some listened; many did not. Consequently, it lay buried for a hundred years. In the next century, Abraham Lincoln made music of another kind—the music of words, eloquence such as no other American has ever equaled, words in which great ideas that went deep into the nature of truth and reality were expressed with such vividness and beauty that the words of no other American can be compared to them. Yet the people were not compelled to listen to him. They were free to listen or not, as they chose. Some chose not to listen. Thank God many did listen, and what they heard, they never forgot.

An opportunity may now stand at your door. You are absolutely free to open the door or to leave it closed. You can accept it, you can rise to its challenge, you can take the risk of it and plunge into the depths of it, or you can stay locked up in your little house, sealed in your private shell, all safe and sound by yourself. You have the freedom to do either.

Some things in life we have no choice about, but when it comes to the great things, we can take them or leave them. We can open the door or leave it closed. When Christ stands before you in any shape or form—in a beggar, in a neighbor, in an enemy, in a friend, in a lover, in a decision, in a choice, in a challenge—you are absolutely free to take him or leave him. There is no compulsion, one way or the other.

The choice the people had to make about Jesus on that first Palm Sunday was not an easy one. Is it ever, do you think? On the one hand, there was something in them that responded to him deeply, sincerely. He had done so much for them: he had opened the eyes of their blind; he had healed their sick; he had cured their mentally disturbed. He had unlocked the gate of heaven for so many of them and shown them things they had never dreamed of, stars they had never seen before. They knew that. There were so many things about him that appealed to them, things that answered some of the deepest needs of the human soul. They knew that, too. And in most cases, in their secret hearts, they knew that he spoke the truth as the truth had never before been so clearly and so unambiguously spoken.

But, if they accepted him, they would surely get in trouble with Rome. If they accepted this man as their real king, they would certainly get in even more trouble with Rome than they were in already. They would be guilty of treason. On the purely local scene, some of them would surely lose their jobs, especially if they worked in the Temple, and there were hundreds employed in the performance of the sacrificial cult. All of them would have to change their ways of life, some of them very radically. They were the victims, you see, of what we have come to know—thanks to the psychiatrists—as ambivalence, which is the co-existence of opposite and conflicting feelings about the same person or object. They wanted him, and they didn't want him. They were drawn to him, and they were repelled by him.

There were some people, of course, who were totally drawn and others totally repelled, but as a people, there was a real, deep-seated ambivalence, and their divided heart was never so vividly or so dramatically exposed as it was on Palm Sunday, when their first impulse was to accept him with open arms and to hail him as their king and deliverer. But when they stopped to think about it, they withdrew; they changed their tune. They began to rationalize along these lines: it is better that one man should die, even though he be the best man that ever lived, than that everybody should get into trouble. That is good rationalization, isn't it? It is good enough for the twenty-first century. It makes sense. So they rejected him. They returned him like a manuscript sent back to its author with a rejection slip on which were three words: *Good, but dangerous!*

The point is, of course, that the same ambivalence is in all of us in one way or another, and this is why we come back again, year after year, to these mighty events—not because we are compelled to but because we are drawn to them, because in the drama of this one Life the issues of every life are set forth. We find ourselves right in the middle of it (that is, if we have the eyes to see), and we find in ourselves the same conflict of feelings that the people had then. For us it is something like this: we accept something good in principle, but when it stands before us incarnate in a person, then we begin to wonder, we begin to count the cost, to add up all the "ifs, ands, and buts," to see the implications, to get frightened and, more than once, reject it.

To make this specific (and there is no point in saying it unless it is specific, is there?), you accept the principle of racial integration. I would be willing to guess that there are very few people in this part of the country who do not accept, in principle, the proposition that all men are created equal and that, no matter what their color or race may be, they should be treated alike, without discrimination. But you want to sell your house. There the principle stands before you, incarnate in a person, and you begin to wonder; you add up all the factors in the situation; you begin to rationalize, and is it not altogether likely that you will end up by saying, it is better that one good family suffer than that this whole neighborhood be ruined? You might not say that, but the chances are that even the best of you would.

Again, you accept the principle of disarmament. I imagine that few people would not say that, in principle, they believe that the nations of the world should put down their arms, for their arms will ultimately destroy the world and all the human beings in it. Then someone presents a plan for disarmament; the plan has risks, and there are questions about it that you cannot answer. And when the principle becomes incarnate in a specific plan, then you begin to wonder, to get cold feet. You begin to think of the safety of the nation, and you rationalize, only you put it the other way around this time, in an even more horrible way. You say it is better that the whole world blow up than that this one nation lose its security (not altogether logical but emotionally satisfying).

Or you accept the principle of religious freedom—the right of every man and woman to worship according to his or her conscience; and you, in your tradition and culture, respect the religion of other people and their beliefs. Then a man who belongs to a church that you fear is nominated for high office. The principle is then incarnate in a person and demands action on your part—a decision, a vote; but you begin to tremble, and to ask questions, and to wonder whether it is right, and what would happen if so-and-so should be elected, whether perhaps it is not better for one person, or one church, to suffer than that the whole nation be exposed to danger.

We could go on like this indefinitely, but we will not. One more example of the ambivalence you are likely to find in yourself will be enough. You accept the principle of Christian marriage—a man and a woman living together in lifelong union with each other, in order to fulfill the life of each partner of the union and to provide the maximum degree of security and happiness for their children. But when an unpleasant or difficult husband or wife faces you every morning at the breakfast table, when that principle becomes incarnate in a person and stares at you in a real situation, then you begin to change your mind, to back down, to rationalize. And you often come to the point where you reject the principle altogether.

This ambivalence that was so vividly dramatized on Palm Sunday many years ago, and that is so much a part of our lives as we live them now, is not, to my way of thinking, so much because we are bedeviled as it is because we are bewildered. Not many people go out deliberately to kill the Prince of Life; not many people deliberately set out to reject the good when it stands before them. They do it because they are caught in the trap of their own conflicts, their own desire for security, their fears and timidities. And when these begin to work against their ideals, their finest insights, their deepest longings, they are more than likely to give up. And the Prince of Glory pays the price, always. The best we have suffers the most. The highest we know is dragged down to the lowest to which we can sink.

I have never before felt so vividly what it meant when the prophet said, as though by anticipation, "And the Lord hath laid on him the iniquity of us all." I am not sure in exactly what sense we can say that the Lord deliberately did it, but I am sure that the iniquity that is the tragic result of our ambivalence inevitably falls on the innocent and good.

The Palm Sunday story ends here, but we cannot stop here—not quite. Jesus was finally rejected, but the rejection was not final. That is the amazing paradox, and the gospel is a grand series of paradoxes, one often becomes the book that the whole world accepts. That is the paradox. And the very rejection may have something to do with the power that wins the final approval. That is the mystery.

Rembrandt was the most popular painter of his day until he was about thirty-five. He had the whole of Holland, virtually the whole of Europe, applauding him, clamoring for his work. He painted everybody of any distinction at all and could command any price he wished. Then when he was about thirty-five, another painter came along—Van Dyke—more elegant than Rembrandt, easier for the general public to grasp and understand, and Rembrandt was rejected in favor of his more elegant successor. Then years before his death, he was forced to sell everything that he had, and he lived the last years of his life in poverty. "And yet," writes an art critic, "most of his finest painting belongs to those difficult years." He was finally rejected, but the rejection was not final. Somehow or other, you cannot help but feel that the rejection had something to do with the greatness that followed, that the rejection, as it were, pierced him and struck open a new vein so that the genius was greater than before.

This is not the time to spell out this side of the truth. We say only this: we are ambivalent creatures at best. We see it so clearly on a day like this, when we look at ourselves in the mirror of Palm Sunday. We often reject those we love the most, and love and hate are so closely interwoven in our hearts that it is sometimes almost impossible to disentangle them. But God has a way of taking our rejections and turning them into life. "The stone that the builders rejected has become the head of the corner. This is the Lord's doing; it is marvelous in our eyes."

Open our eyes, O God, that we may see thy marvelous works, how thou canst take even the evil that is in us and use it for thy good purposes; how Jesus could take the thorns of life and wear them as a crown. Give us the grace and courage to follow in his train.—Theodore Parker Ferris

SUNDAY, APRIL 16, 2006
Lectionary Message

Topic: Resurrection Faith (Easter Sunday)
TEXT: John 20:1–18
Other Readings: Acts 10:34–43; Ps. 118:1–2, 14–24; 1 Cor. 15:1–11

I. *The false report* (20:1–10). According to John's Gospel, the first report about Jesus' Resurrection was a false report. That is not too surprising; none of the disciples were expecting the Resurrection. It was only natural that Mary assumed there was a mundane, if sinister, explanation when she found the stone rolled away from the tomb: "They have taken the Lord out of the tomb, and we don't know where they have placed him!" (20:2). That news was enough to send Peter and "the other disciple whom Jesus loved" running off to the tomb to investigate the matter for themselves. The "other disciple" arrived there first and had the first look at the tomb from without. He saw the linen cloths with which Jesus' body had been wrapped. Nothing more. Had he left then, he might have worried, as Mary did, about what had happened. But when Peter arrived he entered into the tomb after him and took a closer look. There was something unusual about the way in which the cloth that had covered Jesus' face was rolled up by itself in one place (20:7). Perhaps, too, he was struck by the incongruity of someone leaving this cloth behind so neatly while removing the body. Whatever it was, the *bruta facta*—or, more precisely, the in-breaking of a new reality—spoke to him: "He saw and believed" (20:8). This faith arose contrary to his own expectations, first in contradiction to Mary's report and second in contradiction to his own understanding: "*for* he did not yet know [that is, understand] the Scripture" (20:9). He was confronted with a reality from which he could draw only one conclusion: Jesus is risen.

Along with the other Gospels—and Paul (1 Cor. 15:1–11), John's Gospel is not at all shy about pointing to hard evidence for the Resurrection: real phenomena in time and space that themselves speak and cannot be forced into silence (cf. 20:24–29). Something was *there*, sufficient to bring a thinking person to the same conclusion. Something was *there* that did not arise out of the disciples' subjective perceptions, hopes, or wishes. It came crashing in on them, contrary to their expectations and experience. One could never say that Mary's interpretation of the event was just as valid as that of the disciple who believed. She was wrong! In believing the facts, that disciple had to dismiss her report. Both could not be true. That same truth, the evangelist tells us, applies to the Christian witness to the Resurrection: either it is true or false (cf. 1 Cor. 15:17), "if Christ is not raised, your faith is in vain!"

II. *The encounter with the Risen Lord* (20:11–16). Yet mere seeing with the eyes is not sufficient. Mary stands outside the tomb weeping—in unbelief. And as she weeps, she bends over and looks into the tomb. Now she can see all the evidence that Peter and the other disciple had seen—and even more! Two angels appeared, clothed in white, sitting where Jesus' body had been laid, one where his head had been, one where his feet had been. They address her: "Woman, why are you weeping?" (20:13). But Mary remains entirely blind and deaf. She stands outside faith just as she stands outside the tomb, refusing to enter in: "They have taken my Lord away, and I do not know where they have laid him" (20:13). And as she turns away—from the empty tomb and from faith—she has the most unexpected encounter of her life. Jesus himself stands before her. And he asks her the same question as the angels: "Woman, why are you weeping? Whom do you seek?" (20:15). Jesus gently and poignantly attempts again to break through her shell. But to no avail; she is still blind! She imagines that he is the gardener and continues her search for Jesus' corpse (the quests for the historical Jesus, perhaps?). She takes on herself a burden she was not meant to bear: "Sir (Lord!), if you took him, tell me where you laid him, and I shall go remove him" (20:15).

Then comes the decisive word from Jesus: "Mary!" He calls her by name, just as he called Lazarus by name from the tomb (11:43), just as the Good Shepherd calls *all* his sheep by name (10:3), just as at the Last Day he shall call forth his own from their tombs (5:28). Already, on that day of his Resurrection, Mary, who was dead, heard the voice of the Son of God and lived (5:25). "Teacher!" she cried. She had finally found him—no, he had found her. Her eyes were opened through her ears: "the ears alone are the organ of a Christian" (Luther). No matter how long she stood before that tomb and stared the facts in the face, she could not see and believe, because her heart was closed in upon itself and therefore blind. Only the word of the Risen Lord could open her heart. The same was true in a hidden way for the other disciple, who believed when he saw. The same was true for Thomas, who only later believed. The same is true for all who believe the message of Easter. Christian faith is not self-generating, either in terms of its outward evidence or in terms of its inward reality. It is called into being and sustained by the Risen Lord, who calls each of his own by name.

III. *The report of faith* (17–18). Now that Mary's eyes are opened, she is given the task of announcing the good news to others so that their eyes, too, may be opened. Jesus does not permit her to "touch" him, to remain with him in a continuation of their former earthly relationship (20:17). It was quite possible to touch him. In order that he might come to faith, Thomas is invited to do precisely what Mary is denied (20:24–29). But precisely because Mary has believed and because the Risen Jesus must yet ascend to the Father—and thus become present in a new way for all believers—she is not permitted to touch him. Perhaps our English versions have it right when they render the expression as a prohibition against "holding on" to Jesus or "grasping" him. She must let him go, in order for her and all others truly to draw close to him—and to God. The cross has changed the relationship between Jesus and his disciples: by virtue of it, they are now his brothers and sisters. They now share in his relationship with the Father: no longer will he petition the Father for them; they shall petition the Father in his name (16:26). Jesus' God is now their God: they love him and obey him from the heart. He loves them, because they believe in his Son (16:27). Jesus' Ascension is the culmination of this new relation. And this new relation means a new task for Mary and, with her, all of Jesus' disciples: Go and tell!—Mark Seifrid

ILLUSTRATION

When Mary thinks Jesus is the gardener (20:16), she addresses him with the respectful "sir"; when she recognizes his true identity, her address becomes the familiar but still respectful "rabbouni"—"my teacher." The pronoun "my" built into the word is important (see Thomas in 20:28: "*my* Lord and *my* God"). The Christian confession is not in an abstract truth but in the personal God, who knows our name and numbers the hairs of our head (Matt. 10:30). Mary had previously seen the stone rolled away, the empty tomb, two angels, and the Risen Jesus himself, but they did not produce the response of personal faith. The personal address of the Risen Lord himself, the one who calls his sheep by name (10:3), generates authentic faith that overwhelming "evidence," including visions of angels, could not. For John, people come to Christian faith not by weighing the evidence judged by their own criteria (see 7:12) but as a response to the voice of the living Christ that continues to be heard in Christian preaching and the testimony of Christian words, deed, and lives.—M. Eugene Boring and Fred B. Craddock[3]

SERMON SUGGESTIONS

Topic: God's Saving Deed

Text: Ps. 118:1–2, 14–24 (esp. v. 22)

(1) The rejected cornerstone (see John 1:11). (2) The indispensable cornerstone (see John 1:12). (3) Who makes the difference? (see John 1:13).

Topic: If Christ Be Not Risen!

Text: 1 Cor. 15:17, 18, 20

(1) "If Christ be not risen, *your faith is vain*"; you can't trust his love; you can't trust his power; but if Christ be risen from the dead, then faith in God is crowned, justified, vindicated! (2) "If Christ be not risen, *ye are yet in your sins*": then Christ's attempt to be a Savior failed; but—sin is defeated! (3) "If Christ be not risen, *then they also which are fallen asleep in Christ are perished*"; three inevitable conclusions—faith gone, forgiveness gone, immortality gone; but—you have the evidence of the living Christ in yourself.[4]

WORSHIP AIDS

CALL TO WORSHIP.   "O taste and see that the Lord is good; happy are those who take refuge in him" (Ps. 34:8 NRSV).

INVOCATION.   Lord, because no force could block the tomb nor limit the movements of our Risen Savior, we pray no force will prevent nor power negate our worship and our praise.

OFFERTORY SENTENCE.   "He that spared not his own Son, but delivered him up for us all, how shall he not also with him freely give us all things?" (Rom. 8:32)

---

[3]*The People's New Testament Commentary* (Louisville, Ky.: Westminster John Knox Press, 2004), p. 357.
[4]James S. Stewart, *The Gates of New Life* (New York: Charles Scribner's Sons, 1940), pp. 160–169.

OFFERTORY PRAYER.   Grace us, O God, with the insight of the wise and the compassion of the caring because we give today so others may meet our crucified and resurrected Lord.—E. Lee Phillips

PRAYER.   What a day! This is the day that you have made, O God, giving significance to *all* our days. May we come with such faith and expectance as to receive this day in all of its glory and power. Life *is* going somewhere, and even nails and a cross cannot stop it. As you turned the despair of the disciples into hope, so give us faith to believe that every good that has been overcome by evil, and every love that has been buried by hate, and every relationship that has been eclipsed by estrangement shall rise again to *new* life. May we know assuredly that "the stone which the builders rejected *has* become the head of the corner."

For all of us, let this be a day of rejoicing and great gladness—a day when we fully know that although with men the saving of man is impossible, with you all things are possible. Let this be a day when things are possible. Let this be a day when you surprise us with the insight that, in our weakness you can make perfect your strength and, through the foolishness of the cross you reveal *your* wisdom and power. Let this be a day when our every thought and every fiber of our being vibrate with the living hope that the Resurrection of Christ precipitates.

If there are those among us still wrapped by the grave clothes of doubt, of fear, of cynicism, we pray that we may be released to live in the new age heralded by the good news of the first Easter morning: "Christ is risen!" We praise you, O Father, that in the Resurrection we know that all your promises find their "Yes" in Christ. This is of your "doing and it's marvelous in our eyes."

O Father, may we here, and all who are the Church everywhere, pursue with renewed commitment your reconciling love purpose proclaimed in the life, ministry, passion, and living again of Jesus. Bless family and friends with whom we are privileged to celebrate most intimately the meaning of love. Where there is illness, we pray for healing—a wholeness that transcends even physical infirmities. May all of us bereft of loved ones and friends live with the assurance that "life is ever lord of death and love can never lose its own." May we rejoice in a fellowship not limited by time or space—*the communion of saints.* Bless the estranged among us with the sense of your love mediated through the hospitality of this fellowship. For those with civil authority in this country and in all nations, we pray the enlightenment of that Truth, "though crushed to earth shall rise again."

Thanks be to you, who gives us the victory through our Lord Jesus Christ, who is present among us as your eternal Word, teaching us to pray together.—John Thompson

SERMON
Topic: At the End of Your Hope

TEXTS: (1) *Biblical:* "We believe now that we had this experience of coming to the end of our tether that we might learn to trust not in ourselves, but in God who can raise the dead" (2 Cor. 1:9 [Phillips]); (2) *Contemporary:* "Refusal to hope is nothing more than a decision to die."[5]

---

[5]Bernie Siegel, *Love, Medicine and Miracles* (New York: HarperPerennial, 1990).

During Holy Week a mother told me of her daughter who is having a very unholy week in the throes of a divorce. It is the last thing that Susan ever thought would happen to her. It is a kind of living death. It is an end-of-the-world experience for her, and she does not see how she can ever survive such an ordeal—if she could only "curl up and die."

There is the husband who loses his mate of fifty-two years. The shock of his wife's death is just beginning to wear off, and he is realizing now how *final* death is. "Oh, if I could only have died with her," he finds himself saying. "I don't have anything to live for now. It's the end of the world."

There is the woman who has had radical surgery for cancer. She is now having therapy. She is so deathly sick after each treatment, she can't eat. She has lost fourteen pounds in a matter of days. She dreads each treatment. "Life isn't worth living if one has to go through this," she remarks. "Will I ever enjoy health again? Believe me, it is the end of my world!"

I. In every congregation or in everyone's circle of friends, there are persons who have recently encountered these or similar life-threatening circumstances. Such "end-of-my-world" experiences may even have invaded *your* complacency.

No matter how self-sufficient a person may feel, there are contingencies that come to every one of us that are so threatening—so demanding—as to cause us to feel that we have come to the end of our rope—*to the end of our hope.*

It is such an experience that the apostle Paul recalls out of his own life that is recorded in the New Testament lesson: "We should like you, our brothers [and sisters]," Paul writes, "to know something of what we went through in Asia. At that time we were completely overwhelmed; the burden was more than we could bear; in fact, we told ourselves, 'This is the end.' Yet, we believe now that we had this experience of coming to the end of our tether that we might learn to trust, not in ourselves, but in God who can raise the dead" (2 Cor. 1:8, 9).

This experience, as described by the apostle, should not fall on our ears like a rumor from a far country. Who among us, under the stress of some difficulty, has not felt like a tree in a high wind with shallow rootage, like a cistern that has suddenly gone dry, like an army with all its troops in the front line and no reserves. There may be those here this morning who, under the stress and strain of life, feel spiritually exhausted—at the end of *their* hope.

II. It is in retrospect that the apostle sees their difficulties in Asia in true perspective. As he writes, "We believe now that we had this experience of coming to the end of our tether that we might learn to trust, not in ourselves, but in God. . . ." He had learned one of life's most important lessons—that man's extremity *is* God's opportunity.

When looking back over one's own life, as was true with the apostle, who does not see that in every crisis there has been a grace at work that has brought him or her through the stormy seas without shipwreck? As I recall the vicissitudes confronted in my own journey, I see *now* that at every juncture God's grace was present, strengthening the inner person that I could weather every outward threat.

You see, to feel that you have come to the end of your rope need not be a negative; it can be a positive. It was for the apostle, and he frequently comments on it. "In our weakness we are strong," he writes. What a paradox! How can we know strength if we are weak? At first hearing, it may sound like a lot of double talk. But Paul had learned that in his own weakness he became open—available—to receive *God's* strength.

We are not naturally given to humility but to pride. Many a person never looks up until he is flat on his back. That is what happened to a friend. When I knew him, he was an executive for an airline. He was a nominal church member; faith in God was not his forte. He saw himself a very self-sufficient person. At times he was arrogant, frequently playing God. A sudden coronary was the occasion for him to look up for the first time in his life. His extremity became God's opportunity. He learned to wait on him "in whom we live and move and have our being." In his weakness he came to know God's strength, which proved to be his salvation. He became a new person and for many years enjoyed good health and a life of faithful service.

God does not send these life-threatening experiences; many of them we invite ourselves. But God can use them to mediate his saving grace.

III. "We believe that we had this experience of coming to the end of our tether that we might learn to trust, not in ourselves, but in God who can raise the dead."

The God who is at the end of our hope is the God who can raise the dead. For the apostle, the cornerstone of the temple of faith is the Resurrection of Christ. In his first letter to the church of Corinth, the Resurrection is the subject of a lengthy chapter of fifty-eight verses. Paul's argument affirming the Resurrection rose to a grand crescendo in the concluding verses, as he proclaims: "Death is swallowed up in victory." Then he declares the occasion of the victory: "Thanks be to God, who gives us the victory through our Lord Jesus Christ."

Confronted with some end-of-the-world experience—at the end of your hope, God *is*—the God who can raise the dead. Life's shattering circumstances threatening *your* complacency can be the occasion for you to learn some of life's most strategic lessons. Often the beliefs that we profess are not the beliefs by which we live. Until the arm of flesh fails us, we do not learn to rest on the strength of the everlasting arms. Until our beliefs are tested and tempted in the crucible of suffering, they are as hearsay. So Job discerned the meaning of his trial by fire: "Once I knew you by the hearing of the ear but now my eyes see you."

Is not the apostle Paul's experience of coming to the end of his hope the biography of every one of us? When our world seems to be crashing down around us and from all appearances, as with the apostle Paul, it looks like the end, it is only the end of *our* hope. God is not dead. And in the death of our old hope that was limited by our finiteness, we are raised to a new hope as we learn to trust in God and the power of the Resurrection. As someone has aptly put it: "Our hope flies as high as our faith is deeply rooted in the fact of the Resurrection of Christ."

The strategic role of *hope* in therapy is being increasingly realized today, as medical science discovers the psychosomatic nature of many diseases. The importance of hope to the healing process is expressed by Bernie Siegel in *Love, Medicine, and Miracles,* when he writes: "To refuse to hope is to have made the decision to die."[6] In fact, he states that hope may play a very important role in *preventive* medicine—that many of our diseases are self-inflicted; they are a kind of self-fulfillment—we invite them through our negative attitudes, through our anxiety.

---

[6]Bernie Siegel, *Love, Medicine, and Miracles,* (New York: HarperPerennial, 1990).

As we contemplate this matter, we need to realize that God is never through with us; he continually calls us to grow as persons. If we refuse to grow in a healthy, positive way, the body gets the negative message and unhealthy growth can result.

It seems to me that to live with hope begins by accepting the strange new circumstances of one's life in all of their sordidness—their difficulty, their loneliness. No matter how much you may wish that they were different, you must bring yourself to accept the fact that this is the way things are: "This is my reality!" Only in doing this can one make real contact with the grace that heals. Unless we are real with ourselves, how can God be real with us?

When God's grace gets into a situation, the circumstances of one's life are not changed, but he or she is strangely transformed. Problems become opportunities; negatives are turned into positives, liabilities into assets, handicaps into means of grace. What one thought was the end is a new beginning. What one assumed was death—the end of one's world—is the door to a new life. Easter is no longer a fairy tale from some distant land but is happening to you. The stone of fear is rolled from the tomb of your life, and you walk out into the sunshine of an eternal day. And you find yourself saying, with the apostle Paul: "I believe now that I had this experience of coming to the end of my hope that I might learn to trust, not in myself but in God, *who can raise the dead.*"—John Thompson

SUNDAY, APRIL 23, 2006
Lectionary Message

Topic: The Expanding Circle of Joy
TEXT: 1 John 1:1–2:2
Other Readings: Acts 4:32–35; Ps. 133; John 20:19–31

I. *The apostolic witness* (1:1–4). It is the voice of an apostle that opens this letter. The first-person plural "we," with which he speaks, is distinct from the recipients of the letter and all other Christians. The author stands with the other apostles and bears witness. His witness arises from *his* hearing, *his* seeing, *his* handling and touching Jesus, and not only his but also that of all other eyewitnesses.

He announces "the eternal life, which was with the Father and manifest to us" (1:2). This eternal life is that which "was from the beginning" (1:1). It is the "*word* of life" (1:2). It is Jesus Christ, God's Son (1:3), the Messiah who came in the flesh (4:2), who came "not through water only, but through water and blood" (5:6). We miss the thrust of the apostolic witness unless we recognize that it is Jesus Christ, incarnate, crucified, and risen of whom these predications are made. *He* was from the beginning. *He* is "the eternal life." The apostle does not speak of eternal life as an ideal. Nor does he speak of it as a vague "personal relation with Christ" into which one might pour any content one might please. The content of "word of life," the contours of "the eternal life" are defined by the crucified and Risen Lord. In and through him *alone* (2:22–23, 4:15) "we" have fellowship with the Father (1:3).

This fellowship, this participation, this *koinonia* with the Father and the Son cannot remain a private, personal matter. The one who knows and *shares* in God and God's love for us cannot help but announce and proclaim that love (1:3). This fellowship must be shared with others. Therefore the apostle speaks. He speaks that his own joy might be made full, as his readers come to know Jesus Christ, the eternal life, afresh (1:4). The fellowship of joy must be again and again kindled afresh in the hearts of Christians through the apostolic word of witness to Christ. And the fellowship of joy must ever expand its circle.

II. *The light of forgiveness* (1:5–10). The apostolic message is that "God is light: pure, unadulterated light. "In him there is no darkness at all" (1:5). This light is the light of the cross, the Light of Christ, crucified and risen: as we noticed, the apostolic proclamation is not abstract, but concrete. And this proclamation creates *koinonia*—fellowship with the God who is Light. In the center of the light stands the cross. The truth of God is that he is the God who forgives, the God who is love.

In the light, truth and morality meet. What ought to be and what is are one. To walk in the light is to *do* the truth. To walk in the darkness is to lie: here truth and morality are correspondingly absent. The entire question of the passage and of the letter is that *of response* to the apostolic announcement. Not only do the apostles announce "the word of life" (1:1) but human beings speak in response, either in disobedience—the threefold "if we should say" (1:6, 8, 10)—or in *the confession of sin*. Walking in the light therefore is conditioned on our telling the truth about ourselves, and that not merely as the first step of the Christian life but *every* step along the way. Only in the light, only as sinners gathered at the foot of the cross, do we have fellowship with one another. "Our community with one another consists solely in what Christ has done to both of us."

In the light, our sin is cleansed by the sacrifice of God's Son (1:7). "God is faithful and righteous to forgive us our sins and cleanse us from all unrighteousness" (1:9). The condition that is attached—"if we confess our sins"—is not ultimate. Our being forgiven is not finally contingent on what we do, even though our confession is necessary. Our speech, whether it takes the form of a lie or a confession, is nothing other than a response to the announcement that God is light, that he is nothing but redeeming love. In confessing our sins, we step out of darkness into light, into the reality of God and his unconditioned love. God is "faithful and righteous" in that he forgives us our sins and cleanses us from unrighteousness. The apostle here speaks of the truth and morality inherent to the light. Faithfulness is the truth of God in action (1:6; cf. Rev. 3:14, 19:11, 21:5, 22:6). It is also God's righteousness, his rectitude and his justice in dealing with the world. Faithfulness and righteousness, according to this context, find their definition—beyond all human imagination—in God's redeeming love in Jesus.

III. *The aim of the witness* (2:1–2). With respect to its origin and source, the apostolic proclamation seeks to expand the circle of the joy of fellowship with the Father and the Son (1:3–4). With respect to the addressees themselves, the apostle writes, "in order that you might not sin." The statement obviously bears a polemical edge against those who claim "to have no sin" (1:8, 10). It also already anticipates the surprising affirmation that "no one who abides in him [Christ] sins" (3:6; cf. 3:9). The arrival of the light is the arrival of the eschaton. The *non posse peccare* (the impossibility of sinning) has arrived. To believe, to walk in the light, means in the most crucial and fundamental sense to sin no more. Yet the old reality of darkness remains, even if it is passing away: we *do* sin, even though we share in the age to come. This tension between the already and the not-yet is not a meaningless dialectic: the light has conquered the darkness. Sin has decisively been overcome. Jesus Christ, the Righteous One, is our Advocate with the Father; he is the atoning sacrifice for our sins—and not only ours (the apostle turns his attention again to the circle of joy that expands through proclamation) but also those of the entire world.—Mark Seifrid

ILLUSTRATION

EMPATHY.   In the novel *Birdy*, William Wharton's protagonist, Sergeant Alfonso, develops an instant dislike for an obnoxious, overweight enlisted man—a clerk-typist named Ronsky. At the top of his list of gripes about this annoying grunt is Ronsky's revolting habit of continually spitting. He spits all over his desk, his typewriter, his papers, and those who venture too near. Alfonso is only waiting an excuse to punch him out. Then the sergeant learns Ronsky's story. He was an infantryman on D-Day and saw his buddies shot down in the surf before they even reached the beach of Normandy. And his constant spitting, it seems, is a physical manifestation of his attempt to get the nauseous foulness of war and death out of his mouth when anything reminds him, as virtually as everything does, of its acrid smell and putrid taste. Sergeant Alfonso suddenly sees Ronsky with new eyes. What yesterday had irritated him unbearably, today wins his total respect. He sighs with regret and thinks: "Before you know it, if you're not careful, you can get to feeling for everybody and there's nobody left to hate."[7]—David W. Augsberger[8]

SERMON SUGGESTIONS

Topic: Unity
TEXT: Ps. 133
(1) Unity has its rewards at all levels—family, community, nation, world (v. 1). (2) True unity, a blessed fragrance, is from above (vv. 2–3).

Topic: What Can God Do?
TEXT: Matt. 19:26b NEB
(1) God's high standards for us. (2) Our possible and varying failures to measure up. (3) God's power to deal effectively with any and all of our needs: the why; the how.

WORSHIP AIDS

CALL TO WORSHIP.   "This is the day which the Lord hath made; we will rejoice and be glad in it" (Ps. 118:24).

INVOCATION.   Though many high and holy experiences fade soon from our hearts and leave a lingering sadness, grant, O God, that we may know this day the exultation of those who have risen with Christ and are seeking the things that are above, where Christ is, seated at your right hand.

OFFERTORY SENTENCE.   "Whoever shares with others should do it generously" (Rom. 12:8 TEV).

---

[7]Wharton, 1979.
[8]*Hate-Work* (Louisville/London: Westminster John Knox Press, 2004), p. 222.

OFFERTORY PRAYER.   Gracious Father, we have opened our mouths and you have filled them with good things. Now open our hearts to others, we pray, that we may help bring fulfillment to their hopes and prayers. Bless these offerings and direct their use, so that nothing be wasted.

PRAYER.   Eternal Father, because our Lord lives today, we live. But some of us have not felt the lifting power of that truth. We go about as those who know that our Lord was crucified but hardly knowing that he was raised from the dead. We have been told that you have caused us to sit together in heavenly places with him, yet the sights and sounds and smells of Earth are still too much with us. May we hear in your word the trumpet blast of victory and rise with confidence, wide awake to what we are and what we should be doing. Help us to live on this Earth as those whose citizenship is in heaven, but as those who are eager to bring the life of heaven to this Earth. Grant strength to those sorely tempted every day to live as if this world were all. Grant concern and tact to those who see others tempted and wish to help. And give us all a knowledge of your comradeship with us in our pilgrimage.

SERMON

Topic: Value and a World of Change
TEXT: John 20:10–18

I. We live in a world of change, a world of transition. The old world we were born into has ceased to exist, and the new world that our children and grandchildren will inhabit is not yet here, though from time to time we get a glimpse of its outlines. The world has always, of course, been changing. It has never been static. The world is dynamic, its one unchanging constant being its constant change. The difference, however, between our experience of change and that of earlier generations is the rapid rate at which change now occurs. Statisticians tell us (how they know this I can't say) that human knowledge has doubled in the past ten years. There is twice as much knowledge now as there was ten years ago.

With increased knowledge comes increased power—we can do things today that we couldn't do ten years ago because of this exponential growth in knowledge. Doctors announce daily new breakthroughs that hold the promise of eradicating, or at least controlling, our most dreaded diseases. Change is, therefore, good when it promises us conquest over some threatening feature of our world. Yet, ironically, change itself can be a threat. Our world of rapid change upsets our equilibrium because we are not sure what the future is going to be like. And that uncertainty is upsetting because, if we don't know what the future will be like, we can't be sure we will be able to cope with it when it gets here.

But there is another reason why we fear change, why change threatens us. Change threatens what we value most. Change threatens not only our ability to cope with the future but also our discernment of what we are to live for, what we ought to consider important and worthy of our time and energy and effort. We fear that, in the process of change, something of real value may be lost.

The academic world of the university and graduate school (which is largely responsible for the rapid expansion of our knowledge and, therefore, our power and, therefore, the rapid rate of change today) has noted this threat and responded in various ways. The introduction to a popular textbook in ethics, for example, states that one of the purposes of studying ethics is to discover new values to replace the old values that have failed us.[9] Medical students today take courses in medical ethics that raise issues doctors of a few generations ago never faced.

But the perception that real, significant values are threatened by our world of rapid change is not confined to the ivy-covered halls of academe. It is widespread in the marketplace as well. It explains (in part, at least) the rise of reactionary social, political, and religious movements in our century. Fundamentalists, for example, are afraid that the free and critical investigation of the Bible, using the most modern and up-to-date techniques and drawing on our best knowledge, will somehow destroy the authority of the Bible (which to them is perhaps the greatest value of it).

Think of Muslim fundamentalism in Iran, the Marxist Puritanism of Pol Pot in Cambodia, the reactionary dictatorships of Latin America. Catholic churches that offer the Latin mass have so many parishioners respond that they often turn worshippers away for lack of room. And some Episcopal congregations have broken ties with their church because they do not approve of recent changes in Episcopal polity.

Change is threatening, at least in part because we fear that something we value will be lost.

II. Change is a threat, but it is also a fact and will not go away. We know that the world of the future will be different in significant ways from the world of the past. Furthermore, we know that one day our world will undergo the ultimate change—total destruction when the sun in its last stages of existence explodes into a supernova and incinerates the Earth and all that is in it. Think about what that means for things we value. Think about the things that will be gone in the final conflagration.

III. This total destruction of all that we value is (we hope) in the far future, millions and millions of years away. Yet in our reflective moments we must somehow come to terms with this fact intellectually. Why should we value these things if one day they will all be destroyed? Why should we value anything at all, if all ends in death and destruction?

Some people have, in fact, come to this conclusion—that nothing we value is permanent, so we should value only what is pleasing to us, though transitory. Eat, drink, and be merry, for tomorrow we all die. (And if not tomorrow, then the day after.) There is nothing to live for, so let's live for nothing; this is what I call "cosmic despair," and it paints a pretty grim picture of human existence.

There is another, different attitude of despair we might adopt. I call it "heroic cosmic despair." It embodies the despair we experience when we realize that nothing we value has permanence, but it does not degenerate into the "eat, drink, and be merry" variety. No, the one who despairs heroically still clings to the values we all share—truth, beauty, goodness, justice—but does so as an act of heroic (though ultimately futile) defiance against an indifferent or possibly malevolent universe. The hero of cosmic despair says, in effect: "I know that what I value will not last. It will one day be destroyed. I know that truth, beauty, justice, goodness are doomed in the last analysis to be frustrated and thwarted. But I thumb my nose at the universe and its indifference. I will continue to live my life in accordance with these values, even though I know I'm doomed to defeat." No one put this attitude better than Bertrand Russell in an early essay titled "A Free Man's Worship":

---

[9]Raziel Anderson and Marie-Louise Friquegnon, *Ethics for Modern Life*, 2nd ed. (New York: Simon & Schuster/St. Martin's Press, 1982), pp. 4–5.

That man is the product of causes which had no prevision of the end they were achieving; that his origin, his growth, his hopes and fears, his loves and his beliefs, are but the outcome of accidental collocations of atoms; that no fire, no heroism, no intensity of thought and feeling, can preserve an individual life beyond the grave; that all the labors of the ages, all the devotion, all the inspiration, all the noonday brightness of human genius, are destined to extinction in the vast death of the solar system, and that the whole temple of man's achievement must inevitably be buried beneath the debris of a universe in ruins—all these things, if not quite beyond dispute, are yet so nearly certain that no philosophy which rejects them can hope to stand. Only within the scaffolding of these truths, only on the firm foundation of unyielding despair, can the soul's habitation henceforth be safely built.[10]

No one had a keener sense about social and political justice than Russell. And no one worked harder to make the world a better place than he did. Yet he did so believing that all of his efforts would eventually come to naught. "Unyielding despair," he says, must be our attitude, the only "firm foundation" on which to build our lives.

Living in an age of transition threatens us because it threatens that which we value most. We know that one day our Earth and everything in it will be destroyed. We may respond like the reactionary and try to hold change back or pretend that it is not there. Or we may respond with cosmic despair, either in its nihilistic or heroic forms. If these were our only choices, I hope I would opt for heroic cosmic despair like Russell's.

But we have not yet said all there is to say about the future, change, and threats to what we value.

IV. John 20 portrays Mary Magdalene as one threatened by cosmic despair. Her world has crumbled. What she valued most—her relationship to Jesus—has been destroyed by death. She is sorrowful and grief-stricken. She weeps. The Risen Christ approaches her, and she doesn't even recognize him. Her cry is the cry of despair: "The one who meant the most to me, the one whom I loved the most, is gone. He's dead. I'll never see him again. And I don't even know where his body is so that I can honor his memory." She is saying that what she most valued has been taken from her and that she no longer has anything to live for.

Jesus speaks her name, and with that one word she realizes that he is not dead but alive and standing before her. What she cherished most in this world has not been destroyed after all. In joy she reaches out for Jesus to take hold of him and never let him go. But Jesus stops her. "Do not cling to me," he says, "for I have not yet ascended to God." And then Jesus gives Mary a commission: "Go and tell my brothers that I am ascending to God." Mary is ordained to be the first witness to the Resurrection. She is ordained to be the first evangelist, the first bearer of good news. So Mary goes to the disciples and says, "I have seen the Lord!" Her message is that what they all had valued most in this world had not been destroyed or taken from them after all.

V. This is good news. But there is more to Jesus' message than this. There is also the command to accept the fact of change. "Do not cling to me," Jesus says to Mary, when she reaches out to grab hold of Jesus and never let him go. "What I have meant to you has not

---

[10]Bertrand Russell, *Why I Am Not a Christian and Other Essays on Religion and Related Subjects* (New York: Simon & Schuster, 1957), p. 107.

been lost," Jesus is saying, "but what I have meant to you is being changed. I am ascending to God. So, you must not try to cling to me, to hold on to what our relationship was. If you truly want to preserve my value to you, then you must let the old relationship go and accept the new reality of my Resurrection. Nothing essential between us has changed. But there are changes, and you must accept them, or you will run the risk of losing everything."

The Resurrection of Jesus shows that what we value most, if it is what we ought most to value, persists through change. What we value changes, but nothing essential is lost. I do not know how this can be. I do not know how the value of great works of art and literature and music will be preserved. I do not know how people we have loved—parents, children, friends—continue to be real values after the death of their bodies. I have confidence, however, that value—our highest and best values—are preserved, though transformed. And I have this confidence because this is what happened to Jesus. Jesus died. But death did not destroy him. He lives, and he is still with us as our highest value.

Therefore, we need not despair that our work for goodness and beauty and justice is in vain, whether or not we are successful. In some way that we cannot fathom, God will make sure that what we do will be of lasting value. We can have confidence that even the smallest act of "tightness" makes some difference and will not be lost. But if we cling desperately to the old embodiments of value, we will miss the new. Faith in Christ means the willingness to let go of the past in order to have the future. It means the willingness to undergo the transformation from something old to something new, something wonderful. We must lose in order to find.

"All's lost," Godric says at the end of his life, as he realizes that he is about to die and finally meet God face to face. But then he says, "All's found."[11] Godric had to give up his life in order to find it. Another saint put it this way: "If anyone is in Christ, there is a new creation; everything old has passed away; see, everything has become new!" (2 Cor. 5:17).—Bill Thomason[12]

SUNDAY, APRIL 30, 2006
Lectionary Message

Topic: The Center of Scripture
TEXT: Luke 24:36b–48
Other Readings: Acts 3:12–19; Ps. 4; 1 John 3:1–7

I. *The peace of the Risen Lord* (24:36a–43). "Peace be to you!" These are the first words of the Risen Lord to his gathered disciples. They had already heard the report of his appearance to Simon Peter (24:34). The two excited disciples who had encountered him on the Emmaus road had only just recounted their experience. Then he was suddenly there, in their midst.

Yet their reaction to him is just as unexpected as was his appearance to them! Their first response to his words is not peace, but terror. They thought that they were seeing a ghost, a

---

[11]Frederick Buechner, *Godric* (New York: Atheneum, 1980), p. 171.
[12]*Real Life, Real Faith* (Valley Forge, Pa.: Judson Press, 1994), pp. 82–88.

disembodied spirit (cf. Luke 23:46; Acts 23:8–9). The first effect of Jesus' word is the opposite of its intent. Is that not often the nature of our encounter with God in his Word?

Jesus patiently works through their fears. His hands and his feet make it clear that it is he: no doubt the marks of the nails are the telltale sign. He invites them to touch him and see that he has flesh and bones. Not even this evidence is enough! Out of sheer joy, they cannot believe that it is Jesus. He therefore helps their faith further. He requests something to eat from them and eats the roasted fish that they give him in their presence. The sheer physicality of this event must not escape us. Here is the anticipation of our own resurrection. This is what we mean when we confess, "I believe in the resurrection of the dead." Our *bodies* shall be raised!

II. *Christ the center* (24:44–47). What the disciples experienced in that hour with the Risen Lord was the fulfillment of the Scriptures. Everything concerning *Jesus* written in the Law of Moses, the Prophets, and the Psalms had to be fulfilled, especially his Crucifixion but also his Resurrection (24:44).

The crucified and Risen Christ is, in fact, the key to the Scriptures and its center: according to Luke's witness, upon these words Jesus opened their mind to understand the Scriptures. The unbelief of the disciples in Jesus' Resurrection was *disbelief* of the Scriptures, which foretold it. This disbelief, which had to be removed, rested in their failure to reckon with the cross: it was necessary for the Christ *to suffer* and enter into his glory (24:26).

As with Paul, so also with Luke: the cross remains the stumbling block to faith. It is removed by the Risen Lord alone. Jesus' act surely is a prolepsis of the promised sending of the Spirit, which he immediately announces (24:49) and therefore has significance beyond the first disciples. Only Jesus Christ can open the Scriptures to us. Only he can overcome the slowness of our unbelieving hearts and remove the stumbling-block of the cross for us (24:25–26). There is an "inner clarity" of Scripture given only by Jesus Christ, which does not in any way diminish the necessity of the study and interpretation of it.

The fulfillment of Scripture in Jesus Christ extends through the Risen Lord to the world. The proclamation of "repentance for the forgiveness of sins" to all the nations shall yet take place (24:47). This "repentance" is not somehow a requirement added to faith or a supplement to it! It *is* faith, which contains repentance within itself (Luke 24:25; Acts 5:31, 11:18, 20:21). With the fulfillment of the promise to Abraham, which is likewise the fulfillment of the hopes of the prophets, the Gentiles themselves shall come to salvation.

III. *The call to witness* (24:48). The fulfillment of God's purposes in Jesus Christ carries the disciples in its sweep. "*You* are witnesses of these things," Jesus tells them. In the vocabulary of Luke, "witness" is limited to those who are apostles and who have seen the Risen Lord (Acts 1:8 notwithstanding). The physical encounter with the Risen Lord is taken up in this commission. God does not fulfill his promises in words, but in mighty deeds (Luther). The initial proclamation came from those who saw and touched the Risen Lord. Yet the seeing and touching themselves are not enough: the disciples are told to wait in Jerusalem for "the promise of the Father." They are not sufficent for the task. They must be clothed with power from on high. That is the story of the book of Acts with which Luke follows this narrative. It is also the story of the ongoing witness of the Church and of every Christian. We no longer need wait for the Spirit: he has come. But we remain dependent on the power of another to believe, to understand the Scriptures, and to proclaim the gospel to all the nations.—Mark Seifrid

ILLUSTRATION

REPENTANCE.   "Repent!" was not just a word on a sign that crazy, bearded, begowned cartoon characters bannered to announce the coming of the end. "Repent!" was and is the rupturing and then healing turn from present ways to the paths of God. In the end, repentance was a joyful act. The penitent—the one being changed—could say good-bye to his or her old self without mourning. Something new was coming.

Whether Dietrich Bonhoeffer was a prophet, I am not yet ready to say. It's good to allow a hundred years to pass before handing out that label with assurance. Of course, the prophets of ancient Israel *were* prophets. They burned their bridges of security to the larger society, even unto death. I do know that Bonhoeffer spoke and acted prophetically, and went to his death.

So did most of the other people of bygone times who still nag and inspire us today: St. Francis and those strange, medieval women mystics and Abraham Lincoln and Martin Luther King Jr. They lived among apparently hopeless circumstances and projected hope backward, prompting others to follow the new direction.—William Sloane Coffin[13]

SERMON SUGGESTIONS

Topic: God's Peace
TEXT: Ps. 4
(1) A personal confession of faith (v. 1). (2) A yearning for others in their spiritual need (vv. 2–4). (3) A program of help: do what God requires (v. 5); expect God's gracious favor (v. 6). (3) A joyous testimony (vv. 7–8).

Topic: God's New Creation
TEXT: 2 Cor. 5:16–20
(1) It is focused on human beings (v. 17). (2) It brings us into harmony with God (vv. 18–19). (3) It is extended through our Christian witness (v. 20).

WORSHIP AIDS

CALL TO WORSHIP.   "In the morning when I say my prayers, thou wilt hear me. I set out my morning sacrifice and watch for thee, O Lord" (Ps. 5:3 NEB).

INVOCATION.   Our Father, in spite of all our doubts and fears, we keep on coming to you, for in our heart of hearts we do truly believe. Strengthen today the faltering faith of someone who has come to the house of worship in need of hope and help.

OFFERTORY SENTENCE.   "Bring the tithes in full to the treasury, so that there is food in my house; put me to the test now like this, says Yahweh Sabaoth, and see if I do not open the floodgates of heaven for you and pour out an abundant blessing for you" (Mal. 3:10 NJB).

OFFERTORY PRAYER.   Lord of Creation, may our gifts go forth to fall on fallow ground where germination and growth may occur, and blossom toward fruit may flower, and harvest

---

[13]*A Passion for the Possible*, 2nd ed. (Louisville/London: Westminster John Knox Press, 1993, 2004).

in abundance may appear, through Christ Jesus, who died and was buried and rose again, the first fruits of all who believe.—E. Lee Phillips

PRAYER.   Thank you, Father, for the beautiful world that we call home. Even though we have polluted its streams, poisoned its air, and ripped away its abundant forest, you still renew the water, clean the air, and reforest the deserts if we will cooperate in the most meager manner. You have not withdrawn the gentle summer breezes, the soft spring rains, the glorious autumn colors, and the winter stars. You still bless us with sunsets and bird songs, moonlit nights and flower-scented dawns.

Even though we are drawn to the bad news of life, you are constantly injecting the laughter of a child to balance our senses, providing a wise soul to direct our ways, sending music to inspire our souls. While we cower in fear before uncontrollable forces, you set in our midst those who bravely manage pain, people who courageously face earthly life's end, souls who have learned to adjust to crippling situations and live on nobly.

Sometimes our faith is jaded by the invasions of temptation, the failure to live up to the highest we know, the following after personal ambitions that leave God out. Sometimes the joy of early faith seems to go missing after the struggles through which faith leads, and we wonder if that early sense of awe and wonder will ever return. Thank you for teaching us the joy of each small victory, the grace in every kind deed done for us, the love that not only heals but also corrects and lifts. Thank you for those sacred moments when faith is renewed, hope is restored, spirits are lifted, and trust is sealed.

Thank you, Father, for this hour, this gathering of folks suffering loss, folks managing pain, folks dealing with sins, folks filled with joy, folks seeking courage, folks looking for help to manage life. May none be disappointed as we worship here today, we pray.—Henry Fields

SERMON
Topic: Christ Is the Answer
TEXT: 2 Cor. 1:20a

On one occasion Alexander the Great sat to have his portrait painted, but of the artist he made a strange request. He insisted that he be painted in profile, holding one side of his face in his hand, as if to strike a pose of pensive thought. The reason for this strange request lay in the fact that on one cheek Alexander bore a deep and jagged scar—proof positive that at least one enemy's sword had found its mark. This brilliant conqueror was unwilling to be remembered for posterity by the defeats of life.

The Bible—brave book—is not like that. It furnishes a realistic portrait of humanity with no effort to hide the scars! Hence the perversities and perplexities of humanity are spread out for all to see. Even the saints are not spared a relentless exposure of their innermost difficulties. Yet the prevailing mood is never one of pessimism, cynicism, or despair. Despite their defeats, they have discovered the source of victory. Their questions have been answered, their fears have found new courage, their sin has known salvation.

Often we are guilty of glibly offering the answers without bothering to ask the questions. A revival banner announces, "Christ Is the Answer," but if so, then what are the questions? Without an honest look at the questions, we are in danger of prescribing before we diagnose. A better way is to use the Bible as a guide, both to the deepest riddles of human existence and to the deliverance that may be found there. The Bible views life, not in abstraction but in concrete relationships: to oneself (inward), to others (outward), and to God (upward). Three biblical questions focus on the problems that arise in each of these areas and throw into sharp relief the answers we so desperately need to find.

I. *How can I live with myself?* "Wretched man that I am! Who shall deliver me from this body of death?" (Rom. 7:24). This poignant cry issues from inward perplexity. Paul is saying: I do not understand my own actions. I am helpless to carry out my noblest resolves. There is a yawning chasm between my intentions and my accomplishments. I am a paradox: the divine is deep within for I know what I should do, yet the demonic lurks there as well for I am impotent to carry out these very convictions (Rom. 7:15–23). As Goethe's Faust put it: "Two souls, alas, are housed within my breast. And each will wrestle for the mastery there." The Romans sometimes executed by tying a corpse to the condemned person, and Paul may have been alluding to that hideous practice in describing his own soul.

This is every person's dilemma. Not only have we "fallen short of the glory of God" (Rom. 3:23) but our frustration is that we have failed to measure up to our own expectations. Like one of H. G. Wells's characters, we are a "walking Civil War," a spiritual Jekyll and Hyde. A survey of our shabby performance makes us feel much like the little boy who saw an oil slick on a rainy day and cried to his mother, "Look Mommy, there's a rainbow gone to smash."

The result of such futility is "wretchedness." We know that there is a brokenness deep within us that we are helpless to repair. Well-meaning moralists who encourage us to solve the problem by "living better" are like physicians who would tell a person with a broken arm to exercise it and it will get well. No, the break must first be mended.

Someone has said that it would be hell enough to make us live for eternity with the mess that we know we have made for our own lives. Thus we look for a savior. Because we are the prisoners of our past, we cannot open the door to the jail. Because we are sick of soul, we cannot be the physician. To whom shall we look? Paul has it: thanks be to God who provides the deliverance through Christ our Lord (Rom. 7:25).

In Christ we discover one who calls us to abandon the self-rule of our wretched lives and submit to his sovereign sway. He bids us step off the "treadmill to oblivion" and find in him new spiritual power.

His earthly life proved his power both to forgive sin and to fill the "God-shaped blank" within each heart with his own personality. He convinced others that life could have a new beginning in his service.

We can learn to live with ourselves when we make Christ the center of the self. In a radical experience of repentance and obedience, the sinful self abdicates the throne to die in the waters of baptism and life is lived in orbit around the presence of Christ.

II. *How can I live with others?* "Am I my brother's keeper?" (Gen. 4:9). The question of Cain throbs with implications. "I am not my brother's keeper," he sought to imply. The same heresy is with us today: "I walk alone." "Everyone must look out for himself." "He has his own life to live." These cheap mottos of rampant individualism are hollow lies, for our interconnections are inescapable.

Perhaps a second, more subtle overtone was implied in Cain's question: "I am my brother's superior." Some groups still seek to assert their superiority over their brothers: Hitler tried it on the principle of ethnic superiority; the industrial revolution tried it on the basis of economic superiority; other have sought to enforce it by claiming a cultural, racial, or social superiority.

The problem of human relationships lies at the root of the contemporary world tragedy. "Am I my brother's keeper?" This is the question of Jew and Arab, white and black, labor and management. Human history is the sad record of our determined efforts either to forget and banish our brothers or to dominate and exploit them.

Jean Paul Sartre, in his play *No Exit*, probed the dilemma of living with others. Three people, destined for hell, find themselves in a fashionable drawing room far removed from the scorching flames of torment. Feeling that they had been granted a temporary reprieve from hell, they soon discover the deeper torture of perpetual irritation by one another. Finally, the central truth begins to dawn. "Hell" cries one of them, "is others!" We have discovered as much today. Hell is others when we do not know how to live with them.

Christ solved the problem of our relationship to our neighbors by basing it on divine love. We are to love, not according to our inherited prejudices or our personal desires but "as I have loved you" (John 13:34). As Paul put it, "The love of God is shed abroad in our hearts through the Holy Spirit" (Rom. 5:5). Christians love their neighbors with that unique love of God, which was incarnated in the life of Jesus.

This means that all of the hostilities that are foreign to God must be banished. When Dr. S. H. Green, of the Calvary Baptist Church in Washington, D.C., presented for membership a distinguished government official and a Chinese laundryman, he well remarked, "The ground is level at the foot of the cross." The Christian who has been "crucified with Christ" learns to love even his bitterest enemies, as did Christ at Calvary.

III. *How can I live with God?* "If a man die, shall he live again?" (Job 14:14). Many find no answer to this question. "Death," said Aristotle, "is a dreadful thing, for it is the end." There is a futility about death: We don't just die—we have to die. There is a mystery about it: We cannot help but wonder about "the undiscovered country from whose bourn no traveler returns." There is a finality about death; it seems to shatter every plan, making the permanent temporary, stamping all of life with a tragic sense of incompleteness.

Thus death has become the twenty-first-century evasion. "Life can be beautiful!" we glibly say, but life with a dagger in its back cannot finally be beautiful. If life is the climbing ladder that finally leans against nothing, leaving us to topple over its summit into an uncharted abyss, then the rugged climb loses zest and purpose. How may we come to terms with that vast brooding silence that overarches our pilgrimage?

The problem roots in the fact that death always seems to win. It is more than a passing difficulty; it is a permanent fatality. But Christ came back from death to prove by his Resurrection that the grip of death can be broken.

His tomb seemed to seal the fate of every person. If he did not deserve to live, then who does? But when God knocked the door out of his tomb, he made a tunnel into eternity. Thus for all who follow Christ, the tomb becomes a womb, where twice-born believers are refashioned for the future.

His Resurrection was like a hole in a dyke. No one had ever been able to break through the hidden battlements of eternity, but when the dead Jesus did this, he opened a new road to God. He proved decisively that even death is no final barrier to the presence and power of God.

This is why John Wesley could say, "Our people die well." This is why the Christian martyr Perpetua could say as she faced her executioner, "This is my day of coronation." This is why Christian, in *Pilgrim's Progress*, could hear from Hopeful as he came to the deep river before the celestial city, "Be of good cheer, my brother. I feel the bottom and it is good."

Here are the haunting questions that perplex every life. Is there any deliverance from the sickness unto death? Is there some way to live in love with the loveless? Is there a "land beyond the river" that we can call the "sweet forever"? These are the questions that count, for they concern the ultimate relationships of life.

In Christ, an adequate answer is found to every one of these dilemmas. Paul put it simply as he surveyed the vast array of foes that assault and imperil human life: "We are more than conquerors through him who loved us" (Rom. 8:38). In Christ, God answers "Yes" to the deepest questions of life (2 Cor. 1:20). Yes, we can live with self, with others, and with God if, by faith, we let Christ live in us.—William E. Hull

SUNDAY, MAY 7, 2006
Lectionary Message

Topic: How to Show and Know Authentic Christian Love

TEXT: 1 John 3:16–24

Other Readings: Acts 4:5–12; Ps. 23; John 10:11–18

We Christians have heard it ever since we first started going to Sunday school. We have been taught it over and over through all our years in church. We have sung about it so many times we have lost count. We have heard it preached so often, we can quote many of the variations of the admonition (and commandment) by heart:

"You shall love one another."
"They will know we are Christians by our love, by our love."
"If you love your brothers and sisters, you love me."

Everyone knows that Christians are supposed to love each other. Everyone also knows that Christians sometimes have a hard time doing this. Loving has never been as easy as some have made it out to be, and although on the surface it would seem just the opposite, loving folks can even get us into trouble. Why is this? What does it *really* mean to love Christians (particularly) and everybody else (in general)? What happens to us when we fail to love? And more important, what does God make of it? Does God keep a "heavenly checklist" and give us demerits when we do not love the way we should? These questions about love are raised in the text from 1 John, and if we will make them *our* questions, perhaps we will come up with some answers—for own lives and for the world.

I. *What is love, and how do we recognize it?* The author of 1 John makes it very clear that, first, authentic love means that we must follow the example of Jesus and be willing to sacrifice ourselves for other people—the people we meet every day at work or school, or anywhere. Today this standard seems unreal, unlikely, and impossible. Does this mean that we are to *literally* be willing to die for another person or another Christian? Many of us might rationalize that we will never be in a situation where we have to make that choice. The problem is that many church people who call themselves "Christian" have reduced the words "Christian love" to mean nothing more than nice, polite manners—being "sweet" and smiling at everyone at Sunday school. When someone is sick, we might send her a card or flowers, or, if it is convenient, drop by and see her. Or we might call and leave a nice, sincere message, which is much easier on us than actually taking the time and trouble to go and see her.

These mannered acts can be significant, but often they are done with our own feelings and self-esteem in mind, not the other person's. Sometimes we do see love that is special or even extravagant, such as when someone actually takes a person into his home until health comes again, or when a person or church pays all of a hospital bill, or when someone goes the extra mile and shows caring love to another who is particularly unlovable and who "doesn't deserve it." These are special acts of love that God honors, but even they fall short of the cross and what Jesus did for us.

The real key to authentic Christian love—a love that comes close to Jesus' love—is found when our profession (as Christians saved by grace) and our performance (active love modeled after Jesus) work together. The author of 1 John tells us that if we really have God's love in us, then we will help any Christian and any neighbor, when he or she needs to be helped, at any time, whether this involves giving money, time, food, clothes, prayer, counsel, or anything else. God does look at our attitude, and if our attitude is one of wanting to have love and compassion and concern for others, our actions will follow.

II. *Authentic love is a test of who we really are.* Questions that we may have from the idea and practice of authentic Christian love are these:

What if we have doubts about what we are doing in the name of love?
How do we know that what we are doing is real?

Although our feelings and doubts sometimes get in our way, we can know that what we are doing is right and true by simply looking at what we are doing. In other words, God knows when our actions and attitudes are honorable and when our intentions are good and when we fall short. When our loving actions are not what they ought to be, God, in today's terms, "cuts us some slack." The whole point with God is that we are trying and we want to. If we do our best for God, if we love people who are hard to love, if we are willing to sacrifice to help people, then God understands and will not deny his love to us. God will let us know if we pass the test of authentic love, and when we do, our place in his Kingdom is secure.— Perry C. Bramlett

ILLUSTRATIONS

LOVE EQUALS CARE PLUS PERFORMANCE.   C. S. Lewis wrote, in his classic *Letters to Malcolm:* "I am often . . . praying for others when I should be doing things for them. It's so much easier to pray for a bore than to go and see him." It is one thing to talk about love, but it is quite another to actually do it. It is one thing to feel compassion for others; it is quite another to actually do the compassionate act or deed.[1]

THE LOVING CHRISTIAN AND DOUBTS.   "It is not the careless Christian, but more often the carefully conscientious one, who is plagued with a sense of guilt and inadequacy."[2]

---

[1]C. S. Lewis, *Letters to Malcolm: Chiefly on Prayer* (Orlando, Fla.: Harcourt Brace Jovanovich, 1964), p. 66.
[2]D. Moody Smith, *First, Second, and Third John,* Interpretation Commentary (Louisville, Ky.: Westminster John Knox Press, 1991), p. 97.

SERMON SUGGESTIONS

Topic: Two Pictures of God

TEXT: Ps. 23

(1) A loving shepherd (vv. 1–4). (2) A gracious host (vv. 5–6).

Topic: Marks of Christ's Sheep

TEXT: John 10

(1) They know their shepherd. (2) They know his voice. (3) They hear him calling them each by name. (4) They love him. (5) They trust him. (6) They follow him.

WORSHIP AIDS

CALL TO WORSHIP.   "One thing have I desired of the Lord, that will I seek after; that I may dwell in the house of the Lord all the days of my life, to behold the beauty of the Lord, and to inquire in his temple" (Ps. 27:4).

INVOCATION.   This morning, O God, we have come to this place from many ways and with many attitudes. Some eager, some reluctant, some with thanksgiving, some with bitterness, some joyful, some in sadness, some as clean as the morning dew, some burdened with guilt. But we have come, and we are here, all of us, awaiting your help and your blessing.

OFFERTORY SENTENCE.   "God is able to make all grace abound toward you; that ye, always having all sufficiency in all things, may abound to every good work" (2 Cor. 9:8).

OFFERTORY PRAYER.   Gracious Lord, enable us to take up your work with the knowledge that you can give strength to our feeblest abilities. Take the little we have and multiply it by your plenteous grace.

PRAYER.   O God, we stand in awe of your marvelous works. The works of men stagger the imagination. How much greater are the creations of your wisdom and purpose. We do not presume to know all that you are doing in your universe; we do not know even half of what you are doing in the little corner of the world where we live. Yet we are assured that your works are good. The cross of our Lord Jesus Christ, to some an emblem of injustice, has turned out to be the supreme demonstration of your wisdom and your power. When we are tempted to doubt the goodness of your doing, help us to look again at the cross from the viewpoint of the Resurrection and in this way find our faith strengthened, so that we can begin to make sense of the things that are taking place in our lives. We pray, O God, for those who wander in a maze of meaningless activities, seeking happiness and finding little of it. May they realize that the way of faith and obedience is the way to knowledge and fulfillment. Renew the courage of those who are trying valiantly to wrest meaning from their shattered days and ways. Grant that some sense of your presence and power may help them to keep on seeking after you. And grant that they may not demand some spectacular display of your reality. Satisfy us all with a willingness to be faithful, whatever the difficulties.

SERMON

Topic: How Can I Keep a Vital Faith?

TEXT: Rom. 12:11

There is a beautiful word picture of the Christian life in Romans 12:11. James Moffatt renders it: "Never let your zeal flag, maintain the spiritual glow." Eugene Peterson has it: "Don't burn out; keep yourselves fueled and aflame." The image of an "on fire" Christian speaks to us because we so easily lose our fervor, enthusiasm wanes, and the passion for service slackens. How can we keep the radiance of our ardor undimmed?

I. *The problem: A weariness of the spirit.* That question haunts us because Scripture is full of backsliding, of losing one's first love (Rev. 2:4). Think of Abraham in Egypt, passing off his wife as his sister (Gen. 12:10–16); of Moses on Sinai, complaining of his inability to represent God (Gen. 3:11, 13, 4:1); of David and Solomon, yielding to the bewitchments of seductive women; of the exiles in Babylon, unable to sing the Lord's song in a strange land (Ps. 137:1–4); of the twelve at Calvary betraying, denying, and fleeing their Lord; of quitters such as Demas (2 Tim. 4:10) in the early Church. We remember the terrible warnings of apostasy in Hebrews, Jude, 2 Peter, and the letters to the seven churches of Revelation.

Christian history is a sad record of deterioration and decay: the "lapsed" under Roman persecution, the corruption of the Middle Ages, the secularism of the eighteenth century, and alternating periods of awakening and superficiality throughout American history. Theologies come and go; denominations wax and wane in an endless cycle of renewal and retrogression.

Our own personal experience confirms the lessons of the past: we struggle with spiritual burnout; our faith pilgrimage seems to wander in the wilderness for years; we doggedly persevere by force of habit but sink into the blahs! We want so much more for ourselves, for our church, and for our faith than we have been able to claim. How do we overcome this sense of spiritual entropy and maintain the ardor urged by our text?

II. *The promise: A refreshing of the spirit.* We begin where Paul did with the recognition that our glow comes from the Holy Spirit of God (v. 11b). Only the Divine Power that appeared at Pentecost like tongues of fire (Acts 2:3) can bring our lukewarmness to a boil. The verb for "glowing" found in our text is sometimes used to describe metals, such as copper, that become so fiery hot that they glow. We lack the ability to ignite our own hearts with such fervor but, when we are filled with the Spirit, we have within us the one whom John the Baptist promised would baptize us "with fire" (Matt. 3:10), one who himself said, "I came to cast fire upon the earth" (Luke 12:49). Our first imperative, therefore, is to stir up the Spirit within us so that the divine presence of Christ may burn brightly in our lives.

It is neither quick nor easy to stoke the fires of the Spirit, but the process has two main phases. Paul begins the verse with a negative: to "never flag" means to not hesitate in the sense of being tentative, reluctant, or slothful, which means that we must begin by banishing idleness, laziness, or indolence from our hearts. If we treat our service of God as an irksome chore, our hearts will never blaze with passion. In an act of repentance, renunciation, and surrender, we eliminate the spiritual dross that keeps our hearts from catching fire. We purge our lives of pride, self-sufficiency, and tireless ambition so that we may be purified by the divine presence. There is no spiritual glow radiating from within when all we are seeking is to reflect the spotlight of human admiration from without.

Once we have cleansed the heart of the spiritual debris that would snuff out the flame of the Spirit, then we are ready to reach out in wonder and awe for the ultimate energy of the universe. That radical openness to transcendence is called prayer, meditation, and contemplation, by which we get in touch with our own depths in order to commune with the Divine. Our desire is not just to know but to be known, not just to talk but to listen, not just for an encounter but for a relationship that can grow into a ripening friendship. The Spirit dwells within, as we make our hearts hospitable to his presence. The Spirit's presence is enhanced by our life in the incendiary fellowship of the Church where, as Augustine put it, one loving heart sets another on fire. The great prerequisite to a spiritual glow is what Paul, in our text, calls *zeal*—a word that refers to an extraordinary commitment to fulfill one's responsibilities with excellence.

III. *The practice: An eagerness to serve the Lord.* But if that glow is a gift of God's Spirit, why would Paul need to exhort his readers to express such fervor? The answer is that, although only God's Spirit can kindle the fire, we can add the fuel that makes it burn brightly. Note how our text ends: "serve the Lord" (v. 11c). We could paraphrase the entire verse this way: "Work for the Lord with a blazing intensity that results from an eagerness to serve without a trace of hesitation." We give in to the gift of goodness as we replace apathy with action. Passivity tends to create a dormant pattern, while taking the initiative creates a new situation. We can only think and reason and analyze so far, then we must decide, experiment, and risk. Better to act ourselves into a new way of thinking than to think ourselves into a new way of acting. We dare not depend upon a preacher, a church, or a therapist to act on our behalf just because we have given them some money. Instead, we must care deeply enough to take personal responsibility for our actions. Faith involves a commitment to change the world, beginning with oneself, and change requires boldness to be effective.

But even resolute action can become no more than a habit that degenerates into dull routine. Therefore, we may need to replace structure with spontaneity, conformity with creativity. Shake up your settled patterns. Dare to surprise yourself. Seek a serendipitous climate that provides an atmosphere of freedom. Surround yourself with innovative people. Balance obligation with enthusiasm, technique with results, continuity with change. Such a lifestyle is one of understated audacity, a bold defiance of conventional restraints imposed by those who refuse to believe that the best is yet to be.

Lloyd Ogilvie likens this process of self-renewal to the eagle learning to fly (1 Deut. 32:11–12a).[3] Here God is pictured (1) as a *disturber* who stirs up the nest, shakes us out of our security, pushes us to the precipice, and even shoves us over the edge—all in an effort to make us try our wings (which is the only way a bird can learn to fly!) and (2) as a *developer*, who hovers nearby, showing by example how to fly, providing the pattern and thereby proving that birds are made to soar, and (3) as a *deliverer* who spreads his wings and carries us on his pinions if we fall too far (cf. Deut. 33:26–27). If our religion is to stay vital, we must be stirred out of the nest of the status quo. Jesus provided the example of a truly free spirit,

---

[3]*Ask Him Anything: God Can Handle Your Hardest Questions* (Waco, Tex.: Word Books, 1981), pp. 234–242.

soaring above the confines of his contemporaries. With his encouragement we can dare to risk, confident that he is "able to keep us from falling" (Jude 24).

In our day as never before, what matters most in religion is the intensity factor. People no longer submit to the Church as an authority or obey a set of rules in legalistic fashion. They do not stop long enough to reason about the truth of doctrine or to learn philosophical proofs for the existence of God. Most of all, they are turned off by the listlessness of mere routine. Instead, they look for enthusiasm, innovation, and boldness—what I am here calling intensity. If we scream ourselves hoarse at football games, swoon over the latest movie celebrities, go into a frenzy over some TV program or pop singer, but only yawn politely at church, we will not only fail to win the lost, we will not even get their attention! But if there is a spiritual glow about our lives that never fades, the world will come looking for the secret of our incandescence.

Such intensity is difficult, even dangerous, to maintain, for it can easily be confused with fanaticism. Sam Keen has useful guidance on how to temper our religious enthusiasms:

> The value of passion, like fire, is judged finally by the amount of warmth and light it creates. Fanatics, like forest fires, burn bright but destroy all in their path that is tender and green. To be useful, fire must be confined. To live passionately, we must develop discipline; to love powerfully, we must forge bonds of commitment. Passion is inseparable from compassion.[4]

Prayer
Give us a Love that leads the way,
A faith that nothing can dismay,
A hope that refuses to ever tire,
A courage that will burn like fire,
Let us not sink to become a clod,
Make us Thy fuel, O flame of God!
Amen

—William E. Hull

SUNDAY, MAY 14, 2006
Lectionary Message

Topic: What Is a Real Disciple?
TEXT: John 15:1–8
Other Readings: Acts 8:26–40; Ps. 22:25–31; 1 John 4:7–21

In this text Jesus tells us in plain, understandable language that he is "the true vine," that his followers are to "abide in him," that he is the way to God, and that he is the truth.

---

[4]Sam Keen, *The Reader's Digest*, Feb. 1981, p. 17.

Through the centuries Christians have believed this and tried (in various ways) to practice the idea of "abiding in Jesus" or showing that they are *really* Christian.

Christians also strongly believe and have taught and preached that only by loving and trusting in Jesus can we hope to attain authentic personhood, character, and maturity, or what some today call "real life." These are wonderful and abiding ideals, and they are strong cornerstones for our life of faith. But Jesus, as he so often did, added a caveat. John's Gospel includes a strongly worded, ominous note for those who try to follow Jesus—who call themselves Christian but do not bear evidence of discipleship, or, as Jesus put it, "bear fruit." This is one text that you don't hear preached on very often.

The key passage is verse 8: "My father is glorified by this, that you bear much fruit and become my disciples." It may seem obvious, and it is often overlooked, but Jesus here is not assuming that his disciples are actually disciples! It helps to remember that earlier in John (chapter 8), Jesus had told those who followed him that if they "continued in his word," they could call themselves real, or authentic, disciples. It is clear from Jesus' words that he saw a real difference between a "convert" and a "disciple." It is interesting to note that although Jesus knew this, many churches have not followed his words. Many are consumed with the idea of "adding numbers" to the church roll and are not all that interested (as shown by their actual approach to ministry) in making disciples from converts. (How many churches have you attended that included discipleship training in its educational curriculum?)

But in these verses Jesus gave all of us the great clue to the Christian life: that real discipleship (or abiding in Jesus) involves more than just believing; it demands remaining, or constantly maintaining and nurturing, our relationship with God through Jesus. The question for us today is, *What, exactly, is abiding in Jesus?* And the answers to that will tell us what a real disciple is.

I. *Abiding in Jesus is not necessarily validated in "experiences" or rituals.* Throughout history Christians have practiced a number of different approaches to abiding in Jesus. Some feel the presence of God most strongly by meditating upon the Bible and upon songs and writings of other Christians. Another person may find closeness to God in lengthy periods of fervent prayer and meditation. Others keep their focus on Jesus through daily rituals of worship, silence, fasting, or other disciplines. Some experience God in quiet and solitude (often in nature) and some with small group meetings with other Christians. Some just feel God's presence in going to church, being with other Christians, and being involved in a local congregation's myriad events and activities. And all these activities, when practiced faithfully and with a proper attitude, are worthwhile and good! But the gospel is clear. Abiding in Jesus is not just a feeling or a sense of God's presence, and it is not just doing and participating in church events and activities. When Jesus commanded us to bear fruit, he meant much more than feeling pious or going to church or engaging in religious disciplines.

II. *Abiding in Jesus involves ethical action of some kind.* The first Christians were called "followers of the way." This was because they went where Jesus went and tried to do what he did. The first followers of the way were active participants in God's plan to present the Kingdom of God through Jesus and to save and heal the world. In this text the word *fruit* is not explicitly defined. But in the verses following, we can assume that "fruit" is shown by our love, our keeping of Jesus' commandments, and our acceptance of one another as friends. All of these involve and are centered in action. To go into the world we must love the world. And this active love is social, it is physical, and it is redemptive. The Kingdom of God is the real life that we will present to the world if we are truly abiding in Jesus. And this real life, this truth that Jesus said he was, will be pictured for the world in the way we live—the evidence of our abiding in Jesus and being his disciples. This picture will show us helping others, praying for others, forgiving others, feeding others, teaching others, giving money to others, bringing peace to others, and healing others. This is what a real disciple does, and a real disciple performs these loving actions consistently.—Perry C. Bramlett

ILLUSTRATIONS

ALL CHRISTIANS CAN BE DISCIPLES, AND DISCIPLES ARE REALLY MINISTERS.   "When Jesus sent the twelve out into the world, his instructions were simple. He told them to preach the kingdom of God and to heal, with the implication that to do either was in effect to do both. Fortunately for the world in general and the church in particular, our ability to do them is not dependent on either moral character or I.Q. To do them in the name of Christ is to be a minister."[5]

THE CHURCH HELPS US REMAIN IN JESUS.   "We must remain in the community that knows and loves him and celebrates him as Lord. There is no such thing as a solitary Christian. We can't 'go it alone.'"[6]

SERMON SUGGESTIONS

Topic: Astounding Consequences
TEXT: Ps. 22:25–31
When God answers a cry for help, it can mean (1) public praise of God for his help (v. 25), (2) creative influence upon those who hear the story of God's goodness and mercy (vv. 26–29), or (3) unending recognition of "what God can do" (vv. 30–31).

Topic: Always in Debt
TEXT: Rom. 1:14–15
(1) We fear debt. (2) We seek independence and freedom. (3) Acknowledging our debts brings us a strange joy.[7]

WORSHIP AIDS

CALL TO WORSHIP.   "Sing unto the Lord, O ye saints of his, and give thanks at the remembrance of his holiness" (Ps. 30:4).

INVOCATION.   Be our teacher in this hour, O God. Teach us to number our days, that we may live wisely and well. Teach us to believe your goodwill toward us, that we may enjoy our obedience. Teach us to love others that we may be like you.

---

[5]Frederick Buechner, *Wishful Thinking: A Theological ABC* (New York: HarperCollins, 1973), pp. 62–63.
[6]Tom Wright, *John for Everyone*, Part 2, chaps. 11–21 (Louisville, Ky.: Westminster John Knox, 2004), p. 71.
[7]Gerald Kennedy, *Fresh Every Morning* (New York: HarperCollins, 1966), pp. 12–21.

OFFERTORY SENTENCE.   "Blessed are the poor in spirit: for theirs is the kingdom of heaven" (Matt. 5:3).

OFFERTORY PRAYER.   O God, you have made us rich beyond measure, as you have blessed us in all circumstances of life. You have taught us how to be abased and how to abound, how in any and all circumstances to face plenty and hunger, abundance and want. Help us to learn these lessons anew.

PRAYER.   Lord, we are surrounded by walls. There is a wall of guilt between us and those we have hurt, a wall of fear between the present and the future, a wall of suspicion between us and people unlike ourselves, a wall of despair between the world as it is and as it ought to be, a wall of doubt between ourselves and you. Lord, help us to leap over the walls. Turn us into pole-vaulters who, by grasping the strength of your spirit, are hurled over the obstacles we fear into the open field of your grace.—Thomas H. Troeger

SERMON
Topic: The Hope in Today
TEXT: Luke 19:1–10

There are at least three questions that have no answer but the answer of faith. For most of us there are a lot more than three, but regardless of who you are, there are at least these three questions that can be answered only by faith: the question of why we exist, the question of what we are supposed to be doing with our lives, and the question of what happens to us after we die.

(a) First there is the creation question. In the beginning, what? Why is there a creation? The poet asks, "Little lamb, who made thee?" Are we the creation of a loving Power who means us well or the accidental coming together of atoms, sound and fury signifying nothing. *We are the loving creation of a gracious God, who has made us for fellowship with himself.* That is the affirmation of faith. In the beginning, God created—two or three different stories, but they are faith's declaration that in the beginning we are created by God for a purpose.

(b) To the second question: What are we supposed to do with our lives? Here we are. We did not ask to be born. We have been thrown into this time and this place. Some of us have been given lots of stuff; some creatures have been given very little. Some have been made very intelligent; others struggle to get by. Some of those who have been given much seem to think that all they need to do is eat, drink, and be merry. Some who have lots are dedicated to using what they have to help others who have less. Some who are pretty intelligent and resourceful actually use their gifts in ways that hurt and destroy others. So the questions keep coming: How are we to live? What is the purpose of our time on Earth? What difference does it make how we live? And if it makes a difference whether we are good or evil, how do we *know* what is good and what is evil?

It is our claim that God has shown us "what is good, and what the Lord requires of us, but to do justice, and to love kindness and to walk humbly with God." We claim and proclaim that in Jesus Christ God has shown us an example of what we are to be and to do. In the message of Jesus—in the Sermon on the Mount, in the parables, and the teachings—we are told to love God and to love others as much as we love ourselves. We are to attribute to others the same motives and excuses as we give ourselves. If we want the teacher to believe that the dog ate our homework, then when the teacher says that the dog ate our test and we will have to take it again, we have to believe her. Life is a gift of God to us, and we are to use it in a manner that is pleasing to God.

(c) The third question is, What happens to us after death? Where do we go? Is there more, or is this all there is? Is there something different, or do we just go round and round in a circle game of being born and dying, and being born again. And as the singing group "Blood Sweat and Tears" reminds us, we will never know for sure by living, only by dying will we learn.

But it, too, is a question that we answer with faith. In the beginning, God created. In the end, God. Life was created for a purpose. It is given to be lived in a certain way, and it comes to perfection and completion in the love and glory of God.

In faith, I am bold to declare that what God has created in love and redeemed in love through Jesus Christ, God will keep and preserve and perfect in love. In the beginning, God. In life and work, God. In the end, God. And faith has lots of stories to tell about what that new reality in the love of God will be like.

The choir has reminded us this morning of one of the great affirmations of that glory that is given to those who are faithful: "for all the saints who from their labors rest." Heaven is the gift of the Sabbath rest to those who are faithful. The struggle of life is over. All the effort, exhaustion, pain, suffering, conflict, tension, and fears are over, and there is a tranquility, a peace, a calmness and serenity that comes in knowing that the battle is over. I remember even now the great sense of relaxation and relief when I finished my last exam; all those books, all those tests, all those papers, all that effort to keep all those facts, dates, causes and effects, and theorems were now over, and I could let them go—ah, the sheer exhausted serenity of being finished.

Rest is not the only promise or vision we have of the completion and perfection that awaits us. We have lots of stories about heaven because there is so much that we have seen in this life that we would like to see in all its fullness, so much that we have missed that we would like to have satisfied, so much that we have watched cause suffering that we would like corrected. In the great vision of Revelation, heaven is painted as a magnificent city, a glorious city, a grand and glorious fortress city—a walled city like so many of the great cities of Europe. Because as we know so well in the midst of the fear and apprehension, as we live with the threat of terrorism, one of our deepest desires is for security and safety. We frail children of dust, fragile and vulnerable, long and hope for some place where we may be safe. We sing "A Mighty Fortress Is Our God," and we cling to the hope that being with God in his love will give us that place of security.

If we are created by a loving God for fellowship and relationship, then heaven is where that fellowship is made perfect and complete. God is in the midst of the city and dwells with us permanently. There is no need for temple, no need for streetlights, and we will never be separated from that light or love.

And yet so much of our lives is caught up in trying to keep the weeds out of our garden, the water out of our boats, and the oil spill out of our lakes. We are part of creation, and all creation is a struggle—nature raw and tooth and claw. Paul says that creation perished in the fall and all creation is off center; our relationship with nature and animals is violent and destructive. And the stories about heaven talk about heaven as the restoration of the perfection of the Garden of Eden. The lamb shall lie down with the lion. The child shall crawl over the adder's nest. Heaven is the glory, majesty, and wonder of the view from the Rockies, the walk on the beach.

Ina Hughes, whom some of you remember as James A. Jones's daughter and Jim Jones's sister, wrote a tribute to Jimmy in the *Presbyterian Outlook*. For her the vision of heaven to which she entrusts Jimmy is life on the beach. "Now that it has happened, let us send him off on the outgoing tide in front of the beach house at sunset, just as the katydid in the dunes start the lullabies that sweetened the summer dreams during all his childhood and mine." In the beginning God, who creates all things in life, God who redeems all people in death, God who restores and renews all things.

But you and I will not claim these answers of faith to the three great questions without some moment like the one Zaccheus had. All of the telling of these stories about the hope we have in God rests on a moment when salvation came to our house. All of our readiness to trust ourselves to these faith answers about the beginning, middle, and end of life rests on the power of our own experience, like this story about Zaccheus. You remember the pieces of it. Jesus was passing through the town, and Zaccheus was a tax collector. Zaccheus was the person in town that nobody wanted to be seen with. No one visited him; no one talked with him. He was the only New York Yankee fan in all of Boston.

But Zaccheus had heard that Jesus was known to have had fellowship with sinners, and so Zaccheus thought it would be wonderful just to see this man. But like the crowds around political candidates this year, it was pretty hard to get close to Jesus because of the crowd. Zaccheus climbed up a tree. Jesus saw him, told him to come down, and went and had lunch with him. Jesus treated Zaccheus as a human being, included him in the community, accepted him as a person worthy to share a meal with. And Zaccheus's life was changed. He was so overcome with the joy of being acknowledged, recognized, accepted by Jesus that Zaccheus pledged half his income to the poor and promised to restore four-fold if he had defrauded anyone. Jesus turned to the crowd and said, "Here, right before you, now, today salvation has come to this house."

Jesus says this is what salvation looks like. Here is the working of God's redemption and mercy. But look for the coming day of the Lord as the prophets talked about; don't talk about the reward of faith coming in heaven. Salvation looks like this. Salvation is where we received Jesus Christ into our lives and hearts, and know and celebrate the joy of being forgiven and redeemed, and see ourselves as part of the people of God in the Kingdom of God and begin to make our wrongs right, to correct our mistakes, confess our failures, and share the great joy of God's love by caring for others. Today has salvation come to this house. We have all had these moments—"tenth-hour" moments, Gustavo Gutierrez calls them—these tenth-hour experiences that are the intense moments of encounter with the living Lord in which our spiritual lives are nourished and sustained.[8] In the power of the experience of the living Jesus Christ in our lives today, we find the faith to believe that what has been begun in us, in Jesus, will be continued and fulfilled in heaven. It is the power of the coming of salvation into our lives now—today—that gives us the confidence to believe that in life and in death we belong to God.

---

[8]Gustavo Gutierrez, *We Drink from Our Own Wells* (Orbis, Mary Knoll Press), p. 42.

St. Catherine of Genoa described her "today" to her sister. St. Catherine was at confession:

[H]er heart was pierced by so sudden and immense a love of God, accompanied by so penetrating a sight of her miseries and sin and of His goodness, that she was near falling to the ground. In that transport of pure and all purifying love, she was drawn away from the miseries of the world, and she cried out, No more world; no more world. And at the same moment, she felt that had she in her possession a thousand worlds, she would have cast them all away.[9]

The welcome of the love of God in Jesus Christ into our hearts brings us into the family of the people of God, and in the joy of salvation that comes at that moment, there is the assurance that such a love will not cease at death, and yet our concern is to bless, as best we can, those who share our world. In our todays is the reason for our hope for tomorrow.— Rick Brand

SUNDAY, MAY 21, 2006
Lectionary Message
Topic: What Does the Kingdom of God Look Like?
TEXT: John 15:9–17
Other Readings: Acts 10:44–48; Ps. 98; 1 John 5:1–6

If you take a close, reasoned look at the Gospels—the combined witness of Matthew, Mark, Luke, and John—you will discover that their primary intent is to tell us that Jesus came, not to proclaim himself but to announce the coming of the Kingdom of God. This is the gospel, the good news: God's kingship is available to all who will receive it. And if you look at John's Gospel carefully, you will note that John not only echoes the other Gospels in proclaiming God's Kingdom but that it also affirms strongly that, despite all appearances and evidence to the contrary, God is in control of human affairs.

In John's day, a good Jew might have disagreed with this, remembering the tragic history of the Jewish nation, with their constant defeats by past enemies and their current oppression by Rome. And today we might disagree, too, as it seems as if terrorism and war are increasing and things are getting worse, not better, politically. But John says emphatically that God reigns and is in control. John says that God has a Kingdom—that he is the ruler of that Kingdom. And several times in this Gospel, Jesus says that this invisible reality is present and can be experienced by anyone. And he makes it clear that God's Kingdom is spiritual condition, not a physical place, that in some ways it is a mystery, and that we cannot describe it using "everyday" language.

Jesus also said (in this Gospel and the others), in words that are so often ignored or corrupted today, that his Kingdom had nothing whatsoever to do with power and earthly success. And that included power in politics, power in religion, and power in churches. In John's Gospel, Jesus is convinced that his Father's Kingdom will come by peaceful means, not by

---

[9]Friedrich von Hugel, *The Mystical Elements of Religion,* quoted in *The Eloquence of Christian Experience* by Raymond Calkins (New York: Macmillan, 1927), p. 221.

force—the Kingship of God will be present in every true believer's heart and will. Jesus did tell us what the Kingdom of God is like, and what it has to do with—and that is not exactly what many of us might think of.

I. *The Kingdom of God is revealed in our loving relationships.* Jesus knew that, ultimately, his Father's Kingdom would show itself to the world in personal relationships, community, and friendship; it is not a place but a condition of love. But these depend on trust, and often their greatest enemy is fear. Jesus knew that fearful persons tend to retreat from life—from others and themselves. They become less than themselves, less than they were intended to be. Jesus' mission to establish his Father's Kingdom was, in large part, based on his desire to liberate us from our fears and to show us what authentic living is all about. Jesus' own sense of trust in life undoubtedly came from his intimate sense of God's presence and power over all things and events.

So Jesus' command for us to help establish his Father's Kingdom was theologically based; that is, it was based on the vision of God that he had and that he revealed in his teaching. How did he reveal this to us? He gave us a simple and profound command. He told us to love everyone just as he had loved us. And Jesus is our great example, because he loved those deserving of love and also those who were undeserving. He loved everyone, whether they were "lovable" or not. And we are to do the same. We are to love all people, regardless of who they are or whether we can gain something from them or not. This was Jesus' way, not only with his disciples but with everyone. The Kingdom of his Father is revealed in us when we love unconditionally. But when we love half-heartedly, or when our concern for others is self-motivated, the Kingdom of God is a long way off.

II. *The Kingdom of God is revealed in what we do, not in what we feel.* Our love for others is not based on emotions but is an act of our will. When Jesus told us to love one another and even be willing to sacrifice ourselves for them, he was not telling us to react or respond to people with nice, cozy emotional feelings (although these, if sincere, are laudable). But he was telling us that our love for others is something we do, not *necessarily* feel, and that it might possibly mean that we work for their good at the expense of our own. And Jesus' command to love did not mean that we are necessarily to "like" the people we demonstrate love for. By his terms we can love people without liking them. But we are to treat all the people in God's Kingdom as if we did love them; the emotions and feelings and "likings" will follow if we are consistent. Following Jesus and establishing his Kingdom is found, not only in a personal relationship with him but in what we do for others, whether we feel like it or not. A footnote to remember is that although John (and Jesus) do not use the word *church* in this passage, the expressions of love that disciples show and do for others is a mutual undertaking, as disciples are part of the body of Christ, which is the Church.

ILLUSTRATIONS

THE COMMAND TO LOVE.   "But love is never mandated. Love is not available on demand. This command to love has to be Bible language for: 'The Father wills that the children of God's love give themselves to one another freely.' There is no other way to love. It is done freely or it is not love."[10]

---

[10]Gerard Sloyan, *John*, Interpretation Commentary (Atlanta: John Knox Press, 1988), p. 190.

LOVE IS INDISCRIMINATE.   "The gospel is not sectarian, but a call to an indiscriminate, suffering love. The particulars of such love will vary, obviously, with the context, but unlike the principalities and powers, who think it is the power brokers to whom we should cater our concerns, the gospel reminds us that it is particularly 'the least' whom we are called to serve, for in the least is embodied the person of Jesus."[11]

SERMON SUGGESTIONS

Topic: Reasons for Rejoicing
TEXT: Ps. 98
(1) The Lord's saving faithfulness to his people (vv. 1–3). (2) The Lord's saving approach to all the world (vv. 7–9).

Topic: Facing Difficulties
TEXT: Matt. 13:18–23
(1) We are here to maintain that clear-cut distinction between right and wrong. (2) We are here also to exercise that wise patience in dealing with untoward conditions, striving to root out the evil without destroying the good. (3) And most of all, we are here to promote the growth of honest goodness in the common life of the race.—Charles R. Brown

WORSHIP AIDS

CALL TO WORSHIP.   "Be of good courage, and he shall strengthen your heart, all ye that hope in the Lord" (Ps. 31:24).

INVOCATION.   Creator God, alert our senses to your world. Let sight and sound, taste and touch remind us that you have made us and have given us the good Earth as our home. May all that is within us and all that surrounds us glorify your name.

OFFERTORY SENTENCE.   "Let your light so shine before men, that they may see your good works, and glorify your Father which is in Heaven" (Matt. 5:16).

OFFERTORY PRAYER.   Lord of life, who can make of small things, simple deeds, and quiet actions mountains of mercy and rivers of grace, bless our offering this day to its greatest good, for Jesus' sake.—E. Lee Phillips

PRAYER.   Father, some of us come before you with penitent hearts. You have urged us to confess our sins. Gauging our lives by your revealed truth, may we clearly see our sins and, facing them, be courageous enough to own them and deal with them in your presence. Let us have the assurance of forgiveness and be granted the power to break the chains that bind us to our evils and wrongs. Then give us the will to go your way and sin no more.

We come into your presence with intercessions on behalf of others. We have been called by the Lord to bear one another's burdens. Yet we find that our weakness prevents us from

---

[11]Lee C. Camp, *Mere Discipleship: Radical Christianity in a Rebellious World* (Grand Rapids, Mich.: Brazos Press, 2003), p. 191.

carrying such a cumbersome and heavy load. Although in many instances we do our best, we ultimately can only bring them to you and ask for the added presence of your strength and the insight of your wisdom. We ask that you refresh the weary—that feet may move again and tired hands may find new vigor. Comfort the wounded and sorrowful with the light of your presence and relieve their loneliness. Encourage the despairing with added insights that they may overcome despair. Strengthen the weak for the tasks of another day.

We also come, Father, with purpose. Jesus called us to take upon ourselves his yoke and learn of him. We submit ourselves to the instruction of the Holy Spirit. May your word pierce our often-stubborn minds. May it reign victorious over our wills and open before us the highway that leads to life everlasting, we pray in Jesus' name.—Henry Fields

SERMON
Topic: The Heart of a Heartless World
TEXT: Luke 17:7–10

When Jesus preached the Kingdom of God, he did so by telling little stories in which, paradoxically, it was hard to find God, in which God was all but absent. He called them parables. One scholar calls the parables secular stories.

The parables of Jesus resemble the world we live and work in, for it, too, is a world where it's hard to find God. It's a world in which God does not hang out a shingle that says, "I am God. Here is where I am at work."

This is nowhere truer than in the parables found in Luke's Gospel. It is possible even for believers to read these stories and find them offensive. We might even close the book and turn on "Dr. Phil."

In Luke 16, for example, Jesus compares the Kingdom of God to the behavior of a dishonest steward who gets by in this world by means of shady business practices. In Luke 18, the chapter after ours, he compares the Kingdom of God to the behavior of a Crooked Judge and a Nagging Widow.

See if you don't find today's story equally offensive. Listen for its social brutality, which makes no effort to hide itself. Jesus says, "Let's say your *slave* comes in after plowing all day and feeding the animals. Who among you is going to say to him, 'Sit down, my good man. You must be tired. Let me serve you.' Nobody, that's who! You will say, Put on that apron, fix my supper first and serve me. You can eat later. And when he does it (and he will do it), are you going to say, Oh, thank you so much. Of course not!"

When you were a child, your mother might have begun a story, "Once upon a time," and you could relax and prepare to hear a tale from long ago. "Once upon a time, there was a beautiful princess and a frog." Notice, in this parable Jesus doesn't say, "Once upon a time." He begins his story with the phrase, "Who among you?" It is both singular and plural: Which one among you all? It's hard to relax when a story begins like that.

Like the others, this parable reflects a hard and heartless world. This small landowner apparently has one miserable slave who not only has to plow the fields but cook the meals as well. This is not *Upstairs/Downstairs*, with liveried butlers and maids in cute uniforms, but something uglier, less refined. These two personality-less characters are locked in an intimate master-slave relationship that does not include friendship, or even civility.

One could say that this parable reflects a primitive worldview that, thank God, no longer exists. One could say that.

Last evening a young man said to me, "Hi, my name is Brian. I'll be your server this evening. Have you been here before? Let me tell you about our specials." And I said to him, "Brian, you must be tired. I'd love to hear about your specials. So why don't you sit down, have a glass of wine, and tell us about them. Besides, we'd like to get to know you better."

Am I dreaming? Did that really happen? (You are laughing.) Of course it didn't. Who among you would say such a thing—to a server? Who among you would say such a thing to your auto mechanic, your dental hygienist, your flight attendant?

It's a heartless little story because we like to pretend that we (and the world) have a heart after all. We like to pretend that Brian isn't being paid to be friendly, that he really does want to tell us about the specials, that we really do care about him, and that in a democratic society we really are all the same.

It's also a heartless little story Jesus tells because people deserve to be rewarded for their hard work and thanked for it. If there are no rewards, why stay late at the office working on accounts? For the cheap gold watch? For the matched pen-and-pencil set? If there are no rewards, why go into hock to send your child to the best university if you can't expect a payoff somewhere down the line? When she joins the premier firm in the city, is it only a parental fantasy that she will say, "Dad, Mom, you made this possible. Thank you." Is that too much to expect?

They say every parable has a twist, a "gotcha" (that's what makes a parable a parable—it has a gotcha), and this one is no exception. For the first three-quarters of the parable the listeners (you and I) are playing the role of the master. "Who among you will say to your servant . . . ?" But then comes the last verse: "So you also, when you have done all that is commanded of you, say, 'We are unworthy servants; we have only done what was our duty.'"

"Hi, my name is Rick. I'll be your servant this morning. And when you're sick, I'll kneel beside your hospital bed and pray for you; and when you're sad or angry, I'll come to your house and sit at your kitchen table and listen; and when you're hungry and thirsty for redemption, I'll meet you at the table and ask, 'Would you like to hear about our specials?' 'Take, eat, this is the body of Christ for you. Take, drink, the blood of Christ.' No need to thank me at the table. We're both playing roles that have been assigned."

The very work itself is its own reward.

She works for a company called Home Health & Fitness, Inc. Because she is a professional, she makes it a point to wear her blue scrubs every day, as she makes her rounds all over the county. She enters the poorest homes and doublewides, and teaches the infirm, the disabled, the stroke victims how to get dressed, make their beds, and cook breakfast. Sometimes she winds up serving breakfast, even though she is a professional. She is always alone. There is no audience to admire her virtue; she hears no cosmic applause. Even her clients can't always express their gratitude. She does good works in a silent and unresponsive universe.

She is not like many of us, who are also capable of good works so long as they are garnished by applause. It's as if the work itself has a hold on her. In her own quiet way she has broken through the performance-reward syndrome. She knows what is good and does it.

This year our university gave every member of its freshman class two gifts. One was an iPod, which for those of you who dwell in total darkness is a gizmo for organizing your music and making it instantly available to you. The other was a book—the Pulitzer Prize–winning *Mountains Beyond Mountains,* which is the story of Dr. Paul Farmer. Farmer is a Duke-and-Harvard-trained public health doctor who has devoted his entire life and intellect to serving the poor in Haiti.

No wonder the freshmen seem confused. Here is a university that promises its graduates incredible rewards if they do well *and* a university that is encouraging its students to seek a life with no downloadable rewards. The one gift is a critique of the other, just as parts of our lives are critiques of other parts of our lives.

After Dr. Farmer had been serving in Haiti for a while, he began wearing this large wooden cross over his shirt. It was his way of saying, "This work that I do for the sake of others' service is not original with me." Once upon a time there was a man who made this his way of life. He came not to be served but to serve and gave his life as a ransom for many. Who among you wants a life outside his life?

Of all the offensive material in this parable, the greatest offense may be the word *duty.* Just do your duty. Duty alone is a stern taskmaster. Ask the servicemen and women in Iraq or Afghanistan. Ask the mom and dad who give themselves every day for their profoundly disabled child. Ask the home health nurse who goes down the dusty roads and enters the humble homes of strangers. As Annie Dillard says, "How we spend our days . . . is how we spend our lives."

Paradoxically, the only way to do your duty is to discover something greater than duty. Without that something greater, I know that I could not speak so glibly of work, service, duty.

This parable would be unbearable if it taught nothing but duty. It would be unbearably severe were it not for the one who told it. He is the same one who once said *not* "God is Duty" but "God is Love" and then did his duty on the cross to prove it. You know the one—who did not count equality with God a thing to be grasped but emptied himself and took the form of a servant. That one.

He is the soul of our ministry. He is our heart in a heartless world.—Richard Lischer

SUNDAY, MAY 28, 2006
Lectionary Message

Topic: How to Belong to the World
TEXT: John 16:6–19
Other Readings: Acts 1:15–17, 21–26; Ps. 1; 1 John 5:9–13

You might think, after reading the title of this message, that a word was left out. Shouldn't the title be "How *Not* to Belong to the World?" Many people react negatively to the word *world,* because in our thinking it often means something that is evil or sinful or not Christian—that "world" is just the opposite of what many of us believe we stand for. But if we are to understand Scripture correctly and act on it accordingly, we will come to the conclusion that Christians are, indeed, to belong to the world.

We must remember that when we find the word *world* in the Bible, it does not mean the physical world—the world or universe in which we live. *World* in the Bible (especially in the New Testament and the Gospel of John) sometimes means a society, or people, who are organized against God. However, the world does not necessarily consist of people who are blatant deniers of God, the ones we characterize as atheists and agnostics. The world is composed of many people who live as if there were no God—God is not a priority in their lives. John makes it clear that these people are enemies of Jesus and those who follow him.

An important question this text asks is, How did Jesus say his followers should relate to the world? He did not tell his followers to avoid the world, nor did he ask God to take them out of the world. Sometimes people wish this were the case—that Christianity should insulate and protect us from the world and all its problems and tribulations. But Jesus did not say that he wanted his disciples to escape the world, rather that they are to go into it, as he did, and redeem and minister to the world. So Christians are to belong to the world. How do we do this?

I. *Christians are to be* in *the world but not* of *the world.* We should never allow the world—the enemies of Jesus—to conform us to their way of thinking. This means, in plain language, that we do not get our spirit, our message, our ideals, our goals, our attitudes, and our hope from the world. Jesus is literally telling us that we are citizens of two different worlds. We are to love and care for the people who live in and around us. We are to pray for them and forgive them, and we have a responsibility to them. But we are also citizens of the Kingdom of God. It is not always easy to decide what to do while living in these two worlds; so many issues are not black and white but are in the gray areas of life. So we struggle and ask God's guidance, and this is a proof that we are in the world but not of the world.

II. *Being a Christian in the world is not only something we do, it is a lifestyle that says who we are.* Jesus once said that Christians should be the salt of the world. Salt is only good when it is used on something other than itself, and it is not good just by itself. But many Christians sit back and want people to come to them, in effect to "taste" them, rather than the other way around. As Christians, the salt of our life is our faith that we share in the world; we should let our faith come out of its shaker and use it where it will do the most good. Who needs our help? Who needs encouragement? Who needs hope? Who needs a kind word? Jesus prayed for us and asked that we might live in the world, just as he did. And where did he live? He lived where the people were; he lived "out there." He did not seclude himself in a church, nor did he associate just with his friends. He lived and went and ministered where people needed him, where they were hurting, where they were angry, and even where they were hostile.

And we live out there, too. Every day, whether it is at work, or in the shopping mall, or at school, or at the gas station, we are going and living and moving where the people are. The people we meet every day and every week are the people of the world. Some think that all this means is "witnessing" or saying a written-by-someone-else formula of "salvation" to a certain number of people at a certain prescribed (often by someone else) time. But being in the world as a follower of Jesus means much more than programmed words. Our role is the same as it was for Jesus' first disciples: we are missionaries to the world. And our mission in the world—a world that needs us—is our lifestyle of service every day, where we live.

ILLUSTRATION

GOD IS WITH US IN THE WORLD.   Sometimes people worry about being in the world as God's followers; they believe they will be corrupted or tainted and perhaps lose sight of God. C. S. Lewis had a good word for this anxiety when he wrote, in *Letters to Malcolm:* "But in order to find God it is perhaps not always necessary to leave the creatures behind. We may ignore, but we can nowhere evade, the presence of God. The world is crowded with him. He walks everywhere *incognito*."[12]—Perry Bramlett

SERMON SUGGESTIONS

Topic: Preface to Success

TEXT: Ps. 1

(1) The downward steps of sin. (2) The upward steps of righteousness. (3) The great separation.

Topic: Values That Last

TEXT: 1 Cor. 13:13

Why is love the greatest thing in the world? (1) It is the greatest because nothing really arrives without it. (2) But though nothing arrives without love, the least thing arrives with it. The most paltry something takes on real value when it is enriched by love. (3) Finally, love is the greatest thing in the world because it has the most tremendous power to transform.[13]

WORSHIP AIDS

CALL TO WORSHIP.   "Again Jesus said, 'Peace be with you! As the Father has sent me, I am sending you.' And with that he breathed on them and said, 'Receive the Holy Spirit'" (John 20:21–22 NIV).

INVOCATION.   O Lord, because we serve a Risen Savior, who ascended and reigns in glory, we come with special prayers of rejoicing today and ask that our lives might reflect the hope we carry, to God's great glory.—E. Lee Phillips

OFFERTORY SENTENCE.   What good is it, my brothers, if a man claims to have faith but has no deeds? Can such faith save him? Suppose a brother or sister is without clothes and daily food. If one of you says to him, God, I wish you well; keep warm and well fed, but does nothing about his physical needs, what good is it? In the same way, faith by itself, if it is not accompanied by action is dead (James 2:14–17 NIV).

OFFERTORY PRAYER.   Just as our Savior did not leave us comfortless but ascended into heaven to await us, bless this offering with divine power, the explanation of which is known only in the precinct of heaven from which the glory falls.—E. Lee Phillips

PRAYER.   Almighty God, make the nearness of the living Christ become more real so that our coldness may be overtaken by warmth, our stumbling corrected by our being lifted up, and our tears and sorrow wiped away through hope. May we become humble in his presence, and through our surrender to his call may we rise to share in the victory of his will in every decision and crisis of life. Change our lives so that we ourselves may become life-changers who bear others' burdens, offer a cup of water to a thirsty one, and nourish always

---

[12]C. S. Lewis, *Letters to Malcolm: Chiefly on Prayer* (San Diego: Harcourt Brace Jovanovich, 1964), p. 75.

[13]Clovis G. Chappell, *Values That Last* (Nashville: Cokesbury Press, 1939), pp. 49–59.

a vision of the larger good. Help us to work, and pray, and serve until we shall all come "in the unity of faith unto the measure of the stature of the fullness of Christ." Lord, we believe; bear with us through our unbelief. O Risen Savior, lead us to believe in you that we may own your life.—Donald Macleod

SERMON
Topic: More to Come
Text: John 16:12–15

Being one who likes to make sawdust in my shop and occasionally have something emerge out of the sawdust that we can use, I use building images at times. I was talking to a friend about the Christian faith. I suggested that most theology is like boards on a deck that begin to bow and warp. One end comes up—the sovereignty of God—and when you pound that back down, the other end of the board—human freedom and responsibility—comes up. When you try to pound down the "salvation by grace and not by works or law," then up pops the other end of the board, and we are looking at the whole issue of "social responsibility." You are saved by the grace of God. What you do does not save you. So from St. Paul on, some have said, "Hey wonderful! We can do whatever we want because what we do does not matter." As I have lived it, watched it, and proclaimed it, all our talk about God is like trying to keep both ends of the see-saw off the ground. Whenever one end of the see-saw gets stuck on the ground, it is very likely that some evil will come out of that distortion.

So I was talking about the boards coming up on one side, pounding them down, and the other end popping up, and he said if it were him, he would take out the nails, get three-inch galvanized deck screws, and torque that baby right down flat on both sides. And that is why this passage from the Gospel of John this morning is such bad news to most of us. Because most of us would like to drive those screws into life and get it pinned down securely and not have to worry about things any more.

The Bible is the absolute Word of God, and it tells us exactly what we need to know about life, and all we have to do is to turn to it and read it. We would like that. But when you turn to it and take it with absolute seriousness, right here in John we have Jesus telling his disciples that he will send them the gift of the Holy Spirit and that the Holy Spirit will lead them into all truth. The Holy Spirit, which is given to the Church at Pentecost, will speak to the Church things that the Church has not yet heard. The Holy Spirit will be active in the people of God, in the fellowship, in the body of Christ, and the Holy Spirit will declare to the community things that are to come.

See, the more weight, the more importance, the more authority we give to the Bible, the more we have to listen to these words of Jesus telling his disciples that the revelation is not over. There is more to come. Here is the answer to those who wonder from time to time, "How come God talked to all those people back then and has not talked to anybody lately? How come God speaks so clearly and often to Moses, Jeremiah, Ezekiel, Paul, John, and does not speak to anybody now?" If we believe what Jesus says in these verses, the answer has to be that the Holy Spirit is still talking to us. The Holy Spirit is still speaking to the Church. The Holy Spirit is still active and teaching us new truth for new ages. The Holy Spirit is speaking to us about the things to come and is calling us to be the body and witness of Christ in the world now.

The canon of the Bible may be closed, but the revelation of God's grace and truth is not over. It is still happening.

That is the good news—that God has not forsaken us, that God did not just give us an operating manual and leave us on our own. God did not do some special stuff two thousand years ago and leave us on our own with the memory. Jesus says that there will be an ongoing presence of the Holy Spirit with his people. Pentecost is the gift of that Spirit to the Church so that the Spirit may continue to speak God's will and love to the Church in new times and in new places.

The harder we try to nail down and limit the Word of God to the pages of the Scriptures, the more Scriptures themselves tell us that the other end of the board has come up. The revelation is not full or finished: there is the Holy Spirit, which will continue to be teaching us, reminding us, instructing us, and guiding us into the things that are to come. That is why the Church through the ages has, in fact, lifted up and commended, honored and taught various creeds. The creed we say each week is not in Scripture, but we accept that the Apostles' Creed is a powerful summary of what we, as Christians, believe. We Presbyterians have a whole book of confessions written at different times in Church history, and we have affirmed that in those creeds the Holy Spirit has spoken to the people of God about things that were happening and what was to come.

So that is the exciting and glorious good news of this text—that God is still active with us, the Church, and that God, by the gift and through the power of the Holy Spirit, continues to teach us new truths and new understandings of God's purposes and love. When we ask the question, What would Jesus do? we ask for the Holy Spirit to speak to us as to what Jesus would teach us in the new challenge.

But this is one of those good-news–bad-news stories. This is theology, and there is a balance—the see-saw—and there is the demand to keep all the different sides on the ground. Because before we are ready to hear what the Holy Spirit will say to us concerning the things that are to come, it is expected that we will be part of the body of Christ. We will know the family stories of the past. Before the Holy Spirit speaks to us about what God is saying to the future, we have to have been nurtured, shaped, blessed, matured, disciplined, and informed by the stories of the movement of God in the history of his people. To be prepared to hear the Holy Spirit in the speaking of the new revelation, one must have learned the language of the Holy Spirit by listening closely to the revelations of the past. That is why our vision statement says that we will be part of the family of faith by being nourished by the story of God's love in our preaching and in our Christian education program. If we are confused or unable to understand the declaration of the Holy Spirit at this time, it may be because we have not spent much time being shaped and disciplined by the Word of God we already have.

Jesus promises his people that he will send the Holy Spirit so that the revelation of his grace and mercy may continue to bless and guide his people. Pentecost was our celebration that the Spirit has been given to the Church. We have the Holy Spirit. It is at work in our lives and the lives of the people of God. But to hear and understand requires a people who have been soaked and permeated in the Word of God's Spirit in the past.

The other disturbing reality of that good news is that we are rarely guided by the Holy Spirit into things that are to come without a fight, without a lot of argument, controversy, debate, discord, and embarrassment. Those who have been immersed in the stories of the Scripture know that Moses had a constant struggle with his ability to follow God's command to lead the Israelites into the Promised Land. Jeremiah spoke the Word of the Lord and was put in the stockade and humiliated. Amos was cast out of the court of the king by the priest because they did not like the Word of the Lord. Jesus and his sharing of the will and love of God for his people was not exactly received with joy and gladness by everyone. Somebody once said that everywhere Paul went, he caused a riot. The Nicene Creed did not come easily. The Reformation resulted in wars and rumors of war. Why should we think that, when the Holy Spirit speaks to us now, it would not produce controversy, conflict, schism, and great emotion? Perhaps we should look up and rejoice at the size and the energy of the controversy and debate as evidence that the Holy Spirit may be speaking to us yet again.

Certainly, there are significant and future-shaping issues for which we need the guidance of the Holy Spirit. Where the Holy Spirit is speaking to us, the Scriptures suggest there is always contention and conflict. Where the Holy Spirit declares the things that are to come, there has always been conflict, opposition, and controversy. It is the work of the people of God to struggle toward hearing and following what the Holy Spirit says to us, as best we can understand it.

It is the good news of the Scriptures that our calling is to be the body of Christ seeking to make known the love and mercy of God to others. Jesus says that the way we make his love known to the world around us is for us to love one another and care for each other, even as we engage in the disagreeable struggle with each other to hear the Holy Spirit. We do not demonstrate the love and mercy of God by being right. We are not required to have the right solution to all the questions. We are shaped and molded by the Word of God to be the body of Christ, which is willing to love one another, even when we do not agree with one another. Our salvation does not depend on our being right. As the body of Christ, our calling is to struggle to hear what the Spirit is saying to the church in Henderson and to live and love each other, as we argue about what we hear. That is how families live and love.—Rick Brand

SUNDAY, JUNE 4, 2006
Lectionary Message

Topic: This Is That!
TEXT: Acts 2:1–21
Other Readings: Ezek. 37:1–14; Ps. 104:24–34, 35b; Rom. 8:22–27; John 15:26–27, 16:4b–15

On the first page of the Bible it says, "the Spirit was moving over the face of the waters" (Gen. 1:2). On the last page of the Bible, "the Spirit and the Bride say 'come'" (Rev. 22:17). In creation, and throughout the Scriptures, the Spirit is the life-giving principle. In fact, the Bible might be called "the book of the Spirit."

In support of such a possibility, in the New Testament we find the Holy Spirit active at the apex of revelation in the birth of Jesus, then confirming his Sonship again by descending like a dove at his baptism and immediately leading him into the wilderness for the temptation, and there sustaining him. True to the name of Emmanuel—"God with us"—the Holy Spirit is the Comforter who will continue the presence of Christ in the lives of believers after he has ascended (John 15:26, 16:7–11). Accounting for the supernatural phenomenon of Pentecost, Simon Peter cites the prophesy of Joel to the effect that what is happening is what had been spoken about much earlier: "And it shall come to pass in the last days, saith God, 'I will pour out my Spirit upon all flesh.' . . ." (2:28–32). The Holy Spirit, then, is not to be some special gift or experience for a few; the Holy Spirit will be God's presence in the daily lives of all believers (Rom. 8:9).

I. This evident, yet invisible, vitality and power brought unity out of diversity. It has been said that "unity is not found in conformity, or in creedal expression, or in theology, or in ecclesiastical arrangement; it is found at the center of the heart—a place untouched, there lies the common organic nerve that unites Christendom in its worship and hope."[1] Likely each of us has felt the hot breath of certain groups that call for a narrow common denominator in what is believed and practiced, for all others to get on the bus at the same stops where the comparatively few got aboard.

Such a contention may be driven by a culture that is impatient with mystery and that in everything seeks rational explanations. Modernity thrusts upon us competing values with Christianity. It is the threat of this "cognitive contamination"[2] that is imbibed as we stand in line at the supermarket or chat over the back fence; we should be on guard. Since "might makes right," plausibility is sought by some in the strength of the number of adherents. This is not the unity that was the "accord" so prominent at Pentecost. There is no hint of acquiescence in this oneness: "Those devout men out of every nation under heaven" lost nothing singular to their identity but found unity in the midst of diversity in that "melting pot" presided over by the Holy Spirit. Even the wide divergence in language, like other individual and insistent personal notions, was merged so that each person could hear in his own language.

Perhaps this unification that expressed itself in a common language explains why "they were all amazed and marveled" (Acts 2:7). Such commonality is rooted in an upward look that dissipates greed and egotism and instead clothes with a powerful and focused thrust into the world.

II. Consider next the value of a vision. As the men of Galilee watched Jesus ascend into the clouds, "and, while they looked steadfastly toward heaven as he went up, two men stood by them in white apparel, saying, 'This same Jesus which is taken up from you into heaven, shall come again in like manner'" (Acts 1:9–11). So they were never the same: this upward look changed their outlook forevermore; the promise of Christ's return galvanized them into action with power from on high.

At what are you looking? Does the object that holds your gaze inspire you? Does your vision clothe you with spiritual power from on high? The Bible says about Moses that he "by faith forsook Egypt, not fearing the wrath of the king: for he endured seeing him who is invisible" (Heb. 11:27). What is it that grips your sight, that excites your imagination with new resolve until all your courage is focused into a some grand deed? Or has some vision of God's encircling might silenced that raucous anxiety in your soul? When the king of Syria was on the hunt for Elisha, and when the king's soldiers had surrounded Dothan, Elisha's servant

[1]Joseph Parker, *The People's Bible*, Vol. 23 (New York: Funk and Wagnalls), p. 53.
[2]Peter L. Berger, *A Far Glory* (New York: Free Press), 1992, p. 38.

was dismayed and frightened. It was then that Elisha prayed, "and the Lord opened the eyes of the young man; and he saw: and, behold, the mountain was full of horses and chariots of fire round about Elisha" (2 Kings 6:17). Not only is it likely that we become the embodiment of our visions, but we are empowered and made unafraid of life by them. What do you and I see?

We see that Pentecost catapulted that little band of believers into "a world of Spirit" (John 3:6); if the Spirit is lost, the Church loses its main reason for being. Pentecost gave to them, and gives to us, the unifying of energies and the focus of power to change the world.— John C. Huffman

ILLUSTRATIONS

LIGHT SOURCE.   I've heard of a prominent clergyman who was vacationing in New England one summer, when just before nightfall a severe thunderstorm caused a power outage in the little village where he was staying. As the darkness deepened, the townspeople were astonished to see the church building at the top of the hill ablaze with light. They began gathering to discover the explanation of this phenomenon. The secret was that the church had its own power plant.—John Claypool (Crescent Hill Sermons)

GETTING OUR DIRECTIONS.   A pastor tells about his experience driving on the California freeways. He and his wife were attending a convention in San Francisco, and while there, they decided to visit friends in Long Beach. They set out with a carefully noted map. All the exits and entrance ramps were located and numbered. Despite all the care that had been given to their journey, they took the wrong exit—into bumper-to-bumper traffic. They had no idea where they had gone wrong but finally managed to come upon a policeman. They asked for directions to Long Beach. With a déjà vu smile, he noticed the map on the seat between them. Then he said, "If you will give me the map I'll show you where you are." One of the functions of the Holy Spirit, Jesus said, was "to convince of sin." Why? "Because you believe not on me." There the Holy Spirit locates the sinner as lost.—Ralph Henry

SERMON SUGGESTIONS

Topic: Creator—Forever!

TEXT: Ps. 104:24–34, 35b

(1) The beginning of all things is with God (vv. 34, 35b). (2) The sustaining of all things is with God (vv. 24–30). (3) The glory of the Lord encompasses everything: what is beyond our sight and experience (vv. 31–32); what touches our lives and calls forth our praise (vv. 33–34, 35b).

Topic: What Is Man?

TEXT: Ps. 107:8, 15, 21, 31

(1) The Pilgrim, whom God will guide (vv. 4–9). (2) The Prisoner, whom God sets free (vv. 10–16). (3) The Sufferer, whom God makes whole (vv. 17, 22). (4) The Voyager, whom God brings home (vv. 23–31).—James S. Stewart, *River of Life*

WORSHIP AIDS

CALL TO WORSHIP.   "Ye shall receive power, after the Holy Ghost is come upon you; and ye shall be witnesses unto me both in Jerusalem, and in all Judaea, and in Samaria, and unto the uttermost part of the earth" (Acts 1:8).

INVOCATION.   Come upon us Lord, in great power and mighty strength, so that, as on the first Pentecost, we might be enabled to witness with fervor to the Christ of the Ages.—E. Lee Phillips

INVOCATION.   Open the Word to us this hour, O Lord. Increase our acquaintance with Christ. Seal truth in our hearts, and, by thy Spirit, bind us in the fellowship of thy love that knows no end.—E. Lee Phillips

OFFERTORY SENTENCE.   "Offer the right sacrifices to the Lord, and put your trust in him" (Ps. 4:5 TEV).

OFFERTORY PRAYER.   Teach us, good Lord, to serve thee as thou deservest: to give and not to count the cost; to fight and not to heed the wounds; to toil and not to seek for rest, to labor and not to ask for any reward, save that of knowing that we do thy will.—St. Ignatius Loyola.

PRAYER.   O Lord of all truth and love, the source and end of our believing and loving, we gather in your presence this hour as a community of faith and rejoice as we lift our voices in hymns and songs of praise. You alone are worthy of the homage of the whole human creation, and within the courts of this house we unite with those who love your name to sing blessing, honor, glory, and power unto your great Spirit, forever and ever.

We thank you, our God, for this opportunity of separating ourselves from the clamor and clangor of the world, and for the privilege to take time and rest as we await the entrance of your living Spirit. We are your Church on Earth, but our drooping faith tells us we need the baptism of your heavenly fire. We thank you for the gift of your dynamic presence, which can turn this time of worship into an hour of power, especially when souls are moved to aspire to holiness and to union with one another, to become forces of righteousness across the Earth. We remember with gratitude that first Pentecost day, when your Spirit breathed upon desolate and discouraged hearts and launched a movement that has changed the world. We bless you for that little company of disciples and fellow travelers who were of one mind in one place, and for their readiness to receive a living flame from the altar of heaven and to declare to all who would hope that salvation was near through Christ's death and risen power.

And now we ask from your gracious hand those special gifts that we need to extend your Kingdom and to keep our Christian mission strong and great. Purge us from evil and every wrongdoing and anoint us with a sure sense of duty and service. Pour fresh life into every part of our being so that our disordered conduct may give way to the harmony and beauty of your peace. Set our ideals and desires aflame with your undying love so that the reign of Christ may become a reality in every temple, home, and sanctuary, and especially in all the needy places of the earth. Revive, we pray, your Church in the midst of the years to become the means to righteousness and justice among all people everywhere, and bless with abundance the fruits of Christian service now and forever.—Donald Macleod[3]

SERMON
Topic: The Springtime of Hope
TEXT: Pss. 42, 43; 1 Pet. 1:3–9 (esp. v. 3)

Norman Rockwell, in one of his classic paintings of Americana, portrays a sign of spring that is memorable. In this painting a brother and sister have just gotten off the school bus in front of their farmhouse. In what is evidently a daily ritual, they stop by the mailbox to see if the mailman has come. As they take the mail out on this occasion, their eyes light up and expressions of great joy come to their faces, for here is the *seed catalog,* with its brightly colored pictures of flowers blooming, apple trees blossoming. What a sign of *spring* for the farmer and his family! Soon the frigid temperatures will give way to balmy breezes, and the whole landscape will be transformed with the budding, leafing, and blossoming of the new life of spring. Signs of spring are so thrilling, for they are pregnant with hope—with hopefulness.

It seems to me that the ideal climate would be *perennial* spring. One of the attractive things about Costa Rica, among many inviting features, is the climate. An American couple who had moved there from California tempted me on my visit, exclaiming: "It is delightful; it is *eternal* spring."

Is this not the promise of the gospel—perennial spring in the life of the soul? This is the discovery the apostle Paul makes in his encounter with Christ and shares with us when he writes: "Old things are passed away, behold, all things are becoming new." Again he pens: "If any person is in Christ, he is a *new creation.*" Whatever else the meaning of our baptism into the Christian faith is, it is a symbol of the resurrection to *new* life.

I. *Perennial spring: The promise of the gospel.* If perennial spring is the promise of the gospel, why are we so often obsessed by wintry thoughts? Why are we snowed in by our anxieties? Why are we frozen by our fears? Why does a feeling of hopelessness and a sense of helplessness chill us to the bone when some wintry blast blows in our lives?

The psalmist in the Old Testament lesson is thinking wintry thoughts. A snowstorm of doubt has blown into his life. The circumstances of his life have taken a strong turning. He is in exile in Babylon, far removed from his native land and familiar faces. The places of his epiphanies are miles away on the other side of the Jordan River. He is lonely. He is haunted by the seeming godforsakenness of this strange land. He confesses his wintry thoughts and doubts: "As a deer pants for flowing streams, so longs my soul for thee, O God. My soul thirsts for God, for the living God. When shall I come and behold the face of God? My tears have been my food day and night, while my enemies say to me continually, 'Where is your God?'" (Ps. 42:1–3).

Are there any among us who cannot identify with the psalmist in his doubts, in his despondency, in his depression? Sometimes we find ourselves living in a strange land. We have not chosen to be there; at least we were not conscious of the choice. We feel like exiles, far away from home. The occasion for our winter of discontent may be some infirmity, an illness,

---

[3]*Princeton Pulpit Prayers.*

estrangement, even divorce, or the death of someone near and dear to us. We feel lonely, even cut off from God. The heavens are silent. Our prayers seem to rise no higher than our head. A feeling of alienation haunts our every relationship.

While in the hospital calling on a dear friend who has learned she has inoperable cancer—no warning, no pain, but discovered in her annual physical—I find a person in exile. She has always enjoyed robust health. She does not know what it is to be sick. She has not been hospitalized for forty years, and that was a brief stay with an appendectomy. She has always felt that her good living was paying off. But now this? The hospital is like a foreign land to her. All kinds of doubts flood into her mind. She feels cut off from God—alienated, even rejected.

When we become obsessed with wintry thoughts, do we confess our doubts as openly and honestly as does the psalmist? The Psalms are helpful to persons in every generation because they are so honest. They have a universal appeal, for they address the human predicament in its many dimensions. It is helpful to note that the refrains of the 42nd and 43rd Psalms alternate between confession of doubt and affirmation of faith! In his dereliction the psalmist cries: "Why are you cast down, O my soul, and why are you disquieted within me?" As a glimmer of faith breaks through the clouds of doubt, the psalmist affirms: "Hope in God; for I shall again praise him, my help and my God."

A perennial spring for the life of the spirit is the radical promise of the gospel. In saying this, I am not intending to imply that we will not encounter wintry blasts. The winds that blow into our lives may be sharp and chilling. But even in the face of them, we do not need to succumb to wintry thoughts.

This was the experience of Janet, the woman I called on at the hospital soon after she had learned she had cancer. I had some reluctance in making the call, for I anticipated that it would be very difficult. But I should not have been anxious, for I soon discovered in conversation that Janet was not thinking wintry thoughts. She asked me, "John, are the Jacaranda trees in bloom yet? I remember when Fran and I (Fran is her husband) were on the Madeira Island a few years ago, how beautiful the Jacaranda trees were that lined the streets." She continued: "How beautiful the Jacarandas are here when they are in bloom!" Janet was entertaining thoughts of spring, not of winter. She was living out this radical dimension of the Christian hope that the apostle Paul proclaims when he writes: "In everything give thanks, for this is the will of God in Christ Jesus concerning you." He does not say, "in some things, in many things, in most things," but "in all things." The "all" includes death. Janet had passed from death to life. Death no longer had dominion over her. Hers was the miracle of the Spirit, which is the promise of the gospel to every believer.

II. *Fresh from the Word.* This is what I want to say! Our hope is in the Word—the Word of the Lord. God's greatest gift is not the Church and the Sacraments, as important as they are, but the Word. The Word *created* the Church and the Sacraments.

> "In the beginning was the Word and the Word was with God and the Word was God."
> "In the beginning God created the heavens and the earth."
> "Our help is in the Lord who made heaven and earth."
> "In the fullness of time God sent forth his Son."
> "The Word became flesh and dwells among us."

But in the winter of our discontent, many times we are so obsessed with our predicament that we are not conscious of God's Word. Life seems godforsaken. This is the psalmist's predicament: "My soul thirsts for God, for the living God. When shall I come and behold the face of God?"

But there are times when the Word of the Lord is all we have to cling to. In such times the promise of Jesus can mean everything: "Though heaven and earth shall pass away, my Word shall not pass away." No matter how threatening the circumstance of one's life, God's Word of grace, his Word of hope is "an anchor sure and steadfast for the soul."

The occasion for our worship today and every Lord's Day is to celebrate the Word—the Word of the Lord—the Word of God's grace—an amazing grace. From God's Word of grace shines the light that no darkness can ever put out. The dark night of Calvary gives way to the brightness of the Resurrection dawn. This light that Easter beams shines more and more unto the perfect day. Forty days following Easter, it comes into sharp focus in Pentecost, as the apostles receive Christ's promise of the Holy Spirit, and they come out of hiding to become the light of the world, even as the Master had charged them to be.

III. *Pentecost: Living on the right side of Easter.* Pentecost portends that the Church, the believer, can live in the springtime of hope, no matter how fierce the wintry blasts. Pentecost, you see, is all about living on the right side of Easter. The hope to which we are called is rooted in the fact of Christ's Resurrection.

This is the theme of the apostle Peter's sermon on that first Pentecost. To that motley congregation in Jerusalem, the apostle boldly proclaims: "This Jesus whom you crucified and killed God has raised from the dead of which we all are witnesses. . . . Let all the house of Israel therefore know assuredly that God has made him both Lord and Christ, this Jesus whom you crucified."

Some years later this same apostle, writing his first letter to the Church, begins his epistle, as recorded in our text: "Blessed by the God and Father of our Lord Jesus Christ! By his great mercy we have been born anew to a living hope through the resurrection of Jesus Christ from the dead" (1 Pet. 1:3). Our hope is not a theory, but living.

The strong Word of the Lord to every generation is the shout of that first Easter morning when the disciples discover the tomb empty: "He is not here! Christ is risen, even as he said." This is the good news that catapulted the apostles on a world mission. This is the Word that will motivate the Church today to fulfill its mission to a dying world. With the hopelessness of this generation, who can deny that our society is a society sick unto death?

It takes nothing less than this strong Word of the power of God's amazing grace to bring life out of death to minister salvation—wholeness—to your brokenness and mine. There is no other word that can excite and sustain hope in the face of the seeming hopelessness of eventualities that we all encounter sooner or later.

For instance, the other evening I was calling on a member in the Intensive Care unit at the hospital. I held his hand in prayer. When I started to leave, he held my hand tightly; he did not want me to go. He was afraid. There was no family to lean on. I remembered having had the memorial service for his wife several years ago. I gripped his trembling hand, trying in some way to assure him that he was held by the mighty hand of God. Sensing my own weakness and his, I said, Jesus is saying to us: "Let not your hearts be troubled. You believe in God. Believe also in me. . . . Take courage! I have overcome the world. Believe in the Lord Jesus Christ!" To speak a lesser world would be to deny Christ as Lord.

As a woman confessed to her pastor: "Since my divorce, I have died a thousand deaths." We do encounter "end-of-our-world" experiences in life that are as living deaths. We would rather die than go on living. To weather such wintry blasts, how we need the power of the Resurrection that we may live again! We need to hear the assurance of our text: "By God's great mercy we have been born anew to a living hope through the resurrection of Jesus Christ from the dead."

Hope to the New Testament writers is not Pollyanna sweet talk; it is not mere wishful thinking; it is not a whistling in the dark. The sign of perennial spring for the believer is grounded in nothing less than the grace of God, as proclaimed in Christ's Resurrection. This fact is the keystone to the structure of our faith, no matter how we have come to the knowledge of the gospel (and we have all traveled different paths), no matter how many turns we have made along the way, no matter how we view our theological orientation (liberal, fundamentalist, or some place in between). The gospel invites us, tempts us, challenges us to live in the perennial springtime made real for the believer in the power of God in raising Jesus from the dead. If we live on the right side of Easter and Pentecost, we can live in hope, no matter what the death we die.

May the hope of the disciples on that first Pentecost be our faith, for they were not saying *in dismay,* "Look what the world has come to." They were saying *in hopefulness,* "Look what has come to the world!" Amen! And Amen!—John Thompson

SUNDAY, JUNE 11, 2006
Lectionary Message

Topic: The Front End of Salvation
TEXT: John 3:1–17
Other Readings: Isa. 6:1–8; Ps. 29; Rom. 8:12–17

The speaker was addressing the importance of conversion to faith in Jesus Christ. To the raised eyebrows of some, he announced that "conversion" is the *end* of salvation. After a few seconds of questioning silence, he added: "But it's the *front* end!"[4] I've chosen to discuss that placement of "conversion" in the salvation experience, for, as President John Kennedy said in his inaugural, "The longest journey begins with the first step."[5]

That a more thorough understanding of the "first step" taken toward faith in Jesus Christ is essential for Christian discipleship in the modern world meets with little doubt, for the landscape of contemporary Christendom is littered with the wreckage of those who began and didn't finish (Luke 14:28)—some the road-kill of modern science, others the casualties of a corrosive secularism. But my sense of the fundamental cause of the number of "believer body-bags" is the lack of understanding of how one begins the Christian faith, and the basis on which a believer in the gospel can make the audacious claim that she or he has been saved. So I persist with that notion here.

Our text features the encounter of Nicodemus with Jesus. It is one of the best-loved stories in the Bible. Nicodemus ingratiates himself with us and is one of the characters in the New Testament about whom we like to speculate. We warm at his seeking Jesus out, yet we

---

[4]James L. Sullivan said this in a message to the Kentucky Baptist Evangelism Conference.
[5]President Kennedy quoted this Chinese proverb in his inaugural as president of the United States.

wonder why he came in the darkness. Whatever your speculations, put aside any fuzzy feelings for Nicodemus, and see him for the reason he appears in this episode: he is the quintessence of Judaism. He is "a man of the Pharisees, a ruler of the Jews."

I. As a ruler of the Jews, he embodies all the beliefs that are in conflict with the gospel of Jesus Christ. Nicodemus is hung up on the privilege of birth. He reminds me of the Boston matron who had an obsessive interest in biblical genealogies. When asked by her pastor the reason for her fascination, she replied, "When I get to heaven I want to know who's kin to whom." However, Nicodemus's interest went deeper than this: he subscribed to the belief that his Jewish birth qualified him for benefits of a covenant that God had made with Israel (Gen. 12:2–3; Matt. 3:9). Beyond that, he represented a neat system of things that one did *for* God because Judaism espoused the idea that God had a problem that humans could alter by placating and pleasing him. So with meticulous law-keeping and enough sacrifices, God's attitude could be changed.

Jesus engages a belief that had gone astray. No longer will the blood of bulls and goats, and the ashes of a heifer suffice for Nicodemus (Heb. 9:13). He is rattled by Jesus: the problem is not with God; it is with humans (Rom. 3:9f; 2 Cor. 5:19–20). For this reason, "the gospel originates in the love of God for a disobedient world; it centers in the giving of his only Son to and for the world, and its end is that people may not be lost but live under the saving sovereignty of God."[6] Jesus' announcement that it is we who have gone astray startles and confuses Nicodemus, who is a "stand-in" for a self-righteous world. Rather than something one works for, salvation is the gift of God (Eph. 2:8–10). The conflict is joined over what humans can do for God to achieve salvation versus what God has done for humans (John 3:16).

II. To turn around this fatal conceit, not only in Nicodemus but in all of us, the need for repentance is obvious and compelling. But let me disabuse you of the notion that "repentance" means "to stop sinning" (1 John 1:8–10). Common usage of the term may imply that. If so, when one fails the test, disappointment and disillusionment set in. Neither is repentance wallowing in guilt and feeling worthless. A rabbi and the cantor on the Day of Atonement were lamenting their sins at great length, each concluding he was a nobody. Then the sexton, inspired by their example, laments his sins and declares that he, too, is a nobody. Then said the rabbi to the cantor: "Would you just look at who thinks he is a nobody!"[7]

Repentance, as Jesus and John the Baptist used it (Mark 1:15; Matt. 3:2), is a cognitive term meaning to change one's mind. It is a radical term! For Nicodemus to give up the belief that was so deeply ingrained by years of tradition and practice requires the work of the Holy Spirit, for the battle is always between "flesh" and "Spirit." The one thing that is most difficult for the human is to surrender self, to give up our infatuation with the idea that there is some innate goodness within that recommends us to God. Jesus uses several images to depict that. He talked about a "strait gate and narrow way, and the few that find it" (Matt. 7:13–14). The requirement for discipleship, according to Jesus, is to *deny* oneself, and take up his or her *cross* (Matt. 16:24). The object one denies is oneself, in the matter of spiritual salvation, and we must remember that the cross was the instrument of death, and in this instance death to self.

---

[6]George R. Beasley-Murray, *World Bible Commentary* (Nashville, Tenn.: Thomas Nelson Publishers), 1999, p. 51.
[7]Richard John Neuhaus, *Death on a Friday Afternoon* (New York: Basic Books), 2000, p. 16.

I repeat: the hardest thing for the human is to let go of ego! As the gospel song says, "In my hands no price I bring, simply to thy cross I cling."[8] That is the testimony of the penitent.

III. Giving up our false notions is not enough; we must believe the gospel. Jesus told a story about leaving a house empty, and a worse condition occurred (Matt. 12:43–45). The ground-clearing experience of repentance makes an alternative to self possible; then one begins to believe the gospel. The apostle defined the gospel as "Christ dying for our sins according to the scriptures, and that he was buried, and rose from the grave on the third day" (1 Cor. 15:3–4). Richard John Neuhaus said, "If things are to be set right, if justice is to be done, somebody else will have to do it. It is not enough for God to take our part, he must take our place."[9]

The apostle said to the Roman Church and to all the Nicodemuses of the world, "But now the righteousness of God without the law (or anything that is mandatory) is manifested, being witnessed by the law and the prophets, even the righteousness of God which is by faith in Jesus Christ unto and upon all them that believe" (3:21–22). In the prologue of John's Gospel, we read: "to as many as received him, to them he gave the authority of the children of God, even to them that believe on his name" (1:12). Christ then is received as Savior by believing that God, in him, takes your place.

The Bible makes confession of Christ as Savior important. Again, the apostle speaks to the Romans: "That if you will confess with your mouth the Lord Jesus, and believe in your heart that God has raised him from the dead, you will be saved. For with the heart one believes into righteousness, and with the mouth confession is made for salvation" (10:9–10). And as Portia said to Shylock, "The quality of mercy is not strained, it drops as the gentle rain from heaven on the place beneath."[10]

I came to know Christ as my Savior during my teenage years, which were during the Great Depression. We were poor, so poor we couldn't pay attention! But we had time to think about our souls and their relation to the Almighty. In my fifteenth summer I was under conviction that I was lost. Such a burden was it that I tried several ways to find peace. But to no avail. I tried to reform my life; I tried abstinence from profane language; I didn't dance or steal; I tried not to lie. Still, none of these worked for me. One day, on my knees, I said to the Lord in my prayer, "I want you to do for me what I cannot do for myself!" And in that moment, "My sins—O the bliss of that glorious thought—my sins, not in part, but the whole, were nailed to the cross and I bear them no more, Praise the Lord, O my soul!"[11]—John C. Huffman

See p. 478 for Sermon Suggestions.

SERMON
Topic: Let Peace Begin in Me
TEXT: Phil. 4:4–9

Advances in modern surgery are among the wonders of our age. Heart surgery has become so routine that we hardly blink at the successful surgery on two octogenarians in our church

---

[8]A line from the hymn, "Rock of Ages," by Augustus Toplady.
[9]Richard John Neuhaus, *Death on a Friday Afternoon* (New York: Basic Books), 2000, p. 23.
[10]William Shakespeare, *The Merchant of Venice*, Act IV, 1, 82.
[11]A line from the hymn, "It Is Well with My Soul," by H. G. Spafford.

within a week. Who would have thought fifty years ago that major surgery could be done through a laparoscope and skin punctures or that kidney stones could be crushed with sound waves? I have this fantasy about bringing Moses into our world in a time machine, showing him all of the wonders of modern technology, and asking, "What do you think of these miracles?" The man we associate with parting the sea in the exodus might not be as impressed with us as we like to believe.

Moses may have had some vision of our age of surgery. Egyptian carvings dating back to 2500 B.C. picture amazing surgical procedures like the removal of gallstones and the amputation of limbs. Drilling a hole in the skull to relieve pressure on the brain has been traced back to the Neolithic age, as early as 8000 B.C. The Greek surgeon Hippocrates published a manual of surgical procedures in the fourth century B.C. We are aware that surgical circumcision of male babies was a covenant rite of the Hebrews going back to the time of Abraham. Circumcision is still performed by rabbis in Jewish communities.

The appropriate biblical question concerning the miracle of modern medicine is, Where is God in all of this? The question calls us beyond the physical to the unseen spiritual reality of the inner person, whom you cannot reach with a knife. Consider the revelation of God to Samuel before the anointing of David as King of Israel: ". . . for the Lord does not see as mortals see; they look on the outward appearance, but the Lord looks on the heart" (1 Sam. 16:7). And consider the reflection of Paul on calling Corinthians to answer those who, "boast in outward appearance and not in the heart" (2 Cor. 5:12). The Bible does not know about heart-lung bypass machines, but it teaches us things about human anatomy that you cannot learn in medical school. Compared to the ancient world of the Bible, we have made amazing strides in recognizing and understanding the physical world. The human view of the universe has stretched far beyond the wildest dreams of Moses. Our comprehension of the human body has gone far beyond the location and function of organs to the unique structure of cells. Now the Human Genome Project is working to identify and understand the genetic causes behind the physical structures of human anatomy. These are wonderful human accomplishments, most of which have come in my lifetime. What more could we ask?

I. *We are flesh.* The ancient Hebrew could appreciate all of our lessons in human anatomy. Humans are physical beings, like the beasts of the field. Our lives are drawn from the dust, and they return to the dust. The Old Testament knows nothing about natural immortality or of a separate and distinct spirit within the human body. Life after death—the raging debate between Pharisees and Sadducees in the Gospels—was about the resurrection of the body, not the immortality of the soul. Without question, we are flesh; and Jesus was known in the flesh. The incarnation of Jesus Christ proclaimed by John's Gospel is about the Word become flesh. Paul declares that Christ emptied himself of being God to be born in human likeness, and being found in human form, he humbled himself to the point of death. Every time we eat the bread and drink the cup, we are reminded of the flesh-and-blood reality of the man named Jesus.

All human bodies, including the body of Christ, are mortal. From the day we are born, we live under a death sentence. Bodies are fragile. They break when they encounter earthquakes and storms, bullets and bombs, age and disease. We prefer not to think about our mortality, but we cannot ignore the steady approaching end to our physical selves. Reinhold Niebuhr saw our human finitude, the necessity of death, as the root cause of our anxiety in life that produces the worst kind of human evil. The evil escalates in groups in mob behavior. Gangs reinforce and encourage monstrous personal behavior that the individual would never do alone. As he wrote, Niebuhr was observing the demonic behavior of the German nation. The group-think of gangs moves to another level as, "The nation pretends to be God."[12]

In a word, the evil and destruction of World War II was a reflection in the mirror of human mortality. No wonder that Gnostics identified all evil with the human flesh and all virtue with the human spirit. But the human structure is not so simple. The physical event of the Crucifixion of Jesus exposed the most horrible evil that the human mind can imagine and, at the same time, revealed the redemptive grace of forgiveness and compassion. The flesh is not evil; it is the battleground of sin and salvation, the demonic and the divine, the evil and the good. Jürgen Moltmann struggled with the cross in the light of the evil and suffering inflicted on the Jews in the Holocaust. He reminds us: "Anyone who later comes up against insoluble problems and despair must remember that the *Shema* of Israel and the Lord's Prayer were prayed in Auschwitz."

II. *We are more than flesh.* Throughout Philippians, Paul focuses on the inner person—the unseen reality that we associate with the self, the character. For Paul, who you are comes out in what you do. From the beginning, people are created in the image of God and declared from the beginning to be the crowning glory of God's work of creation. The person made from the dust of the Earth is alive by the breath—the Spirit—of God, and the finished product is a living soul. We live in the flesh by the power of the Spirit, and we live in hope beyond the limits of our mortal bodies by the eternal power of God infused into our very being. Human anatomy is unfinished in the flesh. Apart from soul, spirit, mind, and heart—the biblical images of the inner person—human anatomy is incomplete. You cannot get to this part of the human anatomy with any of the wonderful instruments of modern surgery, but they are quite visible and measurable in every person.

Paul challenged the Philippian Christians to "be of the same mind, having the same love, being in full accord and of one mind." He called Christians to transcend themselves, to look beyond self to the interests of others: "Let the same mind be in you that was in Christ Jesus." Although affirming of modern science, Eric Rust notes the inadequacy of science to define the reality of *mind.* You cannot fully describe a person using only the tools of biology. A seminary friend worked in a local hospital as a chaplain, where he not only gained invaluable experience in working with patients, he had opportunities to work with the physicians. Bill told me about a neurologist at the hospital who was absolutely certain that people are just protoplasm. According to the doctor, we do not have all of the answers, but every question has a physical answer. Eventually, we will find a pill for every problem. Who knows what the future may hold? We may be on the verge of medical immortality, or worse, the creation of our own utopia by the genetic engineering of all our children.

As I have come to know physicians through pastoral ministry, I have observed a significant move in recent years toward affirming the Spirit in human nature, the importance of prayer in the process of hearing, and a humility about the transcendent reality of God, before whom we are all accountable. People are moved by spiritual forces that we cannot locate with X-ray. The evidence is the behavior, in doing what is true, honorable, just, pure, pleasing,

---

[12]*The Nature and Destiny of Man: A Christian Interpretations* (Louisville, Ky.: Westminster John Knox Press, 1996), p. 212.

commendable, excellent, worthy of praise. The real you comes out in virtues and vices. "And the peace of God, which surpasses all understanding, will guard your hearts and your minds in Christ Jesus."—Larry Dipboye

SUNDAY, JUNE 18, 2006
Lectionary Message
Topic: What Then Is the Bleating of the Sheep?
TEXT: 1 Sam. 15:34–16:13
Other Readings: Ps. 20; 2 Cor. 5:6–10 (11–13), 14–17; Mark 4:26–34

Without the bleating of the sheep, likely the substance of the text would not have happened. Often the most minute, unexpected sound or event traps us and betrays our overweening ambitions or disobedience. Here the "best laid plans" of King Saul go astray. For him the moment of truth was the bleating of the sheep! On a more optimistic note, however, we are able to bootleg back into this narrative an outcome that helps overcome the barbarism, gore, and clandestine management that fills this section of the Old Testament, namely, the selection and enthronement of David as King of Israel. In addition, we are privileged to have the conviction of Romans 8:28 to the effect that "God is at work in all that is happening to us." At best, though, painful lessons leap out of this passage.

I. Some *signal* always exposes us. The dubious fitness of Saul to be king is being confirmed. Samuel is God's switchboard; through him God tells Saul to avenge an ancestral act of hostility against Israel. A brutal agenda is assigned to Saul: he is to destroy completely the Amalekites—all persons and property. Compliance would vastly improve Saul's job rating with the Almighty. Saul failed the test. Resolutely, and with brimming confidence, Saul meets Samuel with a report of successfully completing the mission. The Amalekites are no more! Even while exaggerating this embroidered tale of conquest, he appears to have no idea of "the tangled web he is weaving." Most of us know that the practice of deceit administers a kind of sedation that blunts the jagged edges of reality and finally creates a euphoria in which we begin to feel at home. But red-handed and red-faced, he is trapped in a lie that was intended to paper over his disobedience when Samuel says, "What then is the bleating of the sheep?"

How often have our misdeeds been exposed by a sudden sound or object that blindsided us from nowhere, or at least we thought it was *from nowhere,* since we had tried to cover our tracks. A fingerprint is left. A rooster crows out of the darkness. An elicit love note is left forgotten in a shirt pocket and discovered when the laundry is done. A small patch of blood on a mattress, with unmistakable DNA, leads police to the door. We may be sure that out of the vast uncertainty that surrounds misdeeds will come the bleating of sheep or the sound of a rooster crowing. It seems our sins invariably find us out!

II. We can't *sanctify* disobedience. Caught in those humiliating jaws of deceit, Saul tries to rationalize the saving of the best herds to be offered as a sacrifice to God at Gilgal. If the truth be told, Saul saved them to glut his greed, and his pious excuse only makes his disobedience more unsavory. And it's not the last time such a ploy has been used. A West Virginia contractor won the lottery in the amount of a hundred million or more, and he justified his participation in such gambling by saying that he would give a tenth of it to his church.

And since the last World War, our churches have prospered financially beyond anything in their histories. It is likely that large amounts of that money, perhaps squeezed out of the misery of folks or gained in some under-the-table fashion have been "baptized" into our churches. To say the least, many folks prefer to give their money rather than the obedience of their lives. It is at this place in the context of our passage that we find the first prophetic criticism of sacrifice when Samuel says to Saul: "Behold, to obey is better than sacrifice, and to harken than the fat of rams" (15:22).

III. Forgiveness of *sin* does not imply that penalties will not be exacted for failure to meet the claims of obligation. Saul's penalty is swift and irrevocable. The kingdom is "rent" from him, as the ripping of a garment. Stunned by this incredible turn of events and with great sorrow, he begs Samuel's forgiveness. A question mark hangs over Samuel's response. However, whether he was forgiven or not, Saul's duplicity takes the inevitable downhill turn. He goes from bad to worse.

There is no mistake that we are affected by our sins. Even though forgiven, the hurt, the disease, the scars, and the crippling effect of sin remains. Shakespeare has Lady Macbeth saying: "If it were done when 'tis done, then 'twere well it were done quickly,"[13] but the problem with sin is that it is never done. My predecessor in a Kentucky church moved from Texas, and his parting gift was a fishing rod and reel. To practice with it, he tied a silver spoon to the line. Soon his competence increased until he could hit a spot on the side of the brick house. Satisfied with his ability, he returned the spoon to the kitchen drawer. When his wife began to set the table for dinner, she found the battered spoon and demanded to know who had damaged it. The children pleaded "not guilty," so finally the preacher owned that it was he who had misused it so thoughtlessly; to placate his upset wife, he offered to replace it with a new one if she wouldn't mention it again. "No," she said, "I don't want a new one. This one was given as a wedding present." The preacher said afterward that, true to her word, she didn't ever mention it again, but at every meal that spoon was at his plate!

(a) We don't diminish sin by blaming others. When caught in the jaws of deceit and selfishness, Saul sought to extenuate his guilt by saying that he feared the people who wanted to keep the best of the herds from slaughter, so he obeyed their voice rather than the voice of God. If nowhere else, in shifting the blame on others he reveals a pettiness that is not befitting a king who adjudicates the affairs of others.

(b) For a half-century now blaming has been epidemic. Youth blame parents. Parents blame schools, and so on. There is competition to see who is the most deprived, unloved, and sinned against so the winner can do the most blaming. As this is written the 9/11 Commission has reported, and the common denominator is blame—enough for everybody! For Saul and for us, blaming is a petty dodge of accountability.

IV. The *selection* of a new king will include a new *standard* for office.

(a) "God spoke to Samuel saying, 'It repents me that I have set up Saul to be king'" (15:10). I don't know what that means exactly, but evidently all concerned came to see that the job was too big for Saul. He had been chosen by the most superficial standards: his height and his looks. Now the Lord had been betrayed by an inadequacy that lay far deeper, and at

---

[13]William Shakespeare, *Lady Macbeth*, Act I, Scene VII, Line 1.

first glance was not as evident as his looks. Perhaps Samuel's grief over Saul's flopping was due to realizing he had been swayed by externals.

(b) David was tanned, "and goodly to look to" (16:12), but this time a new standard for office would operate. The Bible tells us of the human proclivity to look "on the outward appearance"; the judgments of the majority are generally superficial and quickly made. Earlier Samuel had said, "the Lord has sought him a man after his own heart" (13:14), and the search will end in the house of Jesse when the shepherd boy is chosen. Although by no means perfect, David was the man after God's own heart.

V. Quoting from Isaiah, our Lord indicts so many of us when he says, "This people draw near unto me with their mouth, and honor me with their lips; but their heart is far from me" (Matt. 15:8). That was Saul's failure. It is ours, too. When David was anointed by Samuel, "the Spirit of the Lord came upon David from that day forward" (16:13), and he grew into the job. Many of us have been thrust into tasks beyond our reach, but with the help of the Holy Spirit we have grown and been enabled.

> Knowledge we ask not—knowledge Thou has lent,
> But, Lord, the will there lies our bitter need,
> Give us to build above the deep intent
> The deed, the deed.

—John C. Huffman

SERMON SUGGESTIONS

Topic: Praying for Our Nation's Leaders
TEXT: Ps. 20
(1) The occasion may present us with a mixture of problems and possibilities (vv. 1–5). (2) We can be assured of God's will and ability to help (vv. 6–9).

Topic: What Can We Expect from God?
TEXT: Ps. 20
(1) Consider this: the God of King David is our God, too (v. 1). (2) We should expect God to work for us through his people (vv. 2–3). (3) We should pray and plan with confidence in God's ultimate victory (vv. 4–8).

WORSHIP AIDS

CALL TO WORSHIP.   "Awake, awake; put on thy strength, O Zion" (Isa. 52:1).

INVOCATION.   Father's Day. Lord, God, let our faith be firm as is a father's love, and our commitment as mighty as a father's strength, in the power of our Lord Jesus Christ.—E. Lee Phillips

OFFERTORY SENTENCE.   "Give, and it shall be given unto you; good measure, pressed down, and shaken together, and running over. . . . For with the same measure that ye mete withal it shall be measured to you again" (Luke 6:38).

OFFERTORY PRAYER.   Gracious Lord, give us generous hearts, not holding back through fear or selfishness, but imitating your blessed example in our prodigality of love.

PRAYER.   O God, we who are bound together in the tender ties of love, pray thee for a day of unclouded love. May no passing irritation rob us of our joy in one another. Forgive us if we have often been keen to see the human failings and slow to feel the preciousness of those who are still the dearest comfort of our life. May there be no sharp words that wound and scar, and no rift that may grow into estrangement. Suffer us not to grieve those whom thou hast sent to us as the sweet ministers of love. May our eyes not be so holden by self-ishness that we know thine angels only when they spread their wings to return to thee.—Walter Rauschenbusch

SERMON

Topic: How Does Your Garden Grow?

Text: Mark 4:26–32

Remember the nursery rhyme: "Mary, Mary quite contrary, how does your garden grow? With silver bells and cockle shells, and pretty maids all in a row."

That never made any sense to me. There must be more to raising a garden than that.

I. Obstacles arise when planting and growing a garden.

(a) In the parable of the sower and the seed, only one-fourth of the seed fell on good soil, and in the parable of the wheat and the tares that good soil grew with weeds.

(b) Seed needs light to grow, but darkness can hinder growth (hiding our lights under a basket grows ignorance and sin).

(c) Jesus began planting seeds of the Kingdom of God with a ragtag group of twelve disciples who didn't understand his mission.

(d) Sometimes your own weaknesses will make you wonder why God called you.

(e) Be careful to plant the right seeds.

II. Despite hindrances to the Kingdom's growth, God takes over and grows the seed anyway (4:26–29, the seed growing secretly).

(a) Only God can make a seed grow.

The word *automate* means "the automatic earth," so success is inevitable.
God makes sure the Kingdom of God will be mightier and outlast Earth's most powerful
    kingdoms.

(b) We can hinder the process of growth.

It is difficult to let the plant grow by itself.
Growth is gradual, so don't expect immediate results.
The Kingdom of God is not brought in by force or violence.

(c) This doesn't mean we are not to do our share.

Grow roots of faith.
God empowers his followers to spread the growth of his Kingdom.
Remember that "in due season we shall reap if we faint not" (Gal. 6:9).

III. The mustard seed parable gives us two lessons about hope (4:30–32).

(a) How much faith is not as important as where it is directed.

Is our faith in our abilities or in Christ? (see Matt. 17:14–20).

Faith in God can move mountains. What are your mountains?

God will remove or overcome any obstacle to his will.

One purpose of the mustard seed parable is to compare the Kingdom of God at its beginning to its end, from a tiny seed to a fully grown shrub.

Don't wait for conditions to be perfect to do God's will.

(b) The mustard seed requires perennial planting and harvesting.

We both observe and participate in growth, active waiting on God's action.

Jesus said the harvest is plentiful, but the laborers are few (Matt. 9:37–38).

Jesus told his followers that we would do greater things even than he, yet the Church at times seems hopeless to release God's power.

As a pinch of salt flavors a pot of soup, Christians are to be catalysts of change.

The Word of God planted in the heart wants to outgrow its cage and spread.

A plant grows and creates more seeds, likened to the Resurrection.

The same birds that tried to destroy the seed come back for food and shelter.

—Ron Blankenship

SUNDAY, JUNE 25, 2006
Lectionary Message
Topic: Giant in the Valley, Cowards on the Hill[14]
TEXT: 1 Sam. 17:1a, 4–11, 19–23, 32–41
Other Readings: Ps. 9:9–20; 2 Cor. 6:1–13; Mark 4:35–41

Not only is this one of the best-known stories in the Bible, it is, in fact, one of the defining stories of the tradition of David in early Judaism. Here the legitimacy of his choice to be king is confirmed. The heroism of David conquering Goliath did two things: it infused fear in the Philistines so that they never threatened Israel again, and it aroused the slumbering and cowardly energies of the Israelites. David demonstrated one of the prime qualities of leadership.

As the story begins, the Philistines still pose a serious threat to Israel's future. The face-off is typical. The armies are encamped on opposite hills with a valley in between. The selection of a single combatant from each army to fight to the death, with servitude being the price paid by the losing side, was a familiar arrangement in the ancient world.

A fortuitous circumstance sends the boy, David, to the battlefront to carry food to his three brothers and to carry back to Jesse, the father, a report of how his sons are faring in the army of Saul. David arrives just as Goliath banters with the craven-hearted army of Israel to send a man down to fight him. There are no volunteers among the Israelites to meet the menacing challenge of the Philistine. Dismayed by the cowardice of his countrymen, David offers himself.

---

[14]A phrase from a sermon by a prominent Southern Baptist preacher, Dr. H. Franklin Paschall.

I. David learns—all of us learn sooner or later—the hurt and damage *opposition* does when it comes from within.

(a) To his credit, David is not turned from the path of duty by reproach. None of us likes opposition, but it is more poignant and painful when it comes from within our own family or community. Although better things are expected from his brothers, who ridicule him and impugn his motives, he is not deterred from an act of bravery. He seems to understand that angry persons are more desirous of inflicting pain than of uttering truth (Prov. 14:29, 16:32). However, the bitterest and most defeating opposition comes from within. The word *quisling* came into our vocabulary when Vidkun Quisling betrayed his own country. The words of Eliab were intended to damage David in the eyes of others and undermine confidence in him. The reproach of a family member may be the most devastating blow one receives. Opposition within the membership of a church family that leaves "the house divided" has scarred the landscape of nearly every communion. Most readers of this will have experienced similar "slings and arrows" of some outraged fortune somewhere within the circle of a kindred community. For a reason we will come to see, David understands that natural affection vanishes before envy and anger.

(b) In the conquest of life, the first victory is over oneself. And such had been wrought by David on the back-side of his father's field, as he was willing to lay down his life for the sheep. It was there he had learned about weapons that exceeded the reach of technology. The paw of the lion and the paw of the bear God Almighty had delivered into David's hand. He was able to get beyond the sting of this opposition from within because from beyond himself there was a cause: larger than life, the vindication of "the armies of the living God." He belonged to something and to someone that reached beyond the boundaries of his earthly life.

To what do you belong? Is there some overtowering cause, some challenge from some giant objective to which you have foresworn all your loyalties? Then this will be the relentless solvent that diminishes all the opposition of derision and reproach; in fact, it will add fuel to the fire! It is helpful to remember that opportunity is usually matched by opposition.

II. To fight Goliath and redeem the embarrassment of "the armies of the living God" is a providential *opportunity* for David.

(a) How full is life of providential occurrences if we will observe them! The sincerity and rectitude of David's spirit is confirmed by this opportunity. He looks back on his personal history and sees the presence and intervention of God, and he is reassured of the outcome in the face-off with Goliath. We are indebted to the Jewish world for believing that God is One of history, dramatically present in the affairs of humans—that history is an ascending plane that has a culmination, a climax, rather than the Greek idea that history is a vertiginous cycle, "that there is nothing new under the sun."

(b) The story reminds us, too, of the unlikely vessels of God's grace. The basic theme seems to be that God finds possibilities of grace in unlikely places and in unlikely persons. In a full-time carpenter turned itinerant preacher, or in a vengeful Pharisee who becomes his apostle, God turns our prudence and values upside down. As Mary sang in the Magnificat, "He has shown strength with his arm, he has scattered the proud in the imagination of their hearts, he has put down the mighty from their seats" (Luke 1:51–52). David is more than a courageous underdog. Armed with his sling—the equivalent of the Winchester rifle of his day—he goes forth to battle with weapons beyond technology (2 Cor. 10:4). Ultimately, his trust is in the subversive power of truth, and the truth here is that God is in opposition to arrogant and self-serving power and its violence.[15] We must not allow our opposition to evil to become triumphal in a show of bravado and swagger.

(c) Some of the programs and activities of the Church seem to clank around the armor of Saul. It is God who saves, not Goliath or the king, not without human agency, surely, but in ways that are not of this world. To make them so is to lose God's redemptive power.

David's trust in God seemed to nourish hope that there is a way into the future when there seems to be no way. Therefore, we must persist in the notion that the stones of human resistance, well placed, may bring down the impregnable forces of oppression that loom as armored giants. But we must learn once more the lesson of David's God-trusting opposition to all the faces of tyranny. If the truth be told, I never expected to see the at-first pitifully weak "sit-ins," which Dian Nash, James Bevil, and John Lewis, along with a few others, began in the downtown restaurants to overcome the giant oppression and disfranchisement of black people. Neither could I foresee the fall of the elaborate scaffolding of communism or the dismantling of a gigantic apartheid in South Africa. I had left the story of David's God-trusting opposition in the dustbins of the Old Testament. Our nation must not forget his words: "God does not save by sword or spear." Those of us who are "the least of these" need the lesson of this story, as we live under the threat of violent and death-dealing systems.— John C. Huffman

SERMON SUGGESTIONS

Topic: Why We Can Trust God in All Circumstances
TEXT: Ps. 9:9–20
(1) God is all-powerful (v. 9). (2) God is gracious and caring toward those who suffer unjustly (vv. 9–14). (3) God is not to be blamed for the suffering of the wicked (vv. 15–16).

Topic: Caught in Your Own Trap
TEXT: Ps. 9:9–20 (esp. vv. 15–16)
(1) The problem of temptation (vv. 15–16): it is universal; it is deceptive; it is often self-engineered. (2) The solution of the problem (v. 9): the trustworthy power of God; the actual intervention of God.

WORSHIP AIDS

CALL TO WORSHIP.   "This is how we know what love is: Christ gave his life for us. We too, then, ought to give our lives for our brothers! If a rich person sees his brother in need, yet closes his heart against his brother, how can he claim that he loves God? My children, our love should not be just words and talk; it must be true love, which shows itself in action" (1 John 3:16–18 TEV).

INVOCATION.   O divine love, help us today to rise to the challenge of the needs of the world and to do it by making new commitments, followed by faithful service to you and to every soul for whom Christ died. Make us strong in your strength.

---

[15]*The New Interpreter's Bible*, Vol. 2 (Nashville, Tenn.: Abington Press), 1998, p. 1114.

OFFERTORY SENTENCE.   "They gave according to their means, as I can testify, and beyond their means, of their own free will" (2 Cor. 8:3 RSV).

OFFERTORY PRAYER.   God of grace, God of glory, help us understand that we are recipients of your mercy. What we are, your grace has made us. What we have, your providence has given us. And now, do your gracious work also in others, through the gifts we bring.

PRAYER.   Like children we come to you this morning, Father. Reach out and touch us with the finger of your love so that we will stop where we are, sense your presence, and turn to you. Take us and make us what you want us to be, not what we think we ought to be. Call us to adventures that you have planned, not those to which we particularly aspire. Keep us from sin, but when we do sin draw us back to you. Deliver us from small-spiritedness. Help us to know ourselves in truth and to enjoy the person you created us to be.

Help us across the journey of life to use the gifts with which you have endowed us to serve you and our fellow man. Help us to plunge into the mystery of who you are, Father, and to love you above all things. Loving you, may we learn to love without possessiveness. Help us to acquire divine patience, as we live among our fellows. Help us to develop respect for others who do not share our thinking or understand our attitudes. Deliver us from seeking to force others into some mold that fits us well. Rather, help us to be brave and strong enough in our faith to understand that you have made us all unique and special and for your purposes.

As we move through the days of our lives, may we become more understanding of you, wiser in the use of your gifts, and more compassionate in our service to others. Inspire us never to grow tired of telling the grand old story of Jesus and his love so that people from every walk of life may join the journey to follow him, as he leads us into your nearer presence.

Bless us now as we worship and learn and abide for a time in your love and care, we pray in Jesus' name.—Henry Fields

SERMON

Topic: Words and Feelings
TEXT: Prov. 15:4 REB

He came into the room with a smile and a brightness about him that was quite winsome. By previous agreement, those gathered with him had decided to tell him, on every occasion that particular morning, how ill he looked. As the morning progressed, he began to feel ill and before noon had to leave his work because he was too sick to continue.

It all began with a word. So much does. We commonly think of a word as the end product of a thought. It is. But once it us uttered, the word has a certain reflex action and returns to have its effect on the speaker, as well as the one spoken to.

We not only say things because we think them but we think things because we say them or hear them said.

A recent television "doctor" told his listeners that they should always say they are well and never speak of their suffering. They should always assert happiness and success and deny sorrow and failure. He promised that if they would do this, it would be unto them according to their assertion.

Frankly, that little speech turned me off at first. It seemed that listeners were being asked to play the major role in life of a hypocrite and liar. But when you look at that advice and ponder its ramifications for a while, you will discover that there is a smattering of truth in it. What the TV doctor had done was to glimpse the secret power of words.

Physically, a word is a sound vibration. Properly pitch a word, and it has the power to break fine crystal glass. Spiritually, a word also has its vibrations and affects the mind and feelings.

We think in words, especially when we think clearly. We even feel in words. Most of our desires and passions run in channels that have been worn in our brain by the repeated coming and going of certain words. There is sound psychology in saying that words can make us sick or well. Talk of our diseases, and we focus our energies on them in a negative manner, causing them to dominate us. Talk of wellness and health, and a positive power is focused on them, which will take the primary place in our attitudes and thoughts. Speak a positive and uplifting word to another person, and the power of that positive word will begin its work on that person, making him or her more positive. Speak a negative, depressing word to another, and that word will wilt the very spirit of the person to whom it is spoken.

Just as strong, bright, positive, encouraging words reinforce the one spoken to, they also fly back to the one speaking. In every one of them is a seed of feeling. It will fall within the garden of your own heart, as well as that of the other person, and produce a flower.

By the same token, if you produce with your words the expressions of sourness and bitterness, you will sow the briars of despair in the heart of another and increase the productivity of briars in your own heart and soul.

Choose your words wisely. Let them glorify God in you and others, as you plant word-seeds of thoughts and feelings that will produce a garden rather than a briar patch.—Henry Fields[16]

SUNDAY, JULY 2, 2006

Lectionary Message

Topic: Giving God's Way

TEXT: 2 Cor. 8:7–15

Other Readings: 2 Sam. 1:1, 17–27; Ps. 130; Mark 5:21–43

Few subjects in the pulpit generate more controversy than the subject of tithing or giving of offerings. Many people believe that the Church is simply out to take their money and that appeals for giving are actually manipulative and, for the preacher, self-serving. However, the Bible conveys a different perspective from this popular view.

How, then, shall we view the matter of giving? What is involved in giving God's way?

I. *Christian giving is consistent with spiritual abundance* (vv. 7–8). Paul observes here certain spiritual blessings that these Corinthian Christians enjoyed in abundance. He notes that they abounded in faith—the belief of the truth of the gospel. They were able instructors of others. They possessed abundant knowledge of God and his truth. They were diligent in

---

[16]*Rhythms of Life,* pp. 137–138 (text supplied by James W. Cox).

performing their Christian duties, and they were exemplary in their love. However, to that point, they had been careless in the matter of giving. Accordingly, the apostle calls them to be consistent in this matter, with the spiritual abundance they enjoyed otherwise.

The apostle calls giving a *gracious* work. In context with the spiritual blessings identified in these verses, he would have us to understand that giving expresses our awareness of God's grace to us. Thus we realize that when we give, we are acknowledging the undeserved favor we have received from God and are reflecting that favor back to him in sharing with others.

Paul does not press the matter heavy-handedly upon them, as if giving them a command. He realizes that their giving is a matter of their own conscience and must be given freely rather than under compulsion. Nonetheless, he has observed that the Macedonians (who had less ability to give than did the Corinthians) understood the privilege of sharing and had given liberally and sacrificially as a natural consequence of their love for God.

II. *Christian giving is modeled by the Lord Jesus* (v. 9). The supreme example of gracious giving is the Lord Jesus Christ. As an act purely of grace, he exchanged his riches for poverty, so that we might become partakers of the eternal riches that are rightfully his. The reference here clearly is to Jesus' incarnation. He left the splendors of his heavenly glory to take on human form and to live on Earth, with no place to lay his head. At his coming, he did not arrive in a palace, but rather in a manger. He did not live among the powerful, but rather associated with ordinary people at best and with sinners and outcasts at worst. Ultimately, through his sacrificial death on the cross, spiritually impoverished sinners are enabled to become heirs of the glorious riches possessed and given by God alone!

III. *Christian giving reflects Christian commitment* (vv. 10–12). In view of the grace expressed by the Lord Jesus, Christians should be motivated to give of their resources, as he did. Indeed, the Corinthian Christians had apparently understood this and a year previously had promised to give an offering toward the support of the saints (probably those in Judea who were suffering the effects of a famine). However, time had passed, and the offering had not been received. We are not told why this was the case. Perhaps their eager willingness on Sunday was replaced by giver's remorse on Monday. Perhaps they had unexpected expenses that laid urgent claim upon their funds. Perhaps they failed to see any urgency in keeping their commitment. Gently, Paul reminds them that intention must become reality and that the promises they had made should not be taken lightly. He also notes that keeping their pledge to give was to their advantage.

Some might fear that the requirement of this commitment exceeds their ability to give. Paul, however, explains that giving is to be "according to your means." God does not expect us to give beyond what he has provided for us. He does assess the value of our giving according to our ability, as measured by our resources.

IV. *Christian giving achieves equality in the body of Christ* (vv. 13–15). Paul's final line of thought concerning giving God's way implies the fundamental love ethic of Christians for one another—a love that seeks to share from one's own abundance with those who lack. He observes that such sharing is mutual and anticipates the possibility that one day the positions might be reversed. Today's giver may be tomorrow's recipient in this mutual relationship of loving concern.

The principle of shared supply is illustrated in the quotation from Exodus 16:18 (in context of vv. 13–36)—the account of God's provision of manna for Israel in the wilderness.

Equality of provision is clear from that text—though some gathered more and others less, the needs of all were met. Hoarding was futile, because the food would spoil on the second day. Underlying this equality of provision, however, was the more fundamental notion of sufficiency for all, as a matter of God's provision for his people.

The subject of giving may seem distasteful for some, but giving is truly one of the privileges of the Christian life. When we give, we display the glory of God who gives, and who, indeed, has blessed us with his indescribable gift!

ILLUSTRATIONS

Statistics on Christian giving are generally disheartening. Among church members of eleven primary Protestant denominations (or their historical antecedents) in the United States and Canada, per-member giving, as a percentage of income, was lower in 2000 than in either 1921 or 1933. In 1921, per-member giving as a percentage of income was 2.9 percent. In 1933, at the depth of the Great Depression, per-member giving grew to 3.3 percent. By 2000, after a half-century of unprecedented prosperity, giving had fallen to 2.6 percent.[1]

The principles of this text would suggest that such a low percentage indicates anemic spirituality, for our giving is an indicator of our awareness of the spiritual blessings we enjoy, our appreciation of the Lord Jesus, our level of Christian commitment, and our concern for Christian brothers and sisters.

It has been said that the measure of your generosity in giving is not in the amount you give but in the amount you keep for yourself. In Luke 21:1–4, we learn that Jesus one day saw the rich putting their gifts into the temple treasury. He also noted that a certain poor widow put in only two small copper coins. Certainly, the rich gave larger gifts than did the widow, and most people would be more impressed by the giving of the rich. Jesus, however, remarked that the widow put in more than all the others. They, he said, gave from their surplus—money left over after they had done as they wished. The poverty-stricken widow, however, put in all that she had to live on. She did not give from the leftovers; rather she gave sacrificially.—Robert Vogel

SERMON SUGGESTIONS

Topic: When the Bottom Falls Out

TEXT: Ps. 130

(1) We can cry out to God, even in the anguish of desperation. (2) We can believe God hears us, even in spite of our sins (vv. 3–4). (3) We can wait patiently for God's answer, even when immediate solutions seem necessary (vv. 5–6). (4) We can spread abroad faith, hope, and love, because we are assured of God's gracious salvation (vv. 7–8).

Topic: A Portrait of God's Love

TEXT: Hos. 11

(1) An electing love. (2) A molding love. (3) A disciplined love.—Earl C. Davis

---

[1]John L. Ronsvalle and Sylvia Ronsvalle, *The State of Church Giving Through 2000* (Champaign, Ill.: Empty Tomb, 2002), p. 40.

WORSHIP AIDS

CALL TO WORSHIP.   "The Lord is my light and my salvation—whom shall I fear? The Lord is the stronghold of my life—of whom shall I be afraid?" (Ps. 27:1 NIV).

INVOCATION.   As the Earth kissed by the sun finds renewing warmth, so let us be warmed by the rising of your spirit in us today. As the flower opens to receive nurturing power, so let us be open to the power of your grace, we pray. In the promise of forgiveness, we stand before you this morning. In the assurance of your faithfulness, we commit to follow your leading. In the hope of eternal life, we rest our souls with you, even as did those early disciples whom Christ taught to pray: [repeat the Lord's Prayer].—Henry Fields

OFFERTORY SENTENCE.   "Each person should give as he has decided for himself; there should be no reluctance, no sense of compulsion; God loves a cheerful giver" (2 Cor. 9:7 REB).

OFFERTORY PRAYER.   It's offering time, Father. Remind us that our responsibility is to give the first fruits of our labor, not the leftovers. If we are not giving our best, make us brave enough to begin, even now. We pray in Jesus' name.—Henry Fields

PRAYER.   In confession we come, Father. In our more thoughtful moments, we wonder how many times you have looked at us and loved us and wanted us to be filled with Christ's compassion and love for one another, but we were not.

We confess that at times we have felt too busy to answer the cry of another's need. Many times we have answered your call to us, as it was sounded through the cry of another, by saying that their problem was no concern of ours. The world bleeds, children starve, adulterers have no deep comfort in their homes, alcoholics know no salvation but another bottle to dull the remembrance of things past and present for another day, and we do not feel responsibility to them. Most deeply of all, Father, we confess that the cries of the afflicted are so frequent and the injustices of our world are so countless that we have even turned away from listening any longer to the outcry of pain and need. The constant cry for help has dulled our sensitivity and openness to hearing.

This morning, focus our eyes clearly upon the cross, where your love was so freely given. Renew within our hearts the love and compassion we have buried there beneath the many concerns we call our own. Break the bonds that have chained our hearts, and grant us a new dimension of compassion, love, and willingness to let Christ reach out through us to touch the world and make it whole again for those who cry out from the depths of their pain, lostness, struggle, and need. We pray in his name.—Henry Fields

SERMON

Topic: Born Again?

Text: John 3

Jesus lived in and talked about another world known only to those who experience a second birth—a spiritual birth.

I. *Incurably religious people.* The relics and records of all ancient civilizations indicate that people have always been religious. The persistent concern for things of the spirit in all parts of the world today points in the same direction. Nicodemus was a devout leader in the Jewish religion, as practiced in the time of Jesus. He was a Pharisee—a member of a religious order noted for its deep piety. If one sought the best men of the community, one looked among the Pharisees. However, by the time of Jesus, their religion had taken an unfortunate turn. God was sought in rules and regulations. For many of the group, the service of God was a mere form.

Nicodemus was an unusually sensitive and alert man. Familiarity with the laws and language of religion had not destroyed his questing spirit. His native curiosity, his deep sincerity, and his restless sense of need impelled him to seek out Jesus.

II. *Right question, wrong answer.* We have seen in recent years a new interest in religion. Leading universities have added courses of study in this field and have sought the services of outstanding specialists in theology. Billy Graham revivals have been a topic of common conversation, whereas Christianity was only grudgingly mentioned before. Books on religion pour from the presses, and popular magazines carry, without apology, articles having to do with the spiritual life.

Some have found God in spite of the shallowness of much of this talk and action. But they must confess that they have sometimes "used" God and have not honored him, that they have sometimes "explained" God without loving him.

Perhaps we should admire Nicodemus for coming privately to Jesus and for coming at night. Night discussions of the law were signs of deep religious enthusiasm. Furthermore, he spoke to Jesus with moving dignity and courtesy.

Nicodemus approached Christ and the mission of Christ in a factual manner. He inferred that Jesus was a teacher from God because Jesus did things that were impossible apart from divine help (John 3:2). Apparently, the Kingdom of God—a vital theme of Jewish belief— was the topic he intended to discuss.

But Jesus immediately shifted the discussion to a different basis (v. 3). What God is actually doing in the world is known only to those who have had their eyes opened so as to be able to see spiritually. The heart-meaning and importance of Christ for our world is accurately known only by those who have received their facts from God, by those who have been "born again" (v. 3). Otherwise, one cannot see, cannot get the idea of, or cannot experience the Kingdom of God.

III. *An answer you can see.* The mind of Nicodemus struck a snag on the matter of being born again. He continued to think in purely human terms. "How can one go through the birth process twice?" he asked.

In answer, Jesus repeated in more emphatic language what he had just said. He drew more sharply the contrast between natural birth and the "new birth." The first birth is only human. The second is from God—a spiritual birth. The first birth is accompanied by ceremonial defilement (from the Jewish viewpoint); the second is marked by cleansing. The first birth is characterized by weakness, the second by power. Though Jesus had been speaking to Nicodemus in earthly or symbolic terms, he did not understand.

Men like Nicodemus were supposed to be interested in "heavenly things" (v. 12). But such things were the XYZ's of the alphabet of truth, and Nicodemus had not understood the ABC's. How could one be expected to take the last step who had not taken the first?

There are those today who want to travel the last mile of faith before they begin the journey. They want all the questions answered and all problems solved before making any commitment.

Someone has rightly said, however, that we do not follow Jesus head first, but feet first. It is really the simplicities that call forth faith: the love of God, as reflected in the concern for our family; the righteousness of God, as stressed in a father's discipline; the grace of God, as magnified by the presence of a church where we live—all of these things start us toward God; they are earthly things that may lead us to heavenly things. No one is ready to understand the deep things of God until one acts on the simpler things.

IV. *The response required.* The response that God requires is the same for the brilliant Pharisee as for the unschooled man on the street. There must be willing obedience to what God requires and shows to be right and true.

It is then possible to know that through the immeasurable love of God, Jesus Christ came to save those who trust in him and to be assured that God has provided, through Christ, the way of salvation for all people (vv. 16–17).

On the eighty-second birthday of Dr. John R. Sampey, we young preachers in the seminary chapel heard this retired seminary president tell the moving story of his conversion. As a teenage lad, after years of confusion about the way of salvation and with a sense of guilt and need, he turned in the night to Christ, his eyes wet with tears, and said, "Lord Jesus, if I go down, I'll go down trusting you." Joy came to his heart, and from that time on, the reality of God was proved over and over in his life. God proves himself to those who put trust in his Son.

"God sent not his Son into the world to condemn the world; but that the world through him might be saved" (v. 17).—James W. Cox

SUNDAY, JULY 9, 2006
Lectionary Message

Topic: Perspective on Thorns
TEXT: 2 Cor. 12:2–10
Other Readings: 2 Sam. 5:1–5, 9–10; Ps. 48; Mark 6:1–13

Any gardener knows the pain of a thorn. It may be the painful prick from a prolific, aggravating weed. It could be the numbing sensation from the stab of a rose thorn. It may be the sensation of the entangling, flesh-tearing thorns of a wild blackberry bush.

In a passage that is thoroughly personal, Paul chose the metaphor of the thorn to speak of a life difficulty he experienced. He does not say what it was. Speculations have included such things as Jewish persecution, the lingering physical consequences of beatings he had received, chronic problems with his eyesight, or some difficulty with speaking. Knowing the specific problem is not critical to an understanding of the passage, or God would have made its identity clear. It is sufficient to realize that, humanly speaking, it was an undesirable condition.

Like Paul, we can expect to experience thorns in life. Furthermore, like Paul, we need to adopt God's perspective on thorns when they become part of our experience.

I. *When he has given us great privilege, God may give us thorns to keep us humble* (vv. 2–7). Though he speaks in the third person (vv. 1–5), Paul probably is speaking of himself. He recounts a unique experience as a recipient of divine revelation. He was caught up into the third heaven; words, he said, were inadequate to express what he heard and saw. The experience was truly one of great privilege, accorded to few people.

Because of the surpassing greatness of these revelations, to keep him from exalting himself he was given his thorn in the flesh. Although this is not stated, God was probably the one who gave the thorn to accomplish its stated beneficial effect of preventing conceit or pride. At the same time, Paul described it as a messenger of Satan, perhaps because it limited what he believed he might otherwise be capable of doing. Whatever Satan's role in the situation may have been, God's overarching providence always brings good out of difficult circumstances.

II. *Despite our prayers, God may choose not to remove thorns* (vv. 8–9). Three times Paul had asked God to remove the thorn. His prayers surely indicate that he saw his circumstance as a heavy affliction. Yet this was a prayer that God chose not to answer in the way that Paul desired. There is no indication that Paul's prayers were hindered by a lack of faith or an improper motive. Indeed, it is an instance of the fervent prayer of a righteous man. However, rather than grant his petition, God clearly indicates that his greater glory would be accomplished in denying Paul's request.

III. *When God leaves us with a thorn, he provides grace sufficient to bear it* (v. 9). It is striking that the God-given ability to bear the pain of a thorn is a matter of divine grace, one of undeserved favor. Moreover, that grace is provided in abundant and sufficient supply, so that the pain will not be unbearable. Although his grace and power could remove the thorn, it is the ability to bear it that God sometimes chooses to enable.

IV. *God's power is shown most perfectly in the weaknesses of our thorns* (v. 9). The Lord's grace was adequate for Paul in his weakness, precisely because divine power finds its full scope and strength *only in* human weakness. Furthermore, it is apparently a proportional thing: the greater our weakness, the more evident it is that our lives are lived in Christ's power and strength. Thus exists one of the great paradoxes of the Christian life: weakness and strength together. The occasion of our weakness is the occasion of his strength. When we humbly acknowledge our frailty or inability, we find that God accomplishes the extraordinary in and through us, and he alone and clearly deserves the credit!

V. *When we understand God's purposes for our thorns, we will be content to have them* (vv. 9–10). Armed with an understanding of God's good purposes for his thorn in the flesh, Paul can even speak of gladness and glory in his weakness. He can find contentment in weaknesses, insults, distresses, persecutions, and difficulties for Christ's sake, for he has learned that when he suffers such burdens, he is in a position to know, in experience, the strength that comes only from Christ. It is not a matter of an abnormal delight or pleasure in suffering. Rather, it is a way of seeing suffering as a means to a greater end—the manifest glory of God.

Essential to understanding the "why" of some unanswered prayers and the persistent presence of undesired affliction is a divine perspective on thorns. When we understand that thorns are there to serve God's perfect purposes, we will see them as other than intruders to be removed. We will see them, instead, as opportunities to draw close to God in humble dependence and to experience his power made perfect in our weakness.

ILLUSTRATIONS

Evangelist David Ring is a classic example of God's strength manifest in human weakness. From childhood, David has suffered from cerebral palsy. Besides the physical difficulties of the illness, he had to bear the cruelty of taunting remarks directed toward his limitations. He found love in his home, but early in life he was left an orphan. A man with a crushed spirit, unable to talk plainly, bearing the marks of a dreaded disease—and yet a man whom God has used to preach the gospel through his testimony to thousands of people. In David Ring's weakness, God's mighty power is seen.

There was a ten-year-old boy who decided to study judo, *despite* the fact that he had lost his left arm in a devastating car accident. The boy began lessons with an old Japanese judo master. The boy was doing well, so he couldn't understand why, after three months of training, the master had taught him only one move.

"Master," the boy finally said, "shouldn't I be learning more moves?"

"I realize that this is the only move you know, but this may be the only move you'll ever need to know," the master replied.

Not quite understanding, but believing in his teacher, the boy kept training.

Several months later, the master took the boy to his first tournament. Surprising himself, the boy easily won his first two matches. The third match proved to be more difficult, but after some time, his opponent became impatient and charged. The boy deftly used his one move to win the match. Still amazed by his success, the boy was now in the finals. This time, his opponent was bigger, stronger, and more experienced. For a while, the boy appeared to be overmatched. Concerned that the boy might get hurt, the referee called a time-out. He was about to stop the match when the master intervened.

"No," the master insisted. "Let him continue."

As soon as the match resumed, his opponent rushed in on him. Instantly, the boy used his move to pin him. The boy had won the match and the tournament. He was now the champion.

On the way home, the boy and master reviewed every move in each and every match. Then the boy summoned the courage to ask what was really on his mind.

"Master, how could I possibly have won that tournament with only one move?"

The master turned to the boy and answered, "You won for two reasons. First, you have been able to master the most difficult throw in all of judo. And second, the only known defense for that move that you have mastered is for your opponent to grab your left arm."[2]

The boy's biggest weakness had become his biggest strength.—Robert Vogel

SERMON SUGGESTIONS

Topic: Great Is the Lord

TEXT: Ps. 48

(1) God's work in the world is an occasion of praise (vv. 1–3). (2) The evidence of God's work may give rise to fear (vv. 4–8). (3) Careful pondering of the heart of God will give a message for the ages (vv. 9–14).

Topic: Almost Too Late—But Saved

TEXT: Luke 23:32–43

(1) The awful predicament. (2) The ardent plea: made in recognition of his guilt; in light of Christ's forgiveness; while there was still time. (3) The abundant promise: a glorious future; a glorious fellowship.—Hardy R. Denham Jr.

---

[2]"Strength and Weakness" is available from http://members.tripod.com/ ~ robertwells/judo.html; accessed Nov. 16, 2004.

WORSHIP AIDS

CALL TO WORSHIP.   "I will give thanks in the great congregation: I will praise thee among much people" (Ps. 35:18).

INVOCATION.   High thou art and holy, too, God of covenant history. We extol thee; we adore thee, God of all true liberty.—E. Lee Phillips

OFFERTORY SENTENCE.   "Whosoever will save his life shall lose it: and whosoever will lose his life for my sake shall find it" (Matt. 16:25).

OFFERTORY PRAYER.   Because you have given so much to us, O God, we have life, even abundant life. Now help us yield it all up to you that others might find that life.

PRAYER.   O thou that dost pity our infirmity and experience sympathy for us, and behold, and spare, and love, and forgive, what need have we to recite our manifold wickedness and transgressions? It is all before thee. For they who transgress are as shrubs that are full of thorns to men who handle them. We are filled with spines, and yet thou art, as a gardener, constantly tending and pruning us. We pierce thy hands with our sins. We are every day grieving thee. As they who are vulgar in our presence offend us, as they who are rude and boisterous disturb the peace and the quietude of refinement, as they who are selfish are hateful to the beneficent, as the lowly seem to the proud wondrously uncouth, so we, in our unformed nature, are to thee. And yet, with unfolding and enfolding tenderness, wondrous beyond all human conception, thou art patient and dost love unloveliness and dost fashion uncouthness. Thou art the Teacher. We are the poor scholars, learning slowly, still refusing to practice what we learn, too often. And yet, we live by the great bounty of thy sufferance. And thou sparest us, though the work is slow, because there are many summers yet. Thou art still bringing to bear a thousand influences that gradually ameliorate, though we will not hear thy voice. And thou art not judging us as we are now but as thou seest that we shall be when thy work is completed. What strange beauty far off dawns to thine eye behind our ugliness! How wondrous must we seem that are now all blemish, seen as we shall appear when, without blemish or imperfection, thou shalt present us to the throne of thy Father! O wonder-working Savior, still abide with us; still bear our infirmities; still forgive our sins; still give us joy for sorrow—such joy as will lead us above secular sorrow. And grant that the life we now live in the flesh we may live by faith in the Son of God.

We pray that thou wilt bless thy cause in all places of the Earth. Remember our own land. Quicken the hearts of thy people, that they may give liberally and labor abundantly for the spread of knowledge, of intelligence, of virtue. We pray that thou wilt still redeem this land from coarse secular prosperity and build it up in a holy faith and in the purity of the gospel.—Henry Ward Beecher

SERMON

Topic: Who Is Jesus?

TEXT: John 4 (esp. v. 42)

A man said, "I don't go for this business of sending missionaries to people who have other religions. Why not leave them to their own faith? One religion is as good as another."

The one to whom he spoke tactfully pointed out that all people of whatever race or religion probably have some understanding of God, as Paul indicated in the Epistle to the Romans, but that those with a better understanding of God and his ways have a responsibility to those whose knowledge is inferior. As to whether one religion is as good as another, it was shown that some people have sacrificed their own children because of their religion, have eaten their enemies, and actually made sexual orgies a part of their worship experience.

The Samaritans were once a populous race, numbering in the multiplied thousands. They lived in the middle part of Palestine, between Judea and Galilee. Today, not more than a few hundred of these people remain. After Sargon II deported thousands of Israelites in 722–721 B.C., colonies of non-Jews were brought into Samaria from Babylonia, Syria, Elam, and elsewhere. Those deported were chiefly craftsmen and members of the ruling class.

Thousands of the peasant class were left behind. The result was a mixed population that did not observe the Hebrew standards of racial and religious purity. Serious trouble eventually arose when the Samaritans were not permitted to help in the rebuilding of the Jerusalem Temple or allowed to worship there as they had done for centuries. As a result, they built their own temple on Mount Gerizim and developed their own ways of worship. Both Jews and Samaritans felt themselves separately to be the true Israel of God and inheritors of the divine promises. They cast out each other. Therefore, it is accurately stated: "Jews have no dealings with the Samaritans" (John 4:9).

The whole story of Jesus' dealing with the Samaritan woman indicates quite a contrast between the reception given Jesus by the Samaritans and that given by the Jews. It reminds us that the one thankful man out of a group of ten lepers healed by Jesus was a Samaritan and that the hero of one of the most beautiful and compelling parables about Jesus was a good Samaritan.

I. *The water of life.* As Jesus and his disciples were passing through Samaria, they came at noontime to Jacob's well, near the city of Sychar. While Jesus waited for his disciples to return from the city with food, a Samaritan woman came to draw water.

Jesus asked for a drink, and the woman was startled. She looked at him carefully. Her eyes fastened on the tassel on his robe, which marked him as a Jew.

Jesus had violated two taboos, strictly observed by the Jewish people: he had spoken to a woman in public—and a stranger at that—and he had been friendly toward a Samaritan.

Actually, the one asking for water should have been the woman, for Jesus brought in his person the gift of God—living water. The woman, out of deference to her ancestor Jacob, had walked a distance to get water from this well rather than from the spring that was easily accessible in the city. It seemed to her, then, that Jesus was placing himself above even Jacob, offering water to be preferred above what was itself a preference.

Then Jesus made the telling comparison: whoever drinks from the water of Jacob's well will thirst again, but whoever drinks of the water that he himself gives will never thirst. Then the woman, with but a glimmer of understanding of what Jesus was talking about, asked for this water.

Did you ever puzzle about the secret of courage and endurance shown by some people who seem to have little to live for? Sometimes a moist ant heap can be found in the midst of a parched, drought-stricken land. Once such phenomena were "carefully investigated," so we are told,[3] and scientists discovered that the ants had sunk into the earth a shaft sixty-five feet long, "down to a perennial spring," and the ant population stayed busy through the night traveling up and down the shaft carrying their little loads of water to the surface. Thus they moistened their "little fields of fungus crops" and stayed alive. Even so, if you probe carefully, the secret of inner vitality may not be a secret at all. The person simply has a spiritual source of strength.

II. *The nature of God.* When the woman expressed her desire for this gift of God (the water of which Jesus spoke), he led right into the practical aspect of her need. Her life showed a callousness toward moral demands. When Jesus saw to the heart of it, the woman, astonished, recognized him as a prophet. She then revealed her concept of religion as very much a hand-me-down matter. Obviously, she gave lip service to her faith, but she ignored the ethical demands of it. Jesus indicated that he held to the revelation of God as it had come to and through the Jewish nation, but he lifted the subject completely above custom, whether of the Samaritans or of the Jews.

When he said, "God is Spirit" (v. 24 RSV), he took the matter beyond places, times, buildings, and ceremonies, and showed that worship is determined by the very nature of God himself. If God to us is not Spirit, then we may find ourselves prostrate before Venus, Mars, Jupiter, or Mammon, as they appear among us with modern aliases. It is difficult for us to think except in terms of what we already know and deeply desire.

Both the Jews and the Samaritans believed that God is a person. So the Bible teaches, and we believe it, too. But do we not sometimes limit him because we do not understand *how* he is a person? In our narrow view of God, his face has the features of our own race; his thoughts are particularly adaptable to our own political ideas; he becomes a sponsor of our own ambitions. But God is Spirit, as well as person, and we cannot draw a selfish circle around his love, his purposes, and his outreach.

III. *Real worship.* When John Wesley, with his heart strangely warmed, was denied the privilege of preaching in the churches of England, he took to the fields, and in large outdoor gatherings preached the gospel of Jesus Christ to the thousand who would never darken the door of a church building. He went where the people were and where the need was greatest. Lecky, the historian, said that Wesley saved England from revolution in the eighteenth century. Wesley acknowledged, however, that only a few years before he would have considered it a sin to preach anywhere but in a church.

Jesus emphasized to the woman of Samaria that it is not the place of worship that is important but the fact and reality of worship. The greatest lack in our worship efforts is that of faith in the power of the Holy Spirit.

IV. *Christ and divine truth.* The Samaritans looked for a messiah, known to them as "the returning one," whose role it would be to renew the worship on Mount Gerizim, gather together Jews and Gentiles, and rule in glory over them. But the woman made no reference to that exception; she spoke of the messiah as one who would come to "tell us all things," which is to say, *to tell the truth.* Jesus acknowledged that he was this Messiah.

---

[3]Arthur John Gossip, *The Hero in Thy Soul* (New York: Charles Scribner's Sons, 1933), p. 153.

Throughout the Gospel of John, Jesus is pictured as truth manifested in human flesh. Indeed, Jesus told us in terms that we can understand what we need to know about God for our salvation, our service, and our happiness.

All truth is his truth, whether the truth of religion, the truth of government, the truth of economic life, or the truth of science. None of us, eager to know the relevant facts about life and the universe, need ever be afraid to face and to evaluate truth wherever it is found. A Christian's real concern, however, should be to see to it that in one's own thinking and affections, Christ himself, who is the way, the truth, and the life, stands as the very embodiment of truth.

V. *Personal religion.* When the disciples of Jesus returned from the city, the woman left and made her way into the city, saying, "come, see a man, which told me all things that ever I did: is not this the Christ?" (v. 29). The conversation of Jesus with the woman not only made her a believer, it made her a witness of what she had heard and experienced.

This personal evangelism resulted in an astounding religious awakening. Even the statements of an unreliable witness found acceptance. So convinced were the Samaritans of the uniqueness and truth of Jesus and his mission that they persuaded him to stay with them for two days. When they had talked personally with him, their skeptical hope was confirmed by reasoned faith and personal experience. They said to the woman, "Now we believe, not because of your saying: for we have heard him ourselves, and know that this is indeed the Christ, the Savior of the world."

There is no substitute for a personal faith and experience of religion. Thomas Chalmers, the noted Scottish preacher of another generation, was for a time a brilliant lecturer who talked of things of which he had read and studied but not experienced, until a warm and welcome change took place in his heart. He said of this, "Mathematician as I was, I had forgotten two magnitudes—the shortness of time and the vastness of eternity." From that time forward, his ministry demonstrated a new effectiveness, and he experienced a new joy.

The great need of all of us is to be able to say with Job of old: "I have heard of you by the hearing of the ear: but now my eye sees you" (Job 42:5). Jesus Christ accepted, loved, and obeyed is the way to this tremendous transforming experience.—James W. Cox

SUNDAY, JULY 16, 2006
Lectionary Message

Topic: Salvation, the Work of God
TEXT: Eph. 1:3–14
Other Readings: 2 Sam. 6:1–5, 12b–19; Ps. 24; Mark 6:14–29

Salvation is truly a many-splendored thing! As a doctrine, it is found virtually throughout the Scriptures, beginning with the Garden of Eden and culminating in the last times. Its transactions are pictured in the ceremonial law of the Old Testament and explained in the theological strains of the New Testament. As a personal experience, salvation is what transforms us from being dead in sin to being alive to God. Salvation enables us to be at peace with God, when we once were his enemies.

The splendor of salvation, as conveyed in this passage, is that salvation is the accomplishment of God alone. Eleven verses, dense with theological language and concepts, describe a number of transactions involved in our salvation. Although the entire theology of salvation is not given here, the transactions identified cover the breadth of the doctrine, from initiation to consummation. Furthermore, this passage, perhaps uniquely and in significant detail, expresses the involvement of each member of the triune godhead in the glorious plan of salvation. In short, this text teaches that salvation is the work of the triune God alone.

I. *Our salvation was initiated by God the Father* (vv. 3–6). Speaking generally, Paul notes that God has blessed us with every spiritual blessing in Christ. Such a statement is broadly inclusive, expressing the fullness of spiritual benefit provided to us by God's grace. More particularly, however, God the Father is portrayed as the One who planned and initiated our salvation. A number of specific expressions of his role are given. First, he chose us for salvation in Christ before the foundation of the world. Before we were created (even before sin had entered human experience), God, who sees the end from the beginning, chose those who are saved for redemption. His redemptive purposes include setting us apart to himself as holy (positive) and making us to be without blame (negative). Second, he predestined us, in the kind intentions of his gracious, sovereign will, to become his adopted children. As his children, we enjoy the privileges of family standing. Third, the ultimate outcome of God's redemptive plan is that the recognition of God's grace in saving us should call forth abundant praise to his glory.

II. *Our salvation was accomplished by God the Son* (vv. 7–12). The plan initiated by the Father required the redemptive work of the Son, which was accomplished at Calvary's cross. From this work of the Son, many blessings proceed. First, Paul refers to that work as *redemption*—an action that set slaves or prisoners free. The analogy is clear: in Christ, we who were captive in the bonds of sin have been released from that bondage. The price to secure that release was the very lifeblood of Jesus. Second, his redemptive work includes forgiveness of our sins. By this abundant outpouring of his grace, we are released from the guilt of our sins. Third, in Christ's redemption we are granted insight and wisdom to understand his glorious purposes and to act in accordance with them. This insight enables us to grasp God's plan for the ages, as it is summed up in Christ. Finally, beyond all this, Paul says that in Christ we have also obtained an inheritance—the gift of the Father to his children. The specifics of the inheritance are not identified here, but surely they would include the blessings of heaven and eternal life.

III. *Our salvation was sealed by God the Holy Spirit* (vv. 13–14). The role of the third member of the triune godhead is discharged on the occasion of our believing in the gospel of Christ, when we hear the message of the gospel wedded to faith. Specifically, he seals the transaction. The imagery of the seal, as it was used in the ancient world, is instructive, as it is applied to the Holy Spirit. An official might place his seal on a document to guarantee its genuineness. Or a seal could be placed on goods to indicate ownership and to ensure protection from theft.

Not only is the Holy Spirit the One who seals our salvation but the One is also called the *pledge of our inheritance*—a term given as assurance of our full and final redemption. The word was used in commerce to refer to a deposit on a purchase, giving assurance that full payment would follow. The term also was used to refer to an engagement ring. As an engagement ring is given as a pledge of good faith and a promise that marriage will follow, so also the Holy Spirit is given to us as assurance that God will bring to fulfillment all aspects of his glorious plan of redemption, particularly those that lie in the future before us.

From beginning to end, salvation is of the Lord! It is his work completely. He devised the plan, implemented it in his elective grace, paid for it with the blood of the Son, and sealed the covenant with us by his Holy Spirit—all to the praise of his matchless glory!

ILLUSTRATIONS

The Holy Spirit is said to be a pledge of our inheritance (v. 14). This pledge may be compared to the earnest money paid on a real estate transaction. When a buyer decides that he or she wants a particular property, a written offer is made, accompanied by earnest money. The money is a sign that the offer is serious and is made in good faith. It gives assurance to the seller that the buyer truly intends to purchase the property and that when the terms of the agreement have been fulfilled, the remainder of the sale price will be paid. In effect, it promises that the rest will be forthcoming. This analogy is intended to show that the Holy Spirit dwelling in us serves to assure us that God will follow through on his promise to complete our salvation, with its hope of eternal life.

The Holy Spirit is identified as sealing the work of salvation for the believer (v. 13). In the ancient world, a seal could be placed on goods to indicate ownership and to ensure protection from theft. The imagery of the seal is used here to indicate that the Holy Spirit serves to mark us as God's own and to protect us.

When I was a student in seminary, I worked in the stockroom of a department store—one of several in a regional chain of stores. Merchandise was delivered to each location from a central warehouse by a company-owned trucking firm. When a freight delivery arrived at the store, the driver of the truck would present me with a bill of lading. On that bill was a number, corresponding to a seal band that was attached to the latch on the truck's freight door. The first thing I was required to do was to verify that the number on the seal corresponded to the number on the bill of lading. Then I would break the seal, so that we could open the truck door and remove our freight. After our goods were unloaded, I would sign the bill of lading, close the door, and attach a new numbered seal to the latch. This cycle would be repeated at each stop the truck made on its delivery route.

One day, I asked a driver why this procedure was required. He told me that a few years earlier there had been a theft ring involving several drivers for the trucking operation. Between stops, these drivers had been taking some of the freight from the trucks—stealing it. The seal procedure was established, therefore, to secure the goods in the truck between stops. If a seal was broken when the truck arrived, or if the seal numbers did not match, it was an indication that the security of the load had been compromised.—Robert Vogel

SERMON SUGGESTIONS

Topic: When You Come to Church

Text: Ps. 24

(1) Remember your Creator (vv. 1–2). (2) Think of what God requires and provides (vv. 3–6): character (v. 4); salvation as needed (v. 5). (3) Celebrate God's glorious, mighty presence (vv. 7–10).

Topic: Doors into Life

Text: Matt. 11:28–29

(1) Come. (2) Take. (3) Learn. (4) Find.—Charles R. Brown

WORSHIP AIDS

CALL TO WORSHIP.   "Arise, O lord, and come to thy resting-place, thou and the ark of thy power. Let thy priests be clothed in righteousness and let thy loyal servants shout for joy" (Ps. 132:8–9 NEB).

INVOCATION.   O God of light, illumine our way. O God of hope, strengthen our resolve. O God of truth, edify our souls, that we might not only be hearers of the word but doers also, through Christ our Lord.—E. Lee Phillips

OFFERTORY SENTENCE.   "They gave according to their means, as I can testify, and beyond their means, of their own free will" (2 Cor. 8:3 RSV).

OFFERTORY PRAYER.   On this beautiful Lord's Day, we give you thanks for the opportunities we have had this week to be stewards of love, grace, compassion, and patience.

Friend to friend, neighbor to neighbor, community to community, we have extended and joined the hand of servanthood.

Forgive us Lord because we sometimes forget how blessed we are in the face of our immediate inconveniences. We know there are people in your world who cannot imagine even the cool of a shade tree, much less multitudes of trees to cut down; those who cannot imagine enough food to eat, much less enough food to throw away; those who cannot imagine a home, much less one that is adequately heated and cooled.

Help us to remember there are always greater needs to be met, and the opportunities you give us to be your hands and heart are limitless. Let us never lack the courage or the will to do your work.

May these offerings today serve as a reminder to us that our call to stewardship is not weekly at this hour, but daily at your side.[4]

PRAYER.   Father, thank you for today—fresh with sparkling dew, bright with the splendor of the morning sun, and alive with all the livingness of your perennial spirit.

May we receive this day thoughtfully, graciously, and tenderly.

Thank you—for the love of family and the meaning of home, for the joy of good health, for the enthusiasm of youth, for the wisdom of mature years, for the insatiable thirst for the good, the true, and the beautiful, for this season of refreshment to restore body, mind, and spirit, for your Word through which life's meaning is revealed and we are nurtured, for vacations that refresh and help to restore a healthy perspective to year-round tasks, for your love persevering through disappointment, loneliness, failure, and frustration, for the promise of a new Heaven and a new Earth in the presence of the disintegration of the present order.

Oh, to be your person in all the relationships of our every day—as Jesus was. This is our calling! Do not give up on us, O God; call us again and again. In life or in death, may we be faithful to our high calling to be your sons and daughters.—John Thompson

SERMON
Topic: Why Is Christ Our Authority?
TEXT: John 5 (esp. v. 24)

Two men sat together on the bus en route to work. The last time they rode together, they had talked about religion. One of the men had modestly declared his faith in Jesus Christ, saying

---

[4]Deborah Griffin, July 18, 2004 (following the summer storms of 2004).

that he had committed his life to the teaching of Jesus Christ. The other man had thoughtfully nodded his head and listened. This time, the man who had listened was full of questions. "How does Jesus differ from Mohammed, Buddha, or Confucius? Many points of their doctrine were evidently good. Isn't Jesus one among many great teachers?"

I. *Christ challenges custom.* Our Lord accepted no situation in life as necessarily perfect. And he left no situation exactly as he found it. He came into the world that had organized itself into a condition of opposition to God. Sin and its influences were shot through life from top to bottom. Secular life was corrupt. Religious life was a pretense. Many were willing to defend the existing political order as indispensable.

Thus Jesus was often in conflict. There was nothing in the political domain sympathetic with what Jesus was and did. However, the conflict came by way of the religious realm. The political was relatively indifferent to Jesus, but the religious was actively hostile and used the political to further its own purposes.

Jesus condemned sin where it was most despicable. He thrust the surgical knife where it hurt the most—in the heart of the religious life.

Everything was neatly organized. The guardians of religion had a pat answer for every moral question. They had taken fairly simple religious rules and expanded, split, and subdivided them until nothing was left to faith and imagination.

There, for example, stood the noble Sabbath law, given by God in his mercy for human good. But the original law had become overgrown with stipulations that took away its life. At one point and then another, Jesus stripped the heavenly truth of these gaudy parasites. He saw a lame man wanting to be healed. Too many years and days had passed while the man lay in his wretchedness. One more day was too long. Jesus healed him on the spot. And it was the Sabbath! Furthermore, Jesus ordered the healed man to pick up his pallet and carry it home.

That was too much for the law lovers to take. They had their rules, and one of the rules said that it was wrong to carry a burden, such as a pallet, on the Sabbath day. "This was why the Jews used to persecute Jesus, because he did things like this on the Sabbath" (John 5:16 Goodspeed).

We are willing to "let Jesus live" if he will approve the hollow things as they are. But we seek, as it were, to slay the Jesus who would interfere with our entrenched customs, our "glorious traditions," and our selfish interests.

II. *This is authority.* Jesus explained his position. The Father did not quit working on the Sabbath, so why should the Son? (v. 17). As Philo, the Jewish philosopher and interpreter, and various rabbis later recognized, such works were quite different from his labors of creation from which God rested on the seventh day.

Jesus' opponents saw in this only blasphemy. By breaking the Sabbath rules and by calling God "Father," Jesus had, as they saw it, made himself equal with God. To the Jews that meant a separation from God in which Jesus was acting as if he were God and could do with the law as he pleased.

But Jesus carried his explanation further (v. 19). He did not act independently of God. He knew God and God's will directly and acted accordingly.

This tells us a great deal as to what our attitude should be toward Jesus. If we try to worship Jesus and make him Lord of our lives without recognizing him as God's totally obedient Son, then we are guilty of idolatry. But if we worship God and find God's will for us as we worship and obey Jesus, then our devotion is true and right. To the rich young ruler, Jesus said, "Why do you call me good? No one is good but God alone" (Mark 10:18 RSV). This he said, not to deny his divine sonship but to turn the young man's mind to God—the source of all goodness.

Therefore, Jesus Christ is our authority because he speaks for God the Father. Because he does speak for his Father, he can say, "Heaven and earth shall pass away, but my words shall not pass away" (Matt. 24:35).

In our larger Scripture lesson, the authority of Jesus is supported in three ways, according to Professor William Barclay: (1) Jesus claimed to be the Son of Man. That title did not refer to his humanity but to his generous, humane role as the Chosen One of God. (2) Jesus' miracle of healing the paralyzed man was, in itself, a sign and claim that Jesus was Messiah. (3) Jesus' repeated claim to raise and judge the dead indicated his high mission, because in Old Testament times only God can raise the dead, and only God has the right to judge.[5]

III. *Human experience is under his authority.* The authority of Jesus Christ extends over the entire human experience. No part of our pilgrimage escapes him.

He has "the words of eternal life" (John 6:68). The mysteries of redemption we know because of what he was and did while here on Earth and because of what he is and does today in the lives of those who put their trust in him. Through Christ, we have salvation—release from judgment and transition from death to life (John 5:24).

The man who had been a slave to sin at times felt yearnings to be clean and good, but he was bound by physical infirmity on the outside and held down by a weight of guilt inside. Good intentions were beaten back by constant discouragement. At last, he accepted the good news of what God has done for the world in Christ and of what he will do for anyone.

Too often, the appreciation of what our Lord has power to do stops at this point. His salvation we accept, but we are slow to see that the authority of Christ reaches over every relationship and every practice in our lives. It touches our home, our friends, our work, our play, our attitudes toward other people and toward ourselves, our moral behavior, and our worship. Thus right living, dedicated talents, and self-denying love are a part of our salvation, too.

Every aspect of our salvation is under the authority of Christ, including our final destiny. "I have the keys of death" (Rev. 1:18 RSV).—James W. Cox

SUNDAY, JULY 23, 2006
Lectionary Message

Topic: When God Makes a Promise

TEXT: 2 Sam. 7:1–14a

Other Readings: Ps. 89:20–37; Eph. 2:11–22; Mark 6:30–34, 53–56

One of the prominent themes in all of Scripture is that of *covenant.* God periodically makes a promise, binding himself to a course of action or disposition. He made a covenant with Noah, pledging not to destroy the Earth with another flood. He made a covenant promise to Abraham, assuring him an inheritance of land, progeny arising to become a great nation, and

---

[5]William Barclay, *The Gospel of John,* Vol. 2, *The Daily Study Bible* (Edinburgh: The Saint Andrew Press, 1956), pp. 182–185.

peculiar blessing upon him and, through him, upon the whole world. God entered into covenant commitment with the nation of Israel at Mt. Sinai in the Mosaic Covenant. In the Deuteronomic Covenant, God gave Israel assurances of blessing in the Promised Land if they obeyed him and the withdrawal of blessing if they disobeyed.

Second Samuel 7 contains yet another of those covenants. This one is made personally with King David, and it concerned the assurance that God would secure David's dynasty on the throne of Israel.

I. *We may wish to do something to honor God* (vv. 1–7). David had labored long but had arrived at a point of significant achievement in his life. The humble shepherd boy had become the king of Israel. Behind him were the trying days of fleeing for his life from the insanely jealous King Saul. Upon Saul's death, he had succeeded in securing the allegiance of the nation and had led Israel to a point of prominence and security among the nations. At the time of this passage, the nation was at peace. The man after God's own heart was ruling effectively as God's anointed ruler over his theocratic kingdom.

David noted that he lived in a glorious palace in his capital city, Jerusalem. In stark contrast, God's earthly dwelling place—the place in which the Ark of the Covenant was located— was a modest tent. And so David resolved to honor God by building a temple—a permanent and magnificent place of dwelling for him in Jerusalem. Nathan, God's prophet, initially commended David for his plan to so honor God.

God, however, told Nathan that he had a different plan in mind. David was not to be the one to build his temple.

II. *God may choose, instead, to do something for us* (vv. 8–14a). When God does something for us, it will be a grand display of his grace and glory. The surprise that God had in store was that David would not build a house for him; rather, he would build a house for David. In the words of a covenant, God would bind himself to bless David in this fashion.

(a) *God elevated David from shepherd to king* (v. 8). First, God rehearsed things he had already done, by his grace, for David. Those blessings are quickly summed up in the mention of his elevation from the pasture to the palace, from caring for sheep to leading God's chosen nation. The emphatic "I" of the Lord's words underscores the fact that these blessings were intentional and divine. That they were bestowed upon David, the Lord's *servant*, is a striking act of divine condescension.

(b) *God gave David victory over his enemies and promised to make his name great* (v. 9). From his victory over Goliath in his early youth, through his days of trial at the hands of Saul and in his conquests in his early reign over Israel, David's victories had resulted from God's intervention. He had protected David from harm on many occasions, and through these many trying experiences had made David's reputation strong. As God had promised Abraham, he pledged to make David's name great in the Earth. Even the very next chapter (2 Sam. 8) recounts yet another example of this divine enablement in battle and the resultant spread of his fame.

(c) *God promised to establish Israel in security under David's rule* (v. 10). To Abraham God had promised the land. However, he lived in that land as a pilgrim and a stranger. Eventually, his descendants moved to Egypt rather than remain in the Promised Land. Led out of Egypt by Moses in the Exodus and led into the land by Joshua in the Conquest, Israel had begun to realize the promise. However, in the Conquest the people failed to drive out the

Canaanites, and consequently they were troubled by them through the period of the Judges and the early monarchy. Under David's reign, however, God would bring about a stability, in which the foes within the land and surrounding it would be vanquished.

(d) *God promised that David would be succeeded on the throne by his own descendants* (vv. 10–11). The house that God promised to build for David was not a material structure; rather, it was a dynasty. His predecessor, Saul, established a dynasty of one generation. Due to his sin, God decreed that the kingdom would be taken from him and his heirs (cf. 1 Sam. 15). This, however, would not be the case with David. He would be succeeded by a son, and successive generations of kings would also be of his descent. Indeed, this kingdom dynasty would endure forever. One might question the eternal duration of this promise, inasmuch as the dynasty of David came to a close with the destruction of Jerusalem and the capture of King Jehoiachin in 586 B.C. However, the ultimate Anointed One—Jesus Christ—is shown by Matthew to be of the house of David, and the writer of Hebrews asserts that Jesus is the final and eternal heir to the throne of David.

(e) *God promised to establish a unique relationship with David's descendants on the throne* (vv. 12–14a). Unique to the kings of Israel in David's lineage is their relationship to God. He would be as a father to them, and they as his sons. Again, the writer of Hebrews makes clear that this reference is ultimately messianic; Jesus Christ himself is the fulfillment of God's promise to David.

A true servant seeks only to do things to honor his or her master. The surprise is that the Lord, our Master, has graciously done all things for us.—Robert Vogel

ILLUSTRATIONS

PROMISES FROM GOD.   A promise from God is a statement we can depend on with absolute confidence. Here are twelve promises for the Christian to claim:

1. God's presence: "I will never leave thee." (Heb. 13:5)
2. God's protection: "I am thy shield." (Gen. 15:1)
3. God's power: "I will strengthen thee." (Isa. 41:10)
4. God's provision: "I will help thee." (Isa. 41:10)
5. God's leading: "And when He putteth forth His own sheep, He goeth before them." (John 10:4)
6. God's purposes: "I know the thoughts that I think toward you, saith the Lord, thoughts of peace, and not of evil." (Jer. 20:11)
7. God's rest: "Come unto Me, all ye that labor and are heavy laden, and I will give you rest." (Matt. 11:28)
8. God's cleansing: "If we confess our sins, He is faithful and just to forgive us our sins, and to cleanse us from all unrighteousness." (1 John 1:9)
9. God's goodness: "No good thing will He withhold from them that work uprightly." (Ps. 84:11)
10. God's faithfulness: "The Lord will not forsake His people for His great name's sake." (1 Sam. 12:22)
11. God's guidance: "The meek will He guide." (Ps. 25:9)

12. God's wise plan: "All things work together for good to them that love God." (Rom. 8:28)[6]

God's Loving Kindness
Awake, my soul, to joyful lays,
And sing thy great Redeemer's praise;
He justly claims a song from me,
His loving kindness, oh, how free!
He saw me ruined by the fall,
Yet loved me notwithstanding all;
He saved me from my lost estate,
His loving kindness, oh, how great!
Tho' num'rous hosts of mighty foes,
Tho' earth and hell my way oppose,
He safely leads my soul along, His loving kindness, oh, how strong!
When trouble, like a gloomy cloud,
Has gathered thick and thundered loud,
He near my soul has always stood,
His loving kindness, oh how good!
—Samuel Medley[7]

SERMON SUGGESTIONS

Topic: God, on the Way to the Christ
TEXT: Ps. 89:20–37
(1) God chose David and promised him a victorious future (vv. 20–21). (2) God promised to intervene in times of crisis (vv. 22–28). (3) God's promise would reach beyond David's lifetime (vv. 29–37).

Topic: The Living Christ
TEXT: Heb. 15:8
Jesus Christ is the same today: (1) in authority, (2) on power, (3) in love.

WORSHIP AIDS

CALL TO WORSHIP.   "O come, let us sing unto the Lord; let us make a joyful noise to the rock of our salvation" (Ps. 95:1).

INVOCATION.   As we inquire in your temple, O Father, we are reminded of your mercies that have been ever of old: you have been our dwelling place in all generations. Before the mountains were brought forth or ever you had formed the Earth and the sea, from everlasting to everlasting you are God.

---

[6]*Our Daily Bread,* Jan. 1, 1985.
[7]Source unknown.

As we inquire, we are reminded of your mighty acts through your people, Israel, and your mighty Word proclaimed in Jesus, the Messiah.

As we inquire, we are told of an amazing grace by which we live and move and have our being.

For all your goodness to us and to all peoples, we praise you: Father, Son, and Holy Spirit.—John M. Thompson

OFFERTORY SENTENCE.   "Nay; but I will verily buy it of thee at a price; neither will I offer unto the Lord my God that which cost me nothing" (2 Sam. 24:24).

OFFERTORY PRAYER.   We do not give or get, Lord. We give because we have got. In thanksgiving and praise, we bring our offerings. In thanksgiving and praise, we offer ourselves, through Jesus Christ.

PRAYER.   Almighty God—holy, powerful, loving, good. We thank you for yourself whom we have come to know in love—love expressed in generous gifts, love revealed in your Son, Jesus, who called you "Father."

Father of tender mercies, some of us are bruised and battered; we plead for the healing balm of your Spirit. Some of us are anxious and overly ambitious; we ask for peaceful satisfaction in doing your will. Some of us are concerned about family and friends; we seek comfort in the sense of your presence.

Father of forgiving grace, we have sinned against you—your goodness and self-giving love. We have sought to go our own way, refusing to follow your will. We have self-righteously exalted ourselves, ignoring your conflicting righteousness. We ask you to forgive us our sin.

Father of this fellowship, where there is discord, let there be peace. Where there is loneliness, let there be love. Where there is sadness, let there be joy. Where there is sickness, let there be health. Where there is poverty, let there be true wealth.

We are your children—daughters and sons through Christ Jesus. Minister to our needs, we pray, in the name of Jesus.—J. Estill Jones

SERMON
Topic: The Hard Part About Prayer
TEXT: Luke 11:1–13

That you have come to be with God this day—midsummer, midvacation, even when many are cutting church—suggests to me that you want to be here, says to me that you are expecting a pleasant experience here with God this day.

Lord, come to us. God, speak to us. Jesus, show us thy glory. Thus we pray, and thus we are here to be with God.

"Lord, teach us to pray, teach us to be with God, just like John taught us disciples." And Jesus taught, when you come before God, say, "Our Father, thy name be hallowed, thy Kingdom come, thy will be done on Earth just like it is in heaven." Jesus goes on and tells some parable about prayer. But to my mind, this summer Sunday, nothing that Jesus later says about prayer is as challenging, as tough as these words of prayer: "thy name, thy Kingdom, thy will." There's the rub with prayer.

Pat Henry gave me a great business book. I don't read business books, save the ones Pat makes me read. *Fierce Conversation* is the name of the book. It's a book on how to have a significant, substantive conversation with other human beings, because most of business, and just about all of leadership, is a matter of conversation. Here's how to have active, engaging conversation.

The first requirement for a "fierce conversation"? Courage. Guts. The courageous willingness to let the other speak, the openness to enter the deep, unfathomable mystery of another, the risk of having another make a claim on your life.

People have criticized me: "You don't make eye contact, you talk too much and listen too little, you fail to focus on what I'm saying."

And I think, yes, I probably do all those things. And I do them out of an attempt at self-protection. I've had conversations with people before—just talking, just exchanging information, just hanging out—and I came away different, changed.

Years ago, like you, at the beginning of the Sunday service, I'm seated in the pew. A fellow church member at the end of the pew smiles, and I ask, "How are you?" It's a little ritual, a habit: "How are you?" It's what we say when we see somebody—a social convention. It's what we say when we don't mean to say much.

And she says, "Not good, actually. Tom left us last week, and I don't know what the girls and I are going to do."

And I think, "Look, it's just a little social convention. I didn't actually expect you to take me seriously and get intimate with me in church!"

Alas, most of my conversations are facile rather than fierce. I say, "I didn't say anything to him because I didn't know what to say." To tell the truth, I didn't risk the conversation because I didn't know what I might hear.

Jesus said, "When you pray, when you go head-to-head with God, let the very first thing you say be, 'Thy name is holy, thy Kingdom come, thy will be done.'" In others words, prayer "in Jesus' name" is the gutsy willingness to let God be God in your life.

Here is a misconception: prayer is not so much what we say but a determined willingness to let God have his say. Prayer is not so much an articulation of what I want but rather a risk of being exposed to what God wants. Prayer is the possibility that I might be changed in the conversation.

Years ago, I remember, the advertising slogan, "Prayer changes things" was followed by the slogan, "And sometimes what prayer changes is us."

One of the last conversations that Jesus had was in the Garden of Gethsemane—a no-holds-barred, white-knuckled, blood-sweat-and-tears argument—a conversation that ended with Jesus saying, "Nevertheless, not my will but thine be done."

What faith, what courage to pray that and mean it!

I pray, "Lord, take away this cup from me. Deliver me from this distress. Save me from this dilemma. Solve this problem. Save this pain. Er . . . [long pause]. Amen."

I want God to know my will. *My* will be done on Earth—and now.

I told my Freshman Seminar, "We're almost midsemester. I think it would be good to get some feedback on this course. Don't be bashful; give me some midcourse evaluation. How is the course going? How am I doing as your teacher?" Immediately, I heard: "Sometimes you seem kinda disorganized." Another comment: "You let the discussion go on too long. Have you ever taught this course before?"

And I add: "You're just Freshman! What do you know?"

She said to me, going into her third week in the hospital, "Preacher, it's okay if today you don't pray for God to heal me. God knows I want to be healed. But I don't think I'm going to get well. Now, let's pray that God will give me the love to love him no matter what I'm given."

There was a person whom Jesus had taught to pray. One autumn Sunday, shaking hands at the end of the service, a man (a fellow Methodist preacher) came up to me, tears in his eyes. "You haven't heard? Joe has a brain tumor. He goes under the knife tomorrow morning." Joe had graduated with honors from Duke not two years before, had been active in campus ministry. I was devastated.

That afternoon we gathered in Joe's room—parents and me, Joe and his young wife. We were scared. The surgeon appeared. The surgeon told us, in excruciating detail, what was to come in the surgery. And then he said, "Would you like to have prayer?"

We said, "Sure. We've got a couple of preachers right here."

He said, "I'll lead. First I want you to pray for Joe, then I want you to pray for me, then you pray for you." And we joined hands around Joe's bed and this high-powered, Duke neurosurgeon led us in prayer. It was powerful.

At the "Amen," he excused himself and walked out. I followed.

"That was wonderful," I said to the surgeon. "I've been a pastor a long time and I don't know when I've ever had a doctor to lead a prayer like that."

"Do you think it's a good idea?" he asked.

"Well, yes. But I know what you're thinking. This is a secular place. Don't want to intrude on people."

"I wasn't thinking that," said the doctor. "I was thinking that to ask a loving, sovereign God to take charge, to come into this situation—thy will be done—it's a risk. Might not go our way."

And I said, "Yeah, that was just what I was thinking."

Prayer that begins as a projection of my yearnings, desires, and needs upon God ends in an encounter with the living God. We're about to pray. Be careful.—William H. Willimon

SUNDAY, JULY 30, 2006
Lectionary Message

Topic: Anatomy of a Fall

TEXT: 2 Sam. 11:1–15

Other Readings: Ps. 14; Eph. 3:14–21; John 6:1–21

He had done so well. Borne along on the winds of adversity, tried and proven in battle, he had developed heroic qualities. Indeed, he enjoyed a reputation as a mighty warrior. In addition to all of that, he was also a devout man—one who was said to be a man after God's own heart. His fall would not be at the hand of King Saul and his armies, the Philistines and theirs, or any one of a number of other adversaries; rather, his collapse would be one of spiritual failure and of character. In short order (the fifteen verses in this text), in a coldly calculated fashion, he broke at least three of the ten commandments: you shall not covet your neighbor's wife; you shall not commit adultery; and you shall not murder.

It seems impossible that one so close to God should so callously disregard his ways. Yet in a momentary lapse, David unleashed a string of offenses that dishonored God and would prove to be a tragic turning point in his family life and his kingly reign. What went wrong with David? What might go wrong with us? How does a fall progress? This passage is an instructive case study in the anatomy of a fall.

I. *We may take a fall by finding ourselves in the wrong place at the wrong time* (vv. 1–2). David's fall began as he found himself in the wrong place at the wrong time. It was the spring of the year, when kings went to battle. In years previous, David was among them. But this year, he stayed at home—a decision that set the stage for temptation. Rising from his afternoon nap and walking out on the roof of his palace, his eyes fell upon a beautiful woman taking a bath.

The pathway into sin may begin in an apparently incidental or unintentional fashion. At this point in the story, there is no evident intention to act on what was an inadvertent look. Had the impulse been nipped at this point, God's laws would have been upheld. However, the look was not restrained, and moral mayhem followed. We, too, may not immediately realize the peril on our pathway, but no temptation is too small to take seriously.

II. *We may take a fall by taking action to fulfill wrong desires* (vv. 3–4). The snowball began to roll. What David had seen, he determined to have. And so he dispatched messengers from the palace to Bathsheba's home. They took her and brought her to the palace, where David slept with her. We are not told whether she was a willing participant in this act or not, but it is clear that David was the one who initiated the illicit affair. This portion of the passage is brief and unembellished, but there is no mistaking the stark violation of God's law and the sin committed against both Uriah and Bathsheba. We must remember that our sins are always offenses against God, but they often spill over onto innocent people in our pathway.

III. *We may take a fall and seek to cover up our wrongdoing, even with extreme measures* (vv. 6–15). The sin that had been committed in secret was at risk of exposure, when Bathsheba informed David that she was carrying his child. A desperate king saw only one way out: he must try to cover his actions by making it appear that the child Bathsheba had conceived had been fathered by her husband, Uriah. The plan seemed to offer a win-win outcome. By following it, the child would appear to be Uriah's, Bathsheba's honor would be protected, and David's transgression of God's law would be concealed.

The problem was that Uriah was where David should have been—on the battlefield. This fact, however, was no insurmountable object to a man of power. David simply brought Uriah home, so that he could spend the night with his wife, enabling his intimacy with her to provide cover for David's illicit behavior. Moreover, David even manipulated Uriah, plying him with food and drink to lower his inhibitions before sending him home for the night. However, in a way that dramatically displays the contrast between the noble warrior and the treacherous king, Uriah refused intimacy with Bathsheba because his comrades-in-arms could not enjoy such privilege.

With the failure of his plan, David saw no alternative to a most heinous solution. With the reluctant aid of his trusted commander, Joab, David arranged a foolish military maneuver, in which the noble Uriah was killed. A faithful, loyal servant becomes the unwitting victim, simply because he stands in the way of royal lust, embarrassment, and abuse of power.

How far can a person stoop in pursuing his or her sinful desires? More troubling is the question, How far can a person *who professes godliness* fall in unguarded moments? How quickly a circumstantial occurrence can provide an opportunity for a sinful thought or desire to take root and subsequently bring forth the fruit of sin. The matter is only compounded when we seek to cover rather than to repent and forsake our sins. A fully effective cover-up is never possible and will always lead us more deeply into sin.

We must never underestimate the depth of our depravity and must always set a watch on our hearts, that we not take a fall, as David did.

ILLUSTRATIONS

It has been said that in the spiritual life there are no blowouts; there are just slow leaks. A spiritual failure does not happen all at once but rather occurs through a gradual sequence of neglect. This account from the life of David may appear to have been a blowout—a rapidly occurring incident of spiritual disaster. However, in a sense the event is the account of a slow leak. A look became a thought; a thought developed into a few inquiries; a few inquiries brought forth a planned encounter; an encounter became an adulterous affair; an affair required a cover-up; and a cover-up required extremity—a slow leak, compounding itself, with a tragic outcome. The sequence could have been stopped at any point, but as the leak continued, matters went from bad to worse.

Near our home is a thicket of blackberry bushes. The berries are wonderful for making jam, but the vines on which they grow are formidable. They are extremely thorny, long, and entangled with one another. To pick the berries, one must deal with the threat of the vines. A few berries are easily accessible, but soon one must reach more deeply into the vine thicket to get to the berries. At this point, one will quickly learn of the entangling power of a blackberry bush. It starts simply—a thorn snags a piece of clothing. It seems easy to release the thorn, but in the attempt, one becomes entangled with more thorns. The more one tries to get free, the more entangled one becomes. Soon the thorns are tearing clothes and flesh.

Sin works the same way. Initially, it may seem relatively benign, but soon its entangling properties become evident. One may think it a simple matter to pull away, only to find that he or she is deeply entangled, with efforts to break free serving only to make matters worse.— Robert Vogel

SERMON SUGGESTIONS

Topic: The Losers
TEXT: Ps. 14
(1) They dismiss God (v. 1). (2) They ignore the God who seeks them (vv. 2–4). (3) They miss the joy that belongs to the people who know God (vv. 5–7).

Topic: Free—for What?
TEXT: John 8:31–32, 36
(1) The desire for freedom is basic to human nature. (2) The highest expression of our desire for freedom is to be found in the spiritual realm: from the tyranny of the past; from the restraints of legalism; from the enslavements of appetite. (3) Christ can set us free: for personal fulfillment; for the service of God.

WORSHIP AIDS

CALL TO WORSHIP.   "Search me, O God, and know my heart: try me, and know my thoughts: and see if there be any wicked way in me, and lead me in the way everlasting" (Ps. 139:23–24).

INVOCATION.   Blessed art thou, O God, who hast created and dost sustain us, out of whose fullness come blessing and goodness and happiness. Dwell in us as a power of love and of soundness. Heal the disorders of body and soul. Pluck from the memory the rooted sorrow and cleanse the overcharged heart from its misery and pain. Bring thy peace to the troubled conscience. Quench the fires of evil within us, and light a flame of holy love that may warm and purify our lives.—Samuel McComb

OFFERTORY SENTENCE.   "This is the Christ we proclaim; we train everyone and teach everyone the full scope of this knowledge, in order to set everyone before God mature in Christ; I labor for that end, striving for it with the divine energy which is a power within me" (Col. 1:28–29, Moffatt).

OFFERTORY PRAYER.   Lord, help us to understand what we do now in the presenting of our offerings to you: we are, all of us, participants in the preaching and teaching commanded by Christ for the purpose of bringing to maturity in him those who hear and learn. To that end, bless those of us who preach and teach, bless our schools for training ministers and missionaries and lay people, bless those who facilitate the Kingdom work of us all, and make these gifts useful to see your purpose accomplished.

PRAYER.   O God, our true Life, in whom and by whom all things live, thou commandest us to seek thee and art ready to be found; thou biddest us knock and openest when we do so. To know thee is life, to serve thee is freedom, to enjoy thee is a kingdom, to praise thee is the joy and happiness of the soul. We praise and bless and adore thee, we worship thee, we glorify thee, we give thanks to thee for thy great glory. We humbly beseech thee to abide with us, to reign in us, to make these hearts of ours holy temples, fit habitations for thy divine majesty. O thou Maker and Preserver of all things, visible and invisible! Keep, we beseech thee, the work of thine own hands, who trust in thy mercy alone for safety and protection. Guard us with the power of thy grace, here and in all places, now and at all times, forever more.—Adapted from St. Augustine

SERMON

Topic: Are We Evil?
TEXT: John 14:23, 31 (esp. v. 26)

You and I are such slow learners. Just let something happen—the Columbine High School massacre, or the dragging of the black man behind a truck in Texas, or the suffocation of thirty Mexicans in the back of a truck in Arizona, or the surfacing of pictures of the abuse of prisoners in Iraqi—and the question always comes up: How did that happen? Who is responsible for that? Why in the world would anybody act like that? With the picture of the prisoners in Iraq, the question is, once again, on the cover of *Time* magazine: Where does evil come from? Are human beings good or evil (as if we had to be one or the other)?

We are such slow learners because the Christian faith in which we have been brought up, the Christian faith we claim as our hope, the Christian faith we embrace clearly speaks to this question. There is none righteous, no, not one. All have sinned and fallen short of the glory of God. If you ask if we are good, the Scriptures tell us no. Jesus refused to be called good. When the ruler comes to him and says, "Good master," Jesus says there is none who is good but God. The Christian faith from the beginning said we were the wonderful creations of a loving God, and in our divinely given freedom we refused the limits of creaturehood and wanted to be little gods. We wanted to decide for ourselves what was good and what was evil. We have set ourselves up as our own masters, and we do evil. We are the children of God who have fallen. We are walking contradictions, partly truth and partly fiction, partly good and partly evil.

We are always caught up in this struggle between the good that we would do—that we do and not do—and the evil that we do not want to do but somehow slips out and happens. St. Paul talked about the struggle in his heart. All of us are constantly engaged in that conflict. Jesus assures his disciples that he will not leave them alone in the struggle but promises to send them the Holy Spirit to be a help, a guide, a comfort, and an encourager.

The Protestant tradition has always understood that you and I are a mixture. The good things we do always have just a little of the self-centeredness in them. We do amazing things for other people, but we would like our name spelled correctly in the paper. And even in our doing what we know to be wrong, we can find some good to try to justify it. Think of all the jobs the Mafia gives to people. The struggle we have as human beings within the heart and will is to try to keep our evil instincts, desires, and passions under control and to try to enlarge and expand our passions and desires for doing good, to constrain our greed, and to encourage our compassion for others and creation. We pray for God's help to become more Christlike, to grow in love, and to put away the pull of self.

The matching responsibility is to be honest about our actions when evil erupts—the evil that we would not do, that we then do, and then that we need to admit, confess, and repent. The evil simply continues to destroy when it is not admitted and accepted.

We are walking contradictions, partly good and partly evil. And as human beings, we keep setting ourselves up for major disappointments and pain when we try to pretend that we are all good, that we as human beings are moral and just and kind. Just look at the kind of reaction in the world to the pictures of the abuse of Iraqi prisoners, because we had set ourselves up as paragons of virtue. The United States was going to free that country from oppressors. The United States saw the evil in that wicked dictator Saddam, and we alone, of all the nations, were willing to go in and save those people. We were not like other people. We did not fight for conquest. We were champions of justice, truth, freedom, democracy. We were the knights in shining armor. We were goodness coming to fight evil. There was never any public perception that we, as a people, were afflicted with humanity's struggle with evil. So, indeed, when all these pictures appear, there is this horrible gap between our pronouncements and our actions. Now is the time for confession, for apologies, for repentance. Now is the time for humility. Now is the time for embracing our troops with the compassion of people who know how hard it is when pressures are encouraging you to do disgusting things, but you think you are serving your country proudly.

It seems to me that we should hardly ever be surprised by evil. It is in us all, and it erupts and overcomes us in so many unexpected ways. We may be taken off-guard by where and how it shows up, but all of us have within us this power of evil. That is why we need each other in the Church. To encourage us in seeking the power of God to keep this evil under authority, all of us need each other to help us see how the evil and good are intertwined and how to enhance the good and reduce the evil of our actions. All of us need to be in prayer and worship so that the Holy Spirit of God may lead us and guide us.

Why did this happen? Because these wonderfully human soldiers were put into very difficult situations, and the evil in them was permitted to escape in the conviction that they were serving a god. That is why the body of Christ is so important—to give us all a place to ask forgiveness and a place to seek the help of the Holy Spirit for the next struggle.—Rick Brand

SUNDAY, AUGUST 6, 2006
Lectionary Message

Topic: A Model for Ministry
Text: 2 Sam. 11:26–12:13a
Other Readings: Ps. 51:1–12; Eph. 4:1–16; John 6:24–35

What is the best model for ministry in the twenty-first century? Should ministry today be focused on the challenges of the future or on preserving the grand traditions of the past? Should contemporary ministry confront the moral evils of the day or concentrate on encouraging love and justice? Are these things contradictory or complementary?

Second Samuel is the tale of two kings in the same body. David was the best of kings; he was the worst of kings. Chapter 11 records the pivotal event—the change in the tenor of the book. David's sin with Bathsheba changed everything. Before chapter 11, 2 Samuel is high adventure, but afterward the story is tragedy. The first part of the book is Tolkien, the latter part Faulkner. The king who previously had unified his country has now divided his heart. Once he took pleasure in the death of his enemies, but now he has taken part in the murder of his friend. Though God had given David rest from his external enemies, now he has become a man at war with himself. Though he could subdue nations, after his sin he could not control his own sons. The one who initiated the building of the Temple also instigated the destruction of his kingdom. The writer comments on David's sin with Bathsheba and his murder of Uriah with characteristic concision and candor: "But the thing that David had done displeased the Lord" (2 Sam. 11:27).

Chapter 12 focuses on Nathan's confrontation of his sovereign's sin. As the story unfolds, two great movements emerge around the two principals of the narrative.

I. *Nathan provides a paradigm of preaching.* The first thing Nathan did was *confront the crime.* Nathan was a master communicator, because his first step was to open the heart (2 Sam. 12:1–4). By telling David the parable of the wealthy man who stole his neighbor's one little lamb, he got David emotionally involved. He made him feel the anger of injustice and the sting of cruelty. Second, he moved from the heart to the head and changed his mind. Nathan knew, as all good communicators know, that the mind is more effectively changed when the heart is first moved. When David grew incensed at the evil that had been perpetrated in his kingdom, he thundered judgment and condemnation, never realizing that he was the guilty party.

Isn't it amazing that we can watch the evening news and get so angry at all the people in the world who do evil, while we remain oblivious to our own sin? We can get incensed at the lies others tell, yet excuse our own. We suffer anguish over the mistreatment of people we will never know, yet treat those in our own homes with disregard and disrespect. We wonder why the government can't make peace with other nations while we refuse to give any quarter in our own domestic arguments. Like David, our hearts are moved, but until the Holy Spirit points to us and says, "You are the one!" we don't understand our own guilt.

We can be thankful that Nathan's preaching does not end with mere confrontation. He then moves to *confidence of forgiveness* with some of the most precious words in the Bible: "The Lord has put away your sin; you shall not die" (2 Sam. 12:13). God was far more gracious to David than David would have been to the fictitious rich man who stole his neighbor's ewe. Preaching often has to confront the sin in a congregation's life, but what a blessing to also express the confidence of God's forgiveness.

Nevertheless, Nathan had to be honest with David about *the consequences of sin*. God will always forgive, but he will probably not take away all of sin's consequences. Repentant pregnant teenagers still have a baby to care for. Criminals may be forgiven in the courts of heaven but still face incarceration in the prisons of man. One might repent of adultery but still lose one's marriage. But we must not confuse consequences with condemnation.

Indeed, Nathan provides a paradigm for preaching, but no honest reading of the text can claim that the point of the passage is about Nathan or his methodology. No, the point of the text is David's response.

II. *David provides a model for ministry.* Second Samuel 12:13 records the model for ministry that works in any age or in any culture: repentance. David neither offered excuses nor laid blame. He had the power of life and death over Nathan, but he humbly and simply responded, "I have sinned against the Lord." These few words succinctly express the beautiful prayer of confession that David recorded in Psalm 51.

Although we have much to learn from Nathan's paradigm of preaching, the real lesson of the text is what we learn from David. We must be a repentant people. If a primary work of the Holy Spirit is to convict and convince of sin, then a primary work of believers is that we must repent and change our lives if we are to conform to God's will. So when we are incensed at the sin of others, we must first examine ourselves. A repentant spirit and a contrite heart are prerequisite to ministry in an unjust and sinful world. Before we can reconcile others, we must first find forgiveness.

ILLUSTRATIONS

TWO NATURES WITHIN.   "It was the best of times, it was the worst of times, it was the age of wisdom, it was the age of foolishness, it was the epoch of belief, it was the epoch of incredulity, it was the season of Light, it was the season of Darkness, it was the spring of hope, it was the winter of despair, we had everything before us, we had nothing before us, we were all going direct to Heaven, we were all going direct the other way."[1]

---

[1]Charles Dickens, *A Tale of Two Cities*

REPENTANCE.   Suppose you are out driving and develop trouble with your car. If you just sit there doing nothing, your car will not get fixed, and your trouble will not go away. You will just get more and more discouraged. The only other choice you have is to get help from someone who is qualified to fix the problem. That will get your car running, and that will make you happy. So it is with just sitting and feeling bad about your sin; that will never help you. You will only get more and more depressed. What you must do is go to the only one who can fix your sin problem—God.—Hershael York

SERMON SUGGESTIONS

Topic: Honest Confession
TEXT: Ps. 51:1–14
(1) The problem of guilt: because of our nature and tendencies; because of our sometimes gross behavior. (2) The solution of our problem: it resides in God's redeeming purpose; it is available through honest confession; it opens the way to joy and service.

Topic: How Dreams Come True
TEXT: Gen. 37:5–11; Phil. 3:4b–16
(1) Through worthy objectives: by identification with Jesus Christ; by using imagination. (2) Through careful selection: making the right primary choice; moving on with satellite choices. (3) Through staying power: achieved in prayer; strengthened in action.

WORSHIP AIDS

CALL TO WORSHIP.   "Lord, who shall abide in thy tabernacle? Who shall dwell in thy holy hill? He that walketh uprightly, and worketh righteousness, and speaketh the truth in his heart" (Ps. 15:1–2).

INVOCATION.   Lord, we come as we are today: some are cornered by temptation, others are deep in grief, and many are anxious. Help us to cast our burden on the Lord, who knows all about us and longs to hear from us more than we long to be heard. In the Savior's name.—E. Lee Phillips

OFFERTORY SENTENCE.   "Keep your life free from love of money, and be content with what you have; for he has said, 'I will never fail you nor forsake you'" (Heb. 13:5 RSV).

OFFERTORY PRAYER.   Lord, we know that if we love you enough, no other love can compete with what is right. So fix our hearts on you, O God, that everything we gain and control will be under your lordship.

PRAYER.   O merciful Lord, enlighten Thou me with a clear shining inward light, and remove away all darkness from the habitation of my heart. Repress Thou my many wandering thoughts, and break in pieces those temptations which violently assault me. Fight Thou for me, and vanquish the evil beasts; that so peace may be obtained by Thy power, and that Thine abundant praise may resound in Thy holy court, that is, in a pure conscience. Send out Thy light and Thy truth, that they may shine upon the earth; for, until Thou enlighten me, I am but as earth without form and void. Lift Thou up my mind which is pressed down by a load of sins, for no created thing can give full comfort and rest to my desires. Join thou me to Thyself with an inseparable band of love; for Thou even alone dost satisfy him that loveth Thee.—Thomas à Kempis

SERMON

Topic: **"This is My Beloved Son in whom I am well pleased."**
TEXT: Matt. 3:17

They always provoke all kinds of questions. When hurricanes hit the mountains of North Carolina, people ask questions. When four hurricanes in a year hit Florida, people ask questions. When the tsunami hits Asia, people ask questions. One of the first questions is, Why? Then more questions: What happened? What caused that tidal wave? When was the last time something like that happened? Is this the worst one of these we have ever seen? How many people were killed? What can we do to help? These events are always so shocking, so amazing that our first response is questions. And all questions eventually will lead you to the faith question. Where is God in all of this? Why did this happen to them? Is this some kind of punishment from God? Is this some kind of wakeup call to the world, demanding more worldwide cooperation? Is this some kind of revenge of nature on humanity for our abuse of nature?

Questions naturally and normally result in some people trying to give answers. One of the things we seem to be most uncomfortable with is a question to which no one tries to give an answer. Let somebody ask a troubling question in a group, and almost always somebody will immediately try to give an answer. We do not like to look at troubling questions. We do not like to ask the meaning of the question, Why did God let this happen? You mean tsunami? Do you mean the earthquake? Do you mean the survivalist existence on the coast of millions of people? What do you mean by "let"? Is your question whether God intentionally, directly shifted the Earth's plates to cause the tsunami in this place at this day? Do you mean that having created the Earth and put all the forces of heat, expansion, and contraction into play that God should have stopped the waves caused by the earthquake? How do you see God causing this, and how do you think God could have prevented it?

But different people respond to disaster in different ways. Just let questions get out there, and there is almost no end to the different kinds of responses that will be given. We are much too ready to give answers to questions that are too big for answers. One of our greatest sins is the presumption that we have answers for all of God's questions. The great demand of faith is to live in obedience to the call of God's love without all the answers. But we have lots of different people giving a lot of different advice.

I don't know why I let some of the comments bother me so much. Some of the answers, some of the remarks made at times like these, can just irritate the devil right into me. Take, for example, that letter in the paper from the member of the Ayn Rand Institute. Where in the world did that writer ever learn about the way our government works? To declare the amazing concept that George Bush had no right or power to give our tax dollars to relief efforts because every dollar that George Bush gives away is a tax dollar and is not appropriated for charitable causes is almost incredible. Some think money that goes to Halliburton is a charitable contribution. Some think money that goes to tobacco farmers is a charitable gift. To claim that our president cannot use tax dollars for relief efforts would seem to invent a whole new limitation on the executive branch of government.

One hears as well from those who have been engaged in relief efforts of other kinds—the outrage of neglect. Joan Baez has a song on one of her albums about the people who work with unwed mothers and high-risk pregnancies. Their programs are always being cut and squeezed by the lack of public support and money; every year their budget goes down, and the needs grow, and one of the workers says, "Yeah, but they can always find money for floods." The relief effort for these victims may reach $1 to $3 billion. Nelson Mandela just buried his son, who died of AIDS, and the story says that in Africa close to five million people are infected with AIDS, and the world cannot find $1 to $3 billion to help them. Maybe Joan Baez is right. There is always money for floods. I don't know how to explain our reactions. Why does one tragedy become world-shattering and another, even larger place of suffering get no attention? The tsunami has raised questions about what will happen to the children whose parents have died. There is a great fear that they will be rounded up and taken into slavery and prostitution. Our own government reports that every year, year after year, over 800,000 people cross international borders into some kind of slavery, and we never hear a concern expressed.

The tsunami confronts us with so many different questions, so many different needs, so many different challenges! Who gets to say who is being stingy? Whom do we trust to get the help to the people? Fox News happened to have a woman on who just happened to have written a book about "do-gooders." Her basic position seemed to be that most efforts to do good hurt the very people being helped. It sounded something like this: if you feed the poor and the hungry, you only make them live longer, and they end up having to live on the street that much longer; if you give them a jacket, somebody will probably beat them up to take the jacket; if you give them presents, then you just make the expectations for next Christmas higher; if you put people in Habitat for Humanity houses, you just give them more debt and obligations than they can handle. Doing good is really doing harm. That sounded like the premise of her book. If you go in and keep all these victims of the tsunami alive and are only going to be returning them to a life of poverty and subsistence, you are not helping them by returning them to the horrible life they had before.

In these moments when we are confronted by such overwhelming events, and the questions are so great and the answers and the objections and the pronouncements are so confusing, it is important to remember that we have been baptized into a community that is united in Jesus Christ. We are a part of the body of Christ Jesus. We have been baptized and engrafted into the people of God. We have committed ourselves to be part of the people of God, to be in the world in a particular way of being human—a living example, a constant reminder of the true and gracious God-empowered way of life.

In the Old Testament lesson, Isaiah shares with us a way of life that comes to the servant of God when that servant is filled with the Holy Spirit. "Behold, my servant, on whom I have put my Spirit, for he will bring forth justice to the nations." He will bring that justice by faithfully bearing the pain and suffering of those with whom he is one.

Even Jesus has to come to John the Baptist and ask to be baptized by John. Even Jesus wants to be identified with the community of God's people who have been called to be in the world and to live in the world in a way that brings justice. Even Jesus needs to come and show his solidarity with the will and purpose of God by being baptized into the community of faith. Even Jesus says it is appropriate and right for him to be baptized into this community that knows that when the Spirit of God fills his servants, they bring in justice by sharing the suffering of others and by being a part of those people by working with them. When Jesus is baptized by John, the Spirit comes and affirms that this is the Son, the servant, the one who brings justice by suffering with and for others.

In the face of so many questions, in the face of so many different answers and responses, it is good to remember that you and I have been baptized into that same community. The Spirit of God has fallen on us, and we are part of the body of Christ. We are empowered, we are invited, we are called to bring justice to the world by sharing the suffering and pain of others. That is God's notion of justice—that all of us bear the pain and suffering of others. That is God's notion of justice—that all of us bear the pain and suffering of life together. As Robert Fulghum said he learned in kindergarten, "When you go out into the world, it is good to hold hands and help each other."

So I do not know whether it is better to be a do-gooder or a do-nothing. I do not know why some tragedies get more help than others. I do not know why this tragedy happened there and not in Australia or Japan or Hawaii. I do know that the Jesus Christ who is our Lord told his disciples to give drink to those who are thirsty, to feed those who are hungry, to clothe those who are naked, to help those who are homeless, to carry those who are lame, to bear the unbearable sorrows, and to bring justice by sharing the sorrows of the world. You and I do not give to the relief agencies simply because we get tax credits. We will not give and then get great publicity for our gifts. We will not give because we think it will do some good. We simply give in obedience. We give because Jesus told us to give. We give as an act of faithfulness to Jesus Christ our Lord. We give because we are part of the baptized community; we are part of the body of Christ, and Christ has told us that his disciples do these kinds of things.—Rick Brand

SUNDAY, AUGUST 13, 2006

Lectionary Message

Topic: Healing Broken Relationships

TEXT: 2 Sam. 18:5–9, 15, 31–33

Other Readings: Ps. 130; Eph. 4:25–5:2; John 6:35, 41–51

I. *Heal relationships before the break is public* (v. 5). In the later years of his life, David's reign was beset with political unrest and domestic difficulties, almost all of which were the result of his own lack of leadership in his family. Like many of his contemporaries, David departed from the monogamous pattern that God established in the Garden of Eden; he married many wives. They had children, and those children vied for favors and political advantage. The court of Israel became known more for its intrigue and backstabbing than for its devotion to God.

As David grew older, he found himself in unfamiliar territory. He had never been so unsure of himself, never so weak in his leadership. The boy who had killed the lion and the bear to protect his father's sheep could not defeat his own fleshly desires. The self-assured slayer of Goliath had lost his poise, particularly in the face of his generals and his wives. He could command an army, but he could not control his own household.

Little by little, tragedy stole into his life. David's son Amnon raped his own half-sister—David's daughter Tamar. Then Absalom—Tamar's brother—murdered Amnon in revenge.

After Absalom fled to escape his father's justice, he was later brought back by Joab—David's premier military general. Rather than respond in gratitude, however, Absalom interpreted his father's generosity as weakness and began to steal the affection of the people while he plotted to overthrow his own father.

When Absalom gained control of much of the army, David had to flee the capital, running from his own son. In a very public break, Absalom had sex with David's concubines to show all Israel that his break with his father was complete and deep. That forced everyone to choose a side because they knew that this family rift would not be healed.

Second Samuel 18:5 records David's instruction to Joab and his lieutenants to go easy on Absalom. The author of the book dryly notes that all Israel knew of David's instructions. They knew that Absalom was willing to kill his father but that David wasn't willing to utterly destroy his rebellious son.

At some point as David was fleeing Jerusalem, perhaps again as he instructed Joab to spare Absalom's life, he must have wondered where he had gone wrong. Surely, David knew what everyone needs to learn—that broken relationships need to be mended early, before the breach spreads into the lives of others. Parents need to learn to love their children, to spend time with them, to teach them biblical values while they are still small. It might be too late when those children are grown and reject biblical and Christian values. We cannot wait until the private schism becomes public drama to do something about it.

II. *Heal relationships before the breach is permanent.* As long as we have life, we have the ability to change, to heal, to reach out to others, to forgive and to be forgiven. The sad reality that overwhelms us, however, is that sometimes our broken relationships become permanent because people or circumstances intervene and deny us the opportunity to make the changes that we desperately need to make.

As Absalom was on the run from Joab and David's men, his head got caught in an oak tree. When Joab heard about it, he threw three darts into Absalom's body and was joined in the execution by ten young men, who also participated. Each blow signaled not only the death of David's son but the end of any opportunity to repair the relationship. The time had passed.

One of the hardest truths in life to accept is that much of the time, our predicaments are of our own making. Although tragedy that is completely beyond our control may indeed come, most of us struggle far more with the situations that we have created, not those that are thrust upon us. David and Absalom were not victimized by others as much as by themselves. An absent father and a rebellious son, both self-centered adulterers, warred on one another and reaped terrible consequences as a result.

III. *Heal relationships before the break is painful.* When a runner reached the king and told him that his forces had won the battle, David learned that the throne was his once again. He could return to Jerusalem and reclaim all that was his. God had delivered him again.

David did not stage a victory march or throw a party. His own throne did not mean as much to him as the life of his son. Millennia later, one can still hear the bitter pathos in David's voice as he asked a question that he should have asked years earlier: "Is it well with the young man, Absalom?" After he heard of Absalom's demise, it was too late. The pain was too great. He had refused to offer the love and the correction that Absalom had needed years earlier, and now he reaped the bitter harvest. He had not worked to conquer his son's spirit when he was young; now he had to conquer his army and be party to his death.

Although few people today face consequences so stark and obvious as David's, a broken relationship is just as painful, often just as fatal. Parents who realize too late that they did not love and teach their children have to live with broken hearts when they witness their children turn their backs on them and on their values. Husbands and wives sometimes learn too late that the breach has grown too deep, too public, too permanent, and too painful. If the story of David and Goliath stands as a testimony to what faith can accomplish, the story of David and Absalom bears witness to what can be lost—what a lack of faithfulness can lose.

ILLUSTRATIONS

A CLEAN GRIEF.   Death and separation always bring pain, but I have often noticed that people have one of two kinds of grief at the loss of a loved one. First is what I call *clean grief.* This is the pain of separation that has no regret except that caused by separation. The husband who faithfully demonstrated his love for his wife and cared for her during a lengthy illness, the adult child who always showed appreciation for her parents and never missed an opportunity to tell them of her love, the brother who treated his brother as his best friend— these people grieve, but they can handle their grief because they have no regrets. They were loving, faithful, and good to one another.

But then there is that other kind of grief—the pain of regret and missed opportunities. People with this kind of grief mourn not only the loss of one they loved but their own failure to work things out, to express their emotions, and to simply say, "I love you."

WHAT PARENTS WORRY ABOUT.   According to a study cited in *Parents & Teenagers* magazine, parents' concerns include "teenager's academic success" (selected by 15 percent of the parents), "who teenager will eventually marry" (24 percent), "teenager's quality of friends" (32 percent), and "teenager's drug, alcohol, and tobacco abuse" (41 percent). But the leading anxiety for Christian parents is whether their teenagers will stay true to the faith, a worry identified by 56 percent of respondents.[2]—Hershael York

SERMON SUGGESTIONS

Topic: Waiting with Expectation

TEXT: Ps. 130

(1) You may find yourself in desperation from guilt, like the psalmist (vv. 1–3). (2) There is hope for the guilty: because of what we know of the very nature of God (v. 4a, 7); because of what God can accomplish in forgiving us (v. 2b). (3) The scope of God's redemptive love and power is as broad as his people's need (v. 8).

Topic: How Big Is Your God?

TEXT: Isa. 44:9–20

(1) What some of the little gods are like: one that would give us everything we want and fail; one that would rise and fall with weathers and wars and sorrows; one that is the prisoner of a race or a religious denomination; one that excuses everything. (2) Why such gods are

---

[2]Cited in *Parents & Teenagers,* 1990.

inadequate: the human mind grows; the human spirit yearns to expand; the stresses of life require a greater God. (3) How can we believe the right way? Let God be God; don't fear the truth; don't despise revelation; trust God completely.

WORSHIP AIDS

CALL TO WORSHIP.   "Show me thy ways, O Lord; teach me thy paths. Lead me in thy truth and teach me: for thou art the God of my salvation; on thee do I wait all the day" (Ps. 25:4–5).

INVOCATION.   Lord, our God, erase all in us that runs from you; negate in us that which doubts you; break down in us that which holds us back from your leading, in this hour of worship. Conform us to the image of One who was willing to live that we might see the way, and suffer that we might understand the way, and die that we might know the way, who is the truth and life forever.—E. Lee Phillips

OFFERTORY SENTENCE.   "None of us lives for himself only, none of us dies for himself only. If we live, it is for the Lord that we live, and if we die, it is for the Lord that we die. So whether we live or die, we belong to the Lord" (Rom. 14:7–8 TEV).

OFFERTORY PRAYER.   We thank you, Lord, that we can say we belong to you. Make our lives and what we have useful for your purposes, both in this world and in the world to come. To that end, bless us and our offerings, we pray.

PRAYER.   Gracious Father, how often have we had to take refuge in your forgiveness! We have failed in so many ways to measure up to what we know to be right, and we suspect that we have done wrong that we did not recognize as wrong. Help us to see clearly how much we depend on your mercy. Just as we continually stand in need of your grace, so also there are those about us—some as close as members of our own families, some as distant as people in other lands—who need our forgiveness. We sin against one another, and we need as much to forgive as to be forgiven. Grant that we may see that no one has so much sinned against us as we have sinned against you, and yet you offer forgiveness. From this very moment let your forgiveness overflow into our forgiveness of one another, even as you, for the sake of your dear Son, our Savior, have forgiven us.

SERMON
Topic: Prophet with Honor
TEXT: Luke 4:16–30

William Martin's official biography of Billy Graham, *A Prophet with Honor,* is a play on the statement found in each of the Gospels. Martin's book is well documented and quite favorable to Graham, but it is no whitewash. That the famous evangelist chose Martin to write his biography speaks well of Graham. Martin was chosen largely because of his reputation for objectivity in writing about religious subjects, and he was given access to sensitive inside resources. Although Billy Graham has often been at the center of controversy and the target of criticism, Martin's title is right. Billy Graham has garnered in his lifetime a level of respect far beyond the popular acceptance of most religious leaders, including Jesus of Nazareth.

I am sure that Martin was aware of the parenthetical comment attributed to Jesus in John 4:44: "that a prophet has no honor in the prophet's own country." The statement is repeated in each of the Gospels, including Luke's extended story of rejection in Nazareth. I am sure that Graham would readily agree that he is no Jesus and that the Christ was a prophet without honor. But the basic question of the Gospels arises here. Given the fact that Jesus was often despised and rejected, can a true prophet be popular? The truth is, prophets tend to get crucified. Luke observes the irony and perhaps the miracle that Jesus survived a lynching in Nazareth to get crucified in Jerusalem.

Rejection in Nazareth was only a symptom of the larger picture of rejection by the Jews. John sums it up in the first sentences of his Gospel (1:11): "He came to what was his own, and his own people did not accept him." The story stands at the beginning of Luke's Gospel right after the baptism of Jesus and the temptation in the wilderness (4:14): "Then Jesus, filled with the power of the Spirit, returned to Galilee, and a report about him spread through all the surrounding country." Luke describes the scene in detail. Jesus returned to his hometown of Nazareth, entered the synagogue, and opened the Isaiah scroll to a passage strongly associated with the Messiah. The statement of Jesus—"Today this scripture has been fulfilled in your hearing"—was a bit much. The contempt of familiarity was followed by rage, and Luke leaves us in a state of confusion: How could Jesus be the universal Lord, Savior of the world, and not be accepted by his own people?

I. *The scandal of the particular.* We are left to wonder, not only about the scandal of the cross but the miracle of survival. Jesus stirred so much controversy that we can wonder how he survived to be crucified in Jerusalem. What is the problem here? Jesus tended to rub people the wrong way. Before he got to Nazareth, Jesus already had a reputation as a miracle worker and rabbi. It looks at first like the home folks were proud of their native son, glad to have him running for the office of Messiah. It was a high office; it was in the sights of many aspiring young rabbis. The minute Jesus stepped into the role of teacher, they began to get nervous. Why would they have a problem with his proclamation of the good news to the poor, release to captives, sight to the blind, and freedom to the oppressed?

We always expect our messiahs to come floating down from the clouds. The last place on Earth we would expect to hear the Word of the Lord is from the kid who made the birdhouses at vacation Bible school. We prefer a stranger who is a bit more solicitous and less familiar with our prejudices and practices. Homegrown messiahs are too volatile. They know too much, and we know them far too well. It might have been different if Jesus had gone to a foreign school somewhere. He lacked credentials. He was not an educated rabbi. He was a charismatic, who spoke with authority and far too much audacity for anyone's comfort. The scandal of the particular has always been a shadow on the gospel. The story of Nazareth is about a particular man in a particular place with a universal mission. Moltmann strikes the right note when he writes of *The Crucified God*—a peasant preacher from Nazareth, whom we proclaim as Savior and Lord. The scandal of the Gospel focused on the story of a crucified Savior and the message that God was in Christ reconciling the world.

II. *The scandal of the universal.* The salvation of the world presents a problem for folks whose spiritual energy revolves around rejection and division. One of the big battles of early Baptists was waged over this very question. Did Jesus come to save the whole world or just the chosen few who consider themselves among the elect? The message of Jesus extended beyond the lost sheep of Israel. By the time of Luke, Christians were already excluded from the synagogues, and the Gentile mission was well under way. The subtle message of rejection in Nazareth is the story of God's universal love.

Jesus grew up in a rough neighborhood. Galilee had a reputation as a semi-pagan, lower-class community. In John, Nathaniel raises this question about Jesus: "Can anything good come out of Nazareth?" The question has the character of an ethnic joke. Philip offered a correction to the prejudice: "Come and see." It is John's way of showing that Jesus proved to be an exception to the rule. Any criticism of Jesus at Nazareth, therefore, is an indictment of Nazareth. The sword cuts in two directions. The rejection of Jesus is a statement about Nazareth as well as about Jesus. We can no more determine the content of character by the color of skin than people could determine the character of Jesus by his city of origin. The irony of rejection in Nazareth is that Jesus finally gave Nazareth a good name. He not only came to save the folks back home, he came to redeem their bad reputation.

I grew up on ethnic humor. We would have protested that we intended no harm by our jokes about African Americans, Hispanics, and Jews, but the practice was a subtle way of labeling and packaging people so that we did not have to deal with them. Perhaps we *meant* no harm, but unspeakable harm was done to our children, as they developed stereotypes for folks according to race or ethnic identity. Unspeakable harm is done to minority children, as our level of expectation becomes a glass ceiling that limits their self-respect, as well as their opportunity to follow their calling.

Jesus came to set us free, not only from the prisons that surround us but from the prisons that are within us.—Larry Dipboye

SUNDAY, AUGUST 20, 2006
Lectionary Message

Topic: Preparation for Service
Text: 1 Kings 2:10–12, 3:3–14
Other Readings: Ps. 111; Eph. 5:15–20; John 6:51–58

I. *God sometimes uses change to bring opportunity.* David's death signaled not only the end of an era but of a movement. He had united the kingdom torn by Saul's ineffective political and moral leadership. After forty years of David's reign, the nation was at its highest level of national security and wealth. David had raised Israel's stature in the region, and God had given Israel rest from its enemies. Even though the final years of David's reign were tainted with internecine feuds and plots, the epoch of King David had been largely successful and blessed of God.

For years the nation had wondered which of David's sons would succeed him. Absalom had attempted to usurp the throne and had been killed. Adonijah, another son, had likewise tried to ensure that the throne would be his when his father died. All along, however, God's choice was Solomon—the son of Bathsheba and David.

No doubt the average citizen of Israel was disturbed by the death of David. For most of the population, he was the only king they had ever known. For forty years he had been their leader and had ensured a level of stability that now felt increasingly threatened.

But moments of doubt and disturbance are often the precursor to a movement of God. Faith often springs from the fertile soil of crisis. We are forced to decide whether or not we can actually trust God. The very thing that we fear will destroy us is often what drives us to God. The thing that we feel will cast us down lifts us up and produces intimacy with him. Change, even the change of tragedy and loss, can bring the opportunity for growth and renewal.

II. *God sometimes uses opportunity to bring focus.* Solomon was a flawed king. He had been born, after all, to parents whose marriage sprang from adultery and even murder. As a boy he had witnessed all of the palace intrigue and political drama. He had become enamored of the rituals of pagan religions and had already dabbled in religious practices that faithful Jews found odious. Yet the writer pays him one great compliment: he loved the Lord (1 Kings 3:3). He followed the precepts of his father, David; like David, Solomon could get so enraptured by the worship of God that he went beyond the practical. When he went to Gibeon to offer sacrifices to God, he did not offer just a few animals; he offered a thousand animals. His devotion to God was evident.

The night after lavishing such an extravagant gift on the Lord, God appeared to Solomon in a dream and asked him a defining question: What can I give you? What does one ask of the Creator and Sustainer of the universe? God put no limits on Solomon's request; he simply asked what he could do for the new king.

The infinite possibilities that lay before Solomon had a very limiting effect: they forced him to focus. Though God put no boundaries on what Solomon could ask for, he implied that he could ask for only one thing. God's offer forced Solomon to narrow his vision and sharpen his focus. His encounter with the infinite, limitless possibilities led him to discern the one thing he truly needed. Centuries later, the apostle Paul would echo, "This *one thing* I do. . . ." In just such a moment of clarity, the great opportunity that God gave Solomon made him ask himself what he really wanted out of life. For Solomon the answer was as simple as it was profound: he wanted wisdom to lead God's people.

He could have asked for wealth, for pleasure, or for some other material blessing. He could have asked for brilliance, for personality, for friends. Yet Solomon's own personal limitations led him to the conclusion that he needed one thing more than anything else, and that was what he asked for.

God is still infinite, omnipotent, and omniscient. He can answer any prayer, grant any request, fulfill any wish. But what God wants from his people is clarity and focus that leads us to desire one thing more than anything else. Ultimately, that one thing is a relationship with him.

III. *God sometimes uses focus to bring change.* When Solomon responded to God as he did, the Lord not only granted Solomon's request but he gave him all the things he *didn't* ask for. He gave him wealth, long life, and victory over enemies. In the same way, when we "seek first the kingdom of God and his righteousness," God adds all the other things to us. When we seek a relationship with him above all else, God meets needs in a marvelous way, and we learn the sweet but sometimes torturous lesson that Jesus really is enough for us.

Once we focus on living for the Lord, on seeking his wisdom and guidance in life, we find the energy and the desire to make the changes in our lives that we desperately need to make. Wealth doesn't bring wisdom, but wisdom can bring wealth. Long life doesn't guarantee wisdom, but wisdom certainly contributes to long life. As we pursue God's wisdom, we discover that the path is littered with so many things that we never expected—joy, fulfillment, and a different kind of wealth than we ever knew existed.

ILLUSTRATION

"God's little workshop" was the name George Washington Carver gave to his laboratory. According to his own account, it was there the famous scientist asked in prayer to discover the uses of what was then a lowly, unesteemed crop: the peanut. "Dear Mr. Creator," the humble man began, "please tell me what the universe was made for."

"Ask for something more in keeping with that little mind of yours," God answered.

So Carver tried again. "Dear Mr. Creator, what was man made for?"

Again the Lord replied, "Little man, you ask too much. Cut down the extent of your request and improve the intent."

So the scientist tried once more. "Then Mr. Creator, will you tell me why the peanut was made?"

"That's better," the Lord said, and beginning that day Carver discovered over 300 uses for the lowly peanut.[3]—Hershael York

SERMON SUGGESTIONS

Topic: Why Praise the Lord?

TEXT: Ps. 111

(1) Because of his mighty works (vv. 2–4). (2) Because of his providential care: food for us (v. 5); a place to live (v. 6). (3) Because of his very nature (vv. 7–9). (4) Because it is the intelligent thing to do (v. 10).

Topic: Victory Is Yours!

TEXT: Rom. 8:37

(1) Defeats come to all of us: through a bad series of events; through the failures of others; through personal failures. (2) However, we can win: if defeat gives us a truer picture of ourselves (Luke 14:28–33); if we realize that Christ has won the victory before us and for us (2 Cor. 2:14); when the Holy Spirit is at work in our heart.

WORSHIP AIDS

CALL TO WORSHIP.   "The Lord reigneth: let the earth rejoice" (Ps. 97:1a).

INVOCATION.   We rejoice today, O Lord, for we know that you are in control. We do not understand all of your ways, but we know you and trust you. Let that faith pervade all that we do during this time of prayer and praise.

OFFERTORY SENTENCE.   "The earth is the Lord's and the fullness thereof; the world, and they that dwell therein" (Ps. 24:1).

OFFERTORY PRAYER.   It is all yours, O Lord—all that we are and have. Take this portion of our material possessions and glorify your name through a multiplying witness to your love.

---

[3]Paul Thigpen, "No Royal Road to Wisdom," *Discipleship Journal* (Sept./Oct.), 1985.

PRAYER.   Great is your faithfulness, O God our Father. We, the sometimes faithful, come in confession this morning, admitting that we are fickle when we know that you are ever faithful. We know that we practice duplicity, even though as followers we have given our lives to being authentic. We live amid divided loyalties, even as we seek your wholeness. We even come halfhearted into your presence to worship and invoke your presence, when we should be invoking our own. So often we emotionally and even physically saunter into your presence with our hands in our pockets, when you are calling for all that we are and have to stand before you.

Deliver us from our pretense and call us to a commitment that eagerly seeks your face, listens to your counsel, and goes out to do your will. Let us hear the deep in you calling to the deep in us, that we may plumb the depths of what you would have us be. Remind us of your love freely given, that we might be free to attain the highest possibilities you have for us. Assure us that we are acceptable to you, even as we are, when we face our sins, lay them before you in honest confession, and receive your grace and forgiveness.—Henry Fields

SERMON
Topic: The Examination
TEXT: Luke 22:54–62

Then a serving girl, seeing Peter as he sat in the light and, gazing at him, said, "This man also was with him." But Peter denied it, saying, "Woman, I do not know him."

We're in a series of young heroes of the Bible. Today, my hero is actually a heroine. She is an unlikely candidate for this series. She doesn't have a name. She is only mentioned for a few verses and only one place in the Bible. I don't know where she came from or anything about her, except that she is a "servant girl"—a *paidiske*, or a young woman who is in service.

Let me set the scene. It is late at night. It is after the Last Supper, when Jesus has gathered with his disciples in an Upper Room. The Passion of Christ has begun. The soldiers have seized Jesus and led him away to the palace. At the palace, Jesus stands before Pontius Pilate and is on trial. But out in the darkness, in the courtyard down below, another trial takes place. Judge and jury at that trial is a "servant girl." And though we don't know much about her—whether she is a girl or even whether she is a servant—we know that she is a small, insignificant, powerless person. She is not only a woman in a patriarchal culture but she is also a servant woman. And she is young. Some of you are young, and you know that means that you, too, are powerless, on the bottom. And this little, powerless girl is the one who puts Peter—the premier disciple—through his paces.

But when Jesus and his disciples were in the Upper Room at dinner, Peter declared that he would stick with Jesus, no matter what. Jesus had said to his disciples, "All of you will fall away." Peter blurted out, "Though all the rest of these losers will desert you, I am behind you all the way Jesus." As it turned out, he was behind Jesus—far, far, behind Jesus. When the soldiers came to take Jesus, all the disciples fled into the darkness. Peter kept behind at a safe distance. But though he could not closely follow Jesus, he couldn't leave him either. He therefore ended up, in the middle of the night, in a courtyard where some soldiers warmed themselves around a fire.

And there in the courtyard, this "servant girl" put Peter through his paces.

"You also were with the Galilean," she says. And Peter replies, "Woman, I don't know what you are talking about." Note that he doesn't just say, "I don't know what you are talking about." He says, "Woman, I don't know what you are talking about." Perhaps he said this to ridicule her before the bystanders. She is a woman, she is young, she is a servant. What does she know?

Peter is clearly put on the defensive by her statement. She is not necessarily accusing him. She just declares a fact: "You were with Jesus."

And before this assertion, Peter—the one whom Jesus had nicknamed "The Rock," the premier disciple, the one who had been with Jesus from the very first and had heard all of his teaching and observed all of his action—says to her, "I didn't even know him." Three times he says, "Woman, I didn't even know him."

Oh, the power of that young woman! She may have been young, a woman, and a serving woman at that, but in three short sentences she has completely crushed The Rock. She has forced Peter to deny Jesus, not once but thrice. And Peter stumbles out into the darkness beyond the fire and weeps like a baby.

Earlier, on a much brighter, sunnier day, Jesus had asked, "Who do people say that I am?" Peter's hand was the first to go up. "You are the Christ, the son of the God!"

And Jesus had said in response, "I'll build my church on this rock." And from that day on, Jesus had called him Peter, which means, in Greek, rock. Peter's confession is the very rock upon which Jesus will build his church.

And when they were all seated around the table in the warmth of the Upper Room and Jesus predicted that everyone would desert him, Peter blurted out, "Though everyone will desert you, I will stick beside you."

But in the darkness, with the soldiers on the prowl and this impudent young woman— this serving woman—interrogating him publicly, Peter appeared as anything but The Rock.

The power of that woman! There she stood before the best that Jesus could do in the way of disciples—the premier and most powerful of the disciples—and she made him testify, show what he was made of. It was Peter's final and most important exam. And he flunked.

In high school I had this Latin teacher—a mean Latin teacher (perhaps that's a tautology). And part of her meanness was that she gave public exams. Not only did you have to know Latin but you had to know it in front of the whole class which, for me, was an unbearable humiliation—to be made to stand up and, before the whole class, show how little Latin I had in me.

In the course of this service today, you will be asked to "rise and affirm your faith," repeating the words of the Apostles' Creed. And you will be able. It is easy to affirm the faith and to swear to the creed, when we are here in the safe confines of the church. We are protected in this large, fortress-like building, with its thick walls. And we say our creeds, and we sing our hymns, and we affirm our faith. But then we go out. And out there—out there is the exam. And the faith we have tried to keep private is forced to go public. And that's a different story.

The literary critic Eric Auerbach was fascinated by this little interchange between Peter and the serving girls in the courtyard at night. Auerbach says that in all of classical literature, in all of the Greek plays, there is nothing like this. In classical literature, common ordinary people, like serving girls or fishermen, are invariably represented as comic figures, buffoons. But here, in the conversation between Peter and the serving girl in the courtyard, is high drama, tragedy. These ordinary people are being represented as great tragic figures, their conversation ennobled and dignified.

Oh, the power of this woman!

Jesus had chosen Peter as his disciple, and he is clearly depicted as the chief disciple. Jesus named him "Rockie" and said he would build his church upon him. Well, I guess Jesus got that one wrong. Look at him now. All of Peter's great declarations of faith wither in the face of three little questions by a little serving girl. She put him to the test. And he failed it.

Oh, the power of this woman!

A while back a student was telling me that he and his roommate were not getting along too well. I asked him why, and he said, "Because he is a Muslim and I'm not." I asked him how that made a difference. And he said, "When we moved in together, he asked me what my religion was. I told him that I was a Christian—a Lutheran. I told him that my family weren't the very best of Christians, that we only went to church occasionally, and that it wasn't that big a deal to me. My roommate has this nasty habit of asking embarrassing questions."

"What sort of questions?" I asked.

"Well after we had roomed together a few weeks, he asked me, 'Why do you Christians never pray?'"

"I told him, 'We pray a lot. We just sort of keep it to ourselves.'"

"He said, 'I'll say you do. I've never seen you pray.'"

"He prays like a half-dozen times a day on his prayer rug in our room, facing East Durham. When I came in last Saturday morning, he asked me, 'Doesn't your St. Paul say something about joining your body with that of a prostitute?'"

"I told him, 'Look, she is not a prostitute; she is a Tri Delt. I told you I am not the best Christian in the world. You shouldn't judge the Christian faith by me!'"

And I, hearing of his torment, said, "Well, how should he judge the Christian faith? I think I need to write your Muslim roommate a thank-you note. If he keeps working on you with these questions, he may make you into a real Christian."

This little serving girl gave Peter the opportunity to testify to what he believed, to take his faith into the real world. And he flunked. The world is quite right in judging Jesus by the sort of lives he is able to produce. The world is not being cruel or accusatory when it asks us, "Weren't you with Jesus? Does that make a difference?"

I have a friend—an international economist. He grew up in the Church, but he grew away from the Church. But then he came back to the Church and became active. I asked him what propelled him back. He told me that on an academic visit to the former Soviet Union, he had a conversation with a colleague. She was a Communist. In the course of the conversation she asked, "Do you believe in God?"

He said that he did. And then she asked, "What difference does it make in your life that you believe in God? I don't believe, but if I did, it would probably complicate my life. What difference does God make in your life?"

And my friend said that he could not come up with a single thing in his life that was different because of his faith.

He was embarrassed by having no ready answers. Isn't it odd how sometimes these people who don't know Jesus have an uncanny way of knowing more about Jesus than we who do? Sometimes, in the odd workings of Providence, these people expose the limits of our fidelity, and we are forced to say what we believe or else appear embarrassingly out of step with our own professions.

Stanley Hauerwas, who teaches at the Duke Divinity School, says that during his graduate work he became convinced, from a reading of Christian theologians and Scriptures, that

Jesus was a pacifist, that pacifism was the only orthodox Christian way. He had ideas in his head, but he really did not have pacifism in his heart. So in conversation with people, occasionally he would say, "I am a Christian pacifist. I think this is the way of Jesus."

In saying that, he said he met some of the most offensive people—people who would automatically move into their antipacifist arguments: "Well, what would you do if your wife and family were being attacked by somebody? Would you just stand there and not defend them? Were we wrong to declare war against Hitler?" On and on.

Hauerwas says that after a year or so of this interrogation, forcing him to come up with arguments for his profession of pacifism, demanding that he think things through, that he repeat his convictions again and again, after about a year of this, he said, "I was a pacifist. These offensive, antagonistic people, had, through their stupid challenges and dumb questions, made me into a true believer."

Maybe each of us, if we are to follow Jesus, need not only a prayer partner, or the help of a Bible study group, but we also need someone like that little serving girl, who is there to question us, to challenge us, and to make us say what we believe.

In the creed, we mention that Jesus "suffered under Pontius Pilate." Pilate has a place in our creed because he was the one who tried Jesus and condemned Jesus to death on the cross. Pilate unwittingly enabled Jesus to shine forth from the cross, to show the world the depths to which God would stoop to save us.

Maybe we ought to put this little nameless servant girl into our creed. She was the one who put Peter on trial. She was the one who demanded that Peter confess before the world what he held to be true. Of course, Jesus passed the exam that Peter flunked, and maybe that is why we do not give her the credit that she deserves or even remember her name.

In an undergraduate class I was teaching, I asked students to write a short essay on the subject, "What I Believe and Why." By far my most eloquent essay was written by a young man who was Hindu. He was from Little Rock, Arkansas. I marveled at his articulate defense of his faith in his paper. I was somewhat embarrassed by the half-dozen or so papers by Christian students. Many of them had a rather inarticulate view of the Christian faith and obviously found it difficult to say what they believed.

I told him how much I admired his paper and that, as a Christian preacher, I was a bit embarrassed by the papers written by the Christians in comparison.

He said to me, "Remember, I am from Little Rock. I've had to explain my Hinduism my entire life. In Little Rock, no one would say, 'Gosh, you're a Southern Baptist. Tell me about who you are and what you believe.' I got a lot of experience in explaining myself back in Little Rock."

Our faith is strengthened when we have to explain ourselves. All of us need, in the middle of the night, when things are dangerous, to meet some little servant girl, who demands that we say what we believe.

I expect, as you go forth from the safe confines of this fortress of faith, there is a good chance that somewhere, sometime, you will meet someone like this young woman. I call her a "heroine of the faith" because she exposed the vulnerability of our declarations. She forced Peter out into the open. He flunked the test that midnight. But after the Crucifixion of Jesus and after his Resurrection, the Risen Christ appears to Peter. He forgives him, blesses him, and puts him in charge of the fledgling Church. Tradition has it that Peter paid for his faith by being crucified, upside down. When it counted, at the end, Peter was The Rock Jesus had meant him to be.

One reason we ask you to stand to repeat the words of the creed, to affirm your faith, is the hope that if you get enough practice in doing that in the safe confines of this dear church, you will be able to do it when you are tested out there in the world.

Let us stand and affirm what we believe.—William H. Willimon

SUNDAY, AUGUST 27, 2006
Lectionary Message

Topic: Dedication to the Lord
TEXT: 1 Kings 8:1, 6, 10–11, 22–30, 41–43
Other Readings: Ps. 84; Eph. 6:10–20; John 6:56–69

David had always wanted to build a temple for the Lord—a permanent place of worship. The king of Israel had a palace, but the worship of God took place in and around a tent. Second Samuel 7 tells the story of David's plan to build a temple, followed by God's instruction that he wanted David's son to do it, not David himself. So for years David gathered the best materials of the ancient Near East. He had the best wood, gold, and materials that he could find, and he stockpiled them so that his son could one day build a temple for the Lord.

Soon after Solomon's coronation, he began to make good on his father's promise to build a permanent place of worship. He brought the best craftsmen and builders to the task and set them to the work of building what was arguably the most elaborate and ornate building of worship in the world. His care in building and then his great prayer of dedication teach contemporary believers much about the values that God holds dear.

I. *The presence of God has priority over the place of worship.* As soon as Solomon completed the Temple at Jerusalem, he immediately moved to bring the Ark of the Covenant to it. He knew that it would be nothing without the Ark of the Covenant—the symbolic and ritualistic focus of the presence of God. Solomon sent men after the Ark, also known as the Mercy Seat or the Place of Atonement, which had been kept in Bethlehem, his father's hometown; they had a moveable celebration, as they brought the Ark those ten or twelve miles to the new Temple.

Solomon's action says something significant about his values. He had just spent untold millions on the Temple, but he knew it was nothing without the Ark. It is in the act of atonement—the merciful action of God by which he forgives sin through the blood offering—that God dwells with his people. He cannot live with them any other way but through the satisfactory offering for sin. Solomon knew that the most ornate building in the world was empty and useless apart from the presence of God, and the presence of God was inextricably interwoven with the place of atonement. The place of worship was not nearly as important as the presence of God in that place.

II. *The worship of God has priority over the service of God.* When the Ark was carried into the new Temple, something wonderful happened. God inaugurated the work by a visible and tangible presence that filled the Temple. Priests who were doing their ritualistic cleansing had to leave. The presence of God was so great that no man could stand in his presence, and no work could be done in his name.

Serving God is certainly important, even necessary. The Bible places a premium on serving the Lord. Yet worship is and must remain the priority. There are times when God intervenes in our lives and demands that we stop serving and pause long enough to simply worship and adore. Sometimes he may come to us dramatically, palpably. At other times we hear the still, small voice of God. Still, the unmistakable call of God is that we worship him, even more than that we serve him.

III. *The promise of God has priority over the performance of humanity.* First Kings 8:22–30 is one of the most beautiful prayers recorded in Scripture. Solomon certainly knew enough theology to know that God is bigger than the Temple, greater than all other gods, and more faithful than any man. He is the one who keeps covenant. His word endures and is settled forever in the heavens. If this Temple were to endure, it would not be because any person or group of people was good enough or deserved it. It would be only because the Lord chose to put his name there, and it pleased him to be worshipped there.

Though we ought always to strive for holiness, even for perfection, we must realize that any good thing that happens in our life is because every good and perfect gift comes down from above, from the Father of lights. God's presence is not the reward of our goodness but the *cause* of it.

IV. *People have priority over ritual.* Tucked deep in the prayer of Solomon is a fascinating request that has little expression elsewhere in the Old Testament, yet is absolutely foundational to the mission of the New Testament. In 1 Kings 8:41–43, Solomon prays specifically that the Temple—the dwelling place of God—might be attractive and a draw, not only to the Jews but also to the Gentiles, the strangers who might come there. He prayed that even those of other religions and from other countries might know of the God the Jews worshipped, and they might come to the Temple to worship him.

This was a radical notion for Solomon's day, yet Solomon saw the implications of God's greatness. If he is indeed the Creator, then he is the Creator of all and desires and deserves to be worshipped. If indeed he dwells with the Jews, then he can dwell with all people in the same way—through the blood covenant that he keeps. Whatever rites and rules the Jews had, God saw people as more important than ritual.—Hershael York

ILLUSTRATION

WHEN GOD BREAKS THROUGH.   Anyone who was alive in 1963 can probably remember where he or she was when the news of President Kennedy's assassination broke. British novelist David Lodge, in the introduction to one of his books, tells where he was—in a theater watching the performance of a satirical revue he had helped write. In one sketch, a character demonstrated his nonchalance in an interview by holding a transistor radio to his ear. The actor playing the part always tuned in to a real broadcast. Suddenly, came the announcement that President Kennedy had been shot. The actor quickly switched it off, but it was too late. Reality had interrupted stage comedy. For many believers, worship, prayer, and Scripture are a nonchalant charade. They don't expect anything significant to happen, but suddenly God's reality breaks through, and they're shocked.[4]

---

[4]Brian Powley, *Leadership*, Vol. 5, no. 4.

SERMON SUGGESTIONS

Topic: The Pilgrim's Devotion to God

TEXT: Ps. 84

(1) What he hopes for from God is not the fulfillment of specific individual wishes that spring from the human heart. (2) He is satisfied with *God's* grace and *his* glory, toward which he proceeds. (3) He submits to God. (4) He entrusts himself to him.[5]

Topic: Do You Wish to Escape?

TEXT: Heb. 11:35

(1) In the midst of life we find many disconcerting things to torture us: the inconstancy of human friendships; the power of temptation; the inevitability of suffering; the certainty of death. (2) Ways we try to escape or deal with these disconcerting realities: deny them; try to escape them; give up and let them crush us; try to master these things and use them for personal growth and service to others. (3) Can we find a *real* way of escape? Yes, if we can find life's center. Jesus said, "I am the way, the truth, and the life." Yes, if we measure all of life by the greatness, goodness, and love of God (Rom. 8:38–39). Yes, if we live in constant communion with God. Yes, if we join God in living for others.

WORSHIP AIDS

CALL TO WORSHIP.   "Your decrees are wonderful; therefore my soul keeps them. The unfolding of your words gives light; it imparts understanding to the simple. With open mouth I pant, because I long for your commandments" (Ps. 119:129–131 NRSV).

INVOCATION.   Almighty God, we adore you, we praise you, we worship you, we honor you. You give strength to the faint and hope to the weary. You are more than we can comprehend, yet so real that we could never deny you. We honor you with our worship and our praise.—E. Lee Phillips

OFFERTORY SENTENCE.   "Be steadfast, immovable, always excelling in the work of the Lord, because you know that in the Lord your labor is not in vain" (1 Cor. 15:58 NRSV).

OFFERTORY PRAYER.   Gracious Lord, in our offerings may our willingness to give match the measure of your blessing.

PRAYER.   Eternal God, you commit to us the swift and solemn trust of life, and since we do not know what a day may bring forth, but only that the hour for serving you is always present, may we wake to the instant claims of your holy will; not waiting for tomorrow, but yielding today. Lay to rest, by the persuasion of your Spirit, the resistance of our passion, laziness, or fear. Consecrate with your presence the way our feet may go; and the humblest work will shine, and the roughest places be made plain. Lift us above unrighteous anger and

---

[5]Artur Weiser, *The Psalms* (London: S.C.M. Press, 1962), p. 569.

mistrust into faith and hope and love by a simple and steadfast reliance on your sure will. In all things draw us to the mind of Christ, that your lost image may be traced again, and you may own us at one with him, and with you.—Adapted from James Martineau

SERMON
Topic: Secular Communion and Christian Worship
TEXT: Rom. 12:3–5; Matt. 18:19–20

There's a minor character in the movie *Shakespeare in Love* who helps make one of the movie's major points. This moment is a fine example—a paradigm case—of what Ian McEwan calls "public performance" as "a secular communion."[6]

Secular communion at a public performance really happens, and it offers us an analogy for understanding Christian worship, at least in an incipient sort of way. That is, secular communion at a public performance provides us with a beginning point for understanding what is supposed to happen when Christians gather to worship. In both public performance and Christian worship, we are caught up in a story that transcends the individual, particular story of each of us. In Christian worship, both worship leaders and worshippers become actors in the divine drama of redemption—the story of what God has done for us in Christ to save us.

Going to a movie is a little bit like going to a worship service. But only a little bit. This analogy, like all analogies, is not perfect. The most significant difference between performance and worship is that the story proclaimed in Christian worship is true in the most fundamental way something can be true, and *Romeo and Juliet* is not. That is, the kind of truth found in the Christian story is true in a way no other truth is.

So what kind of truth is the truth of the Christian story? How is it true in a way no other truth is true? And what difference does this truth make? The best way to answer these abstract questions is to take a concrete example of Christian truth and see how it is true. Let's take Paul's statement in 2 Corinthians 5:19 that "God was in Christ, reconciling the world to himself." How is this statement true?

First, it tells us something universally and necessarily true about the nature of God—that God is always about the business of reconciliation. It is God's very nature to be ceaselessly acting in ways that reconcile us to each other and to God. It is God's very nature to be grace and love toward us and all creation. Like logical and scientific truth, this truth about God is necessary and universal. God cannot *not* be grace and love.

But second, we do not learn this universal and necessary truth about God by logical reasoning or scientific experiment, as we learn the other universal and necessary truths we know. It is, instead, something we learn by revelation. It is *revealed* to us in the contingent history of a people and the contingent life of a person: the people of Israel and the life, death, and Resurrection of Jesus. God was in *Christ*, Paul says. The very life of God was in the life of a real human being, who lived a real human life at a real period of human history. It is a central part of Christian belief to affirm that Jesus was really human (and it is the oldest of Christian heresies to deny this). This is why the Apostles' Creed contains what is otherwise a

---

[6]*Amsterdam* (New York: Doubleday, 1998), p. 14.

curious statement—that Jesus "suffered under Pontius Pilate." It is our way of confessing that a real human being—Pontius Pilate—condemned a real human being—Jesus Christ—to death.

Revelation is the way we come to the central truths of our faith, and this process is analogous to what happens when we experience the truth of a work of art or the significance of a human life: we see it; we *grasp* the truth in a moment of intuition (or perhaps what really happens is that the trust grasps us). So third, this Christian truth is an aesthetic-ethical truth, which we come to know in the same way we know any other value. Religious truth, in other words, has a way of bringing together all these other kinds of truth. The central claims of our faith unify all the other ways of knowing in what we might call an "epistemological communion"—a union of necessary, contingent, and intuitive truths.

No secular communion resulting from a public performance is true in the comprehensive way Christian belief is true. The truth of the Christian story encompasses all other kinds of truth, and the story Christians are caught up in is true in every way it can be true. Secular communion is, therefore, like Christian worship in that in both we are caught up in the story being told. It is different, however, in that its truth is partial and incomplete and points to the possibility of a deeper truth—the truth of the Christian story.

There is another way secular communion differs from Christian worship: namely, in the quality of the communion it creates. The community we experience in a public performance is at best temporary, fleeting, evanescent. The community this kind of communion creates does not sustain itself but dissipates very quickly after the performance. It may remain a fond, even powerful, memory long after the event. But it has no continuing reality.

The communion created by Christian worship is of a very different quality. To experience Christian communion in a Christian community is to experience an ongoing, living reality. It is ongoing because it depends on God, not on us. Jesus formed a community of people who lived with him as he preached, taught, and healed. These individuals—Peter, James, and John; Mary, Martha, and especially Mary Magdalene, who was the first witness to the Resurrection—became a community of people in communion with Jesus. Jesus incarnates the life of God, because "*God* was in Christ." And by means of this community, Christ began to share the life he had with these first disciples. Gradually, not all at once, they ceased being Peter, James, John, Mary, Martha, and Mary Magdalene and started becoming instead members of the body of Christ and, therefore, members of each other, as Paul said in Romans 12. This means that their individuality became something more than it had been, without becoming lost. Paul was right on this one: to believe in Christ is to begin living the kind of life Christ lived and to share that life with all others who believe.

When we connect with Christ in this way, we are connecting with God's reality, because "God was in Christ." And the life we begin to live connects us with each other in the same way that individual members of a living organism are connected to each other. This means that we give life to each other just as surely as Christ gives life to us. This is why worship with other Christians is so important. It is in our gathering together that Christ is most real among us. "Where two or three are gathered in my name, I am there among them." Worship in community nourishes the new life that we have begun in Christ and helps it grow.

It is true that we can and do experience God in individual private moments—in the beauty of the natural world, for example, or in the overwhelming sense of gratitude and mystery we feel when we witness the birth of a child. These are real experiences of God, and they add immeasurably to our spiritual life. But if they are the *only* ways we know God, then they are very likely to be like the secular communion of a public performance—something that dissipates soon afterward. Spiritual experience of this sort will lack the staying power we need for the long haul of life, and it may not be there for us when we most need it.

To worship God in a community of others makes me aware of the truth that I am not alone as I try to live the Christian life. It reminds me that there are others who believe in God and in Christ as I do, who face the same issues of truth I face. Life is something we give to each other, as well as something that comes from God. By worshiping together, we receive the life of God through Christ and give that new life to each other.—Bill Thomason

SUNDAY, SEPTEMBER 3, 2006
Lectionary Message

Topic: The Ministry of Listening
TEXT: James 1:17–27
Other Readings: Song of Songs 2:8–13; Ps. 45:1–2, 6–9; Mark 7:1–8, 24–15, 21–23

Perhaps you can remember a time when you really needed somebody to talk to—a time when you were not looking for advice but, rather, just a sympathetic ear—a point in your life when you were hoping for someone who would take time to sit down and listen to your problem without passing judgment.

We recall that righteous Job, in the midst of his sufferings, longed for someone who would just listen to his complaints and empathize with him. All of us, like Job, cry out to be listened to.

The apostle James encourages us to be "quick to listen, slow to speak" (James 1:19). True religion is caring for others, including listening to them, in their distress. Listening is a ministry whose importance is being recognized more and more as time goes by. Counseling centers that engage in the ministry of listening and centers of spiritual formation that offer the services of spiritual directors are flourishing like never before. But one need not have a counseling degree or certification in spiritual direction to engage in the ministry of listening. Every one of us can learn to become a good listener; every one of us can learn to exercise the ministry of listening, with a little practice and patience. There are some basic steps to becoming a good listener and exercising the ministry of listening that are accessible to all of us.

I. *Step 1: Encourage verbal sharing.* That is, encourage others to open up and talk to you. Be anxious to let others talk about themselves instead of focusing on your own concerns. Ask open-ended questions, not questions that can be answered with yes or no. Ask "how, what, when, and where" types of questions. Make it your goal to really get to know what the other person is thinking. After the person shares with you, mirror it back to make sure you heard what was being said. That is, repeat back what you think you heard. The way to mirror is to say, "Janey, what I hear you saying is . . ." This will ensure that you are both on the same wavelength.

Now at this point, it is always tempting to jump in and give advice. After we get just a little bit of information, we are always ready to say what we think ought to be done. Right? But this is no place to give advice. When listening, we must learn to keep our "shoulds" to ourselves. Listening is the exact opposite of blaming or judging or giving advice. Remember that James advises, "Be quick to listen, slow to speak" (1:19). We must remember that we are engaged in the ministry of listening, not preaching. So our goal is to encourage verbal sharing.

II. *Step 2: Validate.* Affirm as legitimate the feelings or thoughts that have been expressed. The way we affirm is to say, "Janey, that makes sense to me." By validating what we have heard, we are showing acceptance of the other person. We are letting her know that what she is feeling is not totally off the wall. By validating others' feelings, we are affirming their worth and goodness. We are letting them know that they are not the worst sinner in the world but that what they are feeling is perfectly human and common humanity. We should never be phony in complimenting another person. But at the same time, we can let others know what their unique value is to us. We can compliment and thank them for sharing something so personal with us.

III. *Step 3: Empathize.* Share others' joy and enter into their pain with them. The way to show empathy is to say, "I think I understand how you feel." It is important at this point that there be eye contact. Such emotions as hurt, anger, fear, sadness, and frustration often come out in bodily gestures. In order to fully understand another person so that we may empathize with them, we need to be sensitive to silent body language, as well as spoken words. Our goal should always be to better understand. And sometimes that is all people want: to be understood and accepted, and have their feelings affirmed.

To be a good listener, we need not have all the answers to life's perplexities. A proper response might be, "Well, Janey, that is a difficult problem. Right off, I don't have an answer. But I do understand how you feel. And I will be there with you as a friend, and we will search for the answer together."

I would like to encourage you to study and practice the ministry of listening. It is a ministry that you can perform practically anywhere you happen to be—at work, in the grocery store, at the ball field, at the hospital, or here at church.

Again, the three steps in the ministry of listening are these: (1) encourage verbal sharing; (2) let the other person do the talking, and validate or affirm what has been said; (3) empathize or show that you understand. Listening is a ministry—a ministry that comes from God. The good news is that God listens to us. Listening to our prayers is one of God's good gifts to us (James 1:17). Our ministry, in return, is to listen to others. May God help us all know when to keep silent and when to exercise the ministry of listening.—Randy Hammer

ILLUSTRATIONS

A LISTENING TEST.   Persons preparing for full-time Christian ministry are often given tests on how well they can speak. During my last year in seminary, we had to stand in the chapel and deliver a sermon before our peers and before a video camera. Our peers then critiqued our sermon. We later had to go watch the video with the preaching professor, who critiqued it even more. But no test was given for the ability to listen, even though this is an important ministry in the Church.—Randy Hammer

EMPATHETIC LISTENING.   "God's compassionate, listening heart is seen clearly in Jesus Christ. . . . Because he [Jesus] could hear the full message, he could always respond appropriately. . . . Empathetic listening is one of the best means of expressing unselfish love. Listening says, 'You are important,' or 'Your ideas, problems, and feelings are important to me. I care about you.' Listening is a primary means of modeling God's love. . . ."[1]

---

[1]Norman Wakefield, *Listening: A Christian's Guide to Loving Relationships* (Waco, Tex.: Word Books, 1981), pp. 15, 18.

SERMON SUGGESTIONS

Topic: Safeguarding Love

TEXT: Luke 6:27–38

(1) We want to keep love at its best: love is the greatest hope of peace anywhere; it gives purpose to life; it adds joy and contentment. (2) How to safeguard love: keep love clean, don't use friendship selfishly, don't short-circuit love with lust, don't take the love of God for granted; keep love growing, by taking an interest in others, by using the love you have, by forgiveness.

Topic: A Closer Walk with God

TEXT: Gen. 5:24; John 15:1–17

(1) Things we may fear: enslavement; disapproval; self-reproach. (2) What a closer walk with God involves: changes in thinking and living; new goals; peace that passes understanding; sharing the purpose of God for the world. (3) How we get closer to God: the circumstances of our lives tend to bring us closer; we may aid our growth by constant effort to obey the will of God, as it appears to challenge us day by day.

WORSHIP AIDS

CALL TO WORSHIP.   "My soul shall be joyful in the Lord: it shall rejoice in his salvation" (Ps. 35:9).

INVOCATION.   O God of time and eternity, we know that we never worship apart from a great cloud of witnesses—angels and archangels, as well as your people through the ages who walked this Earth in faith and devotion. Grant that the awareness that our numbers, augmented by all the company of heaven, may embolden us with new confidence and courage.

OFFERTORY SENTENCE.   "He that taketh not his cross, and followeth after me, is not worthy of me" (Matt. 10:38).

OFFERTORY PRAYER.   Lord, sometimes giving is painful, truly painful. Yet, as the wounds of Christ were for the healing of humanity, so let our small sacrifice bless others.

PRAYER.   "I set my bow in the cloud, and it shall be a sign of the covenant between me and the earth" (Gen. 9:13). God of justice and of law, we sign our contracts with indelible ink. Why did you sign your covenant with a rainbow? Why a pastel prism dependent on so fickle an arrangement as the slant of light through droplets of moisture? If you were serious, why didn't you carve it in stone or cast it in bronze? Look, God, at our monuments. We chisel our ideals on public facades, in chambers of state and halls of justice. Do you mock us, God, with your rainbow? Yes, I think you do. You remind us that the strength of a promise is in its keeping and not in the signature of the guarantor. The chromatic-colored cursive that you scrawl across the sky fades with the clearing of the clouds, but the promise of your everlasting care still endures. It is written in hope that cannot be erased. It is scribbled in joy that cannot be washed away. It is printed in the clear, bold character of Jesus Christ. O God, though our ink is indelible, our will is impermanent. Secure our promises with your faithfulness, and we shall be loyal to you forever.—Thomas H. Troeger

SERMON
Topic: The Fruit of the Spirit Is Patience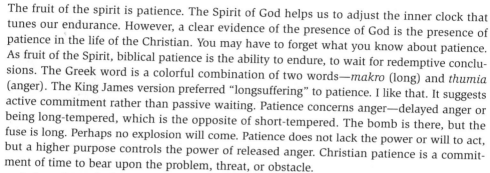
TEXT: James 5:7–11

The fruit of the spirit is patience. The Spirit of God helps us to adjust the inner clock that tunes our endurance. However, a clear evidence of the presence of God is the presence of patience in the life of the Christian. You may have to forget what you know about patience. As fruit of the Spirit, biblical patience is the ability to endure, to wait for redemptive conclusions. The Greek word is a colorful combination of two words—*makro* (long) and *thumia* (anger). The King James version preferred "longsuffering" to patience. I like that. It suggests active commitment rather than passive waiting. Patience concerns anger—delayed anger or being long-tempered, which is the opposite of short-tempered. The bomb is there, but the fuse is long. Perhaps no explosion will come. Patience does not lack the power or will to act, but a higher purpose controls the power of released anger. Christian patience is a commitment of time to bear upon the problem, threat, or obstacle.

I. Impatience is the mark of our busy lives. It was the middle of the busiest intersection during a peak traffic period. Only one lane was open to allow escape from the congestion and noise. The light changed. The car lunged and died. The frustrated driver cranked and cranked, to no avail. In the meantime, the guy behind her began to sound his horn. Finally, the battery expired, and the driver stepped out of the disabled car, walked directly to the door of the trapped motorist behind her, and politely offered, "I know that you must be tired by now. If you will start my car, I will honk your horn." Haven't you always wanted to do that? The story is old. It comes from the good old days when people honked horns instead of shooting each other. We live in an impatient world where time is money, and people want everything yesterday. The computer age has introduced number-crunching and data management, drastically cutting the number of people-hours to do every job, and suggesting that everything ought to be done in an instant. Stories about waiting for the vacuum tubes to warm up on a TV or radio sound like ancient history to our children. Like you, I have grown accustomed to instant-on appliances, instant information from the Internet, instant cash from the ATM. Why should I have to wait for anything or anyone—even God?

I read a church journal, *Net Results*, which is packed with the latest information and trends in church development. The article, "Understanding Generation X," describes the passing of the Baby Boomers to Generation X, "the first 'pure' Postmodern generation." Given the extent to which we are all involved, this may be less about generations than trends. A significant trait of Generation X is the effect of virtual reality—the tendency to confuse fact with fiction, to judge by appearance. Virtual reality is the synthetic, usually electronic, reproduction of images that confuses the sense of reality. Computerized images in the movies are basic examples, but recently CBS did a historical documentary on the first moon walk. The narrator was "Maurice," the fictional astronaut from the TV show, *Northern Exposure*. He stayed in character and spoke as if he had actually participated in the event, deliberately confusing his fictional role with history. Is this real or virtual reality? This is a new twist on the optical illusion. Things are not as they appear. We slip down the slope of illusion. For the Prophets, idolatry was the shortcut to deity. We chisel our gods with electronic illusion, while God endures our play.

II. Do we need patience from God or with God? Jesus came down from the mountain to find his disciples in a quandary of frustration. They had exhausted every resource to heal the epileptic boy. Was the diagnosis or the treatment wrong? "Now let's see; all you have to do is use the right words, hold your hands in the right position, uh, let's see, wave a Bible in the air, hold your breath, that does it. Oops, missed again!"

In Mark, Jesus said this kind must be healed by prayer—no magic words, shortcuts, or instant solutions. The power of healing belongs to the God of creation. Far more miracles flow from the grace of God through the healing power of time than have ever come by a snap of the fingers or by angry demands made on dead demons. The Creator works far more miracles through evolution than through revolution. Even in the Bible, fiat acts of God may be more than they seem. Seven days of creation in Genesis model the weekly cycle of life for the Jews. As time flows, these are poetic days representing billions of years of divine patience. If you think for an instant that the biblical hope is about getting what you want when you want it—instant salvation, turning God into a vending machine dispensing quick, easy answers—look again. The eternal God has all the time in the world. Patience, long-suffering, delayed anger is the divine forte. We had best learn patience with God, for the greatest challenge to human endurance is the forbearance required by faith.

III. Patience is the durable quality of faith. In James "the patience of Job" has become legendary. My first serious encounter with Job was at Baylor. Kyle Yates uttered a shocking heresy: "Job is not patient." All you have to do is read. Job growled at his friends and complained to God and about God. What he did not do was sit in the ash heap scratching his sores in quiet acceptance. But Job endured. Apart from raising some timeless questions about justice, human suffering, and the nature of God, Job's only legitimate claim to fame is endurance. He would not quit. The metaphor should be adjusted to speak of the "tenacity of Job." Faith endures. The NRSV addresses "the endurance of Job." Every last one of the champions of faith in Hebrews 11 "died in faith without having received the promises." But they endured.

The fruit of the Spirit is hardly about getting what you want when you want it. It is about living without what you want, getting what you get, and holding onto God anyway. It is not about instantaneous results. It is about lasting commitments. It is about growing old in grace, allowing others to grow old before you, behind you, and with you. Patience lives toward the ultimate reward: "Well done, good and faithful servant."—Larry Dipboye

SUNDAY, SEPTEMBER 10, 2006
Lectionary Message

Topic: The Problem with People-Labeling
TEXT: James 2:1–10 (11–13), 14–17
Other Readings: Prov. 22:1–2, 8–9, 22–23; Ps. 125; Mark 7:24–37

I am a people watcher. Perhaps you are, too. I enjoy observing people. For instance, whenever I am at a shopping mall and have a few minutes to kill, I enjoy sitting down on one of the benches and just watching the people go by. Once when I was watching people coming and going in the mall, I observed that one shopper seemed to be very physically fit. I thought to myself, "That young man must be an athlete." I saw another person who was very well dressed, and I conjectured that she must be wealthy. One man was sort of suspicious-looking; I judged that he was looking to get into trouble. Another lady seemed to be overly upset and very emotional. It seemed to me that she might be having some emotional problems. Another shopper I decided was stuck-up; another was poor; still another was a foreigner, probably visiting here from a European country. Without even realizing what I was doing, I had started to put labels on people. Without meaning to, I had started forming opinions and judging people by what little I saw of total strangers, solely on the basis of a momentary outward appearance. And I asked myself, "Is this the right thing to do—to put a label on someone or judge someone I have never even met?" Then I realized that this is the way we tend to go through life—putting labels on people we don't even know and drawing distinctions between persons with whom we are not even acquainted.

I. One of the potential problems with people-labeling is that we may set ourselves up as prejudicial judges. In fact, this is what the apostle James is trying to get us to see. James cautions against making distinctions and becoming judges of other people based solely on outward appearances. James warns against showing partiality, especially in the house of God. When we start putting labels on people such as Protestant or Catholic, Christian or Muslim, black or white, rich or poor, foreign or American, ugly or pretty, worthy or unworthy, and so forth, we are showing partiality and passing judgment. A case in point is the fact that a lot of people in our country who are of Arabic descent may be unjustly characterized to be Muslim terrorists. Such is an unfair label.

When we put labels on people on the basis of outward appearances, we allow prejudice to overcome us and fail to see people as they really are. The meaning of *prejudice* is preconceived judgment or opinion without just grounds or before sufficient knowledge. Too often we are tempted to believe that *only* people who look and act just like us are normal. The apostle James is trying to teach us that prejudice is incompatible with Christian faith. The call of Scripture is that we rid ourselves of the distorted glasses of prejudice, and that we be careful about making distinctions, and that we be cautious about putting labels on people on the basis of outward appearance or first impressions. Or to put it another way, it is impossible for the heart to embrace both the Christian faith and prejudice. They are two opposing forces, contrary one to the other. A *prejudiced Christian* is an oxymoron—a contradiction in terms.

II. Another problem with people-labeling and setting ourselves up as judges is that we are not qualified to do that. We don't see—we cannot see—as God sees. As it is written in the book of 1 Samuel, we look on the outward appearance, "but the Lord looks on the heart" (16:7). Too often we are tempted to draw faulty conclusions about someone, based on first impressions. Perhaps you can recall forming a poor first impression of someone, only to later see how wrong you were.

Not long after we moved to West Tennessee, when I started to seminary, I attended a meeting of our local church judicatory. In the course of debate, one of the more "prominent" ministers stood to offer his opinion. I had never met him. But I quickly formed a first impression of him. My first impression was not very positive. But the more I got acquainted with this man, the more I liked him. The more I worked with him, the more my respect for him grew. Three or four judicatory meetings later, this same minister delivered the communion sermon. It was one of the best sermons I have ever heard in my life. I shall never forget it. Today, I hold this minister to be one of the most knowledgeable and talented ministers in the denomination. The story just goes to show how much you can depend on first impressions. Because we cannot see into the heart, we are not qualified to label or judge people.

III. Yet another problem with people-labeling is the fact that God accepts all who love and honor God from the heart. In every nation—every race, every nationality, and every social class—anyone who fears God and does what is right is acceptable in the eyes of the Creator. Are we not sometimes tempted to think that God is partial to persons who are exactly like us in every way and that God has little regard for all others who do not look, live, believe, or worship the way we do? Aren't you glad that God is not partial to a certain kind of people? Aren't you glad that God looks at all people equally, accepting all in the same way? What if God were partial to persons of German descent, as was Martin Luther the reformer, yet you are not German? Or what if God were partial to persons of English descent, as was John Wesley, yet you are not English? What if God were partial to persons of African descent, or Indian descent, or Asian descent? If God were partial to persons of a particular descent, many of us would be doomed.

But God shows no partiality. God loves, cares for, and accepts all the children of the world on the same basis. That includes you and me. Such is the nature of God, as revealed in the person of Jesus Christ. The good news of the gospel—the other side of the coin—is that we don't have to worry about God being partial *against* us. God loves all of us, regardless of where we are from or what we look like.

ILLUSTRATIONS

CLEAN AND UNCLEAN.   The apostle Peter was accustomed to putting labels on people. Peter had been separating people into the clean and unclean. In Peter's eyes, the Jews who ate a certain way and who did certain things were clean, and all others who did not were judged as being unclean. After much soul searching and struggle, Peter finally realized the error of people-labeling. But it took a spiritual vision to correct his thinking and cause him to question his practice of making such distinctions. So Peter could later open his mouth and preach, "I truly understand that God shows no partiality, but in every nation anyone who fears him and does what is right is acceptable to him" (Acts 10:34–35).—Randy Hammer

EYES OF PREJUDICE.   At a railway station, waiting for his train to exchange passengers and continue on its journey, a man looked out the window of his coach and saw people who appeared to have distorted bodies and extremely ugly faces. "I could not believe what I was seeing," the man said. "So to remove my doubts, I lowered the glass window and found that everyone was perfectly normal. The difference was made by the poor and uneven texture of the windowpane through which I had been looking." Likewise, we see a distorted view of others when we look through the eyes of prejudice.—Author unknown

SERMON SUGGESTIONS

Topic: Surrounded
TEXT: Ps. 125
(1) God's people can depend on God's undefeatable purpose for them (vv. 1–2). (2) God is forever at work to help those who want to do what is right (vv. 3–4). (3) Sad to say, those who choose a crooked way engineer their own doom (v. 5).

Topic: Newness of Life

TEXT: Rom. 6:4

(1) A new master (Rom. 6:18). (2) A new freedom (Rom. 7:4). (3) A new law (Rom. 8:2). (4) A new destiny (Rom. 8:6).

WORSHIP AIDS

CALL TO WORSHIP.   "In God is my salvation and my glory: the rock of my strength, and my refuge, I in God" (Ps. 62:7).

INVOCATION.   Gracious Father, as we have turned aside from our usual preoccupations, help us to fix our hearts upon you, that love of you may order our system of values, to give you first place in every important decision of our lives. Transform our idols into servants of your purpose, so that work and money, friends and pleasure, marriage and children may rob us of nothing worthwhile and may increase the treasures of your kingdom.

OFFERTORY SENTENCE.   "The Lord said to Moses, 'Tell the Israelites to make an offering to me. Receive whatever offerings any man wishes to give.'" (Exod. 25:1–2 TEV).

OFFERTORY PRAYER.   O God, we acknowledge that often the more we have to give, the more reluctant we are to part with it. Open our hearts to our greater duty, as we gain larger resources.

PRAYER.   Father, I thank you for him who satisfies the deepest impulses of my nature. He is the only man who ever really lived: gentle, yet brave; confident, yet humble; wise, yet simple; meeting life with calmness, trouble with fortitude, hate with forgiveness, disloyalty with magnanimity, and crucifixion with faith. He has given to my life a savior, a movement, a promise, and challenge. In my saner moments, I know assuredly that somehow the life, ministry, and living again for Jesus is all there is for me! What's new? Life is, when love is renewing it day-by-day. Jesus taught and demonstrated that we can live in the perennial springtime of your love. Hallelujah! Love never gives up. It is always looking for ways to be constructive. It is imaginative. Though one be crucified, even death cannot destroy love. It keeps coming back. Love perseveres. Above all else, may we participate in this love, for it is the fulfillment of all things. Life will never grow stale for us then. Love is ever new, for it is the life of the living God, shared, celebrated. To love and keep on loving is to live a life that even death cannot destroy. What manner of love you have bestowed upon us, O Father, that we should be called your children. Thank you!—John Thompson

SERMON

Topic: The Might of Right

TEXT: Eph. 2:8–10, 6:14b

In his characteristic manner of turning a phrase, Abraham Lincoln inverted conventional wisdom with a challenge to a nation on the brink of war: "Let us have faith that right makes might." Lincoln confronted the philosophy of domination ethics that "might makes right"— a strong power base determines and defines ethics. Morality not only can be legislated, it can be shaped and enforced by the power brokers. At bottom, this ethic is always servant to the principalities and powers. It lives by inversion of the Golden Rule: "Those who have the gold make the rules." Might is a dangerous possession when it is given the priority in life. The first and most prevalent temptation of people in high places is to assume the right to "do as I please." The man who was to guide a nation through the most self-destructive event of its short history, was committed to the priority of principle over power. Like the one he loved to quote, Lincoln died holding to the idealism that right makes might.

I. The strength of right covers the vitality of our lives in the struggle with evil. The military equipment named in Ephesians is archaic at best, but so is the word *righteous*. A nationally famous disk jockey has used the word in jest, in an attempt to create more jargon for the youth culture: a "righteous" song or writer or performer is "cool" or "classy." Before we get too self-righteous about the abuse of a biblical concept, we need to realize that the word, if not the quality of life, is out of style. Being righteous has nothing to do with being right, either ethically or theologically, or with being politically correct. It does not concern leaning to the right in politics or religion, winning my rights, or playing it cool.

Biblical righteousness is the basis of human character. In the Old Testament, the nature of God is the standard, and the measure is obedience to the law—conformity to what God expects. Jesus took a step beyond the Old Testament. He expected his disciples to rise above the righteousness of the scribes and Pharisees. He internalized the law. External matters were secondary to the spiritual struggle within the human heart. Jesus was concerned, not only with the act of murder but the hatred from which murder is born, not only with the act of adultery but with lust. Like the prophets before him, Jesus located the standard of kingdom righteousness squarely in the nature of God: "Be perfect, therefore, as your heavenly Father is perfect." Neither the law nor the gospel draws a line within easy reach of fallible humans. In spite of his rich Jewish heritage, Paul harbored no illusions about his own ability to live up to biblical standards of perfection. The demand of the law exceeded Paul's reach. Thus no one has bragging rights: "By grace you have been saved through faith, and this is not your own doing." The breastplate of righteousness is the armor *of God,* that is, it is God's equipment, a gift from God, grace received by faith. Far from a badge of superiority achieved by disciples, it is a sign of dependence on the God of our salvation.

II. The public forum on values is in session. Today's moral crisis in this country began with the civil rights movement. The issue was racial discrimination. Racial prejudice, if not ethnic hatred, was the accepted standard of behavior for the nation and for most churches. I suspect that the atrocities of the Jewish Holocaust experienced during World War II planted the seed of change in attitudes toward race in America. Many of the issues that disturb the peace today were settled (or undisturbed) in the 1950s. Once the wall of accepted moral behavior was cracked, all of the pieces are open to examination. Civil rights are under discussion for all minorities, including children, women, homosexuals, and fetal life. No matter how you feel about any one of the issues, valid questions have been raised in national forums about the moral standards. We are going through a moral crisis, with forces pulling in two directions. The anything-goes ethic is in mortal combat with the back-to-the-fifties mentality. This is not only an issue of national politics or culture but Christians have never been more divided. Diversity of belief has developed into conflict and schism.

Christians have been trapped in a moral vacuum of ambiguity. What is the standard of righteousness? We are facing numerous issues for which the Bible gives no clear statement of direction. Although Washington, TV preachers, and the media rush in to fill the vacuum, none of the above are qualified to draw the baseline of Christian righteousness. The French Parliament established the language of right-left, conservative-liberal. Supporters of the king sat on the right; advocates of political change sat on the left. The right is not necessarily right, and neither is the left.

III. The standard of righteousness for a Christian is still bound to the nature of God and the leadership of the Holy Spirit. Christians need to work together to find direction. Righteousness does not begin with arrogant certainty on particular issues of theology or ethics, but with absolute dependence on God. Neither political nor theological correctness is the basis of Christian righteousness. Good works are the consequence of a right relationship with God, never the basis or right to a relationship with God. To send your child the message, "Be good, and I will love you," is a violation of love. Love is given, not earned. Love is never the payoff at the end of a performance. Love defined by the nature of God is undeserved and unconditional. To start at the works end of righteousness is to back into our relationship with God. Just as love is not a human creation but a response to being loved by God, loving behavior is not our own creation. Right behavior grows out of right thinking, and right thinking grows out of right relationships. This is the time to confess our need of guidance. Bishop Stephen Neil suggested the clue to Christian holiness in the word of Christ: to love your neighbor as yourself and to love God with all of your being. Righteousness begins in relationship. To be righteous is to be "justified," aligned in loving devotion to God through Christ. The people of God are known by their love for one another in the world around them. If you would be righteous, let the mind of Christ possess you.—Larry Dipboye

SUNDAY, SEPTEMBER 17, 2006
Lectionary Message

Topic: Only Speaking Positively
TEXT: James 3:1–12
Other Readings: Prov. 1:20–33; Ps. 19; Mark 8:27–38

A few years ago, Senator Trent Lott was forced to resign as Senate Republican leader—the first time in history that a party leader in the Senate was driven from his post. You may recall that the scandal that led to Senator Lott being ousted was not embezzlement, not an illicit affair, not obstruction of justice. Oddly enough, Senator Lott's downfall was due to a few careless words that he spoke at Senator Strom Thurmond's hundredth birthday celebration. Simply put, Senator Lott proudly recalled how the state of Mississippi had voted for Thurmond for president in 1948, when he ran as the candidate for the Segregationist Party. Lott's few poorly chosen words evoked a storm of condemnation from many across the country, especially among civil rights advocates, ultimately leading to personal humiliation and his resignation as Senate Republican leader.

I. It is quite amazing when you stop to think about the power a few choice words can have in changing our world so quickly and so drastically. Consider the general's first word, "Attack!" on the battlefield that begins a war. Consider the words, "The stock market has crashed." Consider the words, "The president has been shot." Consider the words, "I'm sorry; we did all we could," spoken by the emergency room doctor. Consider the words, "I now pronounce you husband and wife," spoken by the minister at the wedding chapel. Consider the words, "You're pregnant," or "It's a girl," or "It's a boy." How powerful can be the words that we speak or hear spoken. In a matter of seconds, a few words can drastically change our world.

In recent months, I have come to realize more than ever before the power of words. And I have come to realize how much of what is spoken in the world is negative in orientation. The bad thing is, negative words beget more negative energy. Negative words can be like a cancer that grows, that spreads out and influences others. Once negative words are let loose from the tongue, they tend to spread out of control, causing much damage, as Senator Lott sorely learned.

Negative words can take many forms, such as sarcasm. Your spouse or partner gets up in the morning with his or her hair all disheveled, and you say, "Well, look what the cat dragged in." That is sarcasm, and it starts the course of the day. Negative words can take the form of harsh, cutting remarks like, "I don't love you" or "I hate you." Gossip, which can easily become character assassination, is a form of negative words. Belittling remarks such as, "You're stupid. Don't you know anything?" are negative words. Self-defeating statements like, "I'm no good" or "I'm a failure" are negative words. Negative words rolling off the tongue can lead to discord, fighting, divorce, family breakups, church splits, even war.

There have been many times in my life when I spoke words in haste; sometimes negative words were let loose before I took time to think through the consequences, and then how much I wished I could take them back.

II. The apostle James has a lot to say about the words we speak and about the tongue and how the Christian should work to control it. James compares the activity of the tongue to a wildfire that burns out of control and spreads faster than you can put it out. "How great a forest is set ablaze by a small fire!" James says. One tiny match can set a fire to burn thousands of acres and destroy hundreds of homes. "And the tongue is like a fire. . . . It sets on fire the entire course of our existence" (James 3:6 GNT). So a goal as Christians, as followers of Christ, should always be to be very careful about the words we speak, since our words can have such a powerful impact on our lives and the world around us.

Perhaps you have asked the question, As solitary Christians, what is there that we can do to alter the world for the better? Sometimes we may think there is very little we can do. But one thing we can do is choose our words carefully and wisely. I submit that our aim as Christians should be to always speak helpful, not harmful words; gracious, favorable, and complimentary words; kind and edifying words. We might learn a lesson from some of our Quaker brothers and sisters, who are known for being careful about the words they speak and careful about guarding their tongues. Anyone who can keep his or her tongue in check has achieved self-control of the highest order and can likely keep his or her entire body under control.

III. Consider how each of us could be a positive influence that radiates out into the world like ripples in a pond, if we always made a point to withhold the negative and only speak the positive. Our positive influence could start in our homes. It could radiate out to our extended family and church. It could reach out to the workplace and school. And it could eventually have an impact on the world, as others follow our cue to only speak the positive.

Each of us might do well to look deep within our hearts and determine if we could make a resolution to try to always and only speak positive words. We, perhaps, should never hope for perfection in this regard. But we can hope for positive change and making a positive difference in our lives and in our world by making a personal commitment to never speak negative, but only positive, words. An appropriate challenge for each of us might be to make our daily morning prayer that of the psalmist: "Let the words of my mouth . . . be acceptable in your sight, O Lord, my strength and my redeemer" (Ps. 19:14).

ILLUSTRATIONS

WORDS CAN'T BE TAKEN BACK.   Perhaps you have heard the story of how a church member once started a false rumor about her minister. The rumor spread like wildfire throughout the community, badly damaging the minister's reputation. When the woman realized the damage that she had done, she was sorry and went to the minister to beg his forgiveness and ask what she might do to make things right. He told her to take an old feather pillow, remove the feathers, and take them to the community crossroads, and throw them to the wind. Once she had done that, the woman returned to the minister to report that she had completed her assignment. Then the minister said, "Now go gather all those feathers back up again." Carelessly spoken words, like feathers thrown to the wind, are impossible to take back again.

OSP.   All of us have seen the WWJD bracelets and other forms of jewelry, standing for What Would Jesus Do? I propose that someone design an OSP ring, with the initials OSP standing for Only Speak the Positive. Wouldn't it be great if everyone were to wear an OSP ring to remind us to never speak a negative word about others, or about ourselves, but to only speak the positive? At the very least, we could put a string around our finger as a reminder to only speak the positive.—Randy Hammer

SERMON SUGGESTIONS

Topic: The Story of God's Glory
TEXT: Ps. 19
(1) Nature reveals God's glory. (2) Biblical teaching reveals the will of God. (3) Human response in love and obedience can glorify God.

Topic: The Fellowship of the Convinced
TEXT: John 10:24–33
(1) The true church of our God is made up of those who hear in the voice of Jesus the voice of God. (2) They are convinced of life's spiritual meaning. (3) They are convinced of God's fatherly care.

WORSHIP AIDS

CALL TO WORSHIP.   "Let my mouth be filled with thy praise and with thy honor all the day" (Ps. 71:8).

INVOCATION.   Almighty God, you know all about us. You know when we sit down and when we rise up. You know when we sin and when we obey. May your Holy Spirit purge us of every wrong thing, that our lives may glorify you wherever we are.

OFFERTORY SENTENCE.   "The poor shall never cease out of the land: therefore I command thee, saying, thou shalt open thine hand wide unto thy brother, to thy poor, and to thy needy, in thy land" (Deut. 15:11).

OFFERTORY PRAYER.   O God, we have barely begun to take up the cross of him who had no place to lay his head. Grant that the offerings we bring may be a token of our growth toward true discipleship.

PRAYER.   Almighty God, turn us to Jesus Christ our Lord, that in his presence we may come to life again and know the abundance of thy grace. Set us in the path wherein he walked that we may grow in wisdom and in stature, in favor with our fellow men and women and with thee. Teach us how to forgive as he forgave, bringing souls out of hiding and shame into the light of joy and peace. Help us to put our hands out with the same blessing with which he healed and glorified the least of his brethren. Strengthen our sight to see among our comrades the living glory of the kingdom of heaven. If, or when, we must bear the cross, grant us courage and humility to lift it toward thee. In all our strivings, keep us in remembrance of that life which in Christ our Lord was light indeed.—Samuel H. Miller

SERMON
Topic: We Were Like Those Who Dream
TEXT: Ps. 126

Crushed by sufferings! Zion's enemies in divine judgment had plundered the land (2 Kings 24:18–25:7) Why? Because their "lips have spoken lies," and "no one [went] to law honestly (Isa. 59:3–4). Righteous Job had his vast wealth taken and his children destroyed on the same day. He endured such agonies that he cursed the day of his birth. A friend, David Duke, bore the burden of killer cancer.

Blind, begging Bartimaeus sat in darkness. His future survival depended on the pennies a few generous people might give him. The path of Jesus' obedience led to Gethsemane and Golgotha.

Much of life is learning to endure suffering. At times a part of that endurance is trying to determine whether our sufferings are deserved, like those of Zion, or undeserved, like those of Jesus, Job, and Bartimaeus. "If only I had worked a little harder I would not have been fired from my job." Or, "I did everything they asked. I worked hard, but they still fired me."

"If only we had been better parents, our children would not have forsaken God and us." Or, "We were the best parents we knew how to be, but our children forsook God and us anyway." "Why me?" or "Why not me?" And so on it goes. Part of our struggle dwells on where to assign guilt when we suffer. Usually, we are partly to blame and partly innocent.

Christ and God's mercy form the path to restoration. No matter the causes of our sufferings, renewal is a gift of the merciful God who sent Christ into the world. When we forget about fixing blame and recline in the trust that God will never forsake us, our feet are set on the path to restoration. Bartimaeus cried out for mercy, and Jesus enabled the blind to see. God vindicated innocent Job against all accusations by this "friends." His health and fortune were restored.

God's judgment against Israel was tempered with the merciful promise of renewal. After the Crucifixion, God raised up Jesus from death. As the psalmist so beautifully put it, [read Ps. 126:5–6].

So exhilarating was the experience of renewal that "we were like those who dream" and "our mouth was filled with laughter" (126:1–2). Jeremiah, who suffered as much as any prophet we know about, dreamed of a restoration in which a great company will come weeping for joy and full of consolation (Jer. 31:9).

Renewal! That's something we long for. We read the promises of new heavens and a new Earth. We may remember the promise of 2 Chronicles 7:14. At best, however, our experiences of such renewal come in fragments, incomplete. According to the apostle Paul, our present sufferings are not worth comparing with the glory to be enjoyed in the resurrection day (Rom. 8:18). Jesus, according to Hebrews, "learned obedience through what he suffered" (Heb. 5:7–10). Marcia Duke said they had found "pockets of laughter."

As has been long and proudly proclaimed by the Church, this hope is not based on reason or suggestions from experience. It is based on the gospel proclaimed by the apostles and ratified by Christ's own Resurrection. But there is some reasonableness to hope. Without it, the severe sufferings of the martyrs and the weak ones of the world make no sense at all. So when Jesus says, "Blessed are those who mourn, for they will be comforted," he points not only to our present experience of grace but ahead to the day when we will eat the bread and drink the cup with him again in the resurrection.

Jesus said that unless a seed die and be buried, it cannot rise anew. The apostle Paul said that he died every day (1 Cor. 15:31). Through our sufferings, we learn to die to ourselves and to this world, as it is fallen into sin. Grace operates through our sufferings to bring healing and renewal. It teaches us to cling to the God of mercy revealed in the cross. It teaches us to hope in the powerful God who raised Jesus from death.

Out of this trust and hope, we live to love God and others. Like Israel, crushed by God's judgment, like innocent Job and blind Bartimaeus, we meet up with God's restoring compassion. The psalmist celebrates the restoration that even the nations see.

Restoration is a powerful concept—sometimes a surprisingly powerful concept. It could be a high achievement, such as winning an Olympic medal or returning something to a former state of being (such as restoring a burned-out home). It might be the recovery of something lost (personal health). But it is far more than good luck. Restoration finds its meaning in the process of change—lost to found, captivity to freedom, death to life, danger to safety, exile to homecoming, and forgotten to remembered.

For the psalmist, it came "when the Lord restored the fortunes of Zion" (v. 1). *We were like those who dream!* For a moment, notice the structure of this psalm. It has two parts. Each is introduced by a line that uses the phrase "restore the fortunes" and a simile (vv. 1, 4). "The Lord has done great things" (two times) holds verse 3 to the end of verse 2. In the second part, weeping and joy are correlated with sowing and reaping twice (vv. 5–6).

Words for laughter or joy occur five times in the whole. This for sure gives the psalm its dominant tone. The song is about joy remembered and joy anticipated. In both cases the joy is the work of the Lord. In the first case it is through the restoration of Zion and in the second through the renewal of those who sing the song.

"Restore the fortunes" is a difficult Hebrew idiom to put in English (I am told). It is found mostly in prophetic sayings, where it is used for the radical change from the conditions brought about by divine wrath to those that come from divine favor. It means the restoration of an earlier situation between God and people (see Zeph. 2:7).

The description of the restoration of Zion as a great work of the Lord brought joy to Israel. It caught the attention of the nations. The pilgrims remember it as a time when they were "like those who dream." That is, they were experiencing the opposite of the actual. In Isaiah 29:7–8, dreaming has to do with thinking things are the opposite of what seems to be true. In contrast to verse 8, the meaning in our text would say that the hungry person would dream of being filled, and when he awakes he actually is filled.

C. S. Lewis was, for many years, an atheist. In his description of his conversion, he said, "In the Trinity Term of 1929 I gave in, and admitted that God was God . . . perhaps the most dejected and reluctant convert in all England." But the name of the book is *Surprised by Joy.* He reports that there had never been any hint of any connection between God and joy. He said that there was no strain of music from within, no smell of eternal orchards, when he was dragged through the doorway. But what he found was more than one could dream. Surprised by Joy!

George A. Buttrick, in his sermon from the first two verses of this psalm, says there are three kinds of laughter. The first is childish laughter. This laughter is naïve and natural at times. The second kind is adult laughter, when we laugh at ourselves. The third kind, according to Buttrick, is the laughter of redemption. This laughter is that of childlikeness beyond childishness. Is this what Marcia means by "pockets of laughter"?

What the pilgrims remember about the past, they pray for in the present. The restoration of Zion needs completion in the restoration of the people. In their memory they recall what the Lord can do. They need ever-recurring rhythms of renewal that come like the seasonal rains that make the dry watercourses of the Negev run with water. The prayer for that renewal uses a contrast between weeping-sowing and reaping-laughing. The contrast between tears and laughter tells of the change sought.

In the old religious myths of Egarit and Egypt, seedtime was associated with the death of the god of fertility. Harvest was associated with his revival. Perhaps the psalm intends that the sowers represent the going out of the pilgrims, and those who come carrying the sheaves represent their return.

"Shouts of joy" appears three times in the six verses of Psalm 126. Why all the shouting? In this case it is about redemption—the Lord's restoration of Israel's well-being, something Israel could only dream about. But the dream came true. Some of us (oh, why not say it)—*all* of us should be shouting with joy that the Lord has done more for us than we ever dreamed of. After all, it is pretty humorous that some of us ever got saved. And you can laugh about it, because laughing about it isn't going to undo it! Just makes it better!—Bob I. Johnson

SUNDAY, SEPTEMBER 24, 2006
Lectionary Message

Topic: Dealing with Inner Conflict

Text: James 3:13–4:3, 7–8a

Other Readings: Prov. 31:10–31; Ps. 1; Mark 9:30–37

One evening, an elderly Cherokee man of great wisdom told his grandson a story that has become a classic in Native American literature. The story had to do with the battle that was raging inside himself. The wise elder said, "My son, the battle is between two wolves. One wolf is evil—it is anger, envy, sorrow, regret, greed, arrogance, self-pity, guilt, resentment, inferiority, lies, false pride, superiority, and ego. The other wolf is good—joy, peace, love, hope, serenity, humility, kindness, benevolence, empathy, generosity, truth, compassion, and faith."

The grandson thought about it for a moment and then asked, "Grandfather, which wolf wins?"

His grandfather gently replied, "The one I feed."

I. We can, perhaps, identify with the grandfather's internal struggle and conflict, as often we are torn between what we are tempted to do and what we know we should do. We struggle with our own desires and what others expect of us. We are caught between living for the moment or looking at the big picture and considering the future. We are conflicted over the way we are enticed to go and the right way we know we should go. We are often beset between the past with its failures, regrets, hurt feelings, and disappointments and the future with its hope, promise, and possibilities. And we must choose between resentment and holding a grudge or forgiveness and moving on with our life. Sometimes we feel as though there are fighting wolves within us.

II. The biblical writers put their finger on this inner struggle common to us all. The psalmist, in Psalm 1, speaks about conflicting ways and how we all are faced with a decision. We must decide between two options—two paths—one that leads to happiness and life and the other to despair and death. Often we may struggle or fight within ourselves to decide which way we should go. It is like fighting wolves or a battle raging within us.

And then in the passage that we read from James, we see that he, too, put his finger on this inner conflict—this inner struggle that is common to humankind. James speaks of the constant fighting within the human mind and heart. And he speaks of how this inner conflict—this inner struggle, this inner fighting—often leads to jealousy, bitterness, quarrels, and disorder. The "conflicts and disputes" that plague us, James contends, come from the "cravings that are at war" within us (James 4:1). To put it another way, if we allow the evil wolf within—the wolf of envy, anger, greed, jealousy, and bitterness—to win, we let the evil wolf out into the world. James traces the source of much conflict to unnecessary craving and desire within the human heart.

III. One of our primary goals in life should be to rid our hearts and minds of those negative emotions such as envy, jealousy, greed, bitterness, and hatred that give birth to inner conflict. One of the first steps in dealing with the fighting within, with the inner conflicts that sometimes rage within us, is to realize that such negative feelings are toxic—they are poison, both to us and to those around us. Let us not forget that it was the emotions of jealousy, bitterness, anger, and hatred that nailed Jesus to the cross. After accepting the fact that negative emotions are toxic, then we need to analyze our inner conflict and determine its source. Does our inner conflict result from envy over what our neighbor has, anger over a perceived wrong to us, jealousy of another's success, greed for more than we need, hatred for someone who is not like us, or some other negative emotion? If so, negative conditioning and negative habits need to be replaced with positive conditioning and positive habits. A negative state of mind and negative emotions that are so toxic to our emotional, spiritual, and physical wholeness and well-being need to be countered by fruits of the Spirit and positive emotions that James mentions, such as gentleness, peacefulness, mercy, humbleness, purity, and kindness. The fruits of the Spirit—gentleness, compassion, kindness, and the like—act like antidotes to negative states of mind—envy, anger, jealousy, and hatred. James contends that those who are truly wise are the ones whose lives are guided by humility, mercy, gentleness, and peace.

The question for us to consider is, "Which wolf will we feed?" Will we feed the so-called "evil wolf" that embodies all the negative feelings and emotions that tear at and threaten to destroy our lives and our world—anger, envy, greed, hatred, and the like? Or will we feed the so-called "good wolf" that embodies those positive emotions and characteristics that are becoming to followers of Christ—love, compassion, gentleness, kindness, and the like? The responsibility and the choice are always ours. The challenge for us is to deal with inner conflict—the fighting wolves within—that is common to all of us.

ILLUSTRATION

Peace begins in the human heart.

> If there is to be peace in the world, there must be peace in the nations.
> If there is to be peace in the nations, there must be peace in the cities.
> If there is to be peace in the cities, there must be peace between neighbors.
> If there is to be peace between neighbors, there must be peace in the home.
> If there is to be peace in the home, there must be peace in the heart.—Lao-Tzu

Personal conflict affects the world. Think with me about a man—an ordinary man like the rest of us—who decides he wants a newer, bigger, much more expensive automobile. The man doesn't really need the car, as the car he has is nice enough, but he begins to crave the new one. The man talks with his wife about it, but she doesn't go for it and vetoes his idea. "You don't need it, and we can't afford it right now," she insists.

Well, the man begins to obsess about the car. His desire fills every waking thought and even his dreams at night. The man gets up in the morning all out of sorts. He complains that his breakfast is too cold, yells at his wife, and ruins her entire day. The dog stretches out in front of him, wanting a little attention from his master before he leaves for work, but the man kicks the dog and the poor dog hobbles around all day long.

The man gets on the freeway and impatiently and angrily honks at everyone, curses and raises his hand, liberally giving the universal sign of disdain. The man blasts his coworkers and upsets his boss, who calls corporate headquarters and blasts the CEO of the company.

The CEO has connections to the government and gets short with world leaders, causing friction on the international level. Thus the man's craving and desire for an expensive new car, and the battle going on inside him because of it, reverberates throughout the entire world.

The story is a parable, I grant you. And it may be somewhat exaggerated. But its message is true: how we deal with our inner struggles and conflicts has the potential of drastically affecting the world around us.—Randy Hammer

SERMONS SUGGESTIONS

Topic: Preface to Success
TEXT: Ps. 1
(1) The downward steps of sin. (2) The upward steps of righteousness. (3) The great separation.

Topic: A Step in the Dark

TEXT: Isa. 50:10; 45:1–6

There are some experiences that mere intellect cannot penetrate or produce. (1) Darkness is not always bad: sometimes it is bad; it may be friendly (Isa. 45:3), for it may challenge and call forth the quality of faith. (2) How can we exploit the darkness? Recognize the paralyzing danger of indecision; be willing to make a mistake; recognize the reality of certain spiritual values; act on what you believe; unite with others who believe likewise.

WORSHIP AIDS

CALL TO WORSHIP.   "Be still, and know that I am God. . . . The Lord of hosts is with us" (Ps. 46:10, 11).

INVOCATION.   Lord, speak plainly to us through the Word. Allow prayer to sensitize us to need and the Holy Spirit to prepare us for service, in Jesus' Holy name.—E. Lee Phillips

OFFERTORY SENTENCE.   "A good man out of the good treasure of his heart bringeth forth that which is good" (Luke 6:45).

OFFERTORY PRAYER.   Gracious God, we are sometimes inclined to give an offering from the little that is left after we have enjoyed our necessities and our luxuries. Help us to find joy in giving of the first fruits of our increase.

PRAYER.   We pray for those wandering through wastelands and wildernesses. Keep those whom you love from the mirage of safety. O Lord protect, we pray, those children and adults who have run away from places they can no longer call home. Even now as we ask, cause us to remember those times that we have been delivered from the despair of being lost. Hear our prayer, O Lord. O give thanks unto the Lord, for God is good. O God, who came in the form of one who was condemned to die, cause us not to forget or write off those in prison. Give them hope, as you give us hope, in the hour we are imprisoned by a destructive habit or captive to our own depression. Hear our prayer, O Lord. O give thanks unto the Lord, for God is good. Good and merciful God, be with those who are staggering under the weight of self-inflicted pain. We remember also those whose illness seems so undeserved and unrelenting. Give those in need not guilt, but grace. Hear our prayer, O Lord. O give thanks unto the Lord, for God is good. Lord of the tempest and the calm, quell in us the turbulence that overwhelms and give strength and re-creative power to those whose lives have been torn apart by the storms of nature and the winds of change. We give praise to you for every gentle breeze of your Spirit and the steadfast hope in Christ, which anchors us in the whirlwind. Hear our prayer, O Lord. O give thanks unto the Lord, for God is good.—Gary D. Statman

SERMON

Topic: Life Together

TEXT: Jer. 1:4–5; John 15:5–9, 12–17

I. All of us here today probably have some routine we follow, if we come to church regularly. Recently, I've been wondering, Why? Why did each of us make the decision to get out of bed, get dressed, and come here today? Sunday is a day most of us don't have to work or do anything else. So why do we make the effort to come to this place and worship God?

If I am honest, I have to admit to mixed motives for being here. I want to worship God, but I also know that a big reason I am here is sheer habit. Since childhood, I have usually spent Sunday mornings at church, and old habits are hard to break. Another important reason bringing me back to church each week is the people I hope to see here. I have friends and people who have become models to me of Christian discipleship; if I get to see them at all, it will be at church.

I know that some of us are here today out of desperation. Our lives have hit rock bottom. We've exhausted all of our resources. Nothing has helped. Maybe Jesus is the answer to whatever our questions may be. Since we're at the bottom, we've become desperate enough to give even religion a chance.

Many of us, I know, are here this morning simply because we want to worship God.

II. These are some of the reasons we might give for being here today. They are all different, reflecting our different personalities and circumstances. But they all have one thing in common: they are *our* reasons for being here. They explain our presence here in terms of psychological or sociological facts about us.

These are legitimate explanations of our presence here. But I would like to suggest another, more ultimate reason. Jesus told his disciples in John 15 that they had not chosen him but that he had chosen them. Perhaps each of us has made our way to this place because God called us to be here and called us, *even if only for this one Sunday morning,* to share a life together. Perhaps the real reason we are here today is not habit, or friends, or curiosity, or boredom, or desperation, or even our own desire to worship God. Perhaps the real reason we are here is that God has been working in our lives, leading us to this shared moment of life.

Why does God do this? Why does God call us to be here today together? Why is God at work in our lives (for the most part in hidden, secret ways that we have not even identified as God's) to bring us together at this time and place?

Jesus says in John 15 that God's very nature is grace and love. Grace and love, by their very natures, are things that must be shared. God shares this love with us so that we may abide in Christ—that we may live in Christ. God calls in grace and love to share a life together.

We are utterly dependent on God. In other words, without God's ceaseless, sustaining activity, our world would collapse into nothingness. And no one can be truly alive and truly human, yet at the same time be cut off from significant relationships with others.

III. This need for human community is as real in our religious experience and faith as it is in any other part of our existence. This calls in question the common American assumption that one can worship God without the need for active involvement in a religious community.

Times of solitude are essential for a healthy spiritual life—times when we can concentrate on our inner reality without the distractions of everyday life. Jesus, our model and example, often sought times away from everyone else so he could be alone with God.

But Jesus also formed a community of disciples—women and men who followed him around Galilee, listened to his parables, and saw him heal the sick and forgive sinners. It was a community with whom he ate and drank and shared a life together.

To be Christian means, among other things, to be participating in the life God offers us through Christ and to let that new kind of life grow within us and nurture us and empower us to be our truest, best selves. Individual experiences of solitude certainly contribute to that growth. But without our being rooted in the corporate life of a Christian community, such solitary experiences soon wither and die for lack of nourishment.

"I am the vine," Jesus says, "and you are the branches."

IV. We came to worship, therefore, because deep within us we recognize our need to give and receive spiritual nourishment.

St. Paul likened the Christian community to a body, an organic entity, with each distinct individual nevertheless an integrated part of the whole. "Bear one another's burdens," he wrote the Galatians, "and so fulfill the law of Christ."

V. The grace and love of God, which we experience both as individuals and as a community, require an active response from us. God usually does not overpower us with displays of divine glory, as Moses experienced on Mt. Sinai or Isaiah experienced in the Temple. For the most part, God's activity in our lives is indirect and hidden, always allowing for our free response. God can and sometimes does appear as the awesome, holy, Wholly Other, whose sovereignty requires as the only adequate response that we fall on our knees in awe, adoration, and fear. But such transcendent experiences are best kept to a minimum for special circumstances, when they are most needed. Our spiritual circuits would be blown if this were the only way we could be plugged in to God.

It is a better analogy to think of God's presence in our lives as that of a lover who fell in love with us long before we even knew such love was possible. "Before I formed you in the womb, I knew you," God says to Jeremiah, implying that God's love is intimate and eternal— a love God felt long before we could even recognize or acknowledge it.

When a human lover falls in love, even before the beloved knows it, the lover begins looking for ways to become part of her beloved's life and to show her beloved her passion, desire, and longing to be united forever. So God works in secret and hidden ways to bring us to the moment of recognition when we can finally see God's love for us and recognize it as God's love.

To say yes to love offered, whether human or divine, is an act of faith and trust. So when the moment comes that we realize God is at work in our lives and wants to give us life in a fullness we've not had before, our proper response is to say yes to that life, to believe and trust that it is a real life.

It is, if only implicitly, our faith that God is gracious toward us, that God loves us, and that God desires our good. Even our desperation may be an act of faith and trust—faith that *if* we came here today we would find, in this life we are sharing together at this moment, the God we alone can trust to give us life.

God has been working in my life and your life to bring us to this moment.—Bill Thomason

SUNDAY, OCTOBER 1, 2006
Lectionary Message

Topic: Christ's Boundaries and Ours

TEXT: Mark 9:30–37

Other Readings: Esther 7:1–6, 9–10, 9:20–22; Ps. 124; James 5:13–20

I. *Differences help us define who we are.* More often than not, those who are different from us come out on the short end of the comparison. If I think I am doing something the right way, then it is not hard to conclude that those who do it differently are wrong.

Jesus' disciple John had been following the Master faithfully for years. He had been right there with Jesus as he taught about God's love. He had seen Jesus heal the sick. If anyone should know how Jesus wanted things done in his name, it was John. One day he and the other disciples saw someone they did not know casting out demons in Jesus' name. Someone who had not been with them as they followed Jesus from town to town—a person who had not been instructed at the Master's feet—was taking it upon himself to do Jesus' work.

John tried to stop this outsider. He stood up for the integrity of Jesus. He made sure that the Lord's work was done the right way or no way. He told Jesus what he had done, and he was expecting words of commendation for upholding the standard. But Jesus said, "Do not stop him, for no one who does a deed of power in my name will be able soon afterward to speak evil of us. Whoever is not against us is for us. For truly I tell you, whoever gives you a cup of water to drink because you bear the name of Christ will by no means lose the reward."

II. *Jesus extends a broad welcome.* Does Jesus mean it does not matter what you believe or how you serve him? It is not that there is no need for standards. Elsewhere in the New Testament, the letter to the Ephesians warns us not to be tossed about by every wind of doctrine (Eph. 4:14). Jesus himself warns against false teachers who would lead us astray from a true understanding of him (Mark 13:5). But balanced with that need for true doctrine and right practice is the urgency of his work. People are hurting. People need to hear the good news. It is better that we serve him imperfectly than not serve him at all. It is better that we do something for him than that we do nothing while we wait to make sure it is done flawlessly.

III. *Jesus' mission is urgent.* Jesus went on to say, "If any of you put a stumbling block before one of these little ones who believe in me, it would be better for you if a great millstone were hung around your neck and you were thrown into the sea." Imagine someone running along and tripping over an obstacle and falling on her face. A stumbling block is something that interrupts a person's progress toward a goal. John was placing a stumbling block in front of that outsider. He wanted him to stop healing in Jesus' name. But Jesus' mission is urgent. He compares the urgency of his work with the urgency of saving our lives. Better to live without one hand than not to live at all. Better to see with one eye than be blind. Better to limp on one foot and live than to have both feet and die.

IV. *Our divisions must not hinder us from Christ's work.* Many things divide us in Christ's church, and we spend lots of time focusing on them. Anglicans are divided over ordination standards for bishops. Baptists are divided over issues of biblical interpretation. Presbyterians disagree over how involved to be in social action. The controversies and the divisions are what make the news and take up our time and energy. But today, on this World Communion Sunday, we celebrate those things we have in common. We worship the One who unites us. He has given us the work of showing God's love to all the world. We have stories of God's grace and love to tell. We have children to feed and elderly to care for. We have poor people to comfort, conflicts to resolve, addictions to break.

Jesus wants us to strive to do our very best. He wants us to be true to the traditions we have inherited and the practices we have developed. We need boundaries to help us define who we are. But Jesus is bigger than all our differences. He does not need boundaries to do his work. He works through liberals and conservatives, Catholics and Protestants, people of every nation. His table is large, and we will be surprised at who is joining us when we are gathered together after all our work is done.

ILLUSTRATION

A castaway was stranded on a tropical island. For years he lived in complete solitude. Finally one day, a ship passed close enough that he could get its attention, and the crew sent a rescue party. Before he left the island to return to civilization, the castaway offered to show his rescuers around his encampment, where he had lived without human companionship for all those years. He showed them his house—a comfortable building, considering the primitive conditions under which it was built. Then he showed them the church he had built, where he worshiped regularly. As they were getting ready to leave the island, the rescuers asked him about the third building in the encampment, a building he had ignored during their brief tour. "Oh, that's the other church. I didn't like it so I left and started another one."—Stephens G. Lytch

SERMON SUGGESTIONS

Topic: God and the Dangers of Life

TEXT: Ps. 124

(1) Life has many perils of various kinds. (2) All of us are vulnerable: sometimes we invite danger; often it just happens. (3) In any case, the Lord, the Maker of heaven and Earth, can help us.

Topic: The Perverter of a Nation

TEXT: 1 Kings 14:16

(1) Jeroboam had a meteoric career. (2) Jeroboam perverted the nation. (3) Jeroboam turned back on the threshold of a new vision. (4) There are dragons that rise up on the path of human progress.—Arthur A. Cowan[1]

WORSHIP AIDS

CALL TO WORSHIP.   "Bless the Lord, O my soul: and all that is within me, bless his holy name" (Ps. 103:1).

INVOCATION.   Holy Father, we come together this morning to find our way. Amid all the many diversions of life, we get lost. We lose sight of our purpose as followers of Jesus and need these times apart with you to rediscover who we are and what we are about. Make us bold to do your will in a world where evil often seems to have the upper hand in life and in our hearts. May what we do here today give us the insights needed, as well as the courage to be the heart and hands of truth and righteousness shared in love with the world.—Henry Fields

OFFERTORY SENTENCE.   "Give unto the Lord the glory due unto his name: bring an offering, and come before him: worship the Lord in the beauty of holiness" (1 Chron. 16:29).

---

[1]*Crisis on the Frontier* (Edinburgh: T. & T. Clark, 1943), pp. 32–40.

OFFERTORY PRAYER.   Not the gift, O Lord, the commitment; not the size, the fidelity; not the amount, the motive; not withholding but giving all we can, for Christ, who never stops giving to us.—E. Lee Phillips

PRAYER.   Father of beauty, we cannot but be in awe of the majestic way in which you have daubed color across the landscape to bless us and refresh us in the lingering days of autumn. Each day adds new depth to your artistry and brings renewed inspiration to us, as we revel in your handiwork. Thank you for the undeserved blessings of these days. How could we not be grateful for this house of worship where we can, for a while, be insulated from the demands of daily rigors. Here in the different atmosphere we are refreshed and revitalized in our spirits and thus are made ready to return to the routines that we must honor. Abiding Father, we cannot ably express our gratitude for the evidence of your presence with us at all times and in all circumstances, and especially here.

As we worship today, we pray that you will embrace us with a desire to more ably do your will in the world that we frequent. Open our minds to truth, our eyes to opportunity, our hands to generosity, and our spirits to usefulness by your spirit. Strengthen us to walk in the ugly places of life and the world, where need is so great, and there share the beauty and loveliness of the faith that we know so well. All about us there has been a trend to turn anger and meanness into an art form. So many glory in the opportunity to put another down and to humiliate whenever possible. Where we have engaged in such degrading activity, pray forgive and redeem us and lead us to higher ground that we might live more nobly and usefully.

This morning we pray for those caught in the crossfire of hard business deals, buyouts, and takeovers. We pray for those suddenly without a job or security or hope. Show us how we can help the ones in these circumstances and make us generous with ourselves that they may have enough on which to manage.

Now, please sir, help us to ponder our own lives so that more and more we might be like Christ, meeting others in his fashion and loving them in his name.—Henry Fields

SERMON
Topic: Confidence for the Day of Judgment
TEXT: 1 John 4:17

Dr. Murdo Ewen MacDonald, the distinguished Scottish preacher, related the following story. During an American preaching tour, he felt constrained to give a message in one stately, prosperous church on the theme of judgment—the judgment of Christ. It was a solemn, searching message. Afterward, when the congregation lined up to shake hands with the preacher, one attractive, elegant lady held both his hands warmly and said, "Gee, I guess you're real cute."

As a response to a sermon on judgment, that comment clearly left much to be desired. Perhaps unwittingly, it expressed what so many inside and outside the Church feel about the whole conception of our ultimate accountability to God: treat it lightly, casually—even with amusement, lofty disdain, or supercilious skepticism. It is, after all, only an archaic hangover from more primitive and credulous times. The old-time preachers used to take people by the scruff and hold them over the pit of hell until the smell of fire and brimstone choked them into repentance and faith. Not any longer! Educated preachers like Alexander Pope's "Soft

Dean" never mention hell to polite ears. God is love, which means benign, indulgent, cozy, and grandmotherly.

The truth is that we are right to jettison some of the awful, unbiblical, and almost sadistic concepts of judgment that were once clamorously proclaimed. Former generations tended to interpret with a lurid and unimaginative literalism the symbolic nature of our present knowledge of things unseen and eternal. They presumed to know too much about "the furniture of heaven and the temperature of hell." No doubt they were trying to communicate the urgency of the gospel invitation—a good fault!—but so often they conveyed the idea that they were trying to frighten people into the Kingdom of God.

We must avoid the mistake of taking the pictorial, symbolic language of Scripture *literally*. We must also avoid the greater mistake of not taking it *seriously*. The judgment of God is a great, inevitable reality. Let no one deride it. Let no one forget it. Let no one deny it. The day of judgment—the judgment of a holy God—demands our closest and most reverent attention.

I. "From thence he shall come to judge the living and the dead." Those words in the historic Apostles' Creed, recited by countless men and women across the centuries, are supported by a three-fold witness.

First, there is *the witness of the reason*. The Greeks had no Bible, but they believed in judgment, calling it Nemesis. Why? Why, in generation after generation, have poets, philosophers, and prophets affirmed their belief in an ultimate day of judgment? Because the rationality of the world required it. If there is no judgment to come, then there is no moral law, order, or purpose in life, and conscience has no meaning. We live in chaos, in a world where crime pays, sin is an empty word, and everyone does what is right in his or her own eyes. The ground plan of the universe is unreasonable if we are not accountable, moral beings. Doesn't your mind make that affirmation? It is true that there is a process of judgment in life and history. This is so in the lives of individuals and nations. If they sow in sin, they reap in disaster; if they sow the wind, they reap the whirlwind. But not always in this life. Our minds demand a final accountability—a judgment that corrects the injustices of life.

Second, there is *the witness of the Bible*. If the idea of a future day of judgment is to be discarded, then we must tear out whole pages of the Bible. Prophet, psalmist, and apostle sound the note over and over again:

"If you seek him, he will be found of you: if you forsake him, he will cast you off
  for ever."
"It is appointed unto men once to die, but after this the judgment."
"We must all appear before the judgment seat of Christ, and everyone of us shall give
  an account of himself before God."

One could go on multiplying examples of such declarations in Scripture. If the Bible is our authority, the source book of our holy faith, then every one of us ought to be searching our hearts and asking earnestly:

When thou, my Righteous Judge, shall come
To fetch thy ransomed people home,
Shall I among them stand?

Third, there is *the witness of Jesus himself*. He who was kindness incarnate, who spoke the loveliest words the world has ever heard—Jesus, with all compassion, who said, "Come to me, all you who labor and are heavy-laden, and I will give you rest"—did not hesitate to speak of judgment to come. He spoke of the broad way leading to destruction, of separating some to the right hand and some to the left, of saying to some: "Depart from me, you cursed: I never knew you." We cannot accept some of the sayings of Jesus and reject others because they displease us. In the name of reason, of Scripture, and of Jesus himself we must affirm: "From thence he shall come to judge the living and the dead." A preacher must declare to himself and to the world the whole counsel of God. As David Christie put it: "Rest assured that preaching which has drifted away from divine judgment will inevitably produce superficial people, bored people, unresponsible people. So long as we are called upon to speak to sinful people, we must speak of righteousness and judgment. And when we fail so to speak, men deep down in their hearts know us to be traitors to the truth."

II. But all this is not the gospel! *Gospel* means *good news,* and it is not good news to be reminded that we must give an account one day to a holy and righteous God. It is, in fact, the background of the gospel. Hear now the good news as John records it: "That we may have confidence for the day of judgment." Confidence! Not shivering in terror, not shrinking in shame, but confident! Confident before the righteous Judge, the Sovereign God, the Eternal Throne! Incredible—but exhilarating, exalting, and gloriously true! "That we may have confidence for the day of judgment."

Let no one imagine that the reference here is to self-confidence—a confidence based on our own supposed merit or assumed superiority. That, I'm sorry to say, is a confidence that some Christians appear to have. We presume to judge the spiritual status of others—always to our own advantage. Jesus disposed of such spiritual arrogance in one devastating sentence: "Judge not, that you be not judged." Censorious judgment of our fellows is simply not the human stance.

The grounds of our confidence on the day of judgment are not in ourselves. Far from it! John expounds them for us in this letter. They are in Christ!

> On Christ the solid rock, we stand
> All other ground is sinking sand.

The first ground of our confidence is *our belief in Christ.* John writes in verse 15: "Whoever confesses that Jesus is the Son of God, God abides in him and he in God." We can be confident when we meet Christ as Judge then, if we have met Christ as Savior now. He will confess us as his friends before God the Father then, if we confess him as the Son of God before the world now. "What must I do to be saved?" may be an unfashionable question, but it is as vital as ever. So is the answer: "Believe in the Lord Jesus, and you will be saved." What, then, does it mean to believe in Christ?

Belief certainly involves intellectual consent. For me to confess that Jesus is the Son of God is first an intellectual confession. Because of the historical evidence of the New Testament, the claims of Jesus himself, and my own personal experience of his living presence, I can do no other. It commends itself to my mind. Of course, the mental capacities of us all vary considerably. There is such a thing as "simple faith." But let us be clear about this. Christianity has nothing to fear intellectually. It transcends reason, but it is never irrational. Examine the evidence yourself. Explore the tremendous fact of Christ. Like Thomas in the Gospel record, you may well be compelled to fall at his feet and cry adoringly, "My Lord and my God."

It also involves total commitment. Belief is commitment—the total commitment of the whole personality to the Son of God as Savior and Lord; total commitment to him as One who bore our sins in his own sinless body, who took our place and our rightful judgment upon himself. It is one thing to believe *about* Christ. It is quite another to believe *in* Christ. A merely theoretical or traditional belief is not enough.

The second ground of our confidence is *our union with Christ.* John writes, in verse 16: "He who abides, dwells, in love, abides in God." This thought takes us beyond belief to the idea of a mystical union with Christ, living in close, intimate fellowship with him as he lives in us by his spirit—the spirit of love.

It is a personal union, closer and more personal than any union we can know. In practical terms it means cultivating his presence daily, sharing our lives with him through thought and prayer, letting him refine our natures, mold our character, forgive our sins, heal our wounds. It is well known that two people who love each other very much tend to grow like each other. Abiding, dwelling in love, they grow together. So Christ, who loves us and whom we love, gradually changes us into his own likeness as we say, "I am his and he is mine." We are conformed to his image. The Judge we shall meet at the end is the familiar friend of each returning day!

It is also a social union. We do not abide in Christ alone. United with him, we are united with all who share our love and his risen presence. This means the fellowship of the Church, his body. What brings us together and holds us together in the Church, with all our likes and dislikes and enormous differences, is our common share in Christ. We love one another because Christ loves in us and through us. We help, inspire, encourage, and strengthen one another in Christ. And the climax of this union, its visible expression, is the Lord's Supper—the communion service—where we eat the bread and drink the cup, feeding on Christ by faith with thanksgiving, until he comes again! "That we may have confidence for the day of judgment," we believe in Christ and live in union with Christ, together with all faithful people who find in him their life, their health, their joy and peace.

The third ground of our confidence is *our conformity to Christ.* John says, in verse 17: "Because as he is, so are we in this world." "As he is . . . so are we." That is, we are to be like him, to behave like him, to conform to his mind and purpose and will in the world. To be sure, we can never completely conform to him. He was sinless, morally perfect, utterly obedient—always. But conformity to him, as we are able and enabled, is our goal.

This is an answer to those who think that faith in Christ is a cheap and easy indulgence, a cowardly escape from the consequences of our own sin. No! No! Believing in him, uniting with him, conforming to him is heart-searching, disturbing, challenging. It means obedience at all costs, service at all times, taking up our cross and following in his steps. Cheap and easy? It is the hardest thing in the world. Any fool can conform to the world. Millions do. There are people who drink alcohol, for example, because they are afraid to be different from some friends or social set, craving the approval of others, fearing their ridicule. They will do anything, go anywhere—even renounce their faith rather than risk unpopularity. In other words, such people are more concerned to conform to the world than to Christ, more concerned with the judgment of their friends than they are with the judgment of Christ. It is a curious and sad thing. What does the hollow laughter or bitter hostility of this world mean, compared with the approval of One who loved us and gave himself for us, and before whose burning love we must all stand at last?

Conform to Christ! "As he is . . . so are we." I am always deeply moved when I recall what happened to Samuel Logan Brengle, an American Methodist minister, in 1848. In that year, when William Booth's Salvation Army was enlisting men from all over the world, Brengle felt called to cross the Atlantic and offer his services. A successful minister in a fine church, he gave up everything in obedience to the call. At first, the General accepted him grudgingly and reluctantly. "You've been your own boss too long," he said. To instill humility in him, Booth set Brengle to work cleaning the boots of other trainees. Brengle said to himself, "Have I followed my own fancy across the Atlantic in order to black boots?" He had once dreamed of being a bishop. He had given up so much. Then, as in a vision, he saw his Lord bending over the feet of rough, unlettered fishermen—and washing their feet! "Lord," he whispered, "you wash their feet; I will black their boots."

"As he is . . . so are we." Conformity to Christ!

I walked once with a friend down a busy road, and we saw a man with a doleful expression slowly parading up and down, carrying a poster bearing the words, "Prepare to Meet Thy God." It seemed to me a foolish way of witnessing, and I said: "How awful! Trying to threaten people!" My friend replied: "You interpret those words as a threat! I see them as a glorious hope. How marvelous to meet our God—the God of Creation, of Jesus, of love and mercy! I'm prepared, excited!" The point was well taken. We must all meet God at last. It may seem a threatening prospect—the weak before the Omnipotent, the sinful before the Holy, the mortal before the Infinite. But God has already met us! Rich in mercy, boundless in compassion, he has taken the initiative to give us grounds for confidence on the day of meeting.—John N. Gladstone

SUNDAY, OCTOBER 8, 2006
Lectionary Message

Topic: Faith with No Strings Attached

TEXT: Job 1:1, 2:1–10

Other Readings: Ps. 126; Heb. 1:1–4, 2:5–12; Mark 10:2–16

I. *A challenge to faith.* There is no bigger challenge to faith than undeserved suffering. God is all-powerful. God is love. So how can God tolerate it when good people suffer? Where was God when the trains were rumbling through the gates of Auschwitz? Where is God when hundreds are killed in an earthquake? Where is God when a loved one is dying? If your faith will not protect you from cancer or tornadoes or drive-by shootings, why bother with it?

(a) *Satan's challenge.* That is the question at the heart of the book of Job. It is the question Satan put before God. As Satan went to and fro about the Earth, he noticed that it was easy for people to believe in God when life was going well for them and God's blessings were obvious. But Satan challenged God that the faith of even the most devout person would only go so far. "What will the faithful think of you when they can't see your goodness?" Satan asked God. Is it possible to believe in God with no strings attached? That's the question Job poses for all of us.

(b) *A good and righteous man.* It is important to know one thing about Job. It is so important that we learn it in the very first verse of the book that bears his name. Job was "blameless and upright, one who feared God and turned away from evil" (Job 1:1). At a time when wealth and family were considered signs of God's favor, Job was the richest man in the East. He had seven sons and three daughters.

Job did not take his blessings for granted. He made absolutely sure that nothing ever came between him and God. For instance, his sons liked to party. The morning after each of their parties, while his sons were still sleeping it off, Job would get up early and make a sacrifice to God on their behalf, just in case they had done something the night before that displeased the Lord or had some passing thought that was less than wholesome.

(c) *The worst of it.* One day it all fell apart. Job lost his wealth, his family, and his health. But that was not the worst of it. Oh, you can be sure he cried and grieved the way any of us would do. But what hurt Job most was the sense that somehow he had lost touch with God. Job had built his whole life trusting that if he loved God and did what was right, God would protect him. He and God were friends. How, then, could all of this happen? Where was God in it all? What should a person of faith do?

Job's wife had some advice for him: curse God and die. The way she saw it, if there is a God, it does not make any difference whether you are good or bad. Why should you give God the gratification of acknowledging that God exists? If someone like Job is going to suffer as he did, then why not just turn your back and do whatever you darn well please?

II. *The faith we need.* If we believe we have a credit account with God and God owes us something for our faith, then sooner or later Job's wife is going to make a lot of sense. If prayer is nothing more than the way you let God know what the Holy One is supposed to do for you, then why should you bother if you cannot see the answer to your prayers? If going to church is just another form of life insurance—a way to get brownie points with God so God will pay attention to you when you need God—then something is going to happen that makes Mrs. Job's advice sound pretty good. Sooner or later, God is not going to fit into whatever neat little framework we construct to contain God. If we believe in God because of what is in it for us, then faith cannot help but collapse when our expectations are let down.

But Job's faith did not collapse when his world fell apart. Job did not believe in God as a means to an end. Faith was more than the key to happiness. What Job desired more than anything else was a relationship with his Maker. Job did not plead to have his fortunes restored. He begged to restore his relationship with God. All he wanted was to know that God had not abandoned him in his misery.

III. *The cross as our assurance.* Jesus felt that same absence of God when he was on the cross. Jesus had not done anything to deserve what he got, any more than Job had. Jesus was perfectly sinless, yet he was crucified as a criminal. Stretched on the cross, he cried, "My God, my God, why have you forsaken me?" Jesus affirmed our freedom to scream when we are face-to-face with the powers of death, and God seems far away. But even when he felt forsaken, Jesus could say in faith with his dying breath, "Father, into your hands I commend my spirit"—a final affirmation that no matter what happens, we belong to God.

IV. *God's faithfulness endures.* Job knew that God's faithfulness endures when all else fails, even our understanding of God. Job's life affirmed what Paul wrote hundreds of years later in his letter to the Romans: "For I am convinced that neither death, nor life, nor angels, nor rulers, nor things present, nor things to come, nor powers, nor height, nor depth, nor anything else in all creation, will be able to separate us from the love of God in Christ Jesus our Lord" (Rom. 8:38–39).

ILLUSTRATION

"Why my father? Why Dad?" It was a month after the funeral. Maria's father had contracted a particularly gruesome form of cancer that made his last months a combination of torturous pain and morphine-induced sleep. He died a week before his sixty-fifth birthday. Maria had been stewing over it for weeks, and finally she couldn't hold it in any longer. So there we were in my study—she full of grief and rage and I feeling helpless in the role of defense attorney for God.

"Dad didn't deserve to go that way. Think of all the people who still needed him—my sister and I, his grandchildren, my mother. Look at all he did for this community. And he still had lots of good years left. He was the kindest, most generous man I ever knew. So why did he have to go, when there are so many murderers and drug pushers and awful people who don't get what they deserve?"

When Maria was in my study, I wanted more than anything to be able to offer her a rational explanation that made sense of her father's death. I wanted to be able to answer her question, "Why?" But that is an elusive answer, and it's not one that God promises—at least not in this life. We don't always have the answer. What we do have is the cross. It's not in the answers to my questions that I glory. It's not in a life free from pain. It's in the cross of Christ I glory. That is what stands over the wrecks of time.—Stephens G. Lytch

SERMON SUGGESTIONS

Topic: A Cry for Reassurance
TEXT: Ps. 26 REB
(1) Like the psalmist, we may have our doubts: people may question our integrity; suspect us because of the company that surrounds us. (2) God can see us through our doubts and difficulties: by testing us; by making his house a place of refuge and encouragement.

Topic: The Open Secret of a Great Life
TEXT: Gal. 2:20
(1) It was a life lived under the usual human conditions: "the life which I now live in the flesh." (2) It was a life redeemed from the ordinary by the outworking of a great principle: "I live by the faith of the Son of God." (3) It was a life glorified in its response to the highest sentiment: "who loved me and gave himself for me."—Edwin C. Dargan

WORSHIP AIDS

CALL TO WORSHIP.   "Trust in the Lord with all your heart; and lean not unto your own understanding. In all your ways acknowledge him, and he shall direct your paths" (Prov. 3:5–6).

INVOCATION.   Because of our lack of faith and commitment, O God, we are like wandering sheep. We need your guidance. Help us to seek, above all, your kingdom and your righteousness, so that everything in time will fall into its proper place, and our lives will glorify you.

OFFERTORY SENTENCE.   "With a freewill offering I will sacrifice to you; I will give thanks to your name, O Lord, for it is good" (Ps. 54:6).

OFFERTORY PRAYER.   How can we fittingly thank you, Lord, for burdens lifted, suffering assuaged, sins forgiven, life renewed, differences reconciled, and hopes restored? We bring to you now a token of our gratitude and love, and we pray that because of what we do, others also may know your goodness.

PRAYER.   Heavenly Father, from your vantage point of eternity look afresh into our time—this time—time that you have given to us. You have come into our lives with your love. We have learned to love from that invasion, that incarnation. You know all about us; you know us better than we know ourselves. Teach us to be perceptive and thereby sympathetic with one another. Forgive us, Father, for our waste of time and opportunity. Forgive us the facades of hypocrisy, the masks of pretense. Help us to be honest with ourselves and with one another. We love you, Father, because you first loved us. We love one another and pray for one another. Some of our family suffer, Lord. Free them from their discomfort. Some of us are anxious, Lord. Calm our fears and strengthen our faith. Some of us are in the sorrow of bereavement. Send your spirit of comfort. How grateful we are, Father, for this good day and this opportunity to celebrate your sovereignty as your servants.—J. Estill Jones

SERMON
Topic: Getting Things Straight
TEXT: James 3:1–18

When I say the word *deception*, what comes to mind? What do you see? I see a presidential press secretary carefully shifting his rhetoric from "weapons of mass destruction" to "programs of mass destruction."

Deception. What do you see? I see a man and a woman in a hotel room. They are getting dressed. He tells her he loves only her, but he can't leave his wife—not yet. He assures her that what they have is unique, spiritual. He adjusts his clerical collar and walks out the door.

Deception. I see a preacher in a pulpit in a large church near the beach in Southern California. He tells his congregation that if they are born again, they will experience a great rapture but that many will be left behind in a great tribulation. During this tribulation, every Jew will either be converted or annihilated. He says this in a soft pastoral, matter-of-fact tone of voice. People nod their heads, assenting. Won't it be wonderful?

Deception. What do you see? I see a preacher getting up in front of a small congregation of students in a chapel at a southern university. He rolls out a short list of those who use words to deceive others. The more he points to others and their deceptions, the more certain he is that he and his words are somehow absolved, morally superior. He and his cohort are good at spotting words that deceive—but, of course, they are not participants in this Pelagian-style self-deception. What do you see?

The writer of James sees people like you and me: teachers, preachers, aspiring educators, would-be religious leaders. And he sees all of us under one banner. Written in large red print on this banner are the words: JUDGED WITH GREATER STRICTNESS! That's not a very nice banner to look up and see in our mind's eye in this lovely chapel on this lovely day of beginnings, early in an academic semester. How dare a new preaching professor drag this ugly banner in here this morning!

On the surface of these words, there is indeed a moral wrist slap or two, aimed right squarely at all of us. Teachers, preachers, religious-leaders-in-training, "Watch Your Tongue." Be careful what you say. The principalities and powers in this world cannot wait for you to get up in front of people and open your mouths. As the writer so graphically puts it, "Hell has no greater opportunity than your words to set your congregations, your classrooms, your friends, your culture, even your society 'on fire.'"

At a deeper level, the writer of this epistle is pointing us to what might be called the underside of speaking as believers and religious thinkers in this world. And it is the underside of preaching, if you will, of what I am here to teach you. We know the upper side of preaching: the proclamation of words of hope, liberation, new beginning. That's our positive message, the upper side. But James wants to remind us what we're up against when we try to speak this positive message, that we must attend to the underside of this task: the task of redeeming language and speech itself. He wants us to know that out of the same mouth, at exactly the same time, can come both blessing and curse. At precisely the same instant that we believe we are proclaiming our most positive message, the devil may very well be blinding us to a vicious underside to the words we speak. Because the words of faith, our words of power, our symbols and images have all been used to promote violence and suffering, these words and symbols themselves have to be carefully studied, renewed, and reclaimed, even in the knowledge that reclamation is a task of repair that can harbor new forms of deception.

So much hinges, I suppose, on how we take the word *judgment* on the banner that James wants to fly over our heads this morning. For many of us this is a final word. It indicates closure. End of the story. Period. When the rich young ruler came to Jesus, for instance, and was told that it would be like threading a camel through the eye of a needle for him to enter the reign of God, we immediately give up on him. Case closed. Judged guilty. But we don't know what happened to that rich young ruler, caught up in his wealth-worship, whether his heavier judgment left him in a state of hopeless despair. Maybe this judgment opened out onto a new field of opportunity for him—opportunity to repair, adjust, learn from others. Perhaps the same is true for us today, who stand under this banner of judgment for our word-worship. Maybe we'll find ways to listen to each other and see how words of deception are burning and destroying our faith, our communities, our families, our institutions of learning. Perhaps we will learn to preach and teach and lead in ways that are made wiser by listening to others whose lives are being, in James's words, "poisoned" and "burnt" by our speaking. Perhaps James's words of extreme caution will cause us simply to point the tiny rudder of our ships in a new direction—the direction of the redemption of speech itself.

In order for this to happen, there have to be places of speech-repair, lots of them, in which we allow one another the space to repair our words, thoughts, and speech. If my words are poisoning your life, then I need to think together, with you, about how, with integrity, the venom can be extracted or perhaps used as an antidote. I do not need your final judgment; I need your directional judgment. I hope that you will remember this when you hear my words about your sermons. Judgment for repair. Not judgment for damnation.

Ultimately, at the root of James's vision is not judgment but wisdom. He continues by appealing for "wisdom that comes from above" and whose "heart is peace and making peace."

At the heart of our speech, as people of God, there is a silent, passive voice that wants to speak beyond all of our speaking. It is the voice of wisdom. And this voice wants to say "shalom," "peace," "welcome"—dare I say it—"love." But it knows that once these things are said, once they are given over to feeble, co-opted language, something goes missing.

And so it is a largely silent voice, more a signing than a sign, more a silenced cry than a word. And James wants it at the heart of our speaking with each other and to others, as people of God, people of wisdom—a welcome-word, testifying to divine wisdom and grace in our speaking and our language, even as we speak words that deny what we are trying to say.

This is a kind of vision for us today. That we are signs of peace for each other and for the world, even as we work to resist and repair the signs and words that we use ourselves and that are used in our congregations and cultures. We can sign peace, like the hippies did, I suppose, but at a deeper level we can sign peace in, under, and around these deceiving words that both bless and curse.

How does this word of peace get into our speaking, into our speech? This morning, divine wisdom enters this room as you come face-to-face with me and with each other. I mean really face-to-face, beyond the jockeying for position and competing for grades or status, beyond the ways that I can grasp or reduce you to some manageable piece of my world, face-to-face even beyond our ideas of community and spirituality, which become ways to control identities and relationships. Divine wisdom enters at the point where we experience just our sheer proximity to each other, our being-with each other. It enters when I come face-to-face with you in your vulnerability and in my infinite responsibility for you, and where you experience me in my vulnerability and in your infinite responsibility for me.

This is what I think happened to many people in New York City and around the country in the minutes, hours, days, and weeks after the terrorist attacks of September 11. Many of us began to see each other's face, each other's vulnerability and our responsibility for one another, to feel the proximity, the true nearness, the "neighborness" of everyone in a way that made us want, more than anything in the world, to become signs and sign-givers of peace, compassion, welcome.

Susan Suchocki Brown, a Unitarian Universalist minister from Leominster, Massachusetts, and the chaplain for the local firehouse, watched the planes hit the towers, and she left immediately for New York City. She stayed there for days, at so-called Ground Zero, asking people one simple question: "Are you OK? Are you OK?" And then responding as best she could to their need. When she was interviewed later about her experience, all she could say was, "I feel like my heart is full of a million people."

As religious leaders, this is our testimony as well. "Our hearts are full of a million people." Inasmuch as we can let deep awareness of vulnerability and infinite responsibility be the center, the context of our teaching and learning and speaking, then the word of wisdom, of shalom, will enter our speech and begin the work of redemption. When this happens, then, in our classrooms, our congregations, our communities, and even in our nation and world, our words will be more blessing than curse, more peace than violence, more repair than destruction, more truth than deception. May it be so. May it be so.—John S. McClure

SUNDAY, OCTOBER 15, 2006
Lectionary Message

Topic: Is Anybody Listening?
TEXT: Job 23:1–9, 16–17
Other Readings: Ps. 22:1–15; Heb. 4:12–16; Mark 10:17–31

I. *Our need to be known.* It is liberating to have someone listen to you who can see you in a way that is different from the way you see yourself. There are people who, just by listening to us, can help us see something about ourselves we never noticed, who can help us understand ourselves and what is going on in our lives.

That is one of the things we expect from God—to be heard and understood and accepted. There is something about the freedom to be ourselves without pretense that draws us to God. And that is what makes it so horrible when it seems God does not hear, when our cries for help and our pleas for understanding seem to go no higher than the ceiling.

II. *Job's complaint and his unhelpful friends.* That is what made Job's plight so painful. It was bad enough that he had lost his possessions, his children, and his health. Worse than any of that was the separation he felt from God. He cried out to God for answers, but all he got in return was a vast and empty silence. All he wanted was a chance to plead his case before God, but it was as if there was no one there to listen. Job felt all alone in his suffering.

Job had three friends who came to comfort him. They sat with him for seven days and seven nights without saying a word. For seven days and seven nights, they were completely silent and a comfort to Job—until they started trying to explain things.

One friend, Bildad, saw himself as God's defense attorney. Job or his children must have done something to displease God. God is good and God is powerful, and a God who is good and powerful would not let Job suffer so much without good reason. Bildad's advice was, "Think a little harder, Job. There must be some reason you deserve what you got."

Another friend, Zophar, told Job just to hush because God is wise and knows what he's doing. Zophar told Job that if he would stop being arrogant and try to understand God's ways, his suffering would make perfect sense. Part of us wants to believe Zophar. His answers sound easy and sometimes appealing, but they just do not ring true. Zophar's God sounds coldly rational, discounting human suffering like some mad scientist who pursues abstract notions of good at the expense of innocent human beings.

And then there was Eliphaz—the pious one, who told Job that if he only prayed harder, everything would be OK. The only problem is that Eliphaz did not read the beginning of Job, where it says, "Job did not sin or charge God with wrong-doing." Job did everything right in the first place, and look what it got him.

III. *A friend who does help.* Each of Job's friends thought he had God figured out, and each one tried to squeeze Job's troubles into his notion of how God should operate. None of their answers helped. What Job needed was to know God had not abandoned him. Job needed to know God heard his cries.

Jesus is our assurance that God does hear us when we cry out in our distress. Jesus is the one who walks beside us in worry or pain or anxiety or grief. He is not someone who, like Job's friends, pops into our lives with answers that fit the way we think things ought to be but ignores what we actually experience. Jesus has been where we are.

Even though he is the everlasting Son of God, through whom all the worlds were made, Jesus is just as human as you and I. He knows what it is like to be tired and need a rest. He had to go off into the hills from time to time and recoup. During his forty days in the wilderness, Jesus felt the same temptation we feel to put money and power before commitment to God. He knew what it was like to lose a friend when he mourned the death of Lazarus. He knows what it is like to be abandoned by those we trust. In his hour of greatest need, he stood before Pontius Pilate alone. On the cross, he knew what it was like to suffer unbearable pain. He knew what it is like to feel God has let you down and turned a deaf ear to your cries. Jesus has been through that last obstacle in life that every one of us will experience but none has experienced yet—death.

Jesus assures us that God takes seriously those feelings of loneliness and abandonment, those times when we cry out to God and it seems as though we are talking to the wind. Like Job, we can continue to cry out because we know that no matter how distant God seems, God will not leave us. Jesus is our living promise that every time we cry out to God in faith, God hears us.

IV. *God will answer.* Job did not give up. He kept calling out to God, and he did not stop calling until he heard God's reply. What was true for Job is true for us. God does hear us, and God does answer us. God knows us better than we know ourselves, and the answers God gives us are always given in love and complete understanding.

God does hear us. God does help us. God knows exactly what kind of help we need. Nothing we bring to God is going to make God turn us away. "Approach the throne of grace with boldness," says Hebrews, "and receive mercy and find grace in time of need." Help is here. It is ours for the asking.

ILLUSTRATIONS

THE POWER OF SHARING.   We all know how comforting it is to be heard by someone who has been through the trials we are going through. When you share your problems with someone who has been where you are, you are confident that person will not think that your thoughts and feelings are unreasonable. The success of Alcoholics Anonymous is based on the fact that everyone at an AA meeting has the same addiction. When they tell each other their stories, they know that the people who listen know what they are talking about. Every widow knows there is no support like that of someone who has lost a husband herself. As important as friends and pastors and family members are, no one can listen as well as someone who has actually been there.

FINDING STRENGTH IN OUR WEAKNESS.   Joseph could hardly get out of bed in the mornings, he was so depressed after hearing the doctor's diagnosis that he had a chronic, irreversible, degenerative condition that affected his entire muscular system. He prayed every day for healing, but along with those prayers he lifted his life up to God and asked that in his own weakness he would know even more surely God's strength. The disease continued to progress, but Joseph found a kind of peace and well-being that he had never known before. It was not that his physical condition did not matter. He would have done anything to find a cure. But he was confident that he belonged to someone who is more powerful than his disease, and that changed the whole way he lived his life.—Stephens G. Lytch

SERMON SUGGESTIONS

Topic: The Big Question

TEXT: Ps. 22:1–15 (esp. v. 1a)

(1) God's providence is affirmed in history. (2) God's care is questioned in personal experiences. (3) The worst can be redeemed (Matt. 27:45–46, 28:1–7; 1 Cor. 1:18–31).

Topic: Confidence Before God

TEXT: 1 John 2:28

(1) Shame is a natural part of life. (2) We may be ashamed when we stand before our judge. (3) Yet we may have confidence before God: it is a matter of "abiding in Christ"; how? open the channels, believe, obey, love.

WORSHIP AIDS

CALL TO WORSHIP.   "The eyes of the Lord are upon the righteous, and his ears are open unto their cry" (Ps. 34:15).

INVOCATION.   We come to you, O God, because you call us to come. We pray to you, because you invite our prayers. You assure us that we are not only heard but that our prayers will be answered, though sometimes in ways we do not expect. Help us to be as open to your will as you are open to our cry.

OFFERTORY SENTENCE.   "Let us . . . always offer praise to God as our sacrifice through Jesus, which is the offering presented by lips that confess him as Lord. Do not forget to do good and to help one another, because these are the sacrifices that please God" (Heb. 13:15–16 TEV).

OFFERTORY PRAYER.   As our hearts are attuned to sing your praise, O God, may our hands be accustomed to giving, that the actions of our hands may reveal the song of our hearts and resound to the glory of God.—E. Lee Phillips

PRAYER.   O Father of us all, who is above all, yet in us all, make us grateful for the sense of seeing, of hearing, of smelling, of feeling, of tasting. Make us ever sensitive to all expressions of your grace in the world about us: the glory of the morning hour, the refreshment of the cool breeze that invigorates, the Technicolor of life—in the tree, the shrub, the flower, the sky, the sea. May the matter-of-fact orientation of this scientific age never blind us to the glamour, the romance, the wonder, the mystery of life.

If in the midst of all the excitement, color, and variety of nature about us we find ourselves yawning at life, take the dimness of our soul away. Provoke us from confirming ways that we may be transformed from *within* by the renewing of our minds to all the uniqueness of our creation as persons.

O you, who have called us into being through the creative power of your love and who calls us again and again to be, grant us such attentiveness in these moments of worship that we may hear your call again. May we respond *in faith,* according to our unique opportunity.

In our love and concern for one another, may we discover that we are made whole: "No man lives and no man dies unto himself." For those who anxiously toss on beds of pain, we pray for health; but if death be more merciful, we must pray, "Your will be done." May we who have our work, our families, and our friends not be insensitive to the needs of others for a sense of usefulness and belonging. May we not turn from the pain, the hurt, and what is tragic among us but seek those inexhaustible resources of your love by which we may be the Church to the sick, the lonely, the bereaved, the discouraged, the estranged. With them may we not just survive or merely cope, but win the victory that is present for all of us in Christ.

You are at work in this world. You so love the world and all peoples in it that you have come in person, not to condemn to death but to offer the gift of life. What a day this day can be in the liberation of all humankind from the fears of war and threat of war, from disease, from starvation, from illiteracy—if we have the vision to grasp the "new thing" that you are seeking to do in these tremendous times. We pray for the leaders of nations. We pray for our leaders that they may not just act or react with outmoded clichés of another day but respond to the living Word that you are speaking today. We pray for fledgling leaders in other countries, who struggle with new structures to express and preserve the new-won freedoms of their people.

And now, O Father, grant us the faith, the courage, the grace to live as we have prayed, through whom your Word is complete for men *and* for nations and is among us teaching us to pray and live: [repeat the Lord's Prayer].—John Thompson

SERMON

Topic: Practicing Resurrection
TEXT: Luke 24:1–12

As Arnold Palmer, a four-time winner of the Masters Golf Tournament, walked up the eighteenth fairway for the last time on Good Friday to the sustained applause of the fans, the television commentator said in a low, admiring voice: "He always acted like he was one of us." That spoke volumes about Arnold Palmer's ability to identify with the fans and to turn golf into one of the most entertaining television spectacles. Yet his fame never turned his head from those who paid to see him play.

Long ago on another Friday afternoon, Jesus was condemned to die on a cross on Golgotha's brow, and there, to catcalls and jeers instead of cheers, "the God-man acted like he was one of us." Those last seven lonesome words from the cross are words of identification. The writer of Hebrews puts it this way: "Forasmuch then as the children are partakers of flesh and blood, he also himself likewise took part of the same; that through death he might destroy him who has the power of death, that is, the devil" (Heb. 2:14). The apostle had this to say: "For what the law could not do, in that it was weak through the flesh, God sending his own Son in the likeness of sinful flesh, and for sin, condemned sin in the flesh" (Rom. 8:3). Jesus not only acted like he was one of us but, more important, he acted for us.

Now two thousand years and more have come and gone, yet that death on the cross still marks a precise moment in the extravagant love of God. Jesus dies on that cross for our sin. Molly Marshall said, "the old rugged cross is on a hill—too far away." She was pointing out that when we believe in Jesus for salvation, we are moving that atoning act forward over the years to powerfully change the present. As Paul said, "If any person be in Christ, that person is a new creation" (2 Cor. 5:17).

Just as the atonement of the cross works forward into the present, exercising a creative power to change it, so the future event of fulfillment, which Jesus' Resurrection ensures, works backward, having a powerful influence over things as they are now. The doctrine of "last things" includes the return of Christ in universal glory, the judgment of the world and the consummation of the Kingdom, the general resurrection of the dead, and the new creation of all things. By "last things" is meant these events are to break into this world from somewhere beyond history and to put an end to the history in which all things here live and move. We know this as "the end of time."

Yet it is sad to believe this way. By relegating these events to the "last day," we rob them of the uplifting stimulus and critical significance for all the days that are spent here, this side of the "end." The event of "future salvation" should have a liberating effect on the present, rather than being a mere projection of it. One thing the Resurrection of Jesus means is that eternity is not a continuation of things as they are now, but when God raised up Jesus, he did an incredibly new thing. No wonder Paul said to the Corinthians, "Behold, I show you a mystery!"

Those whose lives have been suffused here and now with this hope of future salvation, when every enemy to the Kingdom has been put down and even the Earth has been redeemed, will be able to "subdue kingdoms, work righteousness, turn to fight the armies of aliens, receive their dead back to life again," as the Bible says. Even if for you this biblical language is astonishing hyperbole, it surely means you can live beyond yourself. How barren the Christian life must be without the stimulus of this hope! Without this hope of the victorious consummation of the ages, reaching back to direct and energize the present for us, all teachings about the "end-time" that overpopulate the bookshelves just now wander off into obscure irrelevancies.

The future consummation, though hidden from view, exhibits its power in the lives of those who trust the promise. To help his hearers grasp the present and prevailing energy of this hope, a preacher recalled the days of his growing up in North Dakota. There the winters were harsh and cruel; the cold ran its fingers deep into the Earth, and snow blanketed the ground for what seemed unending days. But in the town square of the village where he grew up was a huge thermometer. As the winter days moved toward spring, the townspeople would congregate in the square around the thermometer. When finally the mercury moved upward to 33 degrees, there would be a shout of celebration, and joy would prevail throughout the village, for the thermometer had told them that the power of winter was broken. That was all the evidence they had; it was a promise. Ice and snow were still what the people faced, but a sign had been given. And the future prospect of spring gave them, in the midst of snow and ice, the courage to live as though spring had already arrived!

"Death and decay in all around I see," yet the significance of Jesus' Resurrection of long, long ago is that the power of death, with its bondage that paralyzes with fear, has been broken! Can we transport that hope back over time into the present and dare to live now with Paul in "the power of his resurrection" (Phil. 3:10)? "For there were great voices in heaven saying, 'The kingdoms of this world are become the kingdoms of our Lord, and of his Christ; and he shall reign for ever and ever'" (Rev. 11:15). The sovereignty of this world has passed into the hands of our Lord, and he shall reign forever and ever. Let's believe it and live from this day on in its light.—John C. Huffman

SUNDAY, OCTOBER 22, 2006
Lectionary Message

Topic: Putting Your Problems in Perspective

TEXT: Job 38:1–7 (34–41)

Other Readings: Ps. 104:1–9, 24, 35a; Heb. 5:1–10; Mark 10:35–45

I. *The climax of the story.* Job's appeal endures across the millennia because it deals with one of the most enduring of human issues—the problem of suffering. Anyone who has ever felt the grinding deprivation of poverty, the ripping emptiness of death, the helpless bewilderment of disease, or the hopeless absence of God can find in Job the words for which they search to describe their plight. Job has stood as the quintessential spokesperson for human suffering for 2,500 years because he knows every cry and whimper of our pain and gives us a perspective that no amount of introspection can ever attain.

This passage is the climax of his story—the moment for which Job has been waiting and pleading. Once the wealthiest man in the East, renowned for his generosity and his righteousness, Job had lost his entire fortune. All ten of his children had been killed in a terrible storm. He was afflicted with a disease that disfigured him from head to foot. Through thirty-seven chapters, he listened to his friends' feeble attempts to make sense of his pain and his loss. Nothing they said could ease his suffering. All he wanted was a chance to plead his case before God. Job was certain that if God would only hear him, God would bring justice. Job had faith that God would make sense of his situation and put everything back in order. And now, finally, is the long-awaited dramatic moment. At last God speaks to Job.

II. *Not the answer Job expected.* But listen! This is not at all what Job had in mind. Job was waiting for God to vindicate him and show him what his suffering meant. Instead, God reminds Job just who God is and asks Job what his qualifications are for questioning the wisdom and justice of God. For the next four chapters, God takes Job on a verbal tour of the grandeur of nature. "Where were you when I laid the foundations of the earth?" God asks Job. "Did you set the boundaries of the sea that keep it from covering the earth? Did you set the constellations in order? Can you send the rain to water the earth? Does your wisdom order the intricacies of the ecosystem, giving each animal and bird its place? Did you make the lion to roam the savannah? Did you teach the raven how to feed her young?"

No, this is not the response Job expected, and it is not the kind of compassionate listening they taught us in seminary. In fact, it seems almost disjointed. Job wants to know why he is suffering, and God recites the glory of nature. The two do not seem to connect. Nevertheless, it is exactly the response Job needed. God gave Job a new, larger perspective on life that did not ignore or belittle his pain but gave it a context bigger than life itself. God showed Job just how incredibly vast and complex creation is. God reminded Job that God created and sustains every fish in the sea and every star in the sky. If God has the entire universe under control, from the course of the sun to the feeding of the birds, are your problems too big for God?

III. *God puts our lives in the proper context.* Nature reminds us that God is free and independent, completely beyond us and outside our control. It is precisely because nature is so disinterested in us and our problems that we find it so liberating. There is something freeing about looking out over a mountain vista and knowing that it looks the same way it did when your grandparents saw it, and your presence on the Earth has not affected it one bit. There is something refreshing about knowing that the running stream is going to keep flowing whether you are there or not, that the birds are going to build their nests in the spring, regardless of what is going on in your life.

It is in wild, untamed places that people throughout history have met God. God gave Moses the Ten Commandments on remote, windswept Mt. Sinai. Jesus girded himself for his ministry by spending forty days in the wilderness. He showed his disciples just how much they could trust him when he calmed the raging sea. When we remember just how small we are in the vast scheme of creation, we fall back on our Creator, trusting that those things that overwhelm us are not too big for God.

IV. *Majesty in our midst.* When we stand in awe of the majesty of God, it seems all the more remarkable that God should put aside that glory to come among us as a human being, Jesus Christ. God came among us as one of us, not so we can tame God but so we can be drawn into that realm that is far greater than anything we can ever conceive of, that glory beyond human imagination to which tornadoes and sunsets and roaring surf can only point. Jesus himself said it best: "Whoever wants to find their life must first lose it, and whoever loses their life for my sake will find it." Knowing that God is Lord, even of the wilderness, the trackless deserts, the fathomless seas, and the blowing tempests, we can be sure that God is also Lord of the wildest places in our hearts.

God did not give Job an answer to his suffering, but God does give our suffering a place, a context, and an assurance that even though we do not understand why, our pain and our grief and our sorrow are not the last word. God holds us in our sufferings, and nothing—no storm, no drought, no pain, not even death—can wrench us away from God.

ILLUSTRATIONS

DRAWN OUT OF THE VALLEY.   Suffering and grief have a certain inertia that, left to itself, would keep us in that bleak valley. If you have ever experienced a debilitating loss, you have probably felt that swell of indignation when it dawned on you that while you were in deep mourning because your life had a gaping hole ripped in it, the rest of the world was going on as if nothing ever happened. You walk out the door one morning and think, "How dare they?" The children are still going to school, the mail is still being delivered, and the neighbors are still getting in their cars and going off to work. At some point we have to come up out of the valley. Yes, we are forever changed for having been there; we cannot deny that. But God made us to be part of a world that is bigger than ourselves, even bigger than our most devastating losses. Suffering wins when it causes us to lose sight of that, when it will not let us reclaim the part God has for us in something that is bigger than ourselves.

GOD WHOM WE CANNOT CONTROL.   Who wants a god that is like Vernon and Petunia Dursley?

Vernon and Petunia Dursley are characters in J. K. Rowling's best-selling Harry Potter novels. They are Harry's aunt and uncle, with whom he went to live after his parents were killed. Vernon and Petunia treat Harry miserably, but they jump every time their son Dudley looks at them cross-eyed. This is what it was like at breakfast time in the Dursley household on Dudley's birthday:

> Dudley . . . was counting his presents. His face fell.
>
> "Thirty-six," he said, looking up at his mother and father. "Two less than last year."

"Darling, you haven't counted Auntie Marge's present. See, it's here under this big one from Mommy and Daddy."

"All right, thirty-seven then," said Dudley going red in the face.

Aunt Petunia obviously scented danger, . . . because she said quickly, "And we'll buy you another *two* presents while we're out today. How's that, popkin? *Two* more presents. Is that all right?"

"So I'll have . . . thirty . . . thirty . . ."

"Thirty-nine, sweetums," said Aunt Petunia.

"Oh. . . . All right then."[2]

We may fantasize about a god who would treat us like we were Dudley Dursley and give us everything we imagined we wanted, but God knows how unhappy we would be. Our lives would wind up looking like Dudley's room, stuffed with broken toys that bored him.— Stephens G. Lytch

SERMON SUGGESTIONS

Topic: The Magic Scepter

TEXT: Isa. 55:3

Obedience imparts life. (1) It characterizes membership in God's family (Jer. 7:23). (2) It leads to knowledge of truth (John 7:17). (3) It results in purity of life and thought (1 Pet. 1:22). (4) It leads at last to the Celestial City (Rev. 22:14; Matt. 7:21).

Topic: Jesus, Our High Priest

TEXT: Heb. 4:14–16

(1) Has authority conferred by God (see 5:4). (2) Sympathizes with our weaknesses. (3) Provides for our spiritual needs: mercy for past offenses; grace for present and future struggles.

WORSHIP AIDS

CALL TO WORSHIP.   "I will give thee thanks in the great congregation: I will praise thee among much people" (Ps. 35:18).

INVOCATION.   Our Father, let our praise sound forth from joyful hearts. Deepen our faith in what you can do, even as you have already done mighty things for us. Let the victory of our Lord Jesus Christ echo in our gratitude, now and always.

OFFERTORY SENTENCE.   "Each one, as a good manager of God's different gifts, must use for the good of others the special gift he has received from God" (1 Pet. 4:10 TEV).

OFFERTORY PRAYER.   Father of our Lord Jesus Christ, we, who bring what we have, who give what we can, and who pray for your will, ask that this offering be used to bring others to saving faith and bring us to maturing trust, through the sure Word that is the victory!— E. Lee Phillips

---

[2]J. K. Rowling, *Harry Potter and the Sorcerer's Stone* (New York: Scholastic, Inc., 1997), p. 21.

PRAYER.   So often, Father, we take the routines of life for granted. Sunday's activities come and go, and we seldom think of the power of these hours we spend in your presence. This morning we thank you for this hour of worship and all that it brings us of renewal and of strength. The bowed heads about us bear witness to our common need and our common faith. Nowhere in all our living are we closer to one another and to you than in these moments when we, together, offer our prayers and songs to you. Thank you for this fellowship and for the privilege we have of bearing one another's burdens.

In these sacred moments turn our thoughts to Christ. Fill us with his spirit and strength to live after his fashion. Open our eyes to the needs of those whom we daily meet. Generate in us a desire to speak words of encouragement and hope to friends and strangers alike. Lead us to do deeds of grace and mercy, to reach out and lift burdens, and to walk the way with the lonely struggler that he may no longer be alone. Empower us to be more than conquerors, as we manage the multitude of situations that will defeat us without your strengthening presence. Defend us from temptation's grip, even as you deliver us from the evil that we would allow to consume us.

In our weakness empower us; in our fear fortify us; in our loss encourage us; in our lostness find us; and from our sinfulness save us, that we may not only be able servants of the Lord but devout disciples of our Master, in whose name we pray.—Henry Fields

SERMON
Topic: What Is So Bad with Us? Sloth
TEXT: Matt. 25:26

The master returns and calls the servants in to give an account of what they have done with their talents. Those with many talents have done much. The man with the one talent who did absolutely nothing with his talent gets creamed. This is the man Donald Trump fires.

But instead of simply saying, "You're fired," the Master calls him, "Thou wicked and slothful servant." Just that single line in Scripture would be enough for me to put sloth on the list of seven deadly sins. Don't those words just seem like the worst job evaluation you can imagine? Wicked and slothful. Last week we asked the confirmation class to put down some of the things that they would not want anybody to say about them, and none of them worried about being called slothful. They did not even put down lazy. So what is sloth, and what is so bad about it?

At one level sloth is simply laziness—the refusal or lack of willingness to do anything to help, like this one talented servant who did nothing to try to help make things different or better. He just put it in the ground and avoided the whole problem. We have some classic symbols of slothfulness in our society. The teenage boy in the newspaper comic strip "Zits" is one of our models of sloth. The teenager stretched out on the couch, who wants his mother to get him a drink and his sister to bring him the phone, is the laziness that has no interest in doing anything to help. The middle-aged fat man in his undershirt, sitting in front of the TV with beer cans all over the floor, is another classic example of the sin called sloth. The lack of willingness—the lack of interest in life to be willing to do anything—is the common definition of sloth.

Now some people will try to tell you that sloth is the mother of invention, that laziness is a virtue. Just look at all the labor-saving devices that have been created by lazy people. If you really want to find the most efficient and fastest way to do something, hire a lazy person to do the job, and that person will find the easiest and simplest way to do it. Laziness is good.

There was even an attempt to make sloth into a virtue, because look at all the other sins it keeps us from committing. Laziness—this lack of willingness to move, the inertia that keeps us on the couch and prevents us from getting up and doing things—keeps us from all the other sins of passion. This sloth, this lack of interest, this lack of passion in life, keeps us from anger, greed, pride, gluttony. Those are sins of action and passion. So we ought to encourage the sin of laziness and sloth because it keeps us from committing all those sins.

All of that pushes us back to look more closely at what sloth really is. It is not laziness. The laziness that invents labor-saving devices is creative, is involved in life, cares and gets up and does its part to try to make life better. The person who daydreams and spends time sitting on the beach watching the waves has not refused to participate and to take part in the adventure of life. The very creation, invention of tools and devices, is the opposite of sloth.

Sloth is the refusal to be involved in those things that require an effort on our part. Certainly, teenagers and old men in undershirts frequently refuse to be involved in the work of the family or the house. But so also do those who think they are so cool, that they are slicker and smarter and do not need to be involved in the ordinary, daily things of life. They are above caring and doing their part. They might get their hands dirty. They might mess up their hair. They might have to glow. There is a widespread attitude in certain portions of society of an entitlement attitude: from the welfare recipients who have grown up believing that they are entitled to certain benefits without doing anything to those country-club children who believe they are entitled to all the luxuries of life without having to lift a finger to receive them. Somebody is supposed to give those luxuries to them. Sloth is the sin of the spoiled brat. Slothfulness is being unwilling to do what is necessary and appropriate, that is, what God has created and asked us to do, because the effort is more than they want to exert. God has declared that we were created to be stewards of creation, to take care of the Earth; sloth is the refusal to be responsible for the portion of creation in which you live because the effort is more than you are willing to make.

Sloth is laziness. Sloth is being cool and condescending. But sloth is also a deeper, more painful sin. Simon and Garfunkel had a very moving and powerful song, early in their career, about sloth: "I am a rock. I am an island. I touch no one and no one touches me. I am a rock. A rock feels no pain and an island never cries." Maybe that is why the color of sloth is blue, and the animal to represent sloth is a goat. The poet is no longer willing to reach out, to be involved with other people, no longer able or desiring to care for other people; the poet is not willing to risk the pain that such reaching out involves. The poet is suffering from the sadness of sloth. Sloth was originally called the sadness in the face of joy. Here is the sin of shutting up and closing down of life because it does not have the confidence, the hope, the courage to do the things necessary for the joy that it sees.

Jesus invites his disciples to follow him and promises them his presence with them, by the gift of his Holy Spirit, but he calls them to pick up their cross and follow him. Those who look at the joy of salvation and then look at the potential pain of the cross and refuse to follow Jesus because they do not want to have to make the effort of bearing the cross has yielded to the sin of sloth. When we refuse to do our share, when we refuse to make the necessary response to the gift of salvation because it is too hard, too complicated, too much effort, we are slothful people. Paul writes to the Christians at Rome: "For I reckon that the sufferings of this present time are not worthy to be compared with the glory which shall be revealed to us." For Paul there was nothing that would keep him from doing whatever he needed to do to be faithful, so that he might enjoy the glory that was to come. But for so many of us, we have become wicked and slothful servants, because there is in us a faint-heartedness in the matters of difficulty in striving for the good. We will do our part and be involved, as long as the effort required is not great.

Dorothy Sayers, the British mystery writer of the "Lord Peter Wimsey" series and a member of the writers' group with C. S. Lewis, J.R.R. Tolkein, Charles Williams, and others, has described sloth as the sin that believes in nothing, cares for nothing, seeks to know nothing, enjoys nothing, hates nothing, finds purpose in nothing, lives for nothing, and remains alive because there isn't even anything for which to die. If that's all there is, then let's keep dancing.

This is an important sin for us to consider in our community right now. We have talked about it before. But when we look at our community, the first things we see are all of our problems. We see the unemployment and the teenage pregnancies; we see the drugs and the crime; we see the apathy and cynicism in the people's faces. When people talk about what kind of effort we will have to make to become the kind of community we would like to be, it is the sin of sloth that keeps people from being willing to make the effort necessary to get involved and join the struggle to transform this community. The Clean Up Henderson Committee has a vision of a spiritual good: cleanliness is next to godliness, they say. They see a clean, well-kept Henderson as their vision of the Kingdom on Earth. They know the effort and the work that will have to be done, the crosses that will have to be carried. And sloth is the sin that keeps people from getting on board and helping. It is too much work. You will never get adequate code enforcement when the city and county are run by landlords. You will make a lot of people angry. Sloth is the sin that refuses to make the effort necessary for salvation.

The *Henderson Dispatch* carried a story on Friday of a mother and son who were shot at by accused drug dealers, as mother and son were trying to get the drug dealers evicted from a house in their neighborhood. The Committee Against Violence is trying to bring together people to build a community that will not accept violence and crime in its midst. There is the vision of spiritual good. But the dangers are just as visible. Sloth is the fully-aware person renouncing the vision of salvation because the process is too tedious, too disgusting, too dangerous, too impossible, too big, too hard. The joy, the salvation, the Kingdom of God is just not worthy of our effort.

Of course, it is one of the deadly sins because it is the heart afraid of dying that never learns to live. It is the cross of love that Jesus carried that brought life everlasting. The thrill of victory can come only to those who have played the game. The joy of heaven is given to those who have opened their hearts and have done what they could to welcome it.—Rick Brand

SUNDAY, OCTOBER 29, 2006
Lectionary Message

Topic: God's Final Answer
TEXT: Job 42:1–6, 10–17
Other Readings: Ps. 34:1–8 (19–22); Heb. 7:23–28; Mark 10:46–52

I. *The limits of knowledge.* At the beginning of his story, Job lost everything he had—his fortune, his children, his health. The book that bears his name traces his effort to make sense of his troubles and find some rational framework that would explain what happened. Job's friends Bildad, Zophar, and Eliphaz tried to explain his plight, each one offering a different rationale for all the bad things that had happened to Job. None of their answers satisfied. Nothing anyone said made sense. Now, as the story draws to a close, Job gets answers to his questions. God speaks to Job:

QUESTION: Why did I lose everything I had?
ANSWER: Why did God make the ostrich?
QUESTION: Why did all my children have to die?
ANSWER: What is the purpose of the hippopotamus?
QUESTION: Why did I contract this debilitating illness?
ANSWER: Why are there whales?

In other words, there are some things for which we just cannot know the answers.

We are taught from kindergarten that knowledge is the key and that we can do anything if we set our minds to it. There is no problem that does not have an answer, if we work hard enough to find it. Knowledge is power, and understanding gives control. That is why we struggle so mightily to make sense of our suffering. We need our lives to make sense, not only intellectually but also morally.

One of the ways we get some control over life is by trying to impose order on it. Job's friends looked for the bad things Job did that made him deserve his pain. They searched for lessons God was trying to teach Job by making him suffer. But human knowledge is frail. We can be wrong about physical things like nutrition and physics that we can observe and quantify. How much more uncertain is our knowledge of the forces of good and evil that are hidden from our eyes?

In the end, Job realized that some things cannot be explained. At some point we have to accept that injustice and suffering and death make no sense. There are some questions we have to give to God and trust there is wisdom and purpose and order—and love—that are beyond our understanding.

II. *There is an answer.* Those unanswerable questions are not without a final answer, but the answer is not in an explanation; it is in a person. Ultimately, our trust is not in what we know but in the One we know. Jesus gives us the faith to live with those unanswerable questions. His suffering and death were not justified. They made no more sense than the loss and grief Job endured or the loss and grief you and I suffer. Just like everyone else who has ever walked through the valley of the shadow of death, Jesus felt the power of those chaotic forces that harm people who do not deserve it, that rip apart innocent lives, that cause us to question whether there really is a moral foundation to the universe.

Jesus forces us to confront the weakness of every explanation we concoct to explain why people suffer. He did not deserve to suffer. God was not punishing him for his sins. God was not trying to teach Jesus a lesson. Jesus affirms what Job finally knew: God is greater than all our questions and all our suffering. God raised Jesus from death—proof that no matter what happens, God has the last word. That word may be completely different from what we expected to hear, but in the end, God triumphs.

III. *The power of hope.* In Jesus we find hope. The New Testament says, "Hope that is seen is not hope. For who hopes for what is seen? But if we hope for what we do not see, we wait for it with patience" (Rom. 8:24–25). We live in hope of the resurrection to eternal life—our conviction that God is more powerful than all our unanswered questions and undeserved suffering. But hope is more than a conviction that keeps us from falling into despair. Hope is active. It sends us out to proclaim its message. God fills us with the Holy Spirit and sends us out to share our hope with others.

That is why mission is at the heart of the Church. Mission is hope in action. Churches are not the only organizations that do good things for others. Along with everyone else who helps those in need, we share that human desire to relieve suffering and improve lives. But along with the compassion we share with all people of a generous spirit, we have a charge from God. We who follow Jesus have the privilege of showing the world what God is doing. Whenever we feed the hungry, clothe the poor, stand up for the oppressed, or start a new community of faith, we show the world that God is more powerful than anything that can harm us.

We do not have answers to the question of why there is suffering and pain and injustice in the world, in your life or in mine. But we have the good news that there is someone greater than our suffering and wiser than our questions. Jesus Christ is our hope—God's final answer to all our questions.

ILLUSTRATION

Some questions are beyond our understanding. It is one thing to have a medical explanation that your father's family history of heart disease increased the odds he would have a heart attack. But you want to know why a good person like him had to die. Or you can trace the deterioration of a marriage, maybe even pinpoint the places it took irreparable turns. But you wonder why there is such emptiness and a sense of failure so long after the marriage is over. Or you understand the age-old tribal enmities in the Horn of Africa that led to the war between Ethiopia and Eritrea. But you want to know why thousands of children in Africa have to starve to death when there is so much food in the world that the greatest pediatric health hazard in the United States is obesity. Such questions defy knowledge.—Stephens G. Lytch

SERMON SUGGESTIONS

Topic: Making the Right Choice
TEXT: Ps. 34:1–8 (19–22)
The right choice is confirmed: (1) By answered prayer. (2) In continuing experience. (3) Through ultimate deliverance.

Topic: The Heavenly Vision
TEXT: Acts 26:9–23 (esp. v. 19)
There are favorable situations in which we may anticipate having a high level of insight: (1) When doing the common task well (Amos). (2) When in the house of God (Isaiah). (3) When in a personal crisis (Elijah). (4) When another life touches your own (Paul and Stephen).

WORSHIP AIDS

CALL TO WORSHIP.   "O give thanks to the Lord; for he is good; for his loving kindness endures forever" (Ps. 118:1).

INVOCATION.   We swing wide the gate, Lord, as with minds set on the things of God, we enter the challenges set before us. Gather every day of our life unto meaning, that our moments and hours may be God-honoring, beginning with this act of corporate worship.—E. Lee Phillips

OFFERTORY SENTENCE.   "If a brother or sister is naked and in lack of daily food, and one of you say to them, "Go in peace, be warmed and filled; and yet do not give them the things needful to the body; what does it profit?" (James 2:15–16).

OFFERTORY PRAYER.   Receive these offerings, Lord, as part of our worship. In spirit and in truth we seek to worship you. Cleanse our spirits and accept our gifts, we pray, in the name of Jesus.

PRAYER.   O God, for your preparation through Israel, for your coming in person in Jesus of Nazareth, for your purpose expressed in and through the Church, for your continuing presence in the person of your Holy Spirit—for lessons from the past and new beginnings, for the heritage, visions, labors, and sacrifices of the many who have gone this way before us, for victories won, for healings wrought, for difficulties overcome, for estrangements gulfed, for faithfulness to the end—for a living hope not limited by time, or space, or flesh, or any such thing—for the privilege to celebrate on this day, in this place, and with these people your love, mercy, and grace, we give you thanks in an offering of praise, adoration, and joy.

In the spirit of your love—you who so loved the world that you gave your only Son—we would pray for one another and for all others. In the power of your grace to heal, we embrace those who are ill, those facing the loneliness of bereavement, those discouraged with failure, those made anxious with difficult decisions.

We pray for the family of faith; we pray, too, for the families in which our lives are most intimately set. To these we bear an urgent responsibility to share the gospel, but often we are hesitant, even reluctant. Increase your love in us, strengthen our faith, empower us with your spirit to do what we know.

We pray, too, for the family of humankind. How can we worship you—Mother-Father of us all—except our brother, our sister, be with us? We thank you for all who affirm and celebrate your Word, your intention, from the beginning—one world, one people.

We pray for the Palestinians and Israelis that they may find a way to live together as "good neighbors," lest all be lost in mounting tension and widening conflict. We are haunted by our responsibility for the way things are. When frustration to be free and to be treated equally are vented in violent rage, we are there. When we play politics, selfishly seeking our national interest, Lord have mercy.

We pray that we may be more sensitive and courageous and be instruments of your peace and justice.

We pray for those who aspire to lead and for the electorate, that the franchise may be exercised as privilege and responsibility.

Through him who teaches us to pray together as one family: our Father.—John Thompson

SERMON
Topic: A Vocabulary of Faith—Firming a Foundation
TEXT: Deut. 6:4–9; 1 Cor. 8:1–6

John Evans is a pastor in Corvalis, Oregon. He was at a fast-food restaurant with his family, standing in line getting ready to pay. All he needed was a nickel and he would have the correct change. He had a twenty-dollar bill in his pocket, but he didn't want to break the twenty, so he turned to his family and said, "Does anybody have a nickel?" Well, they all knew that four-year old Maya, the granddaughter, had one, because she had been talking about the nickel in her pocket all the way to the restaurant.

Grandpa said, "Maya, may I have your nickel?"

"No!"

Her parents then said, "Maya, won't you give Grandpa your nickel?"

"No."

Her hand went into her pocket, and it was easy to see she was clutching that nickel. Her little lower lip began to quiver. What do you do in a situation like that?

"Why, Maya?"

"Grandpa, it's for the church! It's for the church, Grandpa!"

What do you do when you are the pastor of the church, and you are a grandfather, and your granddaughter wants to give her nickel to the church? You reach in your pocket and you pull out the twenty-dollar bill, and you give it to the cashier, and you get back nineteen dollars and ninety-five cents. Then you take all ninety-five cents in change and you give it to your granddaughter, because you know she has her priorities in order.

What I want us to think about this morning are our priorities—those principles that order our lives. The biblical concept that we are looking at today is order. So far we have talked about wonder, sin, covenant, and deliverance, and today we talk about order.

The book of Deuteronomy is Moses' last statement to his people, his farewell address. He has gathered the people on the plains of Moab. They have traveled for forty years through the wilderness. He is ready to send them into the Promised Land, and this is his last statement to the people. What he does is review what they have been experiencing for the last forty years. A process of review helps with our sense of order. If we look back over our lifetime and we see the significant events, we see where God has interacted with us. We see where we have not been faithful to God. We can begin to develop some sense of priority and direction for our lives. In looking back and reviewing, we can seek an order for the future.

The major purpose of the book of Deuteronomy is to prepare the people for the new land, for the crossing over of the river, and for their occupying of the Promised Land. The major concern is not the people already in the land. Moses doesn't talk about whether Israel can get along with them or not. What Moses focuses on is not to forget the law. Don't forget how God has ordered your life to this point. Moses is helping the people firm their foundation for the chaotic time they will face. One of the things Moses does is to reiterate the Ten Commandments. They were given much earlier, but now he repeats them to the people to remind them of this sense of order from God.

Now it is not in the text anywhere, but I can't help but wonder if, after Moses lists the Ten Commandments once again, somebody in the crowd didn't raise a hand and say, "Moses, is one of those more important than all the rest?" That very question was asked of Jesus generations later.

Our text this morning is Moses' answer to that question, whether it was asked or not.

The whole purpose of this passage is to have the people focused on God when they go into a difficult time of their lives. You and I, in our lives, face difficult times on a routine basis. We need this sense of ordering for our lives as well. We need to make sure of our relationship with God. We need to make sure that our words and our actions teach our children. I don't mean just our biological children. If there are children living anywhere on your street, anywhere they can watch you, you are a teacher of those children. They are watching, and they are seeking guidance always. We are all responsible for all our children. It does take a village to raise a child.

Aldous Huxley said, "God's nature and God's will are one. But our human nature and our human will are two." The Bible refers to that as double-mindedness and repeatedly addresses that situation. In 1 Kings, Elijah says to the people, "How long will you go limping along with two different minds. If Yahweh is God, then worship him. But if Baal is god, then worship him." In the Sermon on the Mount, Jesus said, "Blessed are those who are pure in heart."

SUNDAY, NOVEMBER 5, 2006
Lectionary Message

Topic: She Made Up Her Mind

TEXT: Ruth 1:1–18

Other Readings: Ps. 146; Heb. 9:11–14; Mark 12:28–34

I. *Naomi is left alone.* Can things go worse for Naomi? First there was a famine, so she and her husband and her two sons had to leave their home in Bethlehem and travel south to Moab to find food. There her sons married Moabite women—predictable, but Naomi can't have been too happy about her grandchildren being raised by mothers who did not worship the God of Israel. But then her husband died, and she was left a widow in a land where she owned nothing, where her only protection was her family. Then her two sons died; neither of them had children. When the narrator sums up this part of the story, the words are stark: "the woman was bereft of her two sons and her husband."

II. *Naomi wants to be alone.* This verse says nothing about the two daughters-in-law; Naomi did not think of them as a permanent part of her family, so when she decided to go back to her home and to her own people, she tried to convince the two younger women to stay in Moab and find other husbands. She wasn't angry with them and had no hard feelings against them. Naomi asked God to bless them with a husband and a home, and asked God to treat them as well as they had treated her two sons. But Naomi clearly did not think of them as family, believing instead that the bonds between them were broken rather than intensified by their shared grief. The two women protested: "No, we will return with you to your people." But Naomi had made up her mind.

Why is Naomi so anxious to say goodbye to the two Moabite women? Maybe she was thinking mostly of them, realizing that without a dowry or a male relative who could arrange a marriage, a foreign-born widow would be hard-pressed to find a husband in Israel. Her argument to them was about how she could not provide them with more sons, which would argue that her thoughts were mostly fixed on their hardship. But maybe Naomi was also thinking partly about herself. It would be hard enough for her to make her way in her own hometown as a childless widow, so how could she care for others? How could she take on the responsibility of finding a suitable husband for her daughters-in-law? And then there's her depression over her great loss and her conclusion that God had turned against her; perhaps Naomi wasn't thinking too clearly. Whatever the constellation of reasons, she seems to have made up her mind that she would be completely alone in the world.

It's pretty common after being badly hurt emotionally to want to be left alone. You just don't want to have to interact with people. You don't want to have to talk about what happened or how bad it felt; you don't want to have to answer questions or accept sympathy from those who care about you; everything is hard, and so you resign, withdraw, pull into yourself. You may, like Naomi, even try to tell those who care about you to leave, and you may succeed in isolating yourself. We who minister to those in grief have to respect their need for time to heal, but we also have to watch for those who make themselves into little islands of anger or grief because they make their minds up that life is always going to be awful. Orpah did as Naomi asked, but not what Naomi really needed. Ruth is the better example of how stubborn Christian ministry sometimes must be.

III. *Ruth won't leave her alone.* Naomi got her way with Orpah, but not with Ruth. The beautiful poetry of Ruth's speech, words we sometimes hear at weddings—"entreat me not to leave thee"—should not distract us from what Ruth was saying: "Don't ask me that again!" Ruth does not ask Naomi's permission to tag along on the trip to Bethlehem; she does not propose a plan for her mother-in-law to consider. Instead, she just announces her travel plans ("Wherever you go, I go"), her new living arrangements ("I'm staying with you, wherever that turns out to be"), and the length of the contract ("Until they bury us in the same cemetery plot"). Ruth also says she is claiming Naomi's God, and since Naomi believes God has cursed her, Ruth's saying, "May the Lord do thus to me" means, "Well, maybe God's hand is against you, but I'm choosing to stand with you anyway, and if I ever leave you, then may God do even worse to me than has happened to you." She's made up her mind, and that's that; Naomi has been out-stubborned.

IV. *Ruth and God's Hesed.* The trip back to Bethlehem can't have been much fun, with Naomi grieving, silent, and resigned, and Ruth trying to balance her own grief with her care of Naomi and with her anxieties over what she had gotten herself into. We haven't gotten yet to "they lived happily ever after." But this story is, in the end, about God's *hesed*—a Hebrew word often translated "steadfast love" or "covenant mercy." *Hesed* is that part of God's nature that keeps God faithful to the covenants with humans, even when we are unfaithful. Ruth is a very clear picture of what *hesed* looks like. In the face of death, the destruction of home, and the loss of hope, Ruth's steadfast insistence that she and Naomi were going to live together, make a home together, worship God together, and be a family are embodiments of God's steadfast love. God, who loves us without respect to whether we deserve or even want to be loved, in this story is most like the Moabite widow who told her mother-in-law that she might as well give up on sending her away.

Thanks be to God for God's *hesed*—God's steadfast love that keeps God with us, even when we want to be alone; and thanks be to God for friends and family as stubbornly loving as Ruth.—Richard B. Vinson

ILLUSTRATIONS

I AM A ROCK.   Paul Simon's song describes a person who tries to withdraw from the world, presumably because of the loss of love: "Don't talk of love/ I've heard the word before/ It's sleeping in my memory." The song ends with what we hope for when we draw away because of old hurts: "And a rock feels no pain/ and an island never cries." But it never works out that way, does it?—Richard B. Vinson

IF SHE NEVER LEAVES I WILL BE GLAD.   Ada is speaking to Inman, with whom she has just been reunited after his long journey home from the war: "And there's something you need to know about Ruby, Ada said. Whatever comes to pass between you and me, I want her to stay in Black Cove as long as she cares to. If she never leaves I will be glad, and if she does I'll mourn her absence."[1]

SERMON SUGGESTIONS

Topic: This Business of Trust

TEXT: Ps. 146

(1) Do not put unconditional trust in human beings (vv. 3–4). (2) You can put your complete trust in God (vv. 5–10).

Topic: Sanctification—for You Today

TEXT: 1 Cor. 6:1–9

If we are true Christians, we are sanctified. It is a gift, yet it is something to be achieved. The implications: (1) Deeper prayer life. (2) Greater concern for evangelism and social change. (3) Achievement of clean living (1 Thess. 4:3–7).

WORSHIP AIDS

CALL TO WORSHIP.   "I lift up my eyes to the hills—from where will my help come? My help comes from the Lord, who made heaven and earth" (Ps. 121:1 NRSV).

INVOCATION.   Almighty God, we come to you in weakness and seek your strength. Our temptations are too much for us without your presence. Our burdens are too heavy without your help. Our lives are too empty without your joy. Come to us and stay with us.

OFFERTORY SENTENCE.   "For whosoever would save his life shall lose it; and whosoever shall lose his life for my sake shall find it" (Matt. 16:25).

OFFERTORY PRAYER.   Father, we know that we always have something to give. It might not be money, but whatever we honestly present to you can be used for your glory. As we present our monetary offerings to you now, may they open our hearts even more so that we may daily give to you greater gifts.

---

[1]From *Cold Mountain*, by Charles Frazier (New York: Atlantic Monthly Press, 1997), p. 337.

PRAYER.   "The heavens declare the glory of God and the firmament showeth forth his handiwork." And we mortals look lovingly upward. We thank you for the beauties of your creation. We thank you for the blessings of your providential care. We love you because you first loved us and taught us the meaning of love in the gift of your Son.

We are not worthy of your grace. We have sinned, and we ask your merciful forgiveness.

We thank you for one another, and we pray for one another. Some in our family are ill; we ask your healing. Some are rejoicing; we thank you for that joy. Some are discouraged; we offer our friendship. Some are in turmoil; we pray for your calm. Some are grieving; grant them your comfort.

And outside our family, there's a world out there, fractured and bleeding, hungry and hurting. Grant us the ability and the willingness to help, Lord, and make our help effective.

Today—ah, today, Father—make us good followers of Jesus Christ. We pray in his name.—J. Estill Jones

SERMON
Topic: Redemptive Anger
TEXT: Mark 3:1–6

Walter Wink describes the "food for thought" in a typical movie or TV drama as "the myth of redemptive violence." We are stirred to anger by an oversimplified situation in which the good guys are pitiful victims of the demonic evil of the bad guys. Our anger is stirred as we identify with the victim and feel personally threatened and personally victimized. Finally, the need for revenge is satisfied in a bloodbath of violence poured out on the villains. Violent ventilation of anger is justified by the total depravity of the villains.

We should not be surprised at the growing presence of violence in our world. Some folks move out of the big cities to quiet little communities to get away from the war zone. If we can escape the presence of violence, as Christians we cannot escape responsibility for the persistent warfare in our world.

In the Sermon on the Mount, the description of the righteousness of the Kingdom is set in contrast with the hypocrisy of the Pharisees. Jesus warned about the potential for violence in the powerful human emotion we know too well as anger. He placed anger in context with murder and the humiliating deprecation of another person by name-calling. The connection of anger with the destruction of life and reputation seems to be the real issue. The denial of anger as an acceptable human emotion is not in question here. Jesus condemns the destructive release of anger: nurturing a grudge, hating, attacking another person. Biblical wrath—the anger of God—is a clear mark of divine character. The righteous judgment of God is not petty jealousy if God comes down as judgment on human injustice. On occasions when Jesus is described as an angry man, his anger is like the wrath of God—a drive toward justice. Jesus acted out his indignation toward commerce in the Temple. He drove out the money changers and declared the Temple to be holy—a place of prayer.

I. *Anger is an accepted emotion in the Christian life.* Only once in the Gospels is the word *anger* actually used to describe the emotion of Jesus. In a series of conflicts with the Pharisees over the Sabbath, Jesus irritated his observers by declaring the Sabbath to be a gift of God rather than a burden and citing Old Testament precedence for attending to human need on the Sabbath. Upon entering the synagogue, Jesus encountered a man with a deformed hand, and his critics watched for a technical foul. Healing on the Sabbath would violate the law. Seeking some commitment of response from the watchers, Jesus asked, "Is it lawful to do good or to do harm on the Sabbath, to save life or to kill?" Greeting the question with silence, the critics sit in judgment the way a predator waits for the prey to enter the danger zone. Then Mark describes the emotion of Jesus: "He looked around at them with anger." Only Mark dares to use the word. Perhaps Matthew and Luke were hesitant to portray Jesus with an emotion that causes so much damage in our lives. Luke clearly attributes anger to the Pharisees, and the three Gospels agree that this is an event that leads to the conspiracy of the cross. Mark's statement is valid. In rapid succession Jesus is angry, then he is grieved at the hardness of his critics. Finally, he acts in redemptive love by healing the man. Probably quite by accident, Mark has given us the best mode for the Christian stewardship for anger that can be found anywhere in the Bible. Jesus was angry. He was angry and sinned not. He got angry, and healing took place. This is not the ordinary garden variety of getting mad at someone. This is the holy anger of God at work to bring reconciliation and peace into the world. It is anger that redeems relationships and heals lives.

II. *The power of anger must be managed.* Wayne Oates observed the normal daily eruption of anger in the life of the Christian and warned about the accumulation of resentment into hating and bearing grudges. Paul advised maturity in everything except anger. A child gets angry quickly, expresses that anger directly and clearly, and gets over it completely. The problem is not anger but the poor management of anger. Nurtured, harbored anger often develops into apathy or callous indifference—"hardness of heart," the Bible calls it. Anger is misappropriated when it degrades into blaming accusations of others, including God. Anger is a heat-seeking missile that is not always precise in its choice of target. The object of anger is often transferred from the guilty to the innocent. You are not allowed to yell at the boss, so you go home and cut down your wife with sarcasm, growl at the children, and punish the dog. The back side of anger is self-destructive depression. Anger that is denied or suppressed often turns into acid in the heart and burns from within until self-hatred has replaced the attack on others. The Christian objective is to focus anger on nonmanipulative, responsible love, to move toward understanding and reconciliation, which removes grudges and breaks down dividing walls of hostility.

David Mace concluded, after a long career of marriage counseling to counselors, that the most significant single factor in the development of a healthy marriage is the management of anger. He did not suggest any pretense of avoiding anger, but he warned of a powerful emotion capable of destroying persons and establishing warfare between people who ought to love one another. In 1965 I heard David and Vera Mace address a room full of Christian leaders on the positive process of managing anger in marriage. He defined three steps that he and Vera had adopted as a covenant to keep the fires of love alive. (1) Anger must be acknowledged, the danger identified. Say, "I am angry." (2) Anger must be respected as a dangerous, destructive emotion that can destroy your marriage. Say, "I don't want to be angry. I love you." (3) Finally, anger becomes a grudge only if it is held within one person. When anger becomes the property of a relationship, like marriage, it can become the occasion for a new understanding. Anger may originate in one partner, but it must belong to both of you. Say, "Help me."

Jesus got angry. He wasn't an angry man if the Gospels' use of the word means anything, but he has pointed a way to reconciliation. Jesus got mad and he got over it. He got angry, and he grieved, and he healed.—Larry Dipboye

SUNDAY, NOVEMBER 12, 2006
Lectionary Message

Topic: She Loves You
TEXT: Ruth 3:1–5, 4:14–17
Other Readings: Ps. 127; Heb. 9:24–28; Mark 12:38–44

I. *Ruth works hard.* When we left Ruth and Naomi last week, Ruth had told her mother-in-law that she wasn't leaving her, ever, despite Naomi's attempts to send her home. Ruth made good on her promise, staying with Naomi on the trip back to Bethlehem from Moab. Even when Naomi remarked to all the neighborhood women, "I went away full and came back empty; the hand of the Lord has turned against me," Ruth didn't say, "So what am I, chopped liver?" Instead, Ruth figured a way to put food on the table by going out to the fields to glean behind the harvesters. "Go," says Naomi, not "What a great idea, O best of daughters-in-law!" or "Be careful out there—a single woman can get hurt" or even "Well, if you're going, I'll come, too."

By law, a poor person has the right to scavenge from the grain fields and vineyards, picking up what the landowner's workers left behind; one version of the law commands the harvesters to deliberately leave the edges of the fields for the poor to harvest. But because Ruth happens to land in Boaz's field, she does much better than the scraps and the leavings. As it turns out, he is Naomi's very close kin, so he makes sure that Ruth goes home with plenty every night and that no one bothers her while she works. He's impressed, he tells Ruth, with how kind she has been to her mother-in-law; she suggests that he's pretty kind himself.

II. *Ruth takes a chance.* Now, finally, after Ruth has found Boaz's field all by herself, after she has worked for several weeks bringing home the barley, and after she has impressed Boaz with her strength of character, Naomi has a suggestion for securing Ruth's future. "Tonight is the big winnowing night," she says, "and Boaz will sleep at the threshing floor and have plenty to eat and drink. Put on your best dress and your good perfume and when you see him bed down for the night, you go lie down on his feet, and do what he tells you to do." Not very subtle, eh? Just go throw yourself at Boaz, and leave it to him to figure out what to do about it? Once again, Ruth is taking all the risks here. What about Naomi going to Boaz, since they are kin, and trying to arrange Ruth's marriage to him or to someone in his house?

But Ruth goes to the threshing floor and lies down at Boaz's feet, only she tells Boaz, when he wakes and finds her, that, as next of kin he should marry her. Boaz agrees. There is a little bit of business he has to take care of first, in order to make certain that when he marries Ruth he also buys the field Naomi's late husband owned. But he takes care of that right away, and they get married and have a son.

III. *What we don't know.* Notice what we don't know when we get to 4:14. We don't know what Ruth and Boaz look like; we probably assumed that she caught his eye because she was a "hottie," but the text never tells us that. We don't know if he is marrying her because he is in love with her; the story implies that he is doing it because he believes it is his duty as "redeemer"—the closest male relative to the dead man—to raise up children in the dead man's name. We don't know how Ruth feels about him, either, except that he is kind and a good provider. If we were writing this story, especially if this were a screenplay, we'd want to focus on the romance between Ruth and Boaz, on the growing attraction that leads to a passionate confession of love between them. But nary a word is said about love until almost the end of the book, and when it comes, it isn't from the characters we'd have predicted.

IV. *She loves you.* 4:13 summarizes all the good stuff on which we'd like more information: they get married, they consummate the marriage, and Ruth has a son. The next verse then, perhaps surprisingly, shifts to the neighbor women blessing Naomi—not Boaz or Ruth, but Naomi, whose tragic loss of husband and sons began the book. They tell her that God has been especially good to her, blessing her with a son who will take care of her in her old age. This happened, they say, because she loves you—Ruth, your daughter-in-law, worth more to you than seven sons, loves you.

It's the only time the word *love* is used in Ruth. We're probably not wrong to assume that Naomi loved her husband and two sons, or that Ruth and Boaz love each other, or that the two of them and Naomi are crazy about little baby Obed. But by waiting until 4:15 to use the word *love,* and then having it be an observation of Naomi's community about how Ruth feels about her mother-in-law, the author teaches us something very important about love. Ruth loved Naomi when there was nothing in it for her but a long walk to an uncertain future away from all her natural-born family. Ruth loved Naomi enough to figure out how to support both of them without any help or encouragement from the older woman. Ruth loved Naomi enough to put her reputation and her personal safety on the line, crossing all sorts of boundaries to pop the question to Boaz. And Ruth loved Naomi enough to put her new infant in her mother-in-law's arms, healing the deep grief that begins this story, giving her hope and security at last.

Ruth's love is a picture of God's love—love that gives without restraint, that crosses boundaries, that is not put off by rejection, that works hard for the good of the beloved—love that arises from the core of the lover's self. Blessed be the Lord, who loves us as Ruth loved Naomi.—Richard B. Vinson

ILLUSTRATIONS

THE LOVE OF GOD.   "We must learn to realize that the love of God seeks us in every situation, and seeks our good. . . . For it is God's love that warms me in the sun and God's love that sends the cold rain. It is God's love that feeds me in the bread I eat and God that feeds me also by hunger and fasting. It is the love of God that sends the winter days when I am cold and sick, and the hot summer when I labor and my clothes are full of sweat: but it is God Who breathes on me with light winds off the river and in the breezes out of the wood."[2]

RUTH AND BOAZ.   "They had a son named Obed after a while, and Naomi came to take care of him and stayed on for the rest of her life. Then in time Obed had a son of his own named Jesse, and Jesse in turn had seven sons, the seventh of whom was named David and ended up as the greatest king Israel ever had. With Ruth for his great-grandmother and Naomi for his grandfather's nurse, it was hardly a wonder."[3]

---

[2]Thomas Merton, *New Seeds of Contemplation* (New York: New Directions, 1961), pp. 15, 16–17.
[3]Frederick Buechner, *Peculiar Treasures* (San Francisco: HarperSanFrancisco, 1979), p. 149.

SERMON SUGGESTIONS

Topic: Where God Is Needed

TEXT: Ps. 12

(1) In the building of a house, household, or family. (2) In providing security. (3) In total involvement in life.[4]

Topic: More Room Still

TEXT: Luke 14:22

(1) The curse of complacency. (2) The creativity of concern.

WORSHIP AIDS

CALL TO WORSHIP.   "I lift my eyes to you whose throne is in heaven" (Ps. 123:1 REB).

INVOCATION.   Move deeply in our souls this morning, Father. Call us to praise, to prayer, to learning, and to love after the fashion of the Lord Christ. Let the inspiration of the hour be magnified as we listen to the tone, rhythm, words, and movement of the music that fills this sanctuary today. Indeed, meet us in power, that we may be made keenly aware of your presence with us, even as you were present with those first followers whom you taught to pray: [repeat the Lord's Prayer].—Henry Fields

OFFERTORY SENTENCE.   "[Jesus] said to them, 'Take note of what you hear; the measure you give you will receive, with something more besides'" (Mark 2:24 REB).

OFFERTORY PRAYER.   Lord, let our gifts today be all we can afford in the light of all done for us through our Lord Jesus Christ.—E. Lee Phillips

PRAYER.   All about us we see your handiwork, Father. From the first blush of dawn to the wonder of the starry heavens, we are ever made aware of your creativity and beauty. In these waning weeks of winter, we watch as you prepare the Earth for the freshness of spring. From the silence of bulbs pushing their way through the soft ground, to the swelling of the tree branches with the promise of new growth, to the migration of birds to their nesting places, we see you working through nature and eagerly await the new birth of all of life that so soon will follow. May we never, in our hurry to do the business of life, neglect to take the time to observe your handiwork and be thankful.

In others we see the wonder of your presence, Father. In the hands of the caregiver we see the gentleness of service and love. In the protection and rearing of the child, we see the patient power of growth. In the changing of attitudes and spirits, we see the grandeur of grace. In the forgiveness we both receive and give, we see the glory of your presence. In the salvation we find so near at hand, as we seek and listen and learn, we see the eternal hope for which our very hearts yearn. In our hurry to taste all that we can of life, may we not neglect to see you in the many words, deeds of kindness, and sharing and giving that we experience all along the journey.

As we worship in this small concentration of a moment aside from normal functioning, may we experience you, Father. We do not fully know what that means. For some it may mean simply a quiet hour of regrouping in order to face the world again. For others it may mean finding some anchor, some word, some thought that will sustain them in the midst of a desperate struggle. For yet others it may mean feeling a weight lifted from their souls and hearts so that they can breathe deeply again and breathe free. Still others may long for a word of hope in what is, for them, a hopeless life, a light in their darkness that will illuminate the pathway for them. And there are those who have slipped into this sacred place to find a point of new beginnings, a place of acceptance where confession and restoration and forgiveness can be more than words on a page; they can be experiences in their lives. We all hope for something different as we come into your presence in this special hour. In our hurry to find a fix for our situation, may we not fail to hear and receive whatever truth you want to impart to us as we quietly and expectantly wait, in Jesus' name.—Henry Fields

SERMON
Topic: Triumph in the Desert
TEXT: Acts 8:26

The desert to us is more a place of defeat than of triumph. It conjures up an image of bleak barrenness, unrelieved dreariness, relentlessly blazing sun, hot sand, and weary travelers thirsting for water, frantically chasing tormenting mirages. The desert made the headlines during the long ordeal of the American hostages in Iran. The abortive attempt to rescue them ended in the smoky rubble of the Iranian desert. Two magazine articles reporting the sad details of it were titled "Death in the Desert" and "Debacle in the Desert."

The New Testament records a glorious triumph in the desert, one of the first great triumphs of the Christian Church. It was an unexpected conversion in an unpromising place— the conversion of the treasurer of the Ethiopian court. This conversion marked a further advancement toward the evangelization of the Gentiles and the universality of Christ's Church.

It is a great story, and it speaks to us all today on various levels of our existence.

I. The first thing that meets us here is *the mystery of guidance*. The story begins with Philip. We meet him first in Acts, chapter 6—one of seven men of good report, full of faith and the Holy Spirit, chosen to be deacons with administrative responsibilities in the early Church. Philip had a preaching gift, as well as gifts of organization, and became an effective evangelist. He was in the full swing of a hugely successful evangelistic campaign in Samaria, with many conversions and much joy, when a command of God came to him: "Leave your present work in the city and go to the desert!" This must have seemed a strange, irrational command! Does it make sense to call a man away from the crowded city to the lonely desert if he is a preacher? A preacher needs people, and the more the better! Moreover, success should not be lightly tampered with. But the command was insistent: "Rise and go toward the south to the road that goes down from Jerusalem to Gaza—a desert road." The mystery of guidance!

It speaks volumes for Philip's spiritual sensitivity and unquestioning faith that we read: "And he rose and went." He was open to the guiding hand of God, however strange, even foolish, it may have seemed to his own ideas and preconceptions. He was ready for the risk of faith, going out like Abraham, not knowing where he was going but relying on the promises of a faithful God. The result? A decisive encounter with a seeker after God!

Does God guide us? The Christian answer is an emphatic yes! From generation to generation, men and women have affirmed what Robert Louis Stevenson expressed: "I came about like a well-handled ship. There stood at the wheel that unknown steersman whom we call God." Some of us would put it more evangelically than that, knowing God in Christ through the Holy Spirit. "I being in the way the Lord led me." Sometimes the guidance is obvious and unmistakable. Frequently, it is sensed only in retrospect. Always we must use our own moral and rational judgment. Always we must be ready for one step at a time in faith.

But there is mystery about God's guidance. God's ways are not our ways, his thoughts not our thoughts. So often he seems to lead us into a bleak desert of disappointment, loneliness, failure, bereavement. But then, so often over time, the desert blossoms like the rose! Think of Paul, flung into prison in Rome. That prison became a pulpit from which his words have sounded out to us today. It was in prison that he wrote his letters to the Philippians, Ephesians, Galatians. It all turned out, as he himself claimed, to the furtherance of the gospel. Think of John Bunyan, imprisoned in Bedford Gaol. Within its walls he wrote *Pilgrim's Progress*. Don't judge any situation too early! The mystery may become victory! God moves in a mysterious way, his wonders to perform.

II. The second thing that meets us here is *the inadequacy of religion.* "And behold an Ethiopian, a eunuch, a minister of Candace the queen of the Ethiopians, in charge of all her treasure, had come to Jerusalem to worship, and was returning: seated in the chariot he was reading the prophet Isaiah. . . ." Here was an unlikely congregation of one for Philip the evangelist—a man of the world, of money, of position, yet a religious man, a God-fearing man, a worshipper. And he was searching, looking for some meaning and purpose in life, trying to understand the book of God.

I have met many modern versions of this Ethiopian. I have met them at businessmen's luncheons and dinners (you would be surprised at how many luncheons and dinners I am asked to attend) to say grace. I have met them at weddings and funeral services: unpromising people for a preacher and not always comfortable in a preacher's presence but gropingly religious, seeking for some light and truth, asking questions.

There is a vast amount of this religion in our world. Some of it is bad. Look at it in fanatical action in Iran! Some of it is secular religion—Communism, for example, or the worship of money, status, or so-called charismatic personalities. Some of it is wistful—a genuine search for purpose and spiritual fulfillment. Indeed, however flippant, sophisticated, hard, devil-may-care the pose of men and women may be, basically they are all religious. The dictum of Augustine is profoundly true: "Thou has made us for thyself, and our hearts are restless until they rest in thee."

Dr. Stanley Jones was once approached by a distracted man who had agreed to give an address to a meeting of Theosophists. "How on earth would you address Theosophists?" he asked. And Stanley Jones replied: "I never address Theosophists. I always address men and women." In other words, he ignored outward labels and appearances and went straight for the heart, which is the same in Theosophists, Communists, capitalists, and scientists. The same sins, fears, hopes, loves, and desires jostle within us all. And there is always a God-shaped blank.

This religion, however, is inadequate. It was inadequate for the Ethiopian. It always leaves a big question mark. It is incomplete, unsatisfying. It has no final answers about life and death, sin and suffering, heaven and hell. Religion is man seeking God, groping in the dark. The Christian gospel is God seeking man, God in Christ personally present and redeemingly active—a very different thing! When Philip approached the Ethiopian seeker, asking, "Do you understand what you are reading?" the man articulated the inadequacy of religion: "How can I, unless someone guides me?"

III. The third thing that meets us here is *the word of interpretation*. Philip listened to the Ethiopian reading aloud the matchless words of Isaiah, chapter 53:

> As a sheep led to the slaughter
> Or a lamb before its shearer is dumb
> So he opens not his mouth.
> In his humiliation justice was denied him.
> Who can describe his generation
> For his life is taken up from the earth.

"About whom does the Prophet say this?" he asked. "About himself or someone else?" Here was why God had brought Philip to the desert—to speak the word of interpretation!

"Then Philip opened his mouth and beginning with this Scripture he told him the good news of Jesus." What a sermon it must have been! What would we give for a tape recording of it? It was Bible-based and Christ-centered: good news indeed! Now why was this the word of interpretation? A word is an articulated thought, an expression, interpretation, of the idea in mind. Jesus was "the Word made flesh"—God's very self, expressed in human terms. The New Testament also calls Jesus "the Word of life"—the clue to the meaning of life. So "the good news of Jesus" was a word of interpretation, in three ways.

Jesus is the key to the understanding of all Scripture. How could the Ethiopian understand the words of Isaiah 53 apart from Christ, who offered his life as the Lamb of God? He was the embodiment of the suffering servant. The center and message of all Scripture is Christ. All the great highways of Scripture lead unerringly to him.

Jesus is the fulfillment of all religious longings. "I came not to destroy," he said, "but to fulfill." There are many religions in the world, with their sacred books, rituals, ideals. They are all gathered up in Jesus Christ, the revealer of God to man and guide of man to God.

Jesus is the answer to all human needs. I know that this is a maddeningly complex world, and I have no wish to simplify in a glib, facile way. But take any of our basic problems—personal sin, personal relationships, suffering, bereavement, death. The answer to them all is in the good news of Jesus, the Savior, Lord, and Friend.

This interpreting word is not a philosophy, a code of morality, or an abstract creed but a story—the story of Jesus and his love.

> I know of a world that is sunk in shame,
> Where hearts often faint and tire:
> But I know of a Name, a precious name,

That can set the world on fire:
Its sound is sweet, its letters flame,
'Tis Jesus.

IV. The fourth thing that meets us here is *the seal of baptism*. Clearly, in his sermon Philip told the Ethiopian, as Peter told the Jerusalem audience on the day of Pentecost, that the appropriate response to the good news of Jesus was repentance, faith, baptism, and the reception of the Holy Spirit. As they journeyed, they came to running water. The Ethiopian said, "See, here is water: what is to prevent my being baptized?" And he was baptized. This was the sacramental seal, the outward and visible sign of his inward, spiritual transformation.

The desert stream became a sacramental stream. What is a sacrament? It is two things. It is an ordinary thing that acquires an extraordinary meaning. So ordinary water became a means of grace, spiritually symbolic, as a person of faith is buried with Christ in it and raised again with Christ in newness of life. A sacrament is also an oath of allegiance, a "sacramentum," a vow of love and loyalty. So the Ethiopian sealed his new-found faith in baptism, outwardly expressed it in dramatic action, and pledged his love and loyalty to Christ there and then.

Baptism by itself does not make a Christian. By grace are we saved through faith—the grace of God in Christ, accepted and appropriated by faith. Baptism seals that private, personal relationship and forever witnesses to its reality. When Martin Luther was asked, "How do you know you are a Christian?" he answered, "Because I have been baptized." What he meant was this assurance was founded, not on anything he had done or on any virtues he possessed but on his response to what God had done for him in Christ. Across the years we feel the challenge of the Ethiopian's witness, and face the haunting question he asked: "See, here is water! What is to prevent my being baptized?" We are prevented only by our lack of faith—that leap of trust that makes us one with Christ.

V. The last thing that meets us here is *the joy of commitment*. "He went on his way rejoicing." And no wonder! He was no longer merely the treasurer of the Queen but an ambassador of Christ, the King of Kings! His life faced a new direction, with a new Master and a new purpose. His search was over, his need met, his future sure. A triumphant resurrection had taken place in a barren desert, and the joy he felt was the joy of commitment. "He went on his way rejoicing."

What became of this converted Ethiopian we are not told. Tradition has it that he became a missionary among his own people, and we should expect that. We do know that today, centuries later, he witnesses to us. From him we learn that there is no desert of sin, of need, of agonizing search, of religious formality that cannot be transformed into triumph by the good news of Jesus. To respond to that news by faith, repentance, and commitment is to be surprised by joy![5]

---

[5]John N. Gladstone, *All Saints and All Sorts* (Hantsport, Nova Scotia, 1982), pp. 78–85.

SUNDAY, NOVEMBER 19, 2006

Lectionary Message

Topic: Not Yet!

TEXT: Mark 13:1–8

Other Readings: 1 Sam. 1:4–20; Ps. 16; Heb. 10:11–14 (15–18), 19–25

I. *We want to know.* "Are we there yet?" "How much longer until we can take a break?" "You don't mean I have to read the whole book?" Lots of things seem to go on forever, mostly when they're unpleasant or painful or boring. It helps to know there's an end to it—only twenty-five more miles or fifteen minutes or ten pages to go, and then we'll be free!

Christians have often wanted to know how close we are to the end of the world, and throughout history prophets have obliged, from William Miller, who predicted that the end would come in 1843, to Edgar Whisenant, who wrote *88 Reasons Why the Rapture Will Be in 1988.*[6] Despite these and other failures, writing about the coming end continues to be profitable, as Christians make best-sellers out of "rapture" books. We just want to know, don't we? We want to know that there is an end to all the awful stuff in this world, and we'd like to know that the end will not be too far away.

This passage, however, doesn't get us to the end, nor even to the middle, but only to the very beginning, and it is filled with very unpleasant sorts of things. First the Temple, the glorious house of God in Jerusalem, would be torn down and not a stone left standing. There would be false teachers who claimed to know Christ's will who would lead many astray. There would be wars and earthquakes and famines. All this, says Jesus, is only the start, like the first few labor pains telling a woman that the long hard process of giving birth has only begun.

II. *Institutions will fail, but the end is not yet.* Not very cheery, is it? Don't be alarmed, the text says, but Jesus talks about alarming things. For Jesus' listeners that day, the Temple was the house of God, where prayers and sacrifices were made daily, where the faithful could go to make atonement for their sins and to make offerings required by the law. If the Temple was torn down, then how could they continue to practice their faith?

Jesus' prediction of the destruction of the Temple came to pass in 70 A.D., when the Romans burned it, but the worship of God survived. Jesus' words remind us that no institution, no matter how noble or beautiful, endures forever; all of them eventually die, but the Almighty is not bound by the walls of any house or by the rules of any institution, and the Spirit who raised Jesus from the dead is always drawing us toward life.

III. *Catastrophes will happen, but the end is not yet.* Don't be alarmed, either, when you hear of wars, uprisings, earthquakes, or famines, because those are only the beginning, not the end. To state the obvious, what period of human history has been without these things? Because we live in the age of mass communication and the Internet, we can hear or read something about all these terrible things every day. But when they happen to us, or to someone we know, or in a way that we can imagine clearly how the victims feel, we are

---

[6]Nashville, Tenn.: World Bible Society, 1988.

alarmed, shaken, even sometimes crushed by shock and grief. How can our world continue after something like that?

Not easily, and sometimes not at all. People die in wars and floods and earthquakes and famines, or they are so demoralized that they quit trying to live. Jesus doesn't try to sugar-coat the hard times; in fact, saying that these things will happen but are only the beginning is another way to say that these sorts of things will simply always be a part of life on Earth for Christ's followers. How can life go on after catastrophic tragedy? Not easily, but it can, because the Spirit is always drawing us toward life.

IV. *False teachers will appear, but the end is not yet.* But there will be other voices, too—voices that try to lead us astray. Jesus says that a hard world of fallible institutions and world-shaking catastrophes is made even harder by cynical people who try to take advantage of our desire to hear God's voice. "Listen to me," they will say. "I am the voice of the Lord—I know exactly what God wants you to do!" Beware, says Jesus, because many people will listen and be led farther into the wilderness.

How can we tell the difference between the Spirit's voice and the voices of the pretenders? For one thing, Jesus says that anybody who tries to give you a timetable or outline of events for the end of the world is not speaking for him. For another, those who point to current events—wars, famines, disease, politics—to tell you that the end is close are saying the opposite of what Jesus said. Anybody who tells you that loyalty to an institution is a measure of your faith or that following Jesus will give you a life of material comfort and security is also leading you astray.

Listen and watch for what leads to life for you and for all God's people. God is with us, through the collapse of treasured institutions, through life-shattering calamities, and through the confusion of false teachers. Times are hard, and, according to Jesus, they will never be easy, but the Spirit is always with us, drawing us toward life. Thanks be to God!—Richard B. Vinson

ILLUSTRATIONS

FAILED PREDICTIONS.   Edgar Whisenant predicted that sometime during the period of September 11–13, 1988, Jesus was to return to remove his followers from Earth. When that did not happen, he published a second book arguing that other dates would also fit the prophecies: "Jesus is coming, and I would give it at least a 50% chance in 1989; if not then, an abundance of Scriptures point to 1992."[7]

BAD TIMES NO PREDICTOR OF THE END.   William Butler Yeats's famous poem *The Second Coming* describes vividly how evil things pile up until we lose hope and are certain that the end must be close: "Things fall apart; the centre cannot hold;/ Mere anarchy is loosed upon the world. . . . The best lack all conviction, while the worst/ Are full of passionate intensity./ Surely some revelation is at hand;/ Surely the Second Coming is at hand." Yeats's poem concludes with the prediction that things will only get worse: "And what rough beast, its hour

---

[7]Edgar Whisenant and Gary Brewer, *The Final Shout Rapture Report: 1989* (Nashville, Tenn.: World Bible Society, 1989), p. iii.

come round at last,/ slouches towards Bethlehem to be born?" While cynicism is not an appropriate Christian response, because it connotes a loss of hope, neither is unrealistic optimism, because it can lead to the loss of hope that leads to cynicism.

SERMON SUGGESTIONS

Topic: Contentment
TEXT: Ps. 16
(1) Because of having chosen God (vv. 1–2). (2) Because of supportive friends (vv. 3–4). (3) Because of God's providence (vv. 5–6). (4) Because of God's guidance (vv. 7–11).

Topic: Going the Right Way
TEXT: Col. 2:6
(1) Notice in the text *the fact stated.* Sincere believers have indeed *"received* Christ Jesus the Lord." (2) Notice next *the counsel given:* "So walk ye in him." (3) Notice last *the model that is presented to us:* We are to walk in Christ Jesus the Lord "as we received him."—Charles H. Spurgeon

WORSHIP AIDS

CALL TO WORSHIP.   "I wait for the Lord, my soul doth wait, and in his word do I hope" (Ps. 130:5).

INVOCATION.   Our Father, we come to this place from our often frantic activities, bent as we are to run ahead of you, sometimes ignoring your commandments, sometimes taking matters into our own hands that could be better left up to you. Quiet our racing pulse and restore our jaded spirit, as we, once again, try to put our trust and hope in you.

OFFERTORY SENTENCE.   "I know thy works, and thy labor, and thy patience" (Rev. 2:2).

OFFERTORY PRAYER.   When we have labored on with patience, O God, the reward has come. The joy of honest toil and the products of what we have done have added to our sense of meaning and belonging. Grant that those who have no satisfying work or who can no longer work may not feel that life no longer has meaning or that they are now only in the way. Help them to know that you and we do not forget what they have done in the past and to know that their presence among us is a precious gift of your providence.

PRAYER.   Patient God, we thank you for time, for our life together, for time over coffee, for kids' time—listening to their music, talking. We thank you for lives intertwined through common tasks, for the inns and resting places of the human spirit, for the times, holy places, special people, where we take a breather—a restaurant or coffee shop, a kitchen table, a corner at work.

Adorable God, we thank you for the liturgy of our common ground, the shape of specialness gracing ordinary days, like lilacs about a dilapidated home: an evening out, a weekend away, hunting or fishing, a ball game, needlework, a good book. We give you thanks for new faces; forbid it that we should assume they shall find something of worth and warm us and ours. May we be among them as ones who serve. May we be of some use. We pray for people faithfully tending others, that they may find a pace they can hold, that they may endure, that they may laugh, that they may believe beyond the grave.—Peter Fribley

SERMON
Topic: A God Who Heals
TEXT: 2 Kings 5:1–14

"But when Elisha the man of God heard that the king of Israel had torn his clothes, he sent a message to the king, "Why have you torn your clothes? Let him come to me, that he may learn that there is a prophet in Israel" (2 Kings 5:8).

Nothing gets closer to the core of our essential well-being than the presence, or even the threat, of physical trauma or illness. On the one hand, we feel that we are more than our bodies. Our feelings, thoughts, memories, and plans cannot simply be resolved into the cells and tissues of brains or viscera. On the other hand, we are so intimately bound up with our bodies. When they are fit and healthy, our thoughts and moods follow suit. When they are in pain or disintegrating, the fear and despair can inundate us. When they finally reach the end of their trajectory, life as we know it here on Earth is over.

Often we are angry with our bodies. I remember when I had the detached retina in my right eye. Only a delicate laser surgery stood between me and blindness in that eye. What had I done? Nothing that I knew of. It was like my body had betrayed me. And how does somebody feel who receives the most dreaded diagnosis of all: *cancer?* Your very own body seems to be the enemy. *Where is God in all of this?*

We begin to try and understand by telling a story. Some eight hundred years before Christ, the nation of Israel coexisted uneasily with a powerful neighbor called Aram (2 Kings 5:1). This is the same nation called Syria in other parts of the Old Testament, and their territory was more or less the same as that occupied by the modern state of Syria, bordering modern Israel on the northeast. In those days the Syrians held the upper hand in regional power struggles. The narrator says "the Lord" had given victory to Syria through a general called Naaman, which reflects the growing conviction in ancient Israel that the Lord was not just a tribal God but *the* God of all nations.

But no matter how powerful and victorious Naaman was, the dread presence of leprosy made him feel helpless—so helpless that he would seize the words of an Israelite slave girl, presumably taken as the spoils of war—as a token of hope. Still today, we are often incredibly dependent on those who are humble and weaker than we, as the world counts strength and weakness. Every weekday here in Los Angeles, the "nanny express" drops off housekeepers and caregivers at the homes of the rich and powerful, from Hancock Park to Pacific Palisades, and these privileged families are incredibly dependent on those plucky immigrant women. And the Syrian king was so helpless that he would send his general to the defeated enemy to seek a cure. Disease and death are great levelers—of rich and poor, conquerors and vanquished.

When Naaman arrived in the Israelites' capital, Samaria, with a dazzling foreign aid package (150 pounds of gold and 750 pounds of silver) and a letter instructing the king of Israel to do the impossible (cure him of leprosy) consternation seized the royal court. But as the royal court lay paralyzed with fear, the prophet Elisha, "the man of God," said *"Let* [the general] *come to me, that he may learn that there is a prophet in Israel"* (2 Kings 5:8).

Often all it takes is a little glimmer of hope to get us on our high horses again. Naaman was incensed at the way Elisha received him. Not only did the prophet decline to greet him personally, sending a servant down instead, but his instruction further offended the general's pride. Wash seven times in that muddy Israelite ditch called Jordan? *"Are not Abana and Pharpar, the rivers of Damascus, better than all the waters of Israel?"* (2 Kings 5:12). Once again, the servants saved the day.

Father, if the prophet had commanded you to do something difficult, would you not have done it? How much more when all he said to you was, "Wash and be clean?" (2 Kings 5:13).

Now what insight can we bring from this ancient biblical narrative to our question about God's relationship to human health and illness? Just this: in spite of our fear, our unfaith, our pride and stubbornness, *God wants us healthy.* And yet some of us aren't. We can't simply stop here. Let's push on. Let me put this core conviction—that God wants us healthy—in the midst of several other facts that are supported by both Scripture and experience.

First, all of us will, sooner or later, die. Scripture says, "it is appointed to mortals to die once, and then the judgment . . ." (Heb. 9:27). The apostle Paul connects death explicitly to sin: "For the wages of sin is death . . ." (Rom. 6:23). Furthermore, this sin-wounded world may not be what the Creator intended it to be, but we must acknowledge that death does have a crucial *biological* function. If no creature ever died, the planet would choke and disintegrate under our accumulated mass. And old patterns, life strategies, and ideas could never be challenged or improved. Death "clears the deck" for life to try new strategies.

Yes, we will all die. But in the meantime, think of the marvels that are our bodies. Billions of cells, neurons firing, hearts beating, bones stronger per square inch of load-bearing area than any steel alloy, and even the billions of bacteria that form an ecosystem for thousands of generations in our guts, brokering our digestion. Our brains are more subtle and complex than any computer, our endocrine system more precise and sensitive than any pharmaceutical formula. Indeed, we are *"fearfully and wonderfully made"* (Ps. 139:14).

Which brings us to a second point: Disease is an anomaly—a perversion of God's good creation. Some disease comes upon us as a direct result of sin. It may be our own sin, as when an irresponsible drinker develops cirrhosis of the liver or the sexually promiscuous person contracts a venereal disease. Or we may suffer from someone else's sin. For instance, an infant may be born with fetal alcohol syndrome or children may drink well water polluted by somebody else's toxic wastes. We are all connected, for better or for worse. Sometimes sin is "systemic," as, for instance, when people's lungs are ravaged by polluted air or a child suffers from malnutrition because a third world country is paying down its external debt. Yes, some disease is caused by sin.

Some disease comes because we just seem to wear out. We come with a "limited warranty," and after so many years the cartilage in our joints wears away, the lenses in our eyes cloud with cataracts, and cell systems begin to go awry, producing those irregular and invasive tissues we call cancers. Almost 100 percent of men who live long enough—say, eighty years or more—have some amount of prostate cancer. Usually, we die of something else before it can do us in! Some disease comes because—well, we just don't know! But truly, disease is an anomaly, and the wonderful thing is how healthy and functional most of us are most of the time. Again, God wants us healthy.

Third, look at the centrality of healing stories in the Scriptures, both Old Testament and New. Look at the crucial role of healing in the life and ministry of Jesus. His power to heal was one of the most important signs of his divine authority and identity. And look at the central role of the ministry of healing in the Christian Church down through the generations. Think how many healing angels God has commissioned among our churches. Here in Los Angeles, think of the centers of healing founded in Christ's name: St. Vincent's, Queen of Angles, Good Samaritan . . .

Fourth, God wants us healthy. And God heals. But just as in other areas of life, where God gives us grace, where God resources us but requires from us a response and an accepting of responsibility for our own destinies, so it is with health and healing. There is a *Circle of Health*, so to speak, where our responsibility for our own health—good nutrition, exercise, positive attitude, and so on—meets the contributions of those who pray for us and work to create for us a healthy environment. Think about the doctors and nurses and therapists who care for us. Think about the farm workers who cultivate and harvest our food, the janitors who clean our offices and schools and hospitals, the sanitation workers who keep our neighborhoods clean. It was his *servants,* both at the beginning and the end of the story, who made it possible for proud Naaman to receive God's healing touch.

Finally, let me repeat the all-too-obvious: sooner or later, we all must die. But Christian faith tells us that death is not *ultimate;* it is not truly the end. It is only *penultimate*—a gate through which we all must pass. The Scriptures tell us of a renewed and healed creation, in which death is overcome and we are refitted with "resurrection bodies" for life everlasting.

"Then the angel showed me the river of the water of life, bright as crystal, flowing from the throne of God and of the lamb though the middle of the street of the city. On either side of the river is the tree of life with its twelve kinds of fruit . . . and the leaves of the tree are for the healing of the nations" (Rev. 22:1–2).

And when God, through God's servants, does extraordinary works of healing in this present age, it is to remind us that God's ultimate will is health and healing, our sin notwithstanding, and our ultimate destiny is life.—David L. Wheeler

SUNDAY, NOVEMBER 26, 2006
Lectionary Message

Topic: Famous Last Words
TEXT: 2 Sam. 23:1–7
Other Readings: Ps. 132:1–12 (13–18); Rev. 1:4b–8; John 18:33–37

I. *Famous last words.* There are several "last words" in the Bible. Some of them are prophetic, like Jacob's testament in Genesis 49, where he sometimes criticizes and sometimes predicts what will happen to his sons. Deuteronomy is structured to be Moses' last speech to Israel, but then there is a last song (Deut. 32) that reflects on Israel's history and a testament (Deut. 33) that offers blessings to the tribes. Saul's last words are brief—in order for his armor-bearer to kill him before the Philistines take him captive (1 Sam. 31:4).

How would we characterize this poem titled "The Last Words of David"? It isn't set on David's deathbed; that little speech comes in 1 Kings 2:1–9—a bit of fatherly advice to Solomon, who was set to rule after him. The 1 Kings deathbed speech is a chilling mix of "always obey the Lord your God" and "don't let those traitors Joab and Shimei die in peace." The poem in 2 Samuel reminds us much more of some of the psalms attributed to David: the righteous prosper, but the wicked perish (see Ps. 36:18–20); God is like a rock (Ps. 31:2); a true ruler, ruling under God's direction, is a blessing for his people (Ps. 21). Scripture, in effect, gives us two "last words" for David, each testifying to a real part of the life of the king: the advice to Solomon, showing us the steely-eyed pragmatist who gave orders to kill in order to hold on to power, and this poem, showing us the heart of a man who wanted to speak the words of God's justice.

II. *The Sun King.* The first verse is a long title—long because it keeps adding to David's claims to fame: son of Jesse, exalted by God, anointed by God, God's favorite. The poem itself begins in verses 2 and 3, with the assertion that what he's about to say are the words of the Spirit of the Lord: "A just ruler, who rules according to devotion to God, is like the bright sun." No argument here! Whether we're talking about a king or an elected official or a boss or the leader of a family, anyone who leads by first being a devoted follower of God is "like the sun rising on a cloudless morning."

Unfortunately, it's very hard for anyone, but perhaps especially for those in power, to be as devoted to God as we should be. Second Samuel ends its stories about David with the king's decision to take a census of the people, which displeased God so much that a pestilence fell on Israel and killed seventy thousand. Solomon, the king who would rule after David, was the son of Bathsheba, with whom David committed adultery and whose husband David ordered killed. David may indeed have been "the favorite of the Strong One of Israel," but he was not always "a man after God's own heart."

III. *An eternal covenant.* Verse 5 reflects on the king's house, that is, on the royal line that he began. Because God had made a promise to David that his descendants would always rule (2 Sam. 7:16), the king says, "Will he not cause to prosper all my help and my desire?" Well, no, actually. David's house had not been orderly, always prospering under God. One son, Amnon, raped his half-sister and was, in turn, killed by her brother Absalom, who then led a rebellion against David and had to be hunted down and killed. And it would not always be orderly in the future, eventually coming to an end when the Babylonians destroyed Jerusalem and made Judah a part of their empire. David was God's anointed, but that did not ensure a peaceful household or an eternal dynasty.

Verses 6 and 7 predict the destruction of the wicked; like thorns too sharp to be picked up, they will simply be shoved into a pile and burned. If the bad guys always lost, then the world would be a much simpler place! But then who would be spared? If God's judgment fell without remorse on the wicked, burning them to a crisp, how many of us would still be standing?

IV. *Deconstructing the ideal.* David's poem holds up the ideal of a good king, devoted to God, bringing God's light to everyone, bringing order and peaceful succession, punishing evildoers and protecting the godly. Most kings, presidents, mayors, bosses, and family heads want to do the same thing, but we all fail, because we are weak. Power corrupts us, and we choose to make things better for ourselves or for our favorite people rather than do what's right in God's eyes. That's why we Christians always need to deconstruct the promises and claims of power-holders, and hold them up against the ideal of kingdom and kingship in the teachings of Jesus: not "one who rules over people justly" but "the greatest among you must be like the youngest, and the leader like one who serves" (Luke 22:26); not "will he not cause to prosper all my help and my desire" but "thy kingdom come, thy will be done"; not just "the Spirit of the Lord speaks through me" but "I will pour out my Spirit on all flesh, and your sons and your daughters shall prophesy."

Christ the King Sunday is a good time to consider the inevitable failures of any human ruler or human leader, and how foolish it is to put ultimate faith in political systems of any sort. Today we remind ourselves that ideal kings exist only in poetry that leaves out most of the gritty details and in our hope for God's kingdom to come.—Richard B. Vinson

ILLUSTRATIONS

Other famous last words:

Serene: "Let us cross over the river and sit under the shade of the trees."—General Thomas J. "Stonewall" Jackson

Brave: "Hold the cross high so I may see it through the flames."—Joan of Arc

Sarcastic: "Woe is me, I think I'm becoming a god."—the emperor Vespasian (because of how previous emperors had been declared, postmortem, to be divine)

Sadly mistaken: "They couldn't hit an elephant at this dist. . . ."—General John Sedgwick, killed by a Confederate sniper in the Battle of the Wilderness, 1864[8]

"USA Still on Top, Says Rest of World":

The White House is very, but unofficially, elated over America's top finish in the 1971 Earth standings, announced yesterday in Geneva. The United States, for the twenty-eighth straight year, was named Number One Country by a jury of more than three hundred presidents, prime ministers, premiers, chairmen . . . who hold voting membership in the Association of World Leaders. . . . Except for some lean years in the twenties, . . . the U.S. has dominated the world scene in this century, though it still trails the Roman and British Empires and the Mongol Horde in total wins.[9]

SERMON SUGGESTIONS

Topic: Hope for the Future

TEXT: Ps. 132:1–18

(1) What David promised God (vv. 1–10). (2) What God promised David (vv. 11–18).

Topic: Prayer—Human and Divine

TEXT: Rom. 8:26–27

(1) The human problem: in our weakness we cannot pray as God intends. (2) The divine provision: the Spirit shares our plight by interceding with inexpressible groanings. (3) The ultimate purpose: God searches our hearts to discern the intention of the Spirit's intercession.—William E. Hull[10]

---

[8]From "Famous Last Words," www.geocities.com/Athens/Acropolis/6537
[9]Garrison Keillor, *Happy to Be Here* (New York: Penguin, 1983), pp. 145–147.
[10]In James W. Cox (ed.), *The Twentieth Century Pulpit*, Vol. II (Nashville, Tenn.: Abingdon Press, 1981), pp. 94–104.

WORSHIP AIDS

CALL TO WORSHIP.   "They that wait upon the Lord shall renew their strength; they shall mount up with wings as eagles; they shall run, and not be weary; and they shall walk, and not faint" (Isa. 40:31).

INVOCATION.   Gracious Lord, King of our hearts and ruler of all, we bow before you now and await your promised blessings as we live out our lives in challenging times and situations in the days and years ahead. Let our worship now strengthen us for the doing of your will.

OFFERTORY SENTENCE.   "I do not say this as a command, but I am testing the genuineness of your love against the earnestness of others. For you know the generous act of our Lord Jesus Christ, that though he was rich, yet for your sakes he became poor, so that by his poverty you might become rich" (2 Cor. 8:8–9 NRSV).

OFFERTORY PRAYER.   Accept our Thanksgiving offering Lord, that we bring with gratitude and rejoicing, that others may know the joy of your Lord, where the blessings are inexhaustible and the rewards unending.—E. Lee Phillips

PRAYER.   Eternal God, who watches over the destiny of men and of nations, how can we, who have been so lavishly blessed, appear before you except in thanksgiving? In this season, renew our minds and hearts in the spirit of genuine thanksgiving for all seasons.

O Giver of every good and perfect gift, we thank you:

For seedtime and harvest
For fertile field and productive factory (grove)
For the faith to plant and the strength to harvest
For families where we first experience your love—where the meaning of growing up is interpreted and maturity is encouraged
For faithful friends who with understanding and love call us to our becoming what you intend us to be
For pioneer, pilgrims, frontiersman—who has had the faith to sail unknown seas, to blaze new trails, to follow an idea wherever it leads
"For pilgrim feet, whose stern, impassioned stress a thoroughfare for freedom beat across the wilderness"
For the gift you gave: your strong Word, challenging us to the faith "to give thanks every day for everything"
For your love that never gives up
For your grace inexhaustible—persevering through disappointment, loneliness, failure, frustration, suffering, death

Thanks be to you, O God, for all your goodness to us and to all persons. In our festivities may we not neglect those who suffer anguish of soul, weakness of body, the loneliness of sorrow, discouragement of defeat, fear of tyranny, or pain of poverty.

Bless our homes, O God, with a consciousness of your loving presence, that before you we may fulfill our responsibility, whether husband, wife, child, parent, grandparent. We pray for faith and understanding, love and reconciliation between all nations and peoples, that shalom—being and well-being, peace and joy—may be the blessing of all. We pray for our leaders at all levels of government that their office may be, for them, an opportunity to do justice, to love kindness, and to walk humbly with you, their God.

We pray through him who brings the victory of your abounding grace—thanksgiving every day and in all things.—John Thompson

SERMON
Topic: The Reign from the Cross
TEXT: Luke 23:33–43

This is the last chapter in the story. This is the conclusion to our Christian year. This is where it is all supposed to make sense. This Sunday is called Christ the King, the Reign of Christ. This is where we are supposed to be able to separate the good guys from the bad guys. This Sunday ought to be when we get to celebrate the glorious victory that Christians have. The long journey from Advent comes to a conclusion this Sunday—the Sunday set to celebrate the Kingdom of God. This is the day we celebrate the final victory of Jesus as Lord over all creation. This is the Sunday when we declare Christ the Lord—Christ the winner over evil. And so we shall.

Because isn't that what we are really trying to figure out—how to be a winner in life? Isn't that what most of our efforts involve—how to end up on the side that wins? The good guys win, and we want to be on the winning side. There is a great cosmic struggle between good and evil, and most of the time we are lucky if we think that goodness is holding its own. Most of the time, the feeling I get is that most of us think that goodness is always losing and getting further and further behind. We are struggling where we are to be on the winning side, and we feel like we are getting so tired and our resources are so small and evil looks like it could go on forever.

Just when we think that maybe we have scored one for decency and respectability (CBS was fined $500,000 for the Justin Timberlake–Janet Jackson event), along comes Monday Night Football and another less-than-wholesome scene is aired in our living room. The vice president of the Heritage Foundation, speaking on a talk show, says that everybody feels that his home is being invaded by disgusting and erotic material that he feels he is not able to control. We think then that we are losing the fight.

The more we talk about being winners and achieving the victory over evil, the more some people keep troubling the water by asking what we mean by *winning*. So often the whole process of finding a winner means that most of us end up being losers. In all our sporting competitions, to be a winner means that out of thirty teams, twenty-nine have to go home losers so that one can be a winner. The competition to be a winner results in more pain and suffering for most so that one might be covered in joy.

Dean L. Gregory Jones, dean of the Duke Divinity School in Durham, has a fascinating article in the *Christian Century*. It is fascinating because it is a story about a football program in Baltimore, Maryland, that runs counter to so much of our sport obsession. The program is at Gilman High School, the book is *Season of Life*, and the defensive coach is Joe Ehrmann, a former pro football player. When the players and the coaches huddle, the coach yells to his players: "What is our job?" The players have been taught to yell back: "To love us!" The coach then shouts: "And what is your job?" "To love each other" is the liturgical response. Ehrmann has a different game.

Coach Ehrmann was invited to speak at the University of Maryland football clinic. He was asked what he was going to speak on, and he said philosophy. The speech turned out to be a talk about how to help young boys become men within the context of sports. He said there were three false and deceptive components of bad masculinity: athletic ability, sexual conquest, and economic success. What is really important for real humanity is the capacity to love and be loved, a transcendent purpose of life, and a willingness to accept responsibility, to lead courageously, and to seek justice on the behalf of others. And the way you measure success is the impact you make on the lives of others. Coach Ehrmann wants to free his young men from the bondage of false idols of masculinity.

That is the great problem we have with our passion to be a part of the winning side. We have such confusion as to what it means to win. The bumper sticker says, "The one who dies with the most toys is the winner." That is what we are told by our consumer-driven economy. We have to get more. No wonder we are watching the disappearance in our marketplace of the emphasis on Thanksgiving. What good is Thanksgiving? If we take a moment and reflect upon the blessings that we have, if we stop for a few hours and count our many blessings, count them one by one—count our many blessings and see what God has done— then we might become embarrassed by our desire for more. If we take a moment and look at all the stuff we have, all the piles of stuff, and remember that we have been so much more richly blessed than 80 percent of the world, then we might not feel so compelled to go out after Thanksgiving Day and buy more and more. But how can I be a winner if I don't keep buying more toys?

So it is kind of disappointing to find, on this last Sunday of the Christian year, this story from Luke about Jesus on the cross. We had that sad part during Easter and the Passion of Christ. We had all the struggles in the garden and the bad times. Shouldn't this Sunday be a happy text? Shouldn't this Sunday be a passage about the glories of heaven and the triumph over evil? Why in the world do we have a story about Jesus on the cross and his conversation with the criminals: "Today you will be with me in Paradise"?

Forty years ago the then-famous Bishop J.A.T. Robinson, of the *Honest to God* book fame, said in another place, "What if the cross is all God has to win the struggle of evil? We have an amazing capacity to think that the way of the cross is one strategy God has, and when it will not work, in the end, at the end of time, God will get real and God will send the angels, the tanks, the bombs, and the horses, and clean house. But what if the way of the cross is the way by which God will establish his kingdom? What if that is the only weapon God has to use? Herein is love, that while we were yet sinners, Christ died for us. Be not overcome of evil, but overcome evil with good."

The story from Luke of Jesus on the cross on Christ the King Sunday is here because it is from the cross that Christ reigns. It is on the cross that the victory of God's love over evil is seen. It is in the life of the cross that we are invited to share in the victory of God. It is the way of the cross by which we become winners as well.

The story of Jesus on the cross is the story of the victory of God's way in the world, the victory of the message Jesus spoke to his disciples and the victory of the way of life Jesus lived among his disciples. "If anyone should smite you on the cheek, turn the other cheek. Love your enemies. Pray for those who persecute you. Blessed are you when people revile and persecute you in my name." This is the victory of God's love choosing a way to live in the world that is not conformed to the world's definitions of reality. There is a struggle between good and evil going on around us, and the victory of Jesus over the forces of evil is that the forces of evil do not control, do not dictate to him how we will act. Jesus refuses to exercise his power, his force, his life in ways that are demonic. It is the power of God's love and Holy Spirit at work in Jesus that sets Jesus free from the power and the principalities holding our lives in bondage and requiring us to act in ways we do not like. That is what St. Paul was talking about when he says that the good he wants to do, he can't and the evil that he does not want to do, he does. Those are powers and principalities that we laugh and talk about as powers outside ourselves—as Satan and the devil. We know we ought to lose weight, stop smoking, get more efficient cars, stop consuming so much of the world's resources, care for the poor, help the needy, and yet we keep finding that the power and structure that exist just keep making it impossible. You cannot get a hydrogen-fueled car. These are the powers and principalities of the world that hold us in bondage, and we struggle to become free, to triumph over those forces, to win. And to be victorious over the forces of evil is to be given the power of God's spirit to enable us not to act in evil ways to try to overcome evil.

Here on the cross, Jesus submits to the powers of the lie in order to reveal the lie for what it is and thus to open to all the possibility for truth. By his obedience to the way of God for creation, by his acceptance of God's established way of life—love those who hate us, care for those who persecute us, do no evil to those who do evil to us—Jesus re-established the rule and order of God for all of life. In the obedience and faithfulness of Jesus on the cross, God is made visible to us as the kind of love and mercy that makes its power and grace felt in the world in the way Jesus lives and dies, that the cross of Jesus is the way of God's saving action in history.

There is the thief who still sees the possibility of Jesus calling down the angels with swords and tanks and rescuing him and the two thieves, who wants Jesus to use his power in the old-fashioned way—by force and coercion. The other thief catches something of what is happening here. Here on the cross, by refusing to hate those who are killing him, by refusing to damn them to hell, by asking God to forgive them, by accepting into his life the pain of hate and thus stopping the cycle of hate, Jesus is establishing the Kingdom of God. Jesus there on the cross, not only in the Resurrection but there in the dying, Jesus is reigning as the Lord of Creation, the King of Kings. There, just as in the early temptation stories, there Jesus is refusing to use the power and love of God in any manner contrary to the will and purpose of God. Thus even on the cross he is more than conqueror.

The invitation is always for us to join him in that paradise. The other thief was invited in. We are invited in. Wherever we can, begin to allow the love and mercy of the Spirit of God into our hearts to free us from those forces that keep sneaking out in our speech:

Oh, I have just got to get me one of those new SUVs.
Oh, I really must have a new set of golf clubs.
John has got to go to college.
Mary will just die if she does not get invited.

It is the Jesus on the cross who gives us the courage to resist the power of revenge. Look at the Arabs and Jews, Northern Ireland, and at America and the terrorists. As long as we are tied up in demands of revenge, getting even, blow-for-blow, we have seen that we become as evil as our enemy. Every new act of evil is justified by the latest evil done to us. And we get no closer to peace. Jesus offers us, as individuals and as nations and as a world, the gift of God's love and mercy to invite us to the life of the cross, where we can find ourselves liberated from the bondage of evil and can begin to share in the Kingdom of God—to join Jesus, who reigns from the cross.—Rick Brand

SUNDAY, DECEMBER 3, 2006
Lectionary Message
Topic: The Certainty of God's Promise

TEXT: Jer. 33:14–26

Other Readings: Ps. 25:1–10; 1 Thess. 3:9–13; Luke 21:25–36

Our world is full of insecurity and uncertainty about our daily lives. We feel that we must question everything we try to do and must be prepared for anything and everything. We get up to go to school or to work, and we wonder: Will the water still be in the pipes for washing and cooking? Will the power still be ready for lighting and heating? Will the car start and run? In recent days many people have discovered negative answers to those and a host of other worries and quandaries because of natural disasters, public disruptions, or criminal or terrorist activity. It is a wonderful, satisfying feeling to know that the true basis of our lives is eternally sure and that hope is our daily heritage from God.

I. *What God has promised his people.*

(a) God promised Jeremiah, the prophet, to perform "the Good Thing," previously planned for the two houses or nations of his people—Israel and Judah. From the beginning of his contact with Abraham, God had attached blessed favor and success to the fulfillment of his requests. Abraham was to leave home and continue to Canaan, and God promised to make Abraham's family into a great nation, by which all the Earth should be blessed. And whatever difficulties or obstacles Abraham or his family encountered, God increased their strength, ingenuity, and numbers to enable them to prevail in all the dangers and difficulties, helping them conquer enemies and establish their kingdom under his laws and protection.

(b) But there had always been a challenge to righteousness that the nations had fallen short of achieving; in spite of repeated threats of penalties, they turned to selfish, temporary purposes that led them into suffering and privation, or even conquest. Now Jeremiah receives the promise of the day when the good redemption will come to pass. It will come, says God, through the "Branch of Righteousness," which he will send to David to enforce "judgment and righteousness in the land." That would put within the reach of all the people of God the power to live peaceful, honest, fair, hardworking, worshipful lives—in other words, to be successful children of God. They did then, and we do now, know how to live under the redemptive judgment of God and thus to be blessed.

II. *How the people's fears are answered.*

(a) God further promised Jeremiah that the kingdom of David would never be without a king whom he would bless and that true worship would always be conducted by chosen and dedicated persons who would speak for God to the people and bring the people's sins to judgment and redemption, as they were eradicated in the sacrificial offering of pure, dedicated lives of animals, and, symbolically, by laying personal spiritual suffering upon the mercy of God.

(b) The fear of being a nation without a king was very real among people who had no other way of providing protection, controlling commerce, guiding young people, and creating a manageable community or society. The houses of Israel and Judah had found a strong system through the inspiration of God, and they could only be lost and afraid without the king God had given them, who had a heart for righteousness and for fulfilling all the needs of his nation for God's guidance and blessing.

(c) The people also rightly feared a vacancy in the office of priest. Perhaps the world of today has begun to discover what such an absence of central principle and required, customary consideration of what is just, decent, and right might cause it to degenerate into. The world's surrender to habitual exploitation of the weak, unsuspecting victims of greed, selfishness, and the abuse of power, and to the loss of individual responsibility and respect may, sometime soon, startle the whole population into the realization of our need for what God is here promising to Jeremiah. Although the nation's possessions and even social organization may be threatened by the loss of good central power and true worship of God, his promise still is sure and certain of fulfillment.

III. *Where the power of God's promise lies.* God says the certainty of his promises is in the creation and in the continuing, eternal contract he has made for the sun, moon, and stars, the sequence of the seasons, and the alternation of day and night. All the force of his infinite universe is beneath his promises of good for all his people. The day of the coming of his true redeemer King is as sure as that the sun will rise tomorrow.—John R. Rodman

SERMON SUGGESTIONS

Topic: Is It True?
TEXT: Ps. 25:1–10
(1) Have I been faithful to God? (vv. 1–3). (2) Have I avoided the company of those who plot evil deeds? (vv. 4–5). (3) Have I forgiveness enough to sing about and bear witness to a gracious God? (vv. 6–8). (4) Have I steeled myself against whatever would destroy me? (vv. 9–10).

Topic: Benefits of God's Amazing Grace
TEXT: Titus 2:11–15
(1) Salvation (v. 11). (2) Education (v. 12). (3) Anticipation (v. 13).[1]

WORSHIP AIDS

CALL TO WORSHIP.   "Make me to know your ways, O Lord; teach me your paths. Lead me in your truth, and teach me, for you are the God of my salvation; for you I wait all day long" (Ps. 25:4–5 NRSV).

INVOCATION.   That you are the God who comes and keeps coming in your love that never gives up, we are grateful. For this privilege to celebrate your coming in Word and sacrament, we worship and adore you. May your Word strangely come alive in songs and anthems, through its reading and preaching, through its dramatization in the sacrament. May your spirit

---

[1] Jerry Vines and Jim Shaddex, *Power in the Pulpit* (Chicago: Moody Press, 1999).

quicken mind and heart, that not only in this season but in every season we may practice hospitality to the Highest—the fullness of your grace and truth in the babe of Bethlehem, in Jesus of Nazareth, in the Christ of the cross, in our Living Lord.

Praise be to you, Father, Son, and Holy Spirit.—John Thompson

OFFERTORY SENTENCE.   "Blessed be the Lord, who daily bears us up; God is our salvation" (Ps. 68:19 NRSV).

OFFERTORY PRAYER.   Lord, forgive those who have much and give little; bless those who have little and give much; increase those who would give more if they could, and bring us all to do our part, as you do show us our part to do, for Jesus' sake.—E. Lee Phillips

PRAYER.   We wait upon you, O God, as those who wait for the morning. We wait in faith, knowing that you are the God who comes, and anyone who waits upon you shall never be disappointed. Your coming to the lowliest, the neediest, the weakest is what this season affirms and calls us to celebrate. Your coming is such an advent that Earth cannot contain the glory of it, the rapture of it, the wonder of it, but heaven breaks forth into music and singing.

We praise you for your coming just now in the world—music, song, fellowship of this time and place. Our hearts have been strangely warmed; our minds have been challenged to think new thoughts; our imaginations have been inspired by the not-yet, that in Christ you *are* turned toward us in the eternity of your love; we worship and adore you.

It is of your grace that we, of all people, have been called to the kingdom for such a time as this. In these days, as we are called to commitment and recommitment to the mission of your Church through the life of this congregation, we pray that we may be faithful toward the Word of life, investing of our monies and of our talents, time, and energies. May our stewardship be not a burden but a delight—a joyful response to the fullness of your grace in Christ to us and to all peoples—an offering of praise and thanksgiving for what you have done, are doing, and will continue to do in fulfilling your purpose of love.

Our Father, we find ourselves mourning, but we may not mourn as those without hope, for the dayspring from on high has come, and the dawn of his advent shines more and more unto the perfect day. For those ill and for those loved ones and friends who keep prayerful vigil in their behalf, we pray. Grant us the faith that begets the wisdom to pray for your mercy, where death is a blessing, releasing the spirit from a diseased body. Bless those who are guests among us, that they may experience the comradeship of your people; we pray that together we may rejoice in the wonder of your love, which so quickly removes any strangeness and baptizes us into the communion of your Spirit.

O you who so loves the world that you have given and keep giving yourself for its life, deliver us from the obtuseness of those who persist in brandishing the sword, when you are calling us to put up the sword and live in peace as your family, loving and caring for every person as brother or sister, sharing the Earth and the fullness thereof in life for all. Forgive us when we react to openness with isolationism and to overtures toward peace with suspicion. The shalom you promised through the Prophets is here present in the reconciliation afforded in your coming in Christ, who is here among us, praying for our peace and the peace of the world.—John Thompson

SERMON
Topic: A Different Kingdom
TEXT: John 18:33–37

During the Advent season, we are sure to hear strains of Handel's "Messiah," whether in church or on radio or TV. Especially electrifying are the words that echo the book of Revelation: "King of kings, Lord of lords, and he shall reign for ever and ever. . . . Hallelujah, hallelujah."

When Jesus stood before Pilate, the Roman governor, the question was put to Jesus: "Are you the king of the Jews?" After some sparring, Jesus acknowledged that he was a king but stated that his kingdom was not of this world. By what Jesus Christ was and is, he has given a definition to the name *king* that this world has not seen or known, and his kingdom was and is and will be forever different.

That fact has a life-and-death importance to you and me. How you and I are connected to the Kingdom of God—the reign of Jesus Christ—can determine everything good that we could hope for. It can determine the meaning of our life, our relationship to God and to other people, and heaven itself. We know a lot about the kingdoms of this world, and we need to learn much more, but we need to know more and more about the kingdom that will stand when all the kingdoms of the world have crumbled and fallen. First and foremost we need to know the King!

Napoleon said, "I know men; and I tell you that Jesus Christ is no mere man. Between him and every other person in the world there is no possible term of comparison. Alexander, Caesar, Charlemagne, and I founded empires. But on what did we rest the creations of our genius? Upon force. Jesus Christ founded his empire upon love; and at this hour millions of men would die for him."

When the apostle Paul and Silas brought the good news of Jesus Christ into Thessalonica, many of the citizens were persuaded and joined Paul and Silas. This caused such an uproar among those who opposed their message that they shouted, "These people who have been turning the world upside down have come here also."

As we read the Gospels, we might anticipate such an assessment of what the message of Jesus Christ could do. Of course, those who complained of the revolutionary effect of that message and those who delivered it unwittingly were paying the highest compliment. What do the Gospels tell us that point to such a dramatic effect? It is right there in the parables of Jesus. So many of the parables are prefaced with the words, "The kingdom of heaven (or the Kingdom of God) is like . . ." You will find a different ending to one parable after another—a different ending than you would expect, so much so that one writer has referred to a parable of Jesus as "a holy joke," for it has a surprise ending. Why the surprise ending? For the simple reason that the logic of the parable is the logic of a different kingdom, a higher world—God's world.

Is it any wonder, then, that we hear the apostle Paul saying, "Do not be conformed to this world, but be transformed by the renewing of your minds, so that you may discern what is the will of God—what is good and acceptable and perfect"?

You see, what you and I need to do is to begin to think in different terms about everything. The world has its way of pressing us in its own mold, so that we come out of the mold looking like that world, thinking like it, talking like it, behaving like it. We might even conclude that this way of doing what the world does is all that we ought to do. But we are pulled up short when we consider that other realm—the kingdom of heaven, the Kingdom of God. We belong to that kingdom. The apostle Paul said, "Our citizenship is in heaven." And think of those words of Jesus in his prayer—words that apply to us just as much as they applied to the disciples—when he said, "They do not belong to the world, just as I do not belong to the world" (John 17:16 NRSV).

I can imagine someone saying, "I can't believe that God intends for me to be an oddball and not enjoy my friends and family like other people. I can't believe that God wants me cut off from the innocent joys and pleasures of this life." And I think that someone is right. Jesus said that he came that we might have life and have it more abundantly. Jesus did not come to subtract anything good and helpful and truly meaningful; he came to add to whatever was good and helpful and that gave life meaning. In the case of Jesus himself, it was said that he "for the sake of the joy that was set before him endured the cross, disregarding its shame, and has taken his seat at the right hand of the throne of God" (Heb. 12:2 NRSV).

It sounds like a lot would be expected of us, doesn't it—that we, being who we are as citizens of a higher kingdom, will be different and make a difference in this world we live in right here? Or is Jesus Christ king for nothing?

Well, for one thing, our goals will be different. In one way or another we will see, in the words of the Westminster Confession, that the "chief end of man is to glorify God and enjoy him forever." And both of those goals work together. In one way or another, we live for God whether we intend to or not. We are either God's tools or his partners; that is up to us. We can enjoy God as his partners or miss the joy if we choose not to do his will. In either case, God will be glorified, so that we can sing, "In the cross of Christ I glory, tow'ring o'er the wrecks of time," for the God of the Resurrection can take the worst that human beings can do and transmute it into his glory.

This reminds me of a classic Negro sermon reported by James Weldon Johnson—a sermon that begins with the words, "Young man—Young man—Your arm's too short to box with God." It is a sad fact that we can miss the glory in our personal life, but it is a heartening fact that even our worst deeds cannot put God out of business. We have to "let God be God," recognize that his ways are higher than our ways and that his thoughts are higher than our thoughts. Like it or not, God is and will be God. Jesus, looking ahead to his Crucifixion (and never forget this, his Resurrection) said, "The hour has come for the son of Man to be glorified."

Yes, because Jesus Christ is indeed King, our goals are different. And ways we think about life in all of its aspects are different. Little by little, more and more we learn to think like our Lord and King. It wasn't easy for Jesus' disciples to get some things through their heads, and Jesus often shook his head saying, "O you of little faith!" He compared the Kingdom of God to a mustard seed. It wasn't much to look at as a mere seed, but it became a shrub with large branches that would shade the nests of birds of the air. Whatever else that parable meant, it shatters the notion that bigness and apparent power are the be-all and end-all of our life on this Earth. The philosopher William James captured something of this fact in one long sentence, when he said, "I am against bigness and greatness in all their forms, and with the invisible molecular moral forces that work from individual to individual, stealing in through the crannies of the world like so many soft rootlets, or like the capillary oozing of water, and yet rendering the hardest monuments of man's pride, if you give them time." This truth ought to embolden every one of us, from the youngest to the oldest, whatever our limitations, to give

God our best, assured that service in his kingdom is always important and that God can make of it whatever he will. When God pours his grace and power into our little acts of love and obedience, he will do, as Scripture says, "exceeding abundantly above all that we ask or think."

I heard that truth affirmed a number of years ago by the noted Church historian, Kenneth Scott Latourette. He said that the real makers of Church history were not the popes, the bishops, and such but people like the layman who got up early on a cold winter morning to build a fire in the little country church so that the worshipers would be comfortable when they arrived or like the talented young woman who sang without pay for all the funerals in the community to bring comfort to those who mourned. People like these, he said, were the real makers of Church history, and their names ought to be recorded in the books, but unfortunately we do not know their names. But the king knows, and he will say, "Come, you that are blessed by my Father, inherit the kingdom prepared for you from the foundation of the world."

One other thing needs to be said about this kingdom that Jesus declared is not from this world, not like this world. The citizens of Christ's kingdom do not belong there because they are good or because they have done good deeds. In fact, they have lived as those of whom it was said, "All have sinned and fall short of the glory of God." To some who try terribly hard to win God's favor by their good works, it is offensive to imagine that God would let off some scoundrels who had committed every crime in the books. One cynic called the teaching of Jesus "a slave revolt in morals."

Two days ago, I took part in a roundtable discussion of the criminal justice system. The case of one man came up. He is a known murderer, but he has slipped through the cracks in the system, and he is free. Someone raised the question, "Now where can he go?" A priest at the table said, "To heaven!" Another said, "There is forgiveness." We may not like that idea, if we have not thought the matter through and considered that all of us are sinners needing forgiveness. But thanks be unto God that we, through faith, live in a different kingdom, not a kingdom of this world, and that Jesus Christ is Lord and King, to the glory of God the Father.—James W. Cox

SUNDAY, DECEMBER 10, 2006
Lectionary Message

Topic: God Renews His Promise
TEXT: Luke 1:68–79
Other Readings: Mal. 3:1–4; Phil. 1:3–11; Luke 3:1–6

God's promise, through Abraham and all the sons of the covenant, had always been reiterated by his prophets but now is to be brought to pass, in reality, in the days ahead.

I. *The sufferings of God's people.*

(a) At the hands of their enemies, God's people had suffered heavily, despite the many periods of their strength and independence. From the earliest days and throughout their travels and escapes, from the Egyptians and the Canaanites to the Romans and Babylonians, the Israelites and their families had been enslaved, conquered, displaced, captured, and oppressed by "all that hate" them.

(b) Those who strive to serve God "without fear, in holiness and righteousness before him" (vv. 74, 75) have never found life of that kind easy, and in some times and places it has been impossible. God's people, who do the work he gives them—the work of practice and proclamation—are blessed by those to whom they minister but are scoffed at and rebuked by those who would prefer to violate God's commandments and continue to live in evil ways.

(c) Unfortunately, like the Pharisees and Sadducees who came, driven by curiosity, to hear the preaching of John the Baptist, many today suffer from their sins also. The Pharisees were righteous because they said so, keeping strict outward adherence to laws and ceremonies derived from tradition but not in any numbers receiving God's spiritual renewal to the extent of total personal commitment.

The Sadducees, on the other hand, were highly educated and generally wealthy, holding to close textual accuracy in their doctrines. They held the right of private interpretation.[2] They denied the Resurrection and the eternal punishment of hell, angels and spirits, and any punishment except as the result of one's own action, which each could control. Becoming ever more Hellenized and political, the Sadducees became lumped by John with the Pharisees as "a generation of vipers" (the deadliest of snakes). Hardly anyone today bears their names, but their characteristics appear all too frequently.

II. *The herald of the Lord.*

(a) John prepares the way for Christ by sounding the call to repentance. That must be the first step in anyone's willingness to meet Jesus. Men of John's time and place had a great need to repent. The Greek word translated "repent" is *metanoeo*—"I change, or alter, my mind." They had minds that were upside down, thinking evil was good. They were out of their wits and must return to them. It was then, and still is, the preacher's function and assignment to turn men to a new mental outlook, to convey an upright universe as a challenge to the topsy-turvy world of politics, entertainment, business, and society. Then and not before, that world will see a need to go to the fount of baptism for the realignment of life.

(b) The door of the Church, the haven of forgiveness, must be open to receive all those who repent and take them into fellowship, without asking too many specific, personal questions. When the Gospel says, "Jerusalem, and all Judea, and all the region round about" went out to John, confessing sin and seeking baptism, the meaning probably is not that every single person in the whole land came out to the wilderness but that people of all kinds, races, and ages from every location were crowding about.

It would be very hard to imagine John's hearing a complete auricular confession from each one because of the press of people, but rather to open the baptismal fount—the Jordan—to all who declared themselves sinners and sought the forgiveness thus provided.

God still gives "knowledge of salvation . . . by the remission of their sins" to those who sit in darkness. It is the ministry of all believers to guide feet into the way of righteousness and peace, in order to bring fulfillment in the form of the renewal of God's promise to all his nations.—John R. Rodman

ILLUSTRATIONS

KEEPING IN TOUCH.   A strange and revealing story is sandwiched into the book of Genesis, just after Noah and the flood and immediately before a recounting of Abraham's ancestry: the Tower of Babel story (Gen. 11:1–19). The story is *strange,* because we find God

---

[2]Josephus, *Antiquities,* xviii, pp. 1, 4.

inexplicably alarmed that nomads wandering the desert plan to settle down and build a tower that would reach into heaven; it is *revealing,* because the storyteller clearly believes these desert wanderers could do such a thing. So likely were they to succeed that God had to scramble their speech to interrupt their work. Apparently, the author and early hearers of the story thought that God resides "above," perhaps on a canopy just a few hundred feet above their settlements.

The story, of course ancient, provides a clue to how people over millennia have visualized the spiritual landscape. God, separate from humanity, is *above* in heaven—not too far away to prevent God from listening in and at times intervening, but far enough away to be superior to humanity, to be in command.

The message is: to find spiritual well-being, humans must send praise and pleas "heavenward" while being careful to be earthbound—obedient, humble, docile, tethered down here. The ambition, the striving that drove these settlers to challenge "heaven" must be supplanted by acquiescence to the constraining will of God. Then, and only then, will the connection with God be made.[3]

COMMITMENT.   King did not want to die at all. Early in his public career, he offered a prayer that expressed the sentiments he had held throughout his life: "Lord, I hope no one will have to die as a result of our struggle for freedom in Montgomery. Certainly I don't want to die. But if anyone has to die, let it be me."[4]

SERMON SUGGESTION

Topic: The Easy Way

TEXT: Luke 14:15–24

(1) The gadget age: labor-saving devices; turning Christian service over to a staff of paid workers. (2) With more labor-saving devices, shorter working hours, and more leisure time, living a Christian life will not become easier, but harder. The same excuses prevail today as in olden times.

    I. *Basic requirements of the Christian life:*

(a) That things of first importance be given first place

(b) That a person be prepared for self-denial

(c) That the Word of God be received

    II. *The excuses people make:*

(a) Business

(b) Claims of novelty—surprises

(c) Family obligations

    III. *The irony that such should happen, when it is to a feast we are invited:*

(a) Christianity is a religion of joy.

(b) The Kingdom of God is the pearl of great price.

(c) The road of discipline is the road of mastery.

(d) The highest reward is God himself.

---

[3]James L. Catanzaro, *Ascend: Releasing the Power of the Human Spirit* (St. Louis: Chalice Press, 2003), pp. 67–68.
[4]Michael G. Long, *Martin Luther King Jr., on Creative Living* (St. Louis: Chalice Press, 2004), p. 124.

WORSHIP AIDS

CALL TO WORSHIP.   "The Lord has done great things for us and we rejoiced" (Ps. 126:3 NRSV).

PRAYER OF ADORATION.   That you *are* the God who comes with light and life, that you are turned toward us in the light of your love, that you have identified with us in the flesh and blood of our common humanity, that you are here in the light of your presence in these moments and in every moment in the greatest way you can be, that your spirit, which is holy, is present in our minds and hearts and persons, quickening and renewing life, we worship and adore you. Praise be to you, Father, Son, and Holy Spirit.—John Thompson

OFFERTORY SENTENCE.   "No one has greater love than this, to lay down one's life for one's friends" (John 15:13 NRSV).

OFFERTORY PRAYER.   Lord, let what we give and what we keep, what we share and what we wish we could share, be blessed by the faith that makes intentions possible and hope reality through the Spirit and the Son.—E. Lee Phillips

PRAYER.   As we contemplate the meaning of your advent for us, may we approach its mystery with wonder, its gospel with rejoicing, its meaning with celebration. May we not seek to fashion you after our image but stretch mind and heart to receive the light of the knowledge of your glory in the face of Christ.

You, who so loved the world that you gave your only Son, help us to proclaim and meditate on this love for all. As stewards of the gospel—the good news of Christmas—may we not turn from our responsibility for the life of the *world*. As your Church we are called to be the body of Christ—the flesh and blood of your Word—in this time and place.

O you who watch over the destiny of man and of nations, we pray that all peoples may discover a common humanity and be moved to seek a unity for this world that can lead to peace, that life may continue and flourish on this planet to your glory. Grant to us all such a vision of your coming that the opportunities of this week may be used to prepare the way, for him who is the true and living way.

That our coming and our going—our birthing and our dying—that our successes and our failures, our joys and our sorrows are embraced in the loving intimacy of this community of faith, we are grateful. To include in the embrace of your love, we reach out to those who, in the weakness of mind, body, or of spirit, need the ministry of your grace to become whole. In all the relationships of each day, grant to us the faith, the courage, the love to follow him who was "the man for others" and so teaches us to pray: [repeat the Lord's Prayer].—John Thompson

SERMON

Topic: Why Pray?

TEXT: Luke 2:25–35; Matt. 7:7 RSV

"Ask . . . Seek . . . Knock."

The curse of so much religion," George Meredith is reported to have said, "is that men cling to God with their weakness rather than with their strength."

As I look into my own life, I have to admit, "Yes, it is true—too true. I have often clung to God in weak resignation." I have said, "Why concern myself with this or that? God knows what he is doing." Or I have said, "I'll be satisfied with what I am and what I do. Why be rash and try to play God?"

Many things I read in the Bible disturb me. I read the words of Jesus: "Ask, and it will be given you; seek, and you will find; knock, and it will be opened to you." These words disturb me when I discover that I am to ask and keep on asking; seek and keep on seeking; knock and keep on knocking. Keep on praying? Some of us have hardly prayed about some things the first time!

The need to pray—*prayer* defined by the literal meaning of the English word *pray*—is a basic and continuing need of everyone. More than that, God himself needs our prayers to help him do some things that would not be done without those prayers.

But here is our temptation. We can have our devotional fervor turned on or off by the latest theologian or philosopher we have read. The need to pray, however, is persistent. We may put to sleep that need with a massive dose of hyper-Calvinism, or we may bind and gag it with a brash Stoicism, but the need stays with us.

I. We should not be surprised if an imp sits on our shoulder and whispers, "You can't change God's mind. So why pray?" That assertion is frighteningly close to the truth. Some of the words of the Bible almost say that. "For ever, O Lord, thy word is firmly fixed in the heavens," says the psalmist (119:89 RSV). But he doesn't quite say, "You can't change God's mind." He does tell us that Jehovah differs from the gods of the heathen, for the Lord is predictable. He is faithful and reliable.

Or consider what Paul has to say: "For those whom he foreknew he also predestined to be conformed to the image of his Son. . . . And those whom he predestined he also called; and those whom he called he also justified" (Rom. 8:29–30 RSV). This tells us that God's mind is made up about one thing in particular—the redemption of humankind. His eternal purpose is a purpose of love and grace. When Jesus came, he underscored that fact. Who would want it different? We are resigned to that. No, more than being merely resigned to it, we can welcome it, embrace it, affirm it with our whole being.

However, one aspect of the will of God is not welcomed, not embraced, not affirmed. When God visits us with suffering, sorrow, and death, we indeed "wince" and "cry aloud." Will meets will. Our mind struggles with the mind of God. There is a modern reenactment of the ancient drama of Jacob wrestling with the angel, the Ninevites repenting so that God will repent, or Jesus saying in anguish, "Father, if it be possible, let this cup pass from me" (Matt. 26:39).

The audacity of it is breathtaking. Do I, a mortal, dare put on my shoes and stand up to God? The deed is done when I don't like what is happening to me or to someone else and register my complaint with God, or even when I am bold enough to confront God with the restless yearnings of my heart; am I being blasphemous or insolent to pray like that?

If so, then Epictetus, the Stoic, sounded better than many Christians when he prayed, "Give me what Thou desirest for me. For I know that what Thou choosest for me is far better than what I could choose." Brother Lawrence, who practiced the presence of God, would practically agree with Epictetus, for he said that he regarded the hour spent in the kitchen as valuable as those spent in prayer.

Some philosophers and some saints would make prayer a matter of submission only. Why fight, they seem to say, for the last chapter of this story is already written, and we know how it will come out.

P. T. Forsyth saw it differently. He said, "We need not begin with 'thy will be done' if we but end with it."

Does God really want us to confess our impatience, to ask him questions, and to beat a path of protest to his throne of grace? It should not surprise us if he does. We are not better than our Lord. What more vivid example have we of wrestling in prayer than the picture of a solitary figure—the Son of God—praying through the night hours?

The Bible and our Lord in particular plainly teach that prayer is petitioning—asking—though it may have other meanings, too. It seems clear also that some things simply would not happen apart from our prayers. Theologian Emil Brunner declared, "God awaits our prayer, and because He longs to extend His kingdom not only over men but through men and with men, God accomplishes some things only when they are asked for; God earnestly awaits our prayer. We dare believe that our prayers make possible for us some action of God not otherwise possible."[5]

Can we say that God is any less concerned with the asking than with the receiving? Is he less concerned with seeking than with finding? Is he less concerned with knocking than with the open door? No, "He is the hunger, as well as the food." It is as much Christian to pray *boldly* as it is to yield *graciously*.

II. Now, quite naturally, we are interested in what happens as the result of our prayers. We are practical enough for that! What does happen?

If you pray, something will happen to you. Those who pray find a hand to guide them when the way is dark. We discover we can go on in spite of failure, sickness, and even sin. One hears God say, "Thy sins be forgiven thee" (Matt. 9:5) and "I will never leave thee, nor forsake thee" (Heb. 13:5). We need that! Without seeking and finding the help of God, one might wander a lifetime in the dark or fold up in defeat every time a strong, opposing wind should blow, or despair of ever being at peace with God.

These are perhaps our most urgent needs, these crises of the spirit, but they are not our only needs that God meets through prayer. Some of you may know that as a recent and dramatic experience. Some of you prayed for your daily bread and prayed earnestly. The answer came.

A number of years ago, Dr. H. H. Rowley told a moving story of God's provision through prayer. In response to an appeal for more liberal support of foreign missions, an elderly lady who lived in an almshouse placed in Dr. Rowley's hand an envelope with an extra gift of seven shilling, six pence for foreign missions. Dr. Rowley, who was her pastor, knew that she could not afford such an amount from her meager allowance, since she had already given generously to missions. He begged her to take it back, arguing that as the Lord was pleased with Abraham's willingness to sacrifice Isaac but did not require it after all, so the Lord would be pleased with her willingness without her gift. With quiet dignity she refused, saying that she was not giving the money to her pastor.

---

[5]Emil Breemer, *Our Faith* (London: SCM Press, Ltd., 1949), p. 95.

A few days later a wealthy lady sent Dr. Rowley a check for five pounds for a service he had done for her. She requested that the money be used for his work as he pleased. He went to see the lady in the almshouse. As he was leaving, he asked if she would do him the service of allowing him to leave with her a small gift, telling her of its source.

Immediately, she burst into tears and told him that at the moment when he had knocked at her door she was on her knees, praying that God would somehow send her something to meet her need. She had no food and would receive no more money for three days.[6]

Does this boggle your mind? Perhaps this sort of thing astounds us too much. After all, Jesus said, "You did not choose me, but I chose you and appointed you that you should go and bear fruit and that your fruit should abide; so that whatever you ask the Father in my name, he may give it to you" (John 15:16 RSV). What might appear to be a selfish prayer may be nothing of the kind. It may really be God's indirect way of doing a significant work for his kingdom.

Prayer does cause remarkable things to happen in the life of one who prays. It can also lead to happy consequences in the lives of those one prays for. Pray for a man, and you will come to love him, care what happens to him and, if possible, do something concrete to help him. But that is not the limit of such prayer. God uses our prayers to help those for whom we pray, even though they do not know we have prayed for them, even though we may have no contact with them except through prayer.

One of my seminary professors spoke in a class of the effect of intercessory prayer. He said that God had given him a special ministry of praying for some people whom others had given up praying for and that he had seen some of them become converted. Many people's lives are different today because someone prayed for them, the doctrine of "free will" notwithstanding.

What shall we say of the prayers of those whose concern moves beyond the needs of the individuals they know? Some are distressed by the sins of humankind, by our universal fallen state, by the pain and anxiety that our world, subjected to futility, inflicts on its inhabitants. Are these who mourn in this way truly blessed, as Jesus said they were? Do their lifelong prayers make sense? Will their faith that rebels at last move the mountains of sin, suffering, and death?

Let us turn back the scroll of the centuries. A man of Israel bows to the ground in an agony of prayer. This man had not meekly acquiesced in the humiliation of his people before the world. He had not accepted the perdition of the heathen as a final judgment of God. He found no meaning and redemption in trying to be a well-adjusted personality in the kind of world he lived in. His prayer for a messiah who would change what is mean and spiritually distasteful became the passion of his life. And God gave the man a hope in his striving. God revealed to him that, in his lifetime, he would see the Christ. Years pass. Jesus is born. Inspired by the Spirit, this man Simeon came to the Temple, where the infant Jesus was being presented to the Lord. He took the child in frail arms that now felt new strength. Tears of joy filled the sad, ascetic eyes as he blessed God and said: "Lord, now lettest thou servant depart in peace,/ according to thy word;/ for mine eyes have seen thy salvation/ which thou hast

---

6H. M. Rowley, *The Reverance of the Bible* (New York: Macmillan, 1948), pp. 117–118.

prepared in the presence of all peoples,/ a light for revelation to the Gentiles,/ and for glory to thy people Israel" (Luke 2:29–32 RSV).

This man's prayers poured into the stream of God's purpose, as did the prayers of many others, and surely helped to bring to pass what God had willed. The Redeemer came. At last, he came! What a glorious fulfillment! But there is more.

The last prayer has not been prayed, and the last battle has not been fought. The martyrs pray, "How long, O Lord?" Many other devout hearts pray, "Thy kingdom come, thy will be done on earth as it is in heaven." Some pray in the words of the Seer, "Come, Lord Jesus." And with the whole creation "groaning in travail," nature also mourns for a lost good.

I have often wondered how one could be properly concerned about God's will for the present life and at the same time pray for the hastening of the Lord's return. I knew a pastor who periodically preached and prayed publicly for the second coming of Christ. His concern about it always seemed to coincide with a new crisis in his personal difficulties. He seemed to value the Parousia as a kind of deus ex machina to extract him from the messes he repeatedly got himself into.

Who will be the persons who "have loved and longed for his appearance?" I think it will be those who are so concerned about the ultimate triumph of God's purpose that they throw themselves, their strength, and their prayers into the burning challenges of the hour, with the intrepid expectation that what is but half-finished today will be completely fulfilled in God's great tomorrow.

Why pray? The magnitude of the need of my own life, the incompleteness of the lives of those I love and know, and the burden of the world's sin and suffering leaves me with no alternative but to pray—if I care and God cares. God wants my prayers, asks for them, inspires them, and, amazing though it may seem, will, through those prayers, find his hand strengthened to accomplish his purpose of grace.

Simeon of old fulfilled his stewardship of prayer. Our stewardship is yet unfulfilled. So we and others must pray "until he has put all his enemies under his feet" (1 Cor. 15:25 RSV).[7]

SUNDAY, DECEMBER 17, 2006
Lectionary Message

Topic: The True Fruit of Repentance

TEXT: Luke 3:7–18

Other Readings: Zeph. 3:14–20; Isa. 12:2–6; Phil. 4:4–7

What is the need for repentance? Why bother ourselves with new ideas, much less with getting rid of old patterns of thought and understanding? Fortunately for most of us, we do finally realize that self-centered, exploitative living is counterproductive and detrimental to true personal fulfillment.

I. *Baptism doesn't count without repentance.*

(a) The new life must replace the old, because they cannot exist together. One of the truly great preachers called this "The Expulsive Power of a New Affection." What John the Baptist

---

[7]James W. Cox, *Surprised by God* (Nashville, Tenn.: Broadman Press, 1979), pp. 59–65.

is calling for is a real "complete makeover," which is based on recognition of reality and trust in the truth.

(b) We have heard it said, "There is no free lunch." With any experience, we learn that every "free" gift entails some form of obligation. After leading these Pharisees and Sadducees into the Kingdom of God through baptism, John now instructs them as disciples who must become practitioners of the faith leading to salvation. Life should not be given up, but it should be an exercise of practical righteousness. John calls for them to "bring forth fruits worthy of repentance," not to gain salvation but to give evidence of sincerity in the new life.

II. *Fruits give evidence of true commitment.*

(a) Repentance can yield the fruits, as John suggests to his newly redeemed believers, of generosity, sharing clothes with the needy and food with the hungry; of fairness and honesty in positions of trust, exacting, as publicans, no more than the law requires; of justice and equanimity, protecting, as soldiers, those in their custody, and of unselfish satisfaction with their honest wages instead of complaining.

(b) When faced with the need to give personal evidence of true faith, the repentant person would be false if he tried to rely on family background and national citizenship to prove his worthiness in the sight of God. John uses an extreme example of the uselessness of borrowed reputation of brotherly righteousness: God can make family members or racial forms out of stones. Actually, God did originally create human beings, along with other forms of life, from the dust of the Earth. Therefore, John says, it is no distinction, and certainly no substitute for personal performance, to be of a "good family."

III. *The believer and preacher is the servant of the Master.*

(a) The one who spreads word to the whole nation that new minds and new lives are necessary is not the one who is to be honored and served. He is the one who tells the message, partly by self-sacrifice, as John dressed in skins and lived in the wilderness so as to be of no offense to his fellow citizens. True, he does gain a reputation if his work is good, and sometimes those he leads are very grateful and appreciative. Not often is one compared to, or even imagined to be, as John was, the Christ himself. But the difference, John says, is as great as that between water and the fire of the Holy Ghost. And so it is.

(b) As the servant of God, the bearer of his promise must challenge those who are "dead in their trespasses and sins" by the assurance of being destroyed most completely unless they make truly fruitful use, in a holy and good life, of the gifts of God's power and spirit. As mercy is offered in the gospel, its opposite is in store for anyone who is barren or who bears evil fruit, for as John in his metaphor declares, "every tree which brings not forth good fruit is hewn down and cast into the fire." That fire is the most destructive element known to humanity, and everyone, as an act of kindness and love, should be warned about the destruction of those bearing either no fruit or evil fruit, so that he can follow the Lord in repentance, faith, and good deeds of service.—John R. Rodman

ILLUSTRATIONS

GOD-CONCEPTS—AND THE RESULTS.   "Write a biography of God-concepts in your life." This was the first assignment I gave to a group of experienced pastors and priests who came for a one-week, intensive seminar on the subject "Preaching in a Multicultural Community." I explained the assignment this way: "In the act of preaching, we are working with people's God-images and concepts—evoking them, reclaiming them, affirming them, challenging them, shaping them, reshaping them, and changing them. In order to do this task faithfully, we have to first recover how our own God-concepts have evolved and changed in our lives over the years. In other words, you are invited to explore how God interacted with you during different periods in your lives. In the revelation of God or the in-breaking of the Holy Spirit at significant moments in your lives, you may have been given opportunities to connect with God at a different point and therefore may have gained a view of a different dimension of God. In the process, we might discover what God-concept drives our teaching and preaching, and from where our passion for ministry came."

In other words, this is an exercise for all Christians. It's something we need to do as the first step in our process of learning to communicate the gospel in a pluralistic world.—Eric H. F. Law[8]

THINKING GOD'S WAY.   When I believe in my heart that Jesus Christ is Lord, my outlook toward everything will take on a new tone. That may be long in coming. It may happen gradually, but come it will. When I was a teenager, I heard a man say, "There are some things in the Bible that I wish were not in there." When the pressure of temptation is strong upon us and we want to do a particular thing, we too might wish certain commandments in the Bible were not there. But how foolish! To think like that is like thinking that the guardrails on a winding mountain road should be removed or that all stop signs and traffic signals should be removed. The lordship of Jesus Christ, however, changes such thinking. We begin to think God's way about everything. Our work, our recreation, our politics—everything will be affected. As someone put it a long time ago: "He will be Lord of all or he will not be Lord at all."—James W. Cox

SERMON SUGGESTIONS

Topic: A Sermon You Couldn't Afford to Miss
TEXT: Isa. 61:1–4, 8–11
(1) Because it encourages the oppressed. (2) Because it promises justice for those who have been wronged. (3) Because it celebrates God's deliverance, as if it had already happened.

Topic: How to Prepare for the Coming of Our Lord Jesus Christ
TEXT: 1 Thess. 5:16–24
(1) Attend to your private prayer life. (2) Attend to your public witnessing. (3) Attend to how you live, both publicly and privately.

WORSHIP AIDS

CALL TO WORSHIP.   "Endow the king with your justice, O God, the royal son with your righteousness. He will judge your people in righteousness, your afflicted ones with justice" (Ps. 72:1–2 NIV).

INVOCATION.   Lord, let our lips sing of you, our souls rejoice in you, our wills follow you, because we pause to pray and seek your face and follow the Christ.—E. Lee Phillips

---

[8]*The Word at the Crossings* (St. Louis: Chalice Press, 2004), p. 15.

OFFERTORY SENTENCE.   "Now the God of hope fill you with all joy and peace in believing, that you may abound in hope, through the power of the Holy Ghost" (Rom. 15:13).

OFFERTORY PRAYER.   We thank you, Father, for the joy and peace you give us in our Lord Jesus Christ and for the opportunity to share with others the hope that is ours. May these offerings increase the joy and peace that we experience here and bring hope to the hearts of those who have not yet received our Savior.

PRAYER.   For this privilege to be among your people on this occasion, we give you thanks. What visitations of your grace, all along the way, bring us to this hour. At every juncture in our lives there has been your coming in some guardian angel that has seen us through when it seemed that life had reached an impasse—that we were powerless, mindless, spiritless to negotiate. For all our deliverances by the power of your grace, we praise you.

We praise you for the insight into the meaning and mystery of your coming that has challenged our minds, stirred our spirits, warmed our hearts, as it has been declared through your servant on this occasion.

You *are* the God who comes; you came through your people, Israel, in a special way that all peoples may know of your coming in righteousness and ways of peace. You came conclusively in Jesus of Nazareth that your Word, present from the beginning in creation, declared by prophets through the ages, should be manifested in flesh and blood that no one should miss your love's purpose for all peoples and the world.

You are the God who comes to the weak, the poor, the imprisoned, and we pray that we who are strong, rich, and free may be means of your coming "to the least" in this season and every season. This is our calling. "To whom much is given, of him is much required!"

We *do* pray for ourselves, that we may be discerning of your coming in the fullness of your grace and truth in Christ in all the exigencies of our daily relationships. May we enthusiastically run down the road to tell others of your mighty deeds for our salvation and the salvation of the world.

We pray for the oppressed who have no rights: the thousands living in refugee camps, suffering the subhuman, even antihuman conditions of a barbed-wire imprisonment for half a century. We pray for the oppressors that they may have the change of mind and heart to discover the brotherly and sisterly in their neighbor.

We pray for those participating in the peace process of these days, that they may persevere in ways of justice that peace may come to Jerusalem—and in coming to Jerusalem to all the world.

We pray for the homeless, the jobless. We pray for our leaders the wisdom to make decisions that can alleviate the suffering of so many.

We pray for those among us living in fear because of anxieties over precarious health, that they may discern your coming in their weakness in a strong grace to heal. As "Emmanuel," you are with us in all the dark nights of the soul, enlightening our darkness, dispelling our doubts, conquering our fears.

> Love Divine, all loves excelling
> Joy of heaven, to earth come down,
> Fix in us Thy humble dwelling,
> All thy faithful mercies crown!

Jesus, Thou are all compassion,
Pure, unbounded love thou art;
Visit us with thy salvation,
Enter every trembling heart.

Amen and Amen!—John Thompson

SERMON
Topic: Reaching the Bottom Rung
TEXT: Isa. 61:1–4

During Advent, we need to read Isaiah through the window of the Gospels. Luke tells the story better than Mark or Matthew. Fresh out of the wilderness of temptation, the young carpenter strides into Nazareth, his hometown, and on the Sabbath enters the local synagogue. Luke qualifies the event by the simple statement: "Then Jesus, filled with the power of the Spirit, returned to Galilee." On the surface, nothing about this scene is unusual. Jesus normally attended services at the synagogue, and I suspect he had often read from the ancient scrolls, but Luke reminds us that this ordinary Sabbath was anything but ordinary. Jesus was different. There were rumors, and the gossip may have brought out the rubbernecks on the Sabbath. "Have you heard about Mary's boy? Poor fellow. Thinks he's a rabbi or a prophet. He has been to several synagogues in Galilee, and I hear he is in town."

When Jesus stood up to read the Scriptures, he was handed the Isaiah scroll, and he read our passage. This was a favorite text for Jews under Roman oppression. Everyone recognized the messianic promise, and Jesus might have done well to stop while he was ahead. But he offered an interpretation. "Today this scripture has been fulfilled in your hearing." Then, to compound the offense, he cited the moments in Scripture when revelation had come to Gentiles. James Sanders explains the rage: "Jesus was saying to the congregation that God was not a Jew." His statement was akin to standing on a street corner in modern Jerusalem and preaching that the Messiah will come to release the Palestinians from Jewish oppression.

God is not the prisoner here. "The Faces of Jesus" is a collection of art from around the world, including some drawings by children, depicting the life of Jesus. Every race and culture imagines the Christ in their own costume, with features characteristic of their people. Frederick Buechner provides the narrative for the colorful art photos. He notes that we have no description of Jesus, no sketch from the New Testament. The only portrait of Jesus from the Gospels is a reflection in the faces of the witnesses, and all that we have is the human imagination in centuries of art. Buechner suggests that we look at the face of Jesus, "as the face of our own secret and innermost destiny: The face of Jesus as our face." The beauty of this book is the shocking variety of views and images of Jesus. You begin to get the impression that the Christ who came to his own people comes to each of us in our own time and place. Christ transcends every artistic image.

God is never captive of any culture, any epoch, or any place. Every religion is guilty, and every tribe and nation of every age has been victim of the same myopia. In the process of translating the Scriptures in our dialect and picturing the Christ in our image, we easily slip into the faulty logic of assuming an exclusive possession. Just as Jesus slipped through the crowd trying to throw him over a cliff in Nazareth, he slips through our racial and cultural packages.

We are prisoners and exiles. The prophetic hope was written for exiles on the day of their arrival back in Jerusalem. Taken from the original context, the promised release of prisoners might not sound like good news to us. Unless you count yourself among the captives, you probably are not too interested in a messianic emancipation. I doubt that we could get very excited about opening the gates of Brushy Mountain prison; we would just as soon leave the criminals behind bars. Most of us cannot begin to identify ourselves with prisoners, but the exiles did, and so did the folks in Nazareth under Roman domination.

During Advent we sing Charles Wesley's hymn, "Come, thou long expected Jesus, Born to set thy people free; From our fears and sins release us; Let us find our rest in Thee." Black Americans and early Baptists saw themselves in the mirror of the exodus from Egyptian slavery. People who feel oppressed listen for a gospel of freedom that most of us cannot understand. Where I come from, going to prison is a disgrace. Once the mark is on your record, it is there forever. I recall when one of the kids in my youth group got arrested for stealing hubcaps. The big fancy wheel covers had just become popular on new cars, and they sold at a premium price from junk dealers. Stealing hubcaps did not carry the stigma of robbing a bank or mugging someone. In some youth circles, taking hubcaps was more like a game than a serious felony. But tell that to the judge. That is not how it came down in the courts. The argument that "everyone does it" sinks like a rock. The kid was marked for life.

I recall hearing Whitney Cochran say that successful parenting means your children are not in jail. I know what he meant. Your kids should not have to meet your standards of accomplishment to be loved and accepted, but prison is hardly ever acceptable. That got a bit hard to measure during the civil rights movement, when preachers like Martin Luther King Jr. were thrown in jail for marching with the "wrong crowd."

Prison is not always a stigma. One whole group of epistles in the New Testament clusters around a common experience. They are called Prison Epistles, written by Paul from a Roman prison. I think Paul could identify with the prisoners and the captives whom Christ came to set free, but if you read Paul you will see a much worse prison in the days of his institutional captivity. Paul was never so free as when he was released from his bondage of legalism and set free from his hatred of people he had concluded were the enemies of God.

Jesus came to reach the people at the bottom rung of the social ladder—people of acknowledged need. People of privilege and position are misfits at Advent. God comes to folks who need help, people who can acknowledge that they are missing the mark. Like the people of John's era who claimed freedom based on national heritage, we have great difficulty admitting to need. We are Americans! We are children of Abraham! What is the difference? We are all prisoners of one sort of another, and Christ has come to set us free.—Larry Dipboye

SUNDAY, DECEMBER 24, 2005
Lectionary Message

Topic: The Perfect Offering

TEXT: Heb. 10:5–10

Other Readings: Mic. 5:2–5; Luke 1:47–55; Luke 1:39–45

I. *All offerings of sacrifice have failed.*

(a) When a person does an offensive act, commits a social misdemeanor, or violates a standing stricture of behavior, the suffering felt as a penalty should surely convince him of his error.

He may be made to suffer social ostracism or family disapproval, such as being "grounded." For those who offended against civil laws in the countries where they lived, Jews were penalized, perhaps more than others, but the punishment was according to the laws or to the whim of the king, as in the case of Jerusalem at the time of Herod.

But historically, as well as in the time of Herod and Antipater, the Jews who broke the moral law of God, or violated a Temple code or other Jewish law, or simply as practiced by tradition, were required to offer specific sacrifices at specific times to satisfy the necessary penalties. Depending on a person's private circumstances, these sacrifices could be very costly.

(b) We do not often think of the birth of God's son on Earth as a sacrifice; we look to his death on the cross as the time of sacrifice. However, the birth of Jesus is the beginning of the life of sacrifice for human redemption. One of the major reasons for his coming was to emphasize the need for more than costly payments, the need for a change in the level of sacrifice and of suffering for sins. As stated in the Psalms (40:6) and often elsewhere in the Hebrew Scriptures (Ps. 50; Isa. 1:11; Amos 5:21, 22), it is known that God does not require or want the burnt offerings and ritual sacrifices they practice so well. Amos even records God's despising feast days and assemblies, and even refusing to accept songs and instrumental music.

II. *A satisfactory sacrifice must be holy.*

(a) We see the time when a person must come to do the will of God. The one who does this must be one who first lives by God's will and then teaches others to do so.

Punishment alone is enough to cause a person to realize that an error has been committed, and a good punishment (one that "fits the crime") can even make clear the elements wherein the action was off the mark or the lawless transgression was offensive. Justice requires fair recompense or atonement on the part of the offender; the amount of suffering inflicted as penalty is not allowed to be overly painful or costly for the offender.

(b) The assessment of some form of suitable punishment has always been used as a means of convincing a wrongdoer to try to mend his ways. Along with penalty, however, the wise teacher, parent, or society must offer inducements with pleasurable outcomes to help the erring person not only resolve to cease doing wrong but strongly want to learn to do right.

In others words, everyone must be convinced that obedience or conformity to known rules, laws, or principles yields more and greater satisfaction in the long run than does any amount of thrill or fun in disobedience.

Parents and teachers do have the help of police and judges in impressing a wrongdoer with the evil of his misdeed, but often the law-enforcement agency serves only to anger or inure the sinner against the society.

III. *It is right to please God.*

(a) For most of us sinners, somewhere along the way a conversion is necessary. We must be convinced that a thoroughgoing revision of our concepts of right and wrong—and the necessity of doing right—is essential.

(b) A model of behavior that is acceptable and successful, both for the individual and for the society, is a very desirable element in the development of a life that is pleasing to God. Setting a good example is a strong means of instruction, and the emulation of a beneficial pattern of conduct is a sure means of developing good habits.

(c) For a human being to develop a life pattern of behavior that is pleasing and rewarding, instruction must usually accompany and interpret the example. Rules need to be not only enunciated but also logically justified, as they are illustrated for the learner's adoption.

For a life to be acceptable to God, one must not only know the principles of godly behavior but also realize the gift of God in the coming of Jesus Christ. He "came to do the will of God," and he not only healed the sick and raised the dead but he cured loneliness, selfishness, greed, cruelty, and dishonesty by his instruction and conversation. He also became for us all the perfect offering to God.—John R. Rodman

SERMON SUGGESTIONS

Topic: God Has Not Forgotten
TEXT: Isa. 51:1–8
(1) Questions raised: Ps. 42:9, 77:9, Rev. 6:10. (2) Answers given: God delivers from slavery (Exodus); from exile (return to home); from sin (Jesus); from loneliness (Holy Spirit); from futility (reward).

Topic: The Law in the Heart
TEXT: Jer. 31:31–34 (esp. v. 31:33b)
(1) The law of regeneration. (2) The law of possession. (3) The law of growth.

WORSHIP AIDS

CALL TO WORSHIP.   "And God said, let there be light" (Gen. 1:3).

INVOCATION.   O Father of all lights, who into the darkness of chaos commanded, let there be light, and there was light; and did shine into the world at Bethlehem in the light of the fullness of your love; shine into our minds and hearts and persons that we may be heralds of the coming of your kingdom in this day and place.

OFFERTORY SENTENCE.   "Like good stewards of the manifold grace of God, serve one another with whatever gift each of you has received" (1 Pet. 4:10 NRSV).

OFFERTORY PRAYER.   Lord, may we give cheerfully from all that is entrusted to us as servants of the King of Kings.—E. Lee Phillips

PRAYER.   We wait upon you, O God, as those who wait for the morning. We wait in faith, knowing that you are the God who comes, and anyone who waits upon you shall never be disappointed. Your coming to the lowliest, the neediest, the weakest is what this season affirms and calls us to celebrate. Your coming is such an advent that Earth cannot contain the glory of it—the rapture of it—the wonder of it—but the heavens break forth into music and singing.

Something *has* happened that has never happened before, for almost every home has some symbol of your coming: a candle, a wreath, a tree, bright lights. We praise you for your coming in the *meaning* that enlightens us, in the *mystery* that challenges us, in the *beauty* that inspires us, in the *love* that grasps us and does not let us go.

We praise you for your coming just now in the Word, music, song, fellowship of this time and place. Our hearts have been strangely warmed; our minds have been challenged to grasp new heights and depths of the meaning of your coming; our imaginations have been dared to let go of "that-is" to perceive the "not-yet."

O God of all comfort, we find ourselves mourning, but may we not mourn as those without hope, for the dayspring from on high *is* come and the dawn of his advent shines more and more unto the perfect day. For those ill, and for those loved ones and friends who keep prayerful vigil in their behalf, we pray. Grant us the faith that begets the wisdom to pray for your mercy, where death is a blessing, releasing the spirit from a diseased body. Bless those among us who are guests, that they may experience the comradeship of your people, that together we may rejoice in the wonder of your love, which so quickly removes any strangeness and baptizes us into the communion of your Spirit.

We pray for the peace of Bethlehem and Jerusalem, for we realize that we have neglected or ignored your call for justice for all people.

We pray that somehow the meaning and power of your love to reconcile may invade the minds and hearts of those who are so crazed with self-seeking power that they ruin that which they would rule, and millions are left homeless and starving.

We pray for world leaders who agonize over a strategy that can bring sanity to these troubled areas and for all of those workers and soldiers who have left home and homeland on missions of mercy.

May we faithfully pray and wisely work for that day when all creation will echo back the angels' song of that first Christmas: "Glory to God in the highest and peace on earth to persons of good will."—John Thompson

SERMON

Topic: God Loves the World

TEXT: John 3:16; 1 John 4:7–21

If God loves the world, little else matters. All of the fears and uncertainties in life are met in the confession of faith that grows out of the encounter with Christ Jesus: "God is love." God's love is a steady hint in the Old Testament but not at all a foregone conclusion. Creation is punctuated with the refrain, "God saw that it was good," but the response of the Creator to human failure was harsh and uncompromising. When the "good" creation does not perform as expected, the Creator brings down judgment: expulsion from Paradise is followed with the mark of Cain and eventually a God who "repents" of having created anything. When the reality of evil grows to the point of total divine intolerance, the result is total destruction of the world in a flood. The glimpse of light in the Noachian Covenant and the rainbow is an attempt at a new beginning and a clue to a higher nature in God, but the entire Old Testament struggles with goodness in God. The God of covenant is personal and merciful, but the "demands" side of the covenant proves to be more than mere mortals seem capable of producing. Why does God put more on us than we can bear? The psalmists dare to challenge divine judgment without any satisfactory conclusion. "The Lord is my Shepherd" is a figure that stands for hope, but not even the shepherd image is necessarily loving. In the Psalms, God demonstrates *hesed*—mercy, loving kindness, steadfast love—but we are never sure that God is love. Rather, we get a conflicted picture of a God of wrath who afflicts, who is also the God of compassion who heals.

Questions usually come before answers. Job raises all the right questions about the injustice of life and the goodness of God. Human suffering cannot possibly be a simple matter of settling accounts. Bad things do happen to good people—like Job. Where is God? What is the divine Word? Does the Almighty care? Archibald MacLeish cuts through all of the philosophical chit-chat with the chant of Nickles: "If God is God he is not good, If God is good he is not God." Edgar Brightman poses the conflict: in the face of history, a loving God is an oxymoron. Either God is powerless before the forces of evil and human suffering, or God does not care enough to act. We hang on the horns of a dilemma, between an almighty and all-loving God. Job raises all the right questions but finally comes down on the Old Testament, Augustinian, Calvinistic insistence on the absolute sovereignty of God. The voice from the whirlwind echoes down the corridors of time; "Father knows best," and the perpetual, adolescent rebellion of the children cry, "not enough!" The sovereignty of God is not in question. Finally, the only question that matters is the love of God for the world; more specifically and personally, does God love persons like us?

Long before John, Paul identified three essentials in our relationship with God as faith, hope, and love. In the most beautiful love sonnet of all time, Paul declared that without love the golden tongue of human communication or even the language of the spirit sounds like a gong show. Not only is love the greatest, love is the catalyst that creates faith and hope. So John—perhaps the beloved apostle of the fourth Gospel—reached the grand conclusion about God: God loves the world; God is love. Anyone could take a deep breath and say it, but John said it in the face of the very history that has undercut our confidence in God. The justice of God is revealed in the injustice of the cross. The love of the Son reveals the inner nature of the Father.

The world is measured by the love of God. This is not some utopia—a world without pain, a paradise without death. The Word became flesh and dwelled among us, here in the world of earthquakes, storms, and floods—in the world where people can get shot to death for coming home. With all of the warnings about the evil of this present age, and even in 1 John (2:15), "Do not love the world or the things in the world," we are reassured that God loves the world and that God is love. But whoever said that love is easy? Love is the most costly thing you can do. Forget the cheap stuff that is peddled on the soaps and in the movies. You might have to reassess that moon-eyed romanticism that led you toward marriage. Dietrich Bonhoeffer pointed out that love does not define God. God defines love. Furthermore, the world does not determine its own value; the worth of the world is built in by the Creator. "God so loved the world . . ." You should no more expect to look away from the pain and injustice of the world than you are expected to ignore the cross, but in the face of Christ, the suffering of injustice does not define God. Suffering for someone else in the face of injustice, however, defines love.

We are measured by our love for one another. If God is love, so what? Is that not the usual response to a profound discovery? So what if we can scrape together enough pieces of divine compassion to say with John, "God is love"? Does that change anything? No, the only way our confessions of faith make any difference is when they are confessions of life. Only as faith in a loving God becomes so much a part of ourselves that faith defines us does anything change. For John, the effect of a loving God is a loving people, "Beloved, since God loved us so much, we also ought to love one another." If the identity of God is love, we are the people who are doing something about the cruelty and the apathy of the world. We are possessed with the manifest kindness of God, and our relationship with God has become pure response. We do not initiate anything in this world, much less the power of love. We love in response to the love of God, "not that we love God but that he loved us." Apart from God, love is impossible. Apart from love, God is impossible.

Francis of Assisi was a pampered son of a cloth merchant who discovered in his worldly quests that he was a lost soul without meaning or direction in life. He was a romantic, both self-indulgent and generous with his father's wealth, but he was also empty. One day as he was riding aimlessly, Francis was confronted by a leper. A magnificent compulsion overcame his fear, and he leaped from his horse to embrace and kiss the dying man. This was the beginning of a new life of loving others more than being loved, of giving more than having. Chesterton wrote about the conversion of Francis that Assisi saw a camel go through the eye of a needle. We are witnesses to the love of God, not only in the prayer of St. Francis but in the discovery that it is more blessed to give than to receive.—Larry Dipboye

SUNDAY, DECEMBER 31, 2006
Lectionary Message

Topic: More Than a New Year

TEXT: Col. 3:12–17

Other Readings: 1 Sam. 2:18–20, 26; Ps. 148; Luke 2:41–52

I. The changing period of time offers renewal of life.

(a) We always celebrate the beginning of a new year (and sometimes, even more, the end of an old year). The reason for this kind of celebration, often accompanied by fireworks and feasting, is to add to the joy in the prospect of renewed opportunity to do things as they ought to be done, to start not only a new time in life but even a new life. We have all quite recently celebrated the first days, months, and years of a new century and a new millennium. Each of these periods will, later in history, be referred to by special, specific terms: "That was a great year of recovery"; "That was a century of great production in literature and art"; "That millennium brought civilization to its most advanced point through discovery and learning."

(b) We may someday describe our own times as that description will be worked out over the centuries, but the particular time we're in is not the important element of our life. What we do with that time is immeasurably more significant. Those who accept the gift of Christ's forgiveness as their own must be concerned that their works are in conformity with the character of Christ. So Paul gives a brief outline of the elements that constitute such a Christian character.

II. Believers in Christ who would sincerely "redeem the time" for him can develop the qualities that will mark them and enrich their experiences as followers of the divine King.

(a) Having "a heart of compassion" is an involvement of a person's entire range of emotional feelings and reactions, acknowledging the power of unpleasantness to cause real internal upset or the grip of pity to soften one's actions and impel deeds of kindness. The idea of compassion is that one is emotionally inclined to help and to extend kindness to anyone who is hurt or suffering.

(b) Kindness grows from a compassionate nature. It is the expression of "feeling with" someone else to the point not only of sparing that person from suffering but even of entering into that suffering.

(c) Humbleness results when one compares oneself to higher standards. No matter to what degree one excels in skills or kinds of knowledge, some skills or qualities always remain that are imperfect. Humbleness drives a person to realize that and consider others as deserving of respect.

(d) Meekness and longsuffering are practiced by being self-effacing to a certain point and being patient with others in one's expectations. Meekness and patience result from spending long, regular hours in the company of Jesus Christ, through reading his word and praying.

III. By dedicating the new year to being the kind of person described in our text, a Christian becomes a living exponent of what has been called The Golden Rule, and is, in our text, described as "putting on love" and "forgiving others even as Christ forgave you." It is illuminating to discover the frequency with which this quality of personality is described in the New Testament (Matt. 7:12; Luke 6:31, 37; Gal. 5:14; Rom. 13:8–11; James 2:8–13; 1 Tim. 1:5), and even occasionally in the Old Testament (Hos. 6:6).

(a) A prime characteristic of such a nature is the regularity of praise—praise of God and of Christ in constant recognition of one's new standing before the Lord as a product of his loving gift. A current television ad features people, out of the blue, saying "Thank you!" to a companion. It always startles the companion ("Nothing like that has happened to me!") but is always met with heightened pleasure. God should be thanked more often, perhaps, than most of us usually thank him. Our text describes the use of "psalms and hymns and spiritual song," and there is hardly any better way to do that than by attending the worship services of one's church fellowship, taking part in reading and singing praise. It will make the whole year better.

(b) A life of prayer is a natural accompaniment of following Christ in apostleship. The believer can conceive of no other means of strengthening his life of compassion and love than by speaking with Jesus Christ in a habitual sharing of joy, as well as desires. Prayer is the method by which a believer "gives thanks to God the Father." It is also the means of asking God to apply his loving power to the strong desires of our lives: for the help of our friends, for extensions of his kingdom, for protection in danger, for national unity, and even for forgiveness by and for our opponents, personally and nationally. For these reasons, especially in the busiest kind of life, the believer needs to be a person with a regular prayer life.

(c) In many of the Scriptures mentioned earlier, the phrase justifying the instruction is, "For this is the law and the prophets" or "He that loves has fulfilled the law." God's early law in the Ten Commandments embodies love for one's neighbor and for the whole world. The finest and also most satisfying pattern of life for the new year is the one described in this passage. It may also not only create the best new year but may even result in a "New You."—John R. Rodman

SERMON SUGGESTIONS

Topic: The Word of God

TEXT: John 1:1–14

(1) The pre-incarnate Word (Heb. 1:1–12), we see: Jesus' relation to God; his relation to creation; his relation to humankind; his relation to previous revelations. (2) The incarnate Word: the purpose of the incarnation; the facts of this incarnation; the witness of the incarnation—"full of grace and truth."[9]

---

[9]Compare: Frederick Herman Lindemann, *The Sermon and the Propers*, Vol. I (St. Louis: Concordia Publishing House), p. 73f.

Topic: You Are the Light of the World

TEXT: Matt. 5:14–16 (see also John 8:12; Matt. 14:12; 2 Cor. 4:6)

(1) Our light is borrowed light. (2) If so, our light is a light that needs care. (3) If we are the light of the world, we can be certain that the light will accomplish remarkable things: remove racial ugliness and imperfection; warm and strengthen; guide.

WORSHIP AIDS

CALL TO WORSHIP.   "Praise the Lord. Give thanks to the Lord, for he is good; his love endures forever" (Ps. 106:1 NIV).

INVOCATION.   Lord, there is a sense of finality in our coming together today. We are closing the book on one chapter of our experience and looking forward to another. Help us to look back with penitence for our sins and gratitude for all your blessings. Help us to look forward with awe because of the challenges that face us and with confidence because of the strength we find in you. Help us to look upon this hour you have given us as one more opportunity for worship and for promise.—James M. King

OFFERTORY SENTENCE.   "And when they had come into the house, they saw the young child with Mary his mother, and fell down, and worshipped him; and when they had opened their treasures, they presented to him gifts; gold, and frankincense, and myrrh" (Matt. 2:11).

OFFERTORY PRAYER.   Lord of life, let us not lay up for ourselves treasures on Earth, rather let us lay up treasures in heaven where neither moth nor rust can corrupt nor thieves break through and steal. In the incorruptible name of Jesus, we pray.—E. Lee Phillips

PRAYER.   Your love for us never ends, eternal God, even when by age or weakness we can no longer work. When we retire, keep us awake to your will for us. Give us energy to enjoy the world, to attend to neighbors busy people neglect, and to contribute wisely to the life of the Church. If we can offer nothing but our prayers, remind us that our prayers are a useful work you want, so that we may live always serving Jesus Christ, our hope and our true joy.[10]

SERMON

Topic: Political Refugee

TEXT: Matt. 2:13–23

Somebody once told me there was not very much education in the second kick of a mule. One good kick should be all we need to teach us not to go there. There is not much additional information learned the second time you are kicked. But here is Joseph, facing the second experience of "lie by a dream." You remember that he was told by an angel in a dream to go ahead and marry Mary and to have the child and name it Jesus. He has done that. He has

---

[10]*The Worship Book* (Philadelphia: Westminster Press, 1970).

directed his life on the basis of a dream. Isn't that enough? Like Abraham, hasn't he proved his faith and his obedience? What else does God want to learn about Joseph? Joseph has listened to the prompting of the Holy Spirit, as given by the angel. He has been obedient. What more is there?

What's left is to find out if Joseph knows that faith is not a one-time decision! Faith is the deciding every day to be obedient. Faith is the constant battle between the temptation to live on the basis of the visible, that is, to act and be guided by the principle, "Everybody does it" and to hope and dream for what you know is possible, or to decide to live on the hope of the dreams created by the promises of God. Faith is not just one big decision. Faith is a lifetime of little decisions made over and over, day by day. Will you be faithful today? Will you trust God to guide you? Or will you follow what Wall Street says is the "street wisdom."

Some people answer the question about being saved by describing a particular time and date as the moment they made the decision to follow Jesus Christ, as if the decision of faith were a one-shot deal. But most of us, I think, are more like Joseph. No sooner have we made a great leap of faith and commitment than there comes a second dream—another challenge, another decision to be made on reasonable and normal logic or will be made on the basis of the movement and proddings of the Holy Spirit. Joseph has followed the dream once; now he is facing the question of obedience again. Faith may begin by a turning around of our lives, but all along the journey in the new direction there is the temptation to turn back around. Maybe we were headed in the right direction the first time—the other way seemed so much easier. Am I sure I am on the right road? Faith is a constant trusting oneself to the mystery of the direction of God.

When Jesus was tempted in the wilderness after the forty days of hunger, the devil left Jesus. Scripture does not say that Satan gave up and left him alone completely; it says that Satan left to look for a more opportune time. There is the second dream. Joseph discovers that faith is not a won possession. It is not a deal made and forgotten. It is a renewing of the commitment to follow and obey God's unpredictable spirit. Joseph listens again to the voice of God in the dream and gathers up his loved ones and heads for a strange land, and so becomes a political refugee.

On the way into Egypt, Joseph and his family become part of one of the dark dimensions of life. I dare say most of us are not very familiar with this dark side of life. Maybe we hire them. Maybe we know something about this endless stream of people who are refugees from their homes: migrant workers, immigrants—legal and illegal. Joseph, Mary, and Jesus head toward Egypt because the political powers are killing babies. Joseph, Mary, and Jesus know what the fear tastes like—that fear that runs in the blood because you are not safe in your own place. Joseph takes the baby to Egypt because nobody knows when the knock on the door will be the secret police come to kill the male children under two years old. Jesus came to Earth to share our pains and our sorrows, and from his birth he has known the fear and terror of political violence.

According to a United Nations Development Programs report, there are nearly 125 million people, or almost 2 percent of the world's population, who are living outside their country of birth or where they would want to live. They are refugees from ethnic cleansing, from ancient tribal hostilities in Africa, from Pol Pot political butcherings, from Chinese discrimination against human rights, from Pinochet's secret police, who carry off children and the children are never heard from again.

Jesus came into our world as God's love to share our human struggles and to declare that in the midst of our pain God is present with us. Jesus knows the pain of the dispossessed and the terrorized. Jesus knows the fears at night because the darkness is the best time for cruelty and evil to strike. From his birth Jesus becomes acquainted with our fears and our pains. "Nobody knows the trouble I've seen. Nobody knows but Jesus." Flee into Egypt because Herod is killing the children.

Somebody suggested that most of the time at Christmas we like to take Herod out of the story. Herod is not present among the plastic Santas, reindeer, and nativity scenes. We watch G-rated specials of "Scrooge" and the "Grinch Who Stole Christmas," but we keep Herod way out of the picture. This means we end up offering a sanitized version of the good news. When Herod forces his way back into the story, we are confronted again with the reality of the evil world in which we live and to which God came as grace.

Herod is an important piece in Matthew's story. Herod is part of the pattern:

Joseph, Mary, and Jesus go into Egypt because life where they are is not life-sustaining. Abraham and his family went into Egypt because there was a famine.
Joseph goes to Egypt on a journey with nothing but a promise from God. Abraham set out from Ur with nothing but a promise from God.
The Messiah child is retracing the steps of the chosen people. Jesus is repeating the journey of the covenant children of Israel.

Repeat the sounding joy. Repeat the sounding joy. Beneath the chaos and the violence of Herod, Matthew is pointing us to a larger picture of the pattern of God's grace working for the redemption of history. Slaughter of children, death by famine. Abraham and his family go into Egypt. Joseph, son of David, and his family flee to Egypt. Joseph, son of Abraham, and his virtues are constantly attacked. Goodness is always harassed and attacked by evil. Pharaoh decides to kill Jewish babies because there are too many of them. Herod is killing Jewish babies because they are a danger to his power. It is within Egypt that Moses and Jesus both find protection. The one called by God to bring salvation and redemption is protected and nurtured by the Egyptian government. God calls his people out of Egypt, brings them to Sinai, and creates the covenant with the Ten Commandments. Jesus comes out of Egypt to Calvary and establishes the new covenant on the cross with the one commandment, "that you love one another as I have loved you." Matthew tells the story as a repetition and fulfillment of the old story. Matthew sees beneath the scattered and frightening events around us the hidden hand of God, working and guiding and shaping history.

Looking at the surface of things, we may get tempted just to see Herod's deadly desire to hold on to his political power—a sad bit of partisan politics, a tiny tyrant who must kill any opposition because he knows he cannot rule by popular support. Joseph and his family, just another innocent family caught up in the power politics, who has to flee from Kosovo to save their lives! Political refugees. Events looking out of control. Life is just the struggle to find bread and water, full of suffering, lacking in meaning. But Matthew sees deeper than that. Matthew can see a pattern. Matthew can see a structure to what is happening. Matthew sees the pieces coming together as part of a greater purpose. Matthew sees it all as part of the master purpose of God's grace and redemption.

Did you happen to see the "Foxtrot" comic strip recently, when Jason Fox was making his elaborate Christmas nativity scene? When he came to the crèche, he turned to his sister and said, "And you will see in the manger the savior of our Christmas." Paige says, "Jason, that is a credit card." And Jason says, "Are those storm clouds gathering out there?"

There was another Christmas pageant at another church where the pageant went the way of all such childhood pageants at first. The magi appeared in long robes, carrying large and expensive-looking boxes wrapped in gold and silver foil. There were the shepherds in bathrobes. They all gathered around the manger. Yet the highlight came when Mary unwrapped the babe in swaddling clothes and revealed not a cuddly baby doll but a cross. In silence, Mary held the cross over the manger.

It does not take much faith to look at the world and to see the horrors of Bosnia and Palestine and Pol Pot and Pinochet. It does not take a lot of faith to see the reckless greed of hedge fund investors, putting the economies of the world in danger for a few dollars more.

But to be able to see beneath these harsh realities, to be able to see beyond the cynicism and the sarcasm, to be able to see beyond the slaughter of the innocent and the viciousness of the political tyrants, to see deep down by the light of this child Jesus, whom we welcome again as the Christ, to see and rejoice and affirm that this birth is part of God's great plan, to see that there is a providence and purpose that leads from this manger to the cross for the salvation of the world, to believe that all of the strange and confusing events of the world around us are surrounded by the goodness and mercy of God, and to trust ourselves to the promises of God made in this child, that this child shows us the true nature of the glory and power, majesty and mercy of God, is to see the world as Matthew sees it. The flight into Egypt is part of the deeper, wider, and holy purpose of God—to redeem creation. Our faith in the power of God in Jesus Christ is more than sufficient for all the evils around us. Can you see it?—Rick Brand

CONGREGATIONAL MUSIC RELATED TO THE LECTIONARY

BY PAUL RICHARDSON

The hymns have been chosen for their relation to the Scripture readings for each service. They are not merely compatible with the theme of the pericope but reflect the particular language, imagery, or content of the passage. Several choices are provided for some readings; others have no readily accessible companion in the hymnic literature. Sometimes the scriptural link, though evident, is not that of traditional usage (for example, "Joy to the World," typically sung at Christmas, is a paraphrase of Psalm 98 and is listed with that reading). The use of a familiar text in a different context can prompt new awareness of both Scripture and hymn.

Because hymn texts have often been altered, even in their first lines, the author's surname or the source is provided as an aid to location. No judgments are made as to authenticity of attributions, nor are preferences expressed for particular translations. The texts are listed in alphabetical order within each grouping.

Three hymns appear more than twice during the year and are identified in connection with multiple passages. Learning and repeating these in their various relationships offers a way to expand a congregation's enduring repertory for worship and devotion. These hymns are:

"Blessed Jesus, Living Bread" (Vajda)
"Like the Murmur of the Dove's Song" (Daw)
"O Love, How Deep, How Broad, How High" (anonymous Latin, sometimes attributed
    to Thomas à Kempis; also translated "O Love, How Vast, How Flowing Free")

The first of these—Jaroslav Vajda's "Blessed Jesus, Living Bread"—presents an unusual opportunity. It is based on John 6 and provides stanzas for five consecutive weeks beginning July 30.

If a hymn is widely published, no source is cited. For those found in only one of the hymnals listed here, that book is indicated using the following abbreviations:

BH *The Baptist Hymnal* (Nashville, Tenn.: Convention Press, 1991)
CH *Chalice Hymnal* (St. Louis: Chalice Press, 1995)
HWB *Hymnal: A Worship Book* (Elgin, Ill.: Brethren Press, 1992)
NCH *The New Century Hymnal* (Cleveland: The Pilgrim Press, 1995)
PH *The Presbyterian Hymnal* (Louisville, Ky.: Westminster John Knox Press, 1990)
RS *RitualSong: A Hymnal and Service Book for Roman Catholics* (Chicago: GIA, 1996)

UMH *The United Methodist Hymnal: Book of United Methodist Worship* (Nashville: United Methodist Publishing House, 1989)

WC *The Worshiping Church* (Carol Stream, Ill.: Hope Publishing, 1990)

Particular mention must be made of *Hymns for the Gospels* (Chicago: GIA, 2001), an anthology of texts chosen specifically for use with the Gospel readings for most Sundays in the three-year lectionary. Because of its focus and function, this collection is cited with the abbreviation HG for every relevant text, even if it also appears in one or more of the hymnals.

Another collection of hymns directly related to the lectionary is Carol Doran and Thomas H. Troeger's *New Hymns for the Lectionary: To Glorify the Maker's Name* (New York: Oxford University Press, 1986), which contains hymns for Sundays of Year B—the cycle that runs through the first eleven months of 2006. These hymns, some of which are also found in the hymnals listed, are marked with NHL. Troeger's texts (without musical settings) are also found in his subsequent anthology, *Borrowed Light: Hymn Texts, Prayers, and Poems* (New York: Oxford University Press, 1994). It is instructive for preachers to observe how this prominent practitioner of homiletics has approached the biblical texts. This model—reading hymns for potential insights for preaching—can add new facets to the understanding gleaned from commentaries.

Hymns identified with the Psalm readings are closely related to the corresponding text, in keeping with the design of the Revised Common Lectionary, which intends that the Psalm itself be a response to the first lesson. Because numerous recently published resources, including many hymnals, provide brief responses for use with the reading or chanting of the Psalms, none of these is cited here. Rather, all hymns listed in connection with the Psalms are metrical versions; that is, they are in traditional multi-stanza hymn form. Many of these come from *The Presbyterian Hymnal.* A more extensive collection of stanzaic Psalm settings is found in the Christian Reformed Church's *Psalter Hymnal* (Grand Rapids, Mich.: CRC, 1987), which contains metrical versions of all 150 Psalms.

Those who would use hymns not found in their own congregational hymnal are reminded of the obligation, both legal and ethical, to observe the copyright law. Each of the collections cited provides clear information about copyright owners and agents. Three services make available a wide range of this material without great cost or complex paperwork:

Christian Copyright License International (17201 NE Sacramento Street, Portland, OR 97230; www.ccli.com)

LicenSing: Copyright-cleared Music for Churches (Logos Productions, 6160 Carmen Avenue East, Inver Grove Heights, MN 55076-4422; www.joinhands.com)

OneLicense.net (found on the Web at that address)

Though all three are useful, the last is particularly so with the literature covered here, as it provides access to materials from GIA and Oxford University Press.

January 1

Isaiah 61:10–62:3 "Graced with Garments of Great Gladness" (Franck) NCH; "Jesus, Thy Blood and Righteousness" (Zinzendorf) WC; "Live into Hope of Captives Freed" (Huber) PH; "Now Is the Time Approaching" (Borthwick) NCH

Psalm 148 "All Creatures of Our God and King" (Francis of Assisi); "Creating God, Your Fingers Trace" (Rowthorn); "God Created Heaven and Earth" (anonymous Taiwanese); "Let the Whole Creation Cry" (Brooks); "Praise the Lord! Ye Heavens Adore Him" (anonymous English); "Stars and Planets Flung in Orbit" (Stuempfle) NCH

Galatians 4:4–7 "My God, My Heart Accept This Day" (Bridges) NCH

Luke 2:22–40 "Come, Thou Long-Expected Jesus" (Wesley); "Lord, Bid Your Servant Go in Peace" (Quinn); "Lord God, You Now Have Set Your Servant Free" (Whitney) PH; "Lord, Now Let Your Servant" (Seddon) WC; "My Master, See, the Time Has Come" (Luke 2:29–32) UMH; "Now May Your Servant, Lord" (Westra) PH; "See Mary Setting Out at Dawn" (Vajda) HG; "Sing of Mary, Meek and Lowly" (Palmer) RS; "Though Every Sun Shall Spend Its Fire" (Troeger) NHL

EPIPHANY
January 8

Isaiah 60:1–6 "Arise, Shine Out, Your Light Has Come" (Wren) UMH; "Arise, Your Light Is Come" (Duck); "Keep Awake, Be Always Ready" (Clyde) NCH; "Morning Star, O Cheering Sight" (Scheffler) HWB; "O Splendor of God's Glory Bright" (Ambrose); "Rise, Shine, You People" (Klug) UMH

Psalm 72:1–7, 10–14 "Hail to the Lord's Anointed" (Montgomery); "Jesus Shall Reign Where'er the Sun" (Watts)

Ephesians 3:1–12 [none]

Matthew 2:1–12 "A Star Not Mapped on Human Charts" (Troeger) NHL; "Angels from the Realms of Glory" (Montgomery); "As with Gladness Men of Old" (Dix); "Bright and Glorious Is the Sky" (Grundtvig) HWB; "Brightest and Best of the Sons of the Morning" (Heber; also found beginning "Hail the Blest Morn"); "Famed Though the World's Great Cities Be" (Shanley) HG; "From a Distant Home" (traditional Puerto Rican); "Midnight Stars Make Bright the Sky" (anonymous Chinese) PH; "On This Day Earth Shall Ring" (*Piae Cantiones*); "Sing We Now of Christmas" (traditional French); "The First Noel the Angel Did Say" (traditional English); "The Magi Who to Bethlehem Did Go" (Juncas) NCH; "We Three Kings of Orient Are" (Hopkins); "What Child Is This, Who, Laid to Rest" (Dix); "When Christ's Appearing Was Made Known" (Sedulius) HWB; "Wise Men, They Came to Look for Wisdom" (Idle) WC

January 15

1 Samuel 3:1–10 (11–20) "Open Now Thy Gates of Beauty" (Schmolk); "Speak, Lord, in the Stillness" (Grimes) WC; "When Heaven's Voice Was Still" (Troeger) NHL

Psalm 139:1–6, 13–18 "You Are Before Me, Lord" (Pitt-Watson) PH

1 Corinthians 6:12–20 "Take My Life, and Let It Be" (Havergal); "We Praise You with Our Minds, O Lord" (McElrath)

John 1:43–51 "We Need No Ladder Now" (Stuempfle) HG

January 22

Jonah 3:1–5, 10 [none]

Psalm 62:5–12 "All My Hope on God Is Founded" (Neander) NCH; "God of Our Strength, Enthroned Above" (Crosby) HWB; "My Soul Waits in Silence for God" (Anderson) PH

1 Corinthians 7:29–31 [none]

Mark 1:14–20 "Dear Lord and Father of Mankind" (Whittier); "I Danced in the Morning" (Carter); "Jesus Calls Us, O'er the Tumult" (Alexander); "Lord, You Have Come to the Lakeshore" (Gabaraín); "To Those Who Knotted Nets of Twine" (Troeger) NHL; "Two Fishermen, Who Lived Along the Sea of Galilee" (Toolan); "You Walk Along Our Shoreline" (Dunstan) HG

January 29
Deuteronomy 18:15–20 [none]
Psalm 111 "God's Holy Ways Are Just and True" (Wollett) WC
1 Corinthians 8:1–13 [none]
Mark 1:21–28 "Silence! Frenzied, Unclean Spirit" (Troeger) HG, NHL

February 5
Isaiah 40:21–31 "Arise, Your Light Is Come" (Duck); "Be Strong in the Lord" (Johnson)
Psalm 147:1–11, 20c "Now Praise the Lord, All Living Saints" (Anderson) PH
1 Corinthians 9:16–23 [none]
Mark 1:29–39 "At Evening, When the Sun Had Set" (Twells) HWB; "Beyond the Press and Pull of Crowds" (Troeger) NHL; "By Peter's House in Village Fair" (Albright) HWB; "O Christ the Healer, We Have Come" (Green) HG; "Your Hands, O Lord, in Days of Old" (Plumptre) RS

February 12
2 Kings 5:1–14 [none]
Psalm 30 "Come Sing to God, O Living Saints" (Anderson) PH
1 Corinthians 9:24–27 "Awake, My Soul, Stretch Every Nerve" (Doddridge); "Forth in Thy Name, O Lord, I Go" (Wesley)
Mark 1:40–45 "Jesus' Hands Were Kind Hands" (Cropper); "Shackled By a Heavy Burden" (Gaither); "The Leper's Soul Was No Less Scarred" (Troeger) NHL; "We Give God Thanks for Those Who Knew" (Perry) HG; "Your Hands, O Lord, in Days of Old" (Plumptre) RS

February 19
Isaiah 43:18–25 "Gangling Desert Birds Will Sing" (Troeger) NHL
Psalm 41 [none]
2 Corinthians 1:18–22 "Standing on the Promises of Christ My King" (Carter)
Mark 2:1–12 "I Danced in the Morning" (Carter); "In the Stillness of the Evening" (Ellingsen) HWB; "Now in This Banquet" (Haugen) RS; "Sing Praise to God for Friends" (Stuempfle) HG; "Songs of Thankfulness and Praise" (Wordsworth); "We Have the Strength to Lift and Bear" (Troeger) NHL

February 26
2 Kings 2:1–12 "God of the Prophets, Bless the Prophet's Heirs" (Wortman) NHC; "Swing Low, Sweet Chariot" (spiritual) UMH
Psalm 50:1–6 "Golden Breaks the Dawn" (Chao)
2 Corinthians 4:3–6 "O Splendor of God's Glory Bright" (Ambrose); "Strong Son of God, Immortal Love" (Tennyson) HWB
Mark 9:2–9 "Christ, Upon/Jesus on the Mountain Peak" (Wren); "Jesus, Take Us to the Mountain" (Vajda) NCH; "O Wondrous Sight! O Vision Fair" (*Sarum Breviary*); "Swiftly Pass the

Clouds of Glory" (Troeger) PH; "'Tis Good, Lord, to Be Here" (Robinson) RS; "Transform Us as You, Transfigured" (Dunstan) HG; "We Have Come at Christ's Own Bidding" (Daw) NCH

LENT
March 5
Genesis 9:8–17 "Sing of Colors" (Mexican folk song) NCH
Psalm 25:1–10 "Lord, to You My Soul Is Lifted" (Wiersma) PH
1 Peter 3:18–22 "Thy Holy Wings, O Savior" (Sandell-Berg) UMH
Mark 1:4–15 "Christ, When for Us You Were Baptized" (Tucker) PH; "Lord, When You Came to Jordan" (Wren) PH; "Lord, Who Throughout These Forty Days" (Hernaman); "Mark How the Lamb of God's Self-Offering" (Daw) HG; "Neither Desert Wind Nor Sun" (Troeger) NHL; "O Love, How Deep, How Broad, How High" (anonymous Latin; also translated "O Love, How Vast, How Flowing Free"); "O Radiant Christ, Incarnate Word" (Duck) NCH; "What Ruler Wades Through Murky Streams" (Troeger) NCH; "When Jesus Came to Jordan" (Green)

March 12
Genesis 17:1–7, 15–16 [none]
Psalm 22:23–31 "Amid the Thronging Worshipers" (*The Psalter*, 1912) WC
Romans 4:13–25 "Let Us Hope When Hope Seems Hopeless" (Beebe) NCH
Mark 8:31–38 "Before the Cross of Jesus" (Blanchard); "I Can Hear My Savior Calling" (Blandy); "Make Our Church One Joyful Choir" (Troeger) HG; "Take Up Thy Cross and Follow Me" (McKinney); "Take Up Thy Cross, the Savior Said" (Everest); "Who Now Would Follow Christ in Life" (*Ausbund*) HWB

March 19
Exodus 20:1–17 [none]
Psalm 19 "God's Law Is Perfect and Gives Life" (Webber) PH; "Nature with Open Volume Stands" (Watts); "O Sing Unto the Lord" (Rosas); "The Heavens Above Declare God's Praise" (Webber) PH; "The Stars Declare His Glory" (Dudley-Smith) RS
1 Corinthians 1:18–25 "Ask Ye What Great Thing I Know" (Schwedler); "Darkness Is Gone" (Bell) RS; "Here Hangs a Man Discarded" (Wren) CH
John 2:13–22 "You Strode Within the Temple, Lord" (Stuempfle) HG

March 26
Numbers 21:4–9 [none]
Psalm 107:1–3, 17–22 [none]
Ephesians 2:4–20 "Amazing Grace! How Sweet the Sound" (Newton); "Great God of Wonders! All Thy Ways" (Davies) HWB; "Let Us Plead for Faith Alone" (Wesley) UMH; "Marvelous Grace of Our Loving Lord" (Johnston); "Not What These Hands Have Done" (Bonar); "We Are God's Work of Art" (Haugen) RS; "What Mercy and Divine Compassion" (Hiller) HWB; "Wonderful Grace of Jesus" (Lillenas)
John 3:14–21 "A Spendthrift Lover Is the Lord" (Troeger) NHL; "Alone and Filled with Fear" (Stuempfle) HG; "As Moses Raised the Serpent Up" (NCH editors) NCH; "For God So Loved the World" (Whitney) BH; "For God So Loved Us" (Rische) HWB; "Give to Our God Immortal Praise" (Watts) WC; "God Loved the World" (Lippen and Opfer) NCH; "God Sent His Son"

(Gaither); "Love One Another" (Chepponis) RS; "Of the Father's Love Begotten" (Prudentius); "To God Be the Glory" (Crosby)

April 2
Jeremiah 31:31–34 "Deep Within I Will Plant My Law" (Haas) RS; "O God, Who Gives Us Life" (Daw) HWB
Psalm 51:1–12 "Have Mercy On Us, Living Lord" (Anderson) PH; "Have Mercy in Your Goodness, Lord" (Webber) WC
Hebrews 5:5–10 "In a Lowly Manger Born" (Yuki) NCH
John 12:20–33 "Before the Fruit Is Ripened by the Sun" (Troeger) HG, NHL; "In the Bulb There Is a Flower" (Sleeth); "Lift High the Cross" (Kitchin and Newbolt); "O Jesus, I Have Promised" (Bode); "The Work Is Thine, O Christ" (Preiswerk and Zaremba) HWB; "Unless a Grain of Wheat" (Farrell) RS; "When Christ Was Lifted from the Earth" (Wren) BH

April 9
For the *Liturgy of the Palms*

Matt. 21:1–11 "A Cheering, Chanting, Dizzy Crowd" (Troeger) NHL; "All Glory, Laud, and Honor" (Theodulph of Orleans); "Filled with Excitement, All the Happy Throng" (Avila); "Hosanna, Loud Hosanna" (Threlfall); "My Song Is Love Unknown" (Crossman); "Rejoice, O Zion's Daughter" (Stuempfle) HG; "Ride On, Jesus, Ride" (spiritual and Haugen) RS; "Ride On, Ride On in Majesty" (Milman)
Psalm 118:1–2, 19–20 "Open Now Thy Gates of Beauty" (Schmolck); "This Is the Day the Lord Hath Made" (Watts)

For the *Liturgy of the Passion*

Isaiah 50:4–9a [none]
Psalm 31:9–16 "God of Our Life, Through All the Circling Years" (Kerr); "God of the Ages" (Clarkson) WC; "In You, Lord, Have I Put My Trust" (Reissner) PH
Philippians 2:5–11 "A Hymn of Glory Let Us Sing" (Venerable Bede; also translated "Sing We Triumphant Hymns of Praise"); "Alas! and Did My Savior Bleed" (Watts); "All Authority and Power" (Idle) WC; "All Hail the Power of Jesus' Name" (Perronet and Rippon); "All Praise to Thee, for Thou, O King Divine" (Tucker; also found beginning "All Praise to Christ"); "At the Name of Jesus" (Noel); "Christ, Who Is in the Form of God" (Koyzis) HWB; "Creator of the Stars of Night" (anonymous Latin); "Emptied of His Glory" (Johnson, Cloninger, and Fettke) BH; "Jesus Came, the Heavens Adoring" (Thring); "Jesus, the Name High Over All" (Wesley) UMH; "Let All Together Praise Our God" (Herman) HWB; "Man of Sorrows, What a Name" (Bliss); "Morning Glory, Starlit Sky" (Vanstone) UMH; "My Lord of Light, Who Made the Worlds" (Idle) WC; "O Love, How Deep, How Broad, How High" (anonymous Latin; also translated "O Love, How Vast, How Flowing Free"); "Of the Father's Love Begotten" (Prudentius); "Praise the God Who Changes Places" (Wren) RS; "Sing Praise to the Father" (Clarkson) WC

Matt. 26:14–27:66 "A Purple Robe, a Crown of Thorns" (Dudley-Smith) WC; "A Woman Came Who Did Not Count the Cost" (Leach) NCH; "An Upper Room Did Our Lord Prepare" (Green); "At the Cross, Her Vigil Keeping" (anonymous Latin); "Before the Cock Crew Twice" (Pjeturssen) HWB; "Christ at the Table There with Friends" (Miller) NCH; "For the Bread Which You Have Broken" (Benson); "Go to Dark Gethsemane" (Montgomery); "Here in Our Upper Room with You" (Robinson) HWB; "How Great Your Mercy, Risen Lord" (Stuempfle) HG; "How Shallow Former Shadows Seem" (Daw) HWB; "It Was a Sad and Solemn Night" (Watts) NCH; "Jesus, Take Us to the Mountain" (Vajda) NCH; "My God, My God, Why Have You Forsaken Me?" (Psalm 22) HWB; "Ruler of Life, We Crown You Now" (Hussey) NCH; "Sing, My Tongue, the Glorious Battle/The Song of Triumph" (Fortunatus); "The Time Was Early Evening" (Iona Community) NCH; "'Tis Midnight, and on Olive's Brow" (Tappan); "To Mock Your Reign, O Dearest Lord" (Green) UMH; "O Sacred Head, Now Wounded" (anonymous Latin); "They Crucified My Savior" (spiritual) HWB; "Were You There When They Crucified My Lord?" (spiritual); "When in Our Music God Is Glorified?" (Green); "Why Has God Forsaken Me?" (Wallace) HWB

EASTERTIDE

April 16, Easter Day

Acts 10:34–43 [none]

Psalm 118:1–2, 14–24 "Open Now Thy Gates of Beauty" (Schmolck); "This Is the Day the Lord Hath Made" (Watts)

1 Corinthians 15:1–11 "Christ Is Risen, Christ Is Living" (Martínez); "This Is the Threefold Truth" (Green)

John 20:1–18 "I Come to the Garden Alone" (Miles); "O Mary, Don't You Weep, Don't You Mourn" (spiritual) UMH; "On This Day, the First of Days" (anonymous Latin); "The First Day of the Week" (Green) BH; "The Sun Was Bright That Easter Dawn" (Stuempfle) HG; "Thine Is the Glory" (Budry); "Woman, Weeping in the Garden" (Damon) CH

April 23

Acts 4:34–35 "Heart and Mind, Possessions, Lord" (Sangle) HWB; "O for a World Where Everyone" (Winter) NCH; "O God, the Creator" (Haile and Corbett) NCH; "When God the Spirit Came" (Dudley-Smith)

Psalm 133 "Behold the Goodness of the Lord" (Anderson) PH; "How Good a Thing It Is" (Seddon) HWB; "O Look and Wonder" (Sosa) CH

1 John 1:1–2:2 "Awake from Your Slumber" (Schutte) RS; "Each Morning Brings Us Fresh Outpoured" (Zwick) HWB; "God Is Love, and All Who Live in Love Live in God" (Haas) RS; "I Want to Walk as a Child of the Light" (Thomerson); "We Hold the Death of the Lord Deep in Our Hearts" (Haas) RS; "When in the Hour of Deepest Need" (Eber) HWB; "When We Walk with the Lord" (Sammis)

John 20:19–31 "Breathe on Me, Breath of God" (Hatch); "Chosen and Sent by the Father" (Clarkson) HG; "Jesus, Sovereign, Savior" (Kirkland) NCH; "Jesus, Stand Among Us" (Pennefather); "Not with Naked Eye" (Damon) NCH; "O Sons and Daughters of the Lord" (Tisserand); "Show Me Your Hands, Your Feet, Your Side" (Dunstan) HG; "These Things Did Thomas Count as Real" (Troeger) NCH, NHL; "We Walk by Faith and Not by Sight" (Alford)

April 30

Acts 3:12–19 [none]

Psalm 4 [none]

1 John 3:1–7 "God Is Love, and All Who Live in Love Live in God" (Haas) RS; "I Then Shall Live as One Who's Been Forgiven" (Gaither) WC; "Jesus, Thy Boundless Love to Me" (Gerhardt); "My Song Is Love Unknown" (Crossman); "When the Lord in Glory Comes" (Dudley-Smith) WC

Luke 24:36b–48 "Go, Make of All Disciples" (Adkins); "Jesus, Sovereign, Savior" (Kirkland) NCH; "Jesus, Stand Among Us" (Pennefather); "Joy Dawned Again on Easter Day" (anonymous Latin) NCH; "Prince of Peace, Control My Will" (Barber) HWB; "See the Splendor of the Morning" (Felciano)

May 7

Acts 4:5–12 "A Single Unmatched Stone" (Troeger) NHL; "Christ Is Made the Sure Foundation" (anonymous Latin); "Christ Is Our Cornerstone" (anonymous Latin) HWB; "Come, O Spirit, Dwell Among Us" (Alford) PH; "O Christ, the Great Foundation" (Lew); "The Church's One Foundation" (Stone)

Psalm 23 "My Shepherd Will Supply My Need" (Watts); "The King of Love My Shepherd Is" (Baker); "The Lord My Shepherd Guards Me Well" (Daw) WC; "The Lord's My Shepherd, All My Need" (Webber); "The Lord's My Shepherd, I'll Not Want" (Huber); "The Lord's My Shepherd, I'll Not Want" (Scottish Psalter)

1 John 3:16–24 "Open My Eyes, That I May See" (Scott); "The Church of Christ in Every Age" (Green); "When the Church of Jesus Shuts Its Outer Door" (Green)

John 10:11–18 "Easter Alleluia" (Haugen) RS; "Gentle Shepherd, Come and Lead Us" (Gaither) HWB; "In Heavenly Love Abiding" (Waring); "Praise Him, Praise Him" (Crosby); "Savior, Like a Shepherd Lead Us" (Thrupp); "Shepherd of Tender Youth" (Clement of Alexandria) HWB; "You, Lord, Are Both Lamb and Shepherd" (Dunstan) HG

May 14

Acts 8:26–40 [none]

Psalm 22:25–31 "Amid the Thronging Worshipers" (The Psalter, 1912) WC

1 John 4:7–21 "Enter in the Realm of God" (Bayler) NCH; "God Is Love—His the Care" (Dearmer) WC; "God Is Love, Let Heaven Adore Him" (Rees) WC; "How like a Gentle Spirit Deep Within" (Lincoln); "I Love Thee" (anonymous) BH; "I Sought the Lord, and Afterward I Knew" (anonymous); "Jesus a New Commandment Has Given Us" (Loperena) NCH; "Let There Be Light, Lord God of Hosts" (Vories); "Love One Another, for Love Is of God" (Chepponis) RS; "Many Are the Lightbeams" (Cyprian of Carthage) RS; "My Jesus, I Love Thee" (Featherstone); "Now Let Us Learn of Christ" (Idle) WC; "O God of Love, Enable Me" (Duncan) BH; "O Love of God, How Strong and True" (Bonar) HWB; "Where Charity and Love Prevail" (anonymous Latin); "Where True Love and Charity Are Found" (anonymous Latin) RS

John 15:1–8 "Bread of Heaven, on Thee We Feed" (Conder) PH; "God, Bless Your Church with Strength" (Dalles) PH; "Like the Murmur of the Dove's Song" (Daw); "Many Are the Lightbeams (Cyprian of Carthage) NCH; "O Come to Me, the Master Said" (Dudley-Smith) WC; "The Branch That Bends with Clustered Fruit" (Troeger) HG, NHL; "Thou True Vine That Heals" (Dearmer) NCH; "Unless a Grain of Wheat" (Farrell) RS

May 21

Acts 10:44–48 [none]

Psalm 98 "Joy to the World! The Lord Is Come" (Watts); "New Songs of Celebration Render" (Routley) PH; "Sing a New Song to the Lord" (Dudley-Smith); "Sing a New Song unto the Lord" (Schutte) RS; "To God Compose a Song of Joy" (Duck); "Too Splendid for Speech but Ripe for a Song" (Troeger) NHL

1 John 5:1–6 "Encamped Along the Hills of Light" (Yates) BH (hymns related to earlier passages in 1 John may be appropriate)

John 15:9–17 "Called as Partners in Christ's Service" (Huber); "From Pharoah to King Cyrus" (Troeger) NHL; "Heart with Loving Heart United" (Zinzendorf; also translated "Christian Hearts in Love United"); "Help Us Accept Each Other" (Kaan); "Jesu, Jesu, Fill Us with Your Love" (Colvin); "Jesus a New Commandment Has Given Us" (Loperena) NCH; "Jesus Is All the World to Me" (Thompson); "Let Us Be Bread" (Porter) RS; "My Lord, I Did Not Choose You" (Conder) BH; "O Come to Me, the Master Said" (Dudley-Smith) WC; "Praise the God Who Changes Places" (Wren) RS; "There Is No Greater Love" (Joncas) RS; "There's Not a Friend Like the Lowly Jesus" (Oatman) BH; "This Is My Will" (Quinn) HG; "What a Friend We Have in Jesus" (Scriven)

May 28

Acts 1:15–17, 21–26 [none]

Psalm 1 "How Blest Are They/The One Is Blest Who, Fearing God" (Gower); "Like a Tree Beside the Waters" (Martin) NCH

1 John 5:9–13 "Good Christians All, Rejoice and Sing" (Alington)

John 16:6–19 "For All the World" (Clarkson) HG; "In This World Abound Scrolls" (Yuya) NCH; "O Christ Jesus, Sent from Heaven" (Crawford) NCH

PENTECOST

June 4

Ezekiel 37:1–14 "Let It Breathe on Me" (Lewis-Butts) NCH

or

Acts 2:1–21 "Filled with the Spirit's Power" (Peacey); "Like the Murmur of the Dove's Song" (Daw); "O Breath of Life, Come Sweeping Through Us" (Head); "O Church of God, United" (Morley) UMH; "O Holy Dove of God Descending" (Leech); "O Spirit of the Living God" (Tweedy); "On Pentecost They Gathered" (Huber); "When God the Spirit Came" (Dudley-Smith); "Why Stare at Heaven's Distant Blue?" (Troeger) NHL; "Wind Who Makes All Winds That Blow" (Troeger)

Psalm 104:24–34, 35b "Bless the Lord, My Soul and Being" (Anderson) PH; "Many and Great, O God, Are Thy Ways" (Renville); "O Worship the King, All Glorious Above" (Grant)

Romans 8:22–27 "By Gracious Powers So Wonderfully Sheltered" (Bonhöffer); "Christ Is Coming! Let Creation" (MacDuff); "Eternal Spirit of the Living Christ" (Christierson); "God Is Working His Purpose Out" (Ainger); "If You Will Only Let God Guide You" (Neumark); "In Solitude" (Duck) NHC; "In the Bulb There Is a Flower" (Sleeth); "O God, Great Womb of Wondrous Love" (Loewen) HWB; "Prayer Is the Soul's Sincere Desire" (Montgomery); "Spirit, Come, Dispel Our Sadness" (Gerhardt) HWB; "We Do Not Know How to Pray as We Ought" (Luff) UMH

John 15:26–27, 16:4b–15 "Come, Lord Jesus, Send Us Your Spirit" (Haas) RS; "For Your Gift of God the Spirit (Clarkson) WC; "Holy Spirit, Come, Confirm Us" (Foley); "Holy Spirit, Truth Divine" (Longfellow); "Let Your Spirit Teach Me, Lord" (Clarkson) HG; "Like the Murmur of the Dove's Song" (Daw) HG; "O Trinity, Your Face We See" (Eschbach) NCH; "Spirit of Holiness, Wisdom and Faithfulness" (Idle) WC

June 11

Isaiah 6:1–8 "God Himself Is with Us/God Is Here Among Us" (Tersteegen); "God of Love and Truth and Beauty" (Rees) WC; "Holy God, We Praise Your Name" (Franz); "Holy, Holy, Holy, Lord God Almighty" (Heber); "I, the Lord of Sea and Sky" (Schutte); "Master, Thou Callest, I Gladly Obey" (Crosby) BH; "My God, How Wonderful Thou Art" (Faber) WC; "Stand Up and Bless the Lord" (Montgomery); "The Voice of God Is Calling" (Holmes); "Whom Shall I Send?" (Green)

Psalm 29 "The God of Heaven Thunders" (Perry) PH; "Worship the Lord in the Beauty of Holiness" (Monsell)

Romans 8:12–17 "For Your Gift of God the Spirit" (Clarkson) WC; "O Spirit of God, O Life-Giving Breath" (Niedling) NCH

John 3:1–17 "Alone and Filled with Fear" (Stuempfle) HG; "As Moses Raised the Serpent Up" (NCH editors) NCH; "For God So Loved the World" (Whitney) BH; "For God So Loved Us, He Sent the Savior" (Rische) HWB; "God So Loved the World" (Lippen and Opfer) NCH; "To God Be the Glory" (Crosby); "Suddenly God's Sovereign Wind" (Troeger) NHL

June 18

1 Samuel 15:34–16:13 [none]

Psalm 20 "In the Day of Need" (Idle) PH

2 Corinthians 5:6–10 (11–13), 14–17 "A Charge to Keep I Have" (Wesley); "All Who Believe and Are Baptized" (Kingo) HWB; "Creator God, Creating Still" (Huber); "Now I Have New Life in Christ" (Lee) CH; "O Come and Dwell in Me" (Wesley) UMH; "The First Day of Creation" (Troeger) NHL; "This Is a Day of New Beginnings" (Wren); "Walk On/Go Forth, O People of God" (Gabaraín); "We Are God's People" (Leech); "We Are People of God's Peace" (Simons) HWB; "We Know That Christ Is Raised and Dies No More" (Geyer); "We Walk by Faith and Not by Sight" (Alford)

Mark 4:26–34 "Come, Ye Thankful People, Come" (Alford); "The Kingdom of God Is like a Grain of Mustard Seed" (Grindal) UMH; "We Plant a Grain of Mustard Seed" (Matney) NCH; "What Shall We Say God's Realm Is Like?" (Dalles) HG

June 25

1 Samuel 17:(1a, 4–11, 19–23) 32–49 "The Battle Is the Lord's" (Clarkson) WC; "We Trust in You, Our Shield and Our Defender" (Cherry) WC

Psalm 9:9–20 [none]

2 Corinthians 6:1–13 "O Sun of Justice, Jesus Christ" (anonymous Latin) RS

Mark 4:34–41 "Lonely the Boat, Sailing at Sea" (Kim); "O Sing a Song of Bethlehem" (Benson); "The Sails Were Spilling Wind" (Troeger) HG, NHL; "The Storm Is Strong; We Face the Wind" (Dunstan) CH; "When the Storms of Life Are Raging" (Tindley)

July 2

2 Samuel 1:1, 17–27 [none]

Psalm 130 "Out of the Depths to Thee I Raise" (Luther); "Out of the Depths I Cry to You on High" (*The Psalter*, 1912) WC; "From the Depths of Sin and Sadness" (Jabusch) HWB; "Out of the Depths I Call" (*New Version*) NCH; "Out of the Depths, O God, We Call to You" (Duck) NCH

2 Corinthians 8:7–15 "O Love, How Deep, How Broad, How High" (anonymous Latin; also translated "O Love, How Vast, How Flowing Free")

Mark 5:21–43 "By Peter's House in Village Fair" (Albright) HWB; "God's Word Throughout the Ages" (Barnard) HG; "Heal Us, Emmanuel" (Cowper); "Here, Master/O Savior, in This Quiet Place" (Green); "Immortal Love, Forever Full" (Whittier); "The Scantest Touch of Grace Can Heal" (Troeger) HG, NHL; "There Was Jesus by the Water" (Grindal) NCH

July 9

2 Samuel 5:1–5, 9–10 [none]

Psalm 48 "Great Is the Lord Our God" (*Psalter Hymnal*, 1987, and *The Psalter*, 1887) PH

2 Corinthians 12:2–10 "Jesus! What a Friend for Sinners" (Chapman); "Make Me a Captive, Lord" (Matheson)

Mark 6:1–13 "How Buoyant and Bold the Stride of Christ's Friend" (Troeger) NHL; "O Carpenter, Why Leave the Bench" (Leach) HG; "O Christ, Who Called the Twelve" (Steumpfle) HG

July 16

2 Samuel 6:1–5, 12b–19 [none]

Psalm 24 "Fling Wide the Door, Unbar the Gate" (Weissel) HWB; "Lift Up the Gates Eternal" (Duba) PH; "Lift Up Your Heads, Ye Mighty Gates" (Weissel); "O God, I Want to Enter" (anonymous Spanish) CH; "The Earth and All That Dwell Therein" (*The Psalter*, 1912) PH; "The Earth Belongs to the Lord" (Hopson) WC; "The King of Glory Comes" (Jabusch)

Ephesians 1:3–14 "Christ, from Whom All Blessings Flow" (Wesley) NCH; "Come, Let Us All Unite to Sing" (Kingsbury) HWB; "Here, O Lord, Your Servants Gather" (Yamaguchi); "May the Grace of Christ Our Savior" (Fawcett); "My God, Accept My Heart This Day" (Bridges) NCH; "Redeemed, How I Love to Proclaim It" (Crosby); "Sing Praise to the Father" (Clarkson) WC; "To God Be the Glory" (Crosby)

Mark 6:14–29 [none]

July 23

2 Samuel 7:1–14a [none]

Psalm 89:20–37 "My Song Forever Shall Record" (*The Psalter*, 1912) PH

Ephesians 2:11–22 "Because He Died and Is Risen" (Baughen) WC; "Called as Partners in Christ's Service" (Huber); "Christ, from Whom All Blessings Flow" (Wesley) HWB; "Christ Is Made the Sure Foundation" (anonymous Latin); "Christ Is Our Cornerstone" (anonymous Latin) HWB; "Christ Is the World's Light" (Green); "For We Are Strangers No More" (Morse) HWB; "In Christ There Is No East or West" (Oxenham); "O Praise the Gracious Power" (Troeger) NHL; "The Church's One Foundation" (Stone); "We Are God's People" (Leech);

"We Are God's Work of Art" (Haugen) RS; "We Are People of God's Peace" (Simons) HWB; "What Is the Place Where We Are Meeting?" (Oosterhis)
Mark 6:30–34, 53–56 "They Came, a Milling Crowd" (Stuempfle) HG

July 30
2 Samuel 11:1–15 [none]
Psalm 14 [none]
Ephesians 3:14–21 "Jesus, Thy Boundless Love to Me" (Gerhardt); "Lord, Whose Love in Humble Service" (Bayly); "May the Mind of Christ My Savior" (Wilkinson) WC; "O Love, How Deep, How Broad, How High" (anonymous Latin; also translated "O Love, How Vast, How Flowing Free"); "O the Deep, Deep Love of Jesus" (Francis); "Our Father, by Whose Name" (Tucker); "There's a Wideness in God's Mercy" (Faber); "You Are Called to Tell the Story" (Duck)
John 6:1–21 "Blessed Jesus, Living Bread" (Vajda) HG; "Break Thou the Bread of Life" (Lathbury); "Far from the Markets of Rich Meat and Wine" (Troeger) NHL; "Plenty of Bread at the Feast of Life" (Haugen) RS; "When the Storms of Life Are Raging" (Tindley)

August 6
2 Samuel 11:26–12:13a [none]
Psalm 51:1–12 "Have Mercy on Us, Living Lord" (Anderson) PH; "Have Mercy in Your Goodness, Lord" (Webber) WC
Ephesians 4:1–16 "All Praise to Our Redeeming Lord" (Wesley); "As Sons of the Day and Daughters of Light" (Idle) WC; "Awake, O Sleeper, Rise from Death" (Tucker); "Help Us Accept Each Other" (Kaan); "Here, O Lord, Your Servants Gather" (Yamaguchi); "O Christ the Great Foundation" (Lew); "O Prince of Peace, O Holy God and King" (Saptayaadi) HWB; "Our God Has Made Us One" (Borop) BH; "Out of Need and Out of Custom" (Medema) WC; "There Are Many Gifts, but the Same Spirit" (Shelly) HWB; "When Minds and Bodies Meet as One" (Wren) NCH
John 6:24–35 "All Who Hunger, Gather Gladly" (Dunstan); "Become to Us the Living Bread" (Drury); "Blessed Jesus, Living Bread" (Vajda) HG; "Bread of Heaven, on Thee We Feed" (Conder) PH; "Bread of the World, in Mercy Broken" (Heber); "Christ, Enthroned in Heavenly Splendor" (Bourne) NHC; "Deck Thyself, My Soul, with Gladness" (Franck); "Eat This Bread" (Batastini); "Forever in the Heart There Springs" (Troeger) NHL; "I Am the Bread of Life" (Toolan); "I Hunger and I Thirst" (Monsell) HWB; "I Received the Living God" (anonymous) RS; "In the Quiet Consecration" (Coote) HWB; "Jesus the Christ Says, I Am the Bread" (anonymous Urdu) NCH; "Jesus, Thou Joy of Loving Hearts" (Bernard of Clairvaux); "O Food to Pilgrims Given" (*Maintzich Gesangbuch*) UMH; "You Satisfy the Hungry Heart" (Westendorf)

August 13
2 Samuel 18:5–9, 15, 31–33 [none]
Psalm 130 "Out of the Depths to Thee I Raise" (Luther); "Out of the Depths I Cry to You on High" (*The Psalter*, 1912) WC; "From the Depths of Sin and Sadness" (Jabusch) HWB; "Out of the Depths I Call" (*New Version*) NCH; "Out of the Depths, O God, We Call to You" (Duck) NCH
Ephesians 4:25–5:2 "Awake, O Sleeper, Rise from Death" (Tucker); "For Your Gift of God the Spirit" (Clarkson) WC; "Forgive Our Sins, as We Forgive" (Herklots); "Help Us to Help Each

Other Lord" (Wesley) HWB; "I Then Shall Live as One Who's Been Forgiven" (Gaither) WC; "Let the Truth Shine in Our Speaking" (Troeger) NHL; "O for a Closer Walk with God" (Cowper); "Where Charity and Love Prevail" (anonymous Latin)
John 6:35, 41–51 "Blessed Jesus, Living Bread" (Vajda) HG; "Graced with Garments of Great Gladness" (Franck) NCH; "Let All Mortal Flesh Keep Silence" (Liturgy of St. James); "We Come as Guests Invited" (Dudley-Smith; see also hymns listed for August 6)

August 20
1 Kings 2:10–12, 3:3–14 [none]
Psalm 111 "God's Holy Ways Are Just and True" (Woollett) WC
Ephesians 5:15–20 "Christ, You Are the Fulness" (Polman) PH; "Come, Rejoice Before Your Maker" (Baughen) RS; "Fill the Earth with Music" (Huff) BH; "In Solitude" (Duck) NCH; "With Glad Exuberant Carolings" (Troeger) NHL
John 6:51–58 "Blessed Jesus, Living Bread (Vajda) HG; (see also hymns listed for August 6 and 13)

August 27
1 Kings 8:(1, 6, 10–11) 22–30, 41–43 [none]
Psalm 84 "How Lovely Is Thy Dwelling Place" (*The Psalms of David* in Meeter and Daw) BH; "How Lovely Is Your Dwelling" (Janzen); "How Lovely, Lord, How Lovely" (Duba); "Lord of the Worlds Above" (Watts) HWB
Ephesians 6:10–20 "Be Strong in the Lord and Be of Good Courage" (Johnson); "Christian, Do You Struggle?" (Neale) WC; "Soldiers of Christ, Arise" (Wesley); "Stand Up, Stand Up for Jesus" (Duffield)
John 6:56–69 "Blessed Jesus, Living Bread (Vajda) HG; (see also hymns listed for August 6 and August 13)

September 3
Song of Songs 2:8–13 [none]
Psalm 45:1–2, 6–9 [none]
James 1:17–27 "For the Beauty of the Earth" (Pierpoint); "For the Grace That You Have Given" (Daw) WC; "God, Whose Giving Knows No Ending" (Edwards); "How Clear Is Our Vocation, Lord" (Green); "I Sing the Almighty Power of God" (Watts); "O God, Who Gives to Humankind" (Burns) WC; "Praise God for the Harvest of Farm and of Field" (Wren) WC; "The World Abounds with God's Free Grace" (Mehrtens) NCH; "We Give Thee but Thine Own" (How); "We Plow the Fields and Scatter" (Claudius); "When the Church of Jesus" (Green)
Mark 7:1–8, 14–15, 21–23 "As a Chalice Cast of Gold" (Troeger) HG, NHL

September 10
Proverbs 22:1–2, 8–9, 22–23 [none]
Psalm 125 [none]
James 2:1–10 (11–13), 14–17 "Brothers and Sisters of Mine Are the Hungry" (Morse) HWB; "Help Us to Help Each Other" (Wesley) HWB; "Let Us Plead for Faith Alone" (Wesley) UMH; "When the Church of Jesus" (Green)

Mark 7:24–37 "By Peter's House in Village Fair" (Albright) HWB; "Lord, I Was Blind" (Matson) WC; "We Give God Thanks for Those Who Knew" (Idle) HG

September 17
Proverbs 1:20–33 [none]
Psalm 19 "God's Law Is Perfect and Gives Life" (Webber) PH; "Nature with Open Volume Stands" (Watts); "O Sing unto the Lord" (Rosas); "The Heavens Above Declare God's Praise" (Webber) PH; "The Stars Declare His Glory" (Dudley-Smith) RS
James 3:1–12 [none]
Mark 3:27–38 "Let Kings and Prophets Yield Their Name" (Daw) HG; "Make Our Church One Joyful Choir" (Troeger) HG; "What Fabled Names from Judah's Past" (Troeger) NHL; "Who Is My Mother? Who Is My Brother?" (Murray) CH

September 24
Proverbs 31:10–31 [none]
Psalm 1 "How Blest Are They/The One Is Blest Who, Fearing God" (Gower); "Like a Tree Beside the Waters" (Martin) NCH
James 3:13–4:3, 7–8a "Lord Jesus, Think on Me" (Synesius of Cyrene); "There Is a Place of Quiet Rest" (McAfee)
Mark 9:30–37 "Lord, Whose Love in Humble Service" (Bayly) HG; "Sister, Let Me Be Your Servant" (Gillard; also found with first lines "We Are Travelers on a Journey," "Will You Let Me Be Your Servant," and "Won't You Let Me Be Your Servant")

October 1
Esther 7:1–6, 9–10, 9:20–22 [none]
Psalm 124 "Now Israel May Say, and That in Truth" (*The Psalter*, 1912)
James 5:13–20 "Come, O Creator Spirit, Come" (anonymous Latin); "From the Crush of Wealth and Power" (Gibbons) NCH; "O Christ, the Healer, We Have Come" (Green); "Sweet Hour of Prayer" (Walford); "What a Friend We Have in Jesus" (Scriven)
Mark 9:38–50 "How Clear Is Our Vocation, Lord" (Green) HG; "Where Cross the Crowded Ways of Life" (North)

October 8
Job 1:1, 2:1–10 [none]
Psalm 26 [none]
Hebrews 1:1–4, 2:5–12 "A Hymn of Glory Let Us Sing" (Bede); "Christ High-Ascended" (Dudley-Smith) WC; "Fairest Lord Jesus" (anonymous German); "God Has Spoken by the Prophets" (Briggs); "How Blest Are They Who Trust in Christ" (Green); "Lord, You Sometimes Speak in Wonders" (Idle) HWB; "My Lord of Light Who Made the Worlds" (Idle) WC; "O Splendor of God's Glory Bright" (Ambrose); "Rejoice, the Lord Is King" (Wesley); "The Head That Once Was Crowned with Thorns" (Kelly)
Mark 10:2–16 "Enter in the Realm of God" (Bayler) HG; "Far More Than Passion's Passing Flame" (Troeger) NHL; "God, When Human Bonds Are Broken" (Kaan) HG; "Jesus, Friend So Kind and Gentle" (Gregory) HWB; "Jesus Loves Me" (Warner; the relevant stanza is found in CH, NCH, PH, and UMH); "Tell Me the Stories of Jesus" (Mathams)

October 15

Job 23:1–9, 16–17 [none]

Psalm 22:1–15 "My God, My God, Why Have You Forsaken Me?" (Psalm 22) HWB; "Why Has God Forsaken Me?" (Wallace); "O My God, O Gracious God" (Iona) NCH

Hebrews 4:12–16 "A Man There Lived in Galilee" (Lowry) WC; "Blest Be the Tie That Binds" (Fawcett); "Christ Is Alive! Let Christians Sing" (Wren); "Christ/God Whose Purpose Is to Kindle" (Trueblood); "Come, Ye Disconsolate" (Moore and Hastings); "How Sure the Scriptures Are" (Idle) WC; "My Lord, You Wore No Royal Crown" (Idle) WC; "O Love, How Deep, How Broad, How High" (anonymous Latin; also translated "O Love, How Vast, How Flowing Free"); "Tell Me the Story of Jesus" (Crosby); "The Word of God Is Alive" (Terley) BH; "When in the Hour of Deepest Need" (Eber) HWB

Mark 10:17–31 "All to Jesus, I Surrender" (VanDeVenter); "Spirit of Jesus, If I Love My Neighbor" (Wren) HG

October 22

Job 38:1–7 (34–41) "God Marked a Line and Told the Sea" (Troeger) NCH; "Let All Things Now Living" (Davis); "When the Morning Stars Together" (Bayly)

Psalm 104:1–9, 24, 35a "Bless the Lord, My Soul and Being" (Anderson) PH; "Many and Great, O God, Are Thy Ways" (Renville); "O Worship the King, All Glorious Above" (Grant); "Praise to the Spinner Who Twisted and Twirled" (Troeger) NHL

Hebrews 5:1–10 [none]

Mark 10:35–45 "Are Ye Able, Said the Master" (Marlatt) UMH; "By Gracious Powers So Wonderfully Sheltered" (Bonhöffer); "Lord, Help Us Walk Your Servant Way" (Stuempfle) HG

October 29

Job 42:1–6, 10–17 [none]

Psalm 34:1–8 (19–22) "Taste and See" (O'Brien) RS

or

Psalm 126 "Let Us Hope When Hope Seems Hopeless" (Beebe) NCH; "When God Delivered Israel" (Saward) PH

Hebrews 7:23–28 "Savior of the Nations, Come" (Ambrose)

Mark 10:46–52 "A Blind Man Sat Beside the Road" (Stuempfle) HG; "By Peter's House in Village Fair" (Albright) HWB

November 5

Ruth 1:1–18 "Wherever You Go, I Will Follow" (Cooney) RS

Psalm 146 "I'll Praise My Maker While I've Breath" (Watts)

Hebrews 9:11–14 "Alleluia! Sing to Jesus" (Dix); "The King of Glory Comes" (Jabusch)

Mark 12:28–34 "If All You Want, Lord, Is My Heart" (Troeger) HG; "Jesus a New Commandment Has Given Us" (Loperena) NCH; "Lord of Creation, to You Be All Praise" (Winslow) WC; "The Call Is Clear and Simple" (Duck) HG; "We Praise You with Our Minds, O Lord" (McElrath)

November 12
Ruth 3:1–5, 4:13–17 [none]
Psalm 127 "Unless the Lord the House Shall Build" (*The Psalter*, 1912) PH
Hebrews 9:24–28 "Built on the Rock the Church Doth Stand" (Grundtvig); "Christ, Enthroned in Heavenly Splendor" (Bourne) NCH; "I Want to Walk as a Child of the Light" (Thomerson); "The King Shall Come When Morning Breaks" (Brownlie)
Mark 12:38–44 "The Temple Rang with Golden Coins" (Stuempfle) HG

November 19
1 Samuel 1:4–20 "For All the Faithful Women" (Stuempfle) RS; "O God, Whose Steadfast Love" (Haddix) NCH
Psalm 16 "When in the Night I Meditate" (*The Psalter*, 1912); "You Are All We Have" (O'Brien) RS
Hebrews 10:11–14 (15–18), 19–25 "Built on the Rock the Church Doth Stand" (Grundtvig); "Christ, Enthroned in Heavenly Splendor" (Bourne) NCH; "I Am Thine, O Lord" (Crosby); "Let Us Draw Near" (Clarkson) WC; "Lord, Teach Us How to Pray Aright" (Montgomery); "What Is This Place?" (Oosterhuis)
Mark 13:1–8 "O Day of God, Draw Nigh" (Scott) HG

November 26
2 Samuel 23:1–7 "The Love That Lifted Lyric Praise" (Troeger) NHL
Psalm 132:1–12 (13–18) "Before the Temple's Great Stone Sill" (Troeger) NHL
Revelation 1:4b–8 "Glory Be to God the Father" (Bonar) WC; "Jesus Came, the Heavens Adoring" (Thring) WC; "Jesus/Lo, He Comes with Clouds Descending" (Wesley); "Of the Father's Love Begotten" (Prudentius)
John 18:33–37 "Crown as Your King" (Troeger) NHL

ADVENT
December 3
Jeremiah 33:14–16 "Now Is the Time Approaching" (Borthwick) NCH
Psalm 25:1–10 "Lord, to You My Soul Is Lifted" (Wiersma) PH
1 Thessalonians 3:9–13 "Keep Awake, Be Always Ready" (Clyde) NCH
Luke 21:25–36 "A Charge to Keep I Have" (Wesley); "Christ Is Coming! Let Creation" (MacDuff); "Jesus/Lo, He Comes with Clouds Descending" (Wesley); "Mine Eyes Have Seen the Glory of the Coming of the Lord" (Howe); "The King Shall Come When Morning Dawns" (Brownlie); "Wake, Awake, for Night Is Flying" (Nicolai); "When the Lord in Glory Comes" (Dudley-Smith) HG

December 10
Malachi 3:1–4 [none]
Luke 1:68–79 "Blessed Be the God of Israel" (Quinn) BH; "Blessed Be the God of Israel" (Perry); "Now Bless the God of Israel" (Duck), NCH
Philippians 1:3–11 "Great Work Has God Begun in You" (Birkland) NCH; "Love Divine, All Loves Excelling" (Wesley); "More Love, O Christ, to Thee" (Prentice)

Luke 3:1-6 "All Earth Is Waiting to See the Promised One" (Taulé); "Comfort, Comfort Ye, My People" (Olearius); "On Jordan's Bank the Baptist's Cry" (Coffin); "There's a Voice in the Wilderness Crying" (Milligan) NCH; "When John Baptized by Jordan's River" (Dudley-Smith) RS; "Wild and Lone the Prophet's Voice" (Daw) HG

December 17

Zephaniah 3:14-20 [none]

Isaiah 12:2-6 "Surely It Is God Who Saves Me" (Daw); "With Joy Draw Water" (McKinstry) NCH

Philippians 4:4-7 "Because He Died and Is Risen" (Baughen) WC; "Rejoice, the Lord Is King" (Wesley); "Rejoice, Ye Pure in Heart" (Plumptre); "What a Friend We Have in Jesus" (Scriven)

Luke 3:7-18 "All Earth Is Waiting to See the Promised One" (Taulé); "Christ, When for Us You Were Baptized" (Tucker) PH; "Christ, Your Footprints Through the Desert" (Stuempfle) HG; "Lord, When You Came to Jordan" (Wren; revised version begins "What Was Your Vow and Vision"); "Mark How the Lamb of God's Self-Offering" (Daw); "O Radiant Christ, Incarnate Word" (Duck) NCH; "On Jordan's Banks the Baptist's Cry" (Coffin); "What Ruler Wades Through Murky Streams" (Troeger) NHC; "When Jesus Came to Jordan" (Green); "When John Baptized by Jordan's River" (Dudley-Smith) RS; "Wild and Lone the Prophet's Voice" (Daw) HG

December 24

Micah 5:2-5a "Little Bethlehem of Judah" (Seerveld) NCH; "O Little Town of Bethlehem" (Brooks)

Luke 1:47-55 "All Who Would Claim the Faith of Jesus" (Coles) RS; "For Ages Women Hoped and Prayed" (Huber) WC; "My Heart Sings Out with Joyful Praise" (Duck) NCH; "My Soul Cries Out" (Cooney) RS; "My Soul Gives Glory to My God" (Winter); "My Soul Gives Glory to the Lord" (Mueller) RS; "My Soul Proclaims with Wonder" (Daw) HWB; "Tell Out, My Soul, the Greatness of the Lord" (Dudley-Smith); "Ye Who Claim the Faith of Jesus" (Coles and Tucker) UMH

Hebrews 10:5-10 [none]

Luke 1:39-45 (46-55) "One Wedding Dress Long Put Away" (Leach) HG; "When to Mary, the Word" (Clark) HG

CHRISTMASTIDE
December 31

1 Samuel 2:18-20, 26 [none]

Psalm 148 "All Creatures of Our God and King" (Francis of Assisi); "Creating God, Your Fingers Trace" (Rowthorn); "God Created Heaven and Earth" (anonymous Taiwanese); "Let the Whole Creation Cry" (Brooks); "Praise the Lord! Ye Heavens Adore Him" (anonymous English); "Stars and Planets Flung in Orbit" (Stuempfle) NCH

Colossians 3:12-17 "Blest Be the Tie That Binds" (Fawcett); "Christ, You Are the Fulness" (Polman) PH; "Come, Rejoice Before Your Maker" (Baughen) RS; "Fill the Earth with Music" (Huff) BH; "In Solitude" (Duck) NCH; "With Glad Exuberant Carolings" (Troeger) NHL

Luke 2:41-52 "O Sing a Song of Bethlehem" (Benson); "Our Father, By Whose Name" (Tucker); "Within the Father's House" (Woodford) HG

MESSAGES FOR COMMUNION SERVICES

SERMON SUGGESTIONS

Topic: A Meditation on the Communion

TEXT: Luke 22:7–38; Mark 14:12–36; Matt. 26:17–30

We are commemorating today a meal that took place almost two thousand years ago, and from whatever point of view you look at it, that is an extraordinary fact. When you stop to think about it and remember the circumstances in which the original meal was set, it becomes an even more extraordinary fact. The meal did not take place in Rome, which was the center of civilization in those days, but in one of the condemned cities of the world—Jerusalem. Forty years after the meal took place, the city lay in ruins and has been a virtual battlefield ever since.

The meal did not take place in a palace—one of the Earth's great houses—but in the upper room of a house; we know neither the name of the owner nor the location nor the address. There were thirteen people present at the meal, and only one of them had any public reputation at all; he was not known beyond a radius of a hundred and fifty miles from his hometown and was killed the day following the meal as a disturber of the peace. The other people who attended the meal were young laboring men whom nobody ever heard of and never expected to see again. It was not a banquet; it consisted of the bare necessities of life—bread and wine.

And yet this meal, so hidden, so apart from the great stream of events, so obscure, so apparently local and transient—this meal is now being celebrated and remembered and participated in by people in practically every country in the whole world. That is extraordinary, and the question that comes to mind is this: What gave this meal its lasting quality and its spreading power? Wherein lies the perennial appeal of this meal, whereby it can speak to men and women in all walks of life, through almost two thousand years of time, in very different circumstances and conditions of life? Wherein lies its appeal? What gives the meal its lasting quality and its spreading power? It is along the lines of those questions that we will direct our thought this morning in a meditation on this extraordinary meal.

I. Before we answer those questions, let us pause long enough to make this observation. Events that seem unimportant to us at the time often turn out to be the hinges upon which the doors into the future swing. No one, certainly, would have predicted that on the night the Last Supper took place, when so much was going on in the city of Jerusalem, that the meal would be the one thing to be most often remembered down through the years. For one thing, it was the great Passover festival—the keystone of the Jewish year, the great holiday of deliverance. People came from all over, not only from their own country but from the distant parts of the world to which they had been dispersed to celebrate this great festival. Their best people were there; their greatest minds, their profoundest spirits were gathered together in Jerusalem. Moreover, Pilate was in town. He was the governor representing the occupying power, and Herod was not very far away, so undoubtedly, affairs of state were taking place in the city that might have had to do with the rise and fall of nations. And yet none of these conquered time; in fact, we know about them only as they happen to relate and refer themselves to this meal. Rather, it is a little undistinguished group of young men having supper together under the threat of doom, mind you, that has conquered time.

You never know where the seeds of life may be lying. If you have a son, he may become the savior of his people. If you eat a meal, it may become, in the course of time, a sacrament of salvation. If you say something that seems unimportant and insignificant at the time, it may save a life—or destroy one. If you make a decision, it may turn the tide of history. If you start an idea going, it may change the course of human life for generations to come. And if you die, you may accomplish more than you would if you had lived. In other words, nothing in life is unimportant, at least in this sense: all life is loaded with possibilities. Not all of them are explored, not all materialize, not all reach maturity, but we, as Christians taking part in this extraordinary meal that seemed so unimportant, insignificant, and irrelevant at the time, are reminded that the material of our lives is of the most intense significance, even the most minute details of it, for it is all charged with the possibilities of God.

You say, "Not in my case! Nothing that I could do or could take part in could possibly be as important as that. I'm just an unimportant person who has no position in life, casts no deciding vote, and spreads no great influence. Certainly it's not true in my case." But I ask you, "What would Peter have said if somebody had asked him on the Thursday night before Good Friday what he thought about the Last Supper? What would he have said in answer to someone who said, 'You have just taken part in a meal that will be, through the generations, the center of men's worship and the incentive of their living'"? He would have said, "Poppycock!"

Now let us get back to our question: What gives this particular meal its lasting quality? I have spoken about it so many times at the Maundy Thursday service and on Sunday mornings that I know those of you who have been with us through all the years will not expect something new or exhaustive. My mind goes today to two reasons for the perennial appeal of this meal. I am sure there are others.

First, the people who knew Jesus wanted something to remember him by. Human memory is one of the most mysterious of our faculties and one of the most wonderful; it can reach back through the years that are gone and pluck things out of the past and make them vivid. But at best, the human memory fades as the years go by, and even people we have known well and loved deeply and clearly have a way of slipping from our immediate consciousness. It must have been so with Jesus, and the people who knew him did not want to forget him. They wanted something to remember him by, and they found it in this meal.

For one thing, it was so like him. It seemed to epitomize in brief, dramatic, direct action and word everything that he had said and done and been. It was simple, not complex. That was characteristic of Jesus—always simple, direct, and never complicated by irrelevant facts and ideas that might be interesting but not to the point. So this meal went right to the point in question. Like him also, it was concrete, not abstract, and even more like him it was plain—so plain that the simplest person could grasp it, yet not vulgar. We are hearing a great deal these days of political campaigning about the necessity of speaking in plain language to plain people, and the tragedy is that some of those who try to do that succeed not only in becoming plain but in becoming cheap and vulgar. Jesus had a unique way of being able to be unmistakably plain, yet never cheap and never vulgar.

Also, like him, the meal was somehow entirely surrounded by God; when it began he gave thanks; when it ended they went out on the Mount of Olives and sang a hymn. Also it made them think of him because it had to do with bread and breakage. It had to do with bread because bread was the very stuff of physical existence, and Jesus never tried to skirt around those necessities. But the bread that he gave to his disciples was broken bread; it was not the promise of a perfect body; it was not the ideal of the Greek body without flaw or blemish of any kind; it was a body broken, scarred, marred, and tortured, through which the glory of the infinite came. Bread and breakage, life and death were the two things that concerned Jesus all of his life.

The first Christians then turned to this meal, and it is interesting to notice that they did not remember Jesus in those first days so much by the last words that he spoke, although they preserved those, as they remembered him chiefly by the last supper that he ate—again, characteristically, action before words.

But there is another reason for the perennial appeal of the Last Supper. It condensed the meaning of life and death into unmistakable and comprehensible terms, not only for the people who lived with Jesus in Palestine but for people down through the ages and in the ages to come for whom the questions of life and death will be essentially the same questions that he and his contemporaries had to face and that you and I have to face. Some people have given men and women a discourse on the meaning of life and death in an attempt to answer those questions. Jesus gave them, rather, a simple act in which they could take part, and as we take part in it again, we will perhaps be conscious of the way in which it condenses the meaning of life and answers some of the questions we ask.

For instance, in some way or other, either in an articulate way or an unspoken way, all of us ask the question, Does anybody really care about me? After all my friends have done their bit, and my family has shown me their love and affection, does anything at the *heart of things* care whether I live or die, or am happy or unhappy, or make the most of life or a mess of life? Does anybody care? Then the words of Jesus come to us: "This is my body which is given for you," and you take it in your hand and you feel it and somehow you know that somebody cares that much. Some of us ask the question, Can my sins ever be blotted out? No matter how sophisticated we may be, no matter how conditioned we may be to the idea of sin as a part of human nature, nevertheless we do not like our sins and we are not proud of them. And there comes a time in everyone's life when he or she says, "Can these mistakes that I see so plainly now—these wrongs, these sins—can anything be done to offset them in the balance of life?" And the words come: "My blood was shed for the remission of your sins." Don't ask how. The mystery of one man's sacrifice somehow outweighing the balance of all men's sins is not for our analysis. When we hear the words and see the cup and drink the wine, somehow we have the assurance that our sins are forgiven.

Many of us at one time or another ask, "Have I anything in common with my neighbor? In this extraordinary social world in which I live, often in such close contact with people I don't particularly like, who do not share my point of view, either religiously nor politically, who seem to be miles apart from anything I ever am or hope to be—have I anything in common with my neighbor?" And we come to the altar rail, and we realize that we have in common our empty hands, the needs that are common to all of us, the empty part of our lives that must be filled with a life outside ourselves if there is to be any life there at all. We have that in common with all men, as we raise our empty hands to receive the bread.

And some people ask from time to time, "Is there anything for me to do in the world? I don't seem to count very much; I haven't any position of great importance; I don't exert much influence in the world, and I sometimes feel that I'm a pretty useless person. Is there anything for me to do in the world?" "Do this in remembrance of me," comes the answer. Do in your own imperfect and inadequate way the thing that I did. Let the glory shine through the breakage that men may be able to pick up the pieces of their lives and live better lives because of you.

And finally, many people, at some time during their lives, are likely to ask the question, "In the darkness of my night is there anyone with me? In this darkness am I alone, isolated, a forlorn and forsaken figure without help or companionship or strength?" And the words come to us: "In the night in which he was betrayed he took bread," and we feel him with us in the night, and we say, "Then shall my night be turned to day."

In 1904 James Bissett Pratt was a young student of philosophy; he later became, as many of you know, the beloved and great professor of philosophy at Williams College. In 1904 he did what a great many students attempt to do—he got up a questionnaire to send to all the leading philosophers of his day, in which he asked them for certain kinds of information. He asked question like these: Why do you believe in God? Do you pray, and if so, why? Do you believe in personal immortality? One of the philosophers to whom he sent the questionnaire was William James, who answered all the questions rather carefully. He then came to this item, "Describe a typical spiritual person." William James put down "Phillips Brooks." Certainly, no one would have been better qualified than William James to describe a spiritual person, but he knew that would not mean much to anybody, for the abstract realities of spiritual life are known and understood only as they become concrete in something real—a person.

So sometimes we feel, today especially at this service, that when people ask us to describe the meaning of life—its joy and sorrow, suffering and tragedy, its brevity and all the rest of it—while we perhaps might do it in an abstract discourse on the meaning of existence, we can do it much more plainly, much more completely by saying simply, "the Last Supper—that is the meaning of life, the bread and the breakage."

The meal, of course, as the years have gone on, has become more and more formal. Some people find difficulty with that, and they might say, at a service like this, "Well, there is nothing to suggest the simplicity of that first meal." It is, I think, bound to be so, for you will recognize, if you think a minute, that a certain amount of formality is necessary to protect the things we care most about. A man's wedding, for instance, is not a casual, careless performance but is surrounded by a certain amount of formality. The graduation of a boy or girl from college is not an indifferent affair; it is surrounded by a certain amount of formality. The inauguration of a president or the death and burial of a person is attended with a certain amount of formality, which protects the event and shields it from carelessness and lack of reverence. And so it is only natural that a certain amount of formality has grown up around this meal, more in some traditions than others.

The final word is this: never let the formality, however necessary, hide the reality of what is taking place. And this is the reality that, in dramatic terms, is acted out in this meal of which you are now a part. Listen. To live is to give; to give is to suffer; to suffer is to die; to die to self is to live.

Lead us, O Lord, ever more deeply into the mysteries of life and death, as we see them revealed in the bread and wine of the Last Supper of thy son, Jesus Christ. May we see there plainly, clearly, and simply stated the meaning of our existence and of thy purpose for us and all thy people everywhere. We ask this in the name of Jesus, who died that we might live.[1]

Topic: Supper of Thanksgiving
TEXT: Matt. 26:26–30

Death literally waited outside the door of the Upper Room where Jesus was eating with his disciples. Jesus was nearing his encounter with treachery, hatred, and violence. But first, he had determined to observe the Passover with those closest to him. After the Passover observance, he instituted a new meal for his Church. In the course of the meal, he paused twice to give thanks. I have often wondered what he said in giving thanks on this particular occasion. Some have suggested that he repeated the usual Jewish formula: "Blessed art thou, O Lord our God, king of the world, who dost bring forth bread from the earth."[2] I would like to think that although Jesus' thanks may have included this statement, his prayer was more spontaneous and wider in scope. I would like to think that his expression included his disciples and the events about to take place. The amazing thing in this crisis—other than Jesus' calmness and assurance—is that in moments of chilling threat, Jesus gave thanks.

But then, Jesus' giving thanks, even in crisis, ought not to be surprising. A study of his life reveals that gratitude was an outstanding feature of it. We are given repeated instances in which Jesus expressed his thanks. A number of such instances had to do with food. Before the feedings of the five thousand and the four thousand, he gave thanks. Before eating with the disciples he had accompanied on the road to Emmaus after his Resurrection, he gave thanks; in fact, this characteristic practice caused them finally to recognize him. Before he called Lazarus from the tomb, he gave thanks for the power of God that was about to be revealed. So during his ministry, Jesus expressed his gratitude for simple things, such as food, and he gave thanks for the Father's presence and power.

Because of his total life, particularly because he gave thanks for the bread and the fruit of the vine as he gave his followers a meal to observe, Jesus made thanksgiving an integral part of what we now commonly call the Lord's Supper. One of the terms used to designate this meal is *the Eucharist*, which means "the thanksgiving." Thus each time we meet together to participate in this meal, we make it an experience of reverent gratitude. All collective worship periods and private devotional periods are times for expressing gratitude, but this is especially true of the Lord's Supper. Part of what we do is to express our deep appreciation to God. George Buttrick wrote that this giving of thanks should spread over all of life and our whole world, "for the whole creation is sacramental, but it [our giving of thanks] should focus in . . . Christ."[3] Our thanksgiving centers around the Person who shows us God.

In the Eucharist or Lord's Supper, *we offer thanks for Christ's selfless life and atoning death*. We acknowledge that our reconciliation to God is not the product of our own effort but the result of God's working on our behalf. We can do nothing less than express gratitude for the towering truth expressed so eloquently by Christ's life and death: before we thought

---

[1]Theodore Parker Ferris, *Selected Sermons*, Vol. 1 (Boston: Trinity Church, 1983) pp. 215–220.
[2]Sherman E. Johnson, *The Interpreter's Bible*, Vol. 2 (Nashville: Abingdon Press, 1951), p. 575.
[3]George Buttrick, *The Interpreter's Bible*, Vol. 7 (Nashville: Abingdon Press, 1951), p. 575.

of loving God, he loved us. John wrote in his first letter: "Herein is love, not that we loved God, but that he loved us, and sent his Son to be the propitiation [expiation] for our sins" (4:10). Before we were good, lovely, or gracious, God in his goodness gave of himself to us. Before we desired to relate to him, he sought to bring us to himself. In the Eucharist, we give thanks for Christ and his self-giving, and we echo the words of Paul in 2 Corinthians 9:15: "Thanks be unto God for his unspeakable gift."

In the course of participation in the Lord's Supper, *we offer thanks for the Resurrection—the event that marked the completion of God's redemptive work for us.* The Resurrection is the historical fact that offers irrefutable evidence that God *was* in Christ, reconciling the world to himself. We look back at the Resurrection as evidence that God is able to thwart the attempts of evil to hold the upper hand in life and as evidence that God is capable of giving life. We look back in gratitude at the Resurrection because it validates Christ's words and deeds. We view the Resurrection with thanksgiving because of the promise it holds for us of life beyond death. But most of all, we look to the Resurrected Lord who shows himself to be the Lord of life. One who is living, present, powerful in our todays, he is One who grants triumph over life, wrong, and death to those of faith. And again, we humbly echo Paul's words in 1 Corinthians 15:57: "Thanks be to God, which giveth us the victory."

By our participation in the Eucharist, *we express our gratitude for the Church's beginning and continuation in Christ's life.* The Church's foundation is God's grace seen in Christ's self-giving. The example by which the Church orders its life is his life. The message the Church proclaims is that Christ gives life.

In this meal, we express our awareness of and our thanks for *the commission that our Resurrected Lord gave to his Church:* the charge to make disciples of all people and to nurture them in the faith.

Also we openly thank God for the gracious promise that accompanies his commission—the promise that we do not labor in our strength alone. He sustains his work by his presence with his Church, which works in the confidence that it will be victorious; it shares and will share his triumph.

And so we participate in the Eucharist—the Lord's Supper—with a prayer of thanksgiving. We not only look back in gratitude for what Christ has accomplished at Golgotha on the first Easter morning and in the early Church, but we offer our thanks for what he is doing now in his people's lives and in his Church's life and ministry.[4]

Topic: The Glue That Holds Us Together
TEXT: 1 John 4:7–12

It's a Charles Schultz classic. Linus has just told Lucy that he plans to become a doctor. Lucy stops skipping rope to offer her usual constructive criticism: "That's a big laugh! You could never be a doctor! You know why?" Then, as she turns to skipping rope again, she offers her acid analysis of Linus: "Because you don't love mankind, that's why!" And Linus, with a straight back and obviously disturbed appearance, comes back with his defense: "I love mankind . . . it's *people* I can't stand!"

---

[4]Eli Landrum Jr., *More Than Symbol* (Nashville: Broadman Press, 1983), pp. 36–39.

The kids in *Peanuts* have a way of echoing the culture something like the way our kids reflect the language and values of home. Although Lucy is usually the one to speak with blatant irreverence, Linus describes the world as he sees it. We can stand the ethic of Jesus—the command to love—as long as we can keep love in the abstract, at a healthy distance from the concrete reality of people. But Jesus bordered on the ridiculous. He said, "Love your enemies and pray for those who persecute you."

In his class, Bob Jones speculated last Thursday about how we would hear his calling aloud the name "Osama Bin Laden" in our prayer on Sunday morning. Praying for your enemy, after all, is the gospel. The only problem I see in calling out the names of enemies in our prayer together is the confusion. After a while we won't know whether your prayer is for a friend or a foe.

William Willimon, former chaplain of Duke University, tells of walking across the campus on a Friday afternoon with an old friend and former professor. They stood on the steps of Duke Chapel, as he put it, "and surveyed the breakdown of western civilization." His friends asked, "Do you know what is for me the ultimate proof of our Lord's divinity?" Willimon took the bait. The friend continued that Jesus had to be different from us if he could look on these masses and have compassion.

The point is well taken. The romantic sentiments that we read on Hallmark cards and "Sonnets to the Portuguese" capture a small fraction of the meaning of authentic love. John declared that love finds its source in God and is so close to the nature of God that he suggests the astounding equation: "God is love." The literal reading of John's sentence does not mean, "love is god." You cannot reverse the order. God and love are not really equal in weight, but John is saying that love is at the core of God's being. Love is the essence of God's nature.

An old story has been passed down through the centuries that identifies the author of 1 John with the apostle who sat at the feet of Jesus. According to tradition, John outlived all the others and eventually was the only living soul who had known Jesus in the flesh. Recognizing the passing of an era, Christians urged the old man to tell all that he knew of Jesus, but he refused to say anything more than, "My little children, love one another. There is nothing more." The story is probably legend, but it reflects the law of love taught by Christ following the washing of the disciples' feet and the Lord's Supper: (John 12:34) "I give you a new commandment, that you love one another, just as I have loved you, you also should love one another."

I. *Love is costly.* "God is love." Paul Scherer calls the love that God defines the costliest thing you can say about God and the costliest thing you can say about us. It's bad enough that our love stories are often full of sentimental journeys and feel-good clichés. Now science has gotten into the picture. I recently saw a PBS analysis of animal love connecting humans to other mammals. Biologists have identified a chemical released in the newborn elephant that not only distinguishes the calf from the rest of the herd but stimulates in a cow a need to nourish and protect her young. The biological marker is also found in humans and provides a chemical explanation of "falling" in love and provides literal meaning to all our metaphors about chemistry between us. There is a down side. The chemical is called phenylethylamine. It occurs naturally in the body from the amphetamine family, but we build up tolerance. Chemical love lasts for two to four years.

Duke Professor of Christian Ethics, Stanley Hauerwas, is also a minister. He claims to have given couples a sealed envelope at their wedding to be opened when things get difficult between them—I suppose when the phenylethylamine wears off. The note reads: "Everyone marries the wrong person." This is the point where the work of marriage begins.

The Christian gospel is anything but romance. Hallmark cards and popular love songs seldom get close to the meaning of love as expressed in the story of Christ. John cannot talk about love in the abstract. He can only speak of the kind of love that disciples saw in the cross: "In this is love, not that we loved God but that he loved us and sent his Son to be the atoning sacrifice for our sins." Paul got close to the core meaning of love: (Rom. 5:8) "But God proves his love for us in that while we still were sinners Christ died for us." The beauty of God's love is also stark and frightening. The only way that Christians could find beauty or meaning in the cross was in the consistency with which Christ practiced what he preached. The Rabbi who taught us to love our enemies prayed from the cross: "Father, forgive them; for they know not what they do" (Luke 23:34).

II. *Love stands in contrast with the counterfeits and shams.* John could not describe Christian love just in positive terms. He addressed our phobias, our fears: "perfect love casts out fear." He also addressed hate, but not the hatred that we see in the world. He identified the unthinkable—hatred in the church. Peter Gomes recalled the observation of Walter White, head of the NAACP, in 1929: "No person who is familiar with the Bible-beating, acrobatic, fanatical preachers of hellfire in the South, and who has seen the orgies of emotion created by them, can doubt for a moment that dangerous passions are released which contribute to emotional instability and play a part in lynching." John called it a lie. You can't claim to love God and hate your brother or sister at the same time: "Those who love God must love their brothers and sisters also."

Erich Fromm wrote *The Art of Loving* with a smack at the typical romanticism that dominates our thinking. He prefers to speak of "standing in love" rather than "falling in love." Love demands something from us and cannot be caught in passive ideas of going limp in the arms of some magical force. Love is an art that is practiced rather than an atmosphere that is breathed or just a chemical released. Fromm distinguished the mature from the immature: "Infantile love follows the principle: 'I love because I am loved.' Mature love follows the principle: 'I am loved because I love.' Immature love says: 'I love you because I need you.' Mature love says: 'I need you because I love you'" (p. 34). Fromm comes close to the thinking of John in the lofty comment: "If I truly love one person I love all persons, I love the world. I love life" (p. 39).

III. *Love endures.* The kind of love that God defines hangs on. John repeats the verb *abide*:

"We abide in him."
"God abides in those who confess that Jesus is the Son of God, and they abide in God."
"Those who abide in love, abide in God, and God abides in them."

We have marriage because people who love each other naturally want to live together—to abide with each other. The glue that holds them together is stronger than all of the forces in life that strive to pry them apart. Although sometimes translated "to live with," the verb John employs is much stronger than a casual cohabitation. It is anchored in commitment. Vows are exchanged, promises are made, and a covenant bond is established, "until death alone shall part us." This is not a chemical fix that passes with the biological adjustment of your body clock. The eternal love of God is stronger than death. As love binds us eternally to the

God who is forever, love binds us to each other, "forever and ever, world without end. Amen."—Larry Dipboye

Topic: Hope Unashamed
TEXT: Rom. 5:1–5

Every few years a different religious idea pops up, and it would seem that we almost wear it out talking about it. The idea of hope is one of the latest of those ideas. Just now we are discussing theologies of hope—plural—for there are different kinds of futures that one may hope for. However, even though we are talking about hope much more than we did just a few years ago, this truth has had a durable life; it has never worn out. Hope, as an essential ingredient of the Christian faith, has never completely dropped out of our vocabulary, though it has been sometimes ignored.

In the magnificent thirteenth chapter of 1 Corinthians, the apostle Paul mentions hope, along with faith and love, as one of the abiding realities: "So faith, hope, love abide, these three; but the greatest of these is love" (1 Cor. 13:13 RSV). The symbol that has long stood before the United States Naval Academy chapel in Annapolis is an anchor that also bears the form of a cross. This anchor with the cross is the abiding symbol of hope.

Do we need hope in these days? Since we talk so much about it, it must be especially necessary. We need hope because of our everyday discouragements and vexations and frustrations. When life becomes cluttered, hope offers a way through. Also occasional crises arise, such as illness, persecution, failure, marital difficulty, and bereavement. Hope enables us to survive these seismic tremors at the foundations of our existence. But it is the inevitably of death, which all of us face, that offers the most sweeping challenge of all. Without hope, a pall hangs over the sweetness of every infant, the beauty of every flower, and the grace of every virtue. Therefore, let us examine this shining word that God has thrust among us in the midst of darkness, defeat, and death.

I want to say three simple things. First, hope is ours. Second, hope is hard-won. And third, hope is reliable.

I. First of all, then, the apostle tells us that hope is ours: "We rejoice in our hope of sharing the glory of God" (Rom. 5:2 RSV).

Now there are different levels of hope. When we use the word, we can mean different things. One kind of hope may be only wishful thinking. Charles Dickens's Mr. Macawber is a man who lives impecuniously, hoping that his luck will improve tomorrow. In and out of debtor's prison for nonpayment of his bills, he keeps hoping that his ship will come in, that tomorrow will be better than today. The main problem is that he never undergirds any of his hopes with honest toil. For him hope is a substitute for work. The American humorist Josh Billings once said, "I never knew a man who lived on hope but what spent his old age at somebody else's expense." If the world's leaders keep hoping that problems created by the population explosion in certain parts of the world will go away and yet do nothing significant about it, then we are headed for disaster. If we continue to pollute the air and water, hoping that everything will be all right, and do nothing significant to correct the problem, again, we are headed for disaster. If we continue to waste our natural resources as if they were inexhaustible, hoping that there will always be enough to meet our human needs, once again, disaster awaits us.

Another kind of hope is reasonable expectation. A man is injured in an automobile accident. The family is filled with anxiety about his recovery. He receives the best medical attention, and after a consultation among the doctors, one of them says to the family, "You have every reason to hope for the best." Their experience with similar cases makes it possible for them to offer hope, for there is reasonable expectation of recovery.

However, the hope the apostle speaks of is certainly more than wishful thinking, more even than reasonable expectation. It is confident assurance. Assurance of what? The assurance of sharing the glory of God. That is, through our faith in Jesus Christ, we have the confident assurance that we will partake in God's triumph over sin and death. When Dr. D. E. King, a well-known preacher from Chicago, was asked why the Christians in the black churches have always been so joyful in their worship, even when things were going very badly for them everywhere else, he said, "We rejoice in what we are going to have." Indeed, regardless of what is happening around us, regardless of our discouragements, our crises, and the grim fact of death itself, we can rejoice, not because of our troubles but because of what we are going to have. We can enjoy the confident assurance that we shall share the glory of God. This glorious assurance is ours for the taking.

II. Now let us go a step further. The apostle also tells us that hope is hard-won: "Suffering produces endurance, and endurance produces character and character produces hope" (Rom. 5:3–4 RSV).

Hope at its best lies at the end of a long road.

Hope at its best begins in suffering. If one suffers, hope may seem—and actually be—far, far away. But for Anton Boisen, hope began in a mental hospital where he was a patient. For Dostoevski, the Russian novelist, hope began as he stood before a firing squad for execution and received a last-minute reprieve. For Ernest Gordon, chaplain at Princeton University, hope began in the filth, stench, and death of a Japanese concentration camp during World War II, where, as a prisoner and an agnostic, a new window on life was opened up for him. In still other kinds of suffering, hope for many persons has had its first frail beginnings. Hope followed hard on the heels of failure, of illness, and of discouragement.

On the way to hope, suffering produces endurance. When an athlete is training for the *big* game, it is suffering that produces the endurance necessary for the real performance. Sometimes he may think his lungs will burst and he will almost scream from the agony of his training, but it is this very suffering that produces the endurance necessary to win when the actual contest takes place. Suffering is bearable if it has meaning, if it looks forward to something, if it has a goal. Suffering is transformed by meaning. My maternal grandmother was an invalid for several years. She never complained, but in answer to a question, she said, "I suffer death every minute." Once she said to me, "I don't know why I have to suffer as I do, but I believe I'll understand sometime." Suffering actually produced a triumphant endurance that lasted through those years.

Endurance produces character and brings God's approval. As you endure, your value system changes. Little by little, you learn what is important in life and what is unimportant, what is worth striving for and what is empty of meaning; you learn why what God expects of you and plans for you is more important than what you had planned for yourself. In other words, what you work for and what you expect gradually come into line with what God wills for you. It is little wonder, then, that the poet Keats wrote: "The world is the vale of soul-making." God must look at the souls of men and women who have endured all kinds of sufferings and achieved unusual depths of character and integrity, and say, as he said after he had created the world and human beings, "It is good . . . it is very good."

God's approval creates hope. When we are sure that God has accepted us, that God has affirmed us, that God has said *yes* to us, we have reason to hope. "We belong to God," was Israel's conviction. In all of the nation's shifting fortunes, Israel believed that God was on her side. Even when God opposed the nation, even when God brought the nation into defeat in battle and exile, Israel never ceased to hope, to have the radiant assurance that all of this was the work of God, creating a marvelous future. Of course, the people often doubted and complained. Their prophets remonstrated with God, like Tevye, in *Fiddler on the Roof,* who asked the Lord why he couldn't choose someone else once in a while.

If you know that God is on your side, though God sometimes may punish you, you never have to give up hoping. You may even sing in the words of the Broadway musical, *South Pacific,* "I can't get it out of my heart."

III. And now a final step. The apostle tells us that hope is reliable: "And hope does not disappoint us, because God's love has been poured into our hearts through the Holy Spirit which has been given to us" (Rom. 5:5 RSV).

This hope of which the apostle speaks is reliable because it rests on God alone. True hope is not built on our intelligence, our performance, our character, or our connections. Our wisdom, our works, our goodness, and our friends at some point fall short of the glory of God. Though we are created in the image of God, our humanity is forever showing through and in one way or another dishonoring God and bringing shame to ourselves. The future into which God is leading us can never be built on the foundations of human achievement. God has to work with sin and failure and defeat and death. It was William Manson who said, "The only God the New Testament knows is the God of the resurrection." And just as our character apart from the grace of God cannot determine the Christian's hope, neither can outward circumstances decide the questions of the Christian's hope. "For I am sure," wrote the apostle Paul, "that neither death, nor life, nor angels, nor principalities, nor things present, nor things to come, nor powers, nor height, nor depth, nor anything else in all creation will be able to separate us from the love of God in Christ Jesus our Lord" (Rom. 8:38–39 RSV).

This hope is reliable, also, because it is certified by the Holy Spirit within us. Samuel Johnson, the English author, was once asked by a woman, "How does one know when he has sinned?" Johnson replied, "A man knows when he has sinned, and that's that!" So it is with the presence of the Holy Spirit within us, creating hope. We know when the Holy Spirit is in our heart and life, and that's that! The Holy Spirit, of course, does not make us infallible, does not guarantee that we shall never be discouraged, does not make us perfect beings. But even while we enjoy the knowledge that the Holy Spirit is in us, he is transforming us, making us into new and different and better persons. Assurance, confident assurance, and transformation of our lives go together. If we claim to have the Holy Spirit within us and yet it makes no difference in how we think and live and behave toward other people, then our hope is false. "God's love has been poured into our hearts through the Holy Spirit which has been given to us." God loves us, and we love others. "We know that we have passed out of death into life, because we love the brethren" (1 John 3:14 RSV).

This hope can enable you and me to face life today undaunted. The ultimate enemy—death—cannot destroy our confident assurance that God will create "new heavens and a new earth." The crises that again and again burst rudely into our lives, such as failure in marriage, business, or in health—these cannot destroy the bright confidence that God is doing great things in our lives, even in the hour of our suffering. And certainly the little difficulties and vexations of everyday living are not too much for God; what God has promised will make all of them more bearable and actually shame us for our preoccupation with trivialities while God is offering his glory to us.

Accept the suffering of the present moment. Don't regard as the sign of God's rejection of you the pain that he lets you feel. Rather, look at it as a token of his acceptance. "The Lord disciplines those he loves, and he chastens everyone he accepts as his child" (Heb. 12:6 TNIV). As theologian Karl Barth put it, "The gate at which all hope seems lost is the place at which it is continually renewed."[5]

Topic: Who Shall Sit at Our Table?
TEXT: Acts 10:34–43

Who shall sit at our table? I suppose another way to raise the same question is, With whom shall we have fellowship? Put even more crudely: What kinds of persons do we want sitting in our pews? And I would guess the question behind that question is, Are there limits, even to our Christian love? And what in the world has any of this to do with Easter and the Resurrection?

Now, I'd venture a guess that you've come here this morning convinced that the preacher's message would simply go over familiar ground. After all, we know that the Resurrection of Jesus Christ has something to do with death being vanquished. And most of us are already aware that Easter celebrates the conquest of the cross; those themes, significant as they may be, have been well worn! So what we'll look at this morning is the somewhat neglected theme of faith in Christ as Lord.

How ironic that the Church should drift so far from the conviction that was once the bedrock foundation of her faith! The lordship of Christ was of central importance to the Gospel writers and the early Church. Around the issue of Christ's lordship, congregations locked horns, Christians broke communion with other Christians, and apostles used rivers of ink writing letters to lift up the lordship of Christ as the cornerstone of the whole Christian worship.

And for these apostles the Resurrection was the essential reality confirming Christ's lordship. The Risen Redeemer was the Lord of life—beyond question. There could be no legitimate contenders to the throne! Because the Easter event was God's mark on Jesus as the Messiah—the Lord of creature, creation, and the universal Church.

So, you see, the question of lordship began to loom large, as the gospel started to spread throughout the Gentile world, where there were loads of lords and hoards of gods—all demanding nothing short of absolute devotion!

Of course, you're aware that the Church began as a Jewish sect. It was born in the soils of Semitic peoples. And with good reason these Jews were not all that trusting of Gentiles, primarily because the Jews were—by far—in the minority. And minority mentalities tend to be very protective. It's a simple question of survival!

The Jews wouldn't want to risk losing their faith, their traditions, and their own particular identity. So they tended to stay pretty much to themselves. It's no exaggeration to state

---

[5]James W. Cox, *Surprised by God* (Nashville: Broadman Press, 1979), pp. 87–93.

that they lived with incredible pressures to forsake their faith, to drop their single-minded devotion to God, to trade in their rich traditions for some cheap imitations, to become good citizens of Caesar's empire. But they also knew that with "a bit of pork here and a pinch of incense to Caesar there," before long their faith would be lifeless!

Strange, isn't it? Often in contemporary Christian circles you'll hear heated discussions about whether or not the Jews will be "saved." It's as though we'd forgotten the words of God to father Abraham: "For the promise is to you and to your children and to all that are far off, everyone whom the Lord our God calls to him." Anyway, here's the irony of it all. For the early Church the most pressing question was: Can the Gentiles be saved? And buried beneath that question was a concern about the lordship of Christ.

The apostle Peter is a prime example of a Jew convinced that Gentiles would hardly qualify as recipients of redemption. The very thought of a Gentile being gifted with God's grace, coming under the covenant blessings would, most likely, cause old Peter to bust a gut! I imagine he would've considered that prospect to be nothing short of someone's foolish fantasy. Then again, it was the apostle Paul who once wrote, "God's foolishness is wiser than human wisdom!"

And one day Peter had his faith shaken to the core by an encounter with some of what Paul called, "God's foolishness." While perched on a roof in prayer, a vision made it crystal clear that Peter's prejudice against Gentiles wasn't in God's game plan! In fact, he was told that it was time to take himself to the home of a Roman centurion named Cornelius. And I can just see Peter scratching his head as he tried to make sense of "God's foolishness."

Be that as it may, Peter decided to put in an appearance. And while there, he thought it might help if he preached a portion of the sermon he'd prepared for Sunday. Well, low-and-behold, when he was about half-way through his third major point, the power of the Holy Spirit swept over Cornelius and his entire clan! Had God granted the Gentiles a share in his sacred covenant grace?

That's exactly what God had done! Because if the Risen Redeemer was Lord of all, then the new covenant community of Christ would never be confined to a certain nationality or race. As Saint Paul put the point in a letter: "There's neither Jew nor Greek, slave nor free, male nor female; for you are all one in Christ Jesus!" Talk about a "New world order!"

Here's what the early Church proclaimed to be the promise and power of Easter: now there was a Lord of lords set loose in this universe—a Lord to rule over every ruinous force we could possibly imagine; a Lord of compassion who had conquered every enemy of his people; a Lord out to create a new community where love, forgiveness, and peace could prevail; a Lord who commanded dedication and nothing short of wholehearted devotion from his disciples.

And where did the early Church experience this reality of a reconciled world? First and foremost, at table—that's where! At table they learned to love in the spirit of their Living Lord, as they sat down to a sacred meal. None would be barred from fellowship. The beggar rubbed elbows with the banker. The merchant broke bread with the mariner. And the Jew passed the cup to the Gentile. At this table they learned to love in the spirit of their Living Lord.

Each time they would gather at table, the presence of Jesus would be felt with and within their common friendship. But they were to break bread, as Jesus had done, as an act of acceptance, love, and a bonded companionship. They were to remember his way of eating with those whom society, or the religious establishment for that matter, deemed worthless. In this table fellowship, they came to discover the meaning of Christ's lordship over their lives.

What's more, they were to share table fellowship without turning the meal into a testimonial dinner for super-saints! At this table all were equal in the sight of God, under the lordship of the crucified and Risen Christ. They were to break bread in the spirit of unity and peaceful coexistence.

And before coming to this table, they were to make right the wrongs committed against a brother or sister. There were to be no grudges, bad feelings, or wounded hearts hanging from this table. But if they were brought, they were to be healed!

Breaking bread in this spirit would make the presence and power of the Risen Christ a reality for all. But sometimes they failed to see the presence of their Living Lord in the fellowship of the faithful. And when that happened, heartache wasn't far behind.

Without the reality of that first Easter, this meal we share would consist of nothing more than a portion of bread and a thimble of wine! Easter celebrates the reality of Christ's presence as our Risen and Living Lord. He is here, with us, for us, binding us together in one body of which he—and he alone!—is the head. At the Lord's table we are all one to Christ, in Christ, by Christ, and through Christ! For whenever we eat this bread and drink this cup, we affirm our unity under the lordship of the Risen, Living Christ.—Albert J. D. Walsh

SECTION V

MESSAGES FOR FUNERALS AND BEREAVEMENT

SERMON SUGGESTIONS

Topic: Gentle Prophet
Eulogy for Henlee Hulix Barnette
By Bill J. Leonard

Humanly speaking, Henlee Barnette was what Jesus would have been like if Jesus had lived ninety-three years. Now we are not talking deity here. Indeed, Henlee would scoff at the idea, with one of those great throwaway lines that become keepers, like "I'm really a barbarian with a thin veneer of culture." But, I repeat, humanly speaking, Henlee Barnette was what Jesus would have been like if Jesus had lived ninety-three years. Here's why I think so.

First, he was eccentric to a fault, flaunting convention in religion and culture. Prophets are almost always eccentrics, or perhaps the best of them are so far ahead of the rest of us that we mistake insight for eccentricity. We prefer labels to listening to them. Jesus said it: "For John the Baptizer came neither eating bread nor drinking wine, and you say, 'he is possessed.' The son of man came, eating and drinking, and you say, 'Look at him! A glutton and a drinker, a friend of tax-collectors and sinners!' And yet God's wisdom is proved right by all who are his children."

Second, to the very end he was a teacher-learner—teaching, teaching, learning, learning, learning—reminding human beings who gathered at his home or who read his books of all those letters and op-ed pieces of the things we know or think we know but readily forget. As Mark writes of Jesus: "On the Sabbath he went to the synagogue and began to teach. The people were amazed at his teaching, for, unlike the scribes, he taught as one who knew what he was talking about."

Third, he was ever exposing and exploding hubris, pomposity, self-righteousness, and what he called "theological twaddle" in fundamentalists, liberals, moderates (an anti-Baptist word, he insisted), evangelicals and academics, and every kind of Baptist. Jesus said it: "Alas to you, scribes and Pharisees, hypocrites, you pay tithes of mint and dill and cumin, but you overlook the weightier demands of the law, justice, mercy and good faith." (By the way, academics were not sacrosanct to him either. He called our graduation processions "Peacock Parades.")

Fourth, he went about doing good, with, for, and among the broken and the disenfranchised, even as he became more bent and broken himself. Isaiah and Jesus echo that in the superb text: "The spirit of the Lord is upon me, because he has anointed me to preach good news to the poor, to let the broken victim go free, to proclaim the year of the Lord's favor."

Fifth, throughout those ninety-three years, like Jesus, Henlee was oh, so full of grace—a grace he offered to the people on the margins, a grace that would not let him take himself too seriously, even as he was deadly serious about Jesus and justice. So you see, Henlee Barnette was what Jesus would have been like if he had lived ninety-three years.

338

And here we are in this good place where he worshiped across the years, sending him on his way, celebrating to heaven his long and legendary life. Yes, we are sad as can be that his voice will no longer be heard in the world, but here and now we commit ourselves to living out and passing on the often uncomfortable ideals he nurtured in and around us. Today we say to John and Wayne, Martha and Jim: we share your sadness, but we also join you in celebrating your father's long life, his insatiable curiosity, and his abiding humility. Today we send him on the way already taken with his two beloved spouses, Charlotte Ford Barnette and Helen Poarch Barnette—two grand women dying all too soon, both dear to him and to their children as well.

It was quite a journey, wasn't it? Born on Sugar Loaf Mountain, North Carolina, Henlee (along with lifelong friend Wayne Oates) worked in the textile mills of the Piedmont region factories built on "can-to-can't, dark-to-darker" working schedules, where injuries were inevitable and benefits nonexistent until Franklin Roosevelt's New Deal brought minimum wage and other opportunities. After FDR, did Henlee ever vote for a Republican? Not in *this* world! In and out of school, he found his way to Wake Forest College, studying ethics for the first time with the likes of Hubert Poteat and Olin Binkley, graduating in 1940. In 1998, Wake Forest University gave him an honorary Doctor of Divinity degree. When I called him up in fall of 1997 to tell him that the faculty and trustees had approved the degree, he replied: "Well, tell them to hurry; I'm eighty-seven you know." At a dinner given for honorees by university president Tom Hearn, Henlee of course charmed everyone, including the playwright Romulus Linney, with statements such as, ""You know all those dead people whose pictures are hanging in the Wake Forest library? I knew them all."

Then he came to the Baptist seminary here in Louisville, where he earned two degrees, along with students the likes of Wayne Oates, Clarence Jordan, Carlyle Marney, and other audacious folks who would shape succeeding generations with their pastoral insights and social radicalism. Serving as pastor of a church in Louisville's Haymarket district, the same part of town where his great Baptist mentor Walter Rauschenbusch and dissertation subject also pastored, he lived among the immigrants, street people, and tenement dwellers, challenging slum lords in the name of the exploited. Henlee once told me about the time that Carlyle Marney preached a revival at his church; at the end of one service, an old woman shook Henlee's hand and declared of Marney: "God almighty, pastor, I didn't understand a word he said, but sure seems like that man loves us, don't it?" God almighty, I wish I could have heard Carlyle Marney preaching a revival in Henlee Barnette's church in the Haymarket district of Louisville!

New doctorate in hand, he headed for Birmingham, Alabama, and a teaching position at Howard College (now Samford University) on a one-year contract. It was the late 1940s, well before *Brown* v. *The Board of Education,* and he had no sooner arrived than he began working to form networks that led to Birmingham's first-ever interracial pastor's conference—an act so scandalous and controversial that Howard refused to renew his contract. It was fifty years before Samford hired son Jim Barnette as university minister, and now another Barnette voice echoes across the quad.

He then moved to Deland, Florida, as a professor at Stetson University, where his continued responses to social and political justice led critics to label him a communist. He didn't last long at Stetson, either. Then he returned to the Baptist seminary in Louisville, and all hell broke loose. He marched with Martin Luther King Jr., worked for integration in this city, helped to link black and white Baptists in new ways, and in 1961 joined a group of young Turk professors with names like Ward, Bennett, and St. Amant in inviting Dr. King to speak in seminary chapel. So great was the furor that it was estimated that the school lost over $250,000, no small sum then and now. Today we say it was money well spent. (By the way, the only two SBC-related schools where King spoke in chapel were the Baptist seminary in Louisville and Wake Forest University—Barnette's two alma maters.)

Henlee challenged the Vietnam War and got himself harassed by the FBI for sixteen years, he said. He called for amnesty for draft defectors and helped bring Philip Berrigan, the ex-priest and antiwar activist, to Louisville. Henlee got him out on a pass from prison, as I recall. Berrigan's visit was likewise so controversial that the administration put a statement on the President's Bulletin Board repudiating any responsibility for the activist's visit. Students taped a 3 X 5 card on the glass, repudiating any responsibility for the seminary administration!

When he could not stay at the seminary any longer and was not made senior professor, Henlee developed a second (or was it third?) career, this one with his friend and brother Wayne Oates at the University of Louisville Medical School. There he explored the burgeoning field of bioethics in ways the medical students had not examined.

Through it all there were the stories—legendary, mythic, apocryphal, and hilarious. Some of us have been sharing them in e-mails this week, sent from across the country.

I have so many favorites. One story suggests that when he got letters from uninformed critics he would write back: "Some fool sent me this letter and signed your name. I thought you'd like to know." Another I read in his memoirs goes like this: A student-critic came by his office to say he didn't think Henlee was taking his subject seriously enough and furthermore the lectures were boring: "Well, if you think the lectures are boring, how about me? I have to give them."

Jim Nogalski wrote of his first meeting with Henlee in 1992: "When I met him, I said, 'I have heard stories about you ever since I was at Samford, but I wonder whether some of them are true.' His response: 'Which ones?' I rattled one off about someone from Ohio writing a letter to the editor in the Baptist paper complaining about his Cooperative Program money being spent (wasted) on a professor who obviously did not represent the views of Southern Baptists. So, the story goes, Henlee went to the library, researched the profile of the church from which the person came, gave him the benefit of the doubt that he was a tither, then proceeded to write the man a check to reimburse him for the CP money that went toward Henlee's salary so that the man could rest easy. Henlee, according to the story, sent the man a check for eleven cents. When I told him the story, his eyes lit up. He told me the name of the man, the name of the association in Ohio, the name of the church, and corrected one detail. It was only ten cents. I never doubted another story."

Someone else reminded me of the day a student remarked to another professor, "I'm worried about Dr. Barnette; he looks so thin, and drawn, and boney," to which the professor responded: "Hell, I wouldn't worry; he's looked like that for thirty years."

But perhaps my own favorite story is a personal one from the first moment I met him. He was sitting in the living room of that faculty house at the Baptist Seminary here on a January day in 1975, when I had my final interview for a teaching position—my first ever—at the school. After a barrage of questions from other folks, Henlee looked me square in the eye, with a twinkle in his, and said, "Well, you need to know that Texans don't last more than two or three years here. Think you can outlast them?" I mumbled something about giving it my best shot, but I knew right then that here was a person who would tell you things straight-up. I stayed in that place sixteen years, and he told me later that he was glad I beat the odds; then he added: "I beat them, too."

And that brings me to a final observation about this amazing man and his impact on so many of us near and far. For three straight days after Jim called about his father's death, I could not speak out loud about Henlee to friends, students, or reporters without weeping. At one point my Episcopal colleague Doug Bailey said, "Bill, that man's put his fingerprints all over your soul!" And I guess he did.

Reflecting on my early and enduring tears, I first thought that Henlee's life and witness is a symbol of what we had and what we lost as Baptists in the South. After years of contro-versy and recrimination, I thought perhaps Henlee's death was a double fault because it caused us to probe the depth of multiple losses across the last two decades. But I was wrong in that initial assessment. When I finally realized—and what dried my tears—was this: For me, and I suspect for many of you, Henlee Barnette's life and death are not symbols of what we've lost but abiding affirmation of what we've found. You see, Henlee would not allow a *place* to silence him. That is, for me, his abiding legacy. Places are wonderful, sacred even, but the idolatry of place is idolatry all the same. Like those Baptists of the seventeenth century and some of the best ones since, Henlee understood the power of conscience and the calling to dissent against establishments social, political, and religious. He chose to trust in God, not in institutions, and let the devil take the hindmost.

His memoirs recall his earliest memory—a moment of anger he felt when a bully harassed his sister Maso at the farm on Sugar Loaf Mountain when he was barely three years old. His conclusion: "You can measure the character of an individual by the way they treat defenseless persons." And, he added, "This applies to institutions as well." Somehow the lesson of a three-year-old endured ninety-odd more years. If justice was to roll down like waters and righteousness like a mighty stream, if he, like Jesus, was "anointed" to preach the gospel to the poor and let the broken victim go free, and if, from the heart of Baptist identity, conscience and dissent matter, then Henlee Barnette would not, could not, be silent in places like North Carolina, or Alabama, or Florida, or Kentucky on issues of race and war, gender and bioethics, poverty and exploitation, wherever it appeared. Along with Walter Rauschnebusch and Martin King, Henlee Barnette was on a quest for the elusive "Beloved Community," where the hungry are fed, the naked clothed, the blind see, the speechless speak, and where no one is "left behind." And in that quest his conscience would not allow any *place* to silence him. You see, our tears today are not for what we lost but what Henlee helped us find: our own courage, and conscience, and voice for the remainder of our journeys.

So this week in the home stretch to All Hallows Eve and All Saints Day, we say, "Farewell, Henlee Hulix Barnette—curmudgeon, prophet, father, eccentric, ethicist, saint, and unashamed Baptist radical. We sing out over you the epitaph of Martin Luther, an earlier eccentric who would not be silent either. "My conscience is captive to the Word of God. I cannot and I will not recant, for to go against conscience is neither safe nor right. God help me. Here I stand. Amen."

For all the saints, especially the radical ones like you, Henlee, thank God.

Topic: Reflections
Funeral Service for My Father, William W. Peters Sr.
By William W. Peters Jr.

Note: We held the funeral for my father on January 1, 2005, on a beautifully sunny winter day. A fast-moving cancer cut his life short, but Dad never ventured into any hand-wringing victimization. He understood his lot as simply an acceleration of the human condition to begin with and proceeded to go about doing what he had to do to prepare both himself and us. Dad understood Henry Kissinger's one-time observation that having no alternative yields an astonishing clarity of mind.

As a lifelong minister and pastor, Dad had witnessed many depths and had seen them handled both well and poorly. His "determined acceptance" prepared him for a dual role he fulfilled admirably: first, as the one doing the dying, leading those left behind through the process, and second, showing us how to face our grief while he lived. When he died, his funeral was a graceful denouement instead of an unraveling descent of grief.

Since then, I am impelled to share these observations as a way to honor his life, and, I hope, to serve his aim to have his last moments craft an instructive and uplifting purpose.

So, recall the overarching lesson that Jesus and my father taught us by their examples: that giving strengthens us all and that love, the "greatest of these," is the gift of yourself and God in you. Go on, with love's inspiration and energy, to prove this great truth in the examples of your own lives.

And, "Thank you." There is no better remembrance than one that guides our today and tomorrows.

Message: God asks no man whether he will accept life. That is not the choice. One must take it. The only choice is how (Henry Ward Beecher). The same is true of death.

Our family had an opportunity many of you will not enjoy: a clear alarm *and* sufficient time to prepare. I hope you *will* be fortunate enough that the one living their last can pull you along and guide you as Dad did with us. The natural question for me at this time is to determine what it means that my father was *my father,* so I'd beg your indulgence to share some observations.

First, and on a personal note that we can all appreciate, they say such nice things at funerals, it makes me sad to realize I'm going to miss mine by just a few days (Garrison Keillor).

Second, Dad would have been touched by your many expressions of love and appreciation, but he wrote his own funeral service to minimize the eulogizing. He didn't want that to distract us from what he felt was most important: his final opportunity to craft an instructive message. Fortunately, I am his son, and children have a license to be unpredictable, especially when lovingly disobedient.

With regard to both our admiration and the intrusive discomforts of his cancer, Dad enjoyed the full depth of double meaning in Jack Benny's quip at an awards show when he said, "I don't deserve this award, but I've got arthritis too, and I don't deserve that either."

When we were in Orange, Virginia, in the 1970s, Dad assisted the church there in hosting luncheons for a group of Meals-on-Wheels retirees. For entertainment, and in a role many of us knew and loved, he once brought his guitar and sang. At the conclusion of that program, an elderly black woman commented, "Ain't it nice to have a preacher that can do something useful?"

It is. Let me show you some other ways.

America today is in love with leadership and ambition and will. We seem to believe these qualities are the ultimate product and best expression of our individuality and freedoms. We seem to recognize as leaders only those "authority" figures that love bold and controversial pronouncements. Many "authorities," at least privately, see themselves as self-made men, and worship their creator accordingly. They make prideful public statements about their faith and proclaim that God is on our side. They end up believing that they themselves are the message.

But God gave us free agency, the power to choose, knowing that a willing and *mindful assent to love* was more powerful than *mindless adherence to form*. As humans, our understanding and our worship of God is imperfect. He is greater, his tent is bigger, his mansion has more rooms than any of *us* can grasp. And so, happily, there is another and vastly different model: quieter perhaps, but no less radical.

Among these, leadership is like a small elastic string with which you urge and pull instead of a rod with which you drive and beat. The ambition of these leaders may also be huge, but it is to bring change and growth in the world by moving within a group of many others, who move of their own will, and in answer to the call this leader kindles in their own hearts.

Far from being self-made, these leaders see themselves made and shaped by their guiding mission as it unfolds an ounce at a time, inch by inch in the small and tentative openings they evoke among the many hearts and minds of those they touch with love and care and respect. This cumulative effect is what their guiding power seeks and how it succeeds.

In the Christian tradition, these are the leaders in the paradigm of the "shepherd." We might also call them gentlemen, to use a term that, sadly, I haven't heard mentioned in public discourse for some time. These are the people whose character is honest and strong and realistic enough to be humbled in response to success and recognition instead of being seduced by it.

They are willing to be seen to fail and laugh at themselves on their patient way to their success. As human beings, they cannot take themselves too seriously, and so they embrace laughter and shared merriment as instruments for the journey. They view the principles they serve as their source of strength, not their own personality and ambition. They see themselves as vessels, conduits of greater things. They study how to get themselves *out of the way* of their mission and message, *not* how to stamp their egos and personalities on the front of it.

They do not presume to say that God is on our side. They are instead concerned that *we* are on *God's* side (Abraham Lincoln). They know that we will need his strength upon our journeys, because, as we hear in the book of Esther, "who knows but whether you have come to the kingdom for such a time as this?" You have to be ready to give up the life you planned in order to live the life that is waiting for you (Joseph Campbell). You must dare to fail in order to succeed.

The difference my father made to me is as an example of this gentle but powerful leadership—of how to live and, now, how to leave. The lessons were clear, but the words to describe and list them have been hard to find because he never forced them upon me. There is subtle wisdom in this, for as I am now discovering firsthand, children may or may not do as you say, but they never fail to do as they see (James Baldwin).

Make sure that:

Your conduct proceeds from goodwill, and your self-control is equal to the emergency.

Your manner of dealing with others shows that you recognize and honor the dignity of each individual and the small spark of God that is present in all of his children and his creation.

You always use the smallest tool necessary.

You oppose without bitterness and yield without being defeated.

You offer thanks to those who do not expect it and for what they do not recognize as gifts that they have given.

You honor a giver by your acceptance, but confer your gifts and favors and compliments in ways that make you feel as if you are receiving them.

You realize laughter is a gift we can always give each other, and it's one of the best there is.

You act with courage. If your conscience is clear of offense, you will have nothing to fear.

You look for and teach others opportunities for happiness and wonder in God's creation. This is a window through which we can approach that mindfully childlike state that Jesus extolled and we so struggle to achieve.

Do all these well enough and long enough, and your foe may be defeated in becoming your friend (Abraham Lincoln).

Recently, many of us will have participated in a Christmas candlelight service. These are beautiful spectacles, especially when a transcendent musical program sends cathedrals of sound vaulting upward, lifting our own hearts and minds and prayers along with them. The greatest beauty of these for me lies in a simple but inescapable and extraordinarily powerful observation—that the light of one's candle is *never* diminished by the lighting of another's.

Quite the contrary, in fact. That little point of light grows greater, according to how many others it touches. Which candle is then the *loser?* This is the way my father lived and loved and worked and died, and a way in which we humans, caught up as we are in our own worlds of haste and circumstance, may reclaim and live God's message of love and stewardship.

We don't have candles enough here today to recreate that environment, but I would ask you a gentle favor. I know you will remember how my father's life touched yours, but I'd like to add a small twist. I want to create a new memory here—one that we can all share, a new memory in honor of our father, your husband, your friend, and pastor, a new memory that lives in our hearts and bodies.

Reach out here, now, with your right hand for the arm or shoulder or hand of the person next to you, that fellow traveler you may or may not have yet met. Let it rest there a moment and remember what you feel. Believe that these unexpected points of contact will be there whether you need something to hold onto or whether you can offer support.

Reflect that it is my [father's] and his [our Shepherd's] wish that we go on from here, go on about our journeys.

Before we go from this place and retreat back into the shells of our lives, remember him in this moment, this simple and small new memory.

Be at peace, and know that there is abundant love for you and within you, and it is nearer than you think. Who among us is now weaker, more vulnerable than just a moment ago?

Extract new trust and love and purpose from our shared feelings of loss.

And now, see if you don't agree: "Ain't it nice to know a preacher who can do something useful?"

Topic: My Redeemer Lives
Memorial for Stan Benson
By Larry Dipboye
TEXT: Job 14:7–14, 19:23–27

Job was a good man who appears from nowhere and disappears into the mist of the Old Testament. Some believe that he is an icon who represents all of us. His only claim to fame is the unreasonable suffering that he experienced and the very human problems that he raised. His story addresses two questions in particular: (1) Do people get exactly what they deserve in life? and—a question of hope—(2) What is the point, the purpose of life? Job does not provide us with better answers than you will find in the Gospels or celebrated on Easter morning, but Job raises the right questions to which the death and Resurrection of our Lord gives response.

Life does not run in rigid tracks of precise logic. Sometimes the answer comes too quickly and too easily. Sometimes we are left with unfulfilled longings and unanswered questions before which even God is silent. Paul reminded us that we see in a glass dimly. Like an algebraic equation, the missing element "X" is often on the wrong side of the equal sign. Not only do we not know the answer, we don't even understand the question. That is where Job comes in. Job causes us to face issues in life and death that many of us try to ignore and prefer to avoid. Then we are shocked awake by the sudden death of a dear friend, someone whose very stability and loving character has been on the hope-side of life. With people like Stan in the world, we have a sense, with Browning's Pippa: "God's in his heaven; all's right with the world." But this is a world where good people suffer, and good people are snatched right from in front of our eyes. If that does not raise questions in your heart, you are not paying attention.

Perhaps Job is a mythical character who stands in the Bible as a symbol of unjust suffering that allows a skeptic like Archibald MacLeish to toy with the issues in his play *J. B.* If he is real, I believe his life is real. Even if not historical, I can imagine Job and Stan looking at the questions and standing in awe at the new perspective of seeing face-to-face and knowing as we are known by God. I believe that they would agree.

Nature does not supply the answer. Natural immortality proclaimed by Plato is not the gospel of Christ. Tennyson reminded us that nature is red in tooth and claw. Yet Job, in the same kind of frustration that all of us feel at such times, cried out, "For there is hope for a tree, if it is cut down, that it will sprout again . . . but mortals die, and are laid low; humans expire, and where are they?"

Joyce Kilmer gave us the line, "I think that I shall never see a poem as lovely as a tree." What a magnificent thing of beauty and joy—the tree! Truly a magnificent creation of God, but would you really want to change places with a tree? When life gets to the dregs with Job, perhaps the longevity of a tree is attractive, but God made Adam and Eve in the divine image. Yet Solomon in all of his glory was not arrayed like the lilies of the field that are here today and kindling tomorrow. God feeds the birds of the air. They neither sow nor gather into barns, but God feeds them. "Are you not of more value than they?"

No, Job. Nature falls short of the promise you seek. You must look elsewhere for the vindication of your life and the justification of your existence.

History cannot contain the human spirit. In desperation, Job grasps for the straw of immortality in the archives of human memory: "O that my words were written down! O that they were inscribed in a book!"

Stan and I share a common path that led us through Fort Worth, Texas, and Southwestern Seminary. At different times, both of us worked for the Texas Christian University library for the slave wages allowed by the university. It was there that Stan was inspired to center his ministry in education and the field of library science.

My wife worked at T.C.U. for the department chair of the School of Education. He came into their office one day and opened a discussion of the meaning of life after death. He had been to a funeral, and it was around Easter, and he loved to playfully pick at our Baptist identity. My wife acknowledged that she believed in life after death, and he asked what that meant. He went on to talk about Ammon Carter, the well-known philanthropist whose name was on everything in town, and cynically speculated that his immortality must be superior to everyone else. His name was certainly chiseled in enough stone around town.

Percy Shelly's poem "Ozymandias" describes a mythical Egyptian statue erected as a monument for all future generations to behold. Shelley wrote: "My name is Ozymandias, king of kings: Look on my works, ye Mighty, and despair! Nothing beside remains. Round the decay of that colossal wreck, boundless and bare the lone and level sands stretch far away." If our hope rests on monuments, we are indeed a desperate lot.

Books once viewed as symbols of something lasting have become as abundant and temporary as the birds. As much as Stan loved books, I think that he would advise Job that getting your name in a book does not satisfy the need for immortality.

Our hope rests only in the eternal vigilance of a loving God. Job has all of the questions and none of the answers. He seemed to see through the fog of his suffering long enough to see Easter morning. Handel interpreted that line from Job as a statement of the gospel of Christ: "I know that my redeemer lives" is in line with the hope of the earliest Christians before an empty tomb and fulfilled prophecy. The *goel,* the redeemer, of Job was an avenger of injustice, one who would vindicate him before God and perhaps even rescue him from God. Rather than a cry of victory, this may have been a whimper of defeat. The words, however, betray a hope that transcends the mind and the time of Job.

Murray Joseph Haar was the son of a devout Jewish family. His parents were among the few relatives who survived the Nazi Holocaust, but they did not like to discuss the horrible experience with their son. He grew up in anger and frustration—anger at a God who would allow such things to happen and who remains silent before such atrocity. "No God with an ounce of love or compassion could have watched children being burned alive and have remained silent."

Murray met a Lutheran pastor who not only allowed his questions but suggested that his questions were holy, that questions and faith go together. He learned about another Jew, who died unjustly, shouting questions at God. When asked where Jesus was in the death camps of the Holocaust, the pastor replied, "He was with the dying, relentlessly and unceasingly, screaming the questions at God."

The response of God to Job, to Auschwitz, and to the pain we feel in this moment does not come in mere word, but in the Word become flesh to dwell among us. The Advent we celebrate is God's response. God comes to us in Christ, O, Come Emmanuel.

Topic: "Lord, Keep Me Alive While I'm Still Living!"
By John Thompson
TEXT: John 11:17–27; the Epistle: 2 Cor. 5:16–6:2

Biblical text: Jesus said, "I am the resurrection and the life; he who believes in me, though he die, yet shall he live, and whoever lives and believes in me shall never die."—John 11:25

Contemporary text: "To be eighty years young is sometimes far more cheerful and hopeful than to be forty years old."—Unknown American Poet

Would you bet your life on this man? He is fifty-three years old. Most of his adult life has been a losing struggle against debt and misfortune. A war injury has denied him the use of his left hand. He has had several government jobs, succeeding at none, and he has often been in prison. Driven by heaven-know-what motives—boredom, hope of gain, creative impulse—he is determined to write a book. The book turns out to be one that has enthralled the world for more than 350 years. That former prisoner was Cervantes, and the book was *Don Quixote,* one of the greatest novels ever written.

His story poses an interesting question: Why do some persons discover new vitality and creativity to the end of their days, while others go to seed long before?

Mark Twain commented about this in his characteristic, pithy way: "Let us so live that when we come to die even the undertaker will be sorry." I am sure there are some people whom the coroner finds much difficulty in pronouncing dead because they have never really lived. Their living or dying makes so little difference.

Robert Frost penetrates to this predicament in lines from "The Death of the Hired Man": "Nothing to look backward to with pride, And nothing to look forward to with hope."

One is reminded, too, of Captain McWhirr in Joseph Conrad's novel, *Typhoon.* Captain McWhirr had sailed over the surface of the oceans as some men skim over their years of existence, only to sink gently into a placid grave, never having experienced the heights and depths of existence, ignorant of life to the last.

Seneca, the first-century Roman philosopher, conclusively makes our point when he writes: "The ultimate evil is to leave the company of the living before you die."

In one of Charles Schulz's comic strips, we see Charlie Brown coming downstairs for breakfast. As he sleepily rubs his eyes trying to get them open, he exclaims to his mother: "I think I have discovered my trouble in getting out of bed; I'm allergic to *morning!*" There *are* people who develop an allergy to morning, but the real tragedy is when persons develop an allergy to *life.*

Could this be the predicament of any one of us?

Afraid of life. Do *you* want life? Do you want life with a capital "L"? Do you have a real passion for living? Is life the most important thing in the world to you? Who would not answer, "Of course, I want life. Nothing is so precious to me." Is that so? Are you really sure about that?

One day a young man who thought that he was interested in life came running to Jesus. He asked, "What must I do that I may have eternal life?" The Living Bible has it, "What must I do that I may get to heaven?" However, there is a difference in meaning in the way we use the terms "eternal life" and "heaven." Heaven refers to life after *death;* eternal life denotes life after *birth.*

When Jesus tells the young man how he can enter into life: "Go, sell all that you have and give to the poor and come follow me," he turns away sorrowful.

Evidently, this young entrepreneur was more interested in security than in life. Life was too challenging, too demanding, too dangerous. He was not willing to die—to risk all—that he might *live;* what Jesus holds out to him as life, he interprets as death. To give priority to one's own security is to choose death.

The perennial message of Easter is that there is a life that death cannot destroy. It is not discovered in playing it safe but in risking all, as Jesus did. To choose life is not to evade death but to live life to the fullest—to risk anything and everything. If death comes, it does not destroy such a life but fulfills it.

Is this not the meaning of Dag Hammarskjöld, a former security general of the United Nations, when he wrote in the midst of his dangerous life: "Do not seek death. Death will find you. But seek the road which makes death a fulfillment."

Where had he learned that? From Jesus, whose life and teachings he daily meditated on. Is not Hammarskjöld's "Marking" but a paraphrase of Jesus' statement: "He who saves his life shall lose it but he who loses his life for my sake and for the sake of the gospel shall find it?"

To choose life, you see, is very different from choosing security. To choose life is to live by faith, to adventure, to give to the uttermost, to shoulder whatever cross God's love and purpose commands. To choose life, whatever the risk, is to believe in the Resurrection.

We think that a person, given a choice, will naturally choose life. Not so! We are afraid of life and often live by our fears rather than by faith.

The headlines of that first Easter morning: HE IS RISEN! HE IS RISEN INDEED! Shake the stones from the mouths of the caves where we spend our days in darkness hiding out from life. How many of us here live in the twilight zone of our fears rather than turning about to welcome the light of the Easter dawn into our lives? Does God's judgment upon people in the first century, as depicted by John in the prologue to his Gospel, fall upon us as well: "The Light is come, but men love their own darkness rather than God's life."

The exultation of Easter: The Resurrection is such a challenge to faith—to one's imagination—that when the apostle Paul proclaims that "all things have become new" (not some things, not many things, but all things), who can grasp this? We can only let go and let it grasp us.

There is an insanity about Easter that we who pride ourselves in our sanity will miss every time. The fact of the Resurrection excites, incites—an exultation that betrays our reasonable, prosy, pedantic ways. Of those early leaders in the Church, members of that little apostolic band, the New Testament records that they were as persons beside themselves. In the face of the threat of prison and even death, they shouted, "We can but speak the things which we have seen and heard: "Christ is risen!"

Handel, the composer of the oratorio that includes the "Hallelujah Chorus," was a person beside himself caught up in the rapture of the Christ-event. During the days that he was writing this composition, trays of food were left at the door of his study with a knock so as not to disturb him. But many meals were left untouched because he was so preoccupied in trying to compose music that in some way would express the exultation of the Resurrection, and the "Hallelujah Chorus" is testimony that he succeeded, for it lifts us right out of ourselves until we are more out of this world than in it. Is there a more thrilling musical experience this side of heaven?

What we are asking this morning is this: Does the exultation of the news of the Resurrection die with the fading of the notes and lyrics of that great "Hallelujah Chorus" so spiritually presented by the choirs and instrumentalists?

This seems to me something of the question Eugene O'Neill poses in his provocative drama, *Lazarus Laughed.* As you know or will have guessed, this play is based on the New Testament story of the raising of Lazarus—the Gospel lesson this morning. This drama is a parable illustrating man's fear of life.

God's laughter: The perennial joy of life. Lazarus is all the time smiling, laughing. He even laughs in the presence of death. He is an irresistible joy. He seems to grow younger all the time. He loves everyone. His contemporaries can't stand someone who is so *full of life.* His strange aliveness is as a judgment on their miserable, paltry living. His presence is too disturbing. They burn Lazarus at the stake, only to realize too late, that the darkness is in them. They are *afraid of life.*

O'Neill's theme reminds me of the story of the woman with a feather in her hat (the fact that she had a feather in her hat has nothing to do with this part of the story; I don't know how that got in here) who attended Easter services in another church. As she entered the sanctuary a couple greeted her: "Christ is risen!" To this news she responded with a kind of under-the-breath "Ugh," to be interpreted as "So what?" As she was ushered to her seat, the usher handed her a bulletin saying: "He is risen." To which the perturbed, unflappable worshiper responded: "Yea, I know; that's what they told me back there at the door."

You see, there *can* be an embarrassment in the Resurrection, as the playwright so artfully portrays.

People find difficulty in letting themselves go and being caught up in the rapturous joy this exudes. There is a hesitation, a reticence, even a reluctance to give full expression to the Resurrection joy found on almost every page of the New Testament. We excuse ourselves by saying: "Oh, we are so reserved. We are from New England." But O'Neill proclaims, through Lazarus, that the Resurrection is such an embarrassment because we are afraid of life—we fear *life* more than we fear death. This penetrating insight of the playwright is expressed by the chorus of Lazarus's followers when they chant:

> Men call life death and fear it.
> They hide from it in horror.
> Their lives are spent in hiding.
> Their fear becomes their living.
> They worship life as death.

When in the opening scene of the play, Lazarus repeats the affirmation, "Yes!" one of the characters asks him: "What did you find beyond there, Lazarus?" At this point in the script, the stage instructions for Lazarus are interesting; they read: [Lazarus smiles gently and speaks as if to a group of inquisitive children.] He says: "O Curious Greedy Ones, is not one world in which you know not how to live enough for you?"

But the curious guests keep asking: "What is beyond there? What is beyond?" In a voice of loving exclamation, Lazarus responds to their curiosity: "There is only *life!* I heard the heart of Jesus laughing in my heart; 'There is Eternal Life in No,' it said, 'and there is the same Eternal Life in Yes! Death is the fear between!' And my heart reborn to love of life cried 'Yes!' and I laughed in the laughter of God."

When O'Neill wrote a friend about the theme of his play, he concluded his letter with the statement: "Life itself is the self-affirmative joyous laughter of God." Life is the laughter of God. As I contemplate this meaning, I recall the Genesis story when Abraham laughs at the news that he is to have son in his old age, even though Sara, his wife, is past her childbearing years. Actually, God is laughing through Abraham, for life *is* God's laughter.

Choose life. Through our text comes the laughter of the Eternal Spirit made real through the life, death, and Resurrection of Christ, saying, "I am the *resurrection and the life,* he who believes in me, though he die, yet shall he live, and whoever lives and believes in me, shall never die." "I am the resurrection and the life . . ." For belief in some far-off future event, Jesus substitutes belief in himself. So this affirmation not only addresses the issue of life after death, but life after birth.

To die before you live is the real tragedy. To have spent your allotted threescore years and ten or more and never to have entered into life—this is death. To live out the faith-relationship with him who is the Resurrection and the life is to choose life whether here or hereafter.

Anybody can curl up in self-pity and die, but to live is the challenge. Today is the day of our salvation. Now is the timely time. Choose life, choose death! You choose!

Let us pray: Lord, make me alive while I'm still living. Thank you, God. Amen.

Benediction: And now as we go forth to be and to become, O Father, bless us with your laughter—the perennial joy of life—for today, and tomorrow, and all of life's tomorrows.

SECTION VI

LENTEN AND EASTER PREACHING

SERMON SUGGESTIONS

Topic: The Absolutely Decisive Question

TEXT: Matt. 16:13–25

Matthew watched his world collapse. The Romans, vindictive over Jewish insurrection, sacked Jerusalem, burned the Temple, slaughtered the populace. Amid the carnage and desolation, the symbolic center of Matthew's faith crumbled. But worse, the religious establishment, panicked by rising messianic sectarianism, finally expelled Matthew and his "Jesus movement" from the synagogue. So Matthew is composing his Gospel some fifty years after Jesus' death, wounded by a double blow: the laying waste of his beloved Jerusalem and the stunning rejection by his fellow Jews. The absolutely decisive question facing him: Can we remain faithful to the hope in Jesus Christ when everything else is going down the drain? Can we remain loyal in times like these? That question resonates down the centuries. It is no less decisive now than when Matthew struggled with it nearly two thousand years ago.

I. In that dramatic passage we read this morning, Jesus asks his followers, "Who do people say that I am?" They come up with a variety of answers: "You're a religious genius. You stand right up there with Mary Baker Eddy, the Dali Llama, and Robert Schuller." "Interesting," replies Jesus. "Fascinating."

Now Jesus sharpens the question: "But who do *you* say that I am?" Then Peter (and gender notwithstanding, in the Gospels Peter stands for you and me) confesses: "Yes, we recognize you as a famous religious figure, but more, much more. We perceive you as a genius, and you do belong in the pantheon of the world's dreamers and idealists, but you're more, much more."

And then he blurts out: "You are the Christ, the Messiah, the hope of the world. You bear a future, for all of us, where strife dissolves; you bring to our world of smart bombs, ballistic missiles, and C-130s the reality of mutual servanthood and collaborative vision. You break in among us," Peter confesses, "melting cultural barriers, bridging hostile civilizations, healing grievances, transforming religious hatred into a unified purpose, liberating a world where men and women live under the threat of terror by one another into one where dignity and respect, compassion and the search for justice sustain human solidarity."

And, "yes," says Peter, no less contemporary than ourselves, "in times like these you bring to our world a reality so new that our type will no longer be in charge, not the white faces or the male faces, not the corporate boards, the Ivy Leaguers, or the Western Christians—a world so new that the first is last and the last first, meaning simply that the world's hierarchies of gender, culture, race, weapons, trust accounts, and property are rendered irrelevant. You bring a world so new," confesses Peter, "we can compare its citizenship only to those who slumber in our alley, languish at Cedar Junction, die on an Afghan outback because they represent a different order; they live beyond the outside of our systems, our pretensions, our interests."

You see, amid the devastation of all his treasures, Matthew affirms, through Peter, the presence of a new order, when all the evidence battering him from all sides screams, "No way!" He envisions a global hope, when hope seems on the wane.

II. If Jesus asked us his question—Who do people say that I am?—how might we answer? How does the world answer? How do you answer? How do I?

Joan Vennochi offers a clue in a *Boston Globe* op-ed article. Ms. Vennochi writes of teaching a Junior High boys' Sunday school class, her own son among them. (Already she's my hero!) She writes with love and warmth—the signs of a great Sunday school teacher. But trying to interpret the meaning of Jesus to those boys sounds like Matthew's storied encounter between Jesus and Peter at Caesarea Philippi. Ms. Vennochi tries to answer the question, So who do we say Jesus is? She introduces her students to Jesus, as a person, she says, who "treats everyone politely regardless of wealth or status, who walks away from fights, who is humble and forgiving. Someone who welcomes beggars and lepers." Here, in Jesus, she suggests to her class, you might find a role model.

She hears from the corner of the room one of her cherished twelve-year-olds reply, "What a loser!" She finds herself sobered. Most "uncool," she suggests. "Their role models, after all, are athletes and sportscasters, actors and video stars, and anyone who makes a lot of money fast." She goes on: "Jesus never dunked a basketball, threw a touchdown or caught one, or slapped a home run over the Green Monster. He didn't snowboard or skateboard or do anything that anyone on ESPN would ever do a feature on. He had no fancy digs, splashy sports cars, or bevy of babes prancing around him. Mary Magdalene," she observes, "is not an adolescent's idea of a hot chick. Jesus didn't do rap or hip-hop. He didn't start a company, cash in his stock options, and get out with the big bucks just before the venture crashed. . . ." Their idea of a miracle? An underdog win in the Super Bowl or the World Series. Now *that* is an act of God! She asks, finally, "Do you know anyone who reminds you of Jesus?" Silence. "They cannot think of a soul."

But her point is not about seventh-grade boys; it is what rules in their homes. Are those icons suffusing the atmosphere surrounding them at home? Are these images and models dominating their personal hopes and dreams, the menu for shaping values around where they eat and sleep? She is confident most of them will grow to be goodhearted men. But do we catch a glimpse here of what some of us consider the most important, exciting, inspirational types in our lives? The rage of popular culture—the celeb, the guy wrapped in the flag, the gal with the Academy Award?

You see, we find ourselves confronted by our Lord's question: Who do you say that I am? How shall we answer? "The bearer of a new creation, a new community, a global human family?" Confess and envision *that,* suggests Matthew, in times like these and you can bet your confession arises from no human observation ("not flesh and blood?"). It comes as nothing less than divine gift.

II. And yet, no sooner do we make confession than we discover the startling implications of loyalty to Christ. Matthew vividly demonstrates our dilemma. What a story! Peter makes his confession against all odds. Then Jesus announces his trip to Jerusalem, sparing none of the gory details: suffering and death in the capital city. And what does Peter do? He remonstrates. He rebukes Jesus. "No Lord," he cries. "Jerusalem? No Way! Betrayed? Not by us! Impossible," Peter insists. "We're with you all the way. A failure? Hey, we didn't join this crusade to end up failures. Death? Come off it, Lord. You're only thirty years old; you'll find most everyone on your side; if by some chance things get too hot, we'll slip town and wait 'til everything cools down."

Do you recall our Lord's response? "Out of my sight, you fraud, you seducer, you devil! You mistake your own illusions for Divine purpose."

Oh, Matthew, you know where the major obstacle to the hope for the world lies. It is not the atheists. It is not the ayatollahs, the dictators, corporate thieves, or the prostituted politicians of the world. It is Christians—confessors of loyalty to the Kingdom one moment, then sell-outs at the batting of an eye.

Some of our lesser faithfulness may surface in a minor key—from time to time in worship, for instance. Not long ago I ran across a report from the General Assembly of the Free Church of Scotland; it reminded me of a failure endemic to some congregations. The report spoke to the issue of congregational singing. According to this report, one member of that Scots Assembly learned that the Psalmody Committee was preparing another exhortation to brighter congregational singing. He wished laryngitis on the committee convener. The convener droned on anyway, regretting the "slurring, scooping and other blemishes" marring congregational praise. Another delegate seconded his remarks, convinced that listeners could never tell if a congregation sang a joyful hymn or funeral dirge. He found himself of the opinion, as a matter of fact, that most of us church types sound as if we're singing from the telephone directory. Now to be sure, dolefully singing hymns may not sink us, but for heaven's sake, ours is a joyful, glorious singing faith, and if visitors wander in here and wonder if the news we sing about is really good, then perhaps we get in the way of our Lord.

Or, on a different note, we often use Jesus to bless our unjust *status quo*. We often mistake our class interests for his interests. Harry Emerson Fosdick, writing years ago, ashamed of what Christians have done to Christ, put his finger on this particular problem. Speculating about a person in his Riverside Church congregation who believes Jesus has nothing to do with social problems, expressing his incredulity at such an outlook in light of what Jesus said and did, Dr. Fosdick goes on to say this:

> Almost always the person who believes Jesus has nothing to do with social questions is privileged; almost always he or she sits on a cushioned seat in the *status quo;* they want "what *is*" made secure much more than they want change. To be sure, the person confesses devotion to Christ, and thus wishes Christ to bless her or her *status quo*.

And thus, Dr. Fosdick continues, Jesus becomes spiritualized, disengaged from the hurly-burly of power politics, economic justice, and equal rights. Jesus becomes a massager of our moods, the sanctified of purely personal virtue, the key to a mystical communion with God. And that is OK, but nothing much gets disturbed in this approach. How easy we find it, he writes, to start "by adoring Christ and to end by appointing him chairman of the board-of-sponsors for our own special interests."

"Fraud," cries Jesus. "Devil! You confuse your interests with God's."

And friends, I am not oblivious to how we in the ministry fit perfectly into Peter's shoes. You know it better than we do and yet continue to put up with us. I dare not speak for Lael and Jennifer (ministers at Boston's Old South Church), and I beg your pardon for these self-referential images, but—my soul!—how we in the ministry can become enmeshed in busyness, tantalized by abstractions, infatuated with rhetoric. We can rationalize procrastination, hide ourselves in institutional minutiae, and spend time and money barely coinciding with our Sunday convictions.

"Fraud" says Jesus. "You fail to understand the full dimensions of discipleship; you've got it all upside down and backwards; you've been suckered by the devil."

You see, we confessing Christians present a major obstacle to the future of God in this world, and those of us in liturgical dress are no less culpable.

III. How then do we answer our Lord's provocative and incessant question—Who do you say that I am? How do we remain loyal to our confession in times like these? Matthew offers a clue. "Take up your cross," he insists, "and follow Jesus." Take up our cross? How do we do that? What does Matthew mean? If we want to answer his decisive questions, we do so taking the risks that love assumes. We surrender the loyalties we hold now; we leave the sovereignties ruling our lives and take a step in a new direction. We lay our time, our money, our language, our vocations, our family life, our relationships on the line for the sake of a human community that takes on the image of the crucified Christ.

The absolutely decisive question: Who do *you* say that I am? How to retain loyalty in these times—in any time? In the face of resistance, rejection, cynicism, act with malice toward none, charity for all; take up your cross, assume the heavy risks of love in a world where it can be laughed off by the frivolous and chewed up by the cynical, and follow the courageous, gracious, sustaining, transforming Christ.—James W. Crawford

Topic: Three Ways to Die
TEXT: Luke 23:39–43

Normally, we approach Good Friday with eyes only for that man on the middle cross. Yet three men died that day, each in a dramatically different way. Let us look closely at them all, for they offer us the options from which to choose as we decide how we shall live and how we shall die.

I. *The first cross: Grasping as a way of life.* The first victim lashed out in fury against his plight and took it all out on Jesus. Lacking any sense of remorse or personal guilt, he was ready to blame whoever was nearest at hand, even though Jesus had done absolutely nothing to cause his predicament and obviously had troubles of his own. There was no originality to his railing, for he merely borrowed his hostile attitude from the spectators. Those in the crowd scoffed as they passed by, deriding Jesus and wagging their heads (Matt. 29:34; Mark 15:29). But, more important, the "rulers" jeered at Jesus as well (Luke 25:35). Chief priests and scribes mocked him to one another (Matt. 27:41; Mark 15:31). Even the Roman soldiers joined in the cruel jest (Luke 23:36–37).

Thus did a devilish idea form in his desperate brain: I will agree with those in charge. Indeed, I will outdo them in my contempt for this upstart. Maybe when they see my enthusiasm for their cause they will relent and take me down from this cross. After all, what have

I got to lose? So he began to "blaspheme" Jesus (Luke 23:39). The verb form means that he continued to hurl insults, to rail with sneering rage, to taunt him, abuse him, heap coarse contempt upon the muted head. With vile sarcasm he began: "*You* couldn't be the Christ, could you?" Then he echoed the cry of those at his feet: "Save yourself," as if to say to the crowd, "Look, I don't deserve to be up here with him, but down there with you!"

Could any strategy be cheaper, more expedient, or more callous? Here is a perfect picture of sheer self-interest, an eager willingness to try anything to save his own skin, a complete disregard of justice or truth or even elemental decency. The thief did not know Jesus. He could not check the veracity of his sources, so he condemned outright a perfect stranger on the basis of hearsay. And why did he twist reality so readily to his own advantage? It was but the outcropping of his whole approach to life. He was a taker, a keeper, a robber. Maybe he started down this road with high ideals like the Zealots of his day, but he ended up grasping for whatever he could get for himself, integrity be damned!

Our zeal can become misguided as well. As Americans, we set out to tame a wilderness, conquer a frontier, and settle a new country. But for some, that commendable drive became an obsession with no limits, no scruples, no rules, just all I can get for Number One. How else are we to explain unbridled greed at the highest levels of the business world? When someone comes along to speak up for the oppressed, we call them "bleeding hearts." When they tell us the price tag for compassion, we taunt them as "do-gooders." When they point to a Kingdom that money cannot buy, we revile them as "idealists." It is our way of saying to the rich and powerful, "I'm on your side."

Finally, this attitude becomes blasphemy when we demand that God "prove" himself by dancing to our tune. "Save yourself" reflects no concern for Christ's cause but only a selfish desire to ride victorious coattails, to be on the winning side, to support anyone who can get us out of the mess we are in. In contemporary life this mood of grasping selfishness has been elaborated into a syndrome with three components: (1) narcissism—always looking in a mirror to see only ourselves, (2) hedonism—the drive for pleasure lifted to passion, and (3) privatism—the escape from responsibility for the public good.

We may be more refined than the thief on our first cross, but no less determined to clutch all we can, to claw and scratch and dig for self-interest, to play the blame game if it makes us look better, to turn on innocent victims if it will curry favor with the power brokers, to punish those who have done us no harm. The end of such a lifestyle is utter corruption, a loss of honor, of integrity, of respect for others. Nobody can be trusted or loved or served, for everybody is a potential enemy if they happen to get in our way.

II. *The second cross: Gratitude as a way of life.* We dare not indulge in unwarranted psychologizing, but there are tantalizing hints in the text that cry out for a reconstruction of what was going on inside this second brigand as he hung on the tree. One plausible hypothesis begins with Matthew 27:44, which pictures both criminals reviling Jesus "in the same way" as those around them. So let us suppose that the other thief started out being caught up in the mood of the crowd. But soon he heard Jesus reply to his tormentors, "Father, forgive them" (Luke 23:34). Now he had to choose between the ugly insults being hurled by the mockers and the loving mercy coming from the lips of Jesus.

If the two robbers were Zealots, they may have begun with contempt for Jesus as a weakling who would not use the sword to oppose Rome. By reputation, at least, he seemed not to be patriotic enough, he found too many faults with the leaders of his own people, he was too ready to praise Roman centurions. Zealots had been taught to make heroes out of fighters such as Barabbas and to despise cowards such as Jesus. So what kept him from becoming cynical like his compatriot on the other cross?

Perhaps the turning point was the unwarranted outburst of his partner against Jesus. Even though the second criminal had joined in the jeering, he could see the injustice of Jesus' condemnation (Luke 23:40–41). So twisted was the stream of blasphemy coming from the first cross that it reflected no ultimate fear of God but only a pandering to the approval of others. After all, both of these partners in crime knew that they were guilty of a capital offense, whereas it was obvious that Jesus was utterly different. He had never been seen in their underworld haunts, nor had he allowed his disciples to join their marauding bands. It may well be that the shock of what cynicism had done to his accomplice, combined with the radically different love shown by Jesus from the cross, caused the second criminal to change. In any case, he dared to reach out with open heart for whatever boon the crucified King could confer.

How primitive and immature his faith must have been! "Remember me" was a familiar petition on the tombstones of that day, a plea to be included in the Great Resurrection of the dead. So he cried: "If that sign over your cross has any truth, if you really are our king, then don't forget me when you come to reign. I want a king like you—loving and forgiving—instead of the kind of kings we now have—condemning and cruel. Maybe if we had been ruled by a king like you, I wouldn't be hanging here now!" In response, he got much more than he could ever ask for or think of (Eph. 3:20). Why? Because in his pain and confusion and remorse, he had stumbled upon the secret of "amazing grace." Instead of railing at Jesus with a clenched fist in anger, he had learned to be grateful for anything he could get, since none of it was deserved and none could be reciprocated.

How hard to learn that life has far more to give us freely than we can ever take by selfish grasping. The first criminal clawed frantically and got nothing, while the second criminal quietly pleaded and got everything. How often do we have not because we ask not aright (James 4:2). Friends have so much to offer, but we allow neighbors to remain virtual strangers. The Bible could give so much light and strength, but we leave it closed. Prayer is able to bless and inspire, but we stay too busy to bow our heads. The problem is not that God is stingy with his blessings but that we are seldom open to receive them.

Why are we so reluctant to ask? Because Christ's claim to be King is drenched in blood, a scandal to the thoughtless crowd. It is so hard to believe that a crucified messiah could give us anything. What an astonishing paradox: that by demanding nothing we can have everything; that by depending on a dying Christ, we can live more abundantly than we ever could on our own! The claim is audacious, now as then, and only those willing to take an ultimate risk will ever discover its truth. Our instinct instead is to look for help from winners rather than from losers, to depend on people of influence who can push buttons and open doors and make contacts and peddle power. That was the real difference between the two robbers. The first sided with those in power then—those with the badges and titles and insignia of rank and status, those in control of the Crucifixion rather than those being crushed by it. The second sided with one who had no power then but would come into power when love and truth finally prevailed.

How seldom do we turn to the kind of people who get crucified to ask for help. Yet here is where love is to be found. The Caesars and Pilates of this world have no love. They are looking out for themselves, using raw power to protect their privileges. But turn to those "bleeding heart do-gooders" who follow the crucified Christ and you will find that you matter intrinsically to them because you are loved as a child of God. To be sure, we must swallow pride to hold out an empty hand and say, "I've but failed. Give me what I can never get for myself." Yet the plea of that empty hand is the hope of grace. The old hymn says it well: "In my hand no price I bring, Simply to Thy cross I cling!"

III. *The final cross: Giving as a way of life.* Of all those crucified at Calvary, Jesus had the most right to complain—of injustice, misunderstanding, hypocrisy, and undeserved suffering. He could have easily ignored the robbers as callous brutes with vile tongues, bent only on saving their own skins. Instead he responded by giving the grateful thief far more than he could have ever dreamed of asking for. His response began with "Amen," the preface to a royal edict meaning that what followed was guaranteed by the Sovereign of the universe. From a naked, bloody King came a solemn promise, guaranteed by God himself. What incredible authority he possessed to talk like that amid the sordid insults of the moment! But nothing, not even the curse of a cross, could shake Jesus' assurance that he really was the Lord of life and death.

The next word—*today*—pointed his promise, not to some distant millennium or idealistic utopia but to that very moment as a date with destiny. Now was the dawning of the messianic age of salvation. Jesus would not have to toil for years to rebuild his broken movement. There was no need to wait until he had overcome this horrid failure. For the cross was not a final defeat. He was King then and there. His love was already ruling from the scaffold. He was mightier in spirit than those tormenting his body to death.

What did Jesus have to offer on that day? Only himself: "You shall be *with me.*" Rather than being included in the Great Resurrection after sleeping in the dust for endless years, they would enter glory together! Side-by-side, arm-in-arm, hand-in-hand, death would be their shared coronation. Already this thief who "feared God" had faced his ultimate judgment and been acquitted by the chief criminal in the docket!

His being with Jesus was then described as living "in Paradise," a Persian word referring to a walled garden. Persian kings made favored citizens "companions of the garden," privileged to walk in cool, fragrant seclusion, enjoying intimate fellowship with royalty. Jesus now gave this wretched robber a pass to be his "companion of the garden" in the better world to come. Why so extravagant a response? Because Jesus had done that all of his life, surprising people with more than they dared to request. He was a giving person, not concerned to grasp, or even to receive gratefully what others might give, but to share all that he had with others whether they deserved it or not.

We usually make the thief on the second cross our hero of this story, but he was only a half-way house to the supreme truth revealed on the middle cross at Calvary. To be sure, it is infinitely better to be an open, grateful receiver than a clutching, cynical grasper. But it is even better to learn how to become a lavish giver after the manner of our Lord. Too often we create the impression that Christianity is a matter of Christ doing all the giving while we do all the receiving. But we learn to receive precisely as a first step in learning how to give. Because we have been "graced" by him, we become grace-ful to others. The burden of so many of Jesus' parables was that those who have been "for-given much" must learn to "give for," rather than against, the best interests of others.

The three ways to live traced here constitute a crucial progression in our journey toward spiritual maturity. At first our fists are clenched in a grasping refusal to let go of what is ours.

Then our hands are open and empty, ready to receive gifts of love. But finally, our arms are outstretched to others, as we share the bounty of what we have received. Many shrink back from ever attempting to act like Jesus, but his example here can guide us as we learn to say, with the assurance of the Divine, "Amen"—that "today" we will share life together with the undeserving, we will walk in the garden together as friends, we will let them have a claim on our hearts forevermore.

It was not only from the cross that Jesus offered Paradise as a bliss beyond the curse of Earth. He was forever saying to people, "Today your life can begin anew." Today you can follow me. Today you can know God's love. Today you can be forgiven. That kind of Paradise may be consummated in the life beyond, but it can be inaugurated in the here and now. As that old favorite "In the Garden" puts it, "He walks with me, and He talks with me, And He tells me I am His own." We must learn both to receive that greatest gift from him and then to pass it on to others. How hungry people are for a pass admitting them to the cool of the garden. That is our greatest gift to give: personal fellowship with God through Christ. Jesus was right: it is nothing less than Paradise. And the best place to discover it is on a hill called Calvary.—William E. Hull

Topic: "Go Quickly and Tell . . ."
Text: Matt. 28:7

Have you ever noticed how almost every account of Jesus' Resurrection in the Gospels ends up as the story of a foot race? Once the angelic announcement of the empty tomb sent the startled women in search of the disciples, Matthew says that they "departed quickly . . . and *ran*" (28:8). Mark says that "they went out and *fled*" (16:8). John says that Mary Magdalene *ran* to tell Simon Peter and the beloved disciple (20:2) and they, in turn, both *ran* to see for themselves (20:4).

One of the finest artistic testimonies to the Resurrection is the painting by Eugéne Burnand, "Peter and John Running to the Tomb." The two disciples are bent forward in anticipation, their hair rippling in the wind, their eyes wide with expectancy. Into their eager faces, filled with wonder, Burnand has compressed the trembling hope of the whole world.

Nor could it be otherwise, for the Resurrection is good news, and good news cannot sit or walk—it must run to live. That is why the angel said, "Go *quickly* and tell" (Matt. 28:7). As Gerald Kennedy put it, witnessing to the Resurrection is not like going door-to-door selling a book of home remedies. Rather, it is like standing on the street corner and shouting "Extra! Extra!" What glad tidings do we have to declare that cannot wait?

I. *The power of God.* By far the deepest question in all of life is the problem of evil, which is called theodicy: How can a good God allow so much suffering? That problem came to a climax at Calvary, where the most undeserved agony in all of history was inflicted on an innocent victim. If ever we can solve that tragedy of unjustified heartbreak, then we can solve whatever life may bring.

The Resurrection was God's vindication of Christ, signaling his victory over pain and death. To triumph over the forces that put Jesus in the tomb, God had to be mightier than the evil coalition that conspired against him. Indeed, he had to be powerful enough to overcome the knockout punch of death.

Easter is the gospel's declaration that God is the ultimate power in the universe. How do we know that he is mightier than envy, jealousy, hatred, cruelty, and cowardice? Because Christ came back triumphant when these very passions appeared to have destroyed him. Because he validated his living presence in the hearts of his disciples, even when they faced persecution. Because his vitality continues unabated to this day. Dead people do not transform others after two thousand years. The Caesars of Jesus' day had absolute power, seen clearly in their authority to order crucifixion, yet they are impotent to have any influence on life today. Christ, by contrast, had no power during his earthly life, yet he continues to change even those who resist him. That takes power—ultimate power, God's power!

Make no mistake: veneration of the dead Jesus is no substitute for faith in the Risen Christ. When Eva Perón died in 1952 of cancer at age thirty-three, her embalmed body came to be idolized by the working masses of Argentina as a symbol of their cause. Fearing that her remains would be used to rally the opposition, the military leaders who had overthrown her husband, Juan Perón, confiscated her corpse and sent it to a secret burial site in Italy, where it was interred under a false name. But when Perón regained influence in exile, he demanded that the body of his wife be returned. It was exhumed and transported in a silver coffin to his villa in Madrid, where it was kept in an open casket on the dining room table. His third wife, Isabel, combed the corpse's hair in an act of devotion and, when she became president after Perón's death, had Eva's body brought back to Argentina, where it was finally buried under three plates of steel to prevent further disturbances. But all of this necrophilia approaching adoration did nothing to give Eva Perón the power exercised by an obscure young man named Jesus who was buried in a borrowed grace. What was the one thing she lacked that he had? The power of Resurrection!

II. *The potential of persons.* It is ironic that, for all of our vaunted scientific achievement, we have been diminished by these technological triumphs. Individuals seem to have become little more than a number in the computer, a cog in an impersonal bureaucracy, a perpetual consumer helping somebody else to make a profit. How strange that most "passion plays" of the twentieth century were written, not about Jesus but about us. Think how the plays of Arthur Miller, Tennessee Williams, and Samuel Beckett portray our perpetual frustrations. And what are the crosses on which these modern martyrs are crucified? Blandness, boredom, self-indulgence, mediocrity, and compromise.

Such was the plight of the early disciples, whose weaknesses were exposed so remorselessly by the cross. One betrayed him, another denied him, all fled from him. But it was precisely that motley band that almost immediately regrouped to become the architects of a new age in human history. Indeed, their transformation in life was almost as great a miracle as their Master's transformation in death. In one sense, both leader and followers were resurrected as parts of the same miracle, for their new life came from the Risen Christ living in their hearts. And what was the secret of this vast new potential given to miserable failures? It was his promise, "Lo, I am *with you* always . . ." Life was cheap in the Roman world of that day, but the Risen Christ made it infinitely precious by the gift of his indwelling presence.

The skeptic might attribute such changes to the power of a vivid memory, but how do you pass on such a memory for two thousand years to strangers who have never set foot in Palestine? Some religions claim to transform their followers by obedience to commandments, others by mystical meditation, others by spiritual insight. Only Christianity claims to do it by a personal relationship with one who is as alive today as he was two thousand years ago. His impact is equally great on all who receive him, regardless of their race, nationality, culture, or family background. Every time we baptize another believer, we test the Easter claim: whether each and every person, regardless of background or circumstances, can be raised with Christ to newness of life.

Without Resurrection, where is our source of true hope? As Gil Bailie put it, "Today, it is falling again to Christianity to inspire a hope capable of filling the vacuum left by the collapse of modernity's naïve optimism, on the one hand, and the shrugging hopelessness and cynicism of postmodernity, on the other." Ronald Knox once said, "Whenever faith in the miracle of resurrection strikes deep root, the miracle of the resurrection repeats itself. The challenge Christians face today is that of preparing the soil so that the miracle of the resurrection can strike deep root once again."

III. *The promise of eternity.* If God's life could not be kept out of Christ's tomb, and if that life comes rushing into our inner tombs today with as much potency as ever, then when and where will it stop? Are there any limits to the kind of life that can flourish for two thousand years and show no sign of abating? Does Christ live in more hearts today than ever before because his kind of life is eternal, because it always has been and always will be so?

Test the answer to that question by the experience of those who have lived with that life for many years and have felt it grow stronger, even as their own biological life grows weaker. Those who live with Christ for decades and find his presence to be perpetually fresh, even though their own lives begin to age, become convinced that his is a life that will never die. As John 3:16 puts it, we already *have* eternal life! And why should the death of the body destroy it? After all, that life has never yet been snuffed out, either by the death of Jesus or by the death of his followers. The burden of proof is on the skeptic to explain why a life that has flourished in countless believers for so many centuries would ever die.

Our belief in eternity is based not on the immortality of our souls or on our scientific ability to stay the hand of death but on the quality of our relationship with the risen life of Christ. If his life can be snuffed out by any force on earth then, as Paul said, our faith is in vain (1 Cor. 15:14). For two thousand years every effort imaginable has been made to deny or to destroy his Resurrection, yet he is as much or more alive today than ever before. Nor is his life bound to one body or even to one time or place. So where will his life be when planet Earth is no more? The only answer that makes any sense is that the Living Lord will spend eternity in fellowship with his own.

Easter and death are close companions for me. It was on an Easter morning in 1983 that Marguerite McCall died, then on Easter eve in 1986 that Badgett Dillard died—two of my very closest friends at Southern Seminary. In both cases, the life of Christ indwelling and filling them was the secret of their beautiful lives. They would not have been who they were without that life! It radiated in their personalities. It controlled their motivations. It filled their existence with meaning and value. Now their physical bodies have gone to the grave. But what of the life that animated those bodies? It was the life that brought Christ back from the dead. It was the life that has sustained the Church to this day. Otherwise, neither of them would have known it, but know it they did. So how can I doubt that such life still lives in them and they in it, and therefore that they shall live for all eternity?

There has been an urgency about the glad tidings of the Resurrection gospel ever since the first Easter morn. After all, why wait to claim Christ's presence? Why try to live in our kind of world without a power mightier than death? Why risk dying without such a life as your hope for eternity? What is to be gained by delay? After searching feverishly for other answers, have you found anything better to take its place? Do you know of any other person whose life is as meaningful and as enduring as the life of Christ?

Thus our text carries a twin imperative. First, be quick to tell. One does not dally in blowing fresh breath into the drowning! But there's more: Be quick to take. If one comes running to you with Resurrection tidings, then, like Peter and John, come running back with them to discover its truth for yourself. Claim the life of Easter for your own life and do it right now! If you already have the Resurrection life, *go quickly* and share it! If you still need this Resurrection life, *come quickly* and claim it!—William E. Hull

EVANGELISM AND WORLD MISSIONS

SERMON SUGGESTIONS

Topic: What's a Born-Again Christian?

TEXT: John 3:1–17

The newspapers, television, and magazines are saying today that we have a "born-again Christian" in the White House. Many persons refer to Charles Colson, one of the leaders in the Watergate scandal, as a "born-again Christian." Recently, one of America's leading pornographers, Larry Flynt, is supposed to have had a personal experience with the Lord. The news media are calling him a "born-again Christian."

Our job is not to pass judgment on whether these people are truly born again, but we note with interest that the news media have developed another term in qualifying Christians. They would say that while there are Christians in general who usually belong to the established churches, there are also "born-again Christians." This latter term is reserved for these who aggressively share their faith and claim a personal encounter with God beyond infant baptism and mere church membership.

Which are you? Are you just a Christian in the general sense, or are you a born-again Christian? Your answer is extremely important. Jesus said that unless we have been born again we cannot see the Kingdom of God. In other words, spiritual blindness is still our lot until we experience the new birth of God in Christ. Apparently, millions of people in the world call themselves Christians who only mean they were sprinkled with water as infants or they affiliated with a church at some time in their lives. For some, it only signifies that they happen to have been born in a Christian environment. We can categorically say, on the authority of Christ, that these people will never see heaven unless they experience the new birth.

Let us look into the Scriptures and see what the term *new birth* means. It comes from four great sources. Jesus Christ himself is the first to teach that "you must be born again" (John 3:7). Human knowledge or a computer readout did not invent this. Church leaders or pious monks did not invent it. It comes directly from Jesus! He explicitly says, "You must be born again." The great apostle Peter, who magnified the preaching of the gospel at Pentecost, teaches that true Christians are those who have been "born again, not of corruptible seed, but of incorruptible, by the word of God, which liveth and abideth forever" (1 Pet. 1:23).

The apostle Paul, who wrote much of the New Testament, is another of the great teachers of Christianity who says that we need spiritual rebirth to be children of God. John, perhaps the closest disciple to Christ, teaches that, "Whosoever believeth that Jesus is the Christ is born of God" (1 John 5:1). The idea of a new kind of birth for each of us is not an isolated or obscure teaching of the New Testament. It is one of the most prominent and important ideas of Christianity. To understand this matter more clearly, let's ask the following three questions and seek answers to them from the Bible: (1) Who needs the new birth? (2) What is the new birth? and, (3) How is one born again?

I. *Who needs the new birth?* Who needs to be born again? Let's get the answer to this question abundantly clear, because it may be you and it may be me who needs to be reborn.

In the first place we can emphatically state that all the world's "prodigal sons" need a rebirth. Persons living in immorality and lawlessness need a rebirth. All persons—whoever they are and wherever they may be—who have turned their back on the heavenly Father and gone their own way, need to be born again. They need to depart from the hog pens of immorality and spiritual rebellion against the Father. They need to experience the joy of a new birth that includes oneness with the Creator and spiritual food for the soul.

"That which is born of the flesh is flesh" (John 3:6), said Jesus. Until we have a spiritual birth, we are still just so much ashes to ashes and dust to dust. Without a new beginning given to us by God, we end up in the awful meaninglessness and emptiness of life without God. We can never have the new birth apart from God.

But that is not the end of the story. Good people also need to be born again. Good people need a rebirth of the spirit. Not only the prodigal son needed a rebirth, but so did the pious elder brother who stayed at home. For verification of this, look at Nicodemus in John 3:1–7. Who is this man? Is he some dropout of society or the owner of the local house of prostitution? No. On the contrary, he stands head and shoulders above most of his peers in his morality and religious orthodoxy. He is one of the best men in the community and yet Jesus says to him, "Ye must be born again" (v. 7).

Who was Nicodemus? He was a son of Abraham. He was a Jew. He was one of God's chosen people. He belonged to the special race that God selected to be his instruments of personal revelation to all other nations of the Earth. Nicodemus could say: "I trace my religious lineage back through my father, my grandfather, my great-grandparents, and eventually to Abraham himself. I am a part of the covenant race. I am a part of the great nation of King David. I am a Hebrew, one of God's special persons. But in spite of all this religious heritage and the promises of the Old Testament, Jesus says to Nicodemus: "You need to be born again or else you will never see the Kingdom of God."

This is extremely important. Many persons have the idea that they are saved because they have a godly heritage. Because Grand-daddy was a Catholic, or because Mother was a Bible-believing Methodist, or because they grew up in a Baptist Sunday school, they think they're immune to the need of a new-birth experience. Nicodemus felt the same way. He grew up thinking that because his grandfather was a Jew and because his great-grandfather was pious and because his great-great-grandfather was religious, he was in good shape spiritually. This is false. There is no such thing as inherited new birth. There is no such thing as being "born of God," merely because you are raised in a good Christian home or because you were born in a religious nation.

We have several members of the canine species in our home. That's a nice way of saying we have dogs at our house. We talk to these dogs occasionally, and sometimes they are in the family room when we read the Scriptures. They are around, too, when we pray. They are even close by when we talk about the great things of God and when we sing hymns. But for all the fact that they were born into a Christian home, and they hear the Bible read every day, and they see us down on our knees praying, they still are not Christians. They will always be dogs! We will never be able to convert them.

In like manner, because a person grew up in a Christian home doesn't make that person a Christian. Being born in the United States does not give us the new birth from God. Being a Baptist is not synonymous with being born again. It is something much deeper.

Nicodemus was also a Pharisee. This word has fallen into disrepute in America. We say of a person, "He's a Pharisee," and we look down on him. It wasn't that way in Jesus' time, because if there was anyone who was orthodox, who kept the truth and tried to live it, it was a Pharisee. Pharisees dotted every religious *i* and crossed every ritualistic *t*. They believed in keeping the whole law. Nicodemus was not a drunkard. He probably never gambled. He wasn't on drugs, and he never violated the Sabbath day or women. The word *pharisee* meant "separatist." The Pharisees separated themselves from worldliness and gross sin. They meticulously kept all the laws. When the apostle Paul wanted to emphasize what a religious person he was before he was born again, he wrote, "Don't forget I was a Pharisee" (see Phil. 3:5). The Pharisees were perhaps the most moral and religious people in Jesus' day. Nicodemus was one of them. In other words, having a lot of external goodness and saying: "I don't lie, cheat, or commit adultery" is still not enough. Everyone, even good people like the Pharisees, needs to be born again, according to Jesus.

But Nicodemus was more—he was a leader of the Jews. He served on their judicial board called the Sanhedrin. This was a position of high honor and great respect. It meant he was a judge whose reputation for justice and fairness had probably earned him a seat on the high court of Israel. Still, Jesus said he needed a whole new birth. Social status and moral position is not enough to open our eyes to the kingdom of God.

One other fact about Nicodemus requires our attention. He probably made his living being a professor—maybe even a professor of religion. Jesus says in verse 10, "Are you a professor in Israel and don't know these simple things?" You see, you can be a professor on a university staff and be charged with the responsibility of teaching the great truths of God and still be lost. They can call you "Doctor So and So," or "Reverend So and So, or "Deacon So and So," or "Sunday School Teacher So and So," but if you haven't been born again, Jesus says you shall not see the Kingdom of God! Even teachers and preachers of religion need to be born from above. It is extremely dangerous to take for granted that just because someone belongs to a religious organization that he or she has been born again. We need to encourage each person to reexamine his or her faith. Is your faith in Christ, or is it in self-attainment? Have you been born again, or are you just a church member?

II. *What does the new birth mean?* We move now to our next question. What does it mean to be born again? Being born again means God has chosen to put his Spirit within us and caused us to become his children. It means God has chosen to put his own divine nature in those who ask him into their lives on a permanent basis. It signifies that we have received something more than just a human nature. We've been given something more than just the result of a fleshly relationship. Indeed, being born again means we've been given the divine nature of God, and therefore we're called "Sons" or "Children of God" by the heavenly Father. The important thing about this is that *God does it!*

God is the one who saves. We don't save ourselves. With all of our good works, we cannot pull ourselves up by our bootstraps to God. We are impotent to make ourselves the children of the Almighty. For all of our goodness we can never deserve the new birth. For all of our "Brownie" points that we make through church work and other volunteer services, we are never able to accumulate enough merit to save ourselves.

The new birth is God reaching out to embrace us. He does it of his own free will and accord. It is the redemption work of God, not the work of the church or a preacher. Being sprinkled as an infant or being baptized as a youth or joining a church does not, in itself, make possible the new birth. God and God alone brings about the new birth. God is the sole being of the universe who can transform us out of a mere fleshly existence into a life of spiritual-mindedness.

St. Augustine, a renowned theologian, lived in the fourth century. In his younger days he was self-indulgent. He was part of every gross kind of immorality imaginable. Finally, God saved him while he was in his garden one day. The Holy Spirit imparted to him a new life. He was born again. A few days later, while walking down the street, a prostitute, with whom Augustine had previously been very good friends, met him. He only nodded to her and went his way. She said to Augustine, "Don't you know who I am?" The young Christian turned and said, "Yes, but I'm not who you think I am."

This was Augustine's way of saying to her the change in his life was so radical that, where he formerly thought only in terms of his own selfish desires and the gratification of his fleshly and materialistic appetites, God had now revolutionized his thinking and actions. He now thought as a different person! In essence, he was a different kind of person from the one the prostitute had known before. Prior to his new-birth experience he was always after something for himself. Now his whole standard of values had changed. After surrendering to Christ, he desired praise to God and a lifestyle that verified that praise.

Being born again means that our whole reason for existence is changed. Our entire philosophy of life is turned around. Our motivation for doing things becomes charged with external values by the Spirit of God. It is such a revolutionary change in our thinking, motivation, and lifestyle that it is called by Jesus "born again"—a new life from God!

III. *How is one born again?* This third question is of highest importance. Once again the answer is that we cannot do it ourselves. We simply are incapable of climbing up into God's graces and meriting the miracle of a new birth. No, there's only one way to have this greatest of all experience. It comes by saying to God: "I believe in Christ with all my heart, mind, and strength." "For God so loved the world, that he gave his only begotten Son, that whosoever believeth in him should not perish, but have everlasting life" (John 3:16).

The new birth takes place in us when we come to that place in life where we say, "God, I'm not going to trust in myself or in my good works anymore. I'm not going to trust in my intellectual ability another day. I'm not looking to my contributions to the church or to the religion of my parents or grandparents to save me. Lord, I give all that up. I believe only in you. I throw myself into your arms of mercy."

If you're not believing in God, what are you believing in? Everyone believes in something. Most people simply believe in their own ability and goodness. Someday they will get old. They will wish they hadn't postponed trusting in God. But at this stage in life, they're so successful that they believe in their own strength and leave God out of their lives. Other people trust in their good works. They make themselves their own god.

But God says, "Put everything else to one side and simply put yourself in my hands." When a newborn baby looks at its parents, it doesn't earn its right to be in the family. It doesn't trust in its ability or its good works to be a child of the family. It would be ridiculous if a child thought: "I really need to do something great to earn sonship with these parents. I have to behave like a perfect child to stay in this family circle."

This is the way many people look at God—as if they had to buy their way into his good favor by church membership, or by religious rituals, or by good behavior. The truth of the matter is that we can never be perfect enough or religious enough to merit sonship with God. All we have to do is what babies do—just relax and let God take over, just entrust our lives fully into his loving arms. "Behold, I stand at the door and knock" (Rev. 3:20), said Jesus. He knocks at your heart. He knocks at your mind. He knocks at your will. He says, "Just open up and let me come into the center of your life." The loving wisdom of God is, "Stop depending on yourself; stop thinking you can do it all. Just come to your Creator and let me be God in your life." Too many people push God away into the skies. To them, he is just the God of the universe. They never let him become the God of their lives.

Christ's great appeal is to come into your life. He wants to come through the door of your mind, heart, and will. He wants to be your friend and the Lord of your life. When you accept him by faith into the position of lordship over you and your affairs, he makes you a son of God.

Many interesting stories came out of the tragedy of the sinking *Titanic*. There was a Scotchman who survived that horrible ordeal and recounted his experience afterward. He said he hung onto a small piece of wood and drifted to a Mr. Harper, who was also clinging to another small piece of wreckage. Harper asked him: "Are you trusting in God?" "No, I never have trusted much in God," the Scotchman replied. Harper challenged him to put his trust in God, stating that Christ would transform his life. The waves separated them and they drifted apart. Later, they drifted back together, and Harper asked again if he had given his life to God. Again the Scotchman confessed he still hadn't committed his soul to the Father. The waves separated them again, but not without Harper's appealing with tears for the Scotchman to put his faith in Christ. One more time it fell their lot to drift close together. Harper's voice was weakening, but this time, with the last bit of strength, he asked: "Have you put your trust in Jesus as your Savior?" This time the Scotchman quietly lifted his words heavenward. "God," he said, "if you get me out of this ocean I'll trust you for all of life." This didn't bring him peace either. At a distance he saw Harper slip into the sea and drown. This did something to him. He wept and cried aloud, and his soul longed for satisfaction before God. Finally, he came to that crucial point in life where he was ready to give his all. He shouted with all his might: "God, whether I ever see Scotland again or not, or whether I live or die, I want you to be my God. I trust you and want the forgiveness of Christ's blood for my sins."

Fortunately, he did get home. He spent the rest of his life telling others about the goodness of God. The lesson we learn from this is that we don't bargain with God. We don't make conditions with God. We don't say to God, "If you'll do this, then I'll be yours." God is not somebody's fire escape from problems!

All we have to do is say, "God, in the circumstances just like I am, I trust you." If you have trusted him that way with all you are and all you ever hope to be, if you've trusted him to the best of your ability, you are a born-again Christian! In reality there is only one kind of Christian. Only a born-again person is a Christian. Isn't it great to have that wonderful assurance that you belong in the family of God because you've been born by the Spirit of God? If we are grateful for God's effecting the new birth in us, then why don't we show that gratitude to God and to others? If you haven't the assurance that you have been born again, why not receive Christ into your heart now? Today is the best day of your life to let God be your God! He will give you his very life![1]

Topic: Are You Ready for a Blessed Disturbance?
TEXT: Mark 10:17–31

My intention in this and other sermons is to point us to the future. I am asking you to ask yourselves the "Am I ready?" question. It's about our readiness for something brighter and better. You believe that God has been with you in the past. Do you believe that God wants to be in your future? If so, "you are ready" to move into that future.

(Retell the story of the text.) The story simply mentions a "man" but does not say who he was. Therefore, everyone can identify with him. For centuries those who came to the Temple in Israel had asked the question, "What must I do to enter and to share in life?" The priests would remind them of the commandments, as Jesus does here. Students of the rabbis asked similar questions.

But this story is about a man who wants to accomplish something more than the ordinary person does. It was common in Israel to speak of "inheriting" what God had promised through his gracious love. The person who asks this question must be very serious as he asks this question. Much more than a happy, well-adjusted life is at stake. The question is about "eternal life"—the final existence in the presence of God on the other side of death. That makes it profound dialogue.

In verse 18, the address "Good Teacher" is not customary for either Jew or Greek.[2] Jesus does not accept that name. And that presents a problem for interpreters. One interpretation is that Jesus intended to say it is not fitting to exchange compliments when discussion concerns God and no other. But here, Jesus acts in the place of God. When the man says yes or no to Jesus, he is saying yes or no to God (8:38). In history God encounters the man in Jesus and nowhere else. However, this Jesus always turns people's attention away from himself "to the only one who is good."

Jesus is seeking nothing for himself. He desires that no facet of his life might call attention to himself but that all may point to One who is greater. God wills to encounter the world in his Son (15:39). This has been his will from the beginning (John 1:1–3). Jesus simply reminds him of the commandments without giving any further explanation. He quotes from memory the more practical ones from the second half of the Ten Commandments in a random order.

I think this shows the lack of interest in legalistic discussion. By this, Jesus reminds the ordinary person in the church who might be awed by the achievement of some saintly person, of all the people who are trying to be obedient to God.

Verse 20 says, "Jesus fixes his gaze on the man." Jesus' interest in this man is emphasized greatly. The only thing this man needs is to become a follower of Jesus. Jesus has already

---

[1]John W. Patterson, in *Award Winning Sermons*, Vol. 3, James C. Barry, ed. (Nashville: Broadman Press, 1979), pp. 95–103.
[2]Schweizer, p. 210.

made it clear that not everyone must literally follow Jesus (5:19) by traveling with him. The man who has kept all the commandments must now prove his sincerity by becoming a follower of Jesus in a spiritual sense.

This is not a call for more achievement. It is an invitation to show that the man understands the lesson: *obedience to God must be demonstrated by acknowledging that God meets us in Jesus.* Giving up one's possessions is not a prerequisite for following Jesus. Jesus prescribes no rules that might apply to everyone. For one person it is a fishing boat or tax collector's desk that must be abandoned. For another person it is parents. Whatever it is, there simply is no other way to be close to Jesus.

So the call to discipline is always a matter of total commitment. The divine call gives. It also demands. The man's rejection (v. 22), in light of God's willingness to give him everything he wants, shocks us.

The gloom on his face as he goes away is not that of rebellion but dismay. He simply could not bring himself to the point of being willing to receive. And that is a big issue for us as Christians. Are you willing to be disturbed enough to receive what God has for you in this church?

Mark tells us that when the man heard Jesus tell him to "go and sell . . ." he was shocked. Of course he was. Who wouldn't be? And when Jesus talked about the camel going through the eye of a needle (v. 25), the disciples were "astonished." Astonishment is not a bad thing to think about. If we had more astonishment, we might be more willing to listen to Jesus.

Are you above being flabbergasted? Seat yourself among the disciples. If you are a little uneasy and squirming in your seat, that's good. If you are scratching your head about what seems to be a blanket condemnation of holding on to possessions, then you are in the right place. This story is meant to disturb.

And it does disturb, because many people did give up everything to follow Jesus. Peter said so in verse 28. Let's take him at his word. They left everything behind and went out to tell the world about Jesus. They followed the instructions of Jesus in Mark 6:8: "To take nothing for their journey except a staff; no bread, no bag, no money in their belts." With just the shirts on their backs they went preaching and teaching. They depended on the grace of God and the kindness of the people they met.

We need this story. You know some people who have given up all to follow Jesus. You have seen students and faculty who have given up a lot to follow Jesus. We need this disturbance because we are bothered by the sacrifice of others—sacrifices we have never made. We need to know what it is that following Jesus means for us.

I want to ask a very personal question. What do you have that God wants you to feel disturbed about? When this church does not reach its budget—its goals to support its ministry—are you disturbed? Is there anything down inside that stirs you to do something about it?

I believe this: this church has everything and everyone it needs to fulfill its calling from God right now. God does not expect us to do what we cannot do or give money we do not have. He does not hold us accountable for workers who aren't among us. God does seek to disturb us with this story.

In a practical view, someone has reminded us that the church is often made up of the "pillars" and the "pew sitters." We understand that, don't we? Sometimes the pillars get tired and get viewed as "running the church." Sometimes they burn out. One of the reasons the pew sitters give for sitting is that no one asked them to do anything. Therefore, one of the jobs of the pillars is to make sure that the pew sitters get a chance to follow Jesus through self-giving service, in and through the church.

God also makes a great promise. If you will make yourself open to giving up all that you have, he will give you all that you can receive.—Bob I. Johnson

Topic: Are You Ready for Jesus' View of Righteousness?
TEXT: Mark 7:1–8

There's no debate. Jesus surprised a lot of people when he came out in public. People might have thought that Jesus would be a nice guy, following in the steps of Joseph as a skilled carpenter, and being a good Jew. Who would ever have thought that he would turn our world upside down, especially, in our view of being good? We can never get over what happened. And aren't we glad! Or are we? When Jesus entered his earthly ministry, he brought a different idea about righteousness. The pious religious leaders couldn't swallow it. Those inside the Jerusalem beltway decided that Jesus' view of righteousness was so heretical that Jesus must be brought down. They simply weren't ready for his take on rightness with God.

The text is full of surprises. Jesus has taken his power! He has begun his ministry. Amazingly, he limited it to service. More amazing is that the ministry opens outward to all. Those in our text are interested in keeping God in their box and confining things to "the chosen" that keep the rules.

We know what that is like. We are mostly compelled to seek safety and to be with those we know and like. When we encounter areas of life that won't stand still for us, we look for molds and chains or cages to make sure they stay where we want them. That's fairly natural. *And then comes Jesus!* He rattles every cage. He breaks the chains of religious snobbery. He shatters the mold for judging goodness.

We inevitably mistake our way of thinking and doing for the "real thing." Our *tradition* becomes the rule and guide to the faith. It becomes the inflexible and rigid norm against which we measure everything else. It ought to be a humble attempt to describe what we "see through a glass darkly." But staying with things as we like them is much more comfortable. I am surprised (or am I?) that some religious folk have readily assigned a theological interpretation to the tsunami tragedy that says it is God's judgment on folk who had it coming. Enough of that, however. Lest we become smug in our condemnation of those folk, let us go to the text and summarize.

(Summarize the text.) The Jews knew what the "Law" or "Torah" was. It was God's basic guidance and teaching, which he had given to their ancestors to guide them. The Torah was written down in the OT especially in the first five books. *Torah* is often translated "Law," but that term is misleading for many. It may lead to seeing God as some magistrate or judge rather than as a father who gives guidance to his family.

For hundreds of years the scribes had been adding to the Torah in order to explain its meaning. This was handed down through the generations and became a tradition as important for many Jews as the keeping of the Torah. Some even paid so much attention to the traditions that they forgot the Torah.

Washing hands before a meal is an example of a tradition. Jews washed their hands as a sign that they were God's chosen people. This wasn't a reflection on the modern practice of washing hands as a matter of hygiene. Their explanation was clear: "We may easily have been touched by a Gentile on our way back from the market."

Jesus had two things to teach about that: One, don't think that when you have washed your hands, your hearts are clean in God's sight (vv. 14–23). And two, don't become so interested in this tradition that you begin to think you have kept the whole Torah.

(Emphasize verse 8.) The cost in "abandoning the commandments of God" is *spiritual blindness that affects our relationship with others.* Now I have learned to love this church. I believe that you are an open and supportive congregation. You don't seem to be sticklers on nonessentials.

When the Pharisees observed Jesus and his disciples in action, all they could see was Jesus not conforming to the law—at least as they understood it. Prior to this story Jesus is healing the sick and hurting. All that the Pharisees saw was failure to "fit the mold."

Jesus feeds the five thousand, walks upon the water, and heals the sick. He can hardly walk through a village for the people wishing to touch the hem of his clothes. Yet his opponents point out, "Your disciples don't wash their hands right." Then Mark tells two more miracle stories. Once again Jesus feeds a multitude—just 4,000 people this time.

Now, we could really take off on the religious bigots we know. But I am not going there. (I wouldn't have to help most of you!) I have learned that any theological perspective can house rigidity toward others.

Rather, I want to focus on Jesus' view of righteousness for us in this place. The text tells about a criticism as to how the disciples prepared for a meal. This washing of hands isn't referring to the same one that you mothers or fathers have in mind when your child comes in from playing in the dirt and heads straight for the supper table.

Let us ask ourselves: What do we make of our ritual observances? What are the things that cause us to judge others or even ourselves? Do they have to do with coming to church? What if we shut down here at this house for a month? Would the church be better or worse off? Would we put our faith on hold for that time? Or would we find ways to be the people of God anyway?

I think it is fair to say that most practice of our faith is related to external matters of doing what we are supposed to do. Verse 8 of the text ought always to hang in our minds as a guide, as well as a warning.

I don't think it is my way of operating to beat people over the head with sermons. This Scripture and this sermon call for us to examine our hearts, our relationship with Jesus Christ. That's what I'd like to get across. Is the Savior the most important person in my life? Is his life of nonconformity the norm for me? Is my religion a matter of the heart? Am I ready for Jesus' view of righteousness?

Are you ready to look seriously at what it means to be believers in this place and in this time? Are you ready to find answers to what ministries you should put forth? Can you say, "Here is how we want to be the people of God; here is how we want to be unique in our calling; here is what we want to do to reflect the righteousness Jesus promoted"?—Bob I. Johnson

Topic: My Best Friend: A Spiritual Autobiography
TEXT: Rom. 5:11 TLB; John 15:13–15 KJV

There is a very special friend of mine present today. I would like to introduce him to you, if I may.

We have known each other for twenty-five years now. The friendship we share grows more meaningful and rewarding each year. Over this quarter-of-a-century friendship, we have been in close personal contact.

He and I have shared many wonderful experiences. The first few days of October we were on a hunting trip in Arkansas. We have worshiped and studied together. We have worked together in preaching, visiting, and witnessing. Every moment we've shared has been great.

We first met during my days as a student in Howard Payne College at Brownwood, Texas. I had heard much about this person but had never become personally acquainted with him. My friends offered to introduce us. They told me of what their relation with him had meant.

But before we got acquainted, things began to happen in my life that were not good. I did things that I am very ashamed of. I became worried and depressed because of guilt. My life was filled with doubt. Problems arose that seemed beyond solution. Burdens were heavier than my strength to bear them. The darkness was impenetrable. Sins seemed unforgivable. I was tired of wrestling with it all. I talked with my college friends. I sought the advice of my college professors. I counseled with the pastor of the college church I attended. Nothing helped. I had tried and failed. I felt so helpless. My life was a shambles. Life simply became less tolerable and less desirable. I could see no reason for living.

It was then that the thought came to me that if I could talk with this person others had told me about, he could surely help me with my problems. But I could not find him.

In desperation, I made one last appointment with the pastor. We met during the Church Training hour on Sunday evening. We talked and prayed about my problems. No solutions were effected. I left his office empty and alone.

Since I had been weeping as we talked and prayed, I went by the men's restroom to freshen up before the worship service. As I washed my face, rearranged my tie, and combed my hair, looking into the mirror, I became aware that I was not alone in that small, four-by-six-foot restroom. Another person was there. In this awareness, and looking myself straight in the face in that mirror, I completely turned my life over to Jesus Christ. I asked him to come into my life and take control. He did!

The "peace that passeth understanding" flooded into my soul in an indescribable way. A quiet, holy calm settled upon me, as an inexplicable mystery. A "joy, unspeakable, and full of glory" filled my mind. An assurance came into my life that remains to this very day.

Now you know that the person I want to introduce you to is none other than Jesus Christ. He is my *best friend!*

I left that men's restroom that evening, after my encounter with Jesus Christ, as a new creation (2 Cor. 5:17). I went into the worship period to hear the pastor preach a message entitled "A Dark Night in Babylon." It wasn't dark for me anymore. "For God, who commanded the light to shine out of darkness, [had] shined in [my] heart, to give the light of the knowledge of the glory of God in the face of Jesus Christ" (2 Cor. 4:6).

"In him was life; and the life was the light of men. And the light [shined] in the darkness; and the darkness comprehended it not" (John 1:4–5).

I was "giving thanks unto the Father, which [had] made [me] meet to be [a] partaker of the inheritance of the saints in light: Who [had] delivered [me] from the power of darkness, and [had] translated [me] into the kingdom of his dear Son" (Col. 1:12–13).

"Now we rejoice in our wonderful new relationship with God—all because of what our Lord Jesus Christ has done in dying for our sins: making us friends of God" (Rom. 5:11 TLB).

I have had many doubts since that December evening in 1950. I have doubted my call to the gospel ministry. I have even initiated action to change professions. I have doubted and questioned God's leadership in my life. I have doubted his leading me to this pastorate. I have cried out in complaint because of these doubts concerning God's love and leadership. But *I have never had one single doubt* about the saving work of Jesus Christ in my life. His presence has never been questioned. I have been—and remain—as sure of heaven as if I were there. And sometimes I feel as though I am there.

This, then, is the person who is present with us, to whom I introduce you. He is my *best friend!* There are four reasons for my saying this.

I. *When I am tempted—like Peter—his prayer is offered.* Jesus said to Peter, "Simon, Simon, behold, Satan hath desired to have you, that he may sift you as wheat: but I have prayed for thee, that thy faith fail not" (Luke 22:31).

Peter was tempted. He did sin. The results were tragic. But one shudders to think what the results might have been had not Jesus prayed for him. For after the sin of denying, with bitter cursing, that he knew Jesus, Peter remembered that promise of Jesus to pray for him. Peter wept tears of repentance and was recovered from his sin.

Satan tempts me daily to do things that would adversely affect the friendship I have with Jesus. Sometimes I don't say no when I should. But I know that my friend Jesus has been through the experience before me. Because "he himself hath suffered being tempted, he is able to succor them that are tempted" (Heb. 2:18). Because he was tempted in every way like I am, yet did not sin, he understands the pressure I feel, and knows the weakness I experience, when I am tempted (Heb. 4:15). And the Scriptures say, "He ever liveth to make intercession for them" (Heb. 7:25).

Jesus is my best friend because when I am tempted to sin, he prays for me.

II. *When I sin—like Peter—his provision is available.* Though Jesus prays for me when Satan is tempting me, still I sometimes sin. I do not want to. But I do. And I know it breaks the heart of Jesus when I do. But he doesn't reject me. He, rather, provides the means for forgiveness and restoration to fellowship. Listen to what his Word says: "My little children, these things write I unto you, that ye sin not. And if any man sin, we have an advocate with the Father, Jesus Christ the righteous: And he is the propitiation for our sins: and not for ours only, but also for the sins of the whole world" (1 John 2:1–2).

The word *advocate* means "representative" or "attorney." When we have sinned, Jesus is ready to represent us before God. He does not argue our innocence but confesses our guilt and asks for mercy. He does not present any merits we have as the basis for mercy but presents his own merits in our behalf.

The world *propitiation* means "the place where and the means by which forgiveness may be obtained." It refers to the Ark of the Covenant and the mercy seat of the Old Testament tabernacle (the mercy seat was the golden lid that covered the Ark of the Covenant, which contained copies of the Law). Upon the mercy seat and at its center point, where the gaze of the cherubim met, the high priest put the blood of the Passover lamb to make atonement for sin. Propitiation, then, is a word picture that says that the cross of Christ is the place where forgiveness of sin can be found, and the blood of Christ is the means by which my sins can be cleansed and forgiven.

Out of ancient Greek history comes the story of a man named Aeschylus, a poet. His brother had committed a crime against society and had been found guilty. It was rather certain that he would get the death penalty. The jury was assembled to assess the penalty. Before the jury stood Aeschylus. He had lost an arm when he fought with the Greek army against the Persians in the battle of Salamis. That battle ultimately gave the Greeks victory over the Persians. Aeschylus faced that jury, which was about to sentence his brother to death. He spoke not a word. He simply pulled back his coat and exposed the loss of his arm to the jury. As the jurors looked upon that sight, they were moved to release his brother.

In like manner Jesus shows his wounds as the basis for our forgiveness. Peter said it like this: "For his wounds have healed ours" (1 Pet. 2:24 TLB).

Charles Wesley's hymn expresses it like this:

> Five bleeding wounds he bears,
> Received on Calvary;
> They pour effectual prayers,
> They strongly plead for me:
> Forgive him, O forgive, they cry,
> Nor let that ransomed sinner die!
> And so my best friend provides for my forgiveness when I sin.

III. *When I am tested—like Job—his permission is required.* You know the story. The sons of God presented themselves before the Lord, and Satan appeared among them. God asked Satan where he had been. He replied, "From going to and fro in the earth." God asked if he had considered Job, a man who feared God and shunned evil, a perfect man. Satan accused Job of having ulterior motives for his faithfulness to God. He said Job served God because of all the riches he could get. Satan said if God would take away Job's possessions, Job would curse God. God gave permission for Satan to remove Job's property from him. Satan took away cattle, barns, lands—even Job's seven sons and three daughters. Job remained faithful.

On another day the scene in heaven is repeated. This time Satan accuses God of overprotecting Job. He indicates that if God would touch Job's body, Job would curse God to his face. God allows Satan to touch Job's body but requires him to stop short of taking Job's life. Satan inflicts Job with sore boils from head to foot. In it all, Job remains true to God and praises God for his love.

The truth I draw from the story is that Satan had to have God's permission before he could test Job's faith in God. Before Satan can do anything to me, or against me, he must secure permission from my friend, Jesus Christ.

"There hath no temptation taken you but such as is common to man: but God is faithful, who will not suffer you to be tempted above that ye are able; but will with the temptation also make a way to escape, that ye may be able to bear it" (1 Cor. 10:13).

"Count it all joy when ye fall into divers temptations; Knowing this, that the trying of your faith worketh patience. But let patience have her perfect work, that ye may be perfect and entire, wanting nothing" (James 1:2–4).

"Wherein ye greatly rejoice, though now for a season, if need be, ye are in heaviness through manifold temptations: That the trial of your faith, being much more precious than of gold that perisheth, though it be tried with fire, might be found unto praise and honor and glory at the appearing of Jesus Christ: Whom having not seen, ye love; in whom, though now ye see him not, yet believing, ye rejoice with joy unspeakable and full of glory: Receiving the end of your faith, even the salvation of your souls" (1 Pet. 1:6–9).

IV. *When I die—like Lazarus—his promise is kept.* Lazarus lay at the rich man's gate and begged. One day he "died, and was carried by the angels into Abraham's bosom" (Luke 16:22). But before Lazarus's death, Jesus had made valid promises to him.

Jesus had said to the sister of another man named Lazarus, "Thy brother shall rise again" (John 11:23). He further promised, "I am the resurrection, and the life: he that believeth in me, though he were dead, yet shall he live: And whosoever liveth and believeth in me shall never die!" (John 11:25–26).

What a glorious promise!

But Jesus also promises: "Let not your heart be troubled: ye believe in God, believe also in me. In my Father's house are many mansions: if it were not so, I would have told you. I go to prepare a place for you. And if I go and prepare a place for you, I will come again, and receive you unto myself; that where I am, there ye may be also" (John 14:1–3).

What a glorious provision!

And again I read in Scripture: "For we know that if our earthly house of this tabernacle were dissolved, we have a building of God, a house not made with hands, eternal in the heavens" (2 Cor. 5:1).

What a glorious prospect!

Then I hear this: "Behold, I shew you a mystery; We shall not all sleep, but we shall all be changed, in a moment, in the twinkling of an eye, at the last trump: for the trumpet shall sound, and the dead shall be raised incorruptible, and we shall be changed. O death, where is thy sting? O grave, where is thy victory? The sting of death is sin; and the strength of sin is the law. But thanks be to God, which giveth us the victory through our Lord Jesus Christ" (1 Cor. 15:51–52, 55–57).

What a grandeur of power!

These are "exceeding great and precious promises" (2 Pet. 1:4). And they are mine! And when I die, like Lazarus, or like countless millions before me, these promises, which my friend has made to me, are kept.

"Yea, though I walk through the valley of the shadow of death, I will fear no evil: for thou art with me; thy rod and thy staff they comfort me" (Ps. 23:4).

Jesus is my best friend because:

1. When I am tempted—like Peter—his prayer is offered.
2. When I sin—like Peter—his provision is available.
3. When I am tested—like Job—his permission is required.
4. When I die—like Lazarus—his promise is kept.

I am so anxious for you to meet Jesus. I want you to get to know him as your friend. He wants to be your Savior and Lord. He will be the best friend in all the world to you.

You can meet him through an act of repentance, confession, and faith. Accept him and his offer of forgiveness. He will come into your life and live with you forever. As your best friend, he will give you life more abundantly.

"Oh, that my Savior were your Savior, too."[3]

---

[3]Byron Allen Jr., in *Award Winning Sermons,* Vol. 1, James C. Barry, ed. (Nashville: Broadman Press, 1977), pp. 55–64.

RESOURCES FOR PREACHING FROM 1 PETER

BY THE MINISTERS OF SOUTHEAST CHRISTIAN CHURCH, LOUISVILLE, KENTUCKY

Topic: A Reason to Hope

TEXT: 1 Pet. 1:1–12

What keeps you going when life is desperate? What's your support system when life falls apart? Many place their hope in friends, family, business, or wealth. That is not a satisfactory answer. Friends will desert you, family members will die, and businesses will not last forever.

We better have something more to sustain us during desperate times than the temporary, undependable things of this world. With that in mind, we turn to the book of 1 Peter in search of an everlasting hope, and we will not be disappointed.

I. *We are God's people and are part of his victorious Kingdom.*

(a) We are chosen.

We have been chosen by the Creator to be a part of his Kingdom.

To be chosen means to be given the opportunity to identify with God.

(b) We are being sanctified.

To be sanctified means to be set apart for a godly task.

We are sanctified for a holy purpose at the same time we are saved.

Being sanctified simply means that God has a specific purpose for our lives.

II. *We have been born again and are guaranteed eternal life in heaven.*

(a) How can one be born again?

Hear the Word of God and accept it as true.

Respond in obedience by repenting of sin, confessing belief in Christ, and being baptized into him.

(b) Once you have been born again, you have a living hope.

Our hope of heaven won't perish.
Our hope will not spoil.
Our hope will not fade.

III. *We are protected by God and are exempt from unnecessary pain.*
(a) We are shielded by God's power.

God doesn't shield us from all suffering.
God does shield against vicious, head-on attacks of Satan that would destroy us or render us incapable of fulfilling his will.

IV. *We have purpose in suffering and are thankful it's temporary.*
(a) To be shielded by God's power doesn't mean we're exempt from all pain.

God allows pain that he deems necessary to strengthen us, comfort others, force us to rely on him, and appreciate the suffering of Jesus.
Though none of us would volunteer for it, suffering often serves a positive purpose in our lives.

(b) We can have hope in suffering because it's meaningful and temporary.

You can put up with a lot if you know it's purposeful and temporary.
God temporarily uses pain to deepen us.

V. *We have knowledge of the gospel and understand God's overall plan.*
(a) We are privileged to have a full understanding of God's plan of salvation.

The Old Testament prophets who predicted the coming of a Messiah did not completely understand it.
Even the angels didn't fully understand the plan of salvation until it unfolded.

(b) What was hidden from the prophets, angels, and Satan has now been revealed to us.

We understand that Christ was "pierced for our transgressions."
We understand that Jesus' suffering was his glory.

CONCLUSION: This hope that Peter talks about is one that can be trusted. No one can ever take it from you, but you are the only one who can accept it. It is a hope that is freely given to all who are willing to place their trust in the sacrifice of Jesus Christ on the cross.

He's chosen you; he wants to sanctify you for his purpose and reserve a place in heaven for you. He has chosen you. But will you choose him?—Bob Russell, Senior Minister

Topic: A Reason to Deepen
TEXT: 1 Pet. 1:13–23

Newborn babies are not able to eat, talk, or walk on their own, and definitely they are not able to control their bladders! It's part of being a baby. No one would even expect a small baby to be able to do such things. However, if a child reaches the age of ten and still cannot perform these basic functions of life, there would be some serious concern. It is just assumed that a child will mature with the passing of time. And you and I should have the same expectations for our spiritual life. As a result, in this letter the apostle Peter encourages his readers not to be stunted in their development but to move on to maturity in Christ.

I. *We are to deepen mentally, "preparing our minds for action"* (1 Pet. 1:13–2:3).
(a) Our society places more emphasis on feeling than thinking.

Music, art, and movies are all about feeling.
God has given us emotions as a distinctively good gift.
God also has given us the capacity to reason.
As we deepen in the Christian life, we move from being emotionally driven to being scripturally driven.

II. *We are to deepen morally—"by becoming like God in his holiness"* (1 Pet. 1:15–16).
(a) What is *holiness?* The word *holy* means distinctive, pure, and sacred.

Removing sinful activities is a part of holiness.
Holiness is imitating God's character because we are God's children.
Holiness is not instantaneous.

(b) Four motivations for holiness:

1. A desire to resemble the heavenly Father
2. A reverent fear of judgment
3. Recognition of the futility of unholiness
4. The loving sacrifice of Jesus

III. *We are to deepen socially—"by loving each other deeply"* (1 Pet. 1:22).
(a) We must learn to be unselfish.

Little children think the world revolves around them. The same is true spiritually.
One of the most difficult lessons of the Christian life is to put others ahead of self.

(b) We move from being self-centered to other-centered.

You learn to express love because you realize that life is fleeting.
You must get rid of wrong attitudes that alienate you from people.

An excellent example of someone who noticeably is deepened in all three of these areas is the author of this letter—the apostle Peter. When he first came to Christ he was driven by emotion. He was up and down, confessing Christ as Lord one minute and telling him he was wrong the next. But Peter became a man of obedience and consistency, willing to give his own life to be faithful to Christ.

At first Peter wasn't a very holy man, either. He was egotistical, demanding center stage, known to lose his cool and curse on occasion. But he matured to become more and more like his Father.

Peter did not change on his own accord but through the power of the Holy Spirit. It is because of that same Spirit that we can continue to deepen in our faith as Christians.—Bob Russell, Senior Minister

Topic: A Reason to Live

TEXT: 1 Pet. 2:4–12

What is your purpose in life? That seems like such a simple question, but it is one to which many people do not have an answer. And it is not just young people who seem not to have an ultimate purpose; it seems most adults don't either.

Unfortunately, this futile mind-set has even slipped through the walls of the Church. Why do a number of Christians commit suicide? Why do some Christians drift away from involvement in the local church? Why do some believers fall back into sinful habits and even get entangled in addictive behaviors? Some have clearly lost sight of our ultimate purpose as Christians. In this section of 1 Peter, the apostle reminds us of our ultimate reason for living.

I. *We are living stone, with a significant ministry in God's Church.*

(a) Peter compares the Church to a building.

It is a building composed of many stones.

Jesus is the most important stone.

(b) When you become a part of the Church, you are a part of an institution with eternal significance.

It is an institution much greater than you.

Being a part of the Church magnifies the cost of your mistakes and increases the value of your contributions.

If you are a member of the Church, you have a ministry to perform for the strengthening of the "building."

II. *We are holy priests, with a privileged opportunity to glorify God.*

(a) In the Old Testament, Israel had a priesthood—a special class of religious leaders who, through a cleansing ceremony, were considered holy and given direct access to God.

The common people were considered unholy, unworthy to come into God's presence.

Those priests took approaching God in worship very seriously.

(b) In the New Testament, Jesus is the high priest whose blood has cleansed us from sin. Therefore, every Christian is a priest.

We are each privileged to have direct access to God.

We don't have to confess our sins to a clergyman.

We don't have to pray to God through a saint or a relative.

(c) As a holy priesthood, we have a privileged opportunity to glorify God with worship.

III. *We are God's people, with a crucial responsibility to witness to the truth.*

(a) God has given you an honored status for the purpose of communicating the truth of the gospel to lost people.

(b) You communicate God's truth by living a distinctive lifestyle.

Don't get too familiar with the world. Don't fall in love with the world.

Abstain from sinful desires that war against your soul.

Live such good lives that the world sees your good deeds and glorifies God.

What is your purpose in life? After taking a look at the words of the apostle Peter, you can be certain you have great reasons to live. You have been called to an eternal purpose in his Church, your life matters to God, you are a holy priest, and you belong to God.—Bob Russell, Senior Minister

Topic: A Reason to Submit
TEXT: 1 Pet. 2:13–25

As we pick up in 1 Peter, the apostle has just finished explaining that Christians are aliens in this world. But now he wants his readers to understand that, even though their citizenship is in heaven, they are also to be good citizens on earth. Peter knows that submission is a defining characteristic of great citizens. And so, with that knowledge in mind, Peter begins with:

I. *A difficult command: "Submit yourselves."*

(a) Submission is unnatural.

(b) Submission is unforced.

The verb *submit* is in the middle voice. Literally, it means to "place yourself in submission." Submission comes from a willing spirit.

II. *A compelling motivation: "For the Lord's sake."*

(a) Submitting to others honors God.

(b) When we submit, it enhances our testimony.

A lack of submission is the cause of most division within the Church.

The most powerful testimony we can have as a Church is through submitting and doing what we read in Philippians 2: " . . . treating others better than ourselves."

After Peter lays out this difficult command and helps us understand the motivation behind it, he gives two practical situations to which these principles of submission apply.

III. *Submitting to the government.*

(a) There are a few things to remember as Christian citizens when getting involved in politics:

The government has limited influence. The big political illusion in our day is that there is a political solution for every problem in life. If we truly desire to change lives for Christ, it will not happen through political activity but through proclaiming the Kingdom of God (2 Cor. 10:3, 4).

You stand in the shadow of the cross. Rebellion toward the government will give some people a bad perception of the Christian faith. We have no record of Jesus attacking the government of his day. Be careful that your political involvement doesn't keep people from the only one that truly can save them.

Christians often take two misguided approaches toward the government: (1) they lash out; (2) they cave in.

IV. *Submit in the workplace.*

(a) When Christians don't have a submissive spirit in the workplace, it can ruin their testimony.

(b) Submission in the workplace must be an intentional effort because many people naturally rebel against authority.

CONCLUSION.   For the Christians to whom Peter was writing, the call to submit would not have been an easy pill to swallow. They faced physical abuse and persecution from the government. As if that would not have been bad enough, many of them were slaves, though slavery then was much different than what took place in our country.

Peter follows up his unpopular teaching with a powerful example. Jesus lived a life that was marked by submission and died in the same way. And because Jesus submitted himself to death on a cross, salvation was made possible. Submission in the life of one man changed the world forever, and through lives marked by submission, we can continue to spread the change.—Kyle Idleman, Preaching Associate

Topic: A Reason to Love
TEXT: 1 Pet. 3:1–12

Jesus said that the subject line of every Christian's life ought to be "love."

In John 13:35, Jesus said the world would know we are his disciples by how we love. In 1 Corinthians 13, Paul reminds that we can do a lot of great things: we can put together inspiring worship services, run creative programs, and take courageous stands. But if the Church isn't known first for its love, then we have failed to fulfill our purpose. Therefore, when Peter wrote this section of his letter, he was challenging us to be people who are marked by love in three areas:

I. *What love should look like in marriage* (1 Pet. 3:1–7).
(a) How love looks in the lives of Christian wives.

Submission is not a sign of inferiority or weakness. It is not keeping all of your opinions to yourself and being the silent partner.
Submission is a "voluntary selflessness." It is a submission, not out of fear but out of perfect love.

(b) How love looks in the lives of Christian husbands.

They must be considerate.
They must be respectful.
They must be spiritual.

II. *What love looks like in the Church* (1 Pet. 3:8).
(a) It is unified.
(b) It is sympathetic.
(c) It is compassionate.
(d) It is humble.
III. *What Christian love should look like to the world* (1 Pet. 3:9–12).
(a) Love refuses to retaliate.

It is the government's job to protect our country.
The Church must respond in a spiritual way, such as by sending missionaries and building hospitals.

(b) Love seeks to serve others.

CONCLUSION.   The Christian life should be one marked by love. That should be quite natural for us because the one we have been named after lived in such a way. Not only was his life marked by love, so was his death. He has the scars to prove it.

When we exhibit love in marriage, in the Church, and in the world, we are putting Christ himself on exhibition for all to see.—Dave Stone, Preaching Associate

Topic: A Reason to Witness

TEXT: 1 Pet. 3:13–22

When we are given a chance to witness about Christ, many of us pass up the chance because of fear, uncertainty, or a variety of other reasons. Regardless of the reason, it is never a good feeling to know that we missed an opportunity to share Christ.

Interestingly enough, the author of 1 Peter knew that feeling of missed opportunity quite well. In fact, he passed up a chance to witness about Christ three times within moments of each other.

The same Peter who was so afraid that night in the courtyard, however, ended up being one of the most courageous and bold witnesses for Christ the world has ever known. And because he was, we would be wise to listen to Peter's advice on several different aspects of witnessing.

I. *The method of witnessing.*

(a) Be courageous (1 Pet. 3:13–14).

When you share the truth boldly, remember that it is not your job to cause a person to grow into a saved relationship with Christ.

As a Christian, your responsibility is to plant seeds for Christ.

(b) Be prepared (1 Pet. 3:15).

Share a personal experience.

Know God's Word.

(c) Be respectful.

Evangelism is not to be viewed as a debate to be won.

God called us to win people, not arguments.

II. *The motivation for witnessing.*

(a) God loves us.

(b) God loves others.

If you believe that people are really lost apart from the Lord, then it's the height of selfishness to fail to point them toward the Lord.

The secular world might not be ready to listen to our doctrine, but they simply cannot ignore unselfish love, as demonstrated by Christ's followers.

III. *The result of witnessing.*

(a) Believers receive salvation from sin.

(b) Christians have victory over Satan.

(c) The redeemed have the hope of heaven.

CONCLUSION.   Someone once said, "We ought to talk to God about people before we talk to people about God." If that statement is true, then our prayers about lost people should be abundant.

We live in a lost and dying world that is desperately in need of a cure for the sin problem. Actually, the cure already has been provided. People need to be told that there is hope in Christ. Don't keep the good news to yourself.—Dave Stone, Preaching Associate

Topic: A Reason for Self-Denial

TEXT: 1 Pet. 4:1–11

It has been said that self-denial is actually desire-denial. When said like that, it is easy to see why we so often shy away from self-denial; it's just too easy to subtly make our lives all about us. However, no fulfillment will be found in the lifestyle of self-indulgence. With that truth on Peter's mind and a pen in his hand, he offers us three reasons for self-denial.

I. *Self-denial lets us experience life the way God intends.*

(a) Arm yourself with the attitude of Christ.

(b) Avoid sin rather than approach it.

(c) Pursue obedience, regardless of the consequences.

II. *Self-denial lets us experience eternity the way God intends.*

(a) Self-denial has far better consequences than self-indulgence.

(b) In a life of self-denial, there are no regrets.

(c) We will reap what we sow.

III. *Self-denial lets us experience community the way God intends.*

(a) It allows for a loving community.

(b) It allows for a forgiving community.

(c) It allows for a welcoming community.

(d) It allows for a serving community.

CONCLUSION.   Ultimately, self-denial is the distinctive mark of the Christian life. Jesus Christ plainly said, "If any man would come after me he must deny himself, take up his cross daily, and follow me."

Simply put, self-denial is a choice we made when we accepted the call to follow Christ. The question then that must be asked is this: "Does the life you live match the decision you made?"—Dave Stone, Preaching Associate

Topic: A Reason to Suffer

TEXT: 1 Pet. 4:12–19

Why do bad things happen to good people? That is a question that has been asked often throughout the centuries. In fact, you probably have asked that question yourself, and fairly recently.

Unfortunately, it seems we never receive a satisfying answer. However, though we probably will never completely understand this dilemma until this life has passed, in 1 Peter the apostle shares some helpful insights into the mind of God about human suffering and anguish.

I. *Some suffering is inevitable. Accept it.*

(a) Sometimes we suffer because of our Christian testimony (v. 14).

(b) Sometimes we suffer because of our own sinful behavior (v. 15).

(c) Sometimes we suffer because of satanic attack.

(d) Sometimes we suffer because we live in a fallen world.

(e) Sometimes we suffer because of God's discipline.

II. *All suffering is purposeful. Rejoice in it.*

(a) When you hurt, you can appreciate more deeply what Jesus endured. Physical pain, emotional stress, and alienated relationships are examples of the pain we may endure.

(b) When you hurt, you have the opportunity to mature.

(c) When you hurt, your opportunity to witness is enhanced. Suffering puts the spotlight on you. Nobody wants to go through pain, but once you've been there, your credibility is enhanced.

III. *Patient suffering is commendable. Trust God's justice in it* (v. 19).

(a) God is going to administer justice someday. The righteous who have and do suffer patiently will be commended. The wicked who have prospered but have never given God glory, however, will be punished.

(b) Since we cannot see the future, we only can trust God's providence.

CONCLUSION.   Back to the original question: Why do bad things happen to good people? The truth is, there are no good people. Granted, some people are worse than others, but we know from the Bible that "all have sinned and fallen short of the glory of God" (Rom. 3:23). We all deserve punishment, but the Gospel proclaims that there is a good God.—Bob Russell, Senior Minister

Topic: A Reason to Lead and Follow
TEXT: 1 Pet. 5

Some of the most popular books on the market today are those written on leadership. It is not surprising that those books are so popular, because we are all leaders in some area of our lives. Maybe it's at work, maybe it's at home, maybe it's at church, but regardless of the circumstances we all lead in some way. It is interesting, however, that you hardly ever find a book on being a good follower. We need to be reminded that following well is equally as important as leading well. Just as we all lead in some areas of our lives, we are all followers in other areas of our lives. With that on his mind, Peter writes 1 Peter 5 to describe the godly leader and follower.

I. *The godly leader.*

(a) God's intention for church structure:

God designed that spiritually mature leaders in each congregation would be the overseers of the church.

The church elders are to be shepherds of God's flock, which is entrusted to their care.

(b) The godly shepherd has a three-fold responsibility to the flock:

1. Feed the sheep.
2. Protect the sheep.
3. Guide the sheep.

(c) Four motivations for the good shepherd:

1. "Not because you must, but because you are willing" (v. 2).
2. Not greed for money, but eagerness to serve.
3. Not to lord it over those entrusted to you, but to be an example to the flock (v. 3).
4. Not for the approval of men, but the reward of God.

II. *The godly follower.*
(a) A good follower is humbly submissive.
(b) A good follower is divinely strengthened.
(c) A good follower is fully engaged.
(d) A good follower is mutually inspired.
(e) A good follower is eternally motivated.

CONCLUSION.   The choice to be a good leader, as well as a good follower, is sometimes one of life or death. We have been taken hostage by Satan and are hopelessly trapped in sin. There are a lot of leaders in this world promising health, wealth, and happiness, but only Jesus Christ can lead us out of the bondage of sin and into a relationship with the Almighty God.—Bob Russell, Senior Minister

MESSAGES FOR ADVENT AND CHRISTMAS

SERMON SUGGESTIONS

Topic: The Unexpected Christ

TEXT: John 1:10–11

You say immediately, was anyone ever more expected than Christ? Was anybody ever more looked forward to than he was? You know that on February 15, 1564, Michelangelo died and Galileo was born, and that on the twenty-third of April in the same year, Shakespeare was born. There are three men who shaped our thinking. No one had any reason to expect any one of them. But surely it was not so with Christ; a whole nation was expecting him! They had been waiting for at least two or three hundred years for his arrival. They were looking everywhere for him, and every time they saw someone like John the Baptist, they wondered whether he might be the one. The hope of his coming kept them going through the humiliation and the indignity of their exile and through the coming of the Greeks with their temples and then of the Romans, with their efficient management of government. So, certainly, you can't say that they didn't expect him.

And yet, the fact is that when he did come, they didn't know it, and they didn't know it because he wasn't the Christ they had expected. They expected him to come with a fanfare, to cause a stir. But he didn't. He came quietly. The story tells us that a few shepherds knew it, but no one else. And in Malcolm Muggeridge's extraordinary book in which he describes his own rediscovery of Jesus, he writes, "Probably no child born into the world that day seemed to have poorer prospects than Christ did." They didn't expect that kind of Christ.

They expected (at least most of them did, and I must warn you that when we say "they," we are not including everyone, because there were always exceptions, then as now), but in general, they expected a Christ who would liberate them from Rome. He didn't. He liberated them from Satan—from sin and from guilt. They expected a Christ who would dazzle them by miraculous feats. He didn't. He healed the sick and he fed the hungry, but he didn't jump off the Temple just to dazzle them into belief. He refused to do that.

What is more, they expected a Christ who would instill in the young a love of the *Law*—the Law with a capital L because it was the Law of God that Moses had given them, and it covered every aspect of life with rules and regulations, both ceremonial and moral. People were neglecting it, and they were expecting a Christ who would rekindle a love of the Law with a capital L. He didn't. He talked about the law of Love, which was quite different. He said that love is the fulfilling of all the laws.

They expected a Christ who would make life easier, reduce the taxes, increase the employment, bring down the prices. He didn't. If anything he made it harder. He talked about crosses, not crowns. It is harder, infinitely harder, to change yourself than to change your surroundings. I am not saying that it isn't important to change the surroundings of other people from time to time, for it is, but the essential thing is to change the person, and it is much easier to change the surroundings in which a person lives than to change the person who lives in those surroundings.

Above everything else, they expected a Christ who would be a smashing success. He wasn't. He was a dismal failure. They expected a Christ whom they could keep to themselves as a nation. They couldn't. He was like a river, the current of which is so strong that no bank can contain it. They expected a Christ who would promise a happy ending. Everybody likes happy endings. He didn't promise the kind of a happy ending that all people really long for. He never let them forget about the girls who might have gone to the wedding but didn't because they were too late, and the man who missed the dinner because he was too busy to accept the invitation. He never let people forget the fact that the door can be closed and that it can be closed forever—that there *is* the possibility of missing the bus.

They didn't expect anything like that; only a few of the most perceptive ones could see the possibility of a Christ born in a manger and crucified on a cross. So it is no wonder that they hardly recognized him, because he was not the Christ they expected. They weren't ready for the Unexpected Christ.

Now we come to another Christmas, the middle of another season of Advent. We know that Christmas will come in the normal course of events. It always has come; the calendar always gets around to the twenty-fifth of December, and if we all live for another ten days, we will all have another Christmas. We know that. And we also know that Christ will come, in one way or another, but instinctively we look for him to come in the way we expect him, and there is a sense in which he will come in that way. He will break through, here and there, the crust of our fierce, competitive world; he will soften a hard heart, here and there. He will heal an open wound; he will manage to find a small place on the thousands of cards and messages, even the ones that have not a single reference to himself, because the one who sends it expresses his own love and affection on that card. So he will come that way.

But there is also a sense in which he is always the Unexpected Christ. We expect him to come in the usual place, which for us is either the church, or the home, or both. For many people he may come in neither of those places. He may come in the streets; he may come on the college campus where there doesn't seem to be much sign of him at the moment; he may come on a ski slope where a family spends the holidays. Or he may come like a shining light in a scientist's laboratory, the flickering of a new idea that will open one of the secrets of the world. We expect him to come in the familiar music of the carols we love and have heard all our lives and will hear again next Sunday, and all through the Christmas season. For many of us he will come in that music. But for thousands he may come in the more primitive rhythm of music that is called Rock. I don't understand it, but I am prepared for the fact that that is the way he will come for many people.

We expect him to come in the familiar language of the Bible, especially the King James translation, and the Book of Common Prayer. He may come in our time in some strange, new tongue that sounds to us so like vernacular that it borders on the vulgar. Before you make any judgment about it, remember that the first translation of the Scriptures from Greek into Latin was called the *Vulgate* for that very reason. People thought it was a vulgar language.

We expect him to come in the structure of our long-established manners and morals. He may not. He may come to some little shed completely outside our sheltered lives, in some new way of loving each other in a world in which love has been almost forced out of the picture by the sheer size of the human family.

This is disturbing to people over thirty. It would be so much easier for all of us if he came in the same old place, in the same old way. The old decorations would do and would save us such a lot of trouble and an enormous amount of money. But he won't. He will not leave us alone; that is, he will not let us alone. He wants to keep us alive. Instead of solutions, he gives us problems for Christmas, if you can believe it. A man can settle down and die in a solution, but in a problem he is more sure to stay alive.

Christ comes as the angel who troubles the water. He says something like this to me, and he may say it to you, but he says it to me this particular year. You can't wrap God up in a proof-sheet of logical, rational reasoning. You can't have me gift-wrapped for a Christmas present. You can't preserve me in your theological formulas or even in your ecclesiastical institutions, because I will always be slipping out for a breath of fresh air. He says, if you want the serenity that I can give you, you must take the restlessness that goes with it, without which the serenity would be nothing but smugness. He says, when I come, I come as I am—like the wind, like a breath of life. If you don't expect me, you will not find me. If you do find me, don't be surprised if I am not the one you expected.

George MacDonald, the Scot who left the ministry because it was too tight for his mind, wrote a great many novels and stories for children. In 1883 he published a book of poems, one of which has been included in two of our hymnals. There are only three stanzas. The language is Victorian, but you can see why I end this sermon with these three verses:[1]

> They all were looking for a king
> To slay their foes, and lift them high;
> Thou cam'st a little baby thing
> That made a woman cry.
> O Son of Man, to right my lot
> Naught but thy presence can avail;
> Yet on the road thy wheels are not
> Nor on the sea thy sail!
> My fancied ways, why shouldst thou heed?
> Thou com'st down thine own secret stair;
> Com'st down to answer all my need
> Yea, ev'ry bygone prayer.
> The Unexpected Christ coming down his own secret stair!

—Theodore Parker Ferris

Topic: If Christ Were Born Today
TEXT: Heb. 13:8

In the mid-1950s, England was convulsed by a storm of religious controversy over the BBC lectures of a fortyish schoolmarm, Margaret Knight, on what she called "scientific humanism." Dismissing both God and the devil as outdated beliefs, she urged a view of Jesus devoid

---

[1]George MacDonald (1824–1905). Published in 1883.

of supernatural trappings. Capitalizing on the public outcry that rushed to attack or defend the soft-spoken but opinionated psychologist, the London *Daily Sketch* headlined "the boldest discussion ever attempted by a newspaper," a three-week series by big-name Britons on the subject, "If Christ Comes Back."[2]

What if you were asked to contribute to that symposium? What do you think it would be like if Jesus returned to Earth again, beginning this Christmas? Actually, the New Testament does not leave us in great doubt about that question, for it affirms that people really do not change very much. We are pretty much like the people to whom he came two thousand years ago. Furthermore, we can be certain that he is the same today as he was yesterday (Heb. 13:8). That being so, let us use a biblically controlled criterion to imagine what the incarnation would be like in our day.

I. *He would enter through a lowly door.* Writing in the *Daily Sketch*, Bishop Gorton of Coventry described the sensationalist view, which is probably most popular today: "great headlines would appear in the papers . . . busloads, special trains and gatherings in the Albert Hall. . . ." In other words, Christ would become an instant celebrity because of his reputation through the centuries.

There is much to commend this view, for we live in the "Age of Hype." Promotion of media stars has reached a new level of intensity. Millions are spent to create an atmosphere of hysteria. So it would be easy to see Christ with a booking agent, pursued by television cameras, giving interviews to newspaper reporters, appearing on talk shows, negotiating with publishers screaming for a book, making the cover of *People* magazine.

The only problem is that this scenario does not square with New Testament facts. To begin with, the first century was an Age of Hype also. The Caesars such as Nero were masters of the celebrity cult. But Jesus never accepted the puffery that even the Jews thought went along with being a royal Messiah. Instead, he made his messiahship a "secret"—the very opposite of celebrity ballyhoo.

How do we translate that deliberate incognito into twentieth-century categories? Jesus was born in Bethlehem, a mere suburb of Jerusalem, and lived in Nazareth, which was not even on the map! So would he be born today in some rural hamlet or urban slum? Even worse, Palestine was a remote province of the Roman Empire, so would he be born in a third world country where nothing important ever seems to happen? Would Americans ever accept a savior born in Zimbabwe?

Jesus never once made the news in his day. No written accounts, inscriptions, or statues remain. He did not make the history books until a century later. So what if you learned that the Messiah was actually back on Earth and had never been interviewed by the talk show hosts? Or that the news anchors had never given him thirty seconds to voice a "sound bite" on television news? Or that he did not have a single book in print? Or that nobody important was paying any attention to him, whether politicians, scholars, pundits, or other movers and shakers?

What that would mean is that you would have to decide about Jesus entirely on the basis of who he was, rather than on the basis of what important people thought of him. You would have to base your decision on substance rather than on style, on integrity rather than on image, on reality rather than on reputation! The absence of "hype" would demand that you

---

[2]*Time*, Jan. 24, 1955, p. 44; Mar. 21, 1955, pp. 51–54.

make up your own mind rather than conform to popular opinion reflected by the latest poll. You would have to listen to what he was actually saying rather than catch a "quotable quote" already given media "spin." Strangely enough, you would begin to realize that his is one decision you would have to make entirely by faith rather than because of a successful sales pitch.

II. *He would disturb the status quo.* Before reckoning what your decision would be, realize that this antihero, this antithesis of the celebrity, was a provocation to the caretakers of the power structure. Billy Graham made that point in his contribution to the *Daily Sketch* series: "First, He will disturb the economic life. There are thousands of economic injustices. . . . Second, He will disturb the political status quo. The dictators, the aggressors, the crafty politicians and corrupt political systems . . . will be objects of his wrath. Third, He will disturb the social status quo. . . . Fourth, He will also disturb the religious status quo. The most scathing denunciations that Christ gave two thousand years ago were against religious leaders!"

There is much in the New Testament to support this revolutionary view. Jesus cried out against excessive riches, against political zealotism, against the social segregation of Samaritans, against the enforcers of petty legalisms, as well as against those who had corrupted the Temple. He made enemies as soon as he began to minister (Mark 2:1–3:6). He could not be intimidated by the political or religious establishment. Even at the height of his popularity, he managed to get himself crucified as the Great Disturber.

The amazing thing about Jesus was his combination of complete humility to claim nothing for himself, combined with his complete authority to judge everything by the will of God. His only weapons were words. His only appeal was to conscience. His only strategy was to depend on God to vindicate his indictments. As Pilate instantly recognized, he had no army, no organization, no following in the sense of a rival "movement." In the showdown, even his disciples refused to fight for him, leaving him as one lone man against the entrenched status quo. He lacked what we would call social "leverage" or political "clout."

This picture leaves little doubt that Christ today would not march under any of our commonly accepted banners. He would challenge any economic system, whether it be capitalistic or socialistic, that causes the rich to get richer and the poor to get poorer. He would challenge any political system, whether democratic or totalitarian, that arms a nation to the teeth with nuclear missiles. He would challenge any social system, whether liberal or conservative, that nourishes prejudice against an underclass. Not lowest-common-denominator conformity but prophetic independence would be Christ's stance today.

Hardest of all would be his refusal to fit into the religious establishment. He would denounce lip service masquerading as life service. He would condemn ritual and routine in place of loving relationships. He would ignore mere traditionalism, speculative questions, or orthodoxy, and divisive relations between denominations. Dare we admit that he would be as unwelcome in some of our churches today as he was in the synagogues of the first century?

What this means for us is that he applies no pressure to get a decision from us, yet to make a commitment to his cause requires a break with the status quo. To accept Christ, now as then, is to live out of the future rather than out of the past. It is to join a revolution that goes to the very root of human existence. It is to declare our independence from the mind-numbing and conscience-jading passivity that binds us to the predictable. To follow Christ is to fit no earthly pattern but to pioneer a new one true to the Kingdom of God.

III. *He would give himself to ordinary people.* Most scenarios depict Christ as a mover and shaper of history, thus many assume that if he came back today he would hobnob with the opinion-makers of our time. But we saw precisely the opposite in the original pattern of his coming. Jesus was never comfortable with the flattery of Nicodemus on behalf of the Sanhedrin. Instead, he gave himself to the common folk whom the establishment ignored or even despised.

This is seen in the disciples whom he called: fishermen, tax collectors, misfits all! They offered him no power, no money, no talent. In fact, they were a constant headache to him because of their dullness. But if he could make anything out of them, he could make something out of anybody! They were the least likely candidates to be world-changers, but in response to his call they dared to work a revolution in human affairs.

Would Christ act like that today? He ate with publicans and sinners. Would the socially ostracized flock to him today? He called harlots to follow him then. Would prostitutes welcome him today? He rejoiced over Roman centurions then. Would he attract Chinese army captains today? The blind, the lame, the lepers—would these be in the vanguard of his supporters today?

We often judge leaders by the important people they can influence. In a presidential primary, the key is how many prestigious endorsements a candidate can collect. By contrast, imagine Jesus walking the streets of Birmingham with a crowd of nobodies hanging on to his every word: bums from the Rescue Mission, unwed mothers from abortion clinics, drifters from the Salvation Army, street people from under the viaduct. Many of us would turn Christ off before giving him a chance, not because of who he was but because of the crowd he attracted—those with whom nobody else wanted to associate!

This preference for plain people meant that, for Jesus, faith was devoid of human achievement. These folk had nothing to claim for themselves or to offer him. They could not share with him any brilliance or sophistication. They had no influence or resources to contribute to his cause. All they could do was trust him, cling to him, depend on him, be loyal to him. Out of this fact of history came a revolutionary new understanding of the religious response: faith as sheer openness, dependence, and commitment, free of pride or works or any human merit.

This does not mean that Christ would be able to attract only the simple-minded who were so bereft of ability that they were willing to try anything. Rather, it means that he saw in these forgotten grassroots folk an unrealized potential that others had ignored. He counted on these commoners to launch the greatest religious breakthrough the world has ever seen! They would write the New Testament. They would conquer the mighty Roman Empire "from below." It was not what they could do for him but what he could do for them that mattered most!

The pattern is now sufficiently clear to predict what would happen if Christ came back this year. He would again enter by the back door, largely unnoticed by those who assume that important things happen only in the spotlight. He would create a disturbance by refusing to make sacred cows out of threadbare traditions. A few folk on the fringes would be attracted to him as the only person who had ever noticed them, but that would only widen his credibility gap among those who travel in more select circles. Lest you doubt the picture, let me remind you that this is exactly what happened the first time he came, and little has changed in the two thousand years since then.

So the question is forced: How would you respond if he came back this Christmas? To be sure, you may already be a devoted follower, but are you following the real Jesus, who lived as the Gospels describe? Or are you riding the coattails of his reputation, as it has been sanitized centuries later? It is fairly easy to follow the most acclaimed religious leader of all time, in whose honor an impressive Christian civilization has flourished for two millennia. It is much harder to follow a maverick Jesus whose life has cut across the status quo in every generation, beginning with his own.

In any case, you will have to decide how to respond, for he keeps coming back, not in the flesh as in the long ago, but in the Spirit that dwells among his people. He is neither sealed in an ancient tomb nor is he banished to the highest heavens. Advent means that he comes to us, not just once a year but in the here and now. And when he comes, the next move is up to you!—William E. Hull

SECTION X

A POTPOURRI OF PREACHING

Topic: Wrestling with God
TEXT: Gen. 32:22–32; Gal. 5:22

While in Germany on a recent trip, my friends were taking a long time to eat, so I took a walk and found a beautiful church with stone floors and walls and wooden rafters. I started singing the song, "My Jesus loves me . . . Oh yes he does . . . My Jesus loves me . . . Oh yes he does." Then I got to thinking, "You know it is sad that I have to state that Jesus loves me and that God can't say this to me directly." Then I turned to God and said, "This is kind of sad. In psychology when a father can't say out loud 'I love you,' we call that being dysfunctional." Then I started to sing again, "My Jesus loves me . . ." and at that moment the bells of the church struck twice—ding . . . ding. I broke into tears, as I heard God say, "I do love you! And I can say it out loud!"

I have encountered the living God. Have you ever encountered God?

In our story today an Old Testament patriarch, Jacob, not only encounters God; he wrestles with God. I love this story because instead of me having a problem, God has a problem. You see, God wanted to create a nation. He told Abraham that he would bless the world and create a nation out of Abraham. So Abraham had a son, Isaac, and Isaac had this son, Jacob. And now we have a problem—because Jacob is a scoundrel.

In Hebrew the name Jacob sounds like the Hebrew word for "cheat." And Jacob was aptly named. Jacob cheated his own brother; he deceived his own father; he manipulated his father-in-law. How is God going to bless the world through a fellow who cheats? He must change Jacob.

By the way, isn't there a little of Jacob in all of us? Have you ever manipulated, told a half-truth, fudged the numbers a little? And God wants to use us to change his world. How will God do this? He will have to change us. Jacob is alone because his own brother is trying to kill him. A man starts to wrestle with Jacob. We later learn that this man was a form of God himself. I love this story because Jacob seems to win.

There are those of us who wrestle with God. We struggle to try to figure out God, life, issues, love, hate, betrayal. We struggle to understand a holy God, a profane world, and the meaning of life.

How do you wrestle with God and faith? Have you ever asked questions like these?

Is there a God?
Is God involved in this world?
Is God involved with my life?
Do I believe the Bible?
How literally do I believe the Bible?

What is the meaning of life?
Why is there something instead of nothing?
Where did evil come from?
Why am I here?
Does anyone care about me?
Does God care?
Why is there death?
Is there life after death?
Why did I get cancer?
What is good or bad about divorce?

What should I do or believe about terrible issues that face our world:

Abortion
Death penalty
Gay issue
Euthanasia
A young lady on a respirator
Friends who betray
Should we go to war should we not go to war?
Who do I vote for?
Is this church best or is another church better?
Do I tithe or not?
What should I do with my life?
Is this all there is?

There are only two things in this world: things you can see and things you can't. Things you can't see are, by definition, spiritual. If you have wrestled with life, faith, or any of the problems I just mentioned, you have wrestled with God.

Here are the rules for wrestling with God:

It is OK to wrestle with God: (1) it shows you care; (2) it shows you are thinking; (3) it shows you are growing. Do not buy the ideas of other people. Wrestle with God and life, and find your own answers.

Fighting is a form of love. It may not seem like it at the time. And I don't want to endorse fighting; I know it is not good and I know it hurts. But a lot of people think of hate and fighting as the opposite of love; they are not. The opposite of love is apathy. Hate and fighting are similar to reactions to love. They include passion and interaction and deep care about the outcome of the situation.

This form of fighting and wrestling with God is a form of prayer. Prayer is communicating or talking with God. And yes, we are spending time with God when we wrestle with these issues.

It is OK to tell God everything. He knows your feelings, your doubts, your love and hatred, your fear and your questions. God can handle your anger. Don't be afraid.

It helps to get alone. Jacob spent the night alone. It is then that God speaks to him. Ask questions, seek advice, study books. But in the end you have to get away from people, turn off the noisemakers, and listen to the voice of God. When I have gotten silence, I have never, *ever* failed to hear the voice of God.

Always seek the truth. It is never healthy to settle for what is easy. It is never OK to take the statements of one minister or one professor or one book. It is never healthy to settle for what feels good. Always, *always* seek the truth. You will never go wrong seeking the truth.

Dig deep for the truth. Just remember that the truth is not easy to find. Any problem that you face you must look at from a conservative side, from a liberal side, from a moderate side. Look at it from the top. Look at it from the bottom. Seek out the opinion of many books. Seek out the opinion of many people who have been down that road before.

Don't accept an "easy" truth. When you find someone who has experience, it is easy to accept that as true. Remember that you want to be about seeking the whole truth. I know a CPA who bought two houses and lost money on both of them. I would not recommend taking his advice on real estate. I take advice from people who have done things and been successful. Proverbs 11:14 KJV: "Where no counsel is, the people fall: but in the multitude of counselors there is safety."

Know that God loves you. You cannot do anything that stops God from loving you. Your anger, your questions, your wrestling will never separate you from the love of God.

Don't give up on God. I can tell you there is a God. He loves you, and you can do better with a clear relationship with God.

There is a consequence to wrestling with God. *You will never wrestle with God without being changed.*

Jacob was touched in the hip and walked with a limp the rest of his life.

Abraham and the Jewish people would cut their bodies when they became followers of God to mark that they were different.

Jacob's name was changed to Israel because of his encounter with God.

Jacob changed the name of the place where he met God.

There are parts of our world still today where people who become Christians change their name to mark the new life that they have started in Jesus. To be marked is to be shaped, to have old things cut away and a new shape to be formed. The word *character* means to chip away what is not good and to form something beautiful.

As Christians we are followers of the son of God, Jesus Christ. If we are going to wrestle and grow and be shaped, we will be different from the way we are today.

God wants to do something great with your life. He and you can do it but not without a struggle. Not without wrestling. God wants to form you into his image. God wants to create love, joy, peace, patience, kindness, goodness, faithfulness, gentleness, and self-control. Will you let God do this for you? Will you wrestle with God?

If my father were to stand here beside me, you would notice some very similar characteristics in me and in my father. We both have a potbelly and a bald head, and are just a shade under six feet tall. I bear in my body the marks of my father.

But not just physically. I also bear in my personality the marks of my father. We are both a little feisty; we are both very independent; we are both educated and loving people. You have heard that the acorn does not fall far from the tree—even in my personality I bear the marks of my father.

Those of us who are serious followers of God—who call God our Father—should also bear in our bodies and personalities the marks of God himself.

Are you ready? It's time to wrestle.—Conway Stone

Topic: Once Upon a Dream: Dealing with Disappointment, Dejection, and Deferment
TEXT: Luke 24:13–35

Have you been there—with those two on the road to Emmaus? They followed their dreams and "the dreamer," with expectations of life being changed for the better, forever—only to see their dream vanish like a bubble in the wind, when the one they had followed uttered those dream-ending words: "It is finished."

Have you been there—with nothing left of your dreams but a handful of pieces? Have you been there—when the only thing left of your hopes was a broken heart? Have you been there—bruised and battered on your way back home, with nothing left but empty pockets? Have you been there—on your way from divorce court to nowhere, wondering how in the world did this happen? Have you been there—when the doctor says, "I have bad news—some very bad news"? Have you been there—following a hearse to a fresh-made grave?

You *have* been there, haven't you? I thought so. But if you haven't, you will. Hall-of-Fame country music songwriter Kris Kristofferson had obviously been there when he wrote *Sunday Morning Coming Down*. One verse says: "Then I headed back for home, and somewhere far away a lonesome bell was ringing, and it echoed through the canyon like the disappearing dreams of yesterday."

There are three haunting words in this scriptural narrative: "We had hoped." Heads down, shuffling along, hardly speaking because there was nothing to say except, "We had hoped." Having spent thirteen years in the pastoral ministry and twice that many as a full-time psychotherapist, believe me, I've heard about an endless number of heart-rending broken dreams (meaning no disrespect)—more than you can possibly imagine and more devastating than any human should have to endure.

Dreaming is a basic distinction that separates the human species from those on the short limbs of the evolutionary tree. Dreams, fantasies, hopes, anticipations—all are variations on a common theme: the intrinsic desire of the human being *to have something to look forward to.*

The road to Emmaus scene is a stark reminder of just how fragile life is, how vulnerable we really are, and how quickly our dreams can turn into nightmares. But it's also about the emergence of hope in the face of hopelessness, help in the hands of the helpless, despair that is countered with determination, evildoing that is challenged by goodness, and death that is overpowered by life.

Dreams are about wishes, wants, fantasies, hopes, desires, urges, goals. Dreams are about imagination, visualization, mental imagery. Dreams are about direction, guidance, and where you're headed. Dreams are basically about attitude.

In aviation, the direction of the nose of the aircraft is known as the plane's attitude. Whether the nose is straight and level, pointed down, or pointed up, tells you which way you are headed. Dreams tell us about our attitude—which way we are headed: down, up, straight, level.

Make no mistake about it. Dreams are very important—dare I say, essential. The writer of Proverbs seemed to think they were essential when these words were penned: "Where there is no hope, no anticipation, and no dreams the people fall, but in an abundance of counselors there is safety" (loose translation of Prov. 11:14).

No doubt about this either: life is a Duke's mixture of dreams that encounters crises, contrasts, and contradictions and comes in a variety of sizes, shapes, colors, and content. Examples:

> A *little boy* was dreaming when he said, "I wish I had a watermelon." An older kid replied, "Man if you gonna wish for something, wish for something big." The little kid responded, "I wish I had a *big* watermelon."
>
> A *duck* waddled into a saloon, hopped up on the bar, and said to the bartender, "You got any grapes?" "No," said the bartender. The next day he did it again. "Got any grapes?" Same reply. Third day the same. "Got any grapes?" "Didn't have any yesterday. Don't have any today. Won't have any tomorrow. And if you come back again, I'm gonna nail your feet to the bar." But the persistent little cuss came back again. "You got any nails?" "No," replied the bartender. "You got any grapes?"

The question for the followers of Christ is this: You got any dreams? Sure you do, and if you want them to come true you'll follow the duck's lead: don't argue, don't push, don't get upset, and don't take no for an answer. You just keep on asking questions, asking questions, asking questions.

A *preacher* had some dreams of saving a homeless street person. The street resident was sitting on a park bench, empty Mogen David 20/20 bottle lying beside him, ragged clothes, stinking to high heaven. With both hands shaking while he gazed at the newspaper that had been used for a blanket the night before, the down-and-outer said, "Excuse me Rev, do you know what causes Parkinson's disease?" Seeing this as an opening that was surely the will of God, the preacher decided to scare the man straight.

"Well brother, nobody's sure, but God has laid a word of wisdom on my heart that I'll be glad to share with you. God's leading me to tell you that Parkinson's disease is due to being a wino, doing drugs, gambling, chasing women, and being a sorry good-for-nothing bum. But the Lord can help you, brother, if you just turn your life over to him. What do you think about that?" The street guy replied, "Well, who'd a thought it? I just read in the paper that both the Pope and Billy Graham have Parkinson's!"

For sure, for sure, dreams come in a variety of colors, shapes, and sizes, whether it's a little boy wanting a big watermelon, a duck dreaming of grapes, a preacher trying to save a soul—or you wanting to pay off some debts, or put a kid through college, or buy a boat—a big boat—or a new house, new car; maybe you want early retirement.

But there's another truism on this subject: many of our dreams do not come true, have not become realities—in fact have crashed and burned right in front of our eyes.

The question I pose is this: What do *you* do with disappointments, dejections, and deferments? How do *you* deal with shattered dreams?

That's a question Langston Hughes raised in his marvelous poem, *A Dream Deferred*. What happens to a dream deferred?

Shattered dreams are inevitable for all of us. If you haven't had one already, brace yourself. It's coming. I was in a health club locker room and overheard this conversation between two butt-naked older men. One said, "Roy, you're old, fat, and ugly." Roy responded, "Well, I may be old and fat but I ain't ugly." The other said, "Well, believe me—ugly's coming!"

Well, if you haven't had a broken dream yet, believe me, it's coming. Shattered dreams are a part of life—everyone's life. I know a lot about broken dreams. I've had them personally and professionally. I've been listening to them for nearly forty years. In fact, many of those who come for therapy are backpacking a broken dream.

Martin Luther King had a dream that wasn't realized until after his death. *Danny Thomas* had a dream that came true in his lifetime: St. Jude, the patron saint of hopeless causes, has become the hospital icon for treating children with catastrophic illnesses. And treatment's free! What a dream! What a reality. Yet you can be sure Danny Thomas dealt with numerous shattered dreams on the way to that magnificent reality.

What happens to you when your dreams *don't* come true? How you handle broken dreams has an enormous bearing on controlling your peace of mind. So what can you do with a shattered dream? From my perspective, there are four reactions that pretty much tell the tale of what people do with a broken dream. Today you get the first two; next week, the other two.

I. *Resign from it.* "No more dreaming—it's too painful, too difficult to recover, I've been hurt too many times." I see married couples in this position quite often. "I'm not doing it anymore. I'm giving up," they often exclaim.

Remember the routine the great clown Emmett Kelly did in his hobo tramp outfit? He closed his performance by taking a broom and sweeping the spotlight into a tiny pile. Smaller and smaller until it was gone! That's the way some people deal with broken dreams—they sweep them up and turn out the light and refuse to dream anymore.

A father and his twenty-year-old son were riding down the interstate; the boy was driving. They passed a Cadillac SUV Sport Escalade—that's the one that looks like a tank and sells for about 50K. Son said, "That's the one I want. Right there. And I'm gonna get me one." Dad says, "What? Do you know how much that costs? You're not out of college. You don't even have a job. That's absurd to talk about buying a vehicle like that." It was quiet for a moment and then son said, "Dad, do you know what your problem is? You don't even recognize dreaming when you hear it." Dad had quit dreaming a long time ago and didn't want anyone around him to do it either.

A client of mine stopped dreaming, too. When he was a boy, Landon dreamed daily of playing major league baseball. His coaches said he had the talent and the heart. It was just a matter of time until he played in the Big Leagues. Then, at age fifteen, he contracted polio. He was partially paralyzed on the left side. But the church prayed, and the minister anointed with holy oil, and they laid on hands. But the paralysis remained, and later his leg withered. He never played baseball again, and forty years later a bitter, cantankerous man limped into my therapy room to deal with his long-ago broken dream.

In losing his dream, he lost hope. Without hope, he gave up his faith. In the absence of hope and faith, there was very little capacity to love and be loved. That's a principle that needs to be repeated. *When a person is without faith and hope, the capacity to love is greatly impaired.*

After a few shattered dreams in childhood and some that are added on in adulthood—dare I say many that were added on in adulthood—many people protect themselves by refusing to dream any more. Disappointment is much too painful to take the risk. So they develop a view that lives by the safe beatitude: "Blessed are those who expect nothing from life; they shall not be disappointed!"

II. *Retrieve it.* Dreaming is normal and totally natural. You don't have to teach children how to dream; it's what they are about. When I was a kid we played cowboys and Indians, Tarzan and Jane. Due to the impact of feminism, today's kids don't play Tarzan and Jane; they play Tarzan and Tarzette, and rightly so.

Children dream—they play make believe; they play like they are truck drivers, astronauts, power rangers, firefighters; they talk to imaginary friends. *But* with enough discouragement, dreaming fades and fades to black. During adulthood, with enough disappointments, dejections, and deferments, some have to be coaxed, cajoled, and strong-armed to get them to retrieve their dreams.

Quoting Langston Hughes again, who said, *"Hold fast to your dreams, for if dreams die, life is a broken winged bird that cannot fly."* Well, a lot of you, I suspect, are trying to get back on track and find your way back home, carrying in your bag of experiences a lot of broken dreams. To recover your dreams is like going into your computer and retrieving a very old file that you had long since sent to the junk folder.

Before somebody told you that you had to go to work to make a living, what were your dreams? I asked that question of a man whose net worth is in the twenty-million-dollar range, give or take a million or two, and he responded immediately, "I wanted to teach English literature in a university." "What happened?" I asked. "I was in the first year of my Ph.D. program and got involved with a fellow student. She got pregnant. We got married. I dropped out of school and went to work. Twenty years later—the rest is history." "How does that feel?" I asked. He teared up and said, "I'd still like to teach English literature in a university." "Then retrieve that dream and go for it," I said. After a couple of tissues and a long pause, he smiled and said, "Maybe I will."

How about you? What did you dream of doing or becoming before somebody told you to stop dreaming and start making a living or raising a family? Is it time to retrieve it? I think it is; I believe it is; I know it is; I'm positive it is. And when you don't think you can handle it any longer, remember and repeat those immortal words of Sir Winston Churchill when he stepped to the lectern to give a graduation speech during the darkest times of World War II. Said the old statesman, "Never give up. Never give up. Never, never, never."

You there—with your head down kicking at the dust on the road back to your hometown—don't throw in the towel. Hope is on the way. You there—with a pocket full of broken dreams on your way to downtown, midtown, or out of town. It's time to retrieve your dreams. Hope's a-coming.

In the words of dear Mother Mary, "Let it be, Lord, let it be."—Don Doyle

Topic: Could These Be the Hardest Words to Say?
TEXT: Luke 23:34

That's really what he said: "Father, forgive them, for they know not what they do." Unexpected and out of the ordinary!

Plenty of other voices spoke that day.

Caiaphas for one! In response to the expressed fear that if Jesus were allowed to go on performing signs, people would believe him, and the Romans would come and destroy their holy place and the nation. Caiaphas (the high priest for that year) said, "You know nothing at all! You do not understand that it is better for you to have one man die for the people than to have the whole nation destroyed" (John 11:50). Unbelievable, but that is what he said.

Herod for another! (Luke 23:6–12). Herod, who happened to be in Jerusalem at this time, got an audience with Jesus after Pilate (Herod's old rival). Herod happily received Jesus because for a long time he had hoped to see him for himself. His hope brought out words like these: "Show me one of the signs you have become so famous for." That's the voice of selfish triviality. And Jesus recognizes it as such and answers him not a word. The chief priests were there. Herod and his soldiers joined them in treating Jesus with contempt and mocking. Herod then put an elegant robe on Jesus and sent him back to Pilate. Unbelievable, but that is what happened.

Pilate's voice rises to prominence, too! After having Jesus flogged and seeing the soldiers make their sport by covering Jesus with a crown of thorns and a purple robe, he said, "Here is the man!" Following the demand of the chief priests and the police, Pilate in capitulation said, "Take him yourselves and crucify him; I find no case against him" (John 19:5–6). Inconceivable, but this is what happened.

Mob violence also found press that day! Pilate heard the unified voice of unreasonableness say, "If you release this man, you are no friend of the emperor" (John 19:12b). When Pilate heard these words, he brought Jesus outside to a place called "The Stone Pavement" (in Hebrew *Gabbatha*). He directed his voice to the religious crowd and said, "Here is your King!" The "mob" said, "Away with him! Crucify him!" Beyond us, but that is what they said.

Amidst all these voices the voice of love rang out for the ages to hear. When collected from all the gospel information, seven sayings of Jesus came from the cross that day:

1. The prayer of forgiveness
2. A promise to a dying man
3. Concern for a mother who beheld her dying son
4. A cry of agonizing loneliness
5. A cry of physical anguish
6. A cry of victory in the midst of pain
7. A cry of trust

This message focuses on the astonishing "first word" from the voice at the center cross. What kind of God is this we are dealing with? For some he may be the god who runs from trouble and won't be back. He is the god who abandons in time of need. For others he may be the kind of god who winks at sin or the one who retaliates with an eye-for-an-eye. The question still waves before us in banner-like fashion. What kind of god is this Jesus when he said, "Father, forgive them for they do not know what they are doing?" Hard to grasp, but that is what he said. Could they be the hardest words in the world to say?

These words are spoken against a backdrop of rejection. Isaiah 53:3 reminds us that the suffering servant would be the despised and rejected one, a man of sorrows and acquainted with grief.

Those at the cross were like Judas (Acts 1:25), who went back to his own place. Not to God's place! Not to the realm of forgiveness to which God in Christ was calling them. Not to new faith and hope. Not to the embrace of Christ's redeeming love but to their own place—the place of their own choosing, the place of continued servitude to sin. They went back to where they could shut themselves in and Jesus out—the place of rejection.

The events of the cross were loaded with rejection. The words "Jesus of Nazareth, King of the Jews" were written in

Hebrew—the language of religion, the national language
Latin—the official language, government language
Greek—the language of culture; *koine* or common language

All these elements of life repudiated Jesus. Hebrew demanded his Crucifixion. Latin supplied the power to kill Jesus. Greek ignored him. Sinful religion rejected him; sinful power murdered him, and sinful culture neglected him. Jesus' prayer was uttered in the arena of rejection.

These words were spoken where ignorance flourished. "They do not know what they are doing." We may be inclined to react with surprise.

There's so much they did know:

Judas knew he had betrayed a friend.
Caiaphas knew he had resorted to bribery and tricks.
The chief priests knew their charges were false.
Pilate knew he was allowing an innocent man to be killed.
The soldiers knew he did not deserve this fate.
The crowd knew that to mock him was extreme sadism.

There was so much they did not know:

They did not know how much God was in this event.
They did not know that the cross would help fulfill God's plan.
They did not know that this torture would become a symbol of hope for all.
They did not know that the ugly chasm of their ignorance and sin would be laid bare by this experience.
They did not know how much they needed forgiveness.
They did not know how much this revealed them as God's enemies.

They thought they were doing God's service by ridding their community of this religious trash. But Jesus prayed for them. His saying that they "do not know" meant that they did not know him perceptively in their soul. They had hearsay but not soul knowledge.

The pathos of the situation is seen in the words of Nicholas of Susa, who called us all "doctors of ignorance." Do we not all have Ph.D.'s in not knowing?

These words are spoken with full awareness of sin's seriousness. Humanity's freedom comes into focus; the fact that ignorance can plague us is highlighted here. Jesus was not overlooking our sins. Forgiveness is never an indulgent attitude toward sin but the establishment of a new relationship. That is what is at stake here.

These words by Jesus are spoken to identify his allegiance. His allegiance is to God, and it is also to us, the ignorant. Let me remind you that these words were "shockers" that day.

They did not appear in some manuscript (Vaticanus, for one), although scholars believe them to be valid.

To say these words at least means someone is joining someone—taking sides with someone who otherwise stands in a very bad light. These words speak a remarkable identification of the divine with the human.

What Jesus had preached on a sunny, rural hill of the Galilee he practiced on the grim Golgotha hill of Jerusalem. In Matthew 5:44 he said: "But I say to you, love your enemies and pray for those who persecute you."

And there are still those who reject. For those on that day, there was something—a piece of a leftover coat. Those who looked on divided his coat among them by casting lots. This was all that was left. The rest of him had been spent to identify with us sinners.

Isn't this the kind of Savior you need? Inconceivable, but he is available to all the weary, road-worn travelers whose burden of sin is too heavy to bear and whose hope has darkened until it is hardly visible anymore.—Bob I. Johnson

Topic: The Streaker
Text: 2 Cor. 5:1–10

Last week, I found a metaphor at the heart of this text that may seem a bit strange at first. Years ago, when I was a student in college, there was a fad on campus called streaking. I've noticed that this fad recently made a small comeback on Nike television commercials. In its original form, streaking was an act of protest against the status quo. At some colleges and universities it was not uncommon to look out of one's classroom window and see some entirely or partly naked student racing on foot across campus to make a statement against the establishment.

After reading our biblical text from 2 Corinthians this morning, I almost entitled this morning's sermon "Streaking for Jesus." Paul is talking about "taking it off," by which he means taking off what he calls the "earthly tents we live in." Living in this tent, he says (mixing metaphors beautifully) we "groan," longing to be clothed with "our heavenly dwelling." Like the streaker, taking off this garment of mortality is something of an expression of freedom from the way things are. But unlike the streaker, Paul says that when we have "taken it off," we will not be found naked. In fact, we will find that we are "further clothed" but that the clothes we wear will be an eternal "building" rather than a temporal "tent."

If you're like me, you have some appreciation that you are clothed with what Paul calls "mortality." These bodies of ours are a gift to us, and they need to be defended and maintained in an environment that seems to want to wear them down or even destroy them. Our bodies are finite, fragile, and limited; it is only natural for us to feel in need of some defense against the cold, hard realities of life.

In light of this, the culture of self-help is not all bad. We need to pay attention to our health, and we need a good dose of self-esteem just to get by. And in some situations, our instincts for self-preservation will actually save our lives. Having watched two teenagers get into cars on their sixteenth birthdays and drive away from my house, I am a firm believer in defensive self-preservation. The same is true, of course, in situations of violence or abuse. We don't need someone coercing us into setting aside our good, healthy defense mechanisms.

But this is not what Paul is talking about when he speaks of letting go of, taking off, or releasing the earthly tent in which we live. There are several things that, when taken off, give way to the discovery that we are, in fact, being furthered clothed—clothed with more power for living and being.

The first of these things that Paul says we take off as Christians is the anxiety that we all have about our mortality. Day by day we realize that, as Paul puts it, "our outer nature is wasting away." If you're like me, this is a thought that you would like to deny, or at least avoid. It makes me want to get busy with a thousand distractions in my life. It makes me want to prop myself up with lots of gadgets and things. It drives me to want to achieve things, to make another mark—time for another book, to start another program, to build another building, to establish my legacy. And boy do I want to defend all of these things that are propping me up, to vindicate them, argue for them, praise them. At this point in my life I'm so certain that my form of religion and my lifestyle and my commitments—since they're so necessary for me and my sense of well-being—well, they must be just about as good as they come! How dare you challenge them. What I'm really saying, of course, is *please* don't challenge them, because without them, I would just have to sit here and stare into the ugly yellow face of death. Not a happy prospect.

But Paul is saying to me that because I belong to Christ, I don't have to be controlled by this anxiety about my outer nature wasting away. That anxiety can be taken away from me by Christ, as well as all the forms of idolatry that anxiety has led me into. And when these things are taken off, I don't just stand naked in the face of death, but I discover that in Christ I am further clothed so that, as Paul puts it, "what is mortal" finds that it is "swallowed up in life." I love this image of being "swallowed up by life." As the old earthly tent of anxiety is removed, there's this outer "dwelling" that swallows me up with life—life, as Paul says, that is "guaranteed," not by some thirty-days-or-your-money-back coupon but by the Holy Spirit—the Spirit of Life itself. Do you believe that this dwelling of the Spirit is already coming to roost over your head, descending onto your shoulders like a new garment? I believe that it is. One of the greatest gifts that falls upon us in Jesus Christ is the gift of being free from all the idolatries that creep into our lives—creep in simply because we are scared to death of death.

Tomorrow is our holiday in honor of Martin Luther King Jr. King knew this freedom. Oh, I don't mean that he ceased to worry about his safety. I don't mean that he was fearless. I don't mean that he didn't have human foibles, defenses, or props. But I mean that in Christ he refused to become a victim of his own death. He was able to live *mostly and primarily* into a new garment, to let go of his anxiety because he knew that there was a greater garment wrapped around him—a garment of life, of freedom, and of justice and love—to which his life ultimately bore witness. The guarantee of the Spirit is that mortality will be, can be, and *is* swallowed up by life, and this releases us from lives ruled by anxiety about our mortality.

The second thing Paul says that we "take off" in Christ is our fear of inadequacy. The words Paul uses here for "wasting away" express more than mortality. They express a fear of being inadequate under the weight of our expectations. Will I be adequate as a parent? Will I be adequate as a minister? As a teacher? As a friend? As a spouse? How can I find adequate strength to bear up under my sins or my sufferings, or under the sins and sufferings of the world? How can a dwindling denomination be adequate to the desperate needs for justice and liberation in this world? How do we keep, in Paul's words, from "losing heart"?

It is interesting here that Paul tells us that rather than *fear* our inadequacies, we might almost just *embrace* them! Paul says that the weight of the sin and evil in our lives "prepares" us for an even greater burden of glory. This is not a kind of masochism but a call for hope. As we groan under the weight of our inadequate practices of reconciliation, justice, peace, and love, Paul tells us that if we pay attention we can *begin* to feel the weight of another garment of justice and peace and love—the one yet to come. Last Sunday I watched BBC News as the broadcast covered all the many antiwar protests around the globe, showing clips of speeches, interviewing individuals, panning huge crowds of men, women, and children carrying signs. And there was a part of me that felt the woeful inadequacy of it all—a sinking feeling of futility in the face of principalities and powers set into an almost mechanical motion toward violence and war. It was an interview with a teenager in London's Hyde Park that changed my way of thinking. The interviewer asked, "Why are you here? Do you think that this will do any good?" The teenager said something like this: "Look at all of the people here who care! For me they are a sign of hope."

In the same way, Paul appeals to us to feel how the desperate burden of our present situation of inadequacy is deeply connected to the glorious weight of our future hope. Listen to your life. As a follower of Christ,

> Can you *feel*
> in the way that you and those around you care for the pain in this world?
> Can you *feel*
> in that inadequate care and deep desire for justice and wholeness?
> Can you *feel*
> something of the glorious weight of the hope that Christ promised in the Resurrection?

I can. In fact, I can feel it in my relationships with all of you. I can feel in each of you a *beautifully inadequate testimony* to God's love, justice, and peace. And this gives me hope and power for being—believe me!

The final thing that Paul tells us we take off in Christ is our obsession with sight—our need to have absolute control over everything and everyone. He says that we "walk by faith, not by sight." Paul reminds us that at the heart of our life in Christ is a humble, trusting faith. By "walking by faith and not by sight," Paul means that we simply trust the one who is leading us to get us where we are going.

In his own shorthand, Paul says that the bottom line is that we "make it our aim to please Christ." Make it our aim to please Christ? Now I would not claim to know everything that will please Christ, but I do know, from reading the Gospels, that Christ is pleased where there is mercy and not vengeance, where there is welcome and not dismissal, where there is reconciliation and not division, where the legitimate needs of others *changes* and *defines* both my actions and my identity. Walking by faith means stumbling along in trust behind the one in whom we have faith, practicing the things that Christ practiced.

And so, here we go, fellow streakers: Taking off our anxiety about death, letting it be swallowed up by life; taking off our fears of inadequacy and instead finding in our inadequate efforts a testimony of hope, and taking off our obsession to see and control and putting on the walking shoes of faith, aiming to please Christ in all that we say and do.

Let's go!—John McClure

Topic: The River
TEXT: Mark 1:9–11
In Memory of Flannery O'Connor

When my mother was twelve years old, she got herself baptized. Her mother had been dead for about a year, and her father was a railroad man who was gone most nights. She was essentially raising herself, if a child can do such a thing. One hot summer evening, when she was home alone as usual, she went down to the neighborhood Baptist church where they were holding a revival. At first, she just sat in the back pew and watched. Up front there was a large pool of the coolest and most inviting water you could imagine, and right there in that sweltering church, people were splashing and diving beneath its surface. When the preacher in his waders cried out, "O sinners, come to the river of life," that was all she could stand, and a little twelve-year-old girl bolted toward the water and was baptized. That night her sins were washed away; she joined Jesus and his Church, and she was never alone again.

A baptism of ecstasy, born of loneliness and performed among strangers, is not the usual scenario for the sacrament as we know it. Nor is the baptism that Mark records in his first chapter. For what he describes is a cosmic event. When Jesus comes up out of the water, he sees the heavens open (which is a pale translation of the Greek verb that says they were "ripped apart"). The fabric of the everyday has been torn. Something has been breached. A major revelation has taken place. A voice says to him, "You are my beloved son in whom I am well pleased."

In our tradition a baptism is a grand occasion, but not *that* grand. Relatives gather together in the church. Grandmother's yellowed baptismal dress is brought out. A Camcorder helps us celebrate the moments of our lives. Over it all, the minister presides with a benign expertise. Afterward, the food is wonderful.

We wouldn't have it any other way, but somehow baptism gets reduced to something smaller than it is in the New Testament—to a ceremony of initiation. It becomes the first baby-step on the long road to maturity. How different that is from the strange story in the Book of Acts (19:1–7) in which twelve people living in the Outback of Asia Minor, who had never heard of the Holy Spirit, get baptized and have the Spirit rush upon them and take possession of their speech.

In Martin Luther's discussion of baptism in the *Small Catechism,* he says that baptism conveys to the one baptized forgiveness of sins, life, and eternal salvation. Two sentences later he asks the rhetorical question: "How can water do such great things?" Perhaps Luther's question already betrays the modern tendency to break things down into manageable parts, analyzable by the theologians and sociologists. Many of us know too well the questions about baptism: How old must one be to be baptized? How much *sin* can a child have? How much *faith* can a baby have? And how does the baby's faith relate to the faith of the witnesses? And of course, the most urgent theological question, How *much* water shall we use? Do we need a river, a pool, a font, or a finger bowl? And what does this nice little ceremony symbolize?

In one of her letters Flannery O'Connor tells of a tense little dinner party she attended in Manhattan with a few of the most fashionable writers and literary critics of her day. There she was, the Roman Catholic hayseed writer from Georgia, already feeling out of her element in the literary whirl, when the conversation turns to religion and then to the Eucharist, about which someone at the table says in effect, "What a lovely symbol." O'Connor writes, "I then said, in a very shaky voice, 'Well, if it's a symbol, to hell with it.'"[1] I imagine the party broke up shortly thereafter. She adds, "That was all the defense I was capable of but I realize now that this is all I will ever be able to say about it, outside of a story, except that it is the center of existence for me; all the rest of life is expendable." What she says of the Eucharist we can say of baptism; if baptism doesn't save our lives, if it doesn't fill us with the Holy Spirit, if it doesn't remedy our cosmic loneliness, if it doesn't lie at the center of our identities as human beings—well . . .

One afternoon a strange-looking preacher, dressed up like Elijah the prophet (that is another story), appeared on the shore of the Jordan and said, "O sinners, come to the river," and another young man, his cousin, walked into the water and was baptized. We celebrate the baptism of Jesus in the Epiphany season because an epiphany is a revelation. The ordinary has been rudely breached, however briefly, so that something extraordinary may become visible. We see something about Jesus, namely, that he is the beloved Son of God.

We Christians have always understood our baptism in the mirror of Jesus' baptism. We are in him, we say. We've never been content to know a few facts about Jesus or to entertain selected truths about God. No, we're *in* him or, as Paul puts it, we've *put him on*, the way you slip on a sweater on a chilly day.

Perhaps not many of us were baptized in a river, but if you've received Christian baptism, you have in fact been to the river with him. Baptism is our own trip to the Holy Land (without the home movies), our own sloshing about in the Jordan, when the voice from heaven says to us, "You are my daughter; you are my son. Welcome to my family. You will never be alone again."

As you might expect, a baptism you share with Jesus does not come without a cost. If baptism is only a nice little symbol, it exerts little claim on our lives. About one hundred fifty years ago in America, many slave-holding Protestants effectively reduced the value of baptism to slaves and its cost to themselves. They allowed their slaves to be baptized but only with the explicit, verbalized proviso that baptism would not entail political or social freedom. In other words, it would leave no mark on one's actual life or social practices.

But baptism is bigger than that. Listen in on any one of several baptismal liturgies, and you have a clue to the size of its claims. In one of them, the minister asks the one baptized and the witnesses, "Do you renounce Satan and all the spiritual forces of wickedness that rebel against God?"

I renounce them.

"Do you renounce the evil powers of this world which corrupt and destroy the creatures of God?"

I renounce them.

"Do you renounce all sinful desires that draw you from the love of God?"

I renounce them.

"Do you realize," the minister seems to be asking, "that with this act you are not joining the world but breaking with its values? Do you realize there is such a thing as evil and that you have just been conscripted in the battle against it?" The Christian life begins with a declaration of one's enemies.

---

[1] *The Habit of Being,* p. 125.

In one of Flannery O'Connor's stories there's a little Catholic girl who lives in the South amidst a sea of Protestants. She enjoys visiting the convent, where one of the sisters embraces her. But every time she gets a hug, the crucifix on the sister's belt gets mashed into the child's face, with the result that the gesture of love always leaves a mark. Baptism is like that. God hugs us and makes us his own children, but that act leaves the sign of the cross upon us to remind us of the One whose name we bear.

Children also receive a name when they are baptized. But baptism itself tells us who we *really* are. In baptism you become *somebody*—not a number, a password, or a code; not a name to be misspelled, computerized, merged, and buried with all the other names. But in baptism you become somebody in God's Church, and from that time forward your name stands in relation to another name—that of the Holy Trinity.

The identity based on that relationship is a matter of faith. When our children were small and obligated to take their baths, sometimes they would refrain from actually getting into the water. We learned to do what parents have always done: we would check to see if they were damp. The Christian life is a matter of remaining damp, even when you can't remember your baptism or reproduce the fervor that originally accompanied it. When Luther found himself in a crisis or depression, unable to sense his own salvation, he would stubbornly cling to an act performed outside his remembrance of it. Then he would roar, "I am baptized."

The question of identity is also a matter of context. In your familiar surroundings you're pretty sure you know who you are. But go away to college, enlist in the Marines, or move to a new neighborhood, and your identity seems to be up for grabs. You even look different to yourself. Of course, expensive colleges or big corporations will not be shy about telling you who you are. "Why, you're the brightest and the best, the crème de la crème—and you belong to us." And if you're not careful, you may start to believe that. Or if you're poor, excluded from the in-group, or live in a troubled family, the message you hear may be, "You're nothing but trouble. Worthless. You are nobody."

"I am baptized."

The church, too, will not be shy about telling you who you are: "You are brothers and sisters of the Lord Jesus in this world." As Jesus himself once said, "Whoever does my will is brother and sister and mother to me." But not only that (and this is the hard part), you are also brothers and sisters to *one another.* You haven't chosen these people to be family any more than you chose your natural family, but your baptism has made it so. We have all been washed in the same tub. Christians are bonded to one another by water and the word. *"We are baptized."*

One of the best ways to rediscover your true family is to worship the Lord in another community beside people who don't resemble you, whose ways are not those of your culture. Listen to other preachers; serve in other ministries. See how alike we really are. See how the Word rings out in all settings—how water is water, baptism is baptism, wherever you go and however it's done. Then, trusting in the Church's ancient confession of One Lord, One Faith, One Baptism, and One God and Father of us all, return to your community with a larger sense of your own identity.

In *The River*, Flannery O'Connor tells the story of a little boy named Bevel who seeks baptism in a river that will carry him away from his mother's illness and all the pain of his life. He wants to count for something. In desperation he bounds into the reddish-yellow water, but his river offers only a forgetting, not a redeeming. We do not see Bevel emerge from the river.

Water is willful. It has a mind of its own. As any plumber will tell you, "Water always wins." It can carry you where you do not want to go. When Jesus stepped into the Jordan long ago, he took us with him, but only as a lifeguard enfolds and protects novices in dangerous waters. He took our loneliness and sins with him, as Bevel went "swiftly forward and down" into the loving arms of God. When we all came out—still with him—we were family.—Richard Lischer

Topic: The Despatch of God
TEXT: Rom. 10:9–13

The Biography of a Thief: The Despatch of God is what I call it! The full and immediate response of God, when I called to him with all my heart, was the way he dealt with me. God saved me at the eleventh hour, or you could call it a deathbed confession of faith. The *Apocrypha* gives me the name of Dysmas. Your King James calls me a thief; other references call me a bandit, while others call me a malefactor. My name is Dysmas! Let me tell you about my life's pilgrimage. I was born to poor Jewish parents in Jerusalem. My folks were hard workers and had all they could do to provide for us. They tried to be good parents, but the circumstances of life made it difficult to rear children properly. It did not take them long to find that they had a real "juvenile delinquent" on their hands. Soon after I became a teenager, my parents told me that I would have to leave home if I could not behave myself and quit getting into trouble. My rebellious nature won out, and I left home for good.

I delighted in the fact that I was no longer going to have the restrictions of parental guidance, and I reveled in my freedom. No more did I have to go to the Temple and pretend that I was worshiping Yahweh. No more memorization of the Torah, the Psalms, and a myriad of sanitary and food regulations.

I joined a gang of outlaws headed by a fellow named Barabbas. We plundered the pilgrims making their way from the exotic faraway places to Jerusalem. There were rich spices from the Far East, handcrafted jewelry, caches of gold and silver and other precious metals, fine tapestries, and polished hand weapons to be found in these caravans. Barabbas taught me how to slip a knife under a man's shoulder blade and cause him to empty his purse without so much as a murmur. My name is Dysmas—oh, I've said that already. Often Barabbas bragged that he was my mentor. For sure we were partners in all sorts of criminal behavior.

One night just before the Passover, Barabbas and I were on a drunken spree and became very reckless in our pilfering of the warehouses that belonged to the Roman government. Goods were piled high in these storehouses, and they were the property of those hateful Romans. Representative of all that wealth were three people with a common mind-set—greed, hatred and bitterness! Caiaphas, the Jew, and Herod and Pilate, the Romans. They were a challenge to us, as we sought to find out how some folks could live off the fat of the land, and most of us had little or nothing except for what we took from others. We felt we were entitled to live as well as they.

Our carelessness caused us to be caught by a Roman guard, and we were thrown into prison. The filthy dungeon into which we were cast reeked of human excrement and rotting flesh. At midnight we were taken outside in order for our captors to have some amusement at our expense and pain. Just for the sheer joy they received from it, we were whipped with scourges. This instrument of torture was sometimes called a cat-o-nine tails. Long thongs of leather with pieces of metal, bone, or shards of pottery fastened in the ends made deep cuts and huge welts when they lashed them across our backs, buttocks, and legs. The leather soon became soaked in our blood and sweat, and smarting streaks tore upon the flesh. After this charade, called justified punishment and fun, we were thrown back into a pitch-black hell hole, and the lictors left us with our pain while they went on to more ribaldry. Oh, they did pour salt in our cuts, just for more excitement. Strangely enough, the cool wet dirt was actually a relief after such a severe beating. The blood was attracting the rats, and creeping varmints lapped up the flow. It just added more insult to our injuries.

Even in my suffering I was not sorry for what I had done. A glimmer of hope aroused me to the possibility that I could still escape death if I were chosen to be released on the day of the execution. It was one of their customs, after such a frightening experience, to turn loose only one of the prisoners on the day of the crucifixion. I recalled that a lot of people owed me some favors, as I had robbed the rich and given much of it to the poor folks. They were sure to ask for me to be released.

Make no mistake about it. I knew full well the penalty for stealing. Being impaled upon some rough-hewn timbers and left to die slowly because of the loss of blood and exposure could take several days. The cross beam upon which the victim is nailed through the hands and tied with leather straps was fastened to an upright that was then placed in a hole in the ground. The feet were nailed to the upright. The tearing of flesh from the nails would be horribly excruciating. The body would sag, and the victim would die from suffocation. But to prevent that and make death more prolonged, sometimes a piece of wood was added to form a seat to ease the slumping body and prevent the breast from falling in on the chest cavity; that would prolong the breathing. It was a terrible way to die, and I wanted to avoid it by relying on my friends to get me off. The system had worked before. Influence from those in power could be trusted if enough friends and money were placed just right. I held on to that ray of hope—that I would not die.

In the morning after the night of torture, there was a bit of excitement among the prison guards. I overheard them talking about a new prisoner who came during the night. They said his name was Jesus of Nazareth and that he was thought to be the Messiah. At the name of Jesus, memories came to me about the times that I had seen him. He came to the seacoast towns and villages as an itinerant preacher. I heard him one day. I was standing on a little hill and heard him speak, even though his voice was not too loud. Yet he was so convincing in every word he uttered. He opened his mouth, and people heard him gladly.

"Blessed are the pure in heart, for they shall see God."

Well, he wasn't speaking to me, for I was anything but a person whose heart was filled with right motives.

"Blessed are the peacemakers, for they shall be called the children of God."

Again, I was no peacemaker, for I had so much internal unrest that I could not speak to anyone about being calm and placid in spirit in the face of challenge and opposition.

"Blessed are those who are reviled."

Now, Jesus was saying something with which I could identify. I had certainly been hated and harassed. But he added, "falsely, for my name's sake."

That surely did not fit my lifestyle, for I did things to provoke others for my own self-interests and not for any righteous God. I had always felt that if anything was to be, it had to be me. Look out for number one and do it my way.

Then I remembered another incident about this Jesus. I saw him down at the River Jordan, looking at a person I had seen roaming around in the wilderness on numerous occasions. His name was John, and he bore the nickname "Baptizer," because he preached a stern message that called for repentance, after which he baptized those who confessed their sinful ways. He totally immersed the candidate in water and called it a cleansing bath, "according to God's mercy he saved by the washing of regeneration and renewing. . . ." This John was in sharp contrast to Jesus. John bellowed to the crowds, and he ridiculed them by asking them what they had come out to see and hear from him. Was it because of their curiosity, or was it because they were looking past John to Another who would come, whose shoes John was unworthy to tie. He was such a curious character in his camel's hair clothing, his rough and coarse mannerisms, his rough sandals, and flowing beard. Well, it didn't flow too much because the drippings of wild honey he ate attracted insects, and the mass was quite distasteful. I can't imagine anyone wanting to have him as a guest speaker! His breath reeked of garlic and leeks. Once he pointed his bony finger at me, and I felt the condemnation he preached, even though I was not very close to him. Only this day when he pointed his finger, he waved it toward that lonely person standing by the water's edge—Jesus. When he did he cried out loudly, "Behold, the Lamb of God that takes away the sins of the world." That is what folks thought about Jesus—he was the Lamb of God! I did not know what that meant. Lambs were for sacrifices in the Temple. Could it mean that this was to be an offering for sinners such as I?

I confess that I was taken by the magnetism of this person, Jesus. He was now standing in the Jordan and being baptized by John. I wanted to be a follower of John's because I thought that his cause would surely result in an earthly kingdom and I would be in a favored position when the revolution came.

There were others who felt as I did, whom I remember. Simon the Zealot was one of my friends and a fellow conspirator. Another was Judas from Kerioth, who was so bent on the revolution that he was willing to betray his best friend in order to get what he wanted. I wonder what ever became of him?

Then it is strange how one's memory can force the recall of past experiences that were pleasant. Seeing Jesus, I remembered how he was known for the way he dealt with people. He always treated them with an outward, unconditional love. He called little children to come and sit with him as he taught the people, and he used them as examples of faith and trust. Sick people came to him and wanted to get a glimpse of the Great Physician, for he did miraculous things. One day a woman came to a crowd of folks and begged to get close enough just to touch the hem of his robe. She said that if she so much as did that, the power of his spirit would cure her of a disease that she had had for about thirty years. She believed so much in him that I was envious of her, for I wanted so much to have that kind of belief in him. However, I knew that I could never keep any kind of commitment to become in his life, for it was too much about spiritual matters, and I wanted something for the present. I turned away from him and never followed him again.

In my reverie I had forgotten for a moment that, after all, I was in this dungeon as a condemned criminal. I came face to face with reality when I heard the guards approaching. I foolishly thought that they were coming to release me, for this was the time of the Feast of the Passover. I was so sure that the mob outside had asked for me to be turned loose and pardoned. I spoke to the guard who unlocked my door and told him that it was about time; as

I started out, he hit me full in the face with a blunt instrument and knocked me all the way back to the other side of my cell. As I struggled with consciousness I remember the guard saying, "Barabbas, the people want you to be released." I questioned how they could ever have asked for the leader of this insurrectionist movement, and the only answer I got from the guard was to be hit again; I was senseless.

When I regained consciousness, the guards had left with Barabbas. Other soldiers were coming in the prison, and I knew full well that this time there was no hope, and I must die as a malefactor—one who conceived evil and continued in it (Luke 23:33). I would go to a place outside the city wall to a little hill having the shape of a skull; the name of the site was Calvary. I would be crucified along with others who had been so unfortunate as to have their appeal refused. As the escort took my friend, Gysmas, and me, we were soon joined by another person. In the dim half-light I recognized Jesus, only now he seemed even more tired and weak. We were being forced to carry our cross beam to which we were to be nailed, and he was so weak that a fellow by the name of Simon from Cyrene was forced to take up the burden for him. I could not understand why Jesus would be crucified. Me, I was at least getting what the crime dictated. But he never did anything wrong and didn't deserve to die like this. What was Jesus dying for? Would anyone ever know why?

A person would be less than human if he did not pay some attention to his own demise, but my mind began to wander often to this man Jesus, who was going with us by way of the sorrowful street, the Via Doloroso! He was an itinerant prophet, but he had a gainful job, they said, as a carpenter in Nazareth. He had been terribly beaten, and in mockery his tormentors had placed on his head a mock crown, made of thorny branches. I saw the blood now encrusted on his brow. I had heard about the bizarre treatment the Romans had given him by ridiculing the belief that some held that Jesus was of some kind of royalty. They had draped a purple robe on him and taunted him with the shameful and hurtful thorns that they mockingly called a crown. If he was to be accorded any honor because of his rank as a person with kingly qualities, then the mock robe and crown were certainly fitting. So they reasoned. I cannot understand why they also enjoyed spitting in his face. That seemed to be a disgusting way to treat this lonely, solitary figure. Caiaphas, Herod, and Pilate were rotten pigs, and this only proved how despicable human beings can treat others. Life was so cheap in our world.

The teachings of my childhood came to mind, suddenly. My parents had tried to tell me that the temple was a place of learning and that I would remember those teachings in my later life. My mother had said, "Dysmas, one of these days you will rely upon the teachings you receive at the feet of the rabbis, and they will bring you comfort when you need it the most." I remember one of those sayings from the lessons, "Remember now thy Creator in the days of thy youth. . . . Remember not the transgressions of my youth nor the sins that I have committed. For you, O God, write bitter things against me and my heart is exceedingly troubled and enlarged. O bring me out of my distress. I have sinned against God and have not obeyed the voice of my Lord our God." How strange that I recall these words on the day of my crucifixion.

By now, our terrible procession had come to the top of that little skull-shaped hill called Calvary. My partner in crime, Glysmas, and I were offered a mixture of wine and myrrh to numb the pain that was about to be inflicted upon us. The jeering crowd laughed, joked, and poked fun at us. Our only response was to curse and hurl obscenities at them and our executioners. But the one in between us, Jesus, took all of the shameful shouts and did not put up any resistance at all. He was like a sheep; before its shearers is dumb, so he opened not his mouth. It was as though he were taking all of the guilt of the whole world on himself! When the nails were being pounded into my hands, lashed down with strong strips of leather, I pushed and hollered aloud at the pain as they hammered and pounded into the cross beam. They did the same to Jesus, but he never said a mumbling word, and he felt all of the hurt because he had refused to swallow the potion of myrrh and wine. It seemed that God was forsaking him. If he were truly the Messiah, I could not believe that God would hide his face from his Son at such a time of torture. I heard Jesus say, "I'm thirsty," and then "Father, into thy hands I commit my spirit."

I asked Jesus from my cross, "Are you who they claim you to be?" And, "Are you the Anointed One, God's Son?" If he were, then why did he not save himself and could he not save me as well? I called to him from my cross, to his even a more rugged cross, and asked how I could have the same kind of dying grace that he exemplified. A terrible thought was going through my mind, and my cry to him was from a heart in which heaven and hell itself were beating hard for conquest.

My friend, Glysmas, called out in fiendish ribaldry. He said to Jesus that if he were some kind of god, then he ought to demonstrate his powers by getting us down from our death perches. I said to him, "Don't you fear God, at all? You and I are dying for our sins, and justly so, but this good man is dying for his faith." The divine grief of God concentrated in Jesus— I could sense it! Then I said to Glysmas something like this: "You would do well to believe that his dying can do something for your sins and mine and for all people everywhere who would only believe in him. God did not send his only begotten Son into the world to condemn the world but that the world through him might be saved."

As I lay there on my cross, I knew that Jesus was there to give me solace and by his very presence to provide the comfort that I had been seeking all of my life.

Then the soldiers began to lift high the crosses and for a brief moment we were suspended in midair before the upright beam fell into the hole in the ground. The violent tearing of flesh was compounded by the hammering of nails into our feet to secure us firmly, as though that extra pain was necessary.

Well, the crowd had seen the spectacle, and they began to disperse. There were few faces left about the crosses to watch us die. I turned my head and heard Jesus on his cross saying the first words since this ordeal began: "My God, why have you forsaken me?" Then just as he uttered those words, he spoke others that brought reassurance when he said, "Father, into your hands I commit my spirit." He spoke other words, but he had said enough for me to call out to him, "You are God." His limp chin lay on his sagging breast, and he spoke: "I thirst." Then as though his life's mission were complete, he said, "It is finished."

I knew this was the Son of God! I said to him, "Lord, when you go back to the Father in heaven, remember me."

I took heaven at a leap on that day. That is why I call this autobiographical report the "Despatch of God," for God's immediate response to my cry of penitence was quickly done. Jesus simply said, "This day, you will go with me into heaven." That was the happiest day of my life. Peace at last had come to me, and it had to take this terrifying experience for it to come to me.

Now the soldier came to hasten the deaths of all three because it was the Passover; enough things were happening in Jerusalem besides this public spectacle, which need not continue any longer. The soldier broke my legs with the blunt end of his spear, and with the sharpened end he rammed a gaping hole in my side. He didn't break a bone in Jesus' body, but he did rip open his side, and water and blood flowed from the tear. Another of the sacred writings had Zechariah the prophet say, "In that day a fountain will be opened up. A fountain for the cleansing of sin and unrighteousness, a fountain for the house of David and for all Jerusalem." A fountain opened for me that day, and Jesus' blood became my passport into heaven for eternity.

Then Jesus died. When he died, I imagine that he called for the angels around God's throne to prepare a grand entrance, for the King of Kings and Lord of Lords was coming back and bringing with him a penitent thief by the name of Dysmas. And I was the first person to enter heaven after Jesus went back into his heavenly home.

It had been a most unique day in my life. In the morning I was outside of Christ in my guilt. At noon I was with Christ in grace. And in the evening I was with Christ on the right hand of his Father in heaven.

Well might you sing my song today. Across these nearly two thousand years, your song could be, "The dying thief rejoiced to see, that fountain in his day. And there may I, though vile as he, wash all my sins away."

My final word for you today is this: Don't reject Christ. He will save you now, at this moment, just as he did me. I was saved that no one can say it is too late. It is never too late. Glysmas was not saved because he never believed that Jesus was dying for his sins. I would rather be an ignorant Roman than an intelligent American, if I were determined to reject Christ.

This could be your day, when the swiftness of God's response to your willingness to trust him would be the kind I experienced on Good Friday. It's worth everything!—H. Lloyd Storment

SECTION XI

CHILDREN'S SERMONS

January 1: Promises for the New Year
TEXT: Ps. 118:24
Object: 2006 Calendar
Song: "This Is the Day"

[*Children come to the front.*] Hello boys and girls. I'm glad to see you today and especially glad you chose to attend church. I'm holding a 2006 calendar. Do you know how many months are in a year? That's right—twelve. And how many days? The answer is 365. You may have heard your parents talk about making New Year's resolutions. Can you tell me the definition of the word *resolutions?* [*Wait for response.*] Saying you are "making resolutions" is another way of saying, "I am making changes in my life in the coming months." Or you might say it is "promises you make to yourself."

Often we make promises to eat healthy food, exercise more, and read more books. We would all agree that these are good resolutions, but we may forget about the promises we should make to God. Let's think about how boys and girls can serve God with New Year's resolutions. Think about the following:

- Read my Bible daily.
- Pray for my family.
- Attend church each Sunday.
- Make new friends.
- Help others.

As you begin the New Year, ask God to help you make and keep promises to him. Listen as I read the following verse, found in Psalm 118:24: "This is the day which the Lord hath made; we will rejoice and be glad in it."

> *Prayer:* Father, bless all the children here today. Guide them as they learn more about living for you.
> *Take Action:* Boys and girls, I would encourage you to keep a daily journal, listing one activity per day of the promises you have made to God.

[*Children return to their sets as the pianist plays "This Is the Day."*]—Carolyn Tomlin

413

January 8: Growing into Greatness

TEXT: Prov. 16:3
Object: A bag of peanuts
Song: "Jesus Loves the Little Children"

Hello boys and girls. I'm glad to see you today. I'm holding a bag of peanuts—something you probably enjoy eating. Let me tell you about a man who took the common peanut and produced many products. George Washington Carver was born to slave parents around 1864. A kind family helped raise him and taught him to read. As an adult, he wanted his life to have value—to contribute something to the world so that he would make a difference. He worked hard and graduated from college. Carver loved to experiment with products grown from God's earth. He took the sweet potato, soybeans, and the peanut and made many discoveries that benefited people. Not only did these healthy products provide jobs but they produced many food items we enjoy today.

So the next time you spread peanut butter on a sandwich or eat a sweet potato, remember a young African American boy named George Washington Carver. With God's help, this child grew into greatness. Listen as I read Proverbs 16:3: "Commit thy works unto the Lord, and thy thoughts shall be established."

> *Prayer:* Dear Father, help each child be your servant and make a difference in the lives of others.
> *Take Action:* Develop and prepare an original recipe using peanut butter. Share with your family.

[*Lead the children in singing "Jesus Loves the Little Children." Children return to their seats.*]—Carolyn Tomlin

January 15: Go the Extra Mile

TEXT: Matt. 5:41
Object: A student backpack

Some of you carry a backpack like this when you go to school or day care. This backpack is very heavy; it's full of books. I wouldn't want to carry this load very far.

During Jesus' earthly ministry, Roman soldiers were a common sight. Rome ruled the whole world then, and Roman soldiers enforced the laws and kept the peace by their powerful presence. The soldiers traveled around Israel on foot. In those days there were no tanks or personnel carriers. Only officers had horses to ride. The soldiers carried their heavy equipment with them from place to place and could force someone to carry their gear. An Israelite could be forced to carry a soldier's gear for one mile. After going a mile, someone else had to be recruited to tote the burden. It wasn't a pleasant task. The Israelites tended to gripe and complain, and at the end of a required mile, they might throw the load down and stalk off in anger.

As Jesus was teaching his disciples how to represent his kingdom, he told them to be willing to "go an extra mile." Going an extra mile would impress the hardened soldiers. Instead of griping, the disciple would gladly carry the load and be willing to go farther than the minimum requirement. A surprised soldier might ask why the carrier had a friendly approach when forced to work for them. The disciple could then tell the curious soldier about Jesus.

These days our world is filled with people who gripe and complain. It is easy to take jobs for granted and be willing to do only the minimum amount of work. By going the extra mile today, employers can be impressed with the quality of a believer's work. With so many unwilling to do extra work, the supervisor or owner will begin to think there is something special about the Christian's life.

It's easy to think that in such an arrangement the solider or the employer would be the only one who benefits. But the blessings also flow to the committed believer. Whenever we travel the extra mile, we receive a blessing. Not only do we feel good about our good deed, we have opportunities to tell others about Jesus. Going the extra mile always brings rewards.—Ken Cox

January 22: Thanks
TEXT: Gen. 1
Objects: Large poster board or piece of paper with the letters A–Z and space for responses; marker, pen or pencil, Bible
Song: "Count Your Blessings"

What is your very favorite thing that your mother does just for you? [*Accept answers.*] Those are some very special things. When your mother does something really special just for you, do you remember to thank her?

The first book of the Bible, Genesis, tells us God made everything, and he made it just for us. I've been thinking about some of the things God made for us, and I wondered if you could help me say "thank you" to him. I think together we can do it.

I have here a poster with all the letters of the alphabet on it. Let's see if we can think of something God made that starts with each of these letters. I have already written in a few ideas. For "A," I have that God made apples. What about something that starts with . . . [*Continue through the alphabet until all lines are filled. If an answer does not come quickly and easily, you might suggest one from the list that follows. Have a few of the hardest ones filled out in advance.*]

I knew we could do it! This is a great list. God made all of these things for us. So now let's remember to thank him. Can you say, "We thank you God"? Great. I am going to read a few things on our list. Each time I stop, please say, "We thank you God." [*Work your way through the list, and end with "for all you do to show your love for us, we thank you God."*]

Letter suggestions: A-apple, B-bluebirds, C-cats, E-evening sunsets, F-friends, G-grandparents, H-homes, I-icicles, J-joy, K-kangaroos, L-lakes, M-mountains, N-nuts, O-owls, P-parents, Q-quiet nights, R-rain, S-stars, T-trees, U-uncles and aunts, V-violets, W-wind, X-(Greek for Christ), Y-yellow flowers, Z-zebras.—Janelle Fraze

January 29: David the Spelunker
TEXT: Ps. 57:1
Objects: Pictures of caves, spelunkers

A cave is a deep or shallow hole in a hill or mountain. In some places caves or caverns are entered by holes in the ground where the land is flat. This picture shows the entrance to a cave on a hillside. Some caverns are huge formations that were created by the flowing of underground springs over thousands of years.

A cave explorer is called a spelunker. Spelunkers have to be highly skilled and careful. Never explore a cave without an adult because caves can be dangerous places where poisonous gases accumulate. Also it is easy to get lost in the many passageways of huge caverns.

A man in the Bible spoke about being in a cave. His name was David. This is the same man who defeated the giant, Goliath, with his slingshot. David used a cave for a hiding place from a jealous king of Israel. David went into the cave to be safe. When I was growing up, I had an older sister. When she was mad, I would hide in the closet or under the bed. That's what David did. As a grown man he hid in a cave. David could not fight the king the way he did Goliath.

David wrote this psalm—a song—to describe something he had learned while hiding in that cave. He learned that the safety he gained in the cave was like the protection he received from God. David called God his refuge, or his cave. God was David's hiding place.

Whenever we are in trouble we can seek help from God. In some instances we have to take a stand and directly confront our problems and enemies. In other situations it is best to get to a safe place and wait until the trouble takes care of itself. God wants to be our hiding place, our cave. God always hears us when we are calling for help. He will protect us. God will be our refuge, our cave when we learn to trust in him.—Ken Cox

February 5: God Made You, Sees You, Loves You
TEXT: Gen. 1:31
Objects: Binoculars, Bible
Song: "My God Is Near Me All the Time"

Good morning boys and girls. How many of you wear glasses? [*If you have glasses show them; tell whether you wear them all the time or just sometimes and whether they help you see things up close or far away.*] Many people wear glasses to help them see things that look like they are far away, like maybe the words in a book or a sign along the street.

[*Show binoculars.*] Do you know what these are? Right—they are called binoculars. They help us to see things that are even further away, like in the back of the church, or birds up in trees, or action on a stage, or even a person on the other side of the football field. Those things are always there, but we may not be able to see them without the binoculars. There is another instrument called a telescope. With a telescope even the stars and planets seem close. Without a telescope scientists would not have found out that Mars appears red or that Saturn has rings around it. But they do.

Let's think about something else for a minute. How many of you have grandmothers or grandfathers who live far away, maybe even in another state? If you do, then you know that they are out there somewhere. You cannot see them, but you can talk to them on the telephone or trade news with an e-mail. But the only way you will get to see those grandparents is if they send you a picture or if they visit you or you visit them. You know they love you and are always thinking about you, but you cannot see them.

The Bible tells us God loves you. You cannot see him either. Your glasses won't help you. Neither will these binoculars. Even the most powerful telescopes cannot get a glimpse of God's face for you to see. You don't see God, but he is with you all the time. You can't see him, but he sees and knows everything you do. God doesn't need glasses or binoculars or a telescope. He doesn't even need a camera to see how much you have grown. God made you. God loves you. God knows everything you do, and he will always help you when you ask him to. God is very proud of you. I know that, because the Bible says, "God saw everything He had made, and it was very good."

Prayer: Thank you God for making me, for loving me, and for always being there for me.—Janelle Fraze

February 12: Hearts for Jesus

TEXT: Luke 10:27
Object: Red heart cut from construction paper
Song: "Now I Belong to Jesus"

Hello boys and girls. I'm happy to see you today. The month of February has several holidays. There's Valentine's Day, the birthdays of Abraham Lincoln and George Washington, and Black History Month. All of these are important, and I'm sure you learn more about them in school. But today let's focus on February as National Heart Month. What do you know about your heart? [*Wait for responses.*] Listen to the following facts:

- The heart is a major organ in our body.
- Blood is circulated throughout the body by our heart.
- Normal heart rate for a person in a sitting position ranges from 68 to 72 heartbeats per minute.
- Your choice of food, exercise, and rest affects the health of your body.
- We could say the heart is a vital organ to the overall health of our body.

But there's something else about our heart. The Bible mentions the word *heart* many times. When we give our hearts and lives to Christ, we are called Christians. Listen as I read Luke 2:27: "Thou shalt love the Lord thy God with all thy heart, and with all thy soul, and with all thy strength, and with all thy mind; and thy neighbor as thyself."

So when you see a red heart this month, let it remind you of how much God loves you.

Prayer: Dear Father, may all children present today recognize their need to give their hearts and lives to you.
Take Action: Make a red heart from construction paper and give it to a shut-in in your church or community. Take time to visit and talk with this person.

[*The children return to their seats as the pianist plays "Now I Belong to Jesus."*]—Carolyn Tomlin

February 19: Growing Up

TEXT: Luke 2:52
Object: Bible

Good morning boys and girls. Have you ever wondered what Jesus was like as a little boy? We know he was born in a stable. We know he was visited by shepherds and by wise men from far away. We know when he was two, his family had to run away to another country to protect him from some people who wanted to kill him. We also know that when he was twelve years old he went with his family to visit the synagogue in Jerusalem, and while there he explained the Scriptures to the smartest Bible teachers in town. These things do not sound like things that have happened to any little boys I know. But, after all, he was God's son.

But Jesus was just like you in many ways. [*Open Bible to Luke 2:52.*] The Bible tells us, "Jesus increased in wisdom, in stature, and in favor with God and man." Let's see. The Bible says Jesus increased in wisdom. That means Jesus grew smarter. He went to school. He probably even had homework. He learned to be a carpenter and worked in the shop with Joseph. He watched the world around him, and he learned all about it. Does this sound more like you?

The Bible says, "Jesus increased in stature." That means Jesus grew strong and healthy. What kinds of things do you do to grow strong and healthy? [*Accept responses; possible answers may include eating good food, drinking milk, getting enough sleep, and playing or exercising.*] Jesus must have done all of those things, too.

The Bible says Jesus learned to get along with people. He had friends his own age, and he got along well with the grown-ups around him. He must have been fun, loving, and respectful. Jesus also grew in his knowledge of God's plan for him and in how he could follow that plan.

Maybe, just maybe, you are much more like Jesus than you ever thought possible.

Prayer: Dear Jesus, help us learn as much as we can, to grow tall and healthy, to get along with all those around us, and to follow your plan for our lives.—Janelle Fraze

February 26: Where Is My Coin?
TEXT: Luke 15:9
Objects: A variety of foreign coins

Good morning boys and girls. When Jesus was a boy, there were several different types of coins circulating in Israel. There were Greek coins, like this; there were also Roman and Hebrew coins. One Hebrew coin was called the shekel.

Jesus used a coin to teach how God felt about lost people. Jesus described a woman who had lost a coin in her house. The coin might have been dropped or knocked from a table, but it was missing.

Have you ever misplaced something, and it drove you crazy until you found it? Last week I discovered the flashlight was missing. I was the last one to use the flashlight, and I put it down in the garage somewhere. When I needed it again, I couldn't find it. Soon I forgot my new project because I was so intent on finding the flashlight. I was relieved when it was located.

Jesus said the lady felt that way about the coin she misplaced. Jesus said that she swept the floor and searched everywhere. When she finally found it, she told her friends and neighbors about it.

Jesus said God feels that way about lost people. Jesus said when sinners repent or change their mind about God, the angels rejoice in heaven, just the way that woman was happy about finding the lost coin. The angels are happy because those people really belong to God and needed to be found.

God looks for lost people like that. All people are precious to God because he created them. If they do not know Jesus as Savior, they are considered lost. The Lord invites us to join him in seeking the lost because they belong to him. How do we do it? We look by inviting our friends to Sunday school and church. When they hear the truth of the Bible, they can be found by becoming believers in God's one and only son, Jesus.—Ken Cox

March 5: Make a Difference
TEXT: Ps. 143:10
Object: Red Cross symbol
Song: "Teach Me, O Lord, I Pray"

Hello boys and girls. I'm glad to see you today. I'm holding a symbol that you may have seen in your community. Does anyone recognize this symbol? [*Wait for response.*] This red cross is the symbol used by the American Red Cross. And do you know who started this organization? Clara Barton (1821–1912) believed that all people should get involved and help others. Because she was committed to this belief, she did battlefield relief work during the Civil War. Recognizing the need for nursing care, she organized the American Red Cross in 1881. Today this organization has international respect. You may have seen Red Cross vehicles in your area in times of hurricanes, floods, tornadoes, and other natural disasters. Many people are trained to feed and comfort people during times of stress.

It's true that Barton made a difference during her lifetime, and her efforts continue today. Although you are boys and girls, it isn't too early to ask God to direct your lives so you, too, can make a difference.

Listen as I read from Psalm 143:10: "Teach me to do thy will for thou art my God; thy spirit is good; lead me into the land of uprightness."

> *Prayer:* Dear God, guide each child here today to get involved and lead a life of service to others.
> *Take Action:* This week, read about Clara Barton and how she organized the American Red Cross and led a life of service to others.

[*Children return to their seats as the pianist plays "Teach Me, O Lord, I Pray."*]—Carolyn Tomlin

March 12: Flying on High
TEXT: Gen. 1:1
Object: Kite
Song: "For the Beauty of the Earth"

Hello boys and girls. I'm glad you chose to come to church today. During the month of March, we usually expect lots of wind. There is an old saying, "If March comes in like a lion, it goes out like a lamb." Have you ever heard that saying? Ask your parents; perhaps they have. [*Hold up kite.*] Now, most of you know about kites. How many have flown one? [*Wait for response.*] On a windy day you can fly a kite, and if the string is long enough and the air currents are right, it can sail very high in the sky. Kite flying is a good family activity that everyone can enjoy.

So the next time you see a kite or fly one, remember that it is God who sends the winds and makes this possible. As you look up into the sky, thank God for his beautiful creation—our Earth. We have clean air to breathe, blue skies, green trees, and fertile soil to make plants grow. And remember, we should thank him for our good health to enjoy wholesome activities with our families: "In the beginning God created the heaven and the earth" (Gen. 1:1).

> *Prayer:* Father, thank you for creating a wonderful world in which to live. Thank you for providing good health that allows boys and girls to enjoy family activities.
>
> *Take Action:* Show a friend or sibling how to do one new activity this week.

[*Lead the children in singing one verse of "For the Beauty of the Earth" before they return to their seats.*]—Carolyn Tomlin

March 19: God's Plan for You

TEXT: Gen. 1:24–25
Objects: Several pictures of real animals, Bible
Song: "God Is So Good"

Good morning everyone. [*Show the pictures you have chosen, and ask the children to name the animals. As they name each one, ask them who made that animal.*] The book of Genesis tells us [*read Gen. 1:24–25*].

I've been wondering how God decided which animals to make. Maybe you can help me figure this out. I have noticed that some animals have very special jobs. For example, cows give us milk and meat. What about chickens? Why do you think God made them? [*for eggs and meat*]. What about dogs and cats? [*to be our friends*]. So far so good. What special jobs can an elephant do? [*carry or pull large loads*]. Right again! Did you know there was a very bad earthquake in January of 2005 called a tsunami? Elephants were brought in from the circus to help clear away the damaged buildings and trees! So far this has been pretty easy.

But why did God make tigers, kangaroos, ants, and giraffes? I'm really not sure we could figure those out. But I am sure of one thing: God made no two animals alike, and God had a purpose for every animal he made. I also know that God made you. He made no two people just alike. Even twins who look just alike think and feel differently at times. God made you, he loves you, and he has a plan just for you.

> *Prayer:* Dear God, thank you for loving us. Thank you for creating us. We know you made each of us to be different from anyone else. Thank you for having a special plan just for us. Please help us listen to you and follow your plan for our lives.—Janelle Fraze

March 26: Jesus Cried Because He Cares

TEXT: John 11:35–36
Objects: Pictures of weeping people

Good morning boys and girls. When we see someone crying, like in these pictures, it gets our attention. We can't help but wonder, "Why are they crying? What happened?" If one of your friends begins to weep, you will ask the same question, wanting to know what's wrong. There are many reasons for crying. Tears can be the result of sadness, frustration, or happiness.

The Bible reports that Jesus cried. The Gospel of Luke records Jesus' tears over Jerusalem because the people refused to obey his commands and have peace (19:41). Another time Jesus wept when he was near the burial place of a friend named Lazarus.

Why did Jesus cry? Jesus probably cried at the tomb because the family and friends of Lazarus were so hurt by the death of their loved one. At funerals the sadness of the family is so great it is felt by everyone present. Those in attendance are touched by the power of the emotional distress of the others. Thus Jesus' tears demonstrated how much he was involved with and cared for his followers.

When God doesn't answer our prayers, we might think that God doesn't care about us. It is easy to think, "If God really loved me, he would answer my prayer." When we feel this way, we need to remember this very short verse: "Jesus wept." Jesus wept because he cared. When we are sad, Jesus is sad. When we are distressed, Jesus experiences our frustration and pain the way he did at the grave of Lazarus.

We don't understand why God doesn't answer every prayer, but it is not because he doesn't care. God hears all our prayers. There are millions of prayers said every day. And God loves and cares for each person saying a prayer. Remembering the tears of Jesus in this very short verse helps us remember how much Jesus loves us and is touched by our needs.—Ken Cox

April 2: Planting Seeds That Produce
TEXT: Gal. 6:7
Objects: Flowerpot, soil, bean seeds
Song: "For the Beauty of the Earth"

Hello boys and girls. I'm glad to see you today. This is the month of April—a time when many people plant vegetables and flower gardens. Farmers till the soil and plant seeds, which produce food for people and livestock.

I'm holding a flowerpot filled with good soil and a few bean seeds. Would someone help me punch these bean seeds in this pot? For plants to grow, several sources are necessary. Can someone tell me these things? [*Wait for response.*] Could they be the following?

- Good soil

- Water

- Sunlight

- Healthy seeds

Now let me ask you: Which ones on this list are given by God? [*Wait for response.*] That's right. All these resources are provided by God. We know that God sends the rain. He makes the sun shine to warm the Earth. He provides all soil for plants to germinate and grow. And he provides conditions that produce healthy seeds. God is so good to us. Please bow your heads and let us thank him.

Prayer: Thank you God for sending the rain and sunlight to make plants grow. Thank you for the good soil and healthy seeds.
Take Action: Ask your parents or grandparents to help you plant some seeds this week. You might use a large flowerpot or a sunny place in your yard.

[*Children return to their seats as the pianist plays one verse of "For the Beauty of the Earth."*]—Carolyn Tomlin

April 9: Peace Is by the Cross
TEXT: Jer. 8:11
Objects: Symbols of peace

Hello boys and girls. We all want peace. If we are in a war, we pray for peace to end the violence, loss of life, and devastation. I have on these posters some symbols of peace.

This is a peace *sign;* it is made by lifting two fingers like this. This is a peace *symbol;* inside a circle is an inverted "Y." Another representation of peace is a dove, like this portrayal of the gentle bird.

These are human symbols of peace. Humans tend to seek peace the easiest way possible. Sometimes what is obtained is called a truce—a short period of quietness, a break in the fighting that lasts only while tempers cool. A truce is generally broken when the war that is just beneath the surface erupts through a hostile incident. In such cases the war is not ended, because there is animosity lingering in people's hearts. Their fists are unclenched for a while, but feelings of hatred and desire for revenge soon cause a scuffle.

Jeremiah preached against a false peace or a lull in the fighting. Jeremiah was concerned about solving the war in people's hearts against God. Jeremiah sensed that although the people made some small changes in their behavior, their hearts were still at war with God.

True peace comes only through the grace of God. The root of war in human hearts is the rebellion against God that lurks there. Whenever humans disobey God, they soon find themselves fighting with one another. The war is not limited to military conflicts between countries. War includes the conflict in our homes, schools, and communities.

The true symbol of peace is the cross. [*Show poster of the cross.*] When Jesus died on the cross for the sins of humanity, he made a way for all humans to have peace with God. The cross was God's payment for the penalty for sin. When the problem of sin is settled in the human heart, there is the possibility of peace with God. After we make peace with God through believing in God's son Jesus as our Savior, we can have peace with our fellow man.

There are many symbols for peace, and peace is desired by all. However, there is only one way to a real and lasting peace, and that is the cross.—Ken Cox

April 16: Thanking God for Spring
TEXT: Song of Sol. 2:12
Objects: Branches of spring flowers
Song: "For the Beauty of the Earth"

Hello boys and girls. I'm glad to see you today. Spring is one of my favorite seasons of the year. Do you know why? [*Allow time for responses.*] I think it's because during the winter, the grass and plants have turned brown. But with spring, the sun warms the Earth. Flowers bloom; trees and grass become green. Baby animals are born in the spring. These flowers I'm holding remind me of God's greatness. Only he can make a beautiful flower come from a dried bulb or hard branch. I call that a miracle. When you go outside, look around you and see the wonders of his creation.

There's a verse in Song of Solomon 2:12 that tells about spring: "The flowers appear on the earth; the time of the singing of birds is come, and the voice of the turtle is heard in our land."

Prayer: Dear God, open our eyes to all the wonders of your creation. Thank you for the springtime of the year.

Take Action: During the week, cut out pictures that remind you of spring. Paste these in a notebook to share with a friend.

[*Ask the congregation to join the children in singing "For the Beauty of the Earth." Children return to their seats.*]—Carolyn Tomlin

April 23: Remember All God Has Done

TEXT: 1 Chron. 16:12

Objects: Old church pictures

Hello boys and girls. I'd like to tell you about some of the celebrations and displays by historical societies that help us remember the past. Just recently there was a reenactment of a Civil War battle near here. The men dressed in authentic Union and Confederate uniforms and faced each other as enemies on an old battlefield. The ladies were dressed in the garb of that time, wearing long dresses and bonnets. The sound of the muskets and cannon was like the battle over one hundred years ago.

Reenactments are to help us remember the lessons of the past. Someone has said that those who don't know the lessons of history will repeat the mistakes of the past. In a culture so bent on improving the future, it is easy to regard history as boring, but there is much to learn from history. God instructed his people to remember what had been done in the past through the prophets and patriarchs.

Our church has a long history. This is a drawing of one of the first places the church met. This is a picture of the old church downtown. But of course the church is not the building. The church is the people who belong to the fellowship of believers. These pictures stir memories of worshipping and serving God in those old buildings. We are grateful for the folks who have given financially and through service to bring our church to the point of strength that it has today. We must never forget them.

We can overlook the past and future by being wrapped in the hectic activities of today. By looking back we can come to value the people, like our grandparents, who have made this country and church great. We must serve today, not just thinking of ourselves but of the people who have served in the past.

There is one event in the future that God has planned for the church that we must remember, too—the return of Jesus. Humans are prone to forget the promise of Jesus to personally return for his Church. This coming might be at any moment. We are to live for that day, for it is the future of Christ's Church.—Ken Cox

April 30: Give Forgiveness for Big and Small Wrongs

TEXT: Matt. 18:21–22

Object: A vase of flowers

Hello boys and girls. Giving flowers is something husbands do to seek forgiveness from their wives. For instance, if a husband forgets the couple's wedding anniversary, he might send some flowers, like these, as a way of saying, "I'm sorry; please forgive me."

All of us need forgiveness. First, we need forgiveness from God for our sins, but we also need to forgive one another. We need to forgive little things and big things.

Peter—one of the apostles—asked Jesus about forgiveness. Peter wanted to know how many times he should forgive someone. Jesus answered that forgiveness wasn't limited to a few times or just little things. Jesus taught that forgiveness was to be given for big as well as little things. Like Peter, we have to ask Jesus about forgiveness to understand how to forgive those have committed wrongs against us.

First, forgiveness doesn't include allowing wrongs to continue. If someone is hurting us, we need to get a parent or adult to stop them or call the police. Forgiveness is ours to give after justice has been carried out.

Second, forgiveness is something we do in our hearts. If people wrong us and we are mad at them, we are being unforgiving. It doesn't have to be a big thing; it can be for a little incident known only to us. We can tell we haven't forgiven when we see them and the first thing that comes to mind is the wrong they have committed against us. That feeling is in our heart. That feeling of anger doesn't hurt them; it hurts us. If we don't forgive those who wrong us, that feeling will eat away at us like a physical illness. Forgiveness is something we give to wrongdoers, but it also helps us.

When we understand that God has forgiven us, we can begin to forgive others. To receive forgiveness from God, all we need to do is ask for forgiveness in Jesus' name. To forgive others we need to ask God to give us strength to let go of our anger and not hold it against the person who has wronged us.—Ken Cox

May 7: Don't Tire of Doing Good
TEXT: 2 Thess.
Object: A simple boat shape
Song: "We'll Work Till Jesus Comes"

Hello boys and girls. I'm glad to see you today. As you focus on the boat I'm holding, let's think about the story of Noah and the ark he built. Because man had become evil and the Earth corrupt, God decided to destroy the Earth by a flood. Noah was a good man who loved God. Therefore, God told Noah to build an ark for his family and to take a male and female of every living thing into the ark. After the ark was ready, God would send the rains, which would cover the land. Building the ark required Noah to work very hard. Do you suppose Noah became tired of working? Do you think he wanted to quit?

Did you ever get tired of doing something you should do? Do you suppose your parents get tired of going to work each day? God tells us to never get tired of doing good works. Listen as I read from 2 Thessalonians 3:13: "But ye, brethren, be not weary in well doing."

Prayer: Dear God, help each boy and girl not to grow weary in doing your work.
Take Action: Draw two pictures, one of a chore you enjoy doing and one you don't like.
    Ask God to help you like both jobs.

[*Children return to their seats as the pianist plays "We'll Work Till Jesus Comes."*]—Carolyn Tomlin

May 14: Thanks to Our Moms

TEXT: Prov. 31:28, 31

Objects: Achievement chart, Mother's Day cards

Hello boys and girls. This is an achievement chart like the ones on the walls of your class-rooms here at church and school. It works like this. The names of the members of the class are written on the lines. When an assigned task is completed satisfactorily, like memorizing a verse from the Bible or learning the capital cities of certain states, a star is placed in the square, like this. When students see the stars by their name, they are encouraged to learn. This is called motivation. Recognition of a job well done can be awarded in many ways. This is just one of them. When people are positively motivated, they like their assigned duties and excel in all their tasks.

I think you can relate to the positive or good feelings you get when you are rewarded. A reward can be as simple as a pat on the back or the gift of a dollar bill. Rewards make us feel like we're glowing inside. We walk taller and run faster.

Here are some Mother's Day cards. A couple of these are funny; one is serious. On Mother's Day we give cards to our moms to tell them how much we appreciate and love them. These cards are like the stars that are placed on the achievement chart. Sure, moms take care of their children out of love, not for recognition or stars on a chart, but the approval received on Mother's Day is a reward for them. When we give our moms a card, it tells them that we have noticed their love and hard work for us and we appreciate it. We also communicate how we would be unhappy if we did not receive their loving care.

Our moms are strong and industrious, but they are human and need approval, encouragement, and recognition just like everyone else. If once a year we give them our heartfelt thanks, they are able to gather strength and continue for another year. Watch your mom today. If you give her a card, you'll notice her reading it very closely. She may read it several times during the day, if you write a personal note on the card. Get your dad or a brother or sister to help you write something nice.

The Bible includes a verse that describes the thanks that a good mother should receive. It is a deep sense of gratitude from children that is the mother's reward.

When you get a star by your name in recognition of your achievements, you feel good inside and are ready to do more. Don't forget to say thanks to your mom today, because she feels the same way.—Ken Cox

May 21: God Gives Beautiful Life

TEXT: 2 Cor. 5:17

Objects: A budding bough and a stick

Good morning boys and girls. I want you to notice the differences between these two branches. This one is a dead stick. I picked this up on the ground under a tree. At one time this stick was a living branch on the tree, with leaves growing on it. For some reason the limb died and eventually fell off the tree. This is a living branch. Notice the buds that are present; some have begun to flower. The buds and flower indicate that spring is near. I trimmed this branch off a tree this morning. Until I cut the limb off, it was a living part of the tree.

The two branches look very different. One is dead; the other is still brimming with the power of life. These two branches can illustrate the difference between a person who is alive in Christ and one who is not. The Bible says when we are without Christ and in our sins, it is like we are dead, like this stick (Eph. 2:1). Without Jesus as our Savior and Lord, our lives are broken off from God, the source of all life. And if we are as dead branches, there is no hope for us unless our situation changes.

The Bible also says that when we receive Jesus as our savior we are born again; we become a new creation. Listen to this verse: "So when we accept Christ into our lives we cross over from death to life" (John 5:24). It is like God picks up a dead stick from the ground of the world and attaches it to the living tree that is Christ.

Not only is there a difference in the living status of these two branches, there is a difference in their beauty. This dead stick is very unattractive. The dead limb is useless except to be put on a pile for burning or shredding. In contrast, the living branch is beautiful. This branch could be put into a vase and would finish blooming. The difference is the power of the life in the living branch.

Over the next few weeks as spring begins, the beauty of the flowering ornamental fruit trees will be awesome. It is the same beauty that God can put into every person who is alive in Christ. The life of God is wonderful. We should pray that our lives will be like this branch—full of life and revealing God's power and grace.—Ken Cox

May 28: Memorial Day Tribute
TEXT: Ps. 33:12
Object: American flag
Song: "God Bless America"

Hello boys and girls. I'm happy to see you today. During the month of May we have a special day in which we honor those men and women who have given their lives for our country. On Memorial Day—the last Monday in May—many offices close in honor of these people.

This American flag that I hold is a symbol that represents the United States. The stripes stand for the thirteen original colonies. The fifty stars represent each state. On Memorial Day we fly this flag in honor of those who died to keep America safe and free.

It has been said that America is only as strong as her people. Although you are young, you can still do your part to make our country strong. By keeping God's laws, you will grow up to keep his laws as an adult: "Blessed is the nation whose God is the Lord; and the people whom he hath chosen for his own inheritance" (Ps. 33:12).

> *Prayer:* Lord God, we thank you for those men and women who gave their lives for our country. Help each child here today grow up to keep your laws and to love their country.
>
> *Take Action:* During the coming week, write five things that make you proud to be an American.

[*Lead the children in singing "God Bless America." Children return to their seats as the pianist plays.*]—Carolyn Tomlin

June 4: Summer Pleasures

TEXT: Isa. 48:18
Objects: Sand bucket and small shovel
Song: "I Have Peace Like a River"

Hello boys and girls. I'm glad to see you today. I'm sure you know what I'm holding, and you probably have one of these at home. Where do you use a sand bucket and a shovel? [*Wait for responses.*] When I was a child we often vacationed near the seashore or a river. My friends and I would dig buckets of sand near the shore, and in a few minutes the waves filled the holes back up.

Today, when I'm near a river or ocean I feel a certain peace. In places such as this, I hear God speak to me. I hear his voice in the wind, the cry of the sea gulls, the lapping of the waves on the shore. And I know it was he who created these things for us to enjoy. Listen as I read from Isaiah 48:18: "O that thou hadst hearkened to my commandments! Then had thy peace been as a river, and thy righteousness as the waves of the sea."

> *Prayer:* Dear Lord, help us see your greatness in the whispering winds, the roaring sea, and the music of the birds. May we always be grateful for your bountiful gifts.
> *Take Action:* This week draw a picture of a seashore or river. What colors will you use for your illustration?

[*Ask children to return to their seats as the pianist plays "I Have Peace Like a River."*]— Carolyn Tomlin

June 11: Jesus Spent Quality Time with God

TEXT: Matt. 14:23
Object: A golf club

Good morning boys and girls. This is a nine iron. It's the golf club to use when the ball is close to the green. I've enjoyed playing golf since I was in elementary school. One of the most pleasant things about golf is that I got to know my father while playing. My dad was a very busy man, but we managed to play golf together many times as I was growing up. It was during those times that we established our relationship. We would talk to each other in between shots or while looking for balls in the rough. Some call this spending "quality time" with your kids.

For you and your dad, mom, or grandparents, there are other ways to spend quality time. If you tried to spend quality time playing golf, you might make yourselves miserable. Some people don't like golf at all. Quality time can be found while fishing, camping, attending sports activities, working on cars, quilting, or doing other projects. One granddaughter told me that she and her grandmother became close friends while watching the same television show together every day. That was their special time. It is time that might be discovered by accident.

Jesus spent quality time with God. After an especially busy day Jesus sent the crowds away and went off to be alone with God. During those moments Jesus prayed.

Your heavenly father wants to spend time with you, too. This is done by taking time to read the Bible and by praying the way Jesus did. Other quality time with God is spent during Sunday school and church services. The important step is taking those moments and not overlooking the importance of spending time with God. The result of quality time is getting to know God more closely. It is sad that some people feel that God is far away from them. Actually, there is no place to go where God isn't. He is everywhere, and he knows us individually. It just seems God is distant when we ignore his presence.

Quality time is a blessing and joy. It is great to spend quality time with parents and grandparents. It is even better to spend quality time with God.—Ken Cox

June 18: Wedding Bands
TEXT: Gen. 2:24
Object: A wedding band

Good morning boys and girls. This is my wedding band. I wear my wedding ring all the time. I began wearing it on my wedding day some years ago.

At the wedding ceremonies I perform, I comment on the wedding bands as they are exchanged. My remarks are intended to help the bride and groom understand the special nature of the promises they make to each other in the presence of God. At the end of the ceremony, I have the authority to present the bride and groom as husband and wife.

First, I tell the couple that the purity of the gold stands for the purity of the love the man and wife are to have for each other. To love in purity means there is a self-giving love—a love that looks for the best in their partner. A pure love helps the spouses become all God intends for them to be. Second, I indicate the eternal design of the wedding band. A person can start at any point on the ring's surface and go round and round without ever reaching an end. This infinite shape symbolizes the never-ending vows that are made by the bride and groom. During the wedding the couple promises to love, honor, trust, and serve one another in sickness and in health, in adversity and prosperity, until death ends their relationship.

The exchange of wedding bands is a central part of the wedding ceremony. Each time couples look at their wedding band, they are to remember how important their marriage is in the eyes of God.

The first wedding was in the Garden of Eden. God created Adam and Eve for each other and performed the first marriage ceremony. Because God created the institution of marriage, humans are to regard their marriages as very important. We are to pray for our future husbands and wives before we get engaged and after we are married. Marriage is more than a human contract; it is a divine institution. When we pray for our marriages our homes become happy, and that's what God intended. God wishes to bring us joy through the blessings of good marriages.—Ken Cox

June 25: Beware of Danger
TEXT: Eph. 6:10–11
Object: Sign that says, "Danger"
Song: "Be Strong in the Lord"

Hello boys and girls. I'm glad to see you today. I'm holding a sign that says, "Danger." When you see this sign, you know there is something you should avoid. Recently, I heard several blue jays making a loud noise in my backyard. These birds had discovered a large snake near my home and were alerting me to the danger. You might see a danger sign on a bottle of household cleanser, a warning that a bridge is out on a road, or a flashing blue light on a highway patrolman's car. In order to stay safe, we must know what the danger means.

Sometimes we are tempted to do wrong, and God sends us a danger sign. When this happens, we should listen to our parents, pray about the situation, and find out what the Bible has to say. God wants us to avoid dangerous situations in our life. And often the devil disguises an activity and makes it look harmless; only later do we realize this was something wrong.

Listen as I read from Ephesians 6:10: "Finally, my brethren, be strong in the Lord, and in the power of his might. Put on the whole armour of God, that ye may be able to stand against the wiles of the devil."

> *Prayer:* Dear God, please guide these children to avoid danger in their lives. May they listen to their parents and seek your will.
>
> *Take Action:* Make a list of harmful things in your life. Share these with a sibling or friend.

[*Dismiss the children to their seats as the pianist plays "Be Strong in the Lord."*]—Carolyn Tomlin

July 2: Remembering Our Freedoms

TEXT: Ps. 20:7
Object: Fire crackers or Roman candles
Song: "My Country 'Tis of Thee"

Hello boys and girls. I'm glad you chose to attend church today. During the month of July we celebrate Independence Day, which is July fourth. Do you know why it's known as Independence Day? [*Wait for responses.*] When our country was very young, we were owned by England. Some of the colonists (people who lived in the colonies) thought it unfair to be taxed without having a voice in our government. They decided to form a new government, and a revolution, or war, resulted. Thomas Jefferson wrote the Declaration of Independence, and since 1776 we have been known as the United States. People celebrate this holiday with fireworks and Roman candles.

Yes, America is a country where we enjoy many freedoms. God has given us a great country. We should never forget how fortunate we are to live in America. Listen as I read from Psalm 20:7: "Some trust in chariots, and some in horses: but we will remember the name of the Lord our God."

> *Prayer:* Thank you God for the freedoms we enjoy in our great country. May we remember the cost of these freedoms in the lives of men and women who gave their lives.
>
> *Take Action:* This week, write a poem expressing how you feel about the freedoms you enjoy in America.

[*As children return to their seats, the pianist plays one verse of "My Country 'Tis of Thee."*]—Carolyn Tomlin

July 9: God Is Our Shield

TEXT: Eph. 6:11, 16

Object: Model tank (or picture)

Good morning boys and girls. This is a model of an M1A2 Abrams tank. This kind of tank is currently used by the U.S. Army. There is a hatch on top of the tank, and the soldiers enter the tank through that opening. The outside is covered with heavy steel called armor. The armor in the front, most likely to receive enemy fire, is reinforced and stronger than the back and sides. The armor protects the soldiers inside the tank from bullets and small explosive devices.

The Bible says we need special protective armor. The armor and shield that we need are not made of steel, however. The Bible is referring to spiritual armor to protect us from damaging evil attacks. The spiritual armor and shield are put on by our faith in God. Without the armor and shield of protection, the "fiery darts" of evil in the world would destroy us. The evil that comes against us from our adversary, the devil, is compared to arrows. The thought of being shot through with an arrow is more frightening to me than being shot with a bullet. And the arrows are not plain. They are flaming arrows!

We don't need to fear. We need only put on the armor and use the shield that God intends for all of us to have. God wishes for us to remain safe and sound through the evil attacks of this life. How does the armor and shield of faith protect us?

First, the shield of faith protects us by reminding us of God's love. There is nothing worse than feeling alone and unloved. The creator of the universe loves us. We know this because God sent Jesus into the world to save us.

Second, the armor and shield of faith protects us by truth. The truth protects us by telling us it is always best to be honest, truthful, and caring about others. When we hear the lie that it is OK to steal, be untruthful, or be unkind to others, the truth protects us by reminding us not to accept these falsehoods. Hearing and living the truth always guards and protects us.

On the field of battle a tank's armor protects those inside. In life we are protected by the spiritual armor and shield of faith that God wants us to wear at all times.—Ken Cox

July 16: Avoid Worry

TEXT: Matt. 6:28, 31

Object: A flower

Song: "Have Faith in God"

Hello boys and girls. I'm glad to see you today. I'm holding a beautiful flower in my hand. You know, God made this flower. He made it grow from the soil, from a bud, and open to this particular bloom. And something else: this flower never worried about whether the rains would come, the sun would shine, or insects might eat it before it opens. However, people like you and me worry. Do you ever worry about anything? [*Wait for responses.*] Perhaps you worry about going to school, making friends, or having plans interrupted.

The Bible tells us to avoid worry. Listen as I read Matthew 6:28 and 31: "Consider the lilies of the field, how they grow; they toil not, neither do they spin. Therefore take no thought, saying, What shall we eat? Or, What shall we drink? Or, wherewithal shall we be clothed?"

Prayer: Dear God, please help these boys and girls remember to put their faith in you and to know that worry does not help situations. May they remember the lilies of the fields and how you care for them.

Take Action: Collect pictures of flowers in bloom. Paste them in a scrapbook to remind you of how God cares for the flowers.

[*Children return to their seats as the pianist plays "Have Faith in God."*]—Carolyn Tomlin

July 23: Worry

TEXT: Matt. 6:28–29

Objects: A small bunch of mixed flowers, Bible

Song: "God Will Take Care of You"

Hello boys and girls. Do you ever worry? Can you tell me what kinds of things boys and girls worry about? [*Take responses, which may include such things as storms, schoolwork, illness, or family issues. Validate each contribution. No matter how trivial a concern may seem to you, it is significant to the child, and it is significant to God.*] Did you know the Bible talks about worrying? Let's listen [*read Matt. 6:28–29.*]

[*Show flowers.*] Look at these beautiful flowers. The Bible says God made everything. He made these beautiful flowers. But the Bible also tells us these flowers do nothing for themselves. They just sit there. They do not go to school or work. They do not do kind things for others. They can't even tell God "Thank You" or tell God they love him. But God made these flowers, and he made them to be as beautiful as he could. God takes care of these flowers by sending rain when they are thirsty, by giving them soil to provide the food they need; God sends gentle breezes to keep their leaves and petals clean. He even sends them the sun to help them grow. God takes very good care of the flowers in the fields.

But God loves you even more than he loves the flowers. The next time you are worried, remember that God loves you very much and that he will take care of you.

Prayer: Thank you God for loving each of us. Thank you for knowing everything about us and for taking care of everything we need. Help us to remember that you will always take care of us.

[*If you have enough flowers, give one to each child.*]—Janelle Fraze

July 30: Jesus Satisfies

TEXT: John 4:13–14

Object: A bottle of water

Hello boys and girls. During the summer it is necessary to keep plenty of water available. The heat makes us perspire (sweat), and we get thirsty. We must quench this thirst to replenish the lost fluids by drinking water. When I play golf during the summer months, I keep a bottle of water handy. It seems the more I drink, the thirstier I get.

I've noticed that we have other cravings that are like thirst on a hot summer day. I've discovered this when I eat ice cream. I'll scoop some ice cream into a bowl and top it with chocolate syrup and whipped cream. After devouring the first bowl, I want another helping.

Jesus knew that some desires, like hunger for recognition or popularity, are impossible to satisfy. For instance, a celebrity can be in a movie viewed by ten million people. But that movie star might be jealous of another actor in a film that is seen by eleven million people. Even after earning millions of dollars to buy beautiful cars and homes, such stars are unhappy and sulk around because someone else had a more successful movie. Isn't that silly? But that's the way all of us are. Some of our greatest frustrations come through the desires or appetites we have. Jesus promised that if we dedicate our lives to pleasing him, we would learn to be satisfied.

But some people, including ourselves, are impossible to make happy. We may have noticed how unhappy we are when we are having a very successful season in Little League baseball and lose just one game. Even after beating most of the other ball teams by huge margins, we slip up and lose one game. Afterwards there is crying and discouragement. It's amazing how awful we feel. However, when we dedicate ourselves to honoring Jesus, we will not only please him, we will discover happiness for ourselves.—Ken Cox

August 6: Family Fun Time
TEXT: Phil. 2:14
Object: Road map
Song: "God, Give Us Christian Homes"

Hello boys and girls. I'm glad to see you today. Can you tell me what I'm holding? [*Wait for responses.*] Yes, this is a road map. A road map is used to find the best route when traveling. Towns and communities across our land are connected by roads and highways. When our family takes a vacation to a new location, we check our route with a map.

Spending time together with your parents, grandparents, and extended family is important. God planned for families. Some of you may have single parents; others live with grandparents or foster patents. Did anyone take a family vacation this summer? Or perhaps you have one planned during this month. [*Allow time for responses.*]

So the next time you see a road map, think of the places your family can vacation together. And don't forget to attend church during your trip. "Do all things without murmurings and disputings" (Phil. 2:14).

> *Prayer:* Father we thank you for giving us families. Bless each boy and girl here today and keep them safe as they travel this summer.
> *Take Action:* During the week, ask your parents to help you mark the highways you will travel on a family trip.

[*Lead the children in singing one verse of "God, Give Us Christian Homes" as they return to their seats.*]—Carolyn Tomlin

August 13: "Being" Is as Important as "Speaking"
TEXT: Isa. 29:13a
Objects: Pictures, cartoons, or caricatures emphasizing mouths

Hello boys and girls. Please take a look at these drawings. They emphasize the mouths of their subjects. In this picture the mouth takes up the whole face; the eyes and nose are barely visible. This depiction accentuates the huge lips and the loud sound of laughter coming from the person. These posters indicate the prominence of what is said. A serious insult is to be called a "big mouth." All these drawings depict that major fault.

Jesus told a parable about a father and his two sons that emphasized the importance of what was said versus what was done (Matt. 21:28–31). In the account the father asked one son to go work in the family vineyard, and the son replied, "No, I'm not going." Later that son changed his mind and went and worked in the vineyard anyway. Meanwhile the father asked the second son to go and work in the vineyard. That son said, "Sure, I'll go and work." But the second son never made it to the vineyard. He went and did something else.

After telling the story, Jesus asked the listeners, "Which son did the will of his father, the first or second?" The people answered that the one that initially said, "No" by his words but said, "Yes" by his actions. The answer of the people indicated that what was done was more important than what was said.

As we live as disciples of Jesus, we say many important things. We proclaim the truth of the gospel and offer words of prayer. We may give a testimony of how important Jesus has been in our lives or sing a song with words of adoration and praise. Since speaking is so important to Christianity, it is easy to become all talk and no action. Believers are challenged to let their actions be consistent with, not contradictory to, their words.

It is good to talk about our faith and what we intend to do in obedience to Jesus. But we must remember that we can be quietly obedient and please God, too. Actually, we need to do both. We need to proclaim the good news and live the truth of the Scriptures so the world can have our whole lives pointing to the Savior. We should avoid being a big mouth—talking about our faith but never living up to the standards Jesus proclaimed.—Ken Cox

August 20: Friends
TEXT: Prov. 17:17
Object: Bible
Song: "What a Friend We Have in Jesus"

Good morning boys and girls. I want to tell you about a very good friend. Her (or his) name is [*fill in the blank, first name only*]. My friend and I like to do lots of things together. We like to [*fill in the blank*] and [*another answer*], and once we even [*something fun*]. My friend and I like to spend as much time together as we can.

But I have some other friends, too. Some of my friends are here today. I remember a song that says [*if you know the tune, sing this, or otherwise just repeat the words*], "I have a good friend"; [*name the friend above*] is [*his or her*] name. [*Repeat the same phrase with all the children sitting with you. Look the children directly in the eyes when singing their names. Check names in advance if you need to.*]

I told you about my very good friend. I also named my good friends sitting here with me. But my best friend is Jesus. He is everywhere I go. He is with me all the time. He listens every time I talk with him. He helps me all day, every day. That reminds me of another song. It says [*sing or speak the words*], "My best friend is Jesus, Jesus, Jesus. My best friend is Jesus. I love him."

There is another song that talks about Jesus. It says [*sing or say*], "Oh, how I love Jesus; oh, how I love Jesus; oh, how I love Jesus because he first loved me."

Prayer: Thank you Jesus for loving each one of us. Thank you for always being there. Thank you for always listening. Thank you for always helping me. Thank you for being my best friend.—Janelle Fraze

August 27: Women Give Their Mirrors

TEXT: Exodus 38:8
Object: A hand mirror

Good morning boys and girls. I'd like to show you this mirror. About 160 years ago the process of making a silvered mirror on glass was discovered. These silvered mirrors give a near-perfect reflection of our faces. Prior to that time, mirrors were made out of various metals. If the metal could be made to shine brightly, the reflection was pretty good, but the quality could not compare to the mirrors we use today.

Mirrors have always been important to women. Women use mirrors to fix their makeup and hair because they wish to look their best. Beauty in women has always been as important as physical strength has traditionally been to men. Therefore, mirrors have always been a prized possession of women.

When the children of Israel were making the tabernacle for worship, which was like a huge circus tent, there were parts to be made of bronze. In those days mirrors were made of bronze because of its quality in reflecting images. The Bible says that the ladies who served in the tent of meeting donated their bronze mirrors for this purpose. That means the ladies were willing to give valuable possessions to the Lord.

When we give something to God, we should be willing to give something that is of great value to us. When we do, our actions show how important God is to us. By offering our best we show God how we feel. It also is a testimony to other people who may not know about Jesus. Furthermore, when we give something we prize, and we give it joyfully, that makes us feel very good inside.—Ken Cox

September 3: Workers for Jesus

TEXT: Ps. 90:17
Object: Bible
Song: "We'll Work Till Jesus Comes"

Hello boys and girls. I'm glad to see you today. During the month of September we observe Labor Day—a time to honor our workforce. In our community and all across America, people work each day to make our lives more comfortable, safer, and more interesting. Can you name some of these people who help you? [*Wait for responses.*] What about the police department that works to keep us safe? How does the fire department help us? Then our teachers help educate us. The sanitation department empties our garbage and cleans our streets. When you think about it, you can see that many people in our community make our lives better. When you grow up, you may have a job like these people.

But there is another job that you can participate in now. That is being a worker for Jesus. This Bible that I'm holding is your tool to do the job. To be a good worker, you must know what is inside the Bible. That means you must read and pray. Listen as I read about work from Psalm 90:17: "And let the beauty of the Lord our God be upon us; and establish thou the work of our hands upon us; yea, the work of our hands establish thou it."

> *Prayer:* Dear Lord, let each boy and girl appreciate the work the people in our community do to make our lives better. Help each child be a worker for you.
>
> *Take Action:* Write a letter to a community worker, thanking that person for his or her service.

[*Ask the pianist to play one verse of "We'll Work Till Jesus Comes" as children return to their seats.*]—Carolyn Tomlin

September 10: Knowing and Doing God's Will
TEXT: Titus 1:16a
Objects: A repair manual and tools

Good morning boys and girls. Let me show you this car repair manual. By reading this book, a person can learn how to repair an automobile. With these tools we tighten and loosen bolts, screws, hoses, and clamps, and actually complete the work described in the manual.

However, if a person wants to become a mechanic, more is required than just reading the repair manual. Every chapter in the book can be read, even memorized, but unless there is some hands-on experience and training, a person will never be a good mechanic. Both education from repair manuals and years of experience are necessary to become a first-rate mechanic.

The same is true about doing God's will. We can know the will of God by reading the Bible. But until we take practical steps to become obedient to the truth of God, we will not be within the will of God. The Bible describes some people who read the Bible but don't obey what they have learned. By their actions, these people actually deny God's truth.

Our first step in knowing and doing the will of God involves accepting Jesus as our Savior. We learn about Jesus through Sunday school lessons that are based on the truth of the Bible. However, knowing about Jesus is only part of God's will. When we are old enough to understand, we accept him through prayer and baptism. We know about Jesus and are obedient to his command to be baptized. And we go on from that point. We learn about the great commission from the Bible and then begin to witness so our actions will be in line with our knowledge. We learn about tithing from the Scriptures and then begin to give from our allowances and income. And on and on it goes.

As we learn the truth of God and put it to work in our lives, we discover there is joy in doing the will of God. Because God loves us, he has shown the pathway to unshakeable happiness. God's will enables us to understand how to live in a complicated world. By accepting God's will, we are able to receive the joy that God has promised to all his children.—Ken Cox

September 17: Follow Instructions (Keep Commandments)
TEXT: John 14:15
Object: Board game, "Clue"

Good morning boys and girls. I'd like to show you this game—"Clue." Those playing are like detectives solving a murder mystery. The colorful cover of the box creates interest in playing the game. Here are the board, the pieces for each player, and some other paraphernalia.

To play the game the first time, we take the cellophane off the box, set the board on a table, and put the cards, game pieces, and other objects in place. At that point we are eager to jump right in and start playing, but there is another step we must take. We must read the instructions. That's a boring step. With the game laid out it looks like fun and we can't wait to start, but then we have to stop and read all the instructions! Look at all these words. However, if we don't read the instructions, we will never be able to enjoy the game. We might get in a fight with our friends if we make up the rules as we go. Also we might not even know how to win if we don't read the instructions first. After reading how to play, as tedious as that might be, we can really enjoy the game. The rules are applied fairly to everyone, and the winner can be congratulated at the end of the game.

A similar truth is encountered in each of our lives. God has given us the gift of life, and we are eager to live it to the fullest. However, God has given us instructions about living. The instruction book is called the Bible. When we read and study the instructions, also called commandments, we can truly discover how to live. Jesus said if we loved him we would follow his commandments for life.

Some folks never get around to reading these commandments for life. Others read the instructions but don't play the game of life according to God's rules. These folks will be discouraged by how their lives turn out. They will have many confusing struggles as a result of ignoring God's instructions. However, if we follow the lessons Jesus has given us, we discover that life is abundant and full of joy.

God has given us commandments about life because he loves us. He wants us to know how to truly win in the demands of life. And the more we follow the commands that God has given, the more we truly are able to love Jesus.—Ken Cox

September 24: Color
TEXT: Gen. 9:12 NIV
Objects: Box of basic-colored crayons, Bible
Song: "For the Beauty of the Earth"

Good morning boys and girls. Do you have a favorite color? [*Accept responses.*] Do you think God has a favorite color? Well, let's see.

[*Pull out a corresponding crayon to match each color you name.*] Can you think of something God made that was blue? [*Take several responses for each color, and fill in as needed.*] What about green? What did God make that is green? [*Hear answers.*] Did God make anything red? [*Hear answers.*] How about something yellow? [*Hear answers.*] I know that God made grapes that are purple, and nighttime is black; but what about brown and white? Any ideas for those colors? [*soil and tree trunks, sheep and snow*].

It sounds to me as though God likes all the colors in the world. But then, God did make all the colors in the world, and they are all beautiful. The Bible says God took all the colors and made a rainbow to put into the sky.

Did you know that dogs and cats cannot see colors? Neither can birds or fish. Some people think bulls can see red, but now we know that they just respond to movement. When God made animals, he made them to see only black and white. The only creation God made that sees colors is a human being. God must love us very much to make all of these beautiful colors just for us.

Prayer: Thank you God for loving us so much that you made the world so beautiful for us to look at. Please help us to enjoy your world and to take care of it.—Janelle Fraze

October 1: You Are Special
TEXT: Gen. 1:27; Ps. 139:14
Objects: Bible

Hello boys and girls. The Bible says, "God made me." That reminds me of a song we used to sing when I was young. It says, "I am special, I am special, God made me." Let's see how much alike we are.

If you are a boy, raise your hand. OK, now if you are a girl, raise your hand. It looks like that covers everyone. Now if you have blond hair, raise your hand. What about brown hair? Anyone with red hair? What about black hair? [*If you have a child with no hair, be sure to make that a category.*] It looks like we have a lot in common. Let's try this one. If you have a sister, raise your hand. How about a brother? Do any of you have no sisters and no brothers? I have ____ sisters and ____ brothers [*fill in the blanks*]. Were any of you born in a different country? [*If so, show appreciation for that.*] These are all ways we are different and all ways we are special.

This next part may be a little harder. [*As each section is named, if a child responds in a positive manner, acknowledge that child by name.*] If you are blind, raise your hand. If you have hearing problems, raise your hand. If you use a wheel chair or a walker or crutches to walk, raise your hand. It seems we are not getting as many hands up this time. Let's try one more thing. If you know someone who cannot see, or someone who cannot hear, or someone who needs help in getting around, raise your hand. Many of us have friends in school or in our neighborhood like this.

In the book of Psalms we read, "I am wonderfully made." That means all of us. We are alike in many ways, and we are different in many ways. God loves us all very much. God wants us to love each other, too. The Bible says, "Do unto others as you would have others do unto you." Remember that each person is made by God, and all people are special. If a person seems "different" to you, make an extra effort to get to know him or her. Invite that person to your church. You may just make a new good friend.

Prayer: Dear God, thank you for making each of us different. Thank you for loving each of us. Help us to be kind to others.—Janelle Fraze

October 8: Fall Pleasures
TEXT: Gen. 1:1
Objects: Colored leaves
Song: "For the Beauty of the Earth"

Hello boys and girls. I'm glad to see you today. The colored leaves I'm holding remind me of how God created the seasons. As you know, the year is divided into four seasons: spring, summer, fall, and winter. This is the fall season. What changes take place during this time? [*Wait for responses.*] Squirrels gather nuts and hide them for winter. Leaves turn brilliant shades of red, yellow, and orange. The days grow shorter and the nights longer. Boys and girls have less daylight to play outdoors. You may see people raking leaves, and you may gather a pile to jump on. Families may enjoy sitting around a campfire—singing or telling stories.

Yes, the fall season reminds us of God's greatness. His plan calls for day and night, seasons of the year, and the sun to shine during the day and the moon and stars at night. No one can deny that there is a God. The following verse tells us that God is responsible for everything. "In the beginning God created the heaven and the earth."

Prayer: Dear Father, thank you for the beauty we see during the fall season. Help us use our senses to see your greatness.

Take Action: Take a nature walk with your family and collect colored leaves. Press them between sheets of waxed paper with a warm iron (with adult supervision). Hang these in a sunny window as a reminder of God's greatness.

[*Lead children in singing "For the Beauty of the Earth." Boys and girls return to their seats.*]—Carolyn Tomlin

October 15: God Is Spirit
TEXT: John 4:24
Objects: Pictures of space, space ships, and so forth

Good morning everyone. This is a photograph of a new star being formed in a distant galaxy. Our sun is a star. It is possible that when this new star is formed, other planets may revolve around it the way the earth revolves around our sun.

Because there are so many stars like our sun, scientists wonder if there is other intelligent life in our universe. Next they wonder, If there is other life in the universe, could a spaceship be constructed to carry travelers from earth to visit them? These questions are asked because we have become experts about space, other planets, and "physical" life.

Did you know there are other forms of intelligent life already living here with us? Instead of existing in a physical world, these beings are spiritual. The Bible reveals that God is a spiritual being. He doesn't have a physical body the way we do. God sent his son Jesus to live in a physical body like ours, but God is a spiritual being. The Bible also describes angels as spiritual beings that do God's will. There are also Satan and demons—evil spiritual beings in rebellion against God.

I want us to remember this reality. Our knowledge of physical life has grown tremendously and will increase even more in your lifetimes. We are beginning to understand human DNA and can perform medical scans and tests to detect complex problems in our bodies. However, the more we understand physical realities, the more we overlook or discount spiritual realities.

We must not forget the spiritual realities of the Bible. God created us to have spiritual abilities to relate to him through our understanding and prayer. And for our physical bodies to be strong, we must be spiritually healthy, too. Don't let the reality of spiritual beings frighten you. God, even though he is spiritual, created you and loves you with a powerful, everlasting love. He will protect us from spiritual evil. He will watch over us every day. So the next time you look at the stars at night, it's OK to wonder if there is life out there. But don't forget that there are spiritual beings already here with us, and we're not only physical—we're spiritual, too.—Ken Cox

October 22: Bread Is for Eating

TEXT: Luke 9:18–24 (v. 24): "Whoever loses his life for my sake will save it, but whoever insists on keeping life will lose it."
Object: A piece of stale bread

Good morning boys and girls. How many of you like to eat bread—really good bread? I do, too. Good bread is one of the real joys of life. How many of you like it hot and dripping with butter and jam? I like that, too. Sometimes I like my bread so much that I try to save it and save it. Do you know what happens to good bread when you try to save it for a long time? [*Let them answer.*] That's right; it gets stale. It also molds and turns gray and green. Is there anyone here who likes gray-green stale bread? No one? Not one of you likes that kind of bread? Then why do we save bread? [*Let them answer.*] There is no real reason, because bread is meant to be used and eaten. When you eat and use the bread, it does several good things. For one thing, it tastes good when it is eaten. It also turns into body cells and makes us grow and be strong. That is the way bread was meant to be. It should be used and not saved.

It is the same way with living. A life that is used is a good life. A life that is protected and saved is no good. Jesus taught us a long time ago that we should stop worrying about our lives and that we should use them to do good and to work for God. Some people are afraid to be Christians and to follow Jesus. It sounds dangerous, and they are afraid that he will ask too much from them. They want to save their lives for other things they think are important for them. But whenever you save your life, you lose it, just as you lose bread by saving it.

Jesus wants us to spend our lives—use them and work for him—and he promises us that whatever we give to him will be made into something better. When you eat bread you don't become bread. You become a body. When you work for Jesus and give your life to him, you become something even better. That is a promise of Jesus, and Jesus always keeps his promises. So don't save your life for something that you might think will be important. Give your life to Jesus now, and you will be glad you did.—Wesley T. Runk[1]

October 29: Working at Church

TEXT: 1 Sam. 2:11
Object: Bible
Song: "The Doxology"

Good morning. I've been looking around our church this morning, and there seem to be a lot of people who have a lot of jobs to do. There are people singing in the choir. There are people making announcements. There are people passing the offering plates. There are people handing out bulletins. There are people praying. There are people preaching.

Then I wondered how old you have to be to work for Jesus at church. Let's see. What about our pastor [*fill in the name*]? How old do you think he is? [*Take responses.*] I'm not sure, but I do know he is old enough to have gone to college. He is even old enough to be married and have children. [*Fill in other information that may fit. If you have other staff members the children would know, do a similar thing with their names.*]

---

[1]*God Doesn't Rust* (Lima, Ohio: CSS, 1978), pp. 57–58.

I see in the front pew a whole row of people we call deacons. They don't all seem to be the same age, but they are all grown-ups. So are the people in the choir and those playing musical instruments. And what about your Sunday school teacher? It seems to me that everyone who does something around here is an adult. Does that mean only grown-ups can do things while they are at church to serve God?

In 1 Samuel, the Bible tells of a very young boy named Samuel. When he was only a baby, he went to live at the Temple. He worked very hard to learn from and serve with a man named Eli. While Samuel helped Eli around the Temple, Eli helped Samuel learn about God. We may be just young boys and girls, but there are some things we can do to help out at church. While we are helping, maybe we can find some ways to learn more about God, too.

Here are a few ideas. If we come in quietly and sit down, maybe we will learn what it is like to be with friends in worship together. If we stand up and sing, maybe we will learn some great new songs and learn some very special things about God. If we listen during announcements, maybe we will find there are some real fun things we can do with friends at church, and we can invite other friends to come along. If we remain quiet and still during the sermon, we may just hear God talking to us, too. That is what worship is all about. It is spending time with God.

> *Prayer:* Dear God, we know we don't have to be a grown-up before you love us. You love us right now. We also don't have to be a grown-up to show you that we love you. Help us to start as boys and girls to learn to take time each Sunday morning to be with you and to praise you.—Janelle Fraze

November 5: Hide God's Word in Your Heart
TEXT: Ps. 119:11
Object: A treasure chest (jewelry box)

Good morning boys and girls. This is a small replica of an ancient treasure chest. Before there were banks, people used chests like this to keep their valuables safe. Gold and jewelry were placed inside the chest, and the hasp was dropped over the ring and locked. The chest was then hidden in a place where thieves would not find it. Some treasures were hidden so well they were lost. From time to time an old chest like this is discovered at an old building site; it is called buried treasure.

People are protective of their treasures. Considerable effort is taken to keep valuable things from being stolen or lost. Today most people use banks or safety deposit boxes for their treasures.

Another valuable possession is God's word. God's word is truth and must be protected or it will vanish through ignorance or forgetfulness. Also God's word can be distorted or lost through neglect. It is tragic when that happens.

To treasure God's word we are to hide it in our hearts. What this means is to memorize a verse. I have memorized Matthew 6:33. Listen as I try to recite it [*recite the verse*]. To memorize the verse I had to read it several times and write it out by hand. Then I committed to memory one phrase at a time until I could remember the whole verse. When I was a boy, a preacher came to our church who had memorized the whole New Testament. I will never forget how powerful his memory was for the treasure of God's word.

By memorizing a verse the words become part of our memory. But there is more to learn and understand than the words. As we think and pray about the words and become obedient to what the words say, we have an added depth of understanding. This is called learning the verse by experience. Some people claim to know the Bible, but they only have a surface knowledge of the words. By living the truth of the Bible, it really becomes a part of our families, work, and homes. When we know the Bible's words and meaning, we have a treasure that no one can ever take away from us.

When the treasure of God's word is hidden in our hearts, it really isn't buried. The truth of God's word is there for us to know and see every day. And the most wonderful thing is that the world can see something special in us because of it.—Ken Cox

November 12: Give from Your Heart

TEXT: 2 Cor. 9:7
Objects: Enlarged offering envelopes

Good morning boys and girls. I have enlarged two "pretend" offering envelopes for you to think about. This envelope belonging to Sam Smith indicates an offering of $1,000. The other envelope belongs to Beverly Billings and specifies an offering of $10. From a human perspective there is no question as to who gave the greater amount. Sam Smith gave $990 more than Beverly Billings, but to the Lord the greatness of the amount is determined by looking at the heart.

God looks at many things differently than we do. One day Jesus was in the Temple and many were bringing their offerings to God. A poor woman came and placed two little copper coins, like pennies, in the offering receptacle. Jesus said that the woman gave more than all the others because she gave all that she had (Luke 21:1–4). The woman gave cheerfully and from the heart.

When we give to the Lord, he looks at our heart. In other words, the Lord is interested in why we give. When we give with a true desire to be obedient, God counts that for good. Some give, even though they don't really want to. That kind of grudging offering is not appreciated by God.

So we should always give from the heart. We know that the Lord can take a small gift that is from the heart and use it to accomplish great things. So don't be discouraged in giving a portion of your allowance each Sunday; to the Lord that is a lot. Whatever we give to God is multiplied many times over. We can accomplish tremendous things by giving cheerfully from our hearts.—Ken Cox

November 19: Find Opportunities to Witness

TEXT: James 1:22
Object: Bible
Song: "Holy Bible, Book Divine"

Hello boys and girls. I'm glad to see you today. I'm holding in my hand a book that has been on the best-seller list for years. Why do you think this book is so popular? [*Wait for responses.*] Could it be because this book contains God's plan for living a good life? Jesus used parables, or stories, to illustrate how he wanted people to live. The early Christians realized they must share their faith with others and tell people in other cities about their friend, Jesus.

After he died on the cross and rose again, disciples and apostles went to other places. Today missionaries go to other countries to show people how to become Christians. Your pastor and church staff have committed their lives to telling others about Jesus. Do you ever wonder how you, a boy or girl, could be a witness for him?

Boys and girls do not have to wait until they are adults to share the love of Jesus. By coming to church, reading your Bible, praying, and inviting friends to come to church with you, you are a witness for Christ. Listen as I read from James 1:22: "But be ye doers of the word, and not hearers only, deceiving your own selves."

Prayer: Dear Father, help each boy and girl be a witness for you in their daily life.

[*Lead the congregation and children in singing "Holy Bible, Book Divine."*]—Carolyn Tomlin

November 26: Father, We Are Thankful
TEXT: Ps. 92:1
Object: Cornucopia or basket
Song: "We Gather Together"

Hello boys and girls. I'm glad to see you today. Can anyone tell me the name of the object I'm holding? [*Wait for responses.*] This is a cornucopia, which represents prosperity. These fruits and vegetables represent the good food God provides for us. On the first Thanksgiving, the pilgrims planned a day of celebration and invited their Indian friends for a meal. The Indians taught them how to plant and hunt in this new land. They were thankful to God for his care during difficult days.

What are you thankful for during the Thanksgiving season? [*Wait for responses.*] If you're like me, I'm thankful for God loving and caring for my family. I'm thankful for my home, my church, and friends. We live in a country where all boys and girls can attend school. We have doctors who treat us when we're sick. God has provided for all our needs.

So this cornucopia is only a symbol of Thanksgiving. The real meaning is in our hearts. Listen as I read from Psalm 92:1: "It is a good thing to give thanks unto the Lord, and to sing praises unto his name, O most High."

Prayer: Dear Father, we thank you for all your gifts. We know that all good and perfect gifts come from you.
Take Action: This week, list things for which you are thankful. Share the list with your family.

[*Children return to their seats as the pianist plays "We Gather Together."*]—Carolyn Tomlin

December 3: The Perfect Gift
TEXT: Luke 2:10–11
Object: A box wrapped in Christmas paper with a paper heart inside
Song: "Silent Night, Holy Night"

Hello boys and girls. I'm glad to see you today. Can anyone tell me a special day we celebrate in December? [*Wait for responses.*] Did I hear someone say, "Christmas"? Yes, you are right. But more important, it is the birthday of Baby Jesus. So why do you think I'm holding a brightly wrapped package? And what do you think is inside? I know everyone likes to receive gifts at Christmas, and we enjoy giving presents to others. If you'll help me, let's unwrap this gift and see what it contains. [*Ask a couple of children to help.*] Look—it's a heart. Now why do you think a heart would be in a Christmas package? I think it's because the most important gift we can give Jesus is our lives and our heart. Jesus wants us to love him, and this is the way to show that love.

So as you think of gifts this season, don't forget that the most important gift to give is your heart to Jesus.

> *Prayer:* Dear Father, help each boy and girl know the true meaning of Christmas. May they live each day in a way that honors you.
>
> *Take Action:* Write on a card or draw a picture of something you can do for your parents or family. Wrap this gift and give it as your present on Christmas.

[*Lead the children in singing "Silent Night, Holy Night." Children return to their seats.*]— Carolyn Tomlin

December 10: Joy, Advent-Christmas
TEXT: Phil. 4:4–7
Object: Empty water bottle

Good morning! Does anybody know what special day is coming up this month? That's right, *Christmas!* Raise your hand if you have thought about what gifts you would like to receive at Christmas. There are so many hands raised that I will only choose a few people who haven't raised their hands before. [*Answers will reveal the power of advertising and a few surprises.*] Those are all interesting choices. Now you are all very *grown up* children; you probably can't remember when you were babies. I love watching babies playing with anything that happens to be near them. This empty water bottle is a good example. [*Bounce it off the floor or table and stand it upside down while you are talking.*] While you are opening your popular toys at Christmas, your young sister or brother could be laughing, gurgling, and cooing with joy while playing with an empty water bottle.

For people of all ages, joy comes from inside us and not so much from what we have or don't have. The apostle Paul in the Bible is full of joy, even when he is not with the people he loves, because he *is in the Lord.* That means he depends on the Lord Jesus, and that is where his true happiness—*joy*—is found. He says "let your pleadings be made known to God." [*Squeeze the bottle.*] You can let out all your fears and tears to the Lord, and he will help you. Then the Scripture says to do this with thanksgiving. If you begin to look around you at all your blessings, you will be filled with joy. [*Blow up the bottle with air.*] With that kind of joy you will be better able to celebrate the greatest gift of all—the baby Jesus coming to us.—Gary Stratman

December 17: Enjoy What You've Got
TEXT: Luke 12:13–21 (v. 15): Beware! Don't always be wishing for what you don't have. For real life and real living are not related to how rich we are.
Objects: A bicycle and a lawn mower

Good morning boys and girls. I want to tell you a story today that I hope will teach you something the same way Jesus taught people a long time ago. The story is about a boy who loved to ride his bicycle and dream about being rich. He had the best time just riding around and looking at all of the fancy houses with their huge yards of green grass. In some of the yards there was a swimming pool with fancy chairs and table around the pool. This boy would dream about how he would someday live in a big house, lie in a huge yard, and swim in a beautiful pool.

Then one day the most amazing thing happened. The dream came true. His father told him about the big house that he had bought, with a big yard and a swimming pool. The boy was overjoyed, and he could not wait until he moved into his new house. Every day he would get on his bike and just ride back and forth in front of his wonderful new house. But if you saw that boy today, you would not think he was the happy boy who dreamed of living in a big house with a big yard and a beautiful swimming pool. He is not happy anymore. If you drive by his house you will not see him riding his bike, but instead he is pushing a lawn-mower. His yard is so big that he doesn't have time to ride his bike or play ball or visit with his friends. He cuts the grass, cleans the swimming pool, and takes care of his big bedroom.

It's not a new story. Jesus told it a long time ago about people who were always wishing for something they didn't have. People who dream of being rich forget that this is not what counts here on earth. God promises us that it will be a lot better in heaven than even the life the richest man has here on Earth. God wants us to enjoy the good things about living. When you have a lot of things you have to care for a lot of things, and it doesn't leave much time to enjoy each other, the weather, and the other things, like riding or flying a kite.

That's why Jesus told us not to wish for things that we don't have but instead enjoy the things that are already given to us. I know that my friend who pushes a lawn mower all day wishes he hadn't wished so much, so that he could go back to riding his bike. I hope you won't always be spending your time wishing for things you don't have but rather be happy for the things that Jesus has given you.—Wesley T. Runk[2]

December 24: Does Jesus Love You?
TEXT: John 3:16
Object: Bible
Song: "Jesus Loves Me"

Good morning! I want us to do something very simple today. There is a song that I am sure you know. You have been hearing it and singing it almost your entire life. That song is "Jesus Loves Me." Let's sing it together. [*Sing softly and slowly.*]

The Bible tells us that Jesus loves us very much. He loves us more than anyone possibly could, even more than your mom or your dad. That's hard to believe, isn't it? But it is true. When the song says, "Jesus loves me," who is it talking about? You—that is right. Do you really believe [*insert the name of one child*]—that Jesus loves you? Name each child individually and state "[*fill in name*], Jesus loves you." [*Make sure each child is named. If you do not recognize a child or are unsure of a name, ask when the children are gathering.*]

---

[2]*God Doesn't Rust* (Lima, Ohio: CSS, 1978), pp. 69–70.

You can never do anything bad that will make God love you less, and you can never do anything good that will make God love you more. God made you, and he loves you just the way you are. All that God wants in return is for you to love him too.

When we have a children's sermon, who am I talking to? Just boys and girls—that is right. But I hear that sometimes the adults listen in, too. If any of them are listening today, I would like to tell them, Jesus loves you, too. We are going to sing "Jesus Loves Me" again. If you really believe that Jesus loves you, and if they really believe Jesus loves them, I want you and them to join me as we sing this time. [*Sing softly and slowly.*]—Janelle Fraze

December 31: Following Christ's Example
TEXT: Phil. 3:4
Object: Yardstick
Song: "Amazing Grace"

Hello boys and girls. I'm glad to see you today. This yardstick I'm holding is used to measure. Let's see—what could we measure with this? [*Ask a couple of children to come forward and measure their height.*] What about measuring a wall? Or a floor? A book? I would say this is an important tool if we want to know the length or height of any object.

Did you know that God has a way of measuring our lives? He looks at our hearts and he knows what we are thinking. He knows if we are telling the truth, if we treat people fairly, and if we are honest in everything we do. He also knows how much we love him.

So the next time you see or use a yardstick, let it remind you of how God measures you. Listen as I read Philippians 4:17: "Brethren, be followers of me, and mark them which walk so as ye have us for an example."

Prayer: Father, help all boys and girls look to you as an example of how they should live their life.

Take Action: Write a short note to a senior adult or a grandparent who has been a good example of a Christian. Thank that person for being one who inspires others.

[*Lead children and the congregation in singing "Amazing Grace." Children return to their seats.*]—Carolyn Tomlin

A LITTLE TREASURY
OF ILLUSTRATIONS

ACHIEVEMENT.   Ronald Reagan came from Dixon [Illinois]. Just outside his boyhood home, there's a statue of him, a little larger than life. No doubt his childhood there was child-hood with an alcoholic father, but he seems to have been genuinely fond of the place. He always bragged that as a lifeguard there he saved seventy-seven people, spoke wistfully of the folks who called him "Dutch," and wrote in his autobiography that "one of the benefits of my success in Hollywood was being invited to visit Dixon for the annual Petunia Festival."

Why did stars like Louella Parsons and Ronald Reagan return so readily? There is no evi-dence that they had kept up with friends.

Maybe they just needed to see how far they had come, how high they had risen, and were reassured before they went back home to Beverly Hills or the hills above Malibu.[1]

BURIED RICHES.   Oscar Anderson found it very difficult to eke out a living on his Kansas farm in the Dust Bowl days of the 1930s. In the arid conditions of those days, with little—if any—rainfall, Oscar had many crop failures. Somehow his growing family got by, but barely.

What Oscar did not know is that black gold was buried on his farm. Had he known that and been able to tap it, his economic woes would have been over! In the early 1950s several productive oil wells were discovered on the land where Oscar used to farm.

I see a parallel between Oscar's buried black gold and dormant spirituality. Though every person is endowed with it, spirituality may lie buried and untapped, leaving that person in spiritual poverty.[2]

CHRISTIANS AND JEWS.   The arrogance that the Church developed toward Judaism is one of the great tragedies of history. Teaching Christian congregations to respect Judaism is no mere matter of political correctness. It is a theological necessity. The God of Israel is also the God of the Church and loves both church and synagogue with unconditional love and wills for all people to live together in love.[3]

CHRIST'S RETURN.   My good United Methodist friends, John and Helen Rhea Stumbo, were visiting my husband and me in Washington and came to our Episcopal church with us. Our

---

[1]Lawrence Wood, *One Hundred Tons of Ice and Other Gospel Stories* (Louisville, Ky.: Westminster John Knox Press, 2003), p. 8.
[2]Harold R. Nelson, *Senior Spirituality: Awakening Your Spiritual Potential* (St. Louis: Chalice Press, 2004), p. 1.
[3]Ronald J. Allen and Clark M. Williamson, *Preaching the Gospels Without Blaming the Jews* (Louisville, Ky.: Westminster John Knox Press, 2004), Preface, p. xiv.

closing hymn was one of my favorites—"The Church's One Foundation Is Jesus Christ Her Lord." As we sang the final notes, I turned and saw tears in Helen's eyes. "We don't have that third verse in our hymnal," she said. "And it so spoke to me and what I've been wrestling with."

Consider these words:

> Though with a scornful wonder men see her sore oppressed,
> By schisms rent asunder, by heresies distressed;
> Yet saints their watch are keeping, their cry goes up "How long?"
> And soon the night of weeping shall be the morn of song.

For two thousand years the saints and martyrs have cried, "How long?" Today, across the globe, our suffering brothers and sisters cry, "How long?" I have wept tears outside the House of Bishops and cried, "How long?"

We cling to the promise that soon, soon, soon, the night of weeping shall be the morning of song.[4]

COMPLETELY SECULAR.   On a recent trip I fell into conversation with the man sitting next to me on the plane. After discussing the faith he asked, "If I want to pursue the Christian faith further, what do you suggest I do?" I immediately told him to find a good church in his neighborhood, and then I added, "You should also read the Gospel of John." "Gospel of John," he responded, "what is that?" I briefly explained the origin and meaning of the four Gospels and spoke of them as eyewitness accounts of the life, ministry, death, and resurrection of Jesus Christ. "I've never heard about those books!" he exclaimed. "I'll be sure to get them and read them. They sound fascinating."

This man was a middle-aged, well-educated president of his own company. He was an example of the "secular but interested in spiritual things" kind of person who lives in every strata of our present society.[5]

CONSEQUENCES OF DIVORCE.   Divorce leaves its mark, not just for a brief period of time, but for a lifetime. This does not mean that its effect cannot be surmounted; it does mean that there are real effects to surmount. As one of these children of divorce has said: "Every day I think of my parents' divorce at least once. I consider the ramifications of their decisions and actions. I wish that I could remember the good memories from my childhood. I wonder what my life would be like today if my past were different. . . . I think about what a childhood without adult responsibility would have been like. . . . Every day I relive the pain in some way. Every day."[6]

CONTEMPORARY MUSIC.   Let me confess that my preferences are *still* on the side of the more nearly traditional music, but I wouldn't raise a finger to rob today's young people of

---

[4]Diane Knippers, in *Pilgrims on the Sawdust Trail* (Timothy George, ed., Grand Rapids, Mich.: Baker Academic, 2004), pp. 195–196.
[5]Robert E. Webber, *Ancient—Future Evangelism* (Grand Rapids, Mich.: Baker Books, 2003), p. 55.
[6]David P. Gushee, *Getting Marriage Right* (Grand Rapids, Mich.: Baker Books, 2004), p. 61.

the music they prefer. I have listened to their reasons, and I understand why they like this particular type of contemporary music. I am bearing up bravely, sustained by this assurance: I have seen enough youth generations move into adulthood to know that today's devotees to the rock beat will be tomorrow's devotees to a music type more fully identified with their adult roles. Meanwhile, may Heaven help us all to survive the deafening decibels of today's resounding music with enough hearing to permit us to enjoy once again Tchaikovsky's Fifth![7]

CONVERSION.   Karen Howe of Florida writes: "I became a Christian sitting in a pew, experiencing worship. It wasn't the sermon that did it. No one presented me with the plan of salvation or led me in a prayer of commitment (though that did come later). I simply basked in the presence of God as the worship service progressed around me, and when I left the church I knew that God had entered my life. He was alive. I had encountered Him. That day I was born in the Spirit." The experience of conversion is not dependent on an invitation at the end of the service. Rather, it happens because the unchurched are in church as a result of relationships in which they see faith embodied. Through an association with authentic Christians, truth is assimilated. At some point the Christian faith is internalized and a personal commitment to Christ as Lord and Savior is made public. This may happen in a direct moment of *decision* within worship or with a friend, or conversion may be more gradual and *dawn* on a person who wakes up one day to exclaim, "I'm a Christian!"[8]

CONVERSION—ITS CONSEQUENCES.   For several years, Bob was quite active in the Mafia. He had been raised Roman Catholic but turned his back on his upbringing and became a wealthy leader in the world of organized crime in Chicago. He sold drugs, hired prostitutes, and enjoyed many "courtesans" himself, even though he had married Nancy, a woman who claimed to be a believer but who was not very committed. In fact, Nancy had married Bob more for her enjoyment of the jet set, the fast life, the circles in which Bob operated. Then Bob was dramatically converted through the witness of a fellow mobster. You couldn't have imagined a more changed life. Bob did time in prison and even led several prisoners to the Lord. He continued to be a bold, outspoken evangelist after getting out of jail. Even to this day, he regularly shares his faith, on and off the job, at times with entire strangers. Despite an occasional lack of tact, he has been remarkably successful at bringing countless people to Christ.

Bob's marriage, however, is now on the rocks. At first Nancy claimed to be glad of the wonderful change in her husband. But it soon became clear that he had something she didn't. She got tired of hearing all the talk about spiritual things. Today he no longer tells her much of his evangelistic activity because inevitably she interrupts and starts an argument of some kind. She won't go to church with him, and recently she's been talking about divorce. What really gnaws at her is that God never gave her such gifts as he seems to have given Bob. Nancy has always struggled as an introvert in social situations. Some days she's just not sure how much longer she can take all of this religious stuff.[9]

---

[7]Chester Swor, *The Best of Chester Swor* (Nashville, Tenn.: Broadman Press, 1981), pp. 120–121.
[8]Robert E. Webber, *Ancient-Future Evangelism* (Grand Rapids, Mich.: Baker Books, 2003), pp. 64–65.
[9]Craig L. Blomberg, *Preaching the Parables* (Grand Rapids, Mich.: Baker Academic, 2004), pp. 33–34.

THE ELUSIVE JESUS.   In *Deconstructing Jesus* (2000), Robert Price argues that the biblical representations of Jesus all cancel one another out, since Jesus could not have been an eschatological figure *and* a wisdom teacher *and* a teller of parables *and* a wonder-worker *and* a founder of a new religious community. My conclusion is different. The various aspects of Jesus' image are not fictional. If we have difficulty in applying them to the same person, it is because Jesus is too large to be pigeonholed. The interpreter's most common and most characteristic error regarding Jesus is to narrow down the figure in the Gospels until he fits into some box chosen by the interpreter. My point about the first-century context thus applies to the twenty-first century as well. Jesus does not conform to any contemporary category, whether that of social activist, spiritual guru, alternative healer, ethical teacher, textual scholar, gadfly, hippie, corporate executive, political revolutionary, doomsday prophet, inspirational speaker, or commune founder. Jesus was and is uncategorizable, and this is one reason why he remains a perpetual challenge to believers and nonbelievers alike, a figure instantly recognizable and yet ever elusive.[10]

THE FUTURE.   No human can make good the crimes of the past. But in order to be able to live with this past, with its ruins and victims, without repressing it and without having to repeat it, we need this transcendent hope for the raising of the dead and the healing of what has been broken. Because of the raising of the broken Christ, the Christian hope for the future is at its heart a hope for resurrection. Without hope for the past there is no hope for the future, for what will be, will pass away; what is born, dies; and what is not yet, will one day be no longer. The resurrection hope is not directed toward a future *in* history; it points toward the future *of* history, in which the tragic dimensions of history and nature will be dissolved.[11]

GOD SPEAKS.   Some time ago I was conducting a retreat. During the course of it, one participant asked me why I was interested in spirituality. I told him that I thought the roots of my interest grew out of my childhood fear of death, but there were also other contributors to my passion. Later that day the same man pulled me aside and said, "I am seventy-seven years old, and I have suddenly realized that I'm going to die. I've always known it, but now I feel it. And it has troubled me."

He continued, "But I had a dream that spoke to me. In the dream I saw clearly that the God who made this world and planned all the wonderful things in it has more in store for us in heaven than we have ever been able to comprehend." The man was at peace. Perhaps God did speak to him through the dream.[12]

GOOD NEWS.   The good news with which the Fourth Gospel begins is that humans are neither first in the world nor alone in the world. The *Word* is first, and God has come to us.

The prologue to the Fourth Gospel bears witness to what Jesus Christ meant to a group of people who had come to know him near the end of the first century C.E. Those early Christians saw in Jesus the uncreated light of God, a light that they knew as the Word. Getting to

---

[10]Michael J. McClymond, *Familiar Stranger* (Grand Rapids, Mich.: Eerdmans Publishing Co., 2004), p. 152.
[11]Jürgen Moltman, in *The Future of Hope* (Miroslav Volf and William Katerberg, eds., Grand Rapids, Mich.: Eerdmans Publishing Co., 2004), pp. 17–18.
[12]Ben Campbell Johnson, *The God Who Speaks* (Grand Rapids, Mich.: Eerdmans Publishing Co., 2004), pp. 124–125.

know him was like seeing the dawn break over all creation and in their life as a community. It was like being invaded by grace and truth and life. It was like coming to know God. They set down these words about the Word, to the end that the Word might also become flesh in the lives of those who read this Gospel.[13]

HAPPY WITH GOD—NOW! Even the poorest, most abandoned person can experience the transforming power of God's grace. This is the good news of the gospel—not just that we will be happy with God in the afterlife, but that we can be happy with God right now, however desperate our situation. Christianity is not about rules and laws, guilt and fear of punishment, or extrinsic rewards. It is about grace: the experience of God's transforming love and power in our lives that elevates and perfects our natural abilities and allows us to do more than we thought possible. In this sense, the life of every fully converted Christian moves beyond naturalism. It is God's grace that makes the Christian practice of everyday life possible. And it is this same power of grace that one day will bring us to the resurrection, the ultimate transformation of nature, and to eternal life with God.[14]

HATE. In the novel *Birdy*, William Wharton's protagonist, Sergeant Alfonso, develops an instant dislike for an obnoxious, overweight enlisted man, a clerk typist named Ronsky. At the top of his list of gripes about this annoying grunt is Ronsky's revolting habit of continually spitting. He spits all over his desk, his typewriter, his papers, and those who venture too near. Alfonso is only waiting for an excuse to punch him out. Then the sergeant learns Ronsky's story. He was an infantryman on D-day, and saw his buddies shot down in the surf before they even reached the beach of Normandy. And his constant spitting, it seems, is a physical manifestation of his attempt to get the nauseous foulness of war and death out of his mouth when anything reminds him, as virtually everything does, of its acid smell and putrid taste. Sergeant Alfonso suddenly sees Ronsky with new eyes. What yesterday had irritated him unbearably, today wins his total respect. He sighs with regret, and thinks: Before you know it, if you're not careful, you can get to feeling for everybody and there's nobody left to hate.

Empathy does that. Compassion leaves so few to hate. Once you let them into your inner world of understanding, you change, and they are no longer the people you previously despised. Your world grows larger, the spiritual solipsism breaks open. Solidarity becomes more than a word. Compassion opens us to *things as they are.*[15]

ICONS. The Bible is very skeptical—to put it mildly—about visual images of God: the Ten Commandments forbid God's people to create carved models of the God of Israel like the images of neighboring cultures, and the prophetic words of Second Isaiah contain some savage satire against those who imagine that things they have themselves made can save or help them. In the days of the early Church, one of the things that most surprised non-Christians about Christian worship and places of worship was the lack of images of divine beings; for

---

[13]Lamar Williamson Jr., *Preaching the Gospel of John* (Louisville, Ky.: Westminster John Knox Press, 2004), p. 1.
[14]Terance L. Nichols, *The Sacred Cosmos* (Grand Rapids, Mich.: Brazos Press, 2003), p. 227.
[15]David W. Augsburger, *Hate-Work: Working Through the Pain and Pleasure of Hate* (Louisville, Ky.: Westminster John Knox Press, 2004), p. 222.

most people in that age and area, a place of worship was *essentially* a house for images of the gods. Christians must be atheists, they thought, since they had no gods around.

Yet slowly and steadily, Christian art developed. By the sixth century, places of worship were heavily decorated with painting and mosaic (and embroidered curtains), and pictures on wooden panels were beginning to appear, showing Jesus or his mother or one or more of the saints. These images were increasingly treated with veneration and regarded as instruments of God's work.[16]

INTERCESSION.   A Christian fellowship lives and exists by the intercession of its members for one another, or it collapses. I can no longer condemn or hate a brother for whom I pray, no matter how much trouble he causes me. His face . . . is transformed in intercession into the countenance of a brother for whom Christ died, the face of a forgiven sinner. . . . Intercession means no more than to bring our brother into the presence of God, to see him under the cross of Jesus as a poor human being and sinner in the need of grace.[17]

THE LAST LAUGH.   God has the last laugh. There is an ancient Russian Orthodox tradition that devotes the day after Easter to sitting around a table and telling jokes. Why? According to William J. Bausch, this was the way, they felt, that they were imitating that cosmic joke that God pulled on Satan in the resurrection. Satan thought he had won, and was smug in his victory, smiling to himself, having had the last word. So he thought. Then God raised Jesus from the dead, and life and salvation became the last words. And the whole world laughed at the devil's discomfort. This attitude passed into the medieval concept of *hilaritas,* which did not mean mindless giggling, but that even at the moment of disaster one may wink because he or she knows there is a God.[18]

LIFE EXPECTANCY.   Perhaps the most striking examples of how science and technology have transformed human experience is that, until about two hundred years ago, human life expectancy was less than twenty-five years, whereas it is now about seventy-five years in the wealthiest countries. The fact that life expectancy—the average age to which people lived—was so low in the past does not mean that people somehow died of old age in their twenties but rather that relatively few people died of old age. Widespread infectious disease resulted in extremely high rates of infant and child mortality, so that a majority of the population died before reaching maturity. The application of scientific knowledge to establish public health measures during the nineteenth and early twentieth centuries dramatically reduced the incidence of early death so that now most people in the wealthiest societies live out something close to a full human life span.[19]

LISTENING REQUIRED.   In *Performing the Faith* I argue that the church give no gift to the worlds in which it finds itself more politically important than the formation of a people

---

[16]Rowan Williams, *The Dwelling of the Light: Praying with Icons of Christ* (Grand Rapids, Mich.: Eerdmans Publishing Co., 2004), pp. xi–xii.

[17]Dietrich Bonhoeffer, *Life Together* (New York: HarperCollins, 1954).

[18]Donald McCullough, *The Consolations of Imperfection* (Grand Rapids, Mich.: Brazos Press, 2004), p. 195.

[19]Murray Jardine, *The Making and Unmaking of Technological Society* (Grand Rapids, Mich.: Brazos Press, 2004), p. 17.

constituted by the virtues necessary to endure the struggle to hear and speak truthfully to one another. Note: I do not assume that Christians are in some peculiar possession of the truth that legitimates their imposition of that truth on others. Christians qua Christians have no corner on the truth because, as Bonhoeffer argued, to speak truthfully requires the recognition that the One who is the Truth is the living God who often meets us in the face of the stranger. Christians understand that they are the people who have been claimed by the ultimate stranger, that is, the God who would be known through the Jews. Christians cannot, therefore, ever presume that they will not have to learn from those who are not Christians.[20]

LOVE.   I have often thought I wouldn't have but one text if I thought I could make the world believe that God is love; I would take only that text and go up and down the earth, trying to counteract what Satan has been telling them—that God is not love. He has made the world believe it effectually. It would not take twenty-four hours to make the world come to God if you could only make them believe God is love. If you can really make a man believe you love him, you have won him; and if I could only make people really believe that God loves them, what a rush we would see for the kingdom of God! Oh, how they would rush in! But man has got a false idea about God, and he will not believe that He is a God of love. It is because he don't know Him.[21]

MARTYRDOM AND WITNESS.   We need Bonhoeffer. He can give us the courage to tell the more macabre truths of the last century to the next generation without bringing it to despair. In the disturbing "exhibition hall" of the twentieth century, lined with genocide, abuse of power, forces of cultural disintegration, and sheer hatred for humanity, Bonhoeffer is a witness to God's love, to justice, and to hope. In community, we can open our eyes to the world's evil and still be hopeful for the human race and the world we create and inhabit.

Singer-composer Ken Medema expresses my hope in his provocative song "Dance in the Dragon's Jaws." For according to the Christian way of looking at things, at the center of history, perhaps at the center of reality itself, stands a hellish episode of redemption in which God established life in the jaws of death. Even at the edge of an abyss, perhaps especially there, we can dance.[22]

MONEY CHANGES THINGS.   If my wife and I were to win the lottery, our use of our millions would make a difference to who we are and who we are becoming. If we were to buy our dream house, we could live far from the problems of our neighbors, and near the school of our choice. Each of our children could have their own rooms, TVs, computers, cell phones, and new clothes. No more hand-me-downs. No more sports equipment from yard sales. No more thrift store blenders and crock pots. No more car worries. Perhaps, we would buy a fashionable SUV, and my children would no longer be embarrassed when I drop them off at school. I would not have to embarrass myself with fifteen-year-old jackets and ties. We could

---

[20]Stanley Hauerwas, *Performing the Faith* (Grand Rapids, Mich.: Brazos Press, 2004), p. 15.
[21]Dwight L. Moody (1837–1899).
[22]Craig J. Slane, *Bonhoeffer as Martyr* (Grand Rapids, Mich.: Brazos Press, 2004), p. 10.

correct the things about ourselves that have bothered us for a long time. We could even out imbalances and straighten crooked lines with cosmetic surgery.

With a few million dollars, our everyday lives would not be the same, and we would take a different "place" in the world. When all is said and done, I could not claim that I am simply the same person as before. Such a claim would divide body and spirit—a prideful separation from the very things and way of life that I want to make my own. I could not tell my old friends, "I am just the same guy you used to know." We would change less, I suppose, if we were to give our million dollars away. Such a radical act would bring clarity to our lives. We would have to make a bold decision about who we are and what we want, and with such a decisive act, it is hard to imagine that we would carry on thinking about our lives and living them the same as before. For good or ill, we are changed by our use of money and things.[23]

MORAL VACUUM.   In 1978, Aleksandr I. Solzhenitsyn delivered the 327th commencement address at Harvard University. Titled "A World Split Apart," his speech focused on the growing moral vacuum in Western civilization. In spite of our "abundance of information, or maybe partly because of it," he said, "the West has great difficulty in finding its bearings amid contemporary events." The rising racket of information repeatedly breaks our concentration. We claim to be truth seekers, he argued, but instead we follow simplistic "formulas." We wrongly assume that the overall condition of the world is improving because of our wealth of technology and information. We forget that "truth seldom is sweet; it is almost invariably bitter."[24]

MORTALITY.   It has often been pointed out that in our culture, young people have little sense of their own mortality, something that would not have been the case in premodern societies, with their low life expectancies. Indeed, part of the reason for our current culture's denial of death, as mentioned by Kass, is undoubtedly that so few people have any significant contact with the elderly and the dying. Caring for the elderly would give young people a very different perspective on life.[25]

PERFORMING THE TEXT.   Some years ago Frances Young, the Methodist theologian from Great Britain, wrote a little book called *Virtuoso Theology*. She likened the Christian life to the performance of music. The Word of God is like a musical score. It may be studied and there may be great efforts to establish a clear text and the intention of the text (the work, respectively, of the exegetic or theologian and, by parallel, the musicologist), but the full meaning of the text appears only when it is performed. Fidelity to the text is the bottom line, but there is a difference between a beginner plunking away at Mozart's *Eine Kleine Nachtmusik* and the same piece at the hands of a seasoned performer. Some read so deeply into the mind of the composer that we honor such a person as a musical virtuoso.[26]

---

[23]David Matzko McCarthy, *The Good Life* (Grand Rapids, Mich.: Brazos Press, 2004), p. 167.
[24]Quentin J. Schultze, *Habits of the High-Tech Heart* (Grand Rapids, Mich.: Baker Academic, 2002), p. 25.
[25]Murray Jardine, *The Making and Unmaking of Technological Society* (Grand Rapids, Mich.: Brazos Press, 2004), p. 275.
[26]Lawrence S. Cunningham, *Francis of Assisi: Performing the Gospel Life* (Grand Rapids, Mich.: Eerdmans Publishing Co., 2004), p. 139.

POP CULTURE.   The Rolling Stones began "Sympathy for the Devil" by singing, "Please allow me to introduce myself." Many view pop culture as the devil, as something to shun, avoid, and oppose. Rapper Eminem may be seen as the latest example of evil emanating from pop culture. His songs contain ample evidence of profanity, misogyny, and homophobia. He courts controversy, relishes a fight, openly plays the devil to enrage parents and other guardians of taste. Yet Eminem's film debut, *8 Mile,* also includes some surprisingly inspiring and spiritual undertones. The rap battles in the film take place at "the shelter," in a church basement. They are hosted by Future, a person of prayer who encourages Eminem's character, Rabbit, to "flip the script" onstage. Rabbit wins the rap contest by acknowledging his weaknesses, owning his embarrassments, revealing whatever secrets his opponents may use against him. Eminem's approach is summarized in the Academy Award–winning song from the *8 Mile* soundtrack, "Lose Yourself." He loses himself in the music, but in the principle of self-renunciation—"flipping the script"—finds surprising parallels in the words of Jesus.

In the Gospel of Luke, Jesus challenged his followers to deny themselves, take up their cross daily, and follow him, "For whoever wants to save his life will lose it, but whoever loses his life for me will save it" (Luke 9:24). Jesus' paradoxical teaching flipped the script on people's understanding of power, life, and religion. You find life by losing yourself in Christ. Eminem may be the devil to some, but his *via negativa* has roots in Jesus' surprising strategies. It is easy to identify what's wrong with Eminem, but finding what's right, identifying, and understanding what millions of teens connect with, takes much more work.[27]

PRACTICAL THEOLOGY.   Today, practical theology strives to be fully public in several senses. By making the social sciences its partner in academic dialogue and by taking psychological, societal, and cultural factors into account, practical theology makes its claim to having a voice within the academic world beyond theology and the church. And by addressing issues of public interest and importance, practical theology strives to become involved with the social and political attempts of shaping the future of society or, thinking of current debates, even the future of our globalizing world.[28]

PREACHING.   Francis understood that preaching meant communication. He also understood that the way one lives, the fashion in which a person interacts with others, the picture one presents to the world—these are all forms of communication. He put this theory of communication succinctly in instructions he once gave to some of his brothers as they were about to enter a town: "Preach and, if necessary, use words."[29]

QUARRELING OVER TRUTH.   Our quarreling ancestors were in reality much closer to each other when in all their disputes they still knew that they could only be servants of one truth which must be acknowledged as being as great and as pure as it has been intended for us by God.[30]

---

[27]Craig Detweiler and Barry Taylor, *A Matrix of Meanings* (Grand Rapids, Mich.: Baker Academic, 2003), pp. 7–8.

[28]Richard R. Osmer and Friedrich L. Schweitzer (eds.), *Developing a Public Faith* (St. Louis: Chalice Press, 2003), p. 6.

[29]Lawrence S. Cunningham, *Francis of Assisi: Performing the Gospel Life* (Grand Rapids, Mich.: Eerdmans Publishing Co., 2004), p. 135.

[30]Cardinal Joseph Ratzinger, *Church, Ecumenism, and Politics* (New York: Crossroad, 1988), p. 98.

RESPONSE TO TERRORISM.   The danger terrorism poses may be less in what it can do to harm us than in what it prompts us to do to harm ourselves. If we lose confidence in our own best inclinations, thinking that threats can only be dealt with by mounting counter-threats, that deceit can only be met by clandestine cleverness, surprise only offset by counter-surprise, and violence stemmed only by counter-violence, terrorism will have reshaped us even if we think we have overcome it. If we curtail freedoms in the process of defending freedom, what is the benefit? We need a positive resurgence of our noble convictions rather than the embrace of strategies that merely mirror the stances of those we seek to oppose. Such a response to terrorism is possible only in the context of a very vital practice of a faith deeply rooted in compassion.[31]

RESURRECTION HAPPENS.   We have every reason to believe, on the basis of what happened to Jesus, that God is able and more than willing to take limitations that at best annoy us and at worst fill us with dread and, in ways we cannot yet see or understand, make them serve the purposes of love. This does not make them less painful; this does not make them good in themselves. But it can make them easier to bear, knowing their No! will somehow be turned into a Yes![32]

A SACRAMENTAL UNIVERSE.   Miracles are signs (not proofs) that nature exists within a higher order, an order of love and the fidelity of God. Just as divine grace heals and elevates the human intellect and will, so miracles elevate the activities of physical nature. They thus also reveal the potentiality of nature to exist in transcendent states, not suspected by naturalism. In a miracle, nature becomes transparent to its divine ground, like a window opening onto a higher state of being. Another way of putting this is that miracles are like sacraments: they are visible events in which the divine presence shines forth. If we believe not only in the resurrection of Jesus, but in the universal resurrection of the dead and the consequent transfiguration of nature itself, promised in Romans 8 and in Revelation 21:1 ("I saw a new heaven and a new earth"), then we can look forward to a heaven in which all of nature becomes a miraculous sacrament showing forth the presence of its Creator. Matter itself will be transfigured so that it does not occlude the divine presence, but expresses it. As John Polkinghorne writes: "The ultimate destiny of the whole universe is sacramental."[33]

SALVATION.   Generally speaking, salvation is the experience of the presence of God within the great existential questions of life: bondage and freedom, meaninglessness and meaning, alienation and community, death and life. To be saved is to know that one's life now and forever is held in the eternal life and love of God. For the Christian, this is Christ-centered faith. Jesus has disclosed the fullness of our humanity and its destiny in relationship to God. This experience of the divine presence is the awareness that our life flows from God, in God, to God.[34]

---

[31]Edward LeRoy Long Jr., *Facing Terrorism* (Louisville, Ky.: Westminster John Knox Press, 2004), p. 96.
[32]Donald McCullough, *The Consolations of Imperfection* (Grand Rapids, Mich.: Brazos Press, 2004), p. 194.
[33]Terrance L. Nichols, *The Sacred Cosmos* (Grand Rapids, Mich.: Brazos Press, 2003), pp. 197–198.
[34]R. Lammy Hunter and Victor L. Hunter, *What Your Doctor and Your Pastor Want You to Know About Depression* (St. Louis: Chalice Press, 2004), p. 91.

SOJOURNERS.   If we live as techno-tourists, our primary legacy is technique. If instead we are heartful sojourners, embracing both gratitude and responsibility, we will leave behind a far richer legacy of virtue as a witness to future generations. Our gratitude and the resulting responsibility are both gifts from the past and gifts for the future. They cut through the fog of informational life and open our hearts to faithfulness. As Solzhenitsyn puts it, modernity has "trampled upon" us. "No one on earth has any other way left but—upward."[35]

WITNESSING.   It is, I think, the greatest joy that the soule of man is capable of in this life . . . to assist the salvation of others.[36]

WORK.   A mere hired hand wishes the working day was over, but the person who truly loves the work is not concerned by its difficulty, or suffering, or the length of time it lasts. For this reason it is written, "To serve God and live for him is easy for the one who does it." This is true for the person who does it for love, but it is hard for the person who does it for hire. It is the same with all virtue and good works, as it is with order, laws, and precepts, but God rejoices more over one person who truly loves than over a thousand hired hands.[37]

---

[35]Quentin J. Schultze, *Habits of the High-Tech Heart* (Grand Rapids, Mich.: Baker Academic, 2002), p. 208.
[36]John Donne (1572–1631)
[37]Tony D'Souza (ed.), *The Way of Jesus* (Grand Rapids, Mich.: Eerdmans Publishing Co., 2004), p. 88.

CONTRIBUTORS AND ACKNOWLEDGMENTS

CONTRIBUTORS

Allen, Byron, Jr. Pastor, First Baptist Church, Channelview, Texas

Beck, Peter. Director of marketing, Southern Baptist Theological Seminary, Louisville, Kentucky

Blankenship, Ron. Director, Montgomery Baptist Association, Rockville, Maryland

Bramlett, Perry C. Minister, author, and lecturer, C. S. Lewis for the Local Church Interstate Ministries, Louisville, Kentucky

Brand, Rick. Pastor, First Presbyterian Church, Henderson, North Carolina

Brown, Dick. Canon, St. John's Cathedral (Episcopal), Knoxville, Tennessee

Cox, James W. Senior professor of Christian preaching, Southern Baptist Theological Seminary, Louisville, Kentucky

Cox, Ken. Pastor, First Baptist Church, New Boston, Texas

Crawford, James W. Pastor Emeritus, The Old South Church in Boston, Boston, Massachusetts

Cubine, William. Sociology professor, University of Louisville, Louisville, Kentucky

Dipboye, Larry. Former pastor, First Baptist Church, Oak Ridge, Tennessee

Doyle, Don. Founder and director of the Doyle Family Counseling Center, Memphis, Tennessee

Ferris, Theodore Parker. Former rector, Trinity Church (Episcopal), Boston, Massachusetts

Fields, Henry. Pastor, First Baptist Church, Toccoa, Georgia

Fraze, Janelle. Director of Mother's Day Out program, First Baptist Church, Middletown, Kentucky

Fribley, Peter. Presbyterian pastor, Madison, Wisconsin

Gladstone, John N. Pastor Emeritus, Yorkminster Park Baptist Church, Toronto, Canada

Griffin, Deborah. Lay member of Broadway Baptist Church, Louisville, Kentucky

Hammer, Randy. Pastor, First Congregational Church, Albany, New York

Huffman, John C. Retired Baptist minister, Louisville, Kentucky

Hull, William E. Pastor and former administrator, Samford University, Birmingham, Alabama

Idleman, Kyle. Preaching associate, Southeast Christian Church, Louisville, Kentucky

Johnson, Bob I. Pastor, First Baptist Church, Evansville, Indiana

Landrum, Eli, Jr. Baptist pastor and denominational leader

Leonard, Bill J. Dean, School of Divinity, Wake Forest University, Wake Forest, North Carolina

Lischer, Richard. Professor, Duke Divinity School, Durham, North Carolina

Lytch, Stephens G. Pastor, Second Presbyterian Church, Louisville, Kentucky

Macleod, Donald. Retired professor, Princeton Theological Seminary, Princeton, New Jersey

McClure, John S. The Charles G. Finney Professor of Homiletics, Vanderbilt Divinity School, Nashville, Tennessee

Patterson, John W. Pastor, Hatcher Memorial Baptist Church, Richmond, Virginia

Peters, William W., Jr. Speaker at the funeral of his father, William W. Peters Sr., Sandy, Utah

Phillips, E. Lee. Minister and freelance writer, Norcross, Georgia

Rodman, John R. Retired Presbyterian minister, Louisville, Kentucky

Runk, Wesley T. Lutheran minister and founder of the C.S.S. Publishing Company, Lima, Ohio

Russell, Bob. Senior minister, Southeast Christian Church, Louisville, Kentucky

Seifrid, Mark. Professor of New Testament interpretation, Southern Baptist Theological Seminary, Louisville, Kentucky

Standiford, Jim. Senior pastor, First United Methodist Church, San Diego, California

Stein, Robert H. Professor of New Testament interpretation, Southern Baptist Theological Seminary, Louisville, Kentucky

Stone, Conway. Motivational speaker, Louisville, Kentucky

Stone, Dave. Preaching associate, Southeast Christian Church, Louisville, Kentucky

Storment, H. Lloyd. Associate minister, Broadway Baptist Church, Louisville, Kentucky

Stratman, Gary D. Pastor, First and Calvary Presbyterian Church, Springfield, Missouri

Thomason, Bill. Former professor of philosophy and religion, currently employed in religious book sales, Louisville, Kentucky

Thompson, John. Pastor Emeritus, First Congregational United Church of Christ, Sarasota, Florida

Tomlin, Carolyn. Writer specializing in church curriculum materials, Jackson, Tennessee

Troeger, Thomas H. Professor, Iliff School of Theology, Denver, Colorado

Vinson, Richard B. Dean, Baptist Theological Seminary at Richmond, Richmond, Virginia

Vogel, Robert. Professor of Christian preaching, Southern Baptist Theological Seminary, Louisville, Kentucky

Walsh, Albert J. D. Pastor, Heidelberg United Church of Christ, Heidelberg, Pennsylvania

Wells, J. Kendrick, III. Attorney, Louisville, Kentucky

Wheeler, David L. Pastor, First Baptist Church, Los Angeles, California

Willimon, William H. Bishop of the United Methodist Church for North Alabama

York, Hershael. Lester Professor of Christian Preaching, Southern Baptist Theological Seminary, Louisville, Kentucky

ACKNOWLEDGMENTS

All of the following are used by permission:

Excerpts from John W. Patterson's sermon in James C. Barry (ed.), *Award Winning Sermons,* Vol. 3. (Nashville: Broadman Press, 1979), pp. 95–103.

Excerpts from Byron Allen Jr.'s sermon in James C. Barry (ed.), *Award Winning Sermons,* Vol. 1. (Nashville: Broadman Press, 1977), pp. 55–64.

Excerpts from Eli Landrum Jr., *More Than Symbols* (Nashville: Broadman Press, 1983), pp. 36–39.

INDEX OF CONTRIBUTORS

460

SERMON TITLE INDEX

Children's sermons are marked as (cs); sermon suggestions as (ss).

SCRIPTURAL INDEX

INDEX OF PRAYERS

INDEX OF MATERIALS
USEFUL AS CHILDREN'S STORIES AND
SERMONS NOT INCLUDED IN SECTION XI

INDEX OF MATERIALS USEFUL
FOR SMALL GROUPS

TOPICAL INDEX

The following text was omitted from the June 11 Lectionary Message on pages 146–151:

SERMON SUGGESTIONS

Topic: The Voice of the Lord

TEXT: Ps. 29 (Approach 1)

(1) God's voice commands attention: evoking confession (vv. 1–2a), requiring worship (v. 2b). (2) God's voice signifies his power over all things (vv. 3–10a). (3) God's voice is heard most productively and concretely by his people (vv. 10b–11).

Topic: The Fortunes of Faith

TEXT: Ps. 29 (Approach 2)

(1) Faith exalted (vv. 1–4). (2) Faith challenged (vv. 5–9b). (3) Faith refined (vv. 9c–11).

WORSHIP AIDS

CALL TO WORSHIP.   "Out of my distress I called on the Lord; the Lord answered me and set me free" (Ps. 118:5 RSV).

INVOCATION.   Be all to us we need today, our God, that we may respond by being the persons you need in this place to accomplish the will of God. In the powerful name of Jesus we pray.—E. Lee Phillips

OFFERTORY SENTENCE.   "Lay not up for yourselves treasures upon earth, where moth and rust doth corrupt, and where thieves break through and steal; but lay up for yourselves treasures in heaven, where neither moth nor rust doth corrupt, and where thieves do not break through nor steal; for where your treasure is, there will your heart be also (Matt. 6:19–21).

OFFERTORY PRAYER.   Lord, take our spiritual inclinations and expand them, take our faith-filled impulses and stretch them, take our desire for holiness and increase it, that as we worship we will find more than we thought and love God all the more.—E. Lee Phillips

PRAYER.   Help us to be still and know that thou art God. Give us both the will and the way to renew our spiritual resources, broaden our vision, and enlarge our concept of thy purpose for us so that we may grow daily, steadily, in spirit as well as in body, at home not only in this world of the flesh but in the greater world of the Spirit. We ask this in the name of Jesus, our Lord.—Theodore Parker Ferris